DICTIONARY OF THE ISRAELI-PALESTINIAN CONFLICT

(...)

DICTIONARY
"OF THE ISRAELI-
PALESTINIAN
CONFLICT

CULTURE, HISTORY, AND POLITICS

VOLUME 2: K-Z

MACMILLAN REFERENCE USA
An Imprint of Thomson Gale, a part of The Thomson Corporation

THOMSON

GALE

Detroit • New York • San Francisco • San Diego • New Haven, Conn. • Waterville, Maine • London • Munich

THOMSON

GALE

Dictionary of the Israeli-Palestinian Conflict: Culture, History, and Politics

Since this page cannot legibly accommodate all copyright notices, the acknowledgments constitute an extension of the copyright notice.

While every effort has been made to ensure the reliability of the information presented in this publication, Thomson Gale does not guarantee the accuracy of the data contained herein. Thomson Gale accepts no payment for listing; and inclusion in the publication of any organization, agency, institution, publication, service, or individual does not imply endorsement of the editors or publisher. Errors brought to the attention of the publisher and verified to the satisfaction of the publisher will be corrected in future editions.

LIBRARY OF CONGRESS CATALOGING-IN-PUBLICATION DATA

Faure, Claude.
[Shalom, salam. English]
Dictionary of the Israeli-Palestinian conflict : culture, history and politics / by Claude Faure.
p. cm.
Includes bibliographical references.
ISBN 0-02-865977-5 (set hardcover : alk. paper)—ISBN 0-02-865978-3 (vol 1)—ISBN 0-02-865979-1 (vol 2)—ISBN 0-02-865996-1 (e-book)
1. Israel—Politics and government—Encyclopedias. 2. Jews—Politics and government—Encyclopedias. 3. Israel—History—Encyclopedias. 4. Arab-Israeli conflict—Encyclopedias. 5. Palestinian Arabs—Politics and government—Encyclopedias. 6. Palestine—History—Encyclopedias. I. Title.

JQ1830.A58F3813 2005
956.9405'03—dc22

2004018641

This title is also available as an e-book.
ISBN 0-02-865996-1
Contact your Thomson Gale sales representative for ordering information.

Printed in the United States of America
10 9 8 7 6 5 4 3 2 1

CONTENTS

K

KAʿBA (*Kaaba*; from the Arabic word for "cube"): Also called *Bait Allah al Haram* ("Holy House of God," in Arabic), this is the sacred building in Mecca, square in form, on the corner of which is found the "Black Stone" (*al hajr al-aswad*), which had pre-Islamic religious significance. Built by Adam, according to tradition, and destroyed in the Deluge, the Kaʿba was reconstructed by the prophet Abraham, who made of it a site dedicated to the cult of a singular god, replacing the multitudinous idols in the city. Thereby, the Black Stone, which was white at the beginning and was supposed to have been given to him by the archangel Gabriel, became an object of veneration, thought to eliminate all humankind's impurities. In his turn, Ishmael, the son of Abraham, was thought to have discovered the Zamzam spring, located in the courtyard of Hijr, at the foot of the Kaʿba, a spring that became a symbol of purity. The tombs of Ishmael and his mother, Hagar, are located in this courtyard.

In 630, after having conquered Mecca, Muhammad had all the idols and their temples destroyed, except for the Kaʿba and the Black Stone. Mecca became the goal of a ritual pilgrimage and the pole of orientation of Muslim prayer, wherever it is practiced in the world. On the northwest side of the building is found the "gutter" (*mizab*), coated with gold, called the "gutter of pity" (*mizab al-rahma*). The Kaʿba is covered by a precious drapery, *al-Kiswa al-Sharifa,* black in color, made long ago in Egypt

and offered by the caliph. In the twenty-first century, the upkeep of the Kaʿba is the responsibility of the personnel of the Waqf.

SEE ALSO Abraham; Adam; Ishmael; Muhammad; Waqf.

KABARITI, ABDUL KARIM (1949–): Jordanian political figure, born in 1949, at Amman, descended from an important Aqaba family. After studying geology at the American University of Beirut, Abdul Karim Kabariti obtained a degree in financial management and a master's degree in business administration in the United States. He started on a career in business, particularly in the United States, before being elected a deputy from Ma'an (Jordan), in 1989; in December, he was named minister of tourism and antiquities in the government of Mudar Badran. In June 1990, he joined the National Bloc as an independent deputy, then was renamed to his previous posts, one year later, in the cabinet of Mai Masri. Between November 1991 and May 1993 he was minister of labor in the government of Zayd Bin Shakir. The following November, he was reelected deputy.

In January 1995 he became foreign minister in the cabinet of Bin Shakir. The policies advocated by his ministry allowed Jordan to effect a rapprochement with the United States, and to renew its ties with the Gulf states, interrupted since the war of 1991. On 4 February 1996, anticipating this appointment for more than a year, he was named prime minister, replacing Bin Shakir. The new head of government was also foreign minister and defense minister. On 20 March 1997, his manner of governing and his differences with Crown Prince Hassan led to his being dismissed by King Hussein. Returning to business, Kabariti became president of the administrative council of the Jordan Kuwait Bank, and the following November was named vice president of the Jordanian senate. In March 1999 Kabariti was named head of the Royal Court by the new king of Jordan, Abdullah II, having acceded to the throne after the decease of his father, King Hussein, who had stripped Prince Hassan of the title of crown prince. In January 2000 Kabariti resigned his duties in the Royal Court, to be replaced by the former prime minister, Fayiz al-Tarawneh, and returned to his position of chairman of the Jordan Kuwait Bank.

SEE ALSO Bin Shakir, Zayd.

KABBALAH (Kaballah): Word from the Hebrew, *kabbalah,* which signifies "reception, transmission"; used in the Talmud in the sense of "tradition." Also designates the body of Jewish mystical and esoteric commentaries on biblical writings and their oral tradition. With roots in the period of the Second Temple (first century C.E.), Kabbalah, from the thirteenth century on, developed into a distinct doctrine. The basic idea of this mystical teaching, composed in Aramaic, was to attain to knowledge of the infinite based on an analysis of the finite through all of its elements. Born from this principle was Gematria, a branch of numerology that allows an interpretation of the meaning hidden in each word and letter of the Torah. Cabalistic mysticism, based on ecstasy and meditation, exerted a great influence in the Jewish world and also on Christianity during the Renaissance. The significance of the messianic idea in Cabala was emphasized by Isaac Luria (1534–1572), called Ari the Lion. The great schools of Kabbalah were in Provence, France, in the twelfth century; Gerona, Spain, in the thirteenth century; and Safed, Palestine, in the sixteenth century.

SEE ALSO Christianity; Hebrew; Talmud; Torah.

KACH PARTY ("As it is," "thus!," in Hebrew): Israeli ultranationalist movement. At the beginning of 1968 in New York, Rabbi Meir Kahane announced the coming of the messianic era and the constitution of the theocratic state of Judea during the exultation rising out of the Israeli conquest of the West Bank (the Arab-Israel War of 1967). In 1971, after having emigrated to Israel, he created the ultranationalist

Kach Movement, preaching the creation of a Greater Israel, from which the Arabs would be excluded. This movement attracted a few hundred members, mostly of U.S. origin, and had a militia, Ronen (also known as the "Committee of Road Security"), which was under the direction of Baruch Marzel and Tiran Polack.

In July 1984, Kach won two seats at the Knesset, and, in the following September, Rabbi Kahane proposed a draft bill for discrimination between Jews and non-Jews. On 18 October 1988, confronted with their indelibly racist attitudes, the Knesset passed a basic law outlawing any party whose platform contained racist provisions. As a result, Kach was banned from participating in the 1988 elections. Having returned to the United States, Rabbi Kahane was assassinated in New York on 5 November 1990, which brought on a split in the movement. Some members, under the impetus of Baruch Marzel, decided to keep the name of Kach, while others followed the rabbi's son, Binyamin Ze'ev Kahane, who left the party to found Kahane Hai. On 25 February 1994, Dr. Baruch Goldstein, a member of Kach, killed twenty-nine Arabs praying in the Mosque of the Cave of the Patriarchs at Hebron. On the following 13 March, the Israeli Supreme Court declared Kach and Kahane Hai illegal, and several of their members were placed in preventive detention. So as to keep up the activities of Kach, its supporters decided to create a new clandestine movement, Koach. Accused of inciting to rebellion, Baruch Marzel was interrogated by the police, and then sentenced to house arrest. On 15 May 1995, the Israeli minister of the interior dismissed Baruch Marzel from his duties on the municipal council of Kiryat Arba. On 3 October, approximately twenty Kach members, among them Avigdor Askin, gathered in front of the house of Prime Minister Yitzhak Rabin, praying that he die and accusing him of treason for the accords passed with the Palestinians. The prayer was chanted in Aramaic, under the leadership of Rabbi Yosef Dayan. On the following 4 November, Rabin was assassinated by a Jewish extremist belonging to a splinter group close to Kach.

In July 1997, after he had been sentenced to four months of prison for having organized the ceremony of malediction against Rabin, Askin announced the creation of a new extremist movement, the "Camp of Israel." According to his declarations, this movement "aimed at exploding the myth of peace and substituting a military alternative for it. The people of Israel needed to choose between war or the destruction of Israel." In July 2000, while Israeli-Palestinian negotiations were taking place at Camp

David, members of the movement made death threats against Israeli prime minister Ehud Barak. During the following month of October, confronted by the threat of expulsion hanging over the settlers following the Israeli-Palestinian accords, Kach and Kahane Hai decided to join forces. With Kach officially outlawed (though assembly was still tolerated), Marzel ran unsuccessfully for the Knesset in the 2003 general elections on the Herut Party list. In early September 2004, Marzel and other Kach members announced the creation of a new political party—Hil, an acronym for Jewish National Front—dedicated to preventing the removal of Jewish settlements and transferring 2 million Arabs "over the Jordan River."

SEE ALSO Arab-Israel War (1967); Herut Party; Judea and Samaria; Kahane Hai; Kiryat Arba; Koach.

KADESH OPERATION: Operation launched by Israel against Egypt on 29 October 1956.

SEE ALSO Suez Crisis.

KAFR: Arabic word (sometimes spelled *kufr*) meaning "village." The equivalent word in Hebrew is *kfar*.

SEE ALSO Kfar.

KAHAL (pl. *Kehalim*): Hebrew word meaning "a Jewish congregation."

KAHALANI, AVIGDOR (1944–): Israeli politician; minister of public security (June 1996–July 1999). Born in Mandatory Palestine in 1944, Kahalani was a career officer in the Israel Defense Forces, serving in the Arab-Israel War of 1973 and achieving the rank of brigadier general. He was elected to the Knesset in 1992 as a member of the Labor Party, serving on various committees, including Foreign Affairs and Defense, and Education and Culture. One of the founders of the Third Way Party, he led the party in the 1996 Knesset elections. In June 1996 Kahalani was appointed minister of public security, a post he held until July 1999. In 2001 he was acquitted of charges alleging that during his term as minister he had passed information to publisher Ofer Nimrodi regarding a police investigation against him.

KAHANE HAI ("Kahane lives," in Hebrew): Israeli extremist splinter group, formed in 1991, after a split in the Kach Party, following the assassination of its leader, Meir Kahane. The latter's son, Binyamin Ze'ev Kahane, left Kach to found Kahane Hai, which advocated the instauration of a religious state based

BORN IN VIOLENCE. DEMONSTRATORS SUPPORT EL SAYYID NOSSAIR AFTER HE WAS ACQUITTED OF KILLING MEIR KAHANE, FOUNDER OF THE ISRAELI EXTREMIST GROUP KACH, IN 1991. KAHANE'S SON, BINYAMIN ZE'EV KAHANE (WHO WAS KILLED IN 2000), THEN FOUNDED KAHANE HAI, A SPLINTER GROUP THAT ADVOCATES A RELIGIOUS STATE OF ISRAEL AND VIOLENCE AGAINST OPPONENTS. *(AP/Wide World Photos)*

on observance of the Torah. In March 1994, following the slaughter of Muslim worshipers in Hebron by Kach supporter Dr. Baruch Goldstein, this movement was banned by Israeli authorities. Members were arrested by the police, accused of being responsible for the death of a number of Arabs. Subsequent to the assassination of Yitzhak Rabin on 4 November 1995, members demonstrated publicly in approbation of this act. In October 2000, when the Israeli government was at the point of signing new accords with the Palestinians, Kahane Hai and Kach decided to merge in order to oppose them. On the following 31 December, Ze'ev Kahane and his wife were killed in a Palestinian attack on the Jewish settlement of Ofra.

SEE ALSO Kach Party; Torah.

KALAM: Arabic word meaning "speech" or "discourse." In Muslim usage, *kalam Allah* means "the revealed word of God." *'Ilm al-kalam* means "the science of theology."

KARAITE ("Son of the Bible," in Hebrew): A Jew who rejected the oral tradition and rabbinical law, recognizing only a literal interpretation of the texts of the Bible. This religious sect, founded in eighth-century Iraq by Anan Ben David and Yacub Abu Yussef al-Kirkichani, who contested the oral law codified in the Mishna and the Talmud, existed in perfect harmony with the Muslims. In the early twenty-first century, there are about 30,000 Karaites, approximately 9,000 of which are in Israel, mainly settled at Ramla, Beersheba, and Ashod. The Jewish status of Karaites is ambiguous. In Israel, Karaites have the option of holding identity cards that label them either as "Karaite" or "Karaite-Jew."

SEE ALSO Mishna; Talmud.

KARAME, OMAR (1935–): Lebanese political figure, Sunni, born in 1935. Trained in law, Omar Karame became secretary general of the Arab Liberation Party (ALP) in 1970. On 1 June 1987, Lebanon's prime minister, his brother Rashid, was assassinated. A few days later Omar replaced him at the head of the council of Tripoli, then became president of the coordinating committee for North Lebanon. During the month of July he tried vainly to restart the Arab Liberation Party, with the help of the Syrians. In June 1988, he failed to form a parliamentary bloc with the deputies of North Lebanon in support of the candidacy of Sulayman Franjiyya to the presidency of the republic. On 25 November 1989, he became minister of education in the government of Salim al-Hoss. On 24 December 1990, he was named prime minister by the president of the republic, Ilyas al-Hirawi. In May 1991, he was appointed deputy from Tripoli. In March 1992, he was confirmed at his post of prime minister. On the following 6 May, when a general strike protesting the cost of living turned into a riot, he resigned. He was elected as a deputy in the 1992 election, the first since before the civil war (1975–1990), and reelected in 1996 and 2000. In September 2003 he joined a new political grouping, the National Front, a multisectarian alliance of six prominent politicians promoting reform (in 2004, other members included al-Hoss, former house speaker Hussein Hissein, former minister Albert Mansour, Butros Harb, and Nayla Moawad).

SEE ALSO Hoss, Salim al-; Karame, Rashid.

KARAME, RASHID (1921–1987): Lebanese political figure, ten times prime minister, born in 1921 at Miriata in North Lebanon, into a distinguished Sunni Muslim family, died in June 1987. Between 1948 and 1951, having obtained a degree in law from the University of Cairo, Rashid Karame practiced law. Elected deputy in 1951, several times a minister between 1953 and 1955, he became on 19 September 1955 the youngest-ever prime minister of Lebanon. Opposed to certain policies of President Camille Chamoun, he resigned on 19 March of the following year. In October 1958, converted to the reformism of the new president, Fu'ad Shehab, he formed a new government, which he led until 1964, except between May 1960 and October 1961. Head of the Shehabist parliamentary bloc, he supported the election of Charles Helu to the presidency of the republic in 1964. Once again prime minister between 1965 and 1969, he was confronted by the first violent incidents between the Palestinian resistance and the Lebanese state. His resignation led to a stalemate that lasted six months and was only resolved by the accord between the Palestine Liberation Organization (PLO) and the Lebanese authorities, signed in Cairo on 3 November 1969.

The failure of the Shehabists in the elections of 1970 relegated him to the corridors of political power. On 28 May 1975, when the civil war had just broken out in Lebanon, the Palestinians and their allies forced him on President Sulayman Franjiyya as prime minister. Very quickly, he found himself at odds with the Christian camp, which demanded the intervention of the army in the conflict with the Palestinians. In March 1976, Franjiyya stripped him of all portfolios in favor of Chamoun, but Karame did not present his resignation to the new president, Ilyas Sarkis, until September. Not siding unequivocally either with the Syrians or the Palestinians, he found himself progressively losing influence. In July 1983, a year after the invasion of Lebanon by Israel, he joined a pro-Syrian coalition, which allowed him to return to power and become, the following year, prime minister in a government of national reconciliation. In 1986 he failed to persuade President Amin Jumayyil to endorse a truce agreement signed by the leaders, or warlords, of the three largest sectarian militias. Confronted by hostilities between these militias, the "war of the camps" between the Amal and the Palestinians, plus a significant financial crisis, he offered his resignation on 4 May 1987, but it was not accepted. On 1 June Karame was assassinated in an attack that brought down the helicopter returning him to Beirut from Tripoli. His brother, Omar

Karame, succeeded him politically and became prime minister in December 1990.

SEE ALSO Jumayyil, Amin; Karame, Omar.

KARMEL, AL-: A Palestinian literary journal founded in Beirut in 1981 by the poet Mahmud Darwish. It was relocated to Cyprus in 1982 and to Ramallah in 1996. *Al-Karmel* has an international scope, publishing such writers as Russell Banks, J. M. Coetzee and José Saramago, in addition to Arab and Palestinian writers. Unique among Arab publications, it also regularly publishes the work of Israeli authors. It is run by the al-Karmel Cultural Foundation from offices in the Khalil Sakakini Cultural Center in Ramallah. In 2004, the editor is Hassan Khader, although Darwish remains editor-in-chief. In April 2002, the Israeli army entered the Sakakini Center, including the offices of *al-Karmel,* and destroyed files, papers, and equipment as they vandalized the building, while officially seeking those responsible for recent suicide bombings.

SEE ALSO Darwish, Mahmud.

KASHRUT ("purity," in Hebrew): Body of dietary laws, as defined by the Jewish religious law.

KASSAM

SEE Qassam.

KATA'IB

SEE Lebanon.

KATSAV, MOSHE (1945–): Israeli political figure, born in 1945 in Iran, Moshe Katsav arrived in Israel in 1951, when his family settled in the refugee camp of Qiryat Malachi. While he was a student he became a militant in the Gahal. With degrees in agriculture, economics, and history, he became mayor of the city of Qiryat Malachi in 1969. In 1977, he was elected deputy of Likud. Three years later, he was named deputy minister of housing and construction in the government of Menachem Begin, then minister of labor and social affairs in the Begin-Peres National Unity cabinet. Between 1988 and 1992 he was minister of transportation. In 1992, after the electoral victory of the Labor Party, he became leader of the Likud parliamentary bloc in the Knesset. The following year, after having failed in an attempt to become speaker of the Knesset, he was awarded the number two position in the party, after Benjamin Netanyahu. On 18 June 1996, he was named deputy prime minister and minister of tourism in the government of the

latter. During the following month of October, his name was mentioned for the portfolio of Arab affairs. In May 1999, he was reelected Likud member of the Knesset. On 1 August 2000, he became eighth president of the State of Israel, having carried the second ballot of the vote by 63 votes against 57 for his rival, Shimon Peres. Two days later, on Israeli radio, he announced his conviction that the city of Jerusalem should remain under Israeli sovereignty. On the following 22 August, when King Abdullah of Jordan was visiting, he refused to attend the ceremony that took place in Tel Aviv because, in his opinion, it should have been held in Israel's capital, Jerusalem.

SEE ALSO Begin, Menachem; Knesset; Likud; Netanyahu, Benjamin; Peres, Shimon.

KATZ, YISRAEL (1955–), Likud Party member of Knesset. Born in Ashkelon in 1955, Yisrael Katz received a bachelor of arts degree from Hebrew University. First elected to the Knesset in 1998, he served on several committees, including Finance, Constitution, Law and Justice, and Foreign Affairs and Defense. In February 2003 he was appointed minister of agriculture and rural development.

KEDEM (Rainbow of Eastern Democratic Union, in Hebrew): Israeli political party, created on 27 May 1997, by Maxim Levy, advocating secularism in the Sephardi milieu and the revaluation of eastern culture. This bloc attempts to counter the influence of the SHAS religious party in this community.

SEE ALSO SHAS.

KEREN HAYESOD (also Keren ha-Yesod): Fundraising division of the World Zionist Organization (WZO). Jewish foundation fund for amelioration and assistance, created in 1920 as the major fundraising division and financial institution of the WZO. Prior to 1948, Keren Hayesod was involved in financing immigration, housing, and rural settlement. During the Arab-Israel War in 1948, the agency purchased arms for the Jewish military. After the establishment of the State of Israel in 1948, Keren Hayesod focused on economic development in partnership with the private sector. In the United States, the agency functions as part of the United Jewish Appeal, raising funds for immigration and social services in Israel.

KEREN KAYEMET LE-YISRAEL (KKL; Jewish National Fund; Fund for Land Acquisition): Jewish organization founded in 1901, for the purpose of purchasing land in Palestine for new immigrants wanting to settle there. The political and economic role it played in the construction of the State of Israel was primordial. As the owner of much of the land in Israel, the KKL signed, on 1 August 1960, an accord with the government that stipulated that the land is an inalienable national property, not susceptible to ownership, but only held in trust for a period of forty-nine years, as in the biblical Jubilee.

KFAR: Hebrew word often used in Israeli toponymy, meaning "village"; for example, Kfar-Chabad (pop. 4,000). Often the term is applied to places with large populations; for example, Kfar-Saba (pop. 78,000).

KHADR, HUSAM (1961–): Palestinian political figure born in 1961 in Kufr Ruman, near Hebron in the West Bank, to which his family had fled from Jaffa in 1948. After spending his childhood in the Balata refugee camp near Nablus, Husam Khadr joined al-Fatah in 1978. He was arrested by the Israelis twenty-three times and spent a year and a half in an Israeli prison, as well as a year under house arrest. In the first Intifada, he organized several youth groups that participated in the uprising. After being wounded in a demonstration, he was deported to Lebanon in January 1988. In 1990 he was elected to the executive committee of the Palestine Students General Association, and became a member of the Palestine National Council (PNC), the legislative body of the Palestine Liberation Organization (PLO), and was on its political committee. In 1994, under the terms of the Oslo Accords, he returned to the Palestinian territories. In February 1996 he was elected as a deputy from Nablus to the Palestinian Legislative Council (PLC), and was a member of its political and human rights committees. He also worked in the Palestinian Authority (PA)'s Ministry for Youth and Sports, and was the founder and chairman of the Palestinian Refugees' Rights Defense Committee, which undertook a campaign for the right of return of Palestinian refugees.

In the autumn of 2001, when the al-Aqsa Intifada was intensifying, he denounced the PLO/PA leadership for clinging to their belief in the Oslo process and its various offshoots such as the Mitchell Plan, and called the Intifada a "blessing" for countering Palestinian despair and humiliation. He has been Yasir Arafat's severest critic, denouncing him as corrupt and undemocratic, and calling his cabinet "a bunch of thieves." Khadr was represented widely in the media as a member of a new generation of Palestinian leaders likely to take over from Arafat and his

group. When Israel reoccupied the West Bank cities in 2002, Khadr went into hiding. In March 2003, occupation troops attacked his home in the Balata camp and arrested him, confiscating his computer and files and destroying the contents of his home. He has been imprisoned under extremely harsh conditions ever since, while being "investigated" for "jeopardizing the region's safety" and "engaging in militant activities against Israeli targets."

SEE ALSO Aqsa Intifada, al-; Arafat, Yasir; Fatah, al-; Hebron; Palestine Liberation Organization; Palestine National Council; Palestinian Authority; Palestinian Legislative Council; West Bank.

KHALAF, SALAH (Abu Iyad; 1933–1991): Palestinian, born 31 August 1933 in Jaffa. In 1948 Khalaf and his family took refuge in Gaza, where he joined a paramilitary youth group associated with the Muslim Brotherhood. In 1952, when a student at the University of Cairo, he made the acquaintance of Yasir Arafat and Khalil al-Wazir (Abu Jihad) at the General Union of Palestinian Students, becoming Arafat's deputy and eventually president of the organization. After earning degrees in philosophy and psychology, as well as a teacher's diploma, he decided to devote himself to the Palestinian cause. He returned to Gaza in 1957 to teach, and in 1959 to Kuwait. In October of that year, he participated with Arafat, Wazir, Faruk Qaddumi, and Khalid al-Hasan in the creation of al-Fatah, within which he was responsible for the "mobilization of the masses." From 1960 to 1970 he traveled widely to various Arab countries in the Middle East, as well as to Germany, to sensitize young Palestinians and to win support from the leaders of these countries. At the end of 1967, he was named head of internal security, intelligence, and counterintelligence in the Palestine Liberation Organization (PLO). He was often charged with advocating al-Fatah's positions to the more radical members of the PLO, the Popular Front for the Liberation of Palestine (PFLP) and the Democratic Front for the Liberation of Palestine (DFLP); he was also to some extent their advocate within al-Fatah, protecting them against the hostility of the more conservative members of the leadership.

Although Khalaf advocated peace with Jordanian authorities, they held him largely responsible for the events of Black September 1970, and that month arrested him and sentenced him to death. Egyptian president Gamal Abdel Nasser intervened personally to have him released. He is believed to have created in July 1971 in Lebanon, with Ali Hassan al-Salama, an operational group called Black September, whose object it was to avenge the death of the Palestinian freedom fighters (*fida'iyyun*) killed in Jordan the previous year. In November 1973, he was one of the first Palestinian leaders to advocate the two-state solution, with the establishment of a democratic, secular Palestinian state in the West Bank and Gaza. In October 1974, he was arrested by Moroccan authorities as he prepared an assassination attempt against King Hussein of Jordan, expected shortly in Rabat for an Arab League summit. In July 1981, he was named head of the security departments of al-Fatah and the PLO. In carrying out these functions he was assisted by Khalil al-Wazir, Hayel Abdul Hamid, and Amin al-Hindi (Abu Zuhayr). In this capacity he met often with many leaders of Arab and Western special services; he is said to have supplied them with information about attacks planned by other Palestinian organizations, particularly that of Abu Nidal (Sabri al-Banna), the Fatah Revolutionary Council.

In 1982, when the PLO was forced to leave Lebanon, for the sake of unity in the Palestinian movement, and wanting to remain loyal to Yasir Arafat, he refused to make common cause with al-Fatah and PLO dissidents. Just prior to then he had been to Moscow, asking the mediation of the USSR in resolving the differences between Syria and the PLO. In 1988, when the first Intifada was intensifying in the occupied territories, Khalaf participated in coordinating activities in the West Bank. During the crisis leading to the Gulf War of 1991, Khalaf dissented from the PLO position of support for Iraq, and criticized Saddam Hussein. In the night of 14–15 January 1991, Khalaf and Hayel Abdul Hamid were assassinated in Tunis by a bodyguard who was an agent of the Abu Nidal group, possibly at the behest of Hussein. The death of Khalaf, who was very popular in the Palestinian community, was a heavy blow to the Palestinian central command, and especially to its leader, Arafat. A man of action, and also admired for his intellect, entrusted frequently with the most delicate missions, Khalaf was considered to be Arafat's second in command.

SEE ALSO Arafat, Yasir; Black September 1970; Democratic Front for the Liberation of Palestine; Fatah, al-; Fatah Revolutionary Council; Hindi, Amin al-; Hussein, Saddam; League of Arab States; Palestine Liberation Organization; Popular Front for the Liberation of Palestine; Wazir, Khalil al-; West Bank.

KHALED, LAYLA (1944–): Palestinian activist, born in January 1944 at Haifa. Layla Khaled fled Palestine for Lebanon with her family during the Arab-Israel War of 1948. In 1962 she entered the American University of Beirut, where she joined the Arab Nationalist Movement (ANM). In 1963 she went to Kuwait to teach, and after the Arab defeat in the June 1967 War she joined the Popular Front for the Liberation of Palestine (PFLP) of George Habash. After paramilitary training in Jordan, she led a commando in hijacking a TWA plane from Rome to Tel Aviv, via Athens, on 30 August 1969. During this flight she made the pilot fly over Haifa, so she could see the hometown she was not allowed to visit. The commandos forced the plane to land at Damascus, allowed the passengers to leave, then blew up the airplane. In exchange for the life of the hostages, thirteen Palestinian prisoners were released. Overnight Khaled become a heroine of the Palestinian resistance; her face was so recognizable that she had plastic surgery to disguise it. On 6 September 1970, she participated in a second hijacking, this time of an El Al plane flying between Amsterdam and London. This hijacking was foiled by Israeli guards, who shot her accomplice, and she was arrested when the plane landed in the British capital. Imprisoned for three weeks, she was released as part of a prisoner-hostage exchange deal with another PFLP group that had hijacked three airliners to a remote airstrip in Jordan. Between 1971 and 1978 she participated in various activities in the PFLP. In July 1980 she was part of the Palestinian delegation that went to Copenhagen to attend the United Nations world conference on women. In April 1981, she was elected to the Palestine National Council (PNC), representing the General Union of Palestinian Women. Opposed to the Israeli-Palestinian Oslo Accords, she has lived in Jordan since 1992. Khaled is a member of the central committee of the PFLP and has devoted much of her time to the cause of Palestinian women and of the refugees.

SEE ALSO Arab-Israel War (1948); Arab Nationalist Movement; Popular Front for the Liberation of Palestine; Oslo Accords; Palestine National Council.

KHALIDI, HUSAYN FAKHRI AL-: Palestinian political figure (1894–1962) from a Jerusalem notable family with a tradition of scholarship and public service. Educated as a medical doctor at Beirut and Istanbul, he served in the Ottoman army during World War I but left it to join the Arab Revolt. He served in the department of health of the Syrian government of Emir Faysal ibn Husayn al-Hashem until Faysal was expelled by the French. He held a similar post in the mandatory government of Palestine from 1921 to 1934. From 1934 to 1937 he was mayor of Jerusalem, the last mayor to be elected in the undivided city. In 1935 Khalidi founded a political party, the Reform Party (*Hizb al-Islah*). In 1936 he was a member of the Arab Higher Committee, formed to coordinate the activities of that spring's general strike (that evolved into the Palestine Arab Revolt [1936–1939]). In 1937 Khalidi was deported to the Seychelles Islands by the British for his political activities, although he was allowed to take part in the London Conference of 1939. In 1946 he joined the reconstituted Arab Higher Committee. After the Arab-Israel War (1948), the West Bank was annexed by Jordan, and Khalidi served in the Jordanian government. He was foreign minister in 1953 and 1955, and very briefly prime minister in 1957. Afterward he retired to Jericho where he wrote commentary for a Jerusalem newspaper and also wrote two books, *The Arab Exodus* (*al-Khuruj al-Arabi*) and an unpublished autobiography.

SEE ALSO Arab Higher Committee; Arab-Israel War (1948); West Bank.

KHALIL, AL-: Arabic name for the city of Hebron, meaning "the Friend." This is a reference to the Biblical patriarch Abraham, whose tomb is believed to be located in the city. Abraham is known in sacred Muslim literature as "the Friend of God" or "the Friend of the Merciful" (*Ibrahim al-Khalil al-Rahman*).

SEE ALSO Hebron.

KHATIB, GHASSAN (1954–): Palestinian politician, born 1954 in Nablus. Educated at Bir Zeit University and Manchester and Durham Universities in Britain. Khatib was active in the Palestinian National Front (PNF), a militant organization created by the Jordanian Communist Party in the West Bank, and as a result was jailed by the Israeli authorities from 1974 to 1977. He has worked as a lecturer at Bir Zeit University and was a member of the Palestinian delegation to the Madrid Conference in 1991, as well as a participant in the direct Israeli-Palestinian negotiations of 1991–1993. He has served on the boards of the Arab Development Center (an agricultural organization), the Democracy and Worker's Rights Center, and the Friends Schools in Palestine, and is on the editorial board of the *Israel-Palestine Journal,* which publishes Palestinian and Israeli perspectives on political issues. He is a cofounder and codirector of *Bitter Lemons,* a Palestinian-Israeli Internet-based political magazine. Khatib is director of the Jerusa-

lem Media and Communications Center, which conducts opinion polls and provides support to journalists in the West Bank and Gaza Strip. He is also director of the Institute of Modern Media at Al-Quds University in Jerusalem. An active member of the Palestinian People's Party (PPP), he was appointed Minister of Labor in the PNA in 2002. He has published many articles of political commentary and analysis.

SEE ALSO Bir Zeit University; Gaza Strip; Madrid Conference; Palestinian National Front; Palestinian People's Party; West Bank.

KHUTBA: Arabic word designating the sermon pronounced by the imam, who conducts the Muslim Friday prayer service.

KIBBUTZ (pl. *kibbutzim*; Hebrew for "gathering"): Jewish collective farm, from which all notions of salary and property are excluded. Originally, the land was rented by the Keren Kayemet le-Yisrael and necessary capital was advanced by the Keren Ha-Yessod. The first kibbutz in Palestine was established in 1910 at Deganya, near Tiberias. In a few years there were twenty-five of them, making the kibbutz the principal element in the Jewish population of Palestine before 1948. Attracting people who were totally imbued with Zionist-Socialist ideals, it played a notable role in the creation of the State of Israel. Traditionally, each kibbutz has been socially and economically autonomous. Yet, kibbutzim commonly belong to movements with political affiliations that provide them with services. Kibbutz members and kibbutzim served as solid role models for Israeli youth. Many kibbutz members became political leaders. Over the years, the kibbutz has diminished in significance, due in part to a growing desire of parents to be the primary socializers of their children, with increased educational aspirations for them, as well as the increased industrialization of the larger Israeli society.

SEE ALSO Keren Kayemet le-Yisrael.

KIMCHE, DAVID (1928–): Israeli intelligence officer and diplomat. Born in London in 1928, David Kimche immigrated to Israel in 1948. He received a doctorate from Hebrew University and later worked as a journalist for the *Jerusalem Post.* In 1953 Kimche joined the Mossad, Israel's foreign intelligence service, working in Paris under cover as a journalist. He rose in Mossad's ranks, becoming deputy director under Yitzhak Hofi. Kimche left the Mossad in 1980 after a disagreement over policy concerning Lebanon. Under Israeli prime minister Menachem Begin,

KIBBUTZ YAVNE. VOLUNTEERS FROM OVERSEAS HELP WITH THE APPLE HARVEST IN 1970. ISRAEL EXPORTS SIGNIFICANT AMOUNTS OF CITRUS FRUITS, EGGS, AND PROCESSED FOODS, WITH A SIZABLE PORTION OF THE COUNTRY'S CROPS PRODUCED BY COLLECTIVE FARMS LIKE THIS ONE. (© Ted Spiegel/Corbis)

Kimche was appointed director-general of the Foreign Ministry. He served as chief Israeli delegate at Khalde, Lebanon, in December 1982, at the talks with Lebanon and the United States after Israel's 1982 invasion of Lebanon. After his retirement in 1987, Kimche lectured and authored several books, including *The Last Option* (1991).

KINGS OF JORDAN

SEE Abdullah I ibn Hussein; Abdullah II ibn Hussein; Hashim, al-; Hussein ibn Talal; Talal of ibn Abdullah.

KIRYAT ARBA (*Qiryat Arba;* "City of the Four," in Hebrew): Name of the sepulcher that contains the remains of the great patriarchs of Israel (Tomb of the Patriarchs). Biblical tradition identifies this place with the city of the Hebron. This name is also that of a Jewish settlement on the outskirts of Hebron known for its militant leadership and commitment

to the extension of Jewish sovereignty over disputed territories. Under the 1997 Hebron Agreement, Kiryat Arba retained a link to the site of the Tomb of the Patriarchs in Hebron, while the rest of the city of Hebron was transferred to the Palestinian Authority as part of the Oslo Accords.

SEE ALSO Hebron.

KIRYAT SHMONA: A city in northern Israel, Kiryat Shmona was founded in 1949 on the site of the Arab village of Helsa. Its names means "town of the eight," commemorating Zionist Joseph Trumpeldor, who was killed with seven others in a battle against Arab Palestinians at Tel Hai in 1920. The city had a population of approximately 21,000 in 2003. In April 1974, Kiryat Shmona was the site of a suicide raid by members of the Popular Front for the Liberation of Palestine–General Command, who entered an apartment building, killing all eighteen Israeli civilians who were in the building. Prior to the Arab-Israel

War of 1982, Kiryat Shmona's location, less than 3 miles (5 kilometers) from the border with Lebanon, made it the frequent target of rockets fired from southern Lebanon by Palestinian militants.

SEE ALSO Arab-Israel War (1982).

KNESSET: Hebrew word meaning "assembly." A unicameral parliament, the Knesset is the legislative assembly of the State of Israel. Its name recalls the great legislative assembly of the epoch of the Second Temple, destroyed in 70 C.E. Created in January 1949, the Knesset met for the first time in Tel Aviv, then it was moved to Jerusalem. At the beginning it was supposed to be a constitutional assembly, but the religious parties opposed this, arguing that the Jewish people could have only one supreme law, that of the Torah. The powers of the Knesset were then established by the Basic Law of 1958, amended in 1986, and completed in 1992. Renewed every four years, the Knesset consists of 120 deputies, members chosen wholly on the basis of proportional representation, through a ballot list of candidates, which allows any minority to have at least one representative. To be represented, a party needs only 1.5 percent of the votes cast. The Basic Law, amended in 1992, established a new electoral system, effective for the elections of 29 May 1996. For the first time, Israelis chose, by separate ballots, both the future government leader (prime minister) and the MKs (Knesset members) who would represent them in the Knesset.

In June 1996, when the Likud leader Benjamin Netanyahu became prime minister, having narrowly defeated the Labor Party's Shimon Peres, the composition of the Knesset was as follows: Labor Party: 34 seats; Likud-Tsomet-Gesher Bloc: 32 (Likud: 22, Gesher: 5, and Tsomet: 5); SHAS: 10; Meretz: 9; NRP: 9; Israel be Aliyah: 7; Hadash: 5; United Torah Judaism: 4; United Arab List: 4; Third Way: 4; Moledet: 2. The new electoral reform had produced an anomalous situation in which the left, which had won 53 seats, found itself in the opposition, while the right, which had only 43, but whose candidate for prime minister had been elected, was in power. In the 1999 elections, Netanyahu was soundly defeated by Labor's Ehud Barak (as head of the One Israel coalition), with Barak receiving 56 percent of the vote to Netanyahu's 44 percent. In the Knesset, 26 seats went to One Israel and 19 to Likud. Following Barak's defeat by Ariel Sharon in the prime ministerial election of 2001, Likud regained its prominence. In the 2003 Knesset elections (which abandoned the separate ballot for prime minister instituted in 1996), Likud received 29 percent of the vote (37 seats); the

Labor-Meimad coalition received 14.5 percent (19 seats). The remaining seats were distributed as follows: Shinui: 15; SHAS: 11; National Unity: 7; Meretz: 6; National Religious Party: 6; Torah and Shabbat Judaism: 5; Hadash: 3; Am Ehad: 3; National Democratic Assembly: 3; Israel be Aliyah: 2; United Arab List: 2.

SEE ALSO Netanyahu, Benjamin; Torah.

KOACH ("force, strength," in Hebrew): Israeli ultranationalist clandestine movement, created in March 1994, to replace the Kach Party banned by Israeli authorities.

SEE ALSO Kach Party.

KOLLEK, TEDDY (1911–): Israeli politician; mayor of Jerusalem (1965–1993). Born in Hungary, Teddy Kollek moved to Mandatory Palestine in 1934. He was recruited in 1942 by the Jewish Agency to serve as an intelligence officer in Istanbul. After returning from Istanbul, he continued to work for the intelligence branch of the Jewish Agency, procuring arms, primarily in the United States, for the Zionist movement. Following the creation of the State of Israel, he returned to the United States to work in the Israeli embassy, then in 1949 was made head of the United States desk of the Foreign Ministry. From 1952 to 1964 Kollek was director general of the prime minister's office. Kollek first ran for mayor of Jerusalem as representative of the new Rafi Party in 1965. As mayor, following the Arab-Israel War of 1967, he worked toward the unification of Jerusalem, including overtures to the Palestinian population. In 1988 he received the Israel Prize. During his later years in office, Kollek was criticized for devoting more attention to the development of Jewish Jerusalem than to Palestinian Jerusalem. He was defeated in 1993 by Likud candidate Ehud Olmert.

KOL YISRAEL ("Voice of Israel," in Hebrew): Name of Israeli state radio, established in 1948. Kol Yisrael was government controlled until 1965, when it was replaced by the Israel Broadcasting Authority, a public, nongovernmental body broadcasting in Hebrew and Arabic.

KOSHER ("suitable, apt," in Hebrew): Term describing food that is authorized by Jewish religious law. In general, only the meat of herbivorous animals slaughtered by cutting their throats and drained of their blood is considered suitable for consumption. Scaly fish and ruminants with cleft hoofs are also permitted, although pork, an omnivorous animal, is thought of as a carnivore and, therefore, forbidden. It is forbidden to mix meat and milk or meat and milk products. Equivalent to the Muslim *halal*.

SEE ALSO Halal.

KOTEL

SEE Western Wall Disturbances.

KRAV MAGA (Hebrew for "contact combat"): Kind of martial art taught in the Israeli army.

KREI, AHMED

SEE Qurai, Ahmad Sulayman.

KUFIYYA: A cotton white-and-red or white-and-black headscarf traditionally worn by Arabian, Iraqi, Jordanian, Syrian, and Palestinian peasants and Bedouins. In the 1930s the kufiyya became a symbol of Palestinian national sentiment. Peasants largely led the 1936–1939 revolt, and men in cities were discouraged from wearing the Turkish fez and the Western fedora. It became a nationalist act to wear a kufiyya. It has since become the symbol of the Palestinian cause. Yasir Arafat has made it an internationally recognized icon, wearing it on all occasions.

KUFR

SEE Kafr.

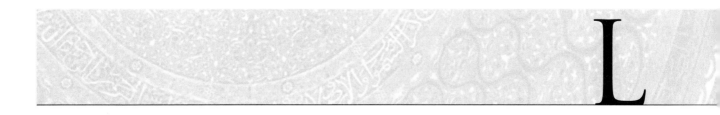

LABIB, ABDULLAH ABD AL-HAMID

SEE Hawari Group.

LABOR PARTY

SEE Israel Labor Party.

LADEN, OSAMA IBN

SEE Bin Ladin, Osama.

LADINO (also called Spanyol or Judezmo): Judeo-Spanish dialect, used by the Sephardim—Jews who settled in the Ottoman Empire and the Maghrib (North Africa) after their 1492 expulsion from Spain. The language makes use of significant Hebrew and Aramaic vocabulary, while its written form uses Hebrew characters. In the nineteenth and early twentieth centuries, Ladino was the primary language of learning among Jews in the Ottoman Empire. In modern times, Ladino has largely been forgotten due to language policies of the post–World War I Republic of Turkey, the significant destruction of Balkan Jewry during World War II, and the migration of most of North African and Levantine Jews to Israel, Spain, South America, and France.

SEE ALSO Ottomans.

LAG B'OMER: Name of a Jewish holiday that is celebrated each May at Meron, near Safed in Galilee, where the tomb of the great Kabbalist, Rabbi Shimon bar Yochai, is located. "Lag" is not actually a word, but it stands for the number 33 in Hebrew. Lag B'Omer takes place on the thirty-third day within a seven-week countdown from the second night of Passover to the day before Shavuot. Every night during this period, Jews recite a blessing and state the count of the *omer* (a unit of measure used in the early days of the temple) in both weeks and days. The countdown itself is a reminder of the connection between Passover, which commemorates the exodus from Egypt, and Shavuot, which commemorates the giving of the Torah, and that redemption from slavery was not complete until Jews received the Torah. During this time of partial mourning, weddings and parties with dancing are forbidden, as are haircuts.

The thirty-third day of the Omer—called the eighteenth of Omer—is celebrated as Lag B'Omer, a holiday to celebrate a break among the deaths of the Torah scholar Rabbi Akiva's 24,000 students by plague. All mourning practices are lifted on this day. In Israel and throughout the diaspora, family and communal picnics, ballgames, and mock bow-and-arrow fights mark the holiday. Also common is the lighting of bonfires, around which signing and dancing take place. Tens of thousands of Jews gather at Meron, the burial place of Rabbi Shimon bar Yochai and his son, Rabbi Elazar ben Shimon. Many parents hold off on cutting their sons' hair until the age of three, and then they do so on Lag B'Omer at the burial place in Meron.

SEE ALSO Diaspora; Iyar.

LAHAD, ANTOINE: Lebanese general, Christian Maronite, born in 1927 at Kfar al'Katra, in the Shuf. Antoine Lahad joined the Lebanese army as an infantry officer in 1948. Between 1954 and 1958 he was assistant to the head of the Deuxième Bureau (military intelligence) and vice commander of the South Lebanon region. In 1966, he was interim head of intelligence for a few months. Four years later, Lahad studied at the general staff school in Paris, and, between 1971 and 1975, was assistant commander, then commander of the Baqaa region of Lebanon. Meanwhile he was following a course of studies at the Ecole Supérieure de Guerre, in Paris. In 1978 Lahad was named brigadier general and assigned to reserve status two months later.

In 1981 Lahad resumed serving and in the following year, participated in the fighting triggered by the Israeli invasion of Lebanon. The Lebanese army, which had been much weakened by desertions during the civil war, functioned in effect as a Christian militia, tacitly supporting the Israelis and their allies in the Lebanese Forces by fighting mainly against the AMAL and Iranian Revolutionary Guards (Pasdaran). During 1983, as the government reorganized the army, Lahad resigned his commission. On 3 April 1984 he was recruited by Israel to become the commander of its proxy force, the South Lebanon Army (SLA), replacing Sa'd Haddad, who had died a few weeks earlier. During the night of 7–8 November 1988, Lahad was wounded in an assassination attempt carried out by a young Lebanese woman, Suha Beshara, a member of the Lebanese Communist Party. He was evacuated to Israel, where he received medical care for a few months. The following year, he traveled to Germany to receive further care, but one arm remained paralyzed. On 17 January 1996 Lahad went to Israel and was received by Shimon Peres, who assured him of the support of Israel. On 23 January Lahad was indicted in absentia by the Lebanese military tribunal for "dealings with the enemy," an accusation that made him liable for the sentence of death. On 6 December of the same year, Lahad was condemned to death, also in absentia, by the same tribunal. At the end of May 2000, following the definitive withdrawal of the Israeli army from South Lebanon and the disbanding of the SLA, Lahad took refuge in Israel. General Lahad belonged to the National Liberal Party (NLP) of Camille Chamoun.

EMILE LAHOUD. YEARS AFTER REORGANIZING THE LEBANESE ARMED FORCES, GENERAL LAHOUD WAS ELECTED PRESIDENT OF LEBANON IN 1998. LAHOUD, WHO SUPPORTS TIES WITH SYRIA, FACED OPPOSITION AND DISCONTENT OVER THE NEXT SIX YEARS. (© 2001 by Jacques Lengevin/ Corbis Sygma)

SEE ALSO AMAL; Lebanese Forces; Pasdaran; Peres, Shimon; South Lebanon; South Lebanon Army.

LAHHUD, EMILE (1936–): Lebanese military and political figure, born in 1936, at B'abda. Emile Lahhud was descended from a family of Lebanese notables, Maronite in confession. His father, Jamal Lahhud, a military officer and labor minister in the presidency of Charles Helu, was nicknamed "the red general," for having legalized the leftist unions.

In 1959 Lahhud entered the military academy of Fayadiyeh. After choosing the navy, he studied for a few semesters abroad: first in Great Britain, where he obtained a degree in naval engineering, then later in France and the United States. In 1980 he was named military staff director in the Lebanese defense ministry. Two years later, under the mandate of President Amin Jumayyil, he was promoted general. In 1984 Lahhud became chief of staff of the defense minister, Adel Osseiran. In September 1988 the interim prime minister, General Michel Aoun, renamed him to this post. A year later, dismissed from his functions, Lahhud rejoined the general staff, President Ilyas al-Hirawi naming him, on 28 November, commander-in-chief of the Lebanese army. This nomination came shortly before Aoun was dismissed from his post as the head of the Lebanese armies. As commander-in-chief, Lahhud undertook a complete re-organization of the Lebanese armed forces, in the hope that they would become a factor in national unification. Having established religious parity within units, he made attempts to reduce political obtrusion into military affairs. At the beginning of 1991, his relations with the defense minister, Ilyas al-Murr, began to deteriorate, and in August 1992, he interdicted military participation in the legislative election campaigns. Supported by the army chief-of-staff, Hikmat Shehabi, his relations with the new Lebanese defense minister, Mohsen Dalloul, improved, and he made attempts to be on good terms with the new Lebanese prime minister, Rafiq Baha'uddin al-Hariri. He was successful also in winning the backing of a majority of the members of the high military council.

On 31 January, 1993 Lahhud went to Damascus, where he was welcomed by President Hafiz al-Asad. Confident because of this support, he did not hesitate to confront the Lebanese prime minister, whom he reproached for relying on internal security forces (ISF), to the detriment of the army. Favoring good relations between Syria and Lebanon, Lahhud worked to improve cooperation between the Lebanese and Syrian general staffs. In April 1994, when he was planning to compete in the presidential election of 1996, the council of ministers voted unanimously to prolong his tenure as the head of the Lebanese army for two years, allowing him to keep his post until the vote. President Hirawi was also a candidate, and relations between the two men deteriorated. The crisis reached its apogee in November 1995, at which time the mandate of President Hirawi was renewed. Three years later, benefiting from the open support of Asad, Lahhud was elected president with 118 of the 128 votes in the Chamber of Deputies—the others, followers of Walid Kamal Jumblatt, boycotted the election. As soon as he entered office, he came up against the opposition of the prime minister, Rafiq Baha'uddin al-Hariri. The latter, when asked by the Chamber of Deputies to stay on in his position, refused to form a new government. Thirty-one deputies then decided to leave the choice of whether or not to renew Hariri as prime minister to the new president. Citing the principle of parity, whereby the president could not himself designate the prime minister, Hariri resigned, replaced by

Salim al-Hoss. There were delays in President Lahhud's effecting the economic reforms expected by the Lebanese population, which resulted in general discontent. In 1999 Lahhud ordered security forces to storm college campuses to stop anti-Syrian demonstrations.

On 3 September 2000, the failure of a number of his supporters in the legislative elections, and the brilliant victory of Hariri's slate in Beirut, weakened Lahhud's position considerably in relation to Hariri and Jumblatt, and Hariri once again became prime minister. In October 2000, Lahhud was scheduled to give a speech at the League of Arab States summit in Cairo, but because President Bashshar al-Asad was late in giving his approval, Lahhud was unable to speak. In 2001 Lahhud found it necessary to execute another campaign of suppression against anti-Syrian nationalists. His prospects for reelection in 2004 were said to be slim.

SEE ALSO Aoun, Michel; Asad, Bashshar al-; Asad, Hafiz al-; Hariri, Rafiq Baha'uddin al-; Hoss, Salim al-; Jumayyil, Amin; Jumblatt, Walid Kamal; League of Arab States.

LAILAT AL-QADR: Muslim holiday, celebrated on 27 Ramadan, commemorating the night of Qur'anic revelation.

SEE ALSO Ramadan.

LAND FOR PEACE: Basic principle of the Israeli-Arab peace process, which first emerged in Resolution 242 and later in discussions surrounding Resolution 338 of the United Nations Security Council. Demands were made that Israel withdraw from "the territories" it had been occupying since 1967 (the Arab-Israel War) as the Arab countries were ready to make peace on condition that Israel restore the lands it occupied. The concept was incorporated into the Madrid Conference on the Middle East in October 1991.

SEE ALSO Arab-Israel War (1967); Madrid Conference; Resolution 242; Resolution 338.

LAND OF ISRAEL

SEE Eretz Yisrael.

LAPID, YOSEF "TOMMY" (1931–): Israeli politician. Born as Tomislav Lampel in Novi Sad, on the border of Hungary and Yugoslavia, Yosef "Tommy" Lapid immigrated with his mother to Israel in 1948, after his father was abducted and murdered by Nazis. A journalist by profession, who also holds a law degree, Lapid first came to public attention as a regular panelist on the talk show *Pop-Politika*. There, he would verbally attack political guests and even fellow journalists, actions that gave him a reputation for being outspoken. In March 1999, the then-sixty-eight-year-old was approached by Shinui Party leader Avraham Poraz to take his place as party head in the Knesset. Under Lapid, the party stressed its opposition to ultra-Orthodox parties and legislation. Lapid has served on various committees, including Foreign Affairs and Defense, Constitution, Law and Justice, and the Parliamentary Inquiry Committee for the Location and Restitution of Property of Holocaust Victims. In February 2003, Lapid gained greater popularity as the appointed minister of justice and deputy prime minister. Some commentators considered him a rival to Ariel Sharon, particularly after allegations of corruption were leveled against Sharon in early 2003.

SEE ALSO Sharon, Ariel.

LARF

SEE Lebanese Armed Revolutionary Faction.

LASHON HA-KODESH ("The holy tongue," in Hebrew): A mixture of Hebrew and Aramaic used in prayer books and holy texts read by all Jews. The term is also used as a name for the classical Hebrew language in ways that emphasize its ancient, holy aspects, rather than its modern incarnations.

LAVON AFFAIR: Political crisis in Israel that eventually led to the resignation of Prime Minister David Ben-Gurion in 1963. The crisis was sparked by what the Israeli press called the "mishap." In 1954, under orders from Colonel Benjamin Gibli (Givly), head of the Intelligence Division of the Israel Defense Forces, a group of Israeli-trained Egyptian Jews were instructed to detonate firebombs in U.S. and British institutions in Cairo and Alexandria, in order to disrupt negotiations on the evacuation of British troops from bases along the Suez Canal. The group was captured by Egyptian security services; two of the leaders were sentenced and hanged, one of the Israeli spies committed suicide in prison, and the others were sentenced to long prison terms. Gibli claimed he had received orders from Pinhas Lavon, who was replacing David Ben-Gurion as minister of defense. A committee of inquiry could not reach a decision on the matter, and both Gibli and Lavon resigned their posts. Four years later, the commander of the special unit in charge of the Egypt operation disclosed that one of the documents presented to the committee had been forged. Gibli admitted to the forgery but claimed that, having received oral orders from Lavon, he had no other recourse to avoid assuming all blame for the incident.

Ben-Gurion insisted on a judicial investigation, while Lavon, then secretary-general of the Histradut (the powerful trade-union umbrella organization), demanded a public exoneration from Ben-Gurion. The incident split not only the Labor Party, but the entire country. Levi Eshkol, then minister of finance, asked Pinhas Rosen, minister of justice, to lead a committee of investigation, which ruled that Lavon had not ordered the operation and that the document had been forged. Ben-Gurion nevertheless insisted on Lavon's resignation of his post at the Histradut. Ben-Gurion's position damaged his already eroding support, and he resigned in June 1963. Eshkol replaced him as prime minister and minister of defense.

SEE ALSO Ben-Gurion, David; Eshkol, Levi; Histradut.

LAW OF RETURN (*Hoq ha-Shvut*, in Hebrew): Passed by the Knesset on 5 July 1950, this Israeli law allowed Jewish immigrants to settle in Israel and obtain Israeli citizenship. On the underlying premise that Israel is a Jewish state and the state of the Jews, the law provides that a Jew is entitled to immigrate to Israel and received the status of *oleh*, an immigrant with automatic citizenship. In 1954, the law was amended to exclude individuals with a criminal past that might endanger public welfare. Citizenship rights were extended to non-Jewish spouses and children of Jews in a 1970 amendment. The law and its amendments have stirred up many debates between Jews and Palestinians, who regard the law as discriminatory, as well as among Jews in Israel and the diaspora. The Law of Return brings into question the definitions of Jewish identity, and there have been periodic calls for the law's repeal from those who believe Israel should hold only to laws that do not discriminate on the basis of religion or ethnicity.

SEE ALSO Diaspora.

LAWRENCE, T. E. (called Lawrence of Arabia, 1888–1935): British soldier, adventurer, and writer, Thomas Edward Lawrence was born on 16 August 1888 at Tremadoc, in Wales, and died in 1935. Early in life, Lawrence became interested in archaeology, which he then studied at Oxford. Under the influence of Professor George D. Hogarth, he specialized in the history of the Middle East. In 1909, after a study trip to Palestine and Syria, he wrote a brilliant thesis on medieval military architecture. Between 1910 and

LAWRENCE OF ARABIA. THE ENIGMATIC BRITISH OFFICER T. E. LAW-RENCE HELPED COORDINATE THE ARAB REVOLT AGAINST THE TURKS DURING WORLD WAR I. ARDENTLY, BUT FUTILELY, ADVOCATING ARAB CAUSES AT THE PEACE CONFERENCE AT VERSAILLES, HE BECAME EMBITTERED BY BRITISH POLICIES IN THE MIDDLE EAST AND SOUGHT OBSCURITY AS A PSEUDONYMOUS SOLDIER—EVEN WHILE GAINING NEW FAME FOR HIS WRITINGS ON ISLAM AND THE ARABS.

1914 he participated in numerous archaeological expeditions in Syria, Palestine, and Mesopotamia, led by Professor Hogarth, and accompanied by Leonard Woolley and R. Campbell Thompson. Lawrence was associated with a number of archaeological discoveries, including some at the site of Karkemish, in Syria. During his travels he formed close ties with members of nationalist movements, particularly with the councils of Armenian and Kurdish revolutionary forces, and he wrote a number of reports on the political situation in these countries.

In January 1914, in his capacity of reserve officer, Lawrence joined the cartographic service of the British army, where he was responsible for establishing an accurate cartography of the Sinai and Syria. In December he was assigned to the military and political intelligence section (MPI), based in Cairo, and

headed by Ronald Storrs. In May 1916, still in Cairo, he was assigned to the Arab Bureau, headed by his former director of archaeological research, Professor Hogarth. On 6 June, Sherif ibn Husayn unleashed the "great revolt" against the Ottoman Empire, placing his Arab troops under the command of his three sons, Ali, Abdullah, and Faisal. In the following October he participated actively in numerous Arab attacks against Turkish troops, allowing the right flank of the British expeditionary force in Palestine to disengage and open the way to the liberation of a part of the Hijaz. Promoted to the rank of major, Lawrence was recommended for the British Order of Bath, and cited for the Order of the French Army. On 11 December 1917, he accompanied Edmund Henry Allenby in the official entrance of British troops into Jerusalem. From January to September 1918, he led a few of the attacks against Turkish positions defending the Hijaz railroad. On 1 October 1918, after entering Damascus in triumph, alongside of the Emir Faisal, Lawrence decided to leave the Middle East and return to England. During January 1919, he accompanied Emir Faisal, who had come to Versailles, at the peace conference. At this meeting, he ardently defended the Arab points-of-view. On 9 March, the American journalist, Lowell Thomas, organized a conference on Lawrence, whom he called "Lawrence of Arabia," and introduced him to the American and British public. In May, Lawrence went to Egypt, to be demobilized. Returning to London, he stayed with Sir Herbert Baker, where he worked on his *Seven Pillars of Wisdom.*

In March 1921, Lawrence became Arab affairs counselor in the British ministry of colonies, headed by Winston Churchill, and, in this capacity, participated in the Cairo conference that year. In October, he was named counselor to Prince Abdullah of Transjordan. On 3 July 1922, confronted by the hostility of Emir Husayn and his sons, who accused him of not having kept his promises of the creation of a "Great Arab empire," he left Transjordan, where he was replaced for a time by Harry St. John Philby. Disappointed in the British policies in the Middle East, Lawrence resigned after having refused the post of British high commissioner in Egypt, offered by Winston Churchill. In the following September, he joined the Royal Air Force (RAF) as a simple soldier, under the borrowed name of John Hume Ross. Obliged to quit aviation in January 1923 because of his fame, which annoyed certain military leaders, he was able to join a tank unit, under the name of T. E. Shaw. Three years later, his major work, *The Seven Pillars of Wisdom,* published in a limited edition, was very successful. He composed a shortened version of it called *Revolt in the Desert*.

In spite of the success of the so-called Arab Revolt of 1916–1918, Lawrence, who narrated his adventures in *Seven Pillars of Wisdom*, thought that his battle for an "Arab cause" was "lost" because "the old men came out again and took from us our victory" in order to "re-make [the world] in the likeness of the former world they knew." Unable to cope with his fractured self and with the historical necessities of British imperialism, Lawrence ultimately stopped believing in a meaningful Arab national movement. He rejoined the air force in 1925 and served as an enlisted man until 1935.

In March 1935, Lawrence resigned definitively from the army to retire to a cottage in Clouds Hill, in Dorset. On the following 19 May, he was killed in a motorcycle accident. Other that the *Seven Pillars of Wisdom*, T. E. Lawrence was also author of *The Womb, Crusader's Castle*, and *Letters*.

SEE ALSO Abdullah I ibn Hussein; Allenby, Edmund Henry; Philby, Harry St. John.

LEAGUE OF ARAB STATES: An international institution, the Arab League (officially the League of Arab States) was founded in Cairo on 22 March 1945. At its creation the Arab League comprised Saudi Arabia, Egypt, Iraq, Transjordan, Lebanon, Syria, and Yemen. The first secretary general of the organization was Abd al-Rahman al-Azzam, an Egyptian diplomat. The Arab League proposed strengthening ties between Arab states and coordinating regional economic and military policy, while refraining from intervening in any conflict between league members. The impulse to create a pan-Arab organization was the product of the ongoing Arab nationalist movement, but during World War II it was also encouraged by the British as a means of influencing Arab public opinion at a time when it appeared that the Germans might well conquer North Africa. With British help, an international conference was convened in Alexandria in September 1944, producing an agreement called the Alexandria Protocol on 7 October. The formal creation of the League—an association of independent Arab states rather than the pan-Arab federation its original promoters had envisioned—followed the next year.

In 1958 the League was recognized by the United Nations (UN) as a regional intergovernmental organization, and it has coordinated with the UN in its various social, cultural, and scientific programs. Headquartered in Cairo, it is the most important Arab venue for official cooperation in matters of education, social, and health issues, mainly through its Education, Scientific and Cultural Organization (AL-ESCO), founded in 1964. In 2004, the League has twenty-two members: the original seven plus Libya (joined 1953), Sudan (1956), Tunisia (1958), Morocco (1958), Kuwait (1961), Algeria (1962), Bahrain (1971), Oman (1971), Qatar (1971), the United Arab Emirates (UAE, 1971), Mauritania (1973), Palestine (originally as the PLO, 1974), Somalia (1974), Djibouti (1977), and the Comoros Islands (1996). South Yemen was also a member from 1967 until 1990, when it united with Yemen. It is believed that the League employs some 540 staff and has a budget of around $27 million.

From its very beginnings the Arab League supported the Palestinian cause, although it was often ineffective due to political differences and rivalries among the Arab states. The League provided for permanent Palestinian representation on the League Council, the main policy-making body; the first Palestinian representative was Musa al-Alami, who had taken part in the Alexandria conference. In September 1946, the League helped to reestablish the Arab Higher Committee (AHC) to represent the principal Palestinian political forces. In July 1948 it attempted to create a civil administration for the areas of Palestine not yet occupied by the Israelis, but was unable to overcome both political dissension within the AHC and opposition within the League by King Abdullah I of Transjordan, who wished to annex those areas. In September 1948, at the insistence of Egypt, which opposed Abdullah's plans, the League helped the AHC to create the All-Palestine Government in Gaza, which lasted only a few weeks. After the 1948–1949 War the League adopted a policy of nonrecognition of Israel and supported the right of the Palestinian refugees to return to their homes. It rejected all later proposals to resettle the refugees permanently outside Palestine. It also cooperated with the United Nations Relief and Works Agency (UNRWA) to assist the refugees. The League declared that, although it supported the liberation of Palestine, it would not use military force to achieve it. In 1950, however, it created the Joint Defense and Economic Cooperation Treaty (JDECT) as a defensive measure against Israel. The League also instituted an economic boycott of Israel, at first (1946) against Zionist-produced goods from Palestine, later (1948) banning all trade between Arab states and Israel or companies doing business with Israel; it established a Central Office for the Boycott of Israel (OB) in Damascus in 1951. Enforcement was voluntary and inconsistent, and the boycott never seriously affected the Israeli economy. Other major actions

Issues at Arab League summits

No.	Date and location	Resolutions, outcomes
1st	January 1964, Cairo	Agreed to oppose "the robbery of the waters of Jordan by Israel."
2nd	September 1964, Alexandria	Supported the establishment of the Palestine Liberation Organization (PLO) in its effort to liberate Palestine from the Zionists.
3rd	September 1965, Casablanca	Opposed "intra-Arab hostile propaganda."
4th	29 August–1 September 1967, Khartoum	Held post-1967 Arab-Israeli War, which ended with crushing Israeli victory; declared three "no's": "no negotiation with Israel, no treaty, no recognition of Israel."
5th	December 1969, Rabat	Called for the mobilization of member countries against Israel.
6th	November 1973, Algiers	Held in the wake of the 1973 Arab-Israeli War, it set strict guidelines for dialogue with Israel.
7th	30 October–2 November 1974, Rabat	Declared the PLO to be "the sole and legitimate representative of the Palestinian people," who had "the right to establish the independent state of Palestine on any liberated territory."
8th	October 1976, Cairo	Approved the establishment of a peacekeeping force (Arab Deterrent Force) for the Lebanese Civil War.
9th	November 1978, Baghdad	Condemned the Camp David Peace Accords between Egypt and Israel, and threatened Egypt with sanctions, including the suspension of its membership if Egypt signed a treaty with Israel.
10th	November 1979, Tunis	Held in the wake of Israel's invasion of Lebanon in 1978, it discussed Israel's occupation of southern Lebanon.
11th	November 1980, Amman	Formulated a strategy for economic development among League members until 2000.
12th	November 1981/September 1982, Fez	Meeting was suspended due to resistance to a peace plan drafted by Saudi crown prince Fahd, which implied de facto recognition of the Jewish state. In September 1982 at Fez, the meeting reconvened to adopt a modified version of the Fahd Plan, called the Fez Plan.
13th	August 1985, Casablanca	Failed to back a PLO-Jordanian agreement that envisaged talks with Israel about Palestinian rights. Summit boycotted by five member states.
14th	November 1987, Amman	Supported UN Security Council Resolution 598 regarding cease-fire in the Iran-Iraq War. Also declared that individual member states could decide to resume diplomatic ties with Egypt.
15th	June 1988, Casablanca	Decided to financially support the PLO in sustaining the Intifada in the occupied territories.
16th	May 1989, Casablanca	Readmitted Egypt into Arab League, and set up Tripartite Committee to secure a cease-fire in the Lebanese Civil War and re-establish a constitutional government in Lebanon.
17th	May 1990, Baghdad	Denounced recent increase of Soviet Jewish immigration to Israel.
18th	August 1990, Cairo	12 out of 20 members present condemned Iraq for invading and annexing Kuwait. Agreed to deploy troops to assist Saudi and other Gulf states' armed forces.
19th	June 1995, Cairo	Held after a hiatus of five years. Iraq not invited.
20th	October 2000, Cairo	Set up funds to help the Palestinians' Second Intifada against the Israeli occupation, and called on its members to freeze their relations with Israel. Iraq was invited.
21st	March 2001, Amman	Held after the election of Ariel Sharon as Israel's prime minister, it appointed Egypt's Amr Mousa as the Arab League's new secretary-general.
22nd	March 2002, Beirut	Adopted the Saudi Peace Plan of Crown Prince Abdullah, which offered Israel total peace in exchange for total Israeli withdrawal from Arab territories conquered in the 1967 war. Opposed the use of force against Iraq.
23rd	March 2003, Sharm al-Sheikh, Egypt	Agreed not to participate in the U.S.-led attack on Iraq, but allowed the United States to use military bases in some of their countries.
24th	May 2004, Tunis	Rejected stand taken by the U.S. and Israel in the Arab-Israeli conflict and supported a peace process founded on international legitimacy, UN resolutions and the principle of land against peace.

taken by the League affecting the Palestinian-Israeli conflict were:

In April 1959, at the urging of Egypt, the League adopted a resolution providing for the expulsion of any member state that negotiated a separate peace with Israel.

In May 1964, at the urging of Egypt, the League supported the creation of the Palestine Liberation Organization (PLO) and the Palestine Liberation Army (PLA). The League regularly supported the PLO's efforts to achieve international recognition.

In September 1967, after the June 1967 War, the League declared its continuing support for the Palestinian cause and established a policy of not recognizing or negotiating with Israel.

In November 1973 the League set conditions to be met for members to engage in talks with Israel. The following November the League recognized the PLO as the only legitimate representative body of the Palestinians, recognized its right to establish a Palestinian state, and admitted it as a full member of the League.

In October 1976 the League agreed to form an Arab Deterrent Force to intervene in the Lebanese Civil War.

In November 1978 the League condemned the Camp David Accords and invoked sanctions against Egypt. They failed to agree on a response to the Israeli invasion of South Lebanon from March to June. In 1979, after the Israeli-Egyptian peace treaty in March, the League expelled Egypt under the terms of the 1959 resolution (member states also suspended diplomatic relations); moved the League's head-quarters to Tunis. This was the beginning of a period of crisis and dissension in the Arab world, in large part over Israel and the status of Palestine, that affected the League's functioning. Some League summit meetings were boycotted by some states, at least one summit was canceled, and few accords were ratified by the Council.

In September 1982 they approved the Fez Initiative, based on the Fahd Plan, disagreement over which had caused the cancellation of a League summit the previous year. It called for withdrawal of Israel from the Occupied Territories and eventual establishment of a Palestinian state in them—amounting to a tacit recognition of Israel within the pre-1967 borders.

In August 1985 the League could not agree to support an agreement between the PLO and Jordan. In November 1987 the League declared that members were free to resume diplomatic relations with Egypt. In June 1988 the League agreed to assist the PLO financially in the Intifada, and in May 1989 readmitted Egypt to membership. They also agreed to mediate a truce in the Lebanese Civil War.

In August 1990 the League was divided over the issue of Iraq's invasion of Kuwait. League headquarters returned to Cairo in October of the same year.

In March 2000 the League passed a resolution reaffirming the right of Lebanon to fight against the Israeli occupation and demanding that the right of return of the Palestinian refugees be respected. In October, after the start of the al-Aqsa Intifada, they called on members to suspend relations with Israel and agreed to financial aid for the Palestinians.

In January 2001 the League accorded its unanimous support to the position of the Palestinian Authority on peace conditions with Israel. On 24 March of that year, Amr Mousa, Egyptian minister of foreign affairs, was chosen, unanimously, as secretary general of the League. (Except for the period 1978–1990, the secretary general of the League has always been an Egyptian.) A restructuring plan was put into effect, with the principal innovation being the establishment of positions of general commissioners. These posts have been given to influential personalities of the Arab world. In July, Hanan Ashrawi, an important Palestinian political figure, became commissioner for information. The following month, the former Jordanian prime minister, Taher al-Masri, was named commissioner for civil society affairs, and the former Egyptian minister of culture, Ahmed Kamal Abul Magd, became commissioner for "dialogue among civilizations."

In late May 2004, while Israeli forces were attacking the Rafah Palestinian refugee camp in the Gaza Strip, in a show of force involving rocket attacks on civilian neighborhoods and mass house demolitions, the Arab League held a summit meeting in Tunis. It was to have been held earlier but had been postponed over disagreements about the issues of democratic reform on the agenda. Some governments skipped the meeting. Although individual governments and politicians had condemned Israel's actions and American support for them, the League summit generally avoided the subject.

SEE ALSO All-Palestine Government; Arab Deterrent Force; Arab Higher Committee; Fahd Plan; Intifada, al-Aqsa.

LEBANESE ARMED REVOLUTIONARY FACTION (LARF): Lebanese armed group, created in 1979 by Georges Ibraham Abdallah, after the breakup of the Popular Front for the Liberation of Palestine–Special Operations (PFLP–SO), of Wadi' Haddad. The hard core of this group was made up of approximately thirty members from five important families from the north of Lebanon. Backed by Syria, the LARF wanted to free Lebanon from all foreign presence. This group was responsible for many attacks, some of which were carried out in the West against Israeli citizens or offices. The LARF ceased to exist in 1986. Abdallah himself has been in prison in France since 1984. He was convicted in 1987 for the killing of an Israeli diplomat in 1982.

SEE ALSO Popular Front for the Liberation of Palestine–Special Operations.

LEBANESE COMMUNIST PARTY (LCP): Lebanese political party, legalized in 1969 by the interior minister, Kamal Jumblatt. The LCP grew out of the Lebanese People's Party, founded in 1924. At the beginning hostile to the Palestinian resistance in Lebanon, the LCP gradually changed its views, conforming to the directives of the Soviet CP, which decided to back the Palestine Liberation Organization (PLO). At its beginning the majority of its members were Christian, but it became mostly Muslim eight years later. In 1971, a splinter group, Trotskyist in tendency, left the party, in order to create the Lebanese Revolutionary Communist Party. The LCP was opposed to the Israeli occupation of South Lebanon and advocated resistance. It has supported Syrian intervention in Lebanese politics. The LCP's influence has shrunk since 1989.

SEE ALSO Jumblatt, Kamal; Palestine Liberation Organization; South Lebanon.

LEBANESE FORCES (LF): Lebanese Christian militia created in 1976 as the militia of the Lebanese Front, an alliance of several right-wing Christian parties, dominated by the Phalange. Its first commander was Bashir Jumayyil, younger son of Phalange boss Pierre Jumayyil. Under his guidance, and with substantial military and financial assistance from Israel and from the Central Intelligence Agency (CIA), the LF became the largest Maronite paramilitary force in Lebanon and a major factor in the Lebanese Civil War. After the Lebanese Front alliance fell apart in 1978, the Lebanese Forces were primarily an arm of the Phalange (and are sometimes referred to as "the Phalange militia"). After the Israeli invasion of June 1982, the LF worked closely, and after Bashir Jumayyil's assassination in September 1982, openly, with Israeli forces, carrying out the brutal Sabra and Shatila massacre in September 1982 and fighting various Palestinian and Lebanese Muslim and leftist factions. Jumayyil was succeeded as commander by Fadi Afram, by Fuʾad Abu Nadr in 1984, and by Samir Geagea in 1985. In 1989–1990 the LF fought the Lebanese Army, then commanded by Michel Aoun, over the Taʾif Accords and the presence of the Syrians in the country, which Aoun opposed. Because of his support of the government, Geagea was included in the first post–civil war government in December 1990. He failed to become Phalange leader, however, and led the LF on a course separate from the party. In 1991, under the terms of the Taʾif Accords, all sectarian militias—with the exception of those in South Lebanon, under Israeli control—were officially dissolved; about two-thirds of the LF's troops were absorbed into the army. The Lebanese Forces then reconstituted itself as a political party, but was discovered to be hoarding weapons. It was banned in 1994 after the bombing of a church in Junieh in which ten people were killed, and the assassination of Dany Chamoun, a rival Maronite militia leader, and a number of other people, were traced to Geagea. Geagea received a death sentence, commuted to life imprisonment, for the Chamoun killing. A rump Lebanese Forces organization remains in the Lebanese Christian community, animated by Strida Geagea, the wife of Samir Geagea. In 2001–2002, Fuʾad Malik attempted to reconstitute the LF as a legal party, but as that necessarily meant accommodating the Syrians, he alienated many LF followers. In 2001 it was reported that LF was still in contact with the Israelis.

SEE ALSO Aoun, Michel; Geagea, Samir; Jumayyil, Bashir; Lebanese Front; Phalange; Sabra and Shatila; Taʾif Accords.

LEBANESE FRONT (LF): An alliance of several right-wing Christian parties and prominent individuals established in 1976. Members included the Lebanese Phalange Party of Pierre Jumayyil, the National Liberal Party of former president Camille Chamoun, the Guardians of Cedars and several smaller groups, as well as former president Sulayman Franjiyya. It was dominated by Jumayyil and the Phalange. The front created a militia called the Lebanese Forces (LF), commanded by Bashir Jumayyil, son of Pierre. Franjiyya left the front in 1978 over the collaboration of Jumayyil and Chamoun with the Israelis, who had invaded Lebanon in March. The alliance distintegrated after that and the Lebanese Forces were thereafter primarily an arm of the Phalange. In June 1978 Bashir Jumayyil had Tony Franjiyya, son of Sulayman, killed along with his family.

SEE ALSO Chamoun, Camille; Franjiyya, Sulayman; Guardians of Cedars; Lebanese Forces; Phalange.

LEBANESE ISLAMIC GROUP

SEE Jamiʿa al-Islamiyya Libnaniyya al-.

LEBANESE KATAʾIB

SEE Phalange.

LEBANESE NATIONAL MOVEMENT (LNM): Lebanese political bloc organized at the beginning of 1975. The LNM, comprised of fifteen political organizations of the left, with the exception of those close to Syria, succeeded the Alliance of National and Progressive Parties, formed in 1969. Among these organizations were: the Progressive Socialist Party (PSP) of Kamal Jumblatt; the Lebanese Communist Party (LCP); the Communist Action in Lebanon Organization of Mohsen Ibrahim; the Syrian Socialist Nationalist Party (SSNP); the Baʿth Party of Abdul Majid Rafei; the Independent Nasserite Movement of Ibrahim Koleilat; the Arab Socialist Union; the Union of Nasserite Forces; the Lebanese Fatah Support Movement; the Kurdish Democratic Party Organization; the Arab Socialist Organization; the Socialist Action Party of Hussein Hamdan; the Christian Patriots Front of Suleiman Suleiman; and the Union of the Forces of the Working People. The Lebanese National Movement was financed mostly by Iraq. It was dominated by Jumblatt's PSP, and its political council was presided over by Jumblatt. Its platform, constituted on 18 August 1975, demanded nonsectarian government, proportional representation, limits on ministerial and parliamentary power, the reorganization of the army, the application of human rights, restructuring of the administration, and adoption of the principle of popular referendum on questions of national interest. These proposals, notably those related to institutional reform and the secularization of the state, were opposed by established Lebanese political figures.

Supporting the Palestinian resistance actions in Lebanon, the LNM created a common command with the Palestine Liberation Organization (PLO) to coordinate the military actions of the two movements. Their success provoked the Syrian intervention on the side of the Christians of the Lebanese Front (LF) in 1976. This made of Jumblatt an enemy of the Syrians. In March 1977 Jumblatt was assassinated by pro-Syrian factions of the SSNP, and his son Walid Kamal Jumblatt took over the leadership of the PSP and the Lebanese National Movement. Walid Jumblatt accommodated himself to the Syrians and attempted to use their support against the Maronites. The Israeli invasion of Lebanon in June 1982, which resulted in the expulsion of the PLO fighters from the country, severely weakened the LNM, which was dissolved in October. In 1983 leading members joined with the Syrians and other Lebanese political factions successfully to pressure President Amin Jumayyil to abandon a proposed Lebanese-Israeli peace treaty, but the the alliance was not revived.

SEE ALSO Jumayyil, Amin; Jumblatt, Kamal; Jumblatt, Walid Kamal; Lebanese Communist Party; Lebanese Front; Palestine Liberation Organization.

LEBANESE NATIONAL RESISTANCE FRONT:
An umbrella organization of leftist parties—the Lebanese Communist Party (LCP), the Organization of Communist Action, and the Socialist Action Party—created after the siege of Beirut in September 1982 to organize resistance against the Israeli occupation of Lebanon. After Israel withdrew from Beirut and the Shuf area to South Lebanon, the movement came—with Syrian assistance—to be dominated by Islamic groups such as AMAL and Hizbullah, and the secular, leftist groups were marginalized.

SEE ALSO AMAL; Hizbullah; Lebanese Communist Party.

LEBANESE PHALANGE
SEE Phalange.

LEBANESE WAR
SEE Arab-Israel War (1982).

LEBANON: Lebanon, like most of the Arab East, was under Ottoman rule until World War I. It was a semiautonomous province, much smaller than the present state, consisting of two districts, one populated mainly by Maronites and the other by Druze. It was governed by a sectarian power-sharing arrangement that had been negotiated in 1861 by the European Great Powers to settle a civil war between the two communities. After World War I, in accordance with the Sykes-Picot Agreement and in breach of the promises made by the Allies to the Arabs during the war, Greater Syria, including Lebanon, was occupied by France.

In 1920 the League of Nations formally gave the French a mandate over Syria, and the French expelled Emir Faysal, an al-Hashim prince who had been chosen by Syrian notables to be their king. (Faysal was the son of King Husayn of Hijaz, Sharif of Mecca, who had led the Arab Revolt against the Ottomans with the encouragement of the British, who promised to support an independent pan-Arab state.) The presence of the French, who, since the mid-seventeenth century, had acted as protectors of the Ottoman Empire's Catholics, allowed the Maronite political elite to reinforce its hold over state institutions. After the Ottoman Empire fell, the Maronites agitated for a Greater Lebanon, and the French annexed to the original Ottoman province of Mount Lebanon the surrounding, predominantly Muslim, districts from Syria. This annex expanded the country to its present borders, giving it relative autonomy under the Mandate. In 1926 a new constitution was promulgated that reformed the administration but preserved the sectarian basis of government (the highest posts were reserved for Maronites), and the country was renamed the Republic of Lebanon, although the French maintained ultimate control through their High Commissioner, the Mandate's chief executive.

In June 1941, during World War II, British and Free French forces captured Lebanon and Syria from the Vichy government, and the Free French, under political pressure, proclaimed the independence of both in November. The independence was only nominal, since the French had no intention of respecting it. In March 1943, Bishara al-Khuri and Riyad as-Sulh, the leading politicians of the Maronite and Sunni Muslim communities, respectively, established the unwritten National Pact. The Pact fixed a ratio for allotting parliamentary seats (six Christian to five Muslim), and assigned the three highest state offices to representatives of three communities: the president would be a Maronite, the prime minister a Sunni, and the speaker of the Chamber of Deputies a Shi'a. No one from the Shi'a, Druze, Greek Orthodox, Melkites or other community was consulted. In September 1943 a new parliament was elected; Khuri became president and Sulh prime minister. That November, parliament amended the constitution to eliminate the position of High Commissioner, and the French arrested the president, the prime minister, and the cabinet. Under pressure from the Lebanese and the Arab world, as well as from Britain and the United States, the French released them on 22 November, tacitly putting an end to the Mandate. The last French troops were finally withdrawn 31 December 1946.

Lebanon expressed its opposition to the creation of the State of Israel in 1948, and sent its small army to join the Arab forces that attacked the Israelis. By the time of the 1949 truce agreement, approximately 100,000 Palestinian refugees had fled into Lebanon, mostly in the south, from which they expected to return. They were welcomed by the Lebanese authorities—partly for domestic political reasons—but not a great deal was done for them. Many Palestinians are still living in camps established at that time. The presence of so many Palestinians, and more, the embedding of the Palestinian issue in Lebanese politics, helped to destabilize the country later on. Meanwhile, Lebanon was ruled by the sectarian elites, for their own benefit and enrichment; Lebanese government was (and still is) legendarily corrupt. In 1952, however, Khuri was forced to resign when the failure to address serious social and economic issues, combined with blatant corruption—including the rigging of the 1947 election to allow him a second term—aroused social unrest and political opposition throughout Lebanese society, culminating in a general strike. Khuri was replaced by Camille Chamoun, who had been expected to be more accommodating toward the Muslim and Druze communities. Instead, Chamoun continued the favoritism toward Christians built into the National Agreement, and aligned Lebanon with the West, adopting its anti-Nasser/anti-Arab nationalist policy. Muslims resented the social and political inequities that underlay National Agreement, which was based on a highly questionable census conducted in 1932. They demanded a new census, but the Christian parties would agree only on condition that Lebanese emigrants in other countries, who were primarily Christians, be counted. Lebanese society, and particularly Muslims, were meanwhile affected by developments relating to the larger world, especially Nasserist pan-Arabism, increasingly strong in the 1950s. Political rivalry between sectarian leaders became intense.

In 1957 Chamoun, needing a constitutional amendment to run for a second term, gained a two-thirds majority in parliamentary elections by what most considered questionable means that eliminated many Muslim representatives from parliament. The result was the civil war of 1958, in which sectarian, social, economic and political grievances all exploded at once. It was set off by the assassination of a journalist. The government blamed outside agitators from the newly constituted United Arab Republic (UAR) and took the matter to the League of Arab States and the United Nations. The simultaneous revolt that overthrew the Iraqi monarchy caused United States president Dwight Eisenhower, at Chamoun's request, to send American forces to Lebanon in July to protect the government. The Americans stayed long enough to oversee the election of a new president, Fu'ad Shehab, former commander of the Lebanese army, who had remained nonpartisan during the 1952 and 1958 disturbances. Shehab, whose first act was to ask the United States to withdraw, made a serious effort to reform government administration, appointing Muslims to his cabinet and increasing the size of the Chamber of Deputies in order to represent Muslim communities more equitably. He also devoted state resources to improving the infrastructure of the country, such as roads, electricity and water distribution systems and rural health facilities. Although he did not directly address the structural issues that had generated the unrest of 1958 and attempted to keep within the terms of the National Agreement, he aroused the opposition of the Maronite leaders. An autocrat rather than a politician, he ruled through the use of the military intelligence apparatus. His successor in 1964, Charles Hilu, a founder of the Phalange who had left that party and who also had not taken sides in 1958, was less able to force through reforms and also ruled with military help. Lebanon did not take part in the 1967 War (the prime minister, Rashid Karame, a Sunni Nasserist, wanted to do so but did not have the support of the president), but the aftermath affected the country deeply. It had become clear that Palestinian refugees would not be allowed to return home, and increasingly politicized Palestinians in the camps turned to armed resistance through guerrilla groups based in Lebanon. Their activities in turn tended to polarize the Lebanese, undermining the National Agreement and government authority, particularly in the south.

On 28 December 1968, in reprisal for an attack on an Israeli airliner in Athens by the Popular Front for the Liberation of Palestine (PFLP), which was based in Lebanon, an Israeli helicopter raid destroyed thirteen Lebanese planes at the Beirut airport, prompting a break between Lebanese supporters and opponents of the Palestinian resistance. In January 1969, a new coalition cabinet was formed that excluded right-wing Maronite parties. This government proclaimed its support for the Palestinian resistance, while allowing the army and police organizations to take measures to repress political activity in the camps and reduce the activity of Palestinian guerrillas on Lebanese territory. Fighting broke out between the army and the *fida'yyun*. Pressure brought by supporters of the Palestinians both inside Lebanon and in other Arab governments prompted negotiations, and in November, accords were signed in Cairo between the government and representatives of the Palestinians, establishing new legal relations between them. Palestinians now had the right to reside, work and travel in Lebanon; the right to govern the camps themselves; the right to police the camps; and the right to maintain military organizations in Lebanon and to use them in the struggle against Israel. In effect, government ceded the Palestinians a kind of autonomous state within the state. Moreover, between the end of 1970 and the beginning of 1971, large numbers of Palestinians arrived in Lebanon, including many Palestine Liberation Organization (PLO) fighters who had been expelled from Jordan in the wake of Black September 1970. Polarization between Lebanese supporters and opponents of the Palestinians increased greatly. Opponents, a coalition of Christians, nationalists and conservatives, objected to the violation of Lebanese sovereignty represented by the Cairo agreement, and particularly feared the consequences of Palestinian guerrilla activity against Israel; as supporters of the National Pact, they also opposed increased access to power for Muslims. Hilu's weakness and attempts to please every faction led to the election of Sulayman Franjiyya as his successor in 1970. Although he had supported the Nasserists in 1958, Franjiyya was a nationalist and an enemy of the PLO, which set up its headquarters in Beirut in 1972. His government also did almost nothing to provide security against Israeli attacks on Lebanese territory in the south, which were indiscriminately hitting Lebanese—predominantly poor Shi'a in that area—as well as Palestinian targets. Tens of thousands of South Lebanese Shiites migrated to Beirut to escape Israeli shelling, and little provision was made for them.

Lebanon remained neutral in the October 1973 War. Franjiyya tried to use the army against the PLO, but when it proved ineffective (many units were Muslim or Druze), he encouraged it to arm and train the Maronite militias, which could be less restrained. On 13 April 1975, unknown persons attempted to as-

sassinate the Phalange leader, Pierre Jumayyil; in retaliation, Phalangists attacked a bus carrying Palestinian civilians through a Christian area of East Beirut, killing twenty-six. Fighting then broke out between armed factional groups and violence spread around the country. Consisting at first of street fighting and random killings, it gradually involved battles between militias, and the country was engulfed in a sectarian civil war. The main antagonists at first were the Phalange and its milita, and the Lebanese National Movement (LNM), which loosely united fifteen organizations of the left around the Progressive Socialist Party (PSP) of the Druze leader Kamal Jumblatt and advocated reform of the Lebanese system. The PLO was aligned with the LNM and established a joint command with its militia. The Phalange was joined by other right-wing Maronite groups (soon to form an alliance, the Lebanese Front [LF], and later a joint militia command, the Lebanese Forces [also LF]). In January 1976 the LF besieged and overran a Palestinian refugee camp at Tal al-Za'atar and destroyed a Muslim neighborhood in East Beirut. Later the PLO and LNM captured a Maronite town south of Beirut. By early 1976 the Lebanese army was disintegrating. In March Muslim troops mutinied and formed the Lebanese Arab Army, which joined with the LNM. It attacked Christian areas of Beirut and forced President Franjiyya to flee. In May Ilyas Sarkis, with Syrian support, was elected to become president in September at the end of Franjiyya's term. At the end of May, when the LF was about to be defeated, Syria, after having for months attempted to mediate a settlement, intervened militarily against the LNM and the Palestinians. This move was supported by Jordan, Israel, France and the United States. By mid-August the Syrian forces had gained control and agreed to a cease-fire. A peace conference in Riyadh and an League of Arab States meeting in Cairo, both in October, resulted in a truce and the creation of an Arab Deterrent Force (ADF) (consisting almost entirely of Syrian troops already in place) to be deployed to keep the peace, under the nominal command of the Lebanese president.

The ADF and Lebanese government authority did not extend to South Lebanon, largely controlled by the PLO (parts of it were known as "Fatahland"), where Israel and Christian militias backed by Israel continued to attack. The diplomatic peace offensive by Egyptian president Anwar al-Sadat toward Israel—Sadat made his dramatic trip to Jerusalem in 1977—drove the Syrians closer to the PLO and away from the Sarkis government. By 1978 the Lebanese Forces (essentially the Phalange militia, the Lebanese Front alliance having deteriorated) were firmly allied with Israel and operating independently of the government, and Syria switched its support to their opponents, the LNM. After a PLO attack within Israel, the IDF invaded South Lebanon in March 1978, intending to destroy PLO bases and drive PLO fighters away from the border by creating a "security zone" on the Lebanese side. The Israelis organized, trained and armed a Christian militia called the South Lebanon Army (SLA) as their proxy to patrol the border area after they withdrew in October. In 1980 and 1981 there was fighting between the LF and the ADF, in which Israel at least once intervened significantly in support of the LF. In June 1982 the Israelis invaded Lebanon again, this time going as far north as Beirut and besieging the city for weeks, using artillery shelling and aerial saturation bombing, including phosphorus bombs. A cease-fire was arranged by the United States, and a withdrawal of the PLO leadership along with about 13,000 PLO and Palestine Liberation Army (PLA) fighters to Tunis was arranged under the supervision of a Multinational (American, British, French and Italian) Force (MF).

Israel's other goal was to ensure that Bashir Jumayyil, the Phalange leader and an asset of both the CIA and the Mossad, became president. Jumayyil was duly elected on 23 August. The MF left Beirut on 10 September. On 14 September Jumayyil was assassinated by Syrian nationalists. Israel then moved in to help the Phalange secure the city. Two days later the IDF helped the Phalange militia enter the Sabra and Shatila Palestinian refugee camps, where from 16–18 September they slaughtered approximately 1,500–3,000 civilians, ostensibly in reprisal for Jumayyil's assassination. On 20 September the Multinational Force was redeployed to Beirut. On 21 September Amin Jumayyil, Bashir's brother, was elected president, and at the end of September the Israelis left the city. In May 1983, under pressure from the United States, Jumayyil agreed to sign a peace treaty with Israel, which was actually ratified by parliament. Opposition to this treaty among Lebanese—and by the Syrians—was so great, however, that Jumayyil felt obliged to refuse to sign it. The Syrians would not negotiate, and the Israelis, who had been protecting Jumayyil's government from its factional enemies, withdrew their forces from the Shuf district southeast of Beirut, a largely Druze area held by the Phalange. Fighting broke out between the Phalange and the Druze militia directed by Walid Jumblatt, which had Palestinian and Syrian support.

These were some of the biggest battles of the war. The "peacekeepers" became involved in the fighting on the Christian side; American warships shelled Syrian positions in the mountains (hitting many civilians). After several months the Phalange were expelled from the area. The MF involvement also provoked retaliation. In October, suicide bombings in Beirut, probably carried out by Hizbullah, killed 241 American and 56 French soldiers. The MF was henceforth kept in its barracks and eventually left Lebanon in the spring of 1984. Jumayyil, with support from Syria, repudiated the agreement with Israel in March 1984. That month a national reconciliation government was formed. In June 1985, Israel withdrew most of its forces from Lebanon, but it maintained the "security zone" manned by the SLA and a battalion of IDF troops. In December an agreement for peace and political reform was signed by the leaders of the LF, the Shi'ite AMAL and the Druze militia, but it never took effect because there was no support for it within the LF leadership. In early 1987 there was fighting between AMAL and the Druze in Beirut. Syria, which had withdrawn its troops from the city as part of the cease-fire in 1982, sent a force in to separate them. In the spring of 1988 there was fighting between AMAL and Hizbullan in the south. In September 1988, just before leaving office and with no successor chosen by parliament, Jumayyil appointed General Michel Aoun, commander of the army, as "interim president." Aoun, a Maronite, turned the army against the Phalange, and in early 1989, the Syrians. In May the League of Arab States sponsored a commission composed of the heads of state of Morocco, Algeria, and Saudi Arabia to resolve the Lebanese civil war. In August a broad coalition of Lebanese political groups opposed to Aoun was formed.

In October the Lebanese Chamber of Deputies (last elected was in 1972) met in Ta'if, Saudi Arabia, and debated the Arab League's proposals, adopting a compromise version called the National Reconciliation Charter, known as the Ta'if Accords. This contained a number of political reforms, chief of which, was an agreement that Muslims and Christians should have an equal number of parliamentary seats; these had previously been apportioned based on the fiction of a Christian majority. (There has still been no census since 1932; it has been estimated that Lebanon is approximately 70–75 percent Muslim.) The president would remain a Christian, but the prime minister would be the executive head of government; the sectarian basis of Lebanese politics was basically unchanged. The presence of Syrian troops was ratified (the League of Arab States mandate had expired in 1982, after several extensions). The Ta'if Accords were accepted by all parties except for General Aoun. On 4 November 1989 parliament elected Rene

Muawad president; he was assassinated on 22 November. On 24 November Ilyas al-Hrawi was elected. A new national unity government was installed in December 1989. From January 1990 on there was fighting between the forces of Aoun and the LF, which was now loyal to the government. In August parliament amended the constitution according to the provisions of the Ta'if Accords. Aoun's forces were isolated, and in October, during the crisis leading to the Gulf War (1991), Syrian forces defeated them. Aoun himself fled to France, where he remains, as of 2004, leading an organization called the Free Patriotic Movement, devoted to opposing Syrian hegemony in Lebanon. An arrest warrant was issued for him in 2003.

The total number of fatalities in the 1975–1990 civil war are estimated to be over 150,000. The Lebanese economy was crippled, and much of Beirut was destroyed, as were many towns in the southern half of the country. No political initiative can be undertaken without the support of the Syrian government. Emile Lahhud was elected president in 1998. Parliamentary elections were held in 1992 for the first time since before the civil war. Rafiq Baha'uddin al-Hariri has been prime minister for all but two years since 1992. Through the 1990s Hizbullah consolidated its influence in South Lebanon and its armed wing launched frequent attacks against Israeli forces there. In 2000 the Israelis at last withdrew from its "security zone," leaving it in occupation only of the disputed Shebaa Farms area. The SLA was disbanded, and its commander, Antoine Lahad, is living in Israel as of 2004.

SEE ALSO AMAL; Aoun, Michel; Arab Deterrent Force; Black September 1970; Chamoun, Camille; Druze; Franjiyya, Sulayman; Gulf War (1991); Hariri, Rafiq Baha'uddin al-; Hashim, al-; Hizbullah; Jumayyil, Amin; Jumayyil, Bashir; Jumblatt, Kamal; Jumblatt, Walid Kamal; Karame, Rashid; Lahad, Antoine; Lahhud, Emile; League of Arab States; Lebanese Forces; Lebanese Front; Lebanese National Movement; Maronites; Melkites; Mossad; Palestine Liberation Army; Phalange; Popular Front for the Liberation of Palestine; Sabra and Shatila; Sadat, Anwar al-; Shebaa Farms; South Lebanon; South Lebanon Army; Sykes-Picot Agreement; Ta'if Accords; United Arab Republic.

LEHI

SEE Lohamei Herut Yisrael.

LEVY, DAVID: Israeli political figure, born in December 1937, in Morocco. After immigrating to Israel in 1957, Levy worked as a mason, then began a career as a union organizer, for the Labor Party, MAPAI. In 1966, he was a member of the municipal council of Beit Shean, and three years later he was elected member of Knesset for the right-wing party, Herut. In 1977, after having failed in a bid to become secretary general of the Histadrut union organization, he became minister of immigrant absorption in the government of Menachem Begin, leader of Herut. Between 1978 and 1980, as minister of housing and construction, he favored the development of Jewish settlements in the Occupied Territories, all the while backing the restitution of the Sinai to Egypt, in exchange for a peace agreement. In 1981, he was once again a losing candidate for the post of secretary general of Histadrut. Between 1981 and 1984, Levy was deputy prime minister and minister of housing in the government of Yitzhak Shamir.

In Herut, where he represented the Sephardi community, David Levy was among the candidates to succeed Menachem Begin as party leader, a position finally won by Yitzhak Shamir. From 1988 to 1990 he was minister of housing and construction, then foreign minister from June 1990 to June 1992, in the Shamir government. In this capacity he participated in the Middle East peace conference, held in Madrid, in 1991, where his relations with Benjamin Netanyahu, spokesperson for the Israeli government and rising star of the Israeli right, were strained. During the first part of 1995, his conflict with Netanyahu, who had meanwhile become Likud leader, prompted him to quit this bloc and create his own party, Gesher "Bridge" Party. On 8 February 1996, in anticipation of the general elections of the following May, he accepted an alliance with Likud and the Tzomet Party, to constitute a common list in support of the candidacy of Netanyahu for the post of prime minister. On 29 May 1996, his party won five seats in the Knesset. On 18 June, he became foreign minister in the government of Benjamin Netanyahu. As soon as his assumed this post, Levy found himself isolated in a cabinet that was dominated by ultranationalists, and where all matters of importance were dealt with by the prime minister himself, which prevented him from having any impact on the course of the Israeli-Palestinian peace process. On 7 July 1997, he was officially mandated to handle negotiations with the Palestinian Authority, which, provisionally, ended his conflict with the prime minister. On 25 August, he became deputy prime minister, all the while keeping his foreign minister's portfolio.

On 5 January 1998, judging that, decidedly, he had no real power, Levy resigned from his positions. During the month of February 1999, looking forward to the general elections of the following May, he joined with the Israel Labor Party and with Meimad to constitute the electoral list of "One Israel," which, on 18 May, won twenty-six seats, while the head of the Labor Party, Ehud Barak, was elected prime minister. On 5 July, he joined the Barak government as foreign minister. On 8 September, three days after the signing of the Israeli-Palestinian Sharm al-Shaykh Summits, the Israeli prime minister asked him to conduct negotiations with the Palestinians on the final status of the Palestinian territories. Five days later, he reaffirmed the determination of Israel to maintain its sovereignty over Jerusalem and to refuse to return to the frontiers of pre-June 1967. At the end of July 2000, he expressed, publicly, his opposition to the offers made by the Israeli prime minister at the Israeli-Palestinian summit which was taking place at the Camp David Accords. On 2 July, following, he resigned his post as minister, and, a few days later, decided to join Likud. When, in March 2001, Likud leader Ariel Sharon was elected prime minister, Levy was not part of the new government. Levy later served as minister without portfolio in Sharon's coalition government, but resigned in July 2002 in protest over planned budget cuts and the exclusion of the cabinet from the decision-making process.

SEE ALSO Barak, Ehud; Begin, Menachem; Camp David Accords; Gesher "Bridge" Party; Herut Party; Histadrut; Israel Labor Party; Likud; MAPAI; Meimad; Palestinian Authority; Shamir, Yitzhak; Sharm al-Shaykh Summits; Tzomet Party.

LF

SEE Lebanese Forces.

LIEBERMAN, AVIGDOR (1958–): Israeli politician.
Born in the Soviet Union in 1958, Lieberman immigrated to Israel in 1978. Chief of staff under Prime Minister Benjamin Netanyahu, Lieberman founded the Israel Beiteinu Party in 1999. An immigrants' rights party, Israel Beiteinu seeks to curb what Lieberman has called the excessive powers of the police and the ministry of justice. He was elected to the Knesset in 1999, and served on the Foreign Affairs and Defense Committee. In March 2001 Lieberman was appointed minister of national infrastructures.

SEE ALSO Israel Beiteinu.

LIKUD (Hebrew for "Assembly" or "Union"): Israeli
political bloc, constituted in July 1973, under the impetus of Ariel Sharon and Menachem Begin. Conscious of the necessity of moving toward the center, the leadership of Herut decided to ally with three other groups: the Liberal Party, the "Free Center," and the State List. This alliance, called the Likud, became the biggest parliamentary bloc in the Knesset.

Representing a threat to the Israeli left, the creation of Likud prompted the Labor Party to adopt a more nationalistic stand. At the end of 1973 through the beginning of 1974, the Arab-Israel War (1973)—which had revealed a certain unpreparedness of the government in facing a major crisis—led to some major changes in the Israeli political configuration. The drift toward the right began to be felt, especially among young soldiers and the less-privileged. In 1976, Sharon resigned from Likud to create his own party, Shlomzion. In the Knesset elections of May 1977, due in part to the Sephardic vote, Likud won forty-three of the 120 seats in Knesset, outdoing the Labor Party, which won only thirty-two. The Labor votes were lost not to Likud but to a new centrist group, Dash, and to the ultra-Orthodox National Religious Party (NRP). The Shlomzion of Ariel Sharon, which had won two seats, rejoined the Likud. The leader of Herut, Menachem Begin, became prime minister, ending thirty years of Labor hegemony. After assuming office, Begin responded to calls by the Soviet Union and the United States to hold an international conference on peace in the Middle East by instead hastening secret bilateral contacts, actions that Anwar al-Sadat took as well. In order to compensate for the extremist image of his bloc, Begin named the Laborite, Moshe Dayan, as his minister of foreign affairs.

When the Likud came to power, inflation had risen to 42 percent, which prompted the Begin government to apply an ultraliberal economic policy. Appointed minister of agriculture, Ariel Sharon favored the development of Jewish settlements in the Occupied Territories, which obstructed the Israeli-Egyptian negotiations that were going on. In September 1978, Israel signed the Camp David Accords with Egypt, and in March of the following year, in spite of disagreement on the Palestinian question, Begin and Sadat initialed the Israeli-Egyptian peace accord. In March 1980, prominent Likud leader Yitzhak Shamir became foreign minister, replacing Moshe Dayan, who had resigned in disappointment over the results of the Camp David Accords. On 30 July 1980, the Knesset passed a law on Jerusalem, "united city, eternal capital of Israel," provoking a

Likud Success. Menachem Begin, head of the ultra-nationalist Herut Party, celebrates with other members of Likud after the May 1977 Knesset elections that brought the right-wing political alliance to power, ending twenty-nine years of Labor Party domination of the Israeli government. Begin was prime minister of Israel until 1983. *(AP/Wide World Photos)*

wave of international protest. Likud came out ahead once more in the Knesset elections of June 1981, but only by a slim margin: it won forty-eight seats in the Knesset, to the forty-seven of the Labor Party. This forced Begin, on 15 July, into an alliance with certain religious groups so as to form a government. In June 1982, under pressure from Defense Minister Ariel Sharon, the Israeli prime minister gave the green light to Operation "Peace for Galilee" in Lebanon, in the course of which the massacres at the Palestinian Sabra and Shatila camps occurred, which aroused widespread outrage in Israeli society and around the world.

On 10 October 1983, succeeding Menachem Begin, who had resigned his post for reasons of ill health and because of his responsibility in the Lebanon affair, Yitzhak Shamir became prime minister. He held onto the foreign ministry, and named David Levy as deputy prime minister and minister of housing and Moshe Arens as minister of defense. In July 1984, Likud finished behind the Labor Party in the

Knesset elections with forty-one deputy seats against Labor's forty-four seats. On 13 September 1985, Likud and the Labor Party signed an accord for a government of national unity, providing for alternation of their parties every two years for the prime ministership. The leader of Herut and Likud, Yitzhak Shamir, was named foreign minister in a government headed by the leader of the Labor Party, Shimon Peres. In 1986, much dissension surfaced in Herut, and at the same time in Likud, provoked by the "war of succession" for the leadership of the party, in the course of which Yitzhak Shamir, Ariel Sharon, Moshe Arens, Benny Begin, and David Levy were all competing against each other. During October, as provided in the accord between Likud and Labor, Shamir became prime minister and Peres became foreign minister. On 22 December, the United Nations Security Council passed a resolution condemning the policies of Israel in the Occupied Territories. On 25 August 1988, the central committees of the Liberal Party and Herut decided to merge their two blocs to found the "Likud-National Liberal Movement" Party, wherein Herut remained the keystone of the organization. In November, Knesset elections confirmed the previous political situation, to the benefit of Likud, which obtained forty deputy seats.

A national unity government was formed under the leadership of Shamir, yet no alternation with the Laborites was going to take place. On 25 December 1988, Benjamin Netanyahu, the new rising star of Likud, was named deputy foreign minister under foreign minister Moshe Arens. Three factions quickly emerged in Likud: The majority view—upheld by Shamir, Arens, and Netanyahu—and two others—one of which was headed by Sharon and Benny Begin; the other by Levy and Yitzhak Modai. On 15 March 1990, a motion of censure, raised by the religious parties, caused the fall of the Shamir "Unity" government. Shamir then formed a cabinet based on an alliance between Likud, the religious parties, and the extreme right. The new government had to confront the crisis of the Gulf War, during which it had decided not to take reprisals against the attacks of Iraqi missiles. Under U.S. pressure, Shamir agreed to participate in the Middle East peace conference in Madrid on 30 October 1991. The Israeli delegation's spokesperson was Netanyahu, which made him appear to some as Shamir's heir. Following this conference, the extremist parties withdrew their support from Shamir's government. The prime minister, no longer controlling the majority in the Knesset necessary to apply his policies, decided to call for new Knesset elections. In the Likud primaries, Ariel Sharon obtained 22 percent of the votes, becoming Shamir's principal rival. In March 1992, a split appeared in Likud following the departure of Yitzhak Modai, who formed his own organization, the New Liberal Party. In June, Likud was defeated in the Knesset elections by the Labor Party of Yitzhak Rabin, who became prime minister. Likud's share of seats dropped from thirty-eight to thirty-two. Weakened by this electoral failure and internal dissension, Likud was taken over by a new generation of militants, who, on 25 March 1993, chose Netanyahu as party leader by 52 percent of the votes of the members against 26 percent for David Levy and 15 percent for Benny Begin.

The first Sabra, or Jew born in Israel, to lead the nationalist right, Netanyahu advocated its core beliefs: maintaining "Greater Israel" from the Mediterranean to the Jordan, keeping the Golan Heights, and not negotiating with the Palestine Liberation Organization (PLO). By the following autumn, Netanyahu was being openly criticized by a majority of

Likud's members, reproaching him for his inability to come up with a credible alternative to the new situation created by the Israeli-Palestinian accord (Oslo Accords). During the first trimester of 1995, in the middle of an upsurge in anti-Israel attacks, Likud was ahead in the polls, though internally it was being weakened by a power struggle between Netanyahu and Levy. The latter resigned from Likud to create his own party, Gesher. On 10 November, following the assassination of Prime Minister Yitzhak Rabin by a Jewish extremist, the popularity of Likud fell in the polls. A majority of politically conscious Israelis blamed Likud for having supported the vilification campaign against the Rabin government, which had contributed to the climate of hate that led to the murder of the prime minister. In January 1996, after Sharon declined to become a candidate for the post of prime minister, Netanyahu began an electoral campaign on the theme of maintaining the territorial unity of Israel and rejecting the creation of a Palestinian state. On 8 February, through the impetus of Sharon, Likud signed an accord with the party of the extreme right, Tzomet, headed by Rafael Eitan, then with Levy's center-right party, Gesher. Netanyahu thus became the unique candidate of the right for the post of prime minister, which was to be filled for the first time by direct universal suffrage against Peres of the Labor Party.

On 25 March, the "hawks" of the party carried the primaries of Likud, organized in anticipation of the Knesset elections. On 29 May, the head of Likud was elected as prime minister, by a slim margin and with only 50.4 percent of the ballots cast. In spite of this victory, the Likud-Tzomet-Gesher alliance won only thirty-two seats in the Knesset, of which twenty-two were Likud, against thirty-four for the Labor Party. The left, which had fifty-three seats, found itself in the opposition, while the right, which had only forty-three, was in control of the government. On 18 June, Netanyahu presented his cabinet, which included, with Likud, two religious parties (National Religious Party and SHAS), a party of the extreme right (Tzomet), and three centrist groups (Gesher, Third Way, and Israel be Aliyah), thereby disposing of the support of sixty-six members of the 120 in the Knesset. On the next 24 September, the Netanyahu government's approval of the opening of an archaeological tunnel near the Esplanade of Mosques in Jerusalem provoked three days of rioting in the Palestinian territories, causing the death of more than eighty people, most of them Palestinians. On 15 January 1997, Netanyahu and Yasir Arafat came to an agreement on Israeli withdrawal from the city of Hebron. This was the first agreement ever signed between the Israeli right and the PLO. Between 1997 and 1998, Netanyahu's policies and his manner of running the cabinet were criticized, even within his own party, which prompted the departure of some important figures, such as Yitzhak Mordechai, Benny Begin, and Dan Meridor. A number of the founding fathers of Likud, called the "princes" of the party, denounced the "duplicity and lack of principles" of the prime minister. Meridor and Mordechai created their own political bloc, the Center Party. On their side, the Sephardim—whose head, David Levy, resigned on 4 January 1998—considered themselves betrayed by the Likud leader for not keeping the promises he made during his electoral campaign, in particular, to appoint more members of their community to positions of responsibility. A number of them turned to the new Center Party, then headed by the former defense minister of the Netanyahu cabinet, the Sephardi Yitzhak Mordechai.

On 9 October 1998, Netanyahu named Ariel Sharon foreign minister, which gave cause to the Palestinians and their partners to fear that the Israeli-Palestinian peace negotiations would be definitively obstructed. On 25 January 1999, the leadership of Likud designated Netanyahu as their candidate for the post of prime minister in the elections that May. In his party's primaries, Netanyahu obtained 75 percent of the votes against his rival, Moshe Arens, but with a voting participation rate of only 30 percent. On 17 May, Netanyahu became a victim of his own mistakes and lost to his adversary of the Labor Party, Ehud Barak, who won 56 percent of the votes. Likud won only nineteen seats, losing three seats compared to the previous Knesset, the worst it had ever done. After these results were known, Netanyahu resigned from the leadership of Likud, and Sharon replaced him, making him responsible for the interim, until new elections could be organized to choose a new party leader. Other than Sharon, among the pretenders to the succession of Netanyahu there figured Ehud Olmert, Moshe Arens, Meir Shitreet, Limor Livnat, and Silvan Shalom. After its electoral failure in the month of May, Likud tried to strengthen its base by recruiting Golan Heights inhabitants and settlers in the Gaza Strip. On 3 September 1999, Sharon was elected to head Likud against his two rivals, Ehud Olmert and Meir Shitreet.

In the framework of the Israeli-Palestinian peace process, Likud began systematically opposing all the proposals of the Barak government. On 31 July 2000, surprising everyone, Likud candidate Moshe Katsav was elected president of the State of Israel by sixty-three votes against fifty-seven for his Labor rival, Shimon Peres. On 28 September, Sharon made a visit to the Temple Mount that provoked anger among the Palestinians, triggering the Intifada in the Palestinian territories. During the election campaign of January 2001 for the post of prime minister, Sharon made efforts to win support from the Netanyahu's partisans. He entrusted his campaign to his son, Omri Sharon, and to Silvan Shalom, assisted by Mrs. Limor Livnat. On 6 February, Sharon was elected prime minister, with 62.5 percent of the votes cast, running against Prime Minister Ehud Barak. The following month, Sharon formed a government uniting eight different political parties, affording him the support of seventy-three of the 120 members of the Knesset. His foreign minister and defense minister were the Laborites Shimon Peres and Benyamin Ben Eliezer, respectively. In his inaugural speech, Sharon declared that peace with the Palestinians could be achieved without "painful compromises." A few weeks later, when the Intifada was intensifying in the Palestinian territories, he undertook a campaign of very harsh reprisals against those responsible for anti-Israel attacks. At the beginning of December 2001, concluding that Yasir Arafat was behind the continuing Intifada, Sharon decided to isolate Arafat by preventing him from leaving his headquarters in Ramallah. After a suicide bombing at a Netanya resort hotel in March 2002, Sharon ordered the invasion and reoccupation of West Bank cities. In May 2002, at a Likud Party conference, the Likud central committee voted—over Sharon's objection—almost unanimously for a resolution, proposed by former Prime Minister Benjamin Netanyahu, to oppose the creation of a Palestinian state. Yet Sharon retained leadership, surviving allegations of financial improprieties. In the 2003 elections, in an apparent endorsement of his policies, voters gave the Likud 29.4 percent of the vote (thirty-eight seats in the Knesset). Some commentators, however, interpreted the vote as an indication of disillusionment with Labor rather than support for Sharon or for the Likud. Under intense pressure from the United States, Sharon's cabinet voted in May 2003 to approve the internationally backed "road map" for peace. Sharon and the Likud continued to attempt to find a difficult balance between right-wing commitment to disputed territories and a more pragmatic approach to an eventual resolution of the conflict.

In 2004, Sharon presented a plan to disengage from settlements in Gaza and parts of the West Bank, which was strongly opposed in a referendum conducted among Likud members. Many questioned the wisdom of Sharon's decision to resort to an internal party referendum, given the unexpected rebuff to his leadership and the overall popularity of the Gaza re-deployment proposal among the general (non-Likud) population of Israel. In July 2004, Sharon sought a coalition with United Torah Judaism and others, while at the same time the hawks of Likud, led by Netanyahu, opposed not only the coalition, but also the disengagement plan.

SEE ALSO Aqsa Intifada, al-; Arafat, Yasir; Barak, Ehud; Begin, Menachem; Ben Eliezer, Benyamin; Camp David Accords; Center Party; Dash; Dayan, Moshe; Gesher "Bridge" Party; Gulf War (1991); Herut Party; Katsav, Moshe; Knesset; Levy, David; Madrid Conference; Mordechai, Yitzhak; National Religious Party; Oslo Accords; Peres, Shimon; Sabra; Sabra and Shatila; Sadat, Anwar al-; Sephardim; Shamir, Yitzhak; SHAS; Sharon, Ariel; Shlomzion; Third Way.

LIPKIN-SHAHAK, AMNON: Born in January 1944, in Tel Aviv, Amnon Lipkin-Shahak began his military career in 1962. During the 1967 War, he served as assistant commander of the Parachute Brigade, and he participated in a special unit (*sayeret*), in which he would remain for six years. In 1972, he was part of a commando unit—along with Benjamin Netanyahu, Ehud Barak, and Dani Yatom—that neutralized Palestinian terrorists who had taken over a Sabena airplane at the Tel Aviv airport with one hundred passengers aboard. In April 1973, Lipkin-Shahak participated, along with Ehud Barak, in an operation in Beirut in which three Palestinian leaders were killed. Rumors abounded that the commandos' initial objective was the elimination of Yasir Arafat or Ali Hasan al-Salama, both of whom were absent on the night of the raid.

In 1976, Lipkin-Shahak was promoted to the rank of colonel and became director of the "deployment" section for parachute troops at the general staff of the Israel Defense Force (IDF). Two years later, as brigadier general, he was given command of an armored division. In 1982, in the context of the "Peace in Galilee" operation in Lebanon, Lipkin-Shahak was in charge of operations in the zones of Beirut and the Shuf. From October 1983 to February 1986, he was in command of the central military region of Israel, and was promoted to the rank of major general during his tenure. He became director of military intelligence in March 1986, succeeding Ehud Barak. Four years later, when Barak became chief of staff of the IDF, Lipkin-Shahak became his assistant. Between 1993 and 1994, Lipkin-Shahak was part of an Israeli delegation that participated in peace negotiations with the Palestinians, as well as with the Syrians. On 1 January 1995, Lipkin-Shahak became chief of staff of the IDF. As such, he supervised the "Grapes of Wrath" operation, launched against the Hizbullah in April 1996, and participated in Israeli-Palestinian negotiations on the withdrawal of the IDF from the Palestinian territories. On 9 July 1998, Lipkin-Shahak resigned from the army, replaced as chief of staff by General Sha'ul Mofaz. In late December, after the Knesset announcement of upcoming elections, Lipkin-Shahak declared himself a "centrist" candidate for the post of prime minister, running against Benjamin Netanyahu, whose policies he denounced as "dangerous." In January 1999, he withdrew his candidacy and joined with Roni Milo, Dan Meridor, and Yitzhak Mordechai to form the new Center Party in time for the May elections.

When the Center Party won six seats in the Knesset, Lipkin-Shahak became a deputy. Shortly thereafter, in July, he was named tourism minister in the government of Ehud Barak. On 5 March 2001, after the electoral defeat of Barak by his Likud adversary, Ariel Sharon, Lipkin-Shahak retired from politics. In 2002 he became the honorary president of the Israel Humanitarian Foundation.

SEE ALSO Arab-Israel War (1967); Arab-Israel War (1982); Arafat, Yasir; Barak, Ehud; Center Party; Grapes of Wrath Operation; Likud; Meridor, Dan; Milo, Roni; Mordechai, Yitzhak; Netanyahu, Benjamin; Sayeret; Sharon, Ariel; Yatom, Dani.

LITANI OPERATION: Code name of the military operation launched by Israel against Lebanon, on 14 March, 1978. The operation followed an attack on a bus, near Tel Aviv, by a Palestine Liberation Organization (PLO) commando group that was based in Lebanon. The PLO assault on the civilian bus, traveling on Israel's Haifa–Tel Aviv highway, resulted in the deaths of thirty-seven Israelis. In response, 20,000 Israeli troops of the Israel Defense Force invaded Lebanon, advancing to the Litani River. The goal of the operation was the destruction of PLO bases south of the Litani and the removal of PLO guerrillas from the area, within range of the Israeli border. An estimated one thousand Lebanese and Palestinian casualties resulted from the invasion, and the United Nations Security Council responded with Resolution 425, calling for Israeli withdrawal and the creation of a United Nations Interim Forces in Lebanon (UNIFIL) as a peacekeeping force. After three months, Israel ceded a 37-mile-long area of Lebanese territory, 3 to 6 miles deep, to UNIFIL and to an Israeli-supported Lebanese militia. The PLO neverthe-less regained a presence in south Lebanon, and the failure of the Litani Operation figured in Israel's sub-sequent invasion of Lebanon in 1982.

LOCAL AID COORDINATION COMMITTEE (LACC): Or-ganization created in 1994, within the context of the Israeli-Palestinian peace process, to coordinate donor policies in the Palestinian territories. This organization worked with the Ad Hoc Liaison Com-mittee on Aid to the Palestinians and the Joint Liai-son Committee (JLC).

LOHAMEI HERUT YISRAEL (LEHI; Hebrew for "com-batants for the liberty of Israel"): Jewish extremist underground organization, founded in Palestine in October 1940, following a schism in Irgun. Support-ers of radical action against the English and Arabs, the LEHI was also called the "Stern Group," after the name of its founder, Abraham ("Ya'ir") Stern, a for-mer Irgun member, who claimed to represent the "true Irgun." In December 1940, seeing in Germany the only power able to rid Palestine of the British presence, Abraham Stern sent Naftali Lubentchik to make contact with representatives of the German Third Reich in Lebanon in order to propose an alli-ance with the German army. Lubentchik was not able to transmit the German reply to Stern after being arrested in June 1941 by French authorities. Stern then sent a second emissary, former Irgun member Nathan Yalin Mor, who was arrested soon after in Syria. This attempt to join up with the Ger-mans prompted a few LEHI members to quit the group. Those remaining faithful to Ya'ir decided to launch a series of attacks against British police forces, as a consequence of which many members of the group were arrested and imprisoned.

On 12 February 1942, the British police killed Stern in Tel Aviv, beginning a crisis period for LEHI. By 1943, the organization had been reconstructed, moving toward the left and openly embracing the Soviet Union and class struggle, under the leadership of Natan Yellin-Mor, Israel Eldad, and Yitzhak Shamir. The LEHI, which considered itself to be the spearhead of the national movement of Hebrew lib-eration, tried in vain to coordinate its actions with those of Irgun. On 6 November 1944, two LEHI members killed the British minister for the Near East, Walter Edward Guinness (Lord Moyne), who was stationed in Cairo. Confronted by the wave of repression unleashed by the British police, the move-ment suspended its operations until the end of World War II. In October 1945, Haganah, Irgun, and

LEHI decided to coordinate their actions against the British forces of order in Palestine by forming a unit-ed front, the "United Hebrew Resistance," directed by Committee X of the Haganah. On 26 June 1946, British authorities—who were unable to put an end to the operations of the movement—launched the "Agatha" operation, in the course of which almost 2,700 people were arrested and a large arsenal of weapons was seized. On 22 July, an Irgun commando exploded part of the King David Hotel in Jerusalem, which housed the headquarters of the civil and mili-tary administration of Palestine. The attack caused ninety-one deaths. Many LEHI and Irgun leaders were arrested, among them was Yitzhak Shamir, who was deported to Eritrea, effectively putting an end to the existence of the United Hebrew Resistance.

In October 1946, after reorganizing their forces, Irgun and LEHI began a wave of anti-British opera-tions, which continued until November 1947, when the United Nations proposed a plan to partition Pal-estine into two states: one Jewish and the other Arab. From this time onward, Arabs became the principal target of Irgun and LEHI operations. On 9 April, more than one hundred Irgun and LEHI men at-tacked the Arab village of Deir Yasin, massacring inhabitants. During the following June, LEHI partic-ipated in a campaign against the proposal of the spe-cial envoy of the UN, Count Folke Bernadotte, who was recommending modifying the plan of partition of Palestine in favor of the Palestinians and Transjor-dan. On 17 September, a LEHI commando killed Count Bernadotte and Colonel Sérot, head of the UN French observers, in Jerusalem. The next day, the Is-raeli army proceeded to arrest members of LEHI en masse, but the perpetrators of the crime were not discovered. Sentenced for belonging to a terrorist or-ganization, the LEHI members later benefited from a general amnesty, and many of them joined Herut, the political party founded by the former head of Irgun, Menachem Begin. Yitzhak Shamir became a member of Mossad from 1955 to 1969, and then after joining Herut, he began a political career, which led him to become Israeli prime minister in the au-tumn of 1983, succeeding Menachem Begin.

SEE ALSO Begin, Menachem; Bernadotte, Folke; Haganah; Herut Party; Irgun; Mossad; Shamir, Yitzhak.

LOVERS OF ZION (English translation of the Hebrew, Hovevei Zion): A group founded in the 1882 by Leo Pinsker, a Russian doctor, and other European Jews living in Europe who dreamed of emigrating to Pal-estine, and who actively organized people to live out that dream. Advocates of Zionism, they organized the creation of Jewish colonies in Palestine. They founded, among others, the cities of Rishon LeTzion and Hadera.

SEE ALSO Zionism.

LUBAVITCHER HASIDIM (Habad, chabad): Important Hasidic movement, founded in Belorussia by Shneur Zalman, at the end of the eighteenth century. At first called Chabad (acronym of "hokhma, binah, da'at": wisdom, reason, knowledge), it developed in the vicinity of the city of Lubavitch, the name of which it adopted. Following the First World War, its epicenter moved to Warsaw, then, after the Second World War, to the United States, specifically to Brooklyn. In 1950, Menachem Mendel Schneersohn took over the leadership of the movement, attempting to maintain its anti-Zionist perspective. At the same time, Israel was becoming the world center of Torah study, and the Lubavitch leader induced some of his faithful to settle there. The movement, which was very quiet for many years, became much more prominent in the middle of the 1980s, when it benefited from the financial support of the Australian millionaire rabbi Joseph Gutnik. Centered around its chief rabbi in Brooklyn, its activity expanded, having vast resources at its disposal, in particular the largest Jewish publishing house in the world, Kehot. Followers of a very strict regimen, the Lubavitch preach the observance of the 613 Torah commandments, and oppose assimilation. After the death, in June, 1992, of Menachem Schneersohn, considered by some as the Messiah ("Moshiach"), two currents surfaced in the movement: the first uniting the messianics, the second uniting the pragmatics. Since then, Rabbi Gutnik has been the political and secular leader of the Lubavitch, while Rabbi Krinsky has been in charge of its overall functions. The Lubavitch movement has opposed any peace accord with the Palestine Liberation Organization (PLO).

SEE ALSO Messiah; Torah.

MAʿABARAH: Hebrew word utilized to designate transit camps for new arrivals to Israel at the time of the great waves of immigration of the 1950s.

MAʿA LOT: An urban community in Upper Galilee, Israel, Maʿa lot was founded in 1956 to replace two temporary settlements of mostly North African Jewish immigrants. Located about 6 miles (10 km) south of the border with Lebanon, Maʿa lot had a population of approximately 20,000 in 2002. It was the site of a terrorist attack on 15 May 1974, when three members of the Democratic Front for the Liberation of Palestine, disguised in Israeli uniforms, took control of a Maʿa lot school building, where a group of ninety children on a field trip were sleeping on the floor. Some of the children were killed on the spot, and some escaped by jumping out a window. The terrorists held the remaining children hostage, threatening to kill them if demands for the release of Arab guerrillas from Israeli prisons were not met by 6:00 P.M. At 5:45 P.M. a unit of the Israeli army's Golani Brigade stormed the building, killing the three terrorists. Sixteen children were killed and seventy were wounded.

SEE ALSO Democratic Front for the Liberation of Palestine.

MAʾARAKH PARTY

SEE Alignment Party.

MAʿARIV (Evening, in Hebrew): Israel daily, center-right, founded in 1948 by journalists who had quit *Yediot Aharonot*. In 1992 its majority stockholder, Robert Maxwell, sold his interest to the Nimrodi family. In September 1995 a telephone-tapping incident, in which *Yediot Aharonot* was also mixed up, obliged its editor to resign. In July 1998 Ofer Nimrodi, president of the administrative council of the newspaper, was sentenced to eight months in prison as a result of this incident.

As of 2004, *Maʿariv* defines itself as an apolitical paper with appeal to both secular and religious Israelis. Although it once had the largest readership of any paper in Israel, its circulation has decreased.

SEE ALSO *Yediot Aharonot.*

MACCABEES (Hammer, in Hebrew): Name of the Jewish family, founders of the Hasmonean dynasty, that led the uprising of the Jews against the Seleucid kings (175–135 B.C.E.), who wanted to impose Greek culture upon them. Mattityahu and his five sons, fighting to rid ancient Palestine of Hellenism, succeeded in restoring the sacrificial altar to the Temple. This event is celebrated during the Jewish holiday Hanukkah. According to legend, during the rededication of the Temple the lamps stayed lit for eight nights, although there was only enough oil for one night's light—a miracle commemorated by the lighting of the menorah.

MADRID CONFERENCE. PRESIDENT GEORGE H. W. BUSH (RIGHT) MEETS WITH PRIME MINISTER YITZHAK SHAMIR OF ISRAEL AT THE MIDDLE EAST PEACE CONFERENCE IN MADRID IN LATE 1991. SEVERAL SESSIONS OF BILATERAL NEGOTIATIONS TOOK PLACE, BUT THE TALKS BROKE OFF WITHOUT ANY CONCLUSIVE PROGRESS. *(© Peter Turnley/Corbis)*

SEE ALSO Hanukkah.

MACCABIAH: Name of the Jewish Olympic games that take place every four years in Israel.

MADRASA: Also medersa, from the Arabic *darasa*, "to learn," and *darrasa*, to teach. The contemporary use of Madrasa designates a school, secular or religious, public or private.

Historically a madrasa was a Qur'anic school, generally established near a mosque. It could be small or a large complex characterized by medieval architectural structure. A typical madrasa had one entrance leading to an interior courtyard with a richly decorated fountain and basin at the center. This couryard was surrounded by tiers of galleries containing openings into student rooms and halls used for prayer and study.

MADRID CONFERENCE: International Middle East peace conference held in Madrid from 30 October to 4 November 1991.

A consequence of the Gulf War, the conference was part of a concerted effort by the United States and the Soviet Union to establish a definitive peace in the Middle East. It took place only after the United States had reaffirmed its commitment to guarantee Israel's security. Because the Palestine Liberation Organization (PLO) was excluded from the discussions, Palestinians were represented by delegates from the occupied territories included in the Jordanian delegation.

The conference, based on UN Security Council Resolutions 242 and 338, comprised three phases:

1) A plenary meeting during which the positions of the participants (United States, USSR, Israel, Egypt, Lebanon, Jordan-Palestinians, Syria, European Union) were argued before the observers (UN,

Gulf Cooperation Council, Maghrib States). Also discussed were proposals for negotiations that set the stage for the two succeeding phases of the conference.

2) Bilateral negotiations (Israel, Jordan-Palestinians, Syria, Lebanon) to resolve territorial conflicts.

3) Multilateral negotiations to solve problems of regional interest (security, economic development, refugees, water resources, environmental protection). During these negotiations, Yitzhak Shamir, the Israeli prime minister, made no concessions to the Arab countries, particularly regarding the Jewish settlements in the Occupied Territories. Under pressure from the United States, however, he was obliged to be more flexible in matters of procedure.

The first direct talks between Israel, Syria, Lebanon, Jordan, and the Palestinians, which began in Madrid on 3 November 1991, were followed by many sessions of bilateral negotiations, but were broken off. While the discussions among the three Arab states were directed toward peace treaties, negotiations between Israel and the Palestinians were based on a two-step formula: agreement about the arrangement of internal autonomy, and negotiations regarding permanent status for the Palestinian autonomous territories. Following the Madrid Conference, although not directly a result of it, two agreements, negotiated through different channels, were finally forged: on 13 September 1993 the Israel-Palestinian Declaration of Principles was signed in Washington; and on 26 October 1994 the Israeli-Jordanian peace treaty was signed at the Araba/Arava crossing between Jordan and Israel.

SEE ALSO Gulf War (1991); Oslo Accords; Resolution 242; Resolution 338; Shamir, Yitzhak.

MAFDAL

SEE National Religious Party.

MAGEN DAVID

SEE Star of David.

MAGHRIB: Geographical term indicating the Arab West—North Africa and, before 1492, Spain. The Arabic word (sometimes rendered "maghreb") means "west" or "place of the sunset." Maghrib is also the name of the fourth Muslim prayer of the day, occuring at sunset, and the Arabic name for the country of Morocco.

SEE ALSO Mashriq.

MAGNES, JUDAH (1877–1948): U.S. reform rabbi, founder and first president of the Hebrew University of Jerusalem.

Born in San Francisco, Judah Magnes received rabbinic ordination at Hebrew Union College in 1900 and his doctorate in philosophy at the Universities of Bern and Heidelberg. He served as rabbi of New York's Temple Emmanuel and later of B'nai Jeshurun. One of the founders of the American Jewish Committee, he also helped found the Yiddish daily newspaper *Der Tag*, as well as the American Civil Liberties Union and the American-Jewish Joint Distribution Committee. Magnes immigrated to Mandatory Palestine in 1922, becoming the first president of the Hebrew University in 1925. He rejected the notion of the "negation of the diaspora," contending that both Zion and the diaspora were of equal importance to Jewish life. He was prominent in the Ihud (unity) movement, a small group of intellectuals who argued for the establishment of a binational state rather than a Jewish state in Palestine. At the end of his life, following the creation of the State of Israel in 1948, he lobbied for a humanitarian resolution to the conflict.

MAHAL: Abbreviation of the Hebrew Mitnadev huts la-Aretz (foreign volunteers), utilized to designate foreign volunteers, both Jewish and non-Jewish, who came to Israel in 1948 to fight with the Israelis against the Arab armies.

MAHDI: Arabic for "the Guided One." The title given the expected deliverer or messianic figure in Islam.

The term and concept are from Muslim eschatological tradition, both Sunni and Shi'a, rather than from the Qur'an. False Mahdis have sometimes arisen at times of crisis in Muslim history. The concept is not current in modern mainstream Sunni Islam, but is sometimes made use of by radical Islamist or Sufi movements to motivate their followers. In Shi'a Islam anticipation of the Mahdi's arrival is a standard component of pious belief.

MAHIR, AHMAD (1935–): Egyptian politician and diplomat, born in 1935. In 1957, Ahmad Mahir joined the Egyptian foreign ministry. Between 1958 and 1970 he was assistant secretary in the Egyptian embassies at Paris and Zurich. Between 1971 and 1974 he was counselor for security affairs to the presidency of the Egyptian Republic. The following year he became bureau chief of community affairs in the Egyptian foreign ministry. Between 1978 and 1980 he was head of the cabinet of the foreign minister,

Kamel Hassan Ali. In this capacity, he participated in the Camp David negotiations.

In 1980 he was named Egyptian ambassador to Portugal. Two years later, he filled the same position in Belgium. In September 1988 he was named Egyptian ambassador to Moscow, then, four years later, to Washington. As such, he participated in much negotiation, making him a known figure in the context of the Israeli-Arab peace process. On 15 May 2001, while directing the Arab and African aid fund of the Arab League, he was appointed foreign minister, replacing Amr Musa, who had just been elected secretary general of the League.

On 27 July 2001 Mahir undertook a European trip that led him to France and Italy as part of the efforts being made to find a solution to the Israeli-Palestinian crisis. He has continued to work toward mediation of relations between Israelis and Palestinians. In December 2003, while visiting Jerusalem in an attempt to improve strained ties between Egypt and Israel, he was shoved and heckled by Palestinian worshippers at the al-Aqsa mosque, who objected to his visit to a holy site under Israeli occupation.

SEE ALSO Camp David Accords; League of Arab States; Musa, Amr Muhammad.

MAHMIR: Word designating a Jew who observes religious commandments in an extremist manner.

MAIMONIDES (1135–1204): Jewish theologian, philosopher, and doctor born in Cordoba in 1135. His real name was Moshe ben Maimon, but he was also known as Ramban and Abu Imran Mussa ibn Maymun.

Forced to leave Spain, Maimonides settled for a time in Morocco, then went to Egypt in 1165 where he was named head rabbi of Cairo and doctor to the vizier of Saladin. A rationalist, he codified the Jewish law and wrote a number of philosophical and theological treatises. His two principal works are the *Mishneh Torah* and the *Guide for the Perplexed (Dalalat al-Ha'irin)*. His encyclopedic work, in Hebrew as well as Arabic, influenced not only Jewish thought, but Christian philosophy as well. He died in 1204 at Fustat (Old Cairo) and is buried in Tiberias.

MAJALI, ABD AL-SALAM (1925–): Jordanian political figure, born in 1925 at al-Karak, Abd al-Salam Majali obtained a diploma in 1949 in general medicine.

Specializing in ENT, Majali was one of the first Jordanian doctors in the Jordanian army where he was director of a military hospital. After resigning from the army at the rank of general, he became personal physician to King Hussein in 1967. In 1969, he was named minister of health, and the following year, minister of the presidency of the Council. Between 1976 and 1979 Majali was minister of education, then counselor to the king. Several times a university president, he was also general director of the Jordan Health Institute in 1990 and 1991.

In October 1991 Majali was named head of the Jordanian delegation for bilateral negotiations with Israel, and on 29 May 1993 he became prime minister while simultaneously holding the portfolios of the defense and foreign ministries. On this authority he participated actively in Jordanian-Israeli peace negotiations and in the Israeli-Palestinian peace process, serving as a signatory on 26 October 1994 to the peace accord between Jordan and Israel. On 8 January 1995 Majali resigned his post as head of government to retake his senator's seat and was again named prime minister on 19 March 1997. On 19 August of the following year, a few days after King Hussein had delegated his powers to his brother, Prince Hassan, Abd al-Salam Majali resigned his posts, yielding his place to Fayiz al-Tarawneh. Today Majali is the vice president of the senate and undertakes semiofficial travel.

SEE ALSO Hassan of Jordan; Hussein ibn Talal; Tarawneh, Fayiz al-.

MAJDAL SHAMS FIRST PLAN: Name of a plan for withdrawal of the Israeli army from the Golan Heights proposed in 1994 by Israeli prime minister Yitzhak Rabin as a prelude to a potential Syrian-Israeli peace treaty.

Based on a partial withdrawal spread over three years, this plan provided for the return of all five of the Druze villages occupied by Israel since 1967, including the important Druze locality of Majdal Shams—thereby testing the security accords that would have been signed with Syria. This plan also provided for setting up a military early-warning system, which would have involved the participation of the United States.

Negotiations began later that year in Washington and continued through early 1996. The Syrians took the consistent position that only a complete withdrawal was acceptable, although they appeared to be flexible about the timing. In February and March of 1996 there was a series of suicide bombings in Israel carried out by Islamist fanatics; and Prime Minister Shimon Peres, who had taken office after Rabin was assassinated in November 1995 by a Jewish fanatic, broke off negotiations with Syria. Peres faced a strong challenge in the upcoming Israeli elections from Benjamin Netanyahu, whose Likud opposed any Israeli withdrawal from occupied land. There were no further negotiations while Netanyahu was in office.

SEE ALSO Golan Heights; Israeli-Syrian Negotiations, 1994–2000; Likud; Netanyahu, Benjamin; Peres, Shimon; Rabin, Yitzhak.

MAJLES AL-SHURA: Arabic for "consultative assembly." By extension it designates the advisory council that is a part of state institutions and most Arab movements or political parties.

MAJLIS AL-SIYASI: Arabic for "political assembly." By extension it designates the political council in state institutions as well as in most Arab political organizations.

MAJMAʿ AL-ISLAMI, AL-: Muslim charity organization ("Islamic Collective") sponsored by the Muslim Brotherhood, started in the Gaza Strip in 1973 by Sheikh Ahmed Yasin who later became the spiritual leader of HAMAS.

SEE ALSO Gaza Strip; HAMAS; Muslim Brotherhood.

MAKHTERET: Hebrew word meaning "underground," used to refer to groups like Etzel and Lohamei Herut Yisrael (LEHI) during the British Mandate. In addition it refers to a Jewish group (also known as "TNT," or Terror Neged Terror, "terror against terror") that in 1984 carried out five attacks against Palestinian mayors in the West Bank, then tried to blow up the Mosque of Omar in Jerusalem.

SEE ALSO British Mandate; Lohamei Herut Yisrael.

MAKI

SEE Israel Communist Party.

MAKTAB AL-SHURA: Arabic for "advisory office," designating one of the infrastructures of a movement or party such as a "consultative bureau."

MAKTAB AL-SIYASI: Arabic for "political department."

MAMLAKHTI'UT: Hebrew word for "statism." it is used to designate the unitary and centralized organization of the State of Israel. The concept is attributed to David Ben-Gurion.

MAMLUKS: Dynasty that reigned over Egypt from 1250 to 1517, after seizing state power following the death of the last Ayyubid sultan. The name derives from an Arabic word meaning "possessed" or "slave"; the Mamluks had first established themselves in Egypt as slave soldiers serving the Ayyubid sultans, who were subordinate to the Abbasid Caliphs in Baghdad. The Abbasids were overthrown by the Mongols, who then moved into Syria and Palestine, where the Mamluks defeated them, thus adding those countries to their Egyptian empire. In 1517, after the occupation of Egypt by the Ottoman Turks, the Mamluks coalesced with the Ottomans. In 1811 the Ottoman sultan Muhammad Ali, sent to Egypt after the Napoleonic expedition, had the Mamluks massacred.

During the era when the Mamluks occupied Jerusalem, it became an important Muslim religious center and many elaborate buildings were constructed, giving a Muslim architectural character to the city. However, the Mamluks took no other interest in Jerusalem; and because of neglect and heavy taxes, the city's economy and population declined under their rule.

SEE ALSO Abbasids; Ottomans.

MAPAI (Mifleget Po'alei Eretz Israel—Workers party of Eretz Israel): Socialist political party, created in 1930 under the impetus of David Ben-Gurion and Berl Katznelson from the merger of two groups, Ahdut ha-Avoda and ha-Po'el ha-Tzaʿir.

Under the leadership of David Ben-Gurion, MAPAI confirmed its reformist orientation by framing the policies that led to the creation of the State of Israel. The first Israeli Knesset elections in February 1949 resulted in MAPAI obtaining 46 seats out of 120, with the radical socialist party MAPAM winning 19. The most important political party in the State of Israel, MAPAI ran the Israeli government for twenty consecutive years. MAPAI supporters had a quasi-monopoly on principal Israeli institutions such as the Jewish Agency for Israel—in charge of immigration—a portion of the army, and Histadrut—the confederation of labor unions. However, because he despised Menachem Begin so deeply, David Ben-Gurion refused to share power with the Herut Party throughout his several terms of office. In December 1953 Ben-Gurion resigned from his post of prime minister to be replaced by Moshe Sharett, but increasing internal frictions led to the emergence of factions within MAPAI, and in February 1955 Ben-Gurion again took office, this time as defense minister. In elections the following June,

MAPAI, weakened by internal quarrels, lost five seats in the Knesset, and it was not until November, after five months of haggling and attempts to build a coalition cabinet, that Ben-Gurion presented his new government.

In June 1956, Ben-Gurion appointed Golda Meir as foreign minister, replacing the "dovish" Sharett, and for the next nine years MAPAI reigned supreme, imposing its policies on the Jewish state and provoking both ideological and personal conflicts. In 1963 Ben-Gurion resigned as prime minister, and from MAPAI, after the Lavon Affair, a controversy that divided the party. In November 1965 MAPAI accepted the participation of the parliamentary oppositional bloc, GAHAL, which had won 26 seats in the government of Levi Eshkol, and in February 1966 Golda Meir was elected secretary general of MAPAI. The party underwent an internal crisis in 1967 with the surfacing of a reformist movement led by Abba Eban, Moshe Dayan, and Shimon Peres. After the War of 1967, this became the majority leaning. In 1968, MAPAI merged with the RAFI and Ahdut ha-Avoda Po'alei Zion parties to create the Israeli Labor Party (ILP). MAPAI remained the most significant element in this alliance although the 1965 election was the last one in which MAPAI ran candidates under its own party name.

In February 1969 Golda Meir became prime minister, replacing Levi Eshkol. The Knesset elections of the following October resulted in the Labor Party–MAPAM alliance winning 56 seats. During the mandate of Meir, MAPAI was confronted by the crisis of the 1973 War, discrediting the entire party. The Knesset elections of December 1973 brought Labor 51 seats, but the Likud bloc grew stronger, winning 43 seats. In April, accused of a negligent defense policy, Meir and Moshe Dayan resigned from the government, yielding to the new Laborite generation centered on Generals Chaim Bar-Lev, Aharon Yariv, and Yitzhak Rabin, with Rabin replacing Meir as prime minister. MAPAI was weakened by dissension in the Labor Party prompted by power struggles and corruption scandals among several prominent leftist politicians. The elections of May 1977 won the Labor front only 32 seats, with the loss of 19 seats, mainly to the centrist bloc, Dash.

SEE ALSO Ahdut ha-Avodah; Begin, Manachem; Ben-Gurion, David; Dash; Dayan, Moshe; Eban, Abba; GAHAL Party; Herut Party; Histadrut; Israel Labor Party; MAPAM; Meir, Golda; Peres, Shimon; Rabin, Yitzhak; RAFI Party.

MAPAM (Mifleget Po'alim Me'uhedet): Israeli radical socialist party, created in 1944 by dissident members of MAPAI. The ha-Shomer ha-Tza'ir ("the Young Guard") later joined this new political party.

In January, 1949 MAPAM won 19 of the 120 seats in the first Knesset elections. This made it the second most important Israeli political party after MAPAI which won 46 seats. During this time, MAPAM, considered to be an extreme leftist group piloted by the ha-Shomer ha-Tza'ir, greatly influenced the Kibbutzim.

In 1954 there was a split in the party with former members of ha-Shomer ha-Tza'ir remaining in MAPAM and former members of Ahdut ha-Avodah-Po'alei-Tziyon forming Ahdut ha-Avodah. Other MAPAM members left to join MAPAI or the Communist Party, further weakening MAPAM, but after creating an alliance with the Labor Party (ILP) in October 1969, the unified parties won a total of 56 Knesset seats, leading to a government coalition. By June 1974 two MAPAM members, Messrs. Shemtov and Rosen, had joined the Rabin government as ministers of health and immigrant absorption. MAPAM continued to back the Labor Party until 1984 when the National Unity accord was signed by the ILP and Likud.

In November 1986 MAPAM leaders participated in an meeting in Romania that brought together Jewish and Arab intellectuals from Israel and Palestine who favored peace. This led to MAPAM basing its platform for the 1988 Knesset elections on the principle of "the territories in exchange for peace." In 1992 MAPAM leadership decided to ally with the Movement for Civil Rights and Peace (RATZ) and the Shinui Party to form the Meretz parliamentary bloc and Labor's primary partner in the government coalition. This left-wing coalition won 61 seats in the June 1992 Knesset elections, with Meretz winning 12 of those seats. Subsequently, four important Meretz figures joined the government of Yitzhak Rabin, one of these being MAPAM leader Yaïr Tsaban, who was appointed minister of immigration.

In October 1993 Hadash and the Progressive List for Peace made common cause with MAPAM during the municipal elections. In the Knesset elections of 1996, which saw the victory of Likud leader Benjamin Netanyahu, Meretz won nine seats, three of which went to MAPAM. Three years later when Ehud Barak, head of the Labor Party, won the elections, Meretz obtained ten seats, two of whom joined the new government as ministers of education and of commerce. This alliance was reversed on 21 June 2000 when Meretz decided to leave the cabinet of

Ehud Barak because of concessions his administration had made to the ultra-Orthodox party SHAS. In the 2003 elections Meretz received 5.2 percent of the vote or six seats in the Knesset.

SEE ALSO Ha-Shomer ha-Tza'ir; Likud; MAPAI; Meretz Party; Movement for Civil Rights and Peace; Progressive List for Peace; Rabin, Yitzhak; SHAS, Shinui Party.

MARONITES: The largest Christian community in Lebanon. They are members of the Maronite Catholic Church, a Uniate Church—affiliated with, but not under the control of, the Roman Catholic Church—that follows its own rites, customs, and liturgy. The church is led by a patriarch, currently Nasrallah Sfeir, who, because of the sectarian political arrangement of Lebanese society, is a politically significant person.

The church was founded in the fifth century at a monastery south of Antioch by followers of the hermit St. Maron. The Maronites emigrated to Mount Lebanon in the seventh century to escape the persecution of the Greek Orthodox Church of Byzantium. They made common cause with the European Crusaders and affiliated with the Roman church in 1182.

The first sectarian struggles between the Maronites and the Druze occurred in 1841. In the following year an era of instability commenced in Lebanon, due to, among other causes, the intervention of European powers into Ottoman politics. Since 1648 France had guaranteed the protection of Catholics in general and Maronites in particular, while Russia supported the Greek Orthodox, and Great Britain, the Druze. In May 1860 an incident between Christians and Druze degenerated into a civil war, which led to the intervention of the French army. A commission of the European Great Powers negotiated an arrangement called the Règlement Organique in 1861 in which the Mount Lebanon province, with a Maronite district and a Druze district, became autonomous within the Ottoman Empire.

Owing to its ties with France, the Maronites experienced significant social, as well as cultural and economic, development. Following World War I and the end of Ottoman rule, France received a League of Nations mandate over Greater Syria, which included Lebanon. At the urging of the Maronites, the French created a Greater Lebanon, taking predominantly Muslim territory from Syria and annexing it to the original autonomous province establishing the current borders. In 1926 the French promulgated a constitution establishing a strong presidential regime headed by a Christian, with a controlling role for the Maronites. The amended constitution of independent Lebanon in 1943 was based on a National Pact agreed to by the leaders of the Maronite and Sunni Muslim communities that reserved the presidency for a Maronite and the prime ministership for a Sunni, and confirmed the sectarian basis of Lebanese politics.

The Maronite political elite dominated Lebanon before the civil war of 1975–1990 and has continued to do so since (with Israeli and Syrian help)—a domination at least partly based on the fiction that the Maronites are the largest confessional community in the country. It is estimated that the population of Lebanon is at least 70 percent Muslim, with 45 percent of that being Shi'a.

SEE ALSO Arab-Israel War (1982); Druze; Jumayyil, Bashir; Lebanese Forces; Lebanese Front; Lebanon; Phalange; Sabra and Shatila; Sfeir, Nasrallah.

MARRANO: Pejorative word used by the Christian populace to designate a Jew ostensibly converted to Catholicism during the fourteenth century persecutions in Spain and Portugal, but who continued to practice Judaism secretly.

MASADA: Fortress, located on a rocky peak beside the Dead Sea, where a historic battle took place between the inhabitants and the Romans from 70 to 73 C.E. and around which an extremely important myth/legend emerged, especially in the twentieth century. Basically composed of Sicarii and Zealots under the command of Elazar ben Yair, the population of Masada (Kasr el-Sebbeh in Arabic), after a three-year siege conducted by the Roman general Flavius Silva, decided to commit suicide rather than surrender to the Romans. According to tradition, two women and three children were excepted, so as to transmit the story of this sacrifice to the Jewish community.

In 1927, the poem "Masada," composed by Isaac Lamdan, became the watchword of Zionist youth. At the end of 1941, when Palestine was threatened by the German troops of General Erwin Rommel, some Jewish leaders proposed a withdrawal of the population to Carmel, where resistance would be organized. The plan was called "Masada." In January 1942 these leaders met on the Masada site to study the plan, but it was not put into effect. The word "Masada" symbolizes the resistance of Israel to invaders of today and yesterday. But it also carries the not-so-acceptable suggestion that suicide is preferable to surrender. Until the end of the 1980s, young recruits to the Israel Defense Force (IDF) were sworn into the service on the site of Masada.

Because of its symbolism, Masada today is the most popular destination after Jerusalem of Jewish tourists visiting Israel. Since the excavation of the fortress in 1964, cable cars have enabled tourists to reach it; now with new larger cars and an elegant tourist center at the base of the mountain, thousands of visitors ascend daily.

MASALHA, NAWAF: Israeli Arab politician, born in November 1943, at Kufr Qara, Palestine.

After studying to be a teacher, Nawaf Masalha joined the Israeli Labor confederation, Histadrut, where he quickly became a member of the central committee and head of the Arab section. In the elections of 1988, he was elected as a Labor Party member and deputy speaker of the Knesset. Re-elected a Labor MK in June 1992, he joined the government of Yitzhak Rabin the following 3 August as a deputy minister of health. In May 1996, after the Right was returned to power, he was again appointed deputy speaker of the Knesset. On 5 August 1999, he was named deputy-foreign minister under David Levy in the government of Ehud Barak, the first appointment of an Israeli Arab to this post. In the Knesset he also sat on the powerful foreign affairs and defense committees.

Masalha gave up his seat in the Knesset in 2003. He has been an ardent defender of equal rights for Israeli Arabs and joined with like-minded Israeli Jews in supporting initiatives for Arab-Israeli peace.

SEE ALSO Barak, Ehud; Histadrut; Knesset; Levy, David; Rabin, Yitzhak.

MASAR

SEE Islamic National Way Movement.

MASHRIQ: A geographical term designating the Arab East, the part of the Arab world in Asia—the Arabian peninsula, and from the Levant to Iraq. The Arabic word means "east" or "place of the sunrise."

SEE ALSO Maghrib.

MASJID: Mosque. The Arabic word means "place of prostration" and indicates the customary place for performing an obligatory ritual prayer.

MASORTI (Conservative, in Hebrew): Traditionalist Jew who is neither Orthodox nor secular and who observes some of the religious commandments for familial, social, or sentimental reasons. This word also designates one of the currents of liberal Judaism, which advocates respect for the halakhah while being in favor of adaptability to modern life. The Masorti Movement in Israel is affiliated with Masorti Olami (the World Council of Masorti/Conservative Synagogues) as well as with the international association of Conservative rabbis and other organizations representing Conservative Judaism throughout the world.

SEE ALSO Halakhah; Rabbi.

MASSAR, AL-: Palestinian political and cultural bimonthly published by the al-Massar Studies Center in Ramallah, Palestine.

MATZPEN (Compass, in Hebrew): Small Israeli political party, founded by students in 1963 after a split with the Communist Party. In 1967 it attracted public attention by protesting Israel's occupation of the West Bank. From then until the early 1970s, when it supported Palestinian resistance in the Occupied Territories, it was Israel's most hated anti-Zionist group. Although it never had more than a few dozen members and nearly dissolved after the 1993 Oslo Accords, former members became increasingly influential, especially with regard to its assertion that Jewish colonization was the primary cause of the Israel-Arab conflict.

SEE ALSO Israel Communist Party; Oslo Accords.

MEAH SHE'ARIM (Hundred Gates, in Hebrew): Name of the main Jewish ultra-Orthodox quarter in Jerusalem, built in the second half of the nineteenth century by Hungarian immigrants. One of Jerusalem's most densely populated neighborhoods, it houses hundreds of yeshivas and synagogues and is known as a center of Orthodox anti-Zionist activity. A majority of its inhabitants devote their time to religious study. Its streets are closed to traffic on the Sabbath.

MECCA: Ancient city (sometimes rendered as Makka) in the Hijaz region of the Arabian Peninsula; the birthplace of the prophet Muhammad and the holiest city in Islam. Mecca has been the spiritual and historical pole of the Muslim faithful since the seventh century; it is the place toward which all Muslims orient themselves during prayer, and the destination of the annual hajj, or pilgrimage, made by pious Muslims. It is the site of the Ka'ba and the well of Zamzam, sites of veneration since, as Muslims believe, Abraham passed by them. Near the Ka'ba are

Mecca. A huge crowd of pilgrims gathers to worship Allah in the most sacred of Muslim holy cities, the birthplace of the Prophet Muhammad. Pilgrimage to Mecca, located in Saudi Arabia, is one of the five pillars of Islam; more than one million Muslims undertake the Hajj every year.

the tombs of Isma'il (Ishmael) and his mother, Hagar.

Mecca is located east of the Red Sea port of Jeddah, and is dominated by Mount Arafat. Once an important commercial station on the road between Syria and Yemen, this city was in ancient times already a place of pilgrimage for Arab tribes, where polytheistic cults abounded, although archaelogical excavations are rarely conducted because of the growth of the city and religious sensibilities.

SEE ALSO Hajj; Ka'ba; Muhammad.

MEDINA: Second holiest city of Islam, after Mecca. This little Arabian oasis, formerly called Yathrib, is where the prophet Muhammad emigrated in 622 C.E., fleeing the hostility of the Meccans, when he began his teaching of the Muslim faith. After the Muslim conquest of Mecca, the oasis changed its name to Medinat al-Nabi (the City of the Prophet, in Arabic).

SEE ALSO Mecca; Muhammad.

MEDO

SEE Middle East Defense Organization.

MEIMAD (Dimension, in Hebrew): Israeli religious political party, created in 1988 by Rabbi Yehuda Amital as a Zionist religious alternative the National Religious Party (NRP), considered to be too nationalist. This center-left party supports the idea of a territorial compromise in exchange for peace with the Palestinians. In the elections of 1988 Meimad obtained no seats in the Knesset. In November 1995, when the Shimon Peres government was being constituted following the assassination of Yitzhak Rabin, Rabbi Yehuda Amital was named minister without portfolio.

Since that time, the leadership of Meimad has hoped to create a center bloc. In February 1996, looking forward to the Knesset elections of the following May, Meimad supported Peres in his candidacy for the post of prime minister against Benjamin Netanyahu, who won the elections. In February 1998 the death of the NRP leader Zevulun Hammer prompted many of the members who had left the NRP in the 1988 split to rejoin. On 22 March 1999, anticipating the Knesset elections, Meimad decided to ally itself with the Israel Labor Party and Gesher to create the "One Israel" (*Israel Ahat*) coalition. The following May, this list won twenty-six seats, while the head of the Labor Party, Ehud Barak, became prime minister. A few weeks later Rabbi Michael Melchior, one of the main leaders of Meimad, was named minister without portfolio in charge of relations with the diaspora.

In 2000 the Gesher members left One Israel, leaving Labor and Meimad allied. In March 2001, when the head of Likud, Ariel Sharon, was elected prime minister, Melchior was named deputy minister of diaspora affairs. The Labor-Meimad coalition had nineteen seats in the 2003 Knesset. As of 2004 the leaders of Meimad are Yehuda Amital, Michael Melchior, Aviezer Ravitsky, Tova Ilan, Benjamin Segal, and Jonathan Shiff.

SEE ALSO Barak, Ehud; Gesher "Bridge" Party; Israel Labor Party; Likud; National Religious Party; One Israel; Peres, Shimon; Rabin, Yitzhak; Sharon, Ariel; Third Way.

GOLDA MEIR. SEEN HERE WITH PRIME MINISTER DAVID BEN-GURION, HER LONGTIME MAPAI COLLEAGUE, C. 1961, MEIR SERVED IN UNION AND GOVERNMENT POSTS FOR DECADES BEFORE BECOMING PRIME MINISTER IN 1969. UNDER PRESSURE FOR FAILURES RELATED TO THE OCTOBER 1973 WAR, SHE RESIGNED IN APRIL 1974. (© Bettmann/ Corbis)

MEIR, GOLDA (Golda Myerson, born Mabovitch; 1898–1978): Israeli political figure, born in Kiev in 1898, died in Jerusalem in 1978. Having been a refugee in the United States since 1906, Golda Meir emigrated to Palestine in 1921, where she was active in union organizations. Rapidly, with David Ben-Gurion, she became one of the leaders of the MAPAI labor party and of the Histadrut union, directing its women's section. In 1934 she was elected secretary of the executive committee of Histadrut. In 1946 she was interim chairwoman of the Jewish Agency for Israel. In 1947, following the United Nations decision on the partition of Palestine (Resolution 181), she went to New York to collect funds for arms for the Haganah. In 1948, as a member of the provisional government, she was the first ambassador of Israel to the USSR after the proclamation of the Jewish state.

From 1949 to 1956 Meir was minister of labor and social affairs in the governments of David Ben-Gurion and Moshe Sharett. In 1955, in the municipal elections, she led the MAPAI list to victory in Tel Aviv. Nevertheless, religious groups opposed her becoming mayor of the city. From June 1956 to January 1966, she was foreign minister in the governments of Ben-Gurion and Levi Eshkol. For ten years she advocated an intransigent foreign policy, in particular toward Arab countries. In February 1966 she was elected secretary general of MAPAI. In 1968 she participated in the creation of the Israel Labor Party (ILP), which came out of the merger of MAPAI with RAFI and Ahdut ha-Avoda Po'alei Zion.

The following year, in February 1969, after the death of Levi Eshkol, she became prime minister. During her tenure (1969–1974), she was confronted with three important crises: the breakup of the national unity coalition, when the Israeli government accepted to consider withdrawal from the Occupied Territories; the tragedy of the assassination of Israeli athletes at the Munich Olympic Games in 1972; and the October ("Yom Kippur") 1973 War. In spite of the victory of Labor in the Knesset elections of December 1973, Meir was unable to withstand accusations that she bore overall responsibility for that war, which caught Israel by surprise and resulted in heavy losses. She was therefore obliged, on 10 April 1974, to resign her post of prime minister; she was replaced by Yitzhak Rabin.

SEE ALSO Ahdut ha-Avoda; Arab-Israel War (1973); Eshkol, Levi; Haganah; Histadrut; Jewish Agency for Israel; MAPAI; Munich; RAFI Party; Resolution 181; Rabin, Yitzhak.

MELKITES: Members of the Melkite (sometimes rendered Melchite), or Greek Catholic, Church. This is a Uniate Church—that is, one affiliated with, but not under the control of, the Roman Catholic Church—which follows its own rites, customs, and liturgy. The name is derived from the Syriac *melek,* which means "belonging to the king" (the Byzantine emperor Marcian), and was possibly derisive when first used. The name was given to the Christians of Syria and Egypt who remained faithful to the Byzantine emperor after the Council of Chalcedon, in 451 C.E. Separated from Rome in 1054, some of them rejoined the Roman family in 1724 when a Roman Catholic was elected patriarch, splitting off from the Greek Orthodox Church, which also follows the Byzantine rite but is not affiliated with the Roman Catholic Church.

MERETZ PARTY: Israeli center-left parliamentary political bloc, separated from the Labor Party, created in 1992 by the union of three political groups: MAPAM, RATZ (Movement for Civil Rights and Peace), and Shinui. The three parties that made up Meretz supported the Israeli-Arab peace process and rejected religious coercion. They were favorable to the existence of a Palestinian entity, coexistence between Israel and Arab states, and opposed to the division of Jerusalem. In the socioeconomic domain, on the other hand, profound differences opposed the Shinui, propounding liberal capitalism, to RATZ and MAPAM, which were openly radical-socialist.

In the elections of June 1992, Meretz won twelve seats in the Knesset, contributing to the return of the Israeli left to power under Yitzhak Rabin, and Meretz became Labor's main coalition partner. Four of its members joined the government of Yitzhak Rabin: Shulamit Aloni (education minister), Amnon Rubinstein (science and energy minister), Yair Tsaban (immigration minister), and Ran Cohen (deputy minister of housing). Tension between Meretz and the SHAS religious party was a factor in the weakening of the Rabin government, which Meretz re-

proached for the absence of "tangible progress in the domain of peace with the Palestinians and with Syria." In May 1993, a cabinet reshuffle allowed Walid Tsadik, Israeli Arab member of Meretz, to join the Rabin government as deputy minister of agriculture, thereby strengthening this party's position in the government coalition. The naming of Meretz member Walid Tsadik provoked resentment on the part of the Arab Democratic Party, which had been supporting the Labor Party since 1988, without obtaining any ministerial post. During the first semester of 1994, Meretz threatened to quit the government, after it was announced that Tzomet would be joining the government and SHAS entering the Rabin cabinet. Internal conflicts, provoked by ideological divergences between the three parties constituting Meretz, and personal differences within each of the parties, resulted in a weakening of Meretz, which emerged from the elections of June 1996 with nine seats in the Knesset.

In August 1997, a delegation of some thirty Israeli Arabs made an official visit to Damascus, where it was received by Hafiz al-Asad. This visit was the first of its kind since the creation of the State of Israel. In the municipal elections of 10 November 1998, Meretz won ten seats on the city council of Jerusalem. On 18 May 1999, in the Knesset elections that saw the victory of Ehud Barak, Meretz strengthened its position, obtaining ten seats. One of these seats was taken by Husniya Jabara, who became the first Arab woman to enter the Knesset. On 6 July, in spite of significant participation of members of SHAS in the cabinet of Ehud Barak, three members of Meretz accepted ministerial portfolios: Yossi Sarid in education, Chaim Oron in agriculture, and Ran Cohen in commerce and industry. On 21 June 2000, facing constant opposition from SHAS members, the Meretz ministers resigned from the Barak government, but the movement decided to continue supporting the government in the Knesset. The principal members of Meretz in 2004 were: Yossi Sarid (RATZ), Ra'an Cohen (RATZ), Anat Maor (MAPAM), Avraham Poraz (Shinui), Yair Tsaban (MAPAM), Chaim Oron (MAPAM), Walid Tsadik, Amos Oz, Husniya Jabara, Shulamit Aloni (RATZ), Zahava Galon. In the 2003 election Meretz received 5.2 percent of the vote (six seats in the Knesset).

SEE ALSO Arab Democratic Party; Barak, Ehud; MAPAM; Movement for Civil Rights and Peace; Rabin, Yitzhak; Sarid, Yossi; SHAS; Shinui Party.

MERIDOR, DAN (1947–): Israeli politician. Born in Jerusalem, Dan Meridor holds a law degree from the Hebrew University of Jerusalem. He served as cabinet secretary under Menachem Begin (1982–1983) and Yitzhak Shamir (1983–1984). Elected to the Knesset in 1984, Meridor served as minister of justice from 1988 to 1992. In June 1996 he was appointed minister of finance, a post he resigned in June 1997. In 2001 he was appointed minister without portfolio, responsible for national defense and diplomatic strategy; he held this post until February 2003. Meridor serves as the international chairman of the Jerusalem Foundation.

MERIDOR, YAACOV (1913–1995): Irgun commander, member of Knesset. Yaacov Meridor was born in Poland in 1913. He immigrated to Mandatory Palestine in 1932. In 1933 he joined the Irgun, later serving as chief commander. In 1943 Meridor relinquished command of the Irgun to Menachem Begin, but he continued to hold senior positions in the Irgun until his capture by the British. He was held in various detention camps until 1948, when he escaped, arriving in Israel on the day statehood was declared. At Begin's request, Meridor assumed responsibility for the integration of the Irgun into the Israel Defense Force. Meridor was elected to the Knesset, serving in the First to the Sixth, and the Tenth Knesset. In 1981 he was appointed minister of economics and planning.

MESSIAH: From the Hebrew word *mashiah*, meaning "anointed, blessed." In the Jewish religion this word means God's envoy on earth, charged with reestablishing universal peace and assuring the resurrection of the dead, still awaited. For Christians this is Christ.

SEE ALSO Christianity.

METO

SEE Baghdad Pact.

MIDDLE EAST: A standard Western term for the area of West Asia and North Africa. The definition is elastic, depending on who is speaking, for what purpose, and whether the context is primarily geographical, political, or cultural. It usually includes the area from Turkey to Yemen, and from Iraq to Egypt. It may also include Iran, the states of North Africa to Morocco, and sometimes Sudan, Ethiopia, Eritrea, Somalia, and Djibouti. "Middle East," "Near East," and "Far East" are not neutral geographical terms, like "West Asia" or "East Asia." They are historical constructions that reflect the worldview and political dominance of those who created it in the course of "discovering" and studying the world, which after all is a globe with no central point on its surface. For the Middle East to be "east," there has to be a (conceptual) center, and that point is Western Europe/North America. The more common term was formerly "Near East" (as distinct from "Far East"), obviously in relation to Europe. The term "Middle East" arose in the United States around the turn of the twentieth century and is now, reflecting the balance of power, the dominant one in the (so-called) West.

MIDDLE EAST DEFENSE ORGANIZATION (MEDO): An international military alliance created in 1950 and comprised of the United States, Britain, France, and Turkey. It eventually failed because of the refusal of Egypt to join. MEDO was a predecessor of the Baghdad Pact.

SEE ALSO Baghdad Pact.

MIDDLE EAST TREATY ORGANIZATION

SEE Baghdad Pact.

MIFLAGAH DATIT LE'UMIT

SEE National Religious Party.

MIFLAGAH KOMUNISTIT YISRAELIT

SEE Israel Communist Party.

MIFLEGET HA-AVODAH

SEE Israel Labor Party.

MIFLEGET PO'ALEI ERETZ YISRAEL

SEE MAPAI.

MIFLEGET PO'ALIM ME'UHEDET

SEE MAPAM.

MILHEMET HOVA: Hebrew word used in the Jewish religion to designate a "war imposed by an aggressor."

MILHEMET MITZVAH: Hebrew word, used to designate a "Holy War, obligatory war," according to the Torah.

MILLET: Turkish word designating non-Muslim religious communities in the Ottoman Empire, officially recognized as having their own hierarchies and legal codes.

SEE ALSO Ottomans.

MILO, RONI (1949–): Israeli politician, minister for regional cooperation (2001–2003). Born in Israel, Roni Milo holds a law degree from Tel Aviv University. The former mayor of Tel Aviv, Milo was a member of the Knesset beginning 1977, serving on various committees, including economics, finance, and foreign affairs and defense. From 1988 until March 1990 he served as minister of the environment, and from March to June 1990 as minister of labor and social welfare. Milo was minister of police from June 1990 until 1992, and from August 2000 to January 2001 he served as minister of health. In August 2001 Milo was appointed minister for regional cooperation. In 2003, having left the Center Party to return to the Likud, he failed to make it into the Knesset on the Likud list. Milo was offered the appointment of Israeli ambassador to London in 2004, which he turned down to opt for a career in business.

SEE ALSO Knesset; Likud.

MI'RAJ

SEE Isra'.

MI'RIJ

SEE Isra'.

MIRO, MUHAMMAD MUSTAFA: Syrian political figure, born in 1941 at Tel Amnin. With a degree in Arab literature and human sciences from the University of Erevan (Armenia), Miro began a teaching career at the end of the 1960s. In 1966, he joined the Ba'th Party. In 1971 he was elected vice president of the teachers' union, then, in 1974, assistant secretary general of the Syrian Arab teachers' union, becoming its vice president four years later. During this period, he was also editor-in-chief of the review, *The Teacher's Voice*. Between 1980 and the beginning of 2000, he was successively governor of Dar'a (1980–1986), al-Hasakah (1986–1993), and Aleppo (1993–2000).

On 7 March 2000, he was named prime minister, replacing Mahmud Zo'bi, accused of corruption. At this time, he was considered a technocrat, and to be in favor of reforming the Syrian civil service. On the following 18 June, after the death of the president, Hafiz al-Asad, he was elected to the command committee of the Ba'th, highest in the hierarchy of the party, while remaining at the head of the government. On 11 August 2001, in the framework of a rapprochement of Syria with its neighbors, undertaken by the new president, Bashshar al-Asad, he traveled

to Baghdad and, in November, to Tehran. On 13 December 2001, at the request of the new Syrian president, he formed a new government, in which changes were made particularly in the economic and social ministries. On 10 September 2003, Miro and his cabinet resigned. The president appointed Muhammad Naji al-Utri, with a mandate to speed the pace of reform.

SEE ALSO Asad, Bashshar al-; Asad, Hafiz al-; Ba'th.

MISH'AL, SHARIF ALI (Abbas Zaki): Palestinian political figure, born in 1943 in the West Bank. After joining Fatah early in the 1960s, Mish'al, better known under the pseudonym of Abbas Zaki, became an ardent defender of the Palestinian cause.

In 1972, he was arrested by Jordanian authorities for his activism, then expelled to Syria. In 1982, Yasir Arafat, to whom he had drawn close, named him al-Fatah representative to Yemen. Four years later, forced to leave Aden, he went to the Palestine Liberation Organization (PLO) headquarters in Tunis, where he became an assistant to Mahmud Abbas, head of the department of national affairs. In 1987 he was in a Palestinian delegation that went to China on an official visit. In August 1989, when the first Intifada was intensifying in the Occupied Territories, he was elected to the central committee of al-Fatah, and he headed the "committee to oversee the uprising in the West Bank," at the same time as he was in charge of affairs in the Occupied Territories on behalf of the executive committee. That year, he accompanied Arafat on many foreign trips. In January 1990, he was in Jordan, in charge of restarting the Palestinian-Jordanian negotiations. In November 1991, in the framework of the Israeli-Arab peace process, started at the Madrid Conference, he went to Damascus to meet with leaders of the Palestinian opposition, members of the Palestinian National Salvation Front (PNSF). In June 1993, at the meeting of the central committee of al-Fatah, he joined with those who criticized the way Arafat was leading the movement. In September, he came out against the Israeli-Palestinian Oslo Accords and Declaration of Principles signed in Washington that month. In February 1996, he was elected a deputy to the new Palestinian Legislative Council (PLC), within which he became president of the commission on education. In 2004 he was head of the International Department of al-Fatah.

SEE ALSO Abbas, Mahmud Rida; Arafat, Yasir; Fatah, al-; Intifada (1987–1993); Oslo Accords;

Palestinian Legislative Council; Palestinian National Salvation Front; West Bank.

MISHMAR HA-GVUL (MAGAV): The Israeli frontier guard, a branch of the Israel National Police deployed throughout Israel and the Occupied Territories. Its organization is similar to that of the Israel Defense Force (IDF) and when necessary it is used to augment the IDF; eighteen-year-old recruits can choose the MAGAV for their mandatory service. Its members receive combat training as well as training in counterterrorism, crowd control, and police work. They serve mainly in rural areas, in Arab villages and towns, near the border and at the West Bank. MAGAV has an excellent record of thwarting terrorist attacks.

SEE ALSO Israel Defense Force; West Bank.

MISHNA ("teaching," in Hebrew): This word designates the traditional teaching of the Jewish religious law by written transmission, as opposed to the Midrash, which involves the interpretation of texts. It designates also the first part of the Talmud, composed by Juda Hanassi (Ha Nassi) in the second century. The latter eschewed apocalyptic traditions to concentrate only on teachings relative to the commandments of the Torah. The Mishna is divided into six "orders" (*sedarim*), or treatises, relating to different subjects of religious law.

SEE ALSO Talmud.

MITCHELL COMMISSION

SEE Mitchell Report.

MITCHELL PLAN

SEE Mitchell Report.

MITCHELL REPORT: Report submitted in May 2001 by the Sharm al-Shaykh Fact-Finding Committee headed by U.S. envoy George Mitchell, which was dispatched to Israel and the Palestinian territories in late 2000 to look into the causes of the al-Aqsa Intifada. This mission's aim was to assess security issues in the Palestinian territories, as had been arranged at the Sharm al-Shaykh Summit of 16–17 October 2000. In addition to Mitchell, a former U.S. senator who was a member of the American Task Force for Lebanon (ATFL), the committee included Suleyman Demirel, ninth president of the Republic of Turkey; Thorbjoern Jagland, minister of foreign affairs of Norway; Warren B. Rudman, former U.S. senator; and Javier Solana, high european representative for

the Common Foreign and Security Policy, European Union.

The report called for an immediate and unconditional halt to the violence and the establishment of a six-week cooling-off period, followed by confidence-building measures leading to resumption of negotiations in view of a final resolution of the status of the Palestinian territories. It stated, "The Sharon visit did not cause the Al-Aqsa Initifada. But it was poorly timed and the provocative effect should have been foreseen."

An unconditional cease-fire being unobtainable, the U.S. CIA director, George Tenet, tried to arrange a cease-fire for 13 June, which would serve as a week's test before the Mitchell Report was put into effect. The Tenet Plan was based on two principles: the immediate resumption of security cooperation and withdrawal of Israeli forces to the positions they occupied on 27 September 2000. At the insistence of Prime Minister Ariel Sharon, the plan assumed a period of seven days without attacks as a condition for its initiation; and since no such period occurred, neither the plan nor the Mitchell Report recommendations could be implemented. By March 2002, when Sharon agreed to forego the week of quiet, Israeli forces had invaded Palestinian territories and the Palestinians were no longer willing to negotiate.

SEE ALSO Aqsa Intifada, al-; Sharm al-Shaykh Summit.

MITHAQ AL-WATANI AL-FILASTINI, AL-

SEE Palestine National Charter.

MIZRACHI (Merkaz Ruchani; spiritual center, in Hebrew): Religious current that surfaced in 1902 in the World Zionist Organization. Twenty years later, this movement gave rise to the worker's party, Ha-Po'el ha-Mizrachi. In 1935, the Mizrachi faction became a major influence in the MAPAI labor party. In 1956 the Mizrachi party merged with other religious Zionist groups to form the National Religious Party (NRP) or Mafdal. Today Mizrachi is a worldwide ideological and educational movement that works to strengthen religious Zionist values both in Israel and among Jewish communities in the diaspora. The Mizrachi youth movement, B'nai Akiva, is the largest youth group in Israel.

SEE ALSO Ha-Poel ha-Mizrachi; MAPAI; National Religious Party; World Zionist Organization.

MIZRAHI (*mizrahi*, pl. *mizrahim*) Hebrew word meaning "oriental(s)," "easterner(s)," that is to say,

Jews from Arab or Muslim countries who have settled in Israel.

SEE ALSO Sephardim.

MOABITES: Nomadic people who settled to the east of the Dead Sea in Moab, in what is now Transjordan, toward the thirteenth century B.C.E. The Moab king feared the invasion of his country by the Hebrews. When the tribes of Israel came from Sinai toward the land of Canaan they circumvented this territory, because of their respect for the determination of its inhabitants to defend themselves. According to the Bible, Moab is the son of Lot.

SEE ALSO Canaan; Hebrew.

MODIʿIN: ("information, intelligence," in Hebrew). Word used to designate Israeli military intelligence, in general.

MOGANNAM, MATIEL: Palestinian feminist (c.1900–1992), born in Lebanon, raised in the United States. She married Mogannam Ilyas Mogannam, a native of Jerusalem who had emigrated to the United States, and returned with him to Jerusalem in the 1920s. She became active in the Palestinian women's movement and was a founder and officer of both the Arab Women's Executive (AWE) and the Arab Women's Association (AWA) in 1929. These groups were begun in the wake of the Western Wall riots and were nationalist as well as feminist organizations. Their primary purposes were to promote the education of girls and the social and economic status of women, but they actively protested the British Mandate and promoted support for the Palestinian national cause. During a demonstration sponsored by the Arab Women's Association in 1933, Matiel Mogannam, a Christian, spoke publicly at the Dome of the Rock, warning of the danger to Palestinians of Zionist immigration. During the 1936–1939 revolt, the AWA provided support for the rebels and aided prisoners. Mogannam was the author of *The Arab Woman and the Palestine Problem,* published in 1937 in London, and of numerous articles in the Palestinian press. She died in the United States.

MOGANNAM, MOGANNAM ILYAS: Palestinian Christian lawyer and political activist. Raised in Jerusalem, he immigrated to the United States before World War I and studied law. Some time in the early 1920s he married Matiel Mogannam and returned with her to Jerusalem (and in 1938 to Ramallah). Mogannam practiced law and was a founding member and offi-

cer of the National Defense Party, a conservative nationalist group favoring compromise with the Zionists and the British, supported by middle-class elites and associated with the Nashashibi family (in opposition to the Palestine Arab Party, equally conservative but opposed to compromise, associated with the rival Husayni family). As a law student, Ahmad Shuqayri, the first head of the Palestine Liberation Organization (PLO), worked in Mogannam's office. The National Defense Party was defunct by 1941, and Mogannam died in 1945.

SEE ALSO Mogannam, Matiel; Palestine Liberation Organization.

MOJHAHED: Shiʿite religious figure, authorized to deliver *fatwas.*

MOKED: A short-lived Israeli political entity. In the Knesset elections of 1973, the two Israeli communist parties, RAKAH (Reshima Komunistit Hadashah) and MAKI (Miflagah Komunistit Yisraelit), formed a joint electoral list as Moked ("Focus"), winning five seats in the Knesset.

SEE ALSO Israel Communist Party; RAKAH.

MOLEDET (Homeland, in Hebrew): Israeli political party of the far right, created in 1988 by the former general Rehavam Zeʾevi, when the Intifada was in its early stages in the Occupied Territories. The Moledet, which upholds the ideology of "Greater Israel," preaches the "transfer" of the Arab population of the Occupied Territories to other Arab countries.

In the Knesset elections of June 1988, this party obtained two seats, filled by Rehavam Zeʾevi and Yaʾir Shprinzak. The following November, Zeʾevi was named minister without portfolio in the government of Yitzhak Shamir. Between 1989 and 1990, Moledet reproached the Israeli government for policies that were "too soft" in the Palestinian territories. In February 1992, for the next Knesset elections, the party allied with ha-Tehiyah. As a result of the ballot, in spite of the defeat of the Israeli right, Moledet strengthened its position, obtaining one more seat than it had in 1988, while ha-Tehiyah disappeared from the political arena altogether. The three Moledet MKs were Rehavam Zeʾevi, Rabbi Joseph Bagad, and Shaul Gutman. Between November 1995 and April 1996, Moledet was weakened by the departure of Gutman and Bagad, who, each in his turn, created their own groups: Yemin Israel and Moreshet Avot, respectively.

For the next Knesset elections Moledet teamed up with the extremist movement Zu Artzenu to constitute a common list. On 30 May 1996, as a result of the Knesset elections, Moledet obtained two seats (Ze'evi, head of Moledet, and Rabbi Benyamin Alon, leader of Zu Artzenu). From 1997 on, the party started recruiting many of its cadres from the ranks of the Russian immigrants, disappointed in Israeli society, where they have problems fitting in. In February 1999, for the general elections of the following May, Moledet decided to join with the extreme right organization, Tekumah, whose key figure was Benny Begin, so as to constitute a common list, the "National Union." As a result of the ballot of 17 May, which saw the victory of the leader of the Labor Party, Ehud Barak, the National Union obtained four seats in the Knesset. In March 2001, when Ariel Sharon, leader of Likud, was elected prime minister, Rehavam Ze'evi was named minister of tourism in the new government. On 17 October, following, while the Intifada was raging in the Palestinian territories, Ze'evi was assassinated by a commando of the Popular Front for the Liberation of Palestine (PFLP).

SEE ALSO Aqsa Intifada, al-; Barak, Ehud; Greater Israel; Ha-Tehiyah; Intifada (1987–1993); Knesset; Likud; Shamir, Yitzhak; Tekuhmah Party; Yemin Israel; Ze'evi, Rehavam; Zu Artzenu.

MORASHAH PARTY (Hebrew, "heritage"): Name of an Israeli electoral alliance between the Zionist religious right and the Po'alei Agudat Israel. Under the leadership of Rabbi Chaim Druckman, it broke away from the National Religious Party in 1984; in 1986 it was reincorporated into that party.

SEE ALSO Po'alei Agudat Israel.

MORDECHAI, YITZHAK (1944–): Israeli politician, minister of defense (1996–1999). Yitzhak Mordechai was born in Iraq in 1944. He immigrated to Israel with his family at the age of five. Mordechai received a master's degree in political science from Haifa University. He served in the Israel Defense Forces for thirty-three years, retiring in 1995 with the rank of major general. Upon his retirement, he joined the Likud Party and was elected to the Knesset in May 1996. Within a month, he was appointed minister of defense, holding that position until early 1999, when he was fired by Prime Minister Benjamin Netanyahu. Mordechai joined a new Center Party and became its candidate for prime minister in the May 1999 elections, but withdrew just before the election. He was reelected to the Knesset in May 1999 as head of the Center Party. In July of that year, the new prime minister, Ehud Barak, appointed Mordechai minis-

ter of transport and deputy prime minister. He resigned after accusations of sexual assault. In March 2001 he was convicted of sexually assaulting and harassing two women and was given an eighteen-month suspended sentence.

SEE ALSO Center Party.

MORESHET AVOT (Ancestral patrimony, in Hebrew): Small Israeli religious political party, created in April 1996 by Rabbi Joseph Bagad, a dissident of Moledet, in anticipation of the May Knesset elections. Rabbi Bagad, a member of the Knesset since 1992 and considered to be a bit eccentric by many members of the Knesset, withdrew his candidacy a few days before the elections; but he ran again in 1999, gaining less than 1 percent of the vote. In 2003 the party again dropped out just before the elections.

SEE ALSO Knesset; Moledet.

MORIAH: Name of a small ultra-Orthodox Israeli party, created in 1990 by Rabbi Yitzhak Peretz-Haim, a dissident from SHAS. For the Knesset elections of June 1992, this party joined with the electoral bloc of United Torah Judaism and won a seat in the Knesset.

SEE ALSO Knesset; SHAS; United Torah Judaism Party.

MORIAH, MOUNT: Biblical name of a hill in Jerusalem, which, by tradition, is the place where Abraham prepared Isaac for sacrifice on a rock. The hill is known to Jews as the Temple Mount. At the top of the hill is Haram al-Sharif (the Noble Sanctuary), an enclosure containing the al-Aqsa Mosque and the Dome of the Rock, enclosing Abraham's rock, which Muslims also believe is the place to which the Night Journey of the prophet Muhammad brought him, and from which he was taken to receive a message from God. It is the third holiest site in Islam. The Dome of the Rock, which replaced the earlier Mosque of Omar, is built upon what is said to be the site of the Temple of Solomon and the Second Temple, or Temple of Herod, of which the Western Wall, or Kotel, is believed by pious Jews to be the remnant.

SEE ALSO Abraham; Aqsa, al-; Haram al-Sharif; Western Wall Disturbances.

MORISCOS: Spanish Muslims who converted to Christianity.

SEE ALSO Christianity.

MORRISON-GRADY PLAN: An Anglo-American proposal made in July 1946 to deal with the post–World

War II problem of Jewish refugees needing to immigrate to Palestine, following upon the report of the Anglo-American Committee of Inquiry. A commission headed by Herbert Morrison, representing Britain's Labour government, and Henry Grady, representing the United States, drew up a report that called for the partition of Palestine into semi-autonomous Arab and Jewish regions, leaving the British high commissioner in charge of defense, foreign relations, customs, and immigration. This plan was rejected by both Arabs and Jews because it would have meant an increase in British control.

MOSAIC LAW: The Law promulgated by Moses, the Torah.

MOSES (Musa, in Arabic; Moshe, in Hebrew): Hebrew prophet. His existence has been reported in three sources, corresponding to different oral traditions: the elohist tradition (the Eternal is Elohim), the Yahvist tradition (God is Yahweh), and the sacerdotal tradition of the Jewish priests. Moses is considered as the unifier of and lawgiver to the Jewish people, leading them to adopt monotheism and the worship of Yahweh, and the author of the basic elements of the Torah.

According to Biblical tradition, Moses, a descendent of Jacob, great-great grandson of Abraham, was born in Egypt around 1300 B.C.E. His father, Aram, was a son of Levi, himself the third son of Jacob. Some scholars believe Moses was the illegitimate son of the pharaoh and a young Jewish girl, Yokebed. To erase the evidence of this, pharaoh ordered all newborn Hebrew males to be put to death. But the child escaped from this fate, due to the intervention of Bitya, a daughter of pharaoh, who then decided to oversee his education. Come of age, Moses entered the court of pharaoh, where he became Mosi (Moses). Around the age of forty, for various reasons, obliged to become an exile, Moses sought refuge in the land of Midian, a region ruled by Jethro, situated east of Sinai. Become a shepherd, Moses married one of the daughters of Jethro, Zipporah, with whom he had two sons, Gershom and Eliezer.

One day, when he was watching over his flock at the foot of Mount Horeb (Mount Sinai), he noticed a bush in flames, but which was not being consumed, from which a supernatural voice arose, demanding that his people be led out of Egypt. Moses asked what name he should cite to motivate the Israelites to leave the land of pharaoh. The voice replied to him "*Ehyeh asher ehyeh* (I am he who is)." The third person form of this was "Yahweh" (He is).

Accompanied by his brother, Aaron, Moses returned to Egypt to try to convince the Israelites to leave this country for the Promised Land, Canaan, and to persuade pharaoh (Rameses II) to allow the Hebrews to leave. The latter denied the request and even added to the backbreaking labor required of the community. A little later, the kingdom of pharaoh was assailed by a series of catastrophes (ten plagues). When darkness covered the land (ninth plague), Moses renewed his demand to pharaoh, who still refused. Then Moses announced that soon "all the firstborn would die in the land of Egypt." To protect themselves against this tenth plague, Moses asked the Jews to sacrifice a lamb and to sprinkle blood on their doors; "so, Yahweh, passing by, will recognize his own and spare the children of Israel." (This "passage" of Yahweh, preceded by a special meal, was commemorated later on as the Jewish Passover or Pesach.) After the death of a number of firstborns, pharaoh decided to let the Jews leave Egypt.

On 15 Nissan, around 1250 B.C.E., the Hebrew people set out on an exodus through the Sinai desert. One day, when his people, confronted by famine and the attacks of the Amalekites, began to doubt the existence of God and the Promised Land, Moses climbed to the top of Mount Sinai, to reflect and try to find a solution. There, after a retreat of forty days (a number that had remained symbolic), Yahweh appeared to him for the second time and transmitted the Table of the Law, inscribed in his own hand. This was an ensemble of Ten Commandments that his people were obliged to obey, renewing thereby the covenant that had passed between God and Abraham a few centuries earlier. Returning to his people, he noticed that the latter had lost their faith, and were worshipping a golden calf, a survival of the Egyptian cult of the bull, Apis. Moses broke the holy Tables. At a loss for what to do, he renewed his ties with the clan of Levites. Many of those close to him implored him to return to Yahweh to ask his forgiveness. After having ascended again to the top of Mount Sinai, Moses, "his face shining," returned with new Tables of the Law on which he himself had engraved the Ten Commandments previously inscribed by Yahweh. He proclaimed the judgment of Yahweh to his people: those who had betrayed him will not come into the Promised Land, only their children will be allowed in. Thereupon, according to Biblical texts, the Hebrews were condemned to wander for forty years, before coming within sight of the land of Canaan. On the twelfth day of the seventh month of the fortieth (symbolic number) year of wandering, having come to Mount Nebo, from which he saw Jericho, Moses showed his people "the land of milk and

MOSES. THIS MANUSCRIPT ILLUMINATION, FROM A TENTH-CENTURY BIBLE, DEPICTS A KEY MOMENT FROM THE BOOK OF EXODUS: "MOSES RELEASING THE WATERS OF THE RED SEA AFTER SAFE PASSAGE OF HIS PEOPLE." THE HEBREW PROPHET IS CONSIDERED THE UNIFIER AND LAWGIVER OF THE JEWISH PEOPLE, THE LEADER WHO BROUGHT THEM OUT OF EGYPT TO THE PROMISED LAND. *(© Gianni Dagli Orti/Corbis)*

honey," promised by Yahweh. A few days later, after having transferred his power to Joshua, Moses died on Mount Nebo, on the threshold of the Promised Land.

According to some scholars, the story of Moses might have been based on Mesopotamian legends. For example, the mystery that surrounds his birth and youth is very similar to the story of Sargon of Akkad, founder of Babylon (twenty-third century B.C.E.). Many resemblances exist between the story of Abraham and that of Moses; the two personages could even have been one. On the other hand, if Moses advocated monotheism, this could be because he revived the idea of a single god, imposed by Pharaoh Amenophis IV (1350–1334 B.C.E.), who supplanted the principal Egyptian divinity, Amon-Re, in favor of Aton, the only god, symbolized by a solar disc. Many Jews having adhered to this new religion,

in spite of the interdiction of the cult of Aton after the death of Amenophis, it is possible that it was maintained in the Jewish community. Finally, an error in translation of Saint Jerome, author of the Vulgate, the Latin version of the Bible, led to an unfortunate artistic interpretation of the personage of Moses, which held sway for a period of ten centuries: Jerome confused the Hebrew word for the "shining" of the face of Moses, on his descent from Sinai, with another word meaning "horns," with the result that statues and paintings of Moses were equipped with horns, an attribute possessed by some pagan divinities!

SEE ALSO Abraham; Canaan; Covenant; Jacob (Biblical); Jericho; Nissan.

MOSHAV (*moshav*; pl. *moshavim*): Jewish community village, where each household is responsible for its

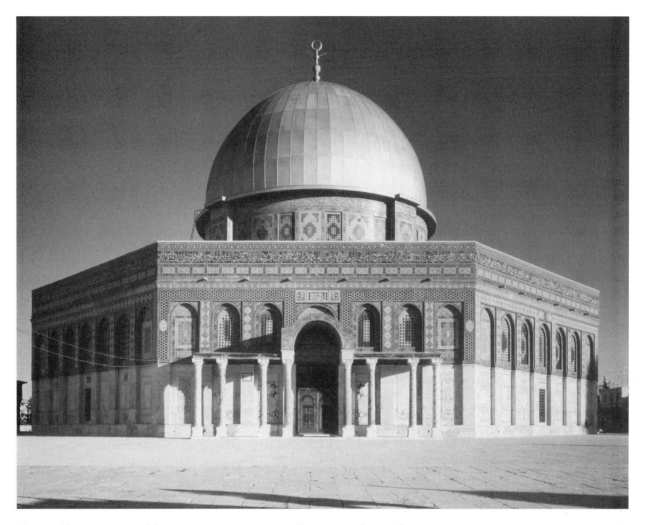

MOSQUE. THE MOST FAMOUS MUSLIM PLACE OF WORSHIP IS THE DOME OF THE ROCK IN JERUSALEM, COMPLETED IN 691 ON THE TRADITIONAL SITE OF THE PROPHET MUHAMMAD'S ASCENSION TO HEAVEN. *(© Scala/Art Resource, New York)*

farm, but the land belongs to the state. The members of the moshav are committed to help each other mutually, while the product of each farm is sold by the central organization of the village, which in return, supplies the equipment and technology necessary for production.

MOSHAV SHITOUFI: A variant of the moshav, based on a collective property and economy, like those of the kibbutz, with the difference that each household manages its own family budget.

    SEE ALSO Kibbutz; Moshav.

MOSHIACH (Mashiah): Hebrew and Yiddish word designating the messenger of God, announced by the sacred texts of the Hebraic law. Equivalent to the Mahdi for Muslims (and the Shi'ite Hidden Imam),

or the Messiah for Christians. Whereas Christians believe that Jesus Christ is the Messiah already come, Jews are still awaiting the coming of their Messiah. Some members of the Lubavitch sect, however, believe that the previous Lubavitcher Rebbe, Menachem Mendel Schneerson, was the Moshiach.

    SEE ALSO Hidden Imam; Lubavitcher Hasidim; Mahdi; Messiah.

MOSQUE: The mosque is a place of worship where Muslims gather to pray. The building is composed of a prayer hall where the mihrab and the minbar are located, very often including a closed court, in the middle of which is found a fountain for ablutions (*mida*). Mosques often have a minaret (from the Arabic *manara*), from which the call to prayer is made.

    SEE ALSO Minbar.

MOSSAD (Mossad Le Biyyun U-le-Tafkidim Meyuhadim; Institute for Espionage and Special Tasks, in Hebrew): Founded in 1951, during the regime of David Ben-Gurion, Mossad is the organization charged with the external security of the State of Israel. This service has been known for many operations involving assassination, in particular those responsible for the murder of the Israeli athletes at the Munich Olympic Games in September 1972. Despite claims as "the best intelligence service in the world," Mossad has known many reversals. If it has shown itself capable of realizing audacious operations, the incompetence of some of its members has been equally notable, and it has gone through periods of obvious internal dysfunctionality. Along with its failure to foresee the 1973 Arab-Israel War, between 1984 and 1989 Mossad endured the fiasco of the Jonathan Pollard affair and found itself implicated in the U.S. Irangate scandal.

At the end of 1997, an internal report alluded to the lack of serious preparation for certain operations. Additionally, there was a series of failures that led to the resignation, in February 1998, of its director, Dani Yatom, replaced by two directors, charged with reforming the service. The successive heads of Mossad have been: Reuven Shiloah (1951–1953), Isser Harel (1953–1963), Meir Amit (1963–1968), Zvi Zamir (1968–1974), Yitzhak Hofi (1974–1982), Nahum Admoni (1983–1990), Shabtai Shavit (1990–1996), Dani Yatom (1996–1998), Ephraim Halevy and Amiram Levine (1998–2002), and Meir Dagan (2002–). The Mossad has been criticized for failing to anticipate the outbreak of the al-Aqsa Intifada in September 2000. At the same time, senior Mossad officials have been increasingly involved in the peace process.

MOSSAD L'ALIYAH BETH "Institution for Immigration B" (so-called illegal immigration): Service in charge of organizing illegal immigration of Jews into Palestine during the British Mandate.

SEE ALSO British Mandate.

MOULID: An Arabic word referring to the popular celebrations surrounding the commemoration of the birthdays of any Muslim holy men and women. Moulid al-Nabi is a Muslim religious holiday commemorating the birth of the prophet Muhammad.

SEE ALSO Muhammad.

MOUSA, AMR MUHAMMAD (1936–): Egyptian political figure, born in October 1936, in Cairo. With degrees in law from universities in Cairo and Paris, Amr Mousa joined the Egyptian foreign ministry in 1958. Twenty years later, at the ministry of foreign affairs, he participated in the Camp David negotiations with Israel. In November 1983, a member of the Egyptian delegation, he became its interim leader, representing his country at the UN. Having returned to Egypt, he rejoined the department of international organizations. In 1987, he was named Egyptian ambassador to India. Three years later, in January 1990, he became permanent representative of Egypt at the UN. While at the United Nations, he invited the State of Israel to join the treaty of nonproliferation (TNP) of weapons of mass destruction in the Middle East.

In March 1991, he participated in activities of the Gulf Cooperation Council (GCC). On the following 20 May, he became the Egyptian foreign minister, replacing Esmat Abdul Meguid, who had been named secretary general of the Arab League. As soon as he entered office, Amr Mousa strove to have his country once more play a central role in the Israeli-Arab peace process. In November 1991, he participated in the Middle East peace conference, which was held in Madrid. In February 1993, with the Djibouti minister, Abdu Bolok Abdu, he co-presided the joint Egyptian-Djibouti commission, which dealt with the Somali problem, among others. During the following April, he made many attempts to reconvene Israeli-Palestinian peace negotiations, which had been adjourned four months earlier, following the expulsion to Lebanon of 415 Palestinians, presumed fundamentalists. Between 1994 and 1995, he campaigned against the Israeli nuclear program, as well as against the proliferation of nuclear arms to certain countries in the Middle East that were starting to want them. On 21 May 1995, he was present in Paris when an accord on arbitrage was signed, in the context of the dispute between Yemen and Eritrea on the Hanish Islands Archipelago in the Red Sea, in which his role as a negotiator was significant. In December 1996, at the Lisbon conference, he spoke in favor of strengthening cooperation between the European Organization for Security and Cooperation (EOSC) and the five Mediterranean countries that were considered as "partners" of the EOSC: Israel, Egypt, Tunisia, Algeria, and Morocco. In November 1997, he was an intermediary in the negotiations between diverse Somali factions, which led to a reconciliation between the parties concerned, signed on 22 December. In February 1998, he became the architect of a rapprochement between Egypt and Iran. During the following October, he served as a mediator in the dispute between Syria and Turkey, concerning Syrian support for the Kurdistan Workers' Party (PKK). His intervention enabled the two parties to come to an agreement.

On 27 July 1988, he met in Paris with his French counterpart, Hubert Vedrine, to discuss possible ways of restarting the Middle East peace process, in particular, the Franco-Egyptian idea of an international conference, which Presidents Mubarak and Chirac had recommended the preceding May. On 19 August 2000, following the failure of the July Israeli-Palestinian summit of Camp David, he received the American envoy, Dennis Ross, in an attempt to oversee the continuing of negotiations toward a final accord between the Israelis and the Palestinians. On 24 March 2001, after ten years at the head of Egyptian diplomacy, Amr Mousa was elected unanimously as secretary general of the Arab League, succeeding his predecessor in the Egyptian foreign ministry, Esmat Abdul Meguid.

As soon as he assumed his new functions, Amr Mousa put into effect a plan for restructuring the organization, the principal innovation consisting in the establishment of positions of League general commissioners of important areas. These posts have been given to influential personalities of the Arab world. In July, Hanan Ashrawi, an important Palestinian political figure, became commissioner for information. The following month, the former Jordanian prime minister, Taher al-Masri, was named commissioner for civil society affairs, and the former Egyptian minister of culture, Ahmed Kamal Abul Magd, became commissioner for "dialogue among civilizations." In August, Mousa called on the world conference against racism, meeting in South Africa, to condemn the policies of Israel toward the Palestinians. In late May 2004, while Israeli forces were attacking the Rafah Palestinian refugee camp in the Gaza Strip, in a show of force involving rocket attacks on civilian neighborhoods and mass house demolitions, the Arab League held a summit meeting in Tunis. It was to have been held earlier but had been postponed over disgreements about the issues of democratic reform on the agenda. Some governments skipped the meeting. Although individual governments and politicians had condemned Israel's actions and American support for them, the League summit generally avoided the subject.

SEE ALSO Ashrawi, Hanan Daouda; Camp David Accords; Gaza Strip; Gulf Cooperation Council; League of Arab States; Ross, Dennis B.

MOVEMENT FOR CHANGE

SEE Shinui Party.

MOVEMENT FOR CIVIL RIGHTS AND PEACE: Israeli political entity, dissident from the Labor Party, founded in 1973 by Shulamit Aloni, Raanan Cohen, and Yossi Sarid. Favoring peace with Arab countries, the Movement for Civil Rights and Peace (RATZ) upheld human rights, and favored the separation of state and religion. In the elections of 1973, it obtained three seats in the Knesset. In June 1974, Aloni joined the government of Yitzhak Rabin as minister without portfolio. In the Knesset elections of 1977 to 1981, RATZ won only one seat, filled by Aloni. Progressively the leader of RATZ succeeded in becoming visible in the Israeli political arena and, as a result of the elections of 1988, her party captured five deputy seats. In 1992, the leadership of RATZ decided to merge with the Shinui Party and MAPAM, to create a new Parliamentary bloc of the center left, the Meretz Party, which obtained twelve seats in the next Knesset elections (June 1992). The two main figures in RATZ joined the government of Yitzhak Rabin: Aloni (who became minister of education) and Sarid (minister of the environment). The stalling of the peace process with the Palestinians and personal conflict between Aloni and Sarid led to a weakening of RATZ, while also prompting Aloni to resign. Sarid succeeded her as the head of the party. In August 1999, the latter was named minister of education in the Barak government, while Ranaan Cohen was given the portfolio of commerce and industry.

SEE ALSO MAPAM; Meretz Party; Shinui Party.

MOVEMENT FOR THE TRADITION OF ISRAEL

SEE TAMI.

MOVEMENT FOR THE ZIONIST RENAISSANCE

SEE Tzomet Party.

MOVEMENT OF THE DISINHERITED: Lebanese Shi'ite organization, created in March 1974 by the Imam Musa al-Sadr, so as to exert pressure on the Lebanese regime to favor the economic development of South Lebanon and the Baqaa Valley, inhabited by a majority of Shi'a. This movement is a branch of the Foundation of the Disinherited (Mustadafin), created in Iran in 1971. Confronted by the lack of responsiveness of the Lebanese government and the degradation of the situation in South Lebanon, the leaders of the movement, in July 1975, decided on armed struggle and created AMAL, the Lebanese Resistance Brigade.

SEE ALSO AMAL; South Lebanon.

MUBARAK, HUSNI (1928–): Egyptian military and political figure, born in May 1928 at Kafr al-Musilha. Having chosen a military career, Husni Mubarak graduated with a degree from the Egyptian Military Academy in 1949, then from the Air Force Academy the following year, obtaining his fighter pilot's credentials. From 1952 to 1957 he was an instructor in the Air Force Academy. Between 1960 and 1964, he studied in the Soviet Union, including courses on piloting heavy bombers, while taking general staff training. In November 1967, he became commandant of the Egyptian Air Force Academy. On 23 June 1969, promoted general, he was named chief of staff of the Air Force, a post he kept until 1971, when he became commander in chief of the Air Force and vice minister of defense.

On 27 April 1972, he accompanied the new Egyptian president, Anwar al-Sadat, to Moscow, where they negotiated an agreement for the Soviet Union to supply arms to Egypt. Improvements he made in the Egyptian Air Force allowed the latter to demonstrate a certain measure of efficacy in the 1973 Arab-Israel War. He was promoted air marshal on 19 February 1974, and Sadat named him vice president of the Egyptian state on 15 April, replacing Hussein Shafi. From then on, Mubarak filled the same role for Sadat that the latter had for Gamal Abdel Nasser. As soon as he was appointed, Mubarak began taking an active part in Egyptian political life, in particular in the domains of defense, and foreign relations, which necessitated much travel. In April 1976, shortly after the abrogation of the Egypt-Soviet friendship treaty, he went to Beijing, where he signed a protocol of a military accord with China. In the following October, he was confirmed in his post of vice president.

In 1977, when the Egyptian president took the initiative of starting a dialogue with Israel, he defended Sadat to Arab countries. On 14 October 1981, following the assassination of Sadat, Mubarak became president. He affirmed that he would continue the policies of his predecessor at a time when Egypt was isolated from the Arab world, following the peace accord signed with Israel. Internally, Egypt was going through a difficult period economically, and in the domain of security, Islamist groups had proved, with the assassination of President Sadat, their determination and capacity to strike at the head of the state. In January 1982, he was named secretary general of the National Democratic Party (NDP). In March 1983, in the corridors of the seventh summit

HUSNI MUBARAK. THE COMMANDER OF THE EGYPTIAN ARMY AIR FORCE, MUBARAK BECAME VICE PRESIDENT OF EGYPT IN 1976 AND THEN PRESIDENT AFTER THE ASSASSINATION OF ANWAR AL-SADAT FIVE YEARS LATER. SINCE THEN, HE HAS ENCOURAGED THE ISRAELI-ARAB PEACE PROCESS AND MAINTAINED TIES WITH THE UNITED STATES, SUPPORTING ITS ACTIONS IN AFGHANISTAN TO COMBAT TERRORISM. *(AP/Wide World Photos)*

of nonaligned countries, held at New Delhi, he spoke with many leaders of Arab countries. These were the first meetings between an Egyptian head of state and Arab leaders since the break in relations between Egypt and the Arab states, provoked by the Israeli-Egyptian peace accords. Reelected president of the Republic of Egypt on 5 November 1987, Mubarak proposed a five-point plan on 22 January 1988 for starting a process of peace negotiations between Israel and the Palestinians.

In February 1989, under his leadership, Egypt joined the Arab Cooperation Council, with Jordan, Iraq, and Yemen. At the time of the Gulf crisis, in August 1990, Egypt backed the Western coalition against Iraq. On 31 October, the headquarters of the

Arab League returned to Cairo, thereby allowing the Egyptian president to assert the hegemony of his country over this organization. Thereafter, in whatever concerned the Israeli-Palestinian peace process, he maintained his leadership of the Arab camp that was supporting the Palestinian cause. On 15 May 1991, his foreign minister, Ismat Abdul Meguid, was elected secretary general of the Arab League, which strengthened the role of Egypt and, by the same token, that of the Egyptian president, in the Arab world. Concurrently, Mubarak launched an economic program meant to reduce inflation and his country's budget deficit, while opening the way to privatization.

On 21 July 1992, he received the Israeli prime minister, Yitzhak Rabin, who had just come to power in Israel. In April 1993, he participated in many meetings with U.S., Israeli, and Palestinian political figures, in an attempt to advance Israeli-Palestinian peace negotiations that had been stalled for several months following the expulsion by Israel of 415 Palestinians, presumed Islamists, to Lebanon. On 13 September, at the time of the signature of the Oslo Accords between Israel and the Palestinians, the Egyptian president affirmed his support for this new phase in the global Israeli-Arab peace process. On 4 October 1993, for the third time, Mubarak was re-elected president of Egypt. On 2 February 1995, he organized a regional summit, in which the participants were King Hussein of Jordan, Israeli prime minister Yitzhak Rabin, and Yasir Arafat, for the purpose of restarting the Israeli-Palestinian peace process. On the following 27 June, he escaped an assassination attempt while on an official visit to Addis Ababa, on the occasion of a summit of the Organization for African Unity (OAU). According to the Egyptian authorities, this attack was carried out by a Sudanese Islamist group. From 13 to 16 March 1996, he presided over the international Summit on Terrorism of Sharm al-Shaykh, which assembled twenty-nine world leaders, of whom twenty were heads of state and government, who had determined to combat terrorism. In the following June, with the advent to power in Israel of the leader of Likud, Benjamin Netanyahu, leading to a blocking of the peace process and a chill in Israeli-Egyptian relations, Mubarak decided to step up his efforts to try to restart Israeli-Palestinian negotiations.

On 3 June, he received the Syrian president, Hafiz al-Asad, with whom he discussed the new regional situation, then, on 18 July, he met with the new Israeli prime minister, who was visiting Cairo. During the mandate of Netanyahu, the Egyptian president was tireless in denouncing, before international organizations, the Israeli leader's evasions. On 4 November, following, he was in Damascus, for talks with the Syrian president. On 17 May 1998, Mubarak was in Paris, where, with President Jacques Chirac, he launched the idea of a conference of countries, "determined to achieve peace" in the Middle East. At the end of April 1999, he led the efforts to mediate the conflict between Ethiopia and Eritrea. On the following 9 July, after Ehud Barak was elected prime minister of Israel, he visited Mubarak, so as to reassure him on the Israeli will to pursue the Israeli-Arab peace process to a successful resolution. On 5 September, at Sharm al-Shaykh, along with the U.S. secretary of state, Madeleine Albright, and the King of Jordan, Abdullah II, the Egyptian president initialed an Israeli-Palestinian peace accord. Two days later, Mubarak was slightly wounded by an man who attacked him with a knife while he was on an official visit to Port Said. On 26 September, reelected with nearly 94 percent of the ballots cast, he began his fourth presidential mandate, with a majority of Egyptians in favor of his designating a vice president. On 5 October, he appointed a new prime minister, Atef Ebeid, an economist, whose main task would be to lift Egypt to the rank of "middle income countries." On 19 February 2000, the Egyptian president made a quick trip to Beirut, so as to demonstrate his solidarity with the Lebanese people following Israeli raids that had destroyed several electricity stations. On 25 February, following, he welcomed Pope John Paul on an official visit to Egypt. On 15 November, the National Democratic Party, led by Mubarak, won the legislative elections, owing to the rallying to it of 209 independent deputies (members or otherwise close to the NDP). Thereby, the NDP obtained 388 of the 444 seats in Parliament. However, these elections were marked by the electoral defeat of some prominent figures in the NDP and by the return of the Muslim Brothers to the political arena, with seventeen deputy seats. On the following 21 November, the Egyptian president decided to recall his ambassador from Israel, following raids of the Israeli army on Palestinian territories, where the al-Aqsa Intifada was in full force. Five days later, he received an advisor of the Israeli prime minister, Ariel Sharon, with whom he discussed the situation in the Palestinian territories and possible ways of restarting the negotiations between Israelis and Palestinians.

Between 24 and 28 April 2001, the Egyptian president was on a European trip, which took him to Germany, Romania, and Russia. On 13 September, two days after the attacks on the World Trade Center in the United States, caught between the U.S.

economic aid necessary to Egypt and public opinion which opposed U.S. strikes in Afghanistan, President Mubarak declared that his country supported the United States in its efforts to combat terrorism, but called for an international conference to deal with the issue. He also called upon the United States to change its policy toward Israel, saying that Israeli occupation is the obstacle to peace. Mubarak strongly opposed the Iraq War of 2003 and predicted that "this war will have horrible consequences. Instead of having one [Osama] bin Ladin, we will have one hundred bin Ladins."

SEE ALSO Albright, Madeleine; Arab Cooperative Council; Arafat, Yasir; Asad, Hafiz al-; Barak, Ehud; Hussein ibn Talal; League of Arab States; Likud; Netanyahu, Benjamin; Oslo Accords; Rabin, Yitzhak; Sharm al-Shaykh Summits.

MUFTI ("judge," in Arabic): Islamic law scholar or jurisconsult who pronounces religious judgments (*fatwas*).

SEE ALSO Fatwa.

MUFTI OF JERUSALEM

SEE Husayni, Hajj Amin al-.

MUHAJIRUN, AL-: Saudi Islamist movement ("Exiles" or "Migrants," in Arabic) started in 1983 by Shaykh Umar Bakri Muhammad. Based in London, this organization is affiliated with the International Islamic Front (IIF), partially financed by Osama Bin Ladin. Its name is a reference to the early Muslim community that followed the prophet Muhammad into exile at Medina.

SEE ALSO Bin Ladin, Osama; International Islamic Front; Muhammad.

MUHAMMAD: The prophet (al-Nabi) and founder of Islam. Muhammad ("he who is praised") ibn Abd'Allah ibn 'Abd al-Muttalib al-Hashimi is thought to have been born in September 570 C.E., in Mecca, in Arabia, in the clan of Hashim of the tribe of Quraysh. In fact, his date of birth remains uncertain, situated by historians during the "year of the elephant" between 569 and 571, a period marked by an attack against Mecca led by the Christian Abyssinian viceroy of Yemen, Abraha, whose troops had a few elephants at their disposal. His father died before he was born and his mother died when he was around six.

Brought up by his uncle Abu Talib, Muhammad, as a youth, accompanied caravans to Syria, affording him the opportunity to meet Jews and Christians, among whom was the monk Bahira, in the city of Basra. The latter has been thought to have seen the future prophet in Muhammad. In 595, Muhammad married a rich widow, Khadija, fifteen years older than he was. In the night of 26 to 27 Ramadan of the year 610 (or 611) he had his first revelations in a cave on Mount Hira, near Mecca. Through the intermediary of the archangel Jibra'il (Gabriel), God charged him with transmitting the Qur'anic message to all of humanity, a message based on the oneness of God. The archangel asked him to be the prophet of the God of Abraham and of Moses. As soon as he started preaching, Muhammad came up against the hostility of the Quraysh, who were afraid that his words might compromise their commercial relations with the people of Mecca, who were polytheists. This hostility prompted him to emigrate to the oasis of Yathrib, a city with a large Jewish community, in July 622. He made a pact with twelve inhabitants of the city (the Oath of Aqaba), allowing him to benefit from the protection of their clan. This emigration marks the beginning of the Islamic calendar named after the emigration (hijra). It was during this epoch, in 622 or 623, that his "Night Journey" (*isra'*) to Jerusalem took place, in which he rode, according to Qur'anic tradition, on a mare that had a woman's head and a peacock's tail. When he arrived in Jerusalem he "ascended to Heaven," where he had been expected by God, who had a message for him. The relations of the first Muslims with the Meccans worsened, leading to a veritable war between the two communities, following which, on 11 January 630, the followers of Muhammad took control of Mecca, emptying the Ka'ba of its idols, leaving only the Black Stone in place. Meanwhile, the Muslims also fought with and banished or killed those who betrayed their army in the battles, in particular many members of the Jewish tribes of Yathrib (renamed Madinat al-Nabi, the "City of the Prophet," or Medina). At Medina, he founded the first Islamic city-state and the first Islamic constitution. The house of the prophet Muhammad in Medina became the first mosque, and Bilal, an emancipated black slave, was charged with calling the Muslims to prayer.

On 7 March 624, the Battle of Badr, south of Medina, marked for Muslims the end of pagan Arabia. The prophet Muhammad remained monogamous until the death of Khadija, following which he married, successively, Sauda, A'sha, Hafsa, Zaynab bint Khuzayma, Umm Salama, Zaynab bint Jahsh, Juwayriya, Umm Habiba, Safiyya, and Maymuna. He had four sons who died early: Qassim, Tayyib, Tahir, and Ibrahim, and four daughters with Khadija:

MUHARRAM. THIS ILLUSTRATION DEPICTS A CELEBRATION OF MUHARRAM, THE FIRST MONTH OF THE YEAR, WHICH INCLUDES ASHURA, THE HOLIEST DAY FOR SHI'ITE MUSLIMS, WHO COMMEMORATE THE DEATH OF THE PROPHET MUHAMMAD'S GRANDSON HUSAYN WITH ACTS OF REPENTANCE. (© *The Art Archive*)

Zaynab, Ruqaya, Umm Kulthum, and Fatima. On 8 June 632, Muhammad died at Medina. For Muslims, Muhammad is the last of the prophets (nabi), after, among others, Noah, Abraham, Moses, and Jesus.

SEE ALSO Abraham; Isra'; Jesus; Mecca; Medina; Moses.

MUHARRAM (*Moharam, muharram*; "forbidden, sacred," in Arabic): Name of the first month in the Islamic calendar. The first of Muharram is New Year's Day; the tenth of Muharram, the Feast of Ashura, commemorates at once the meeting of Adam and Eve, the end of the deluge, and the death of Husayn. Among the Shi'a, Ashura is celebrated in distress, since they commemorate on this day only the death of Husayn. Before the Islamic epoch, the month of Muharram corresponded to a period of sacred repose. Concerning New Year's Day, the Iranians continue to celebrate the "Naw Rouz" (new light), the Sassanid New Year's Day, having survived the coming of Islam, which falls after the spring equinox, 21 March.

SEE ALSO Calendar, Muslim.

MUJAHID (pl., mujahidin; "combatant," in Arabic): Arab word used to designate a militant engaged in armed struggle to liberate a territory or to fight against injustice.

MUJTAHID (*mojtahed*): Someone erudite about Islam, a specialist of religious law, qualified to pronounce an opinion on the law and to interpret it.

SEE ALSO Islam.

MUKHABARAT: Arabic word for intelligence services, in general.

MULLAH: Title given to a Shi'ite religious figure.

MULTILATERAL GROUP FOR REFUGEES

SEE Multilateral Working Group on Refugees.

MULTILATERAL WORKING GROUP ON REFUGEES (MWGR): One of five working groups formed according to the recommendations from the Middle East peace conference held in Madrid in 1991. Its purpose is to deal with the problem of the Palestinian refugees who left Palestine during the various Israeli-Arab conflicts. Its most recent meeting, held on 6 February 2000, was attended by the foreign ministers of Israel, Egypt, and Jordan, plus a representative of the Palestinian Authority.

MULTILATERAL WORKING GROUP ON REGIONAL ECONOMIC DEVELOPMENT (MWGRED): One of five working groups formed according to the recommendations from the Middle East peace conference held in Madrid in 1991. Its purpose is to address issues of infrastructure, trade, finance, and tourism development in the region, including the West Bank and Gaza. Among its goals are the encouragement of the free movement of people, goods, services, capital, and information among the partners in the region and the promotion of the region's integration in global markets.

MUNAZAMAT AL-TAHRIR AL-ISLAMIYYA

SEE Islamic Liberation Organization.

MUNICH: On 5 September 1972, while the Olympic Games were taking place in Munich, eight men belonging to the Black September faction of the Palestine Liberation Organization (PLO) broke into the Olympic Village and killed two Israeli athletes, taking another nine hostage. They demanded the liberation of two hundred Palestinians imprisoned in Israel and safe passage for themselves out of Germany. The Israeli government refused to yield to blackmail and asked the German authorities for permission to intervene to liberate the hostages, but this was not granted; instead, during lengthy negotiations, a plan was made under which the terrorists and their hostages would be flown to Cairo. Although German police intended to kill the terrorists at the airport, they were not aware of how many there were and did not bring a force large or well-equipped enough to do so. As a result, during a bloody firefight during which five terrorists and a policeman were killed, one of the helicopters carrying the hostages was blown up

OLYMPIC TERRORISM. TWO PHOTOGRAPHS SHOW PALESTINIAN TERRORISTS (ONE AT BOTTOM MEETING WITH A MEMBER OF THE INTERNATIONAL OLYMPIC COMMITTEE) AFTER EIGHT OF THEM SEIZED ELEVEN ISRAELI ATHLETES, KILLING TWO, DURING THE 1972 OLYMPIC GAMES IN MUNICH. AFTER A TENSE STANDOFF, A RESCUE ATTEMPT BY GERMAN AUTHORITIES ENDED DISASTROUSLY. (© Bettmann/Corbis)

by a terrorist grenade and the rest of the hostages were shot.

A day later, Israel retaliated by launching simultaneous air strikes on at least ten PLO bases in Syria and Lebanon. Three of the terrorists were captured. On 26 October, more terrorists hijacked a Lufthansa airliner, demanding that the Munich killers be set free, and the Germans let them go. The Israeli prime minister, Golda Meir, then gave the order to Mossad to eliminate all the terrorists who participated in the killing. This operation, which came to be known as "Operation Wrath of God, " was designed not only to see justice done but to send a message to all who might contemplate future terrorist acts. One by one the killers were tracked down and assassinated. As of 2004, only the planner of the Munich attack is still alive.

SEE ALSO Black September Organization; Mossad.

MUQAWAMA AL-ISLAMIYYA, AL-: "Islamic Resistance," the military arm of the Lebanese Hizbullah. In 1993, the leaders of this militia attempted to gather under their banner militants of a number of organizations, sometimes opposed to each other, to strengthen the struggle against the Israeli presence in South Lebanon.

SEE ALSO Hizbullah; South Lebanon.

MUQAWAMA AL-MU'MINA, AL-: "Believer's Resistance," a component of the Lebanese Hizbullah.

SEE ALSO Hizbullah.

MURABITUN ("Vigilants," in Arabic): The origin of this word goes back to the fifteenth century, to the epoch of the Almoravids, Spanish descendents of a nomadic Saharan tribe, who, in the name of a renewed and purified Islam, undertook to drive heretics from North Africa and Spain. The founder of this movement, Abdallah ibn Yassin, professed the rules of his order in a military convent (*ribat*), situated on an island in the Senegal River. There, the warriors (*al-murabitun*, people of the *ribat*) lived austerely and strictly.

MURDJITES: Members of a theological movement of Islam, opposed to the expulsion from the Muslim community of believers who have been guilty of grievous faults with respect to the Qur'anic law.

SEE ALSO Islam.

MURID: Arab word meaning "adept, novice, messiah."

MUSA MURAGHA, SA'ID (Abu Musa): Palestinian military figure born in 1927 in Silwan, Palestine. Sa'id Musa Muragha began a military career in the Jordanian army in 1948, training at the British military academy, Sandhurst. In 1969 he was commander of an artillery battalion. In October of the following year, after the confrontations of Black September 1970 between the Palestine Liberation Organization (PLO) and the Jordanian military, he resigned to join with the Palestinian resistance.

A member of al-Fatah after 1971, he attained the rank of colonel. He was in command of a battalion of the "Yarmuk" brigade in South Lebanon from 1972 to 1977, and fought the Syrians during their intervention in the Lebanese Civil War in 1976. In 1978 he escaped a Syrian attempt to assassinate him. From 1977 to 1982 he was assistant to General Said Sayel (Abu Walid), head of PLO military operations in Lebanon, and directed the PLO's defense in Beirut during the siege of the city by the Israelis in 1982. In February 1983, he was admitted to the Palestine National Council (PNC), but in May he had a falling out with Yasir Arafat, whom he reproached for cor-

ruption and nepotism, promoting incompetent officers based solely on their loyalty to him. Muragha's criticism soon became more generally political, and in November he was expelled from the military command of the PLO, along with Muhammad Tariq al-Khadra, Muhammad Zahran, Mahmud Hamdan, and Yusef al-Ajouri, all accused of conspiracy against the authority of Arafat. From then on, Muragha obtained support from Syria, to consolidate, with Khaled al-Amlah (Abu Khaled), his movement, the Fatah–Temporary Command (or Fatah-Intifada), in opposition to Fatah.

In 1985, he joined the Palestinian National Salvation Front (PNSF), which unified all Palestinian movements that were opposed to Arafat. In 1989, when a split occurred in his own movement, Muragha began to lose his influence over it, and he turned to Iran for financial help. In October 1993, opposing the Israeli-Palestinian Oslo Accords, he and his movement joined the Alliance of Palestinian Forces (APF). Muragha has not been active since the early 1990s.

SEE ALSO Alliance of Palestinian Forces; Arafat, Yasir; Black September 1970; Fatah, al-; Oslo Accords; Palestine Liberation Organization; Palestinian National Salvation Front.

MUSLIM: From the Arabic *muslim*, which means "submitted to the divine faith; believer, faithful." Designates those who believe in the Islamic religion.

SEE ALSO Islam.

MUSLIM BROTHERHOOD: Sunni fundamentalist movement (Jama'at al-Ikhwan al-Muslimin) created on 11 April 1928, in Ismailia, Egypt, by a young teacher, Hassan al-Banna, who had been influenced by the ideas of the reformer Rashid Rida. The doctrine of this brotherhood stressed the refusal of cultural, political, or economic subservience of the Muslim community toward foreign powers; the establishment of an Islamic political, economic, and social order; the restoration of the *shari'a* (Islamic law) in the juridical domain; and the rejection of all nationalism. In the middle of the 1930s, the Muslim Brotherhood started focusing on political action, to the detriment of social action, in opposing the Wafd Party.

Between 1945 and 1948, the radical wing of the party orchestrated a number of attacks on highly placed Egyptian political leaders, notably against the prime ministers Ahmad Mahir and al-Nuqrashi Pasha. Reacting to the Arab defeat at the hands of Israel in 1948, the brotherhood, allied with the communists, became a threat to the Egyptian regime. On 12 February 1949, Hassan al-Banna was executed by the police. In the early 1950s, the movement became more radical, under the direction of Sayyid Qutb, who introduced a political doctrine based on the theory of an Islamic and socialist state. He recruited many officers in the Egyptian army, and in so doing, participated in the coup d'état of July 1952. Relations were tense between the Muslim Brotherhood and the new Egyptian regime, which led to its banning by Gamal Abdel Nasser, in January 1954. The following 26 October, a member of the Brotherhood, firing several shots with a revolver, tried to assassinate President Nasser.

The failed attempt led to massive repression of the movement, which nevertheless succeeded in establishing itself in the Egyptian political picture. Fearing a new attempt on his life, Nasser had nearly 20,000 Muslim Brothers arrested in 1957. Seven years later, they benefited from a general amnesty, which was annulled in August 1965, after another plot against the state was uncovered. Sayyid Qutb, theoretician of the movement, was hanged by Egyptian authorities. According to the indictment, the accused had received financial help from Saudi Arabia via Sudan. Between 1970 and 1981, the policy of openness promulgated by President Anwar al-Sadat allowed the Muslim Brotherhood to reconstitute itself and to become very active, particularly in the universities and among the middle classes. The movement benefited from the religious revival that surfaced after the Arab defeat in the June 1967 war. In spite of their opposition to his policy of reconciliation toward Israel, their activities were tolerated by Sadat as a counterweight to the Nasserists and the extreme left. Brothers were allowed to return to al-Azhar University, from which they had been forced out. Although Sadat would not legalize the Brotherhood as a political party, they ran candidates in the elections of 1976, supported by a popular base and a significant financial network, either as independents or as members of the Arab Socialist Union (ASU), the ruling party in which Sadat allowed factions of left, center, and right to organize and run separate lists. Nine Muslim Brothers were elected deputies as independents and six as ASU members, including one who became the leader of the center faction. Branches of the Muslim Brotherhood were formed in the Palestinian territories, in Jordan, Syria, Sudan, Kuwait, Yemen, and Algeria. In 1979, the installation of an Islamic regime in Iran and the signature of an Israeli-Egyptian peace accord strengthened their position, particularly in the Palestinian territories, Syria, and Jordan.

The assassination of President Sadat, on 6 October 1981, by a conspiracy of Islamist officers, resulted in new repression of the Brotherhood. In Syria, threatened by a revolt spearheaded by the Muslim Brotherhood, the Syrian president, Hafiz al-Asad, undertook a very harsh campaign of repression. In Aleppo and Hama in early 1980 general strikes were broken up by the security forces with mass arrests and summary executions. After an unsuccessful attempt on Asad's life in June 1980, membership in the Brotherhood was made a capital offense, and the regime attacked again, putting an end to the rebellion. (Two years later there was an Islamist uprising in Hama that was put down even more brutally by the army, resulting in the death of as many as 10,000 people.) In the Egyptian legislative elections of 1987, the Muslim Brotherhood was present on the lists of the Socialist Workers Party, which won fifty-six deputy seats. In December 1987, when the first Intifada began in the Palestinian territories, members of the Muslim Brotherhood formed HAMAS, an armed resistance organization.

In the 1990s, implicated in terrorist actions that were becoming more common in Egypt, the Brotherhood found itself marginalized from Egyptian political life, especially after the vain attempts of one of its moderate currents to form a political party in conjunction with the Copts. Although banned, the movement has been tolerated by the Egyptian regime. In 1990, when it held thirty-seven deputy seats, the movement decided to boycott the legislative elections, and to withdraw provisionally from parliament. At the time of the Gulf War of 1991, the Brotherhood denounced the invasion of Kuwait by Iraq, but opposed a foreign presence in the region. In 1995, when the Muslim Brotherhood accounted for sixteen of the twenty-four seats among the Egyptian Attorneys Union, the government passed a law allowing it to exercise control over the principal union organizations. The Brotherhood won no seats at the legislative elections of the same year. In the spring of 2000, the government suspended the activities of the Socialist Labor Party, which had welcomed into its ranks numerous Islamists. As a result of the legislative elections of the following November, while the party of President Husni Mubarak, the National Democratic Party, had won the majority of the 454 seats of the Assembly, the Muslim Brotherhood gained 17 seats, thereby becoming the largest opposition bloc. As of 2004, the Muslim Brotherhood is headed by Mustafa Mashur, seconded by its spokesperson, Maamun al-Hodibi.

> **SEE ALSO** Arab-Israel War (1967); Asad, Hafiz al-; Azhar, al-; Banna, Hassan al-; Gulf War (1991); Intifada (1987–1993); HAMAS; Nasser, Gamal Abdel; Sadat, Anwar al-; Wafd.

MUSLIM CALENDAR

> **SEE** Islamic Calendar.

MUSLIM RELIGIOUS HOLIDAYS: 'Id al-Adha (Feast of the Sacrifice; falls on 10 Dhu al-hijja); 'Id al-Fitr (End of Ramadan; falls on 1 Shawwal); Mawlid al-Nabi (Birthday of the prophet Muhammad; falls on 12 Rabia al-awwal); Ashura (commemorates the death of Husayn, grandson of the prophet Muhammad) falls on 10 Muharram.

> **SEE ALSO** Ashura; 'Id al-Adha; 'Id-Fitr.

MUSLIM WORLD LEAGUE (MWL): International organization (Rabitat al-Alam al-Islami) founded in May 1962, at the Islamic summit organized in Mecca, by King Faysal of Arabia. Its goals are to explicate and disseminate Islamic principles of culture and faith, to consolidate unity and solidarity within Islam, and to uphold the rights and interests of Muslims in the world. The League publishes the weekly *The Muslim World* (*Da'wat al Haqq*).

> **SEE ALSO** Mecca.

MUSTADAFIN

> **SEE** Movement of the Disinherited; Sadr, Musa al-.

MUT'AZILITES: Followers of an ascetic and rationalist Muslim school, heavily favoring the freedom of the human will before God.

MWL

> **SEE** Muslim World League.

NABI: Arabic word meaning "prophet."

NABLUS: Economically important Palestinian city, forty miles north of Jerusalem in the West Bank. It was called Flavius Neapolis by the Romans, who established it in 72 C.E. near the site of the Biblical Shechem (its name in Hebrew). The 2004 population of the city, eight surrounding villages, and three refugee camps (Balata, Askar, and Camp Number 1) is about 165,000. A number of Israeli settlements and an Israeli military base surround the city on confiscated land (the first was established in 1976). Nablus has been an important center of Palestinian resistance in the 1936–1939 Revolt (it was the birthplace of the Arab Higher Committee); during the period of Jordanian control, when it was a center of guerilla activity; and under Israeli occupation. Al-Najah National University is located in Nablus, as is Jacob's Well, Joseph's Tomb, and, near Mount Gerizim outside town, a community of about half of all remaining Samaritans, 200 to 300 people. Mount Gerizim is said by the Samaritans to be the place where Abraham prepared to sacrifice Isaac, and where Moses received the Ten Commandments. Nablus was part of the Palestinian "autonomous" area under the Oslo Accords and was turned over to the Palestinian Authority on 11 December 1995. Like other West Bank cities, it was invaded and reoccupied by the Israelis in April 2002 with great force and destruction—much of the Old City was damaged by tanks, and the an-cient casbah was destroyed—as well as with many civilian deaths and injuries, and it has been subject to curfews and violent repressive actions.

SEE ALSO Arab Higher Committee; Oslo Accords; Palestinian Authority; West Bank.

NAHAR, AL- ("day," in Arabic): A pro-Jordanian Palestinian daily newspaper founded in 1987 in Jerusalem. A separate newspaper of the same name also is one of the most important of the Lebanese Arabic dailies.

NAHDA ("awakening," in Arabic): Word used to designate the Arab cultural renaissance, from about 1830 on. This was a period of cultural and intellectual development that arose in response to the economic reforms of Muhammad Ali, the Ottoman governor of Egypt from 1805 to 1849 and coincided with the development of Arab nationalist ideas and feelings. Muhammad Ali's reforms represented an effort to revive the declining empire after the short-lived but traumatic Napoleonic invasion of Egypt of 1798 to 1801. Palestinians, like other Arabs in the Mashriq, participated in the *nahda* by renewing their interest in Arabic literature and poetry, creating new forms of literature and theater, creating an Arab and then Palestinian (as distinct from an Ottoman or Muslim) identity, and pursuing political self-representation.

CLASH IN NABLUS. YOUNG PALESTINIANS THROW STONES AT AN ISRAELI TANK IN THE WEST BANK TOWN, A CENTER OF ARAB NATIONALISM, IN EARLY 2002. UNDER PALESTINIAN AUTONOMOUS CONTROL SINCE 1995, NABLUS HAS BEEN THE SCENE OF VIOLENCE BETWEEN PALESTINIANS AND ISRAELIS, IN PART BECAUSE OF THE PRESENCE OF WHAT IS BELIEVED TO BE THE ANCIENT TOMB OF JOSEPH, A JEWISH HOLY SITE. *(AP/Wide World Photos)*

SEE ALSO Mashriq.

NAJAH UNIVERSITY, AL-: Palestinian university located in Nablus, in the West Bank. Founded in 1918 as an elementary school, it became a secondary school in 1941 and a two-year community college in 1963. In 1977 it was reconstituted as a university and renamed. Today al-Najah has ten undergraduate faculties, a graduate faculty and a number of technical and professional centers, and continues to operate a separate community college. In addition to the main campus, there is an agricultural campus in Tulkarm and a new campus under construction west of Nablus that will house the medical school, a teaching hospital and a number of other facilities. Al-Najah is the largest university in the West Bank, with over 10,000 students. The student body at the university, as at most Palestinian schools, is politically engaged. As a large school drawing from a wide area of the West Bank, it is greatly affected by the obstacles placed in the way of travel by Palestinians, as well as by the depressed economy. During the first Intifada (1987–1993) the university was declared a "closed military area" by the Israelis; no classes were held from 1988 to 1991. It has also been the object of military action more recently, particularly during the Israeli reoccupation of West Bank cities in 2002.

SEE ALSO Intifada (1987–1993).

NAKBA, AL- ("catastrophe" or "disaster," in Arabic): Word used by Palestinians for the consequences of the 1948 War, which included the disappearance of their country and the dispossession, expulsion, and exile of hundreds of thousands of Palestinians. From 700,000 to 750,000 Palestinians became refugees outside the 78 percent of Palestine that became Israel, living in temporary camps that soon became permanent, surviving on relief supplied by the United Nations through the Relief and Works Agency for Palestine Refugees in the Near East; another 150,000 were displaced within the territory that became Israel: more than 400 Palestinian villages were physically destroyed—bulldozed out of existence, their names disappearing from the map.

SEE ALSO Arab-Israel War (1948); United Nations Relief and Works Agency for Palestine Refugees in the Near East.

NAMIR, ORAH (1930–): Israeli politician. Born in Hadera, Israel, Orah Namir served in the Israel Defense Force in the Arab-Israel War of 1948, then worked for the Israeli delegation to the United Nations in New York, where she attended Hunter College, earning a bachelor of arts degree. She returned to Israel, marrying Mordekhai Namir (1897–1969), a Labor Party leader and mayor of Tel Aviv (1956–1969). Namir was first elected to the Knesset in 1973 on the Labor Party list. She chaired the Education and Culture Committee (1974–1977) and the Labor and Social Affairs Committee (1977–1992). In 1992 Prime Minister Yitzhak Rabin appointed Namir minister for the environment; a year later she was appointed minister of labor and social affairs. In 1996 Prime Minister Shimon Peres appointed her Israel's ambassador to the People's Republic of China, and she held that post until 2000.

NAQIB AL-SAGGADA: Honorific title given to a personal representative of the shaykh of a Sufi brotherhood.

SEE ALSO Shaykh; Tasawwuf.

NAQSHBAND, MUHAMMAD BAHA' AL-DIN AL- (1317–1388): Sufi mystic, founder of the order of Naqshbandiyya. After having been initiated into Sufism along with Muhammad Baba al-Sammasi, who designated him his caliph, he spent twelve years in service to the sultan Khalil at Samarkand, where he participated, in spite of himself, in the all-conquering proselytism of Tamburlaine. Naqshbandiyya is still a significant force in a parallel form of Islam in Central Asia.

SEE ALSO Tasawwuf.

NAQSHBANDI (Naqshbandite): Member of the Sufi order of Naqshbandiyya.

NASHASHIBI, FAKHRI (1899–1941): Palestinian politician. A member of one of Jerusalem's most prominent families and nephew of Raghib al-Nashashibi, Fakhri Nashashibi was employed in various positions in the British Mandate government until the late

1920s, when he became his uncle's chief assistant, organizer, and propagandist. Although the Nashashibis' National Defense Party was represented on the Arab Higher Committee in the first year of the 1936–1939 Arab Revolt, they broke with it, and with Hajj Amin al-Husayni and his supporters, over a British partition plan of 1937. Hajj Amin, a strong nationalist, opposed the plan, and the Nashashibis favored compromise. Raghib al-Nashashibi became the main organizer of the Palestinian opposition to Hajj Amin and accepted help from the British and the Zionists in forming "peace gangs" while doing so. Fakhri was assassinated in Baghdad.

SEE ALSO Arab Higher Committee; Husayni, Hajj Amin al-; Nashashibi, Raghib al-; Palestine Arab Revolt (1936–1939).

NASHASHIBI, RAGHIB AL- (1883–1951): Palestinian politician. Raghib al-Nashashibi was born into one of Jerusalem's most prominent families and studied engineering. He was elected to the Ottoman parliament for Jerusalem and served as an officer in the Ottoman army in World War I. He was a founder of the Literary Society, an important political association, in 1918, and of the Palestinian Arab National Party in 1923. In 1920 he was appointed mayor of Jerusalem by the British, replacing a member of the rival Husayni family, a nationalist whom the British suspected of instigating anti-British demonstrations. In 1934, after being voted out of office, Nashashibi founded the National Defense Party, which advocated compromise with the British and the Zionists. He was a member of the Arab Higher Committee from 1936 to 1937 but left because of disagreements with Hajj Amin al-Husayni and his supporters over British proposals to partition Palestine. He attended the London Conference of 1939 and wanted to accept the terms offered by the 1939 MacDonald White Paper. After the West Bank was annexed by Jordan in 1950, he was appointed governor by the government of Abdullah I and later served as a cabinet minister in charge of the Haram al-Sharif.

SEE ALSO Abdullah I ibn Hussein; Arab Higher Committee; Haram al-Sharif; Husayni, Hajj Amin al-; West Bank; White Papers on Palestine.

NASI (pl. *nessim*): Hebrew word meaning "prince, patriarch." Ancient title of the chief of the Sanhedrin, or of the president of the State of Israel.

NASRALLAH, HASAN (1960–): Lebanese Shi'ite political leader, born in 1960 in East Beirut, where his family had moved from Bazuriya, near Tyre in South Lebanon. The family returned to Bazuriya in 1975 when the Lebanese Civil War broke out. During this period he also joined the ranks of the moderate Islamic movement, AMAL. In 1976 Nasrallah began a course of Shiʿite religious studies at Najaf, Iraq, where he was the student of Muhammad Bakr al-Sadr and Abbas al-Musawi. Influenced by Musawi, he became a political follower of the more radical Islamist Shaykh Muhammad Husayn Fadlallah. In 1978 he returned to Lebanon with Musawi and taught in a school established by Musawi in Baʾalbak in the Baqaʾa Valley. In 1982 he became the leader of AMAL in that district, but when the Israelis invaded Lebanon in 1982, Nabi Berri, the leader of AMAL, agreed to join a national "Salvation Committee" that included right-wing Maronites.

Musawi left AMAL to found a splinter group called Islamic AMAL, and Nasrallah joined a group of followers of Fadlallah who were associated with the Iranian Revolutionary Guards who had been sent to fight the invasion, and helped to create the organization that in 1985 was officially named the Hizbullah (*Hizb Allah*, Party of God). By 1989 Nasrallah had become an important Hizbullah leader and militia commander. In 1989, after an internal dispute over Hizbullah's relation to Syria, he traveled to Iran to complete his religious training. On 18 February 1992, Nasrallah was designated secretary general of the Lebanese Hizbullah, replacing Musawi, who had been assassinated two days earlier by an Israeli commando. The policy of openness that Nasrallah advocated was severely criticized within the movement, in particular by Subhi Ali al-Tufayli. Nasrallah, in effect, wanted Hizbullah to participate actively in Lebanese politics, and favored ceasing operations against Israel, in case of Israeli withdrawal from South Lebanon.

In 1995 Nasrallah was reelected secretary general of Hizbullah for a term of three years. In September 1997, his son Hadi was killed in South Lebanon in a confrontation between Hizbullah members and Israeli soldiers. In November he launched an appeal to volunteers of all faiths to enlist in a new multiconfessional brigade formed for the struggle against the Israeli occupation of South Lebanon. In January 1998, the expulsion of Subhi Tufayli from the leadership council (*shura*) allowed Nasrallah to consolidate his position at the head of the movement. On 24 May 2000, the definitive retreat of the Israel Defense Force from South Lebanon made Nasrallah a hero in the eyes of the Arab world and a formidable political figure in Lebanon. He is said to have made Hizbullah

autonomous from both the Syrians and the Iranians, who support it, and is admired and respected by the leaders of both countries. On 7 August 2001, he was reelected to a fourth term as the head of Hizbullah; Nawaf al-Musawi is the organization's foreign minister. Nasrallah has defended the use of suicide bombings in Israel, although Hizbullah condemns terrorism elsewhere. In January 2004 Nasrallah won the release of 429 Lebanese prisoners and the bodies of fifty-nine fighters, in exchange for an Israeli hostage and the bodies of three Israeli soldiers, after negotiations lasting several years through an intermediary. Nasrallah has transformed Hizbullah in Lebanon into a social movement and political party, the largest in the Shiʿa community; it and holds nine seats in the Lebanese parliament. The movement has about 50,000 members (and many more supporters), its armed militia, a satellite television station, and a social service network that benefits the largely poor Shiʿa population of Lebanon who are not served by the state. Nasrallah is usually known by the honorific *Sayyid*.

SEE ALSO AMAL; Berri, Nabi; Fadlallah, Shaykh Muhammad Husayn; Hizbullah; Israel Defense Force; South Lebanon; Tufayli, Subhi Ali al-.

NASSER, GAMAL ABDEL (Jamal Abd al-Nasir; 1918–1970): Egyptian military and political figure, born in Upper Egypt. Starting in 1935, Gamal Abdel Nasser criticized the monarchy and demonstrated in favor of applying the constitution of 1923. In 1937 he entered the military academy of Cairo, where he became friends with Anwar al-Sadat. An earnest nationalist, in 1942 he founded, along with Zakariya Muhyi al-Din, the clandestine Free Officers group to combat British intrusion in Egyptian affairs. In May 1948, with the Egyptian army, he participated in the first Arab war with Israel. On 23 July 1952, as the head of the Free Officers, he took part in the coup d'état, supported by the Muslim Brotherhood, which brought General Muhammad Naguib to power. The Council of the Revolution exiled King Farouk.

In January 1953, after the abolition of political parties, Nasser became secretary general of the only authorized group, the Assembly of the Liberation. On 18 June the Republic of Egypt was proclaimed. In November 1954 Nasser became prime minister, and then president in June 1956, after shunting aside General Naguib. In his *Philosophy of the Revolution* he expounded his doctrines, which were based on pan-Arabism and support for movements of national liberation.

GAMAL ABDEL NASSER. AN EGYPTIAN NATIONALIST, HE LED THE "FREE OFFICERS" MOVEMENT IN A 1952 COUP AGAINST THE MONARCHY AND, BY 1956, BECAME PRESIDENT OF THE REPUBLIC OF EGYPT. BEFORE HIS DEATH IN 1970, NASSER NATIONALIZED THE SUEZ CANAL, ENGAGED IN TWO UNSUCCESSFUL ARAB-ISRAELI WARS (IN 1956 AND 1967), AND CREATED A SHORT-LIVED UNITED ARAB REPUBLIC WITH SYRIA AND YEMEN. *(United Nations)*

The Lavon Affair in 1954 and Israeli attacks on Gaza in 1954 and 1955 convinced Nasser that the Egyptian armed forces had to be built up. His refusal to join the Baghdad Pact or take sides in the Cold War—in 1955 Egypt joined the Nonaligned Movement, of which Nasser became a leader, along with India's prime minister Jawaharal Nehru and Yugoslavia's president Josip Broz Tito—as well as Egyptian aid to the Algerian nationalists then rebelling against French rule, made it impossible to obtain Western arms and prevented an agreement in ongoing negotiations with Britain over its occupation of the Suez Canal zone, which continued under a 1936 treaty. Nasser concluded an arms deal with Czechoslovakia, then part of the Soviet bloc; the United States withdrew its offer to finance the Aswan High Dam, an important economic project. Nasser's response was to seize and nationalize the Suez Canal. Although he offered financial compensation, the

British and French attempted to break him militarily and colluded with Israel to provoke the Suez War, which ended, mostly because of American pressure, in the humiliation and withdrawal of the British and French and the increased Egypt status in the world, and especially among Arabs. Also under American pressure, the Israelis withdrew from the Sinai, destroying roads and military installations as they left.

In 1958, partly as a result of the popularity of Nasser's Arab nationalism, Syria and Egypt created the United Arab Republic (UAR), with Nasser at its head. Political differences with the Syrians (there was a coup d'état in Syria) led to the dissolution of the UAR in 1961. In 1962 Egypt became involved in a civil war in North Yemen, where a coup d'état had overthrown the Saudi-supported monarchy. The conflict was a drain on Egyptian resources for several years.

Internally the constitution of the charter of May 1962, as well as the agrarian reform and social measures Nasser undertook, assured him great popularity among the Egyptians. To consolidate his position, he created a single party, the Arab Socialist Union in December 1962. 0n 9 March 1962 he proclaimed the independence of the Gaza Strip, over which Egypt had exercised administrative control since the Israeli-Egyptian armistice of 1949. In April 1963 he failed in his project of a tripartite union of Syria, Iraq, and Egypt. In 1964 Egypt, with Syria and Iraq, sponsored the Arab League's creation of the Palestine Liberation Organization (PLO) as a means to channel—and keep under control—the activities of Palestinian nationalists. It was largely beholden to Egypt for material support, although its leader, Ahmad Shuqayri, indulged in belligerent rhetoric, to the detriment of Palestinian as well as Egyptian interests, particularly in the months before the 1967 War.

On 18 December 1964 Nasser named Anwar al-Sadat vice president. In autumn 1966 he was severely criticized by Arab countries, who reproached him for a lack of determination toward Israel; that year Egypt entered into a mutual defense treaty with Syria. In the spring of 1967 the Israelis began massing troops along the Egyptian border. In mid-May the tension between Egypt and Israel was at its peak. After an Israeli raid on a Syrian unit in the Golan, Nasser mobilized the Egyptian army, moving troops to the border. He requested the removal of the United Nations Emergency Force, which had guarded the border since 1956, and on 21 May blockaded the Straits of Tiran. Egypt and Jordan then signed a mutual defense treaty.

These acts were the culmination of the long period of tension and provocation that led to the 1967 War. Israel began the hostilities on the morning of 5 June by destroying the Egyptian air force on the ground. The war was a disaster for Egypt, Syria, Jordan, and the Palestinians: The Arab armies were routed and Israel was left in possession of the Golan Heights and the Sinai Peninsula as well as the Gaza Strip and the West Bank; hundreds of thousands of new Palestinian refugees were created. Nasser's government and international prestige were undermined, and the PLO began to distance itself from Egypt, beginning with the resignation of Shuqayri. Nasser resigned, but his resignation was refused by the National Assembly. Nevertheless, in his weakened position he was constrained to reconcile with King Faysal of Saudi Arabia, who had been supporting the other side in the North Yemen dispute. Nasser also accepted massive aid from the Soviet Union.

Gradually Nasser's stature as leader of the Arab world diminished. On 8 January 1969 his party obtained the quasi-totality of the seats in the Assembly. In April he began the War of Attrition against Israel in the Sinai, although later that year he accepted the Rogers Plan providing for a cease-fire, which went into effect on 7 August 1970 along the Suez Canal. His last action was to negotiate a cease-fire in the Black September conflict between Jordan and the PLO in September 1970. On 28 September 1970 Nasser died of a heart attack. He was replaced at the head of the Egyptian state by his vice president and army colleague Anwar al-Sadat.

SEE ALSO Arab-Israel War (1948); Arab-Israel War (1967); Baghdad Pact; Black September; Gaza Strip; Golan Heights; Lavon Affair; League of Arab States; Muslim Brotherhood; Palestine Liberation Organization; Rogers Plan; Sadat, Anwar al-; Suez Crisis; United Arab Republic; United Nations Emergency Force; West Bank.

NATIONAL AGREEMENT CONCERNING NEGOTIATIONS FOR A FINAL SETTLEMENT WITH THE PALESTINIANS: An Israeli document edited in January 1997 by several Likud and Labor Party representatives. Signed by Likud members Yehuda Lancry, Ze'ev Bo'm, Eliezer Zandberg, Meyer Sheetrit, and Michael Eytan, and by Labor Party members Yossi Bellin, Haim Ramon, and Shlomo Ben-Ami, this document established the minimum that Israel was prepared to accept in preparation for talks on the definitive status of the Palestinian territories. The document provided notably that most of the Jewish settlers in the West Bank and the Gaza Strip would stay "in territorial contiguity" under Israeli sovereignty and that no settlement would be dismantled. Settlers living in territory that was to come under Palestinian control would be accorded "special arrangements, guaranteeing their specific ties with Israel." The settlements situated in the Jordan Valley would be considered a "special security zone," either to be annexed by Israel or to serve as a base for Israeli troops. Jerusalem would remain the capital of Israel, "united under Israeli sovereignty recognized by the Palestinians." In exchange, Israel would "recognize the center of government of the Palestinian entity, situated within the frontiers of this entity, but outside of the current town lines of Jerusalem."

SEE ALSO Gaza Strip; Israel Labor Party; Jerusalem; Likud; West Bank.

NATIONAL CONSTITUTIONAL PARTY: Jordanian political party, created in May 1997 on the impetus of Abdul Hadi Majali, brother of Prime Minister Abdul Salam Majali. A union of nine pro-monarchy centrist parties, formed at the behest of King Hussein, the National Constitutional Party was meant to strengthen the king's hand in dealing with the demands of the Jordanian-Palestinian movements in future negotiations on the definitive status of the Palestinian territories.

SEE ALSO Hussein ibn Talal.

NATIONAL DEMOCRATIC ALLIANCE

SEE Democratic National Alliance.

NATIONALIST ALLIANCE

SEE Fatah-Intifada; Fatah Revolutionary Council.

NATIONAL PROGRESSIVE FRONT (al-Jabha al-Taqaddumiya al-Wataniya, in Arabic): A coalition of Syrian political parties established on 7 March 1972. The National Progressive Front consists of six parties led by the Ba'th Arab Socialist Party. The other five are the Syrian Communist Party, the Arab Socialist Union, the Socialist Unionist Party, the Arab Socialist Party, and the Socialist Unionist Democratic Party. The front plays a significant role in Syrian decision-making.

NATIONAL RELIGIOUS PARTY (Miflagah Datit Le'umit, in Hebrew): Israeli religious party, founded in 1956 by the merging of two religious blocks, Mizrachi and Ha-Poel ha-Mizrachi. The objective of the

Mafdal, or National Religious Party (NRP), was to restore Jewish sovereignty over all of Palestine as it existed in the time of King Solomon. Supporting the expansion and development of Jewish settlements, the NRP opposed restitution of even the tiniest piece of the territories occupied by Israel. In 1974, a new current in Mafdal, rising from the 1973 War, led to the creation of the Gush Emunim movement, which became the spearhead in settling the Occupied Territories. Mafdal's support of the Labor Party waned until it broke with Labor in 1977, contributing to Likud's coming to power. In 1981, a split caused by opposition between the Sephardim and the Ashkenazim in the NPR led to the creation of a new bloc, the TAMI. During the Knesset elections of July, the NRP obtained six deputy seats. Two party members, Yossef Burg and Zevulun Hammer, joined the government of Menachem Begin, the former in the ministry of the interior, the latter in education. In March 1989 two members of the party received appointments in the Yitzhak Shamir government: Hammer as minister of religious affairs and Avner Shaki as minister without portfolio. Between 1994 and 1996, as a consequence of the Israeli-Palestinian accord of September 1993, the NRP was radicalized and obtained nine seats in the Knesset elections of May 1996. Three of its members joined the government of Benjamin Netanyahu: Hammer became deputy prime minister and minister of education, Yitzhak Levy became minister of transport, and Yigal Bibi became deputy minister of religious affairs. Nahum Lagental, political secretary of NRP, was named general director of the ministry of transport.

In February 1998, after the death of Hammer, the NRP named Yitzhak Levy its party leader but his extremist positions prompted some members to resign, joining the Meimad, a religious party of the center-left. On 18 May 1999, in the Knesset elections that brought Laborite Ehud Barak to power, the NRP won only five seats. Three members of the party joined the Barak government: Levy as minister of housing, Bibi as deputy minister of religious affairs, and Shaul Yahalom as deputy minister of education. The following December, the party's leadership threatened to withdraw its support from the government if it retreated from the Golan Heights. On 9 July 2000 the NRP ministers, along with those of Israel be-Aliyah and SHAS, resigned, reproaching Barak for the concessions he was about to make to the Palestinians in the Israeli-Palestinian peace negotiations at Camp David. In March 2001, after Ariel Sharon's election as prime minister, no member of the NRP figured in the new government. However, the party leadership assured the new prime minister

of its continued support for him in the Knesset. In the 2003 elections the NRP received 4.2 percent of the vote and six seats in the Knesset.

SEE ALSO Arab-Israel War (1973); Ashkenazi; Barak, Ehud; Begin, Menachem; Israel be-Aliyah; Israel Labor Party; Likud; Meimad; Mizrachi; Netanyahu, Benjamin; Sephardim; Shamir, Yitzhak; Sharon, Ariel; SHAS; TAMI.

NATIONAL RENAISSANCE

SEE ha-Tehiyah.

NATIONAL UNION (*Ha-Ihud Ha-Leumi*, in Hebrew):

Israeli electoral list, constituted in February 1999, anticipating the general elections scheduled for the following May. The National Union was comprised of the extreme right party, Tekumah, headed by Benny Begin, and the extreme right party, Moledet, led by Rehavam Ze'evi, and Israel Beiteinu, headed by Avigdor Lieberman. As a result of the ballot of 17 May 1999, this list won four seats in the Knesset, taken by Michael Kleiner, Benyamin (Benny) Elon, Hanan Porat, and Rehavam Ze'evi, while the head of the Labor Party, Ehud Barak, was elected prime minister. In March 2001, after the election of the leader of Likud, Ariel Sharon, to head the government, Ze'evi was named tourism minister. On the following 17 October, the latter was assassinated by a Popular Front for the Liberation of Palestine commando. The National Union coalition opposes concessions to the Palestinian Authority and the creation of a Palestinian state. In the 2003 elections, the National Union received 5.5 percent of the vote (seven seats in the Knesset).

SEE ALSO Barak, Ehud; Elon, Benny; Kleiner, Michael; Moledet; Popular Front for the Liberation of Palestine; Porat, Hanan; Sharon, Ariel; Tekumah Party; Ze'evi, Rehavam.

NATUR, MAHMUD AHMAD AL- (Abu Tayib; 1945–):

Palestinian activist. Mahmud Ahmad al-Natur joined the Palestine Liberation Organization (PLO) security services in 1970. In 1979 he became assistant to Sa'ad Sayel (Abu Walid), the new leader of Force 17 whose former chief, Ali Hassan al-Salama, had been assassinated by the Mossad. Force 17 was mainly responsible for the security of Yasir Arafat and his close associates, as well as for missions connected directly to the PLO leader. It was also in charge of security for PLO representatives abroad. Between 1979 and 1981 Natur was the target of several assassination attempts. At the end of 1982 he became the leader of Force 17 when Sayel was assassinated by a Syrian commando. In 1984 Force 17 took the name Presidential Security Service (Amn al-Ri'asa). During the 1980s it carried out numerous attacks on Israeli interests and Palestinian opponents. On 25 September 1985 a Force 17 commando assassinated three Mossad agents at Larnaka, Cyprus, one of whom was Sylvia Raphael, who was considered responsible for Salama's death. In August 1987 Natur reorganized the security service, in which a number of Arafat's opponents had assumed leadership positions. Between 1988 and 1992, in coordination with the Western Sector of al-Fatah, he organized a number of terrorist operations in the Occupied Territories.

During the spring of 1992, when he was hoping to head the al-Fatah security services following the assassination, a year earlier, of Salah Khalaf (Abu Iyad), Arafat shunted him aside. Between 1993 and 1994 he was stripped of his command in response to demands of the Israeli authorities, who refused to negotiate with Palestinians who had been involved in terrorist acts. At the beginning of 1995 al-Natur went to the Palestinian autonomous territories, unofficially taking control of the Presidential Security Service, which was officially headed by Faysal Abu Shar'a.

SEE ALSO Arafat, Yasir; Fatah, al-; Force 17; Khalaf, Salah; Mossad.

NAW ROUZ: Baha'i New Year festival, celebrated on 21 March.

SEE ALSO Baha'i.

NCP

SEE National Constitutional Party.

NEBIM: Hebrew word meaning "annunciators," used to designate the prophets.

NE'EMAN, YUVAL (1925–): Israeli scientist and military and political leader. Born in Mandatory Palestine, Yuval Ne'eman graduated as an engineer from the Technicion Institute in Haifa. He was a member of Haganah, the Jewish paramilitary organization, and participated in the 1948 Arab-Israel War, remaining in the Israel Defense Force (IDF) until 1961. As head of the IDF strategic planning department from 1954 to 1955, Ne'eman created the Lavie File, which dramatically changed Israel's security policy from defensive to offensive. From 1958 to 1960 Ne'eman served as Israeli military attaché in London, where he resumed his studies in nuclear physics. He later pursued research in nuclear physics in the Unit-

ed States, gaining international recognition for his work. He taught at Tel Aviv University in the 1970s, serving as university president from 1971 to 1975. Ne'eman entered politics as one of the founders of ha-Tehiya, a right-wing party. He served in the Knesset from 1981 to 1990 and was minister of science and technology from 1982 to 1984, then minister of energy and infrastructure as well as science and technology from 1990 until 1992. He retired from politics in 1992.

SEE ALSO Arab-Israel War (1948); Haganah; Israel Defense Force.

NESTORIAN: A follower of the doctrine of Nestorius, the patriarch of Constantinople, who taught that there were two persons in Christ, the man and the son of God. Condemned by the Council of Ephesus in 431, the Nestorians rallied in Syria-Mesopotamia, from where they evangelized some of Asia.

SEE ALSO Christianity.

NETANYAHU, BENJAMIN: Israeli politician, born in 1949, in a family of university academics close to the Zionist right. His father, Benzion Netanyahu, was the secretary of Vladimir Ze'ev Jabotinsky. In 1968, after studying in the United Sates, Benjamin Netanyahu enlisted in the Israel Defense Force (IDF) and volunteered to perform his military service in an elite Israeli unit, in which he remained for five years. In May 1972, at the Tel Aviv airport, he participated in neutralizing a Palestinian group that that taken over a Sabena airliner, with some hundred passengers aboard. In the same combat unit were also Ehud Barak, future prime minister, Amnon Lipkin-Shahak, future Army chief-of-staff, and Dani Yatom, future head of Mossad. He was discharged from the IDF in 1972 having reached the rank of captain following the Yom Kippur War. After the army, he completed his studies at the Massachusetts Institute of Technology (MIT), receiving his master's degree in management studies in 1976. He remained in the United States where he was involved in various commercial activities.

During the summer of 1976, after the death of his brother Yonatan, during the famous Israeli raid on Entebbe, Netanyahu joined the party of Menachem Begin, the Herut. The following year, in memory of his brother, he founded the Jonathan Institute for Terrorism Research, at Jerusalem. In 1982, recommended by Moshe Arens, an important figure in Herut and Israeli ambassador to the United States, he joined the staff of the Israeli embassy in Washington, then filled, from 1984 to 1988, the post of Israeli

BENJAMIN NETANYAHU. AFTER SERVING IN AN ELITE MILITARY UNIT, NETANYAHU BECAME A RISING STAR IN THE RIGHT-WING LIKUD PARTY, ITS LEADER IN 1993, AND PRIME MINISTER THREE YEARS LATER. HE SUPPORTED ISRAELI SETTLEMENTS AND OPPOSED AN INDEPENDENT PALESTINIAN STATE, YET HE ALSO AGREED TO ISRAELI WITHDRAWAL FROM HEBRON AND OTHER OCCUPIED TERRITORIES. NETANYAHU LOST A REELECTION BID IN 1999. *(AP/Wide World Photos)*

ambassador to the United Nations. His tenure at the UN took place under the Israeli Likud-Labor coalition, with alternation of the prime ministers, Shimon Peres and Yitzhak Shamir. On 1 November 1988, having returned to Israel, he was elected a Likud member of Knesset, then was named, on 25 December, deputy foreign minister in the coalition government led by Yitzhak Shamir, becoming thereby the rising star of Likud.

Within this party, Netanyahu belonged to the current of Herut, led by Shamir and Arens, while two other tendencies were significant, one headed by Ariel Sharon and Benny Begin, the other by David Levy and Yitzhak Modai. In October 1991, he was the spokesperson of the Israeli delegation to the Middle East peace conference, at Madrid. The tone of his remarks there made many think of him as the heir-apparent to Yitzhak Shamir. In November 1991, he

joined the cabinet of Prime Minister Shamir, to handle specifically the peace process. This appointment was a consequence of some differences that had surfaced between Shamir and the new foreign minister, David Levy. In April 1992, Netanyahu's name came up as a replacement for Levy, thought likely to resign.

After the Labor Party came to power, in July, 1992, Benyamin Netanyahu focused all his efforts on becoming the leader of Likud. On 25 March, 1993, he was elected to lead this party, with 52.1 percent of the votes, against 26.3 percent for Levy. The first *sabra* to head Likud, he committed himself to upholding the dogmas of the nationalist right. At a congress of the party, which took place between 16–18 May, he consolidated his position at the top of Likud by obtaining control of its executive organs. On 19 October, following, after the Israeli-Palestinian accord, signed in Washington in September, he conceded that the peace process with the Palestinians was irreversible, but insisted on maintaining Israeli sovereignty over the Occupied Territories. During the first six months of 1995, his quarrels with Levy weakened Likud, intensifying personal animosities and social-ethnic cleavages. During the month of November, following the assassination of Yitzhak Rabin, his popularity dropped in public opinion, which reproached him for having contributed, through his extremist political rhetoric, to a climate of hate, with the end result that the prime minister was assassinated.

In February 1996, in anticipation of Knesset elections, in the course of which the prime minister would be, for the first time, chosen by direct universal suffrage, Likud joined with the ultranationalist party, Tzomet, headed by General Raphael Eitan. A few weeks later, it expanded this alliance, to include the Gesher "Bridge" Party of Levy, who had resigned from Likud. Thereby he became the sole candidate of the Israeli right, confronted by that of the Labor Party, Shimon Peres, favored to win. On 31 May 1996, Netanyahu was proclaimed prime minister, elected with 50.4 percent of the votes cast, against 49.5 percent for Peres. He became the youngest prime minister ever of the State of Israel and the first head of government chosen by universal direct suffrage. On 18 June, he presented his government, constituted around the Likud-Gesher-Tzomet alliance, along with representatives of two ultra-Orthodox religious parties (SHAS and the National Religious Party) and two centrist groups (Third Way and Israel be-Aliyah). In his program, the new prime minister affirmed his desire to pursue the peace process, but announced his intention of redefining the Oslo Accords, signed between the Israelis and Palestinians. Opposing the creation of an independent Palestinian state, he advocated the development of Jewish settlements, upheld the unity of Jerusalem, and favored maintaining Israeli sovereignty over the Golan Heights. Between 1996 and 1997, his intransigence and many turnabouts wound up blocking the Israeli-Palestinian negotiations on the application of the Oslo Accords, leading to much criticism from the international community and a part of Israeli society. On 15 January 1997, Netanyahu and Yasir Arafat signed an accord on Israeli withdrawal from the city of Hebron. This was the very first accord signed between the Israeli right and the Palestinians.

On the following January, the "Bibigate" scandal burst out, when Netanyahu made a public statement that he had cheated on his wife and his political opponents were trying to blackmail him. On 8 January 1998, David Levy, his foreign minister and rival for leadership of the party, resigned in response to the charges concerning the alleged blackmail. Pressed to make some concessions, Netanyahu signed, on 23 October 1998, the Oslo Accords II, providing for the withdrawal from an additional 13 percent of the territories to the Palestinians. On 21 December, when he was being repudiated for his policies, particularly concerning the Palestinians, both by the opposition as well as by some of his supporters, the Knesset passed a motion authorizing elections, by 81 votes of the 120 in the Knesset, a vote confirmed in a final ballot, on 4 January 1999, by 85 votes. Previously the Knesset had rejected, by majority vote, the five conditions Netanyahu intended to impose on the Palestinians before putting into effect the withdrawal, provided for in the Oslo Accords II. On 25 January 1999, as a result of the primaries of Likud, he obtained 75 to 80 percent of the votes cast, running against Moshe Arens, becoming again his party's candidate for the post of prime minister. On 17 May following, defeated by the candidate of the Labor Party, Ehud Barak, and having obtained only 43 percent of the votes against 56 percent for his adversary, Netanyahu resigned from the leadership of Likud, where he was replaced by Ariel Sharon. His party had won only nineteen Knesset seats. On 28 March 2000, an investigation of him was opened, for embezzlement of funds, breach of trust, and obstruction of Israeli justice. On the following 27 September, the justice department declined to prosecute him, for lack of sufficient evidence. Netanyahu returned to the Knesset in the elections of 2003 and was appointed minister of finance by Sharon. Within the Likud, Netanyahu assumed a leadership role among the "hawks," opposing Sharon's proposed plan for disengagement from disputed territories and opposing the prime minister's apparent acceptance of the eventual creation of a Palestinian state.

SEE ALSO Barak, Ehud; Begin, Menachem; Gesher "Bridge" Party; Golan Heights; Herut Party; Israel be-Aliyah; Jabotinsky, Vladimir Ze'ev; Knesset; Levy, David; Likud; Lipkin-Shahak, Amnon; National Religious Party; Oslo Accords; Oslo Accords II; Peres, Shimon; Rabin, Yitzhak; Sabra and Shatila; Shamir, Yitzhak; Sharon, Ariel; SHAS; Third Way; Tzomet Party.

NETUREI KARTA ("guardians of the [holy] city," in Hebrew): Extremist Jewish anti-Zionist movement, which opposes Zionism prior to divine redemption and considers the existence of the State of Israel a heresy. The movement favors the peace process with the Palestinians and some of its leaders have been in contact, from 1975 on, with the Palestine Liberation Organization (PLO). When the PLO proposed creating a government-in-exile, one of the leaders of the Neturei Karta, the rabbi Amram Blau, offered to be part of this government.

SEE ALSO Palestine Liberation Organization; Zionism.

NEW WAY PARTY: Parliamentary group formed during the Fifteenth Knesset in 2001 by Dalia Rabin-Pelossof, a dissident from the Center Party, along with two other MKs, Amnon Lipkin-Shahak and Uri Savir, both of whom resigned from the Knesset two days later. After some time Rabin-Pelossof joined One Israel, and the New Way ceased to exist.

SEE ALSO Rabin-Pelossof, Dalia.

NEW ZIONIST ORGANIZATION (NZO)

SEE Jabotinsky, Vladimir Ze'ev.

NPF

SEE National Progressive Front.

NRP

SEE National Religious Party.

NUSABAYA, SARI (Nuseibeh; 1949–): Palestinian academic and activist, born in Jerusalem into an old and distinguished upper-class Palestinian family. From the epoch of Caliph Omar (638 C.E.), the Nusabayas, along with the Judeh family, were in charge of opening and closing of the gates of the Holy Sepulcher every day. The father of Sari, Anwar Nusabaya, was defense minister in the Jordanian government. With degrees from Oxford and Harvard, Sari Nusabaya became a professor of political science at Bir Zeit University in the West Bank. Close to al-Fatah and in favor of dialogue with Israel, from 1987 on he participated in many encounters with important Israeli figures, both intellectual and political. In September 1987 he was expelled from the teachers' committee of Bir Zeit for having suggested that since neither the Israelis nor the Palestinians could crush each other Palestinians should ask that the West Bank be annexed by Israel so that they could become Israeli citizens, forcing Israel to give them the rights it was currently denying them.

On 8 January 1988, when it became clear that the Intifada would not be a short-lived phenomenon, he helped organize the Unified National Leadership of the Uprising and participated in composing its first communiqué. Considered one of the main organizers of the Intifada by Israeli authorities, he was forced to close his office at the Palestinian Academic Society for the Study of International Affairs (on whose board he continues to sit). U.S. intervention saved him from being imprisoned. In January 1991, in the context of the Gulf War, he was imprisoned for three months, accused of having transmitted information meant for Iraq to the Palestine Liberation Organization. After he was freed, he laid the groundwork, along with Faysal al-Husayni and Hanan Ashrawi, for the negotiations that took place at the Madrid Conference on Middle East peace. In 1992, during the peace process that started at this conference, he was named head of the technical committees, setting up structures that would be charged with preparing for autonomy in the Palestinian territories.

In 1991, with Mark Heller, he published *No Trumpets, No Drums: A Two-State Settlement of the Israeli-Palestinian Conflict.* In January 1994, while Palestinian autonomy was being established as provided for in the Oslo Accords, he was named assistant director of the governing committee of Palestinian Economic Council for Development and Reconstruction. He has been president of al-Quds University in Abu Dis in East Jerusalem since 1995. In October 2001 Yasir Arafat named him to replace Faysal al-Husayni, who had died in May, as minister of the Palestinian Authority responsible for Jerusalem. He proposed organizing a general assembly of representatives of East Jerusalem to uphold the interests of its Palestinian inhabitants. His position is usually referred to as the Palestinian Authority's diplomatic representative in Jerusalem; he dovotes himself to activities designed to create dialogue with Israelis of good will. In 2001 Nusabaya published an essay proposing that, if there were to be a two-state settlement of the Israel-Palestine issue, Palestinians would have to give up the right of return to anyplace within the boundaries of the State of Israel. This point of view was and continues to be extremely controversial among Palestinians, and it provoked outrage and condemnation, with many calling for Nusabaya to be dismissed from his post.

SEE ALSO Abu Dis; Arafat, Yasir; Ashrawi, Hanan Daouda; Bir Zeit University; Fatah, al-; Husayni, Faysal al-; Intifada (1987–1993); Madrid Conference; Oslo Accords; Palestine Liberation Organization; Palestinian Academic Society for the Study of International Affairs; Palestinian Authority; Palestinian Economic Council for Development and Reconstruction; Quds University, al-; West Bank.

NUSEIBEH, SARI

SEE Nusabaya, Sari.

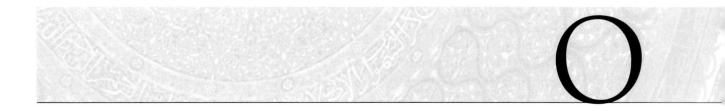

OAPEC

SEE Organization of Arab Petroleum Exporting Countries.

OCCUPIED TERRITORIES: The Palestinian, Jordanian, Egyptian, and Syrian territories occupied by the Israeli army since the 1967 War: the West Bank, which includes East Jerusalem, the Gaza Strip, and the Golan Heights.

SEE ALSO Arab-Israel War (1967); Gaza Strip; Golan Heights; West Bank.

ODA

SEE Organization for Democratic Action.

ODEH, MUHAMMAD (Abu Daud; 1937–): Palestinian activist, born in Silwan, Palestine. Muhammad Odeh studied law in Damascus, where he joined the Ba'th Party. Between 1962 and 1967 he taught in Jordan and Saudi Arabia, then obtained a post in the justice ministry in Kuwait. In 1968, having returned to Jordan, he joined al-Fatah and in 1970 was elected to the revolutionary council. In 1971 he was one of the main leaders of the Black September group, created to avenge Palestinians who died in September 1970 in confrontations with the Jordanian forces. On 5 September 1972 he participated in taking hostage a number of Israeli athletes competing in the Munich

Olympics; eleven of the athletes were killed. On 10 February he was arrested in Jordan with a group of Palestinians accused of planning to assassinate King Hussein. On 1 March a Palestinian commando demanding his release took over the embassy of Saudi Arabia in Khartoum. Three Western diplomats died in the course of the operation. On 8 March the Soviet Union asked King Hussein to pardon him. On 5 September a Palestinian commando took the members of the Saudi embassy in Paris hostage, demanding Odeh's release. Sentenced first to death by Jordanian justice, and then to life imprisonment, he was amnestied by the king on 19 September 1973. Banished from Jordan, Odeh joined the ranks of a Jordanian National Revolutionary Movement that was demanding that King Hussein be deposed.

On 7 January 1977, while he was in Paris for the funeral of a Palestinian leader who had been assassinated a few days earlier, he was arrested by the French internal security service on an international arrest warrant. He was freed four days later, provoking a wave of international outrage. He returned to Lebanon but traveled widely in the Eastern bloc countries, escaping a 1981 assassination attempt in Warsaw. In 1996 Israel allowed him to return to the Palestinian territories to participate in a meeting of the Palestine National Council. In June 1999, after publishing his memoirs, in which he acknowledged his responsibility in the massacre at the Munich Olympic Games, he was named on an international arrest warrant from Germany and was banned from returning to the Palestinian territories.

SEE ALSO Ba'th; Black September Organization; Fatah, al-; Hussein ibn Talal; Palestine National Council.

OIC

SEE Organization of the Islamic Conference.

OLMERT, EHUD (1945–): Israeli politician, born in Binyamina, Mandatory Palestine. Ehud Olmert served in the Israel Defense Force and holds a law degree from the Hebrew University of Jerusalem. First elected to the Knesset on the Likud list in 1973, Olmert served on various committees, including housing, law and justice, and education. He served as minister without portfolio from 1988 to 1990, and from 1990 to 1992 as minister of health. Elected mayor of Jerusalem in 1993, Olmert resigned from the Knesset in 1998. He was reelected to the Knesset in 2003 and was appointed deputy prime minister and minister of industry and trade.

SEE ALSO Israel Defense Force; Knesset; Likud.

ONE ISRAEL (*Israel Ehad*, "One Israel" in Hebrew): Israeli electoral coalition, formed on 22 March 1999, by the leader of the Labor Party, Ehud Barak, in anticipation of general elections the following May. This bloc united the Labor Party, Gesher of David Levy, and the Meimad of Yehuda Amital. As a result of the elections of 17 May, this list won 26 seats in the Knesset, and the leader of the Labor Party was elected prime minister. For the Labor Party, this result represented, nevertheless, a relative failure compared to the 1996 elections, when it won 34 seats for itself alone, even though party leader Shimon Peres had been defeated by Benjamin Netanyahu in the election for prime minister. On 20 February 2001, One Israel was weakened by the defeat of Ehud Barak in the election for prime minister, running against the head of Likud, Ariel Sharon. While seven members of the Labor Party joined the national unity government of Sharon, and Rabbi Michael Melchior of Meimad became Deputy Minister for Diaspora Affairs, no member of Gesher had any part in it.

SEE ALSO Barak, Ehud; Gesher "Bridge" Party; Israel Labor Party; Knesset; Levy, David; Likud; Meimad; Netanyahu, Benjamin; Peres, Shimon.

ONE NATION

SEE Am Ehad Party.

OPEC

SEE Organization of Petroleum Exporting Countries.

OPERATION DESERT FOX

SEE Desert Fox.

OPERATION DESERT SHIELD

SEE Gulf War (1991).

OPERATION DESERT STORM

SEE Gulf War (1991).

OPERATION PEACE FOR GALILEE

SEE Arab Israel War (1982).

ORGANIZATION FOR DEMOCRATIC ACTION (DAO, Da'am in Arabic): Heir to the Trotskyite ideas of Matzpen, this Israeli political entity was founded in April 1996 by Assaf Adiv, in anticipation of the Knesset elections of the following May. Its aim is to organize the working class, especially Arab workers, whom it considers victims of discrimination by the Israeli government. Opposed to the existence of the State of Israel as such, the DAO rejected the Israeli-Palestinian accords of 1993. This movement has not been represented in the Knesset, and in the 2003 elections it received only 1,950 votes.

SEE ALSO Matzpen.

ORGANIZATION OF ARAB PALESTINE: Palestinian movement founded in 1968 following a split in the Popular Front for the Liberation of Palestine–General Command (itself the result of an earlier split with the Popular Front for the Liberation of Palestine) under the impetus of Ahmad Za'rur. Za'rur was a Nasserist and his organization was supported, at least until Gamal Abdal Nasser's death, by Egypt. In 1971 the organization was incorporated into the Palestine Liberation Organization.

SEE ALSO Nasser, Gamal Abdel; Palestine Liberation Organization; Popular Front for the Liberation of Palestine; Popular Front for the Liberation of Palestine–General Command.

ORGANIZATION OF ARAB PETROLEUM EXPORTING COUNTRIES (OAPEC): International organization created in 1968 under the aegis of the Arab League to strengthen cooperation among member states. Members were Algeria, Bahrain, Egypt, Iraq, Kuwait,

Libya, Qatar, Saudi Arabia, Syria, Tunisia, and the United Arab Emirates. Tunisia left the organization in 1986. Seven of these states also belong to the Organization of Petroleum Exporting Countries (OPEC). On 17 October 1973, when the 1973 War had just begun, OAPEC became involved in the conflict by reducing its exports by 25 percent and cutting off the United States and the Netherlands entirely. Exempt from the embargo were Britain (partially), France, Spain, and the Muslim countries. OAPEC announced that the measure would be in effect "until the territories occupied by Israel are liberated and the Palestinian people regain their rights." The embargo was lifted in March 1974, by which time the world price of oil had quadrupled.

SEE ALSO Arab-Israel War (1973); League of Arab States; Organization of Petroleum Exporting Countries.

ORGANIZATION OF COMMUNIST ACTION OF LEBANON

(OCAL; Munazzamat al-ʿAmal al-Shuyuʾi fi Lubnan, or Organisation de l'Action Communiste du Liban): Organization created in 1970 from the merger of two small movements of the extreme left: the Lebanese Socialist Movement and the Organization of Socialist Lebanon. The former had been the left wing of the Lebanese Arab Nationalist Movement and the latter rallied intellectuals from the Lebanese Communist Party and the Baʿth. After April 1971 the OCAL supported the Palestinian resistance in its confrontation with Lebanese authorities. The OCAL advocated a popular war of liberation, rejecting UN Resolution 242 because it made no mention of the Palestinian people. Between 1971 and 1977 the OCAL, which was allied with the Lebanese National Movement, actively supported the Palestinian resistance, within which it had especially close ties with the Democratic Front for the Liberation of Palestine. Pro-Chinese when it was founded, the OCAL has drawn progressively closer to the Lebanese Communist Party. It publishes the newspaper *al-Hurriyah*.

SEE ALSO Arab Nationalist Movement; Democratic Front for the Liberation of Palestine; Lebanese Communist Party; Lebanese National Movement; Resolution 242.

ORGANIZATION OF PETROLEUM EXPORTING COUNTRIES

(OPEC): Cartel of oil-producing states created in September 1960 in response to several rounds of unilateral price cuts by the big multinational oil companies. The founding conference in Baghdad was attended by delegates from five countries: Saudi Arabia, Iraq, Iran, Kuwait, and Venezuela. Subsequently eight additional countries joined. Formed to halt the fall in crude oil prices, OPEC eventually took over the international pricing system from the oil companies after the Arab oil embargo that followed the 1973 Arab Israel War. For years, although often affected by political events such as the Iranian revolution of 1979, its members were able to exercise control over crude oil prices by controlling production. The Iran-Iraq War of 1980–1988, however, caused a serious division in the organization and limited its control of the market. In the late 1980s an extended period of lowered oil prices caused economic problems in oil-producing countries, which responded by increasing production above OPEC quotas, resulting in even lower prices. This overproduction was a contributing factor in the Iraqi invasion of Kuwait in 1990 and the subsequent Gulf War of 1991: Iraq owed huge amounts of money (to Kuwait, among other states) because of its war with Iran and needed higher oil prices to pay its debts. Between 1997 and 1998, torn by internal competition, OPEC went through a crisis, provoked by Saudi Arabia, which was facing serious economic difficulties and obtained an increase in the Gulf states' production quotas, leading to lower prices. New problems for OPEC include potential new sources of production in Central Asia and increasing competition for existing resources from the West and from expanding East Asian economies, particularly China.

SEE ALSO Arab-Israel War (1973); Gulf War (1991); Iran-Iraq War; Organization of Arab Petroleum Exporting Countries.

ORGANIZATION OF THE ISLAMIC CONFERENCE

(OIC): Cooperative organization of Islamic countries created on 25 September 1969 at the special Islamic summit in Rabat following the fire at the al-Aqsa Mosque in Jerusalem. Sponsored by King Faysal of Saudi Arabia and including twenty-three Muslim heads of state, the Rabat summit founded the OIC to safeguard the holy sites of Jerusalem. Among the goals of the organization were "the safeguarding and protection of the holy sites of Islam, of which Jerusalem is one of the essential elements; support for the just cause of the Palestinian people, deprived of its legitimate rights; support for peoples and populations that are victims of oppression and racial discrimination." The OIC has headquarters in Jeddah and includes three decision-making organs: the summit of heads of state, the conference of ministers, and the office of the secretary general; it controls fourteen institutions, including the al-Quds Committee, presided over by the King of Morocco; the Committee of

Six on Palestine; the Islamic Development Bank; and the Islamic Solidarity Fund. In 1972 the OIC adopted a charter fixing the promotion of Islamic solidarity as a principal objective of the organization. As a religious entity, the OIC has been amenable to contacts with the Catholic Church. On 7 April 1981 its secretary general, Habib al-Shatty, was received by Pope John Paul II. On 28 June 2001, as a gesture of support for the al-Aqsa Intifada in the Palestinian territories, the OIC ended its annual summit, which was being held in Bamako, Mali, with an appeal to Muslim countries to break off relations with Israel. Since 2001 the secretary general of the OIC has been a Moroccan, Abdelouahed Belkeziz. In 2004 the OIC included fifty-seven member states.

SEE ALSO Aqsa, al-; Aqsa Intifada, al-.

ORIENT, L'– LE JOUR: Lebanese francophone daily, born of the merger of two French-language newspapers, *L'Orient* and *Le Jour*.

ORIENT HOUSE: Constructed in 1897 in East Jerusalem by Ismaʿil Musa Husayni, Orient House (Bayt al-Sharq) became a center of Palestinian activities following the Madrid Conference in November 1991. After the signing of the Oslo Accords in September 1993, the building was transformed into a symbol of Palestinian nationhood, designated by the Palestinian Authority (PA) as the future seat of government to signal its legitimate presence in Jerusalem. In May 1994 Faysal al-Husayni, owner of the Orient House and the head of the Arab Studies Society, which was also housed there, was made a minister of the PA and assigned the Jerusalem dossier by Yasir Arafat; he became the Palestinian Authority representative in Jerusalem. Israel, which had annexed East Jerusalem in 1967, considered it Israeli territory and disputed the PA's right to be there at all. On 31 May 2001 Husayni died in Kuwait of a heart attack. In August Israeli authorities seized Orient House, closed the Arab Studies Society and the PA offices, and seized all archives, documents, books, and property.

SEE ALSO Arafat, Yasir; Husayni, Faysal al-; Madrid Conference; Oslo Accords; Palestinian Authority.

ORR COMMISSION REPORT (2003): Israeli report on the violence of October 2000, following the outbreak of the al-Aqsa Intifada, in which thirteen Israeli Arab citizens were killed while protesting. The commission was appointed by Prime Minister Ehud Barak under public pressure, primarily from Palestinians. The report was written by Theodor Orr, a Supreme Court judge; Shimon Shamir, former Israeli ambassador to Egypt and Jordan; and Hashim Khatib, a district judge from Nazareth, representing the Arab minority. It was the result of three years spent compiling evidence, including interviews with over three hundred witnesses, and it deplored the failure of all Israeli governments to deal with the social and economic inequalities facing Palestinian citizens of Israel, cited the inadequacy of police response in the past and the overreaction of police forces in October 2000, and condemned several Palestinian politicians for inciting violence. It also criticized the prime minister's office for not anticipating the possibility of the violent outbreak. It recommended the removal of Shlomo Ben Ami, minister of internal security, and criticized the National Police for the use of rubber-coated bullets and live ammunition to quell riots. The two highest ranking police officers, Rav Nitzav and Yehudah Wilk, were barred from holding high office in the National Police, and the Department of Police Investigations in the Ministry of Justice was instructed to review cases of possible unlawful manslaughter.

SEE ALSO Aqsa Intifada, al-; Barak, Ehud.

ORTHODOX JUDAISM: The form of Judaism practiced by Jews who accept as divinely inspired the totality of Jewish law as recorded in the Torah (both the Written and Oral Laws), as codified in the *Shulhan Arukh,* and as observed in practice according to the unchanging principles of the Halakhah. Orthodox Judaism looks upon attempts of other branches of Judaism to adjust to the contemporary "spirit of the time" as incompatible with a strict adherence to normative Judaism which considers the revealed will of God as a permanent and immutable authority and standard. Orthodox Jews may be Ashkenazi or Sephardi, depending on their geographic and cultural origins.

Orthodox Jews are a small minority both in Israel and in the United States (estimates vary between 10 percent and 30 percent), but in Israel they enjoy disproportionate power in government and social institutions, placing legal restrictions deriving from Halakhah (for example, regulations governing marriage, divorce, and conversion) not only on Israel's large secular Jewish population but also on members of the growing Reform and Conservative (Masorti) movements. Orthodox Jews believe that traditional religious commandments should play an important part in shaping government policy, leading to frequent conflicts with secular Israeli Jews who believe in religious pluralism or who wish to limit the role of religion in the state. Many Orthodox Jews believe that Biblical promises entitle Jews to full control over Greater Eretz Yisrael (Land of Israel), and are unwilling to consider territorial concessions to the Palestinians.

SEE ALSO Ashkenazi; Eretz Yisrael; Haredi; Hasidism; Masorti; Rabbi; Reform Judaism; Sephardi.

OSLO ACCORDS: Agreement between Israel and the Palestine Liberation Organization (PLO) negotiated secretly in Oslo, Norway, and signed at the White House on 13 September 1993. These negotiations were begun in February 1993; on 20 August, they resulted in an accord on the provisional autonomy for the Gaza Strip and Jericho ("Gaza-Jericho First" option). The agreement was followed by the Declaration of Principles on Interim Self-Government Arrangements for the Palestinian Territories. This document was signed in Washington under the sponsorship of the United States and Russia (the former USSR). The signing was the occasion of a historic handshake between Israeli prime minister Yitzhak Rabin and the leader of the PLO, Yasir Arafat.

The text of the accord established a schedule of negotiations over a five-year period leading to the establishment of a permanent status for the Palestinian territories. Until then provisional autonomy would exist in the West Bank and the Gaza Strip. The specified phases were: a) 13 October 1993, transfer of administrative powers from the Israelis to the Palestinians; b) 13 December 1993, beginning of Israeli military withdrawal from the Gaza Strip and Jericho, and formation of a Palestinian police force; c) final withdrawal of Israeli forces from the Gaza Strip and Jericho; d) 13 July 1994, elections in the territories of a Palestinian council with jurisdiction over the West Bank and the Gaza Strip, with the exception of East Jerusalem and the Jewish settlements; e) 13 December, 1998 to 13 April 1999, establishment of a definitive and permanent status for the West Bank and the Gaza Strip. But in the months that followed, many incidents took place that prevented the application of the measures. Leaders of the Likud party in Israel, such as Ariel Sharon, stated that if they came to power they would not honor the agreement, while violence erupted between Jewish settlers of the Gaza Strip and Palestinian radicals.

On 29 April 1994 in Paris, Israelis and Palestinians signed a protocol on Israeli-Palestinian economic relations. On 4 May in Cairo Prime Minister Rabin and Arafat signed a provisional agreement on the application of autonomy in the Palestinian territories,

countersigned by Egyptian president Husni Mubarak, the Russian foreign minister, and the American secretary of state. Six days later the first Palestinian police arrived in the Gaza Strip. On 12 May, after the representatives of the right wing walked out of the Chamber, the Israeli Knesset approved the Cairo Accord by a vote of 55–0. On 13 May the Israeli Army gave the keys of the city of Jericho to the Palestinians, and on 12 July, Arafat arrived in Gaza to set up his headquarters. On 29 August the accord was signed on the transfer by Israel of civil powers to the Palestinians.

SEE ALSO Arafat, Yasir; Gaza Strip; Intifada (1987–1993); Knesset; Mubarak, Husni; Sharon, Ariel; West Bank.

OSLO ACCORDS II: On September 28 1995, after much negotiating, Israeli prime minister Yitzhak Rabin and the leader of the Palestine Liberation Organization, Yasir Arafat, signed an agreement in Washington, called Oslo II, dealing with the extension of Palestinian autonomy over the West Bank. The agreement provided for Israeli evacuation of six cities in the West Bank, a partial withdrawal from the city of Hebron, the deployment of Palestinian police, and the organization of elections for the Palestinian Legislative Council. The Gaza Strip and the West Bank were to be divided into four zones. Zone A, which comprises 3 percent of the West Bank, would include the Gaza Strip and eight cities of the West Bank (Jenin, Tulkarm, Qalqilya, Nablus, Bethlehem, Jericho, Ramallah, and Hebron—the latter becoming the focus of special negotiations). In this zone the Palestinian Authority (PA) would be responsible for civil matters and security. Zone B, which comprises 24 percent of the West Bank and is essentially rural in character, includes West Bank villages where the PA would be responsible for civil affairs and for public order, with Israel reserving control of security. Zone C, which comprises 73 percent of the West Bank and where the majority of the Jewish colonies are located, would be entirely under the control of the Israel. Zone D is made up of frontiers, road interchanges, and military outposts responsible for the security of the Jewish colonies. On 6 October the Knesset approved the agreement by a vote of 61 to 59.

The Oslo peace process generated a number of subsequent Israeli-Palestinian agreements. On 23 October 1998, at the Wye Plantation in Maryland, after months of stalled negotiations, Arafat and Israeli prime minister Benjamin Netanyahu signed an agreement on continued Israeli withdrawal from the

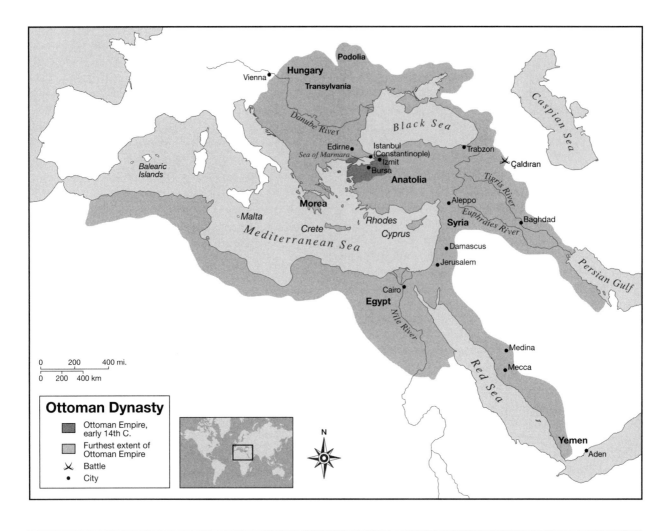

West Bank under the sponsorship of U.S. secretary of state Madeleine Albright. Israel would transfer approximately 13 percent of the territory of the West Bank to the Palestinians: 1 percent of Zone A, and 12 percent of Zone B. The PA would gain control over 60 percent of the Gaza Strip and approximately 10 percent of the West Bank. On 18 November, the Knesset ratified the Wye River Accords, owing to the votes of the Left, by 75 to 19 with 9 abstentions and 17 absent. After Israel withdrew from almost 2 percent of the territory, under criticism by a portion of his majority, Netanyahu refused to continue applying the accord as long as the Palestinians declined to submit to five demands: 1) a commitment from the PA to respect its promises; 2) renunciation of any unilateral proclamation of an independent state with Jerusalem as capital; 3) cessation of all incitements to violence; 4) recognition that the Wye River Accords did not oblige Israel to release Palestinian "murderers"; 5) PA confiscation of illegally obtained arms in territories under its control, imprisonment

of "murderers" and pursuit of security cooperation with Israel.

On 21 December 1998, by a vote of 81 to 30 with 4 abstentions and 5 absent, the Knesset rejected these propositions. The vote prompted the dissolution of the Knesset and the preparation of early general elections. Israeli-Palestinian accords were once more stalled. In August 1999 negotiations on the application of the Wye Plantation Accords, undertaken between Albright, new Israeli prime minister Ehud Barak, and Palestinian negotiators once more snagged over the question of Palestinian prisoners. In the night of 4–5 September, Arafat and Barak signed the Sharm al-Shaykh Memorandum in Egypt, which it was thought would open the way to negotiations on an Israeli-Palestinian peace settlement. The Wye Plantation treaty was endorsed by the Knesset on 8 September by a vote of 54 to 23 with 2 abstentions. The 17 SHAS representatives did not participate in the vote. On 19 September Israel transferred an additional 7 percent of the West Bank to the Palestine Authority.

SEE ALSO Albright, Madeleine; Arafat, Yasir; Barak, Ehud; Gaza Strip; Hebron; Knesset; Netanyahu, Benjamin; Palestine Liberation Organization; Palestinian Authority; Palestinian Legislative Council; Rabin, Yitzhak; Sharm al-Shaykh Memorandum; SHAS; West Bank.

OTTOMAN EMPIRE

SEE Ottomans.

OTTOMANS: Turkish dynasty created by Osman (Othman) the First. From the fourteenth to the sixteenth century, the Ottomans created a vast empire in western Asia, eastern Europe, and north Africa. In 1453 their troops took Constantinople, ending the reign of the Byzantine Christian empire. They controlled Palestine for four hundred years beginning in 1516.

Under Ottoman rule Palestine was divided into three *mutasarrifiyahs*: Nablus and Acre, linked with Beirut, and Jerusalem, which dealt directly with the Ottoman government in Istanbul. Within the Ottoman Empire non-Muslim religious communities were organized into units called millets, each of which collected its own taxes, established its own educational institutions, and administered its own laws relating to personal affairs; thus Jews and Christian sects had full religious freedom during this period. In 1831 the Egyptian viceroy Muhammad Ali Pasha and his son Ibrahim invaded Palestine, establishing a harsh regime while opening the area to Christian and other Western influences. In 1840, however, the British, Austrians, and Russians forced the Egyptians out and Palestine was restored to the Ottoman Empire, which adopted widespread reforms and encouraged foreign colonies. Among these were a few Zionist agricultural settlements, the earliest of which was established by Russian Jews in 1882.

Ottoman control over Palestine ended in 1917–1918, with the arrival of British troops during World War I, and officially ceased in 1922, when the Ottoman Empire, which had been allied with Germany, was formally dismantled. At that time the modern nation of Turkey was created and Palestine came under British Mandate.

PA

SEE Palestinian Authority.

PADICO

SEE Palestine Development and Investment Company.

PAEAC

SEE Parliamentary Association for European-Arab Cooperation.

PAI

SEE Po'alei Agudat Israel.

PALESTINE: Arabic *Filastin*, from the Greek; Hebrew *Peleshet*; "historical" Palestine today is the Palestine of the British Mandate after the separation of Transjordan, the area east of the Jordan River. It encompassed the state of Israel, the West Bank, and the Gaza Strip. Politically, Palestine today consists of the projected Palestinian state in the West Bank and Gaza Strip whose true status is reflected in the name by which it is more usually known, the Occupied Territories.

Palestine derives its name from the Philistines who arrived in what was then Canaan in the fourteenth century B.C.E. and eventually occupied the Mediterranean coastal plain from Jaffa to the Sinai.

In 135 C.E. the Romans changed the name of their province *Syria Judaea,* the southern part of the province of Syria, to *Syria Palaestina.* The name was also used by seventh-century Arab armies, who conquered what they called *Filastin* from the Byzantine Empire. Palestine was ruled by the Ottomans from 1517 until World War I as part of the region known as Syria, or Greater Syria, covering the area between Turkey and Egypt, from the Mediterranean to the Syrian Desert. It was contained in several provinces and administrative districts, none named Palestine or coterminous with the territory known by that name; it had never been a discrete political entity or claimed precisely defined borders.

British forces occupied Palestine in 1917–1918. In 1920, the postwar San Remo Conference ratified the agreement between the French and British to divide the Ottomans' Arab territories between them. The French received a Mandate for Syria, including Lebanon; Britain was given Palestine/Transjordan and Iraq. The borders of these territories were all created by the British and French, with these borders and Mandates approved by the League of Nations in 1922. Britain set up a civil government in Palestine in 1920 and separated Transjordan in 1921–1922, closing Transjordan to Jewish immigration.

Zionists had been establishing colonies in Palestine since 1878, and during World War I the World Zionist Organization (WZO), established in 1897, was particularly successful in lobbying the British government for support of its project to establish a Jewish state. In the 1917 Balfour Declaration the British made a commitment to the WZO to create a "national home for the Jewish people," and the British Mandate for Palestine was written to permit the Zionists to take over the whole territory. The Mandate referred to the indigenous population of Palestinian Arabs as "non-Jewish communities," but in 1918 the population of native Palestinian Jews and European Zionist immigrants numbered roughly 66,000 people, or only about 10 percent of the populace.

Opposition to European Jewish immigration and suspicion of Zionist intentions had grown before the war, but with the advent of the Mandate and the massive postwar immigration and economic changes it brought, Jewish occupation grew to become the major theme of Palestinian politics. Zionists were buying land which, once purchased, was under restriction for use and resale only to Jews. Organizations such as the Muslim-Christian Association, founded in 1918, and the Arab Executive, founded in 1920, tried—largely through attempts at personal persuasion by the leadership—to convince the British to curtail both land purchases and immigration, and to encourage policies leading to Palestinian independence. Palestinian leaders consistently rejected British proposals for political representation in a legislative assembly, since all the proposals fell short of true self-government and required Palestinians to accept the legitimacy of the Mandate with its built-in promotion of the Zionist project. For their part, the Zionist leaders either rejected or reluctantly agreed to these same solutions because they wanted to put off resolution until they had achieved a majority.

Displeasure with the situation led to rioting in 1920, with 47 Jews and 48 Palestinians killed in Jaffa, and again in 1929, with the Western Wall Disturbances claiming 133 Jewish and 116 Palestinian lives in Jerusalem, Hebron, and elsewhere. Commissions of inquiry, including a League of Nations commission, the British Shaw Commission, and the Hope-Simpson Commission, studied aspects of the Zionist-Palestinian problem in 1929–1930. Because of these studies, the British government issued the Passfield White Paper recommending changes to the Mandate favorable to the Palestinians. By 1929 the Jewish population in Palestine was over 156,000—about 16 percent of the population—and under pressure from the Zionists and their allies, the proposed changes were rejected by the government in the MacDonald Letter of 1931.

From the beginning the Zionists, with much help from abroad, had successfully engendered strong, flexible, well-organized civic and political institutions. Palestinian organizations, in contrast, operated according to the customs of late Ottoman politics: the notables—prominent, influential members of the social and economic elite, often from wealthy landowning or merchant families—attempted to discuss matters in private with the authorities and reach a private agreement. The Western Wall episode and its aftermath proved to be a catalyst for more modern political organizing, as well as for more radical and sometimes violent opposition. Several political parties were founded in the years after 1929. The Istqlal (Independence) Party, formed in 1932 by Awni Abd al-Hadi and others, was the first, calling for a boycott of Jewish businesses; and in 1933 a general strike called by the Arab Executive led to violence in which 24 people died. In 1935, Shaykh Izz al-Din al-Qassam, who had fought the French in Syria and had a following among the poor and recently landless Palestinians in Haifa, took an armed group of eight hundred dispossessed peasants to the mountains near Jenin to begin a revolt. He became a martyr when he was killed by British forces.

A series of violent incidents followed, and in early 1936 a shipment of arms to a Zionist group was discovered. In April 1936 Palestinians in Nablus formed a "national committee" and called for a general strike, demanding the suspension of Jewish immigration and the establishment of a democratic national government; similar Palestinian committees were soon formed all over the country. At this point, the Jewish population was about 370,000—28 percent. Prominent leaders of the political elite formed the Arab Higher Committee, headed by Hajj Amin al-Husayni, head of the Supreme Muslim Council, to coordinate and control the strike. At first it was nonviolent, but when the British announced that they were raising the Jewish immigration quota, the strike escalated into a general insurrection known as the Arab Revolt of 1936–1939, in which over 5,000 people were killed, over 14,000 wounded, 5,600 put in detention and thousands forced into exile. Some Zionists formed guerrilla groups, such as the Irgun and the Stern Gang, to attack and terrorize Palestinians. The strike was called off after six months, and the British sent the Peel Commission to investigate the causes of the uprising. In July 1937 the commission recommended the partition of Palestine.

Under the Peel plan, the Zionists would be awarded one-third of the country, including the most fertile and prosperous part, Galilee, where there were few Jews. The Zionist areas would become a self-governing state, while Palestinian areas would be annexed to Transjordan, with Palestinians subject to "compulsory" resettlement if necessary. The Palestinians found this unacceptable, and there was universal anger over this proposal. The violence, which had died down when the general strike ended, resumed.

In September the British district commissioner for Galilee was assassinated, leading the British to impose severe repressive measures against the Palestinians, including collective punishments such as house demolitions and mass detentions in camps. Most of the Arab Higher Committee either was arrested and deported or fled into exile. In 1938 the Woodhead Commission, created to study the partition issue, reported that the Peel Commission's plan was impractical, and the British government announced that it would reexamine the entire question. In March and April 1939 a conference was held in London attended by Zionist, Palestinian, and Arab leaders; it was not a success, but in May the government issued the MacDonald White Paper, which rejected partition and the idea of a Jewish state (although not the "national home" idea), proposed a limit to Jewish immigration and land purchase, and favored the creation of a single independent Palestinian state after a ten-year transition period. The Zionists rejected this plan since it was still their intention to create a Jewish state out of Palestine; the Palestinians rejected it because there were no guarantees regarding statehood; and Hajj Amin, Great Mufti of Jerusalem and the most prominent Palestinian leader, then in exile, did not trust the British to keep their word. A substantial segment of the Palestinian public, however, believed that the White Paper should have been accepted, because the terms represented a serious change of heart by the British. By 1939 the Jewish population in Palestine was 445,456, almost 30 percent of the populace.

During World War II the British banned political activity. The Palestinians were politically disorganized in any case, and Hajj Amin had fled from Lebanon to Iraq to Germany—apparently hoping to find support from the enemies of the British, he collaborated with the Germans in attempting to raise a Muslim army in the Balkans. When the Arab League was being formed in 1946, it appointed Musa al-Alami as Palestinian representative and took control of Palestinian nationalist affairs, including refounding the Arab Higher Committee. Although Hajj Amin was named to head it, the British would not permit him

to return to Palestine. By 1946 the Jewish population of Palestine in was roughly 608,000, or 33 percent.

At the Biltmore Conference in New York in 1942, the WZO had for the first time publicly committed itself to establishing a Jewish state in all of Palestine, although it later was willing to consider partition. The Anglo-American Committee of Inquiry of 1945–1946 recommended establishing a single unpartitioned state, an end to restrictions on land purchases by Jews, and the admission of 100,000 Jewish refugees from Europe. The British felt that they had lost control of the situation after the war and announced their intention to give up the Mandate, turning the problem over to the United Nations. In 1947 the UN Special Committee on Palestine (UNSCOP) recommended partition based on "a realistic appraisal of the actual Arab-Jewish relations in Palestine." The population at that time was approximately 1,131,000 Palestinians and 508,000 Jews, with Jews owning seven percent of the land; the UNSCOP plan called for a Zionist state on 55 percent of the territory—with a substantial Palestinian minority population—a Palestinian state on 40 percent—with a few thousand Jews—and five percent—the city of Jerusalem and suburbs—as an international zone under UN trusteeship. The Zionists accepted the plan; the Palestinians and other Arabs opposed it, but were without power, organization, unity of purpose, or an effective strategy to prevent its adoption. The proposal was passed by the UN Security Council as Resolution 181 in November 1947. The UN vote caused public outrage in Palestine and was followed by another outbreak of communal violence and guerrilla warfare.

In December Palestinian leaders made an effort to revive the "national committees" that had run the 1936 general strike, but it was too late; the Zionists had a modern, well-equipped army, paramilitary organizations, and an entire well-organized, well-run and well-funded state structure that had been building for several decades. After several months of fighting, Israel declared its statehood on 14 May 1948. The next day the Arab states declared war, but the Palestinian guerrillas, allied with the armies of Egypt, Transjordan, Syria, Lebanon, and Iraq, were no match for the Israelis. Moreover, the Arabs were not truly united; Abdullah I, although ostensibly part of the Arab coalition, had previously come to a secret agreement with the Zionists to refrain from fighting with them in territory allotted to them by the UN with the understanding that he would annex to Jordan the territory allotted to the Palestinians. The 1948–1949 War ended with Israel occupying 78 percent of the territory of Mandatory Palestine, all but the West Bank and Gaza Strip; nearly 750,000 Palestinians expelled from Israeli territory became homeless refugees in the West Bank and Gaza Strip, Egypt, Jordan, Lebanon, and Syria; the obliteration of more than 350 Palestinian villages; Jordan's annexation (formalized in 1950) of the West Bank; the destruction of the Palestinian political community; and the permanent presence in Palestine of a European settler state regarded by most Arabs as a tool of Western imperial power. The 1948–1949 War, known to Palestinians as *al-Nakba*, the Catastrophe, was the end of Palestine; since then Palestinians have resisted and struggled to reconstitute their community and to recreate a true Palestinian state.

> SEE ALSO Abd al-Hadi, Awni; Abdullah I ibn Hussein; Alami, Musa al-; Anglo-American Committee of Inquiry; Arab Executive; Arab Higher Committee; League of Arab States; Balfour Declaration; British Mandate; Gaza Strip; Husayni, Hajj Amin al-; Irgun; Jordan River; Lohamei Herut Yisrael; Occupied Territories; Palestinian Statehood; Qassam, Izz al-Din al-; Resolution 181; West Bank; Western Wall Disturbances; World Zionist Organization.

PALESTINE ARAB REVOLT (1936–1939): Palestinian armed insurrection against the British Mandatory government and its support for the Zionist project. It grew from a number of roots: continuing rule by a foreign power; that power's support for foreign colonization (the "Jewish National Home") and its continuing disregard for Palestinian national and civil rights; the failure of any Palestinian group, particularly the Arab Executive, with its cautious methods and its ties to the conservative (and mutually hostile and factionalized) interests of the landowning notable families, to influence the British to change their policies; the rapid increases in Jewish immigration and land purchases and the growth of Zionist civil institutions since the late 1920s; the demonstration of Zionist power to block the reforms called for after the Western Wall Disturbances.

Palestinian politics took a more radical and activist tone in the early 1930s; popular opinion began to force change from below, new political parties and other groups were formed, and demonstrations and boycotts were undertaken. In October 1935 Shaykh Izz al-Din al-Qassam, who had fought the French in Syria and who preached to the poor and recently landless in Haifa against the British and the Zionists, took an armed group of eight hundred dispossessed

Palestinian peasants to the mountains near Jenin to begin a revolt. He became a martyr when he was killed by British forces in November. On 15 April 1936 some of Qassam's followers killed two Jews traveling on the Tulkarm-Nablus Road. The next day a retaliatory killing of two Palestinians took place near Petah Tikvah. On 17 April the funeral of the two dead Jews in Tel Aviv turned into a Zionist riot, with inflammatory speeches, stoning of police, and beating of Palestinians in the streets. On 19 April a Palestinian mob attacked Jews in the first of four days of rioting in which sixteen Jews and five Palestinians were killed. On 20 April Palestinians in Nablus formed a "national committee" and called for a general strike, demanding the suspension of Jewish immigration and the establishment of a democratic national government. Similar committees were soon formed all over the country.

The most prominent leaders of the political elite formed the Arab Higher Committee, headed by Hajj Amin al-Husayni, head of the Supreme Muslim Council, to coordinate the strike and try to keep it under the control. Many groups, including labor organizations, women's committees, and boy scouts, took part. A national conference on 7 May called for nonpayment of taxes and other forms of civil disobedience. Virtually all Palestinian businesses were closed; Palestinian civil servants in the British administration signed a petition endorsing the aims of the strike. The British response was to raise the Jewish immigration quota and announce the creation of an all-Jewish port in Tel Aviv, which would put the old port in Jaffa out of business. Most strikers followed the National Committees' nonviolent strategy, but the strike grew into a popular insurrection and there was violence, including arson, sabotage, burning of crops, mining of roads, derailing of trains, and attacks against suspected strikebreakers. Guerrilla groups formed in the countryside and occasionally fought with British troops, with a very high rate of casualties.

The British responded with collective punishment, including house demolitions (one such action in the center of Jaffa made 6,000 people homeless) and mass arrests. The British offered to form another royal commission to investigate, but after the British government's failure to respond to the findings and recommendations of the Shaw Commission, the Hope-Simpson Commission, or the Passfield White Paper with any serious change, the Palestinians were not mollified. The strike was ended after six months, when the leaders realized that their activities were benefiting Zionist economic interests, when the government sent a new army division, when the orange crop had to be harvested to avoid the loss of the country's biggest export earner, and when the Arab states made a face-saving appeal.

A royal commission, the Peel Commission, did conduct an inquiry and concluded in July 1937 that the mandate was ultimately impracticable and unjust to the Palestinians but made a recommendation that proved unacceptable to them: that the country be partitioned. Under the Peel plan the Zionists would be awarded one-third of Palestine, including the most fertile and prosperous part of the country, the Galilee, where few Jews lived. The Zionist areas would become a self-governing state. Palestinian areas would be annexed to Transjordan, and Palestinians would be subject to compulsory resettlement if necessary. Palestinians greeted this proposal with universal anger, and the violence that had died down when the general strike ended began again. In September the British district commissioner for Galilee was assassinated. The British arrested hundreds of nationalist leaders, banned the Arab Higher Committee and the National Committees, and removed Hajj Amin from the leadership of the Supreme Muslim Council. Members of the Arab Higher Committee were either deported to the Seychelles Islands or, for those who had managed to escape arrest by fleeing the country, forbidden to return. These actions stimulated resistance. Small guerrilla groups united into larger regional ones and the Arab Higher Committee, whose available members, including Hajj Amin, had collected themselves in Damascus, made efforts to supply them with arms.

Coordinated attacks took place all over Palestine on 14 October. Violence spread through the country, and rebel guerrillas controlled large parts of it, including most of the countryside and many of the towns. Roads were mined and other acts of ambush and sabotage took place, as did both skirmishes and pitched battles between the guerrillas and both the British and Zionist forces whose creation the British had allowed. Both sides were responsible for massacres. The British conducted house demolitions and summary executions and created detention camps that held hundreds without trial. This continued into the autumn of 1938.

Violence began to wane as the British, now with more than 20,000 troops and an air force, gained the upper hand militarily and guerrilla leaders were either killed or fled the country. In November 1938 yet another royal commission, the Woodhead Commission, created to study the partition issue, reported that the Peel Commission's plan was impractical and

the British government announced that it would re-examine the entire question. In March and April 1939 it held a conference in London, attended by Zionist, Palestinian, and other Arab leaders, including representatives from Egypt, Iraq, Transjordan, and Saudi Arabia. Hajj Amin was not allowed to attend. The conference was not a success, but in May the government issued the MacDonald White Paper, in which it rejected partition, rejected the idea of a Jewish state (though not the "National Home"), proposed to limit Jewish immigration and land purchases, and favored the creation of an independent Palestinian state after a ten-year transition period, "conditions permitting."

The White Paper was rejected by the Zionists, since it was their intention to create a Jewish state and they did not want the Palestinians to be in a position to thwart them; it was rejected by Hajj Amin because it contained no guarantees of a Palestinian state and because he did not trust the British to keep their word in any case. Other Palestinians, including a substantial part of the public, felt that the White Paper should have been accepted since the terms represented a serious change of heart by the British.

The results of the 1936–1939 Revolt were some 5,000 Palestinians killed, over 14,000 wounded, 5,600 in detention, and thousands in exile. The Palestinians were weaker economically and politically, their leadership was divided, and they had no military force. The Zionists became stronger in every area: 463 Jews were killed, as were 101 British.

SEE ALSO Arab Executive; Arab Higher Committee; Husayni, Hajj Amin al-; Qassam, Izz al-Din al-; Western Wall Disturbances; White Papers on Palestine.

PALESTINE ARMED STRUGGLE COMMAND: Structure (*qiyadat al-kifah al-musallah*) created in Jordan on 18 February 1969, by Yasir Arafat and the executive committee of the Palestine Liberation Organization (PLO) to coordinate the military activities of the Palestine Liberation Army (PLA) with those of other Palestinian armed groups within the PLO. Political differences between the various movements rapidly led to the paralysis of the Palestine Armed Struggle Command (PASC). In Lebanon in the 1970s under the Cairo agreement signed by the PLO and the Lebanese government, PASC evolved into a military police organization, keeping order in the Palestinian refugee camps, attempting to prevent provocative acts against the Lebanese and intervening between opposing Palestinian groups.

SEE ALSO Arafat, Yasir; Palestine Liberation Army; Palestine Liberation Organization.

PALESTINE COMMUNIST PARTY:
Created in January 1922 in Palestine by Jewish immigrants from the Soviet Union who had become disaffected with Zionism. The Palestine Communist Party (PCP) was recognized by and accepted into the Comintern, the international organization of communist parties directed from Moscow, in 1924, and thereafter found itself divided between the directives of the Comintern leadership and the nationalist demands of both the Arab and Jewish communities. In the late 1920s Arabs began to join, and in the 1930s the party, at the direction of the Comintern, began to "Arabize" the party and bring Arabs into the leadership. There were ideological purges in 1932 and 1936, and the party also fractured along ethnic lines during the Arab Revolt of 1936–1939, after which it favored Arab nationalism and denounced Zionist imperialism. In 1943, tensions between Jews and Arabs prompted a breakup, and in 1944 most of the Palestinian membership joined the newly created National Liberation League (NLL) (*Usbat al-Taharrur al-Watani*).

Four years later, Soviet support for the partition of Palestine caused a break between Jewish communists and Palestinian Arab communists. After the Arab-Israel War (1948) the by then mostly Jewish PCP became the Israel Communist Party, and many Palestinians inside Israel, including members of the NLL, joined it. In the Gaza Strip, NLL and former Palestinian PCP members created the Communist Party of Gaza. The NLL continued in the West Bank until 1951, when many of its members joined with Jordanian communists to form the Jordan Communist Party (JCP). The JCP after 1967 became active in resistance to Israeli occupation, and in 1975, its West Bank branch became the Palestine Communist Organization (PCO). In 1982, after internal fighting, the JCP split, and the Palestinians in it, and in the PCO, formed a new Palestine Communist Party, which gave its support to the Palestine Liberation Organization (PLO). In April 1987 the Palestine National Council (PNC) elected a PCP representative to the PLO's executive committee. In 1991, as a consequence of the fall of communism in the Soviet Union, the PCP changed its name to the Palestinian People's Party (PPP).

SEE ALSO Arab-Israel War (1948); Gaza Strip; Palestine Liberation Organization; Palestine National Council; Palestinian People's Party; West Bank.

PALESTINE DEVELOPMENT AND INVESTMENT COMPANY:
Palestinian holding company, registered as a limited liability corporation in Liberia, founded in October 1993 following the Israeli-Palestinian Oslo Accords. Founded by Palestinian businessmen such as Hassib al-Sabbagh, Abdul-Mohsin Qattan, and Munib al-Masri, the Palestine Development and Investment Company (PADICO) raised initial capital of $172 million, to be invested in the Palestinian autonomous territories "to provide competitive financial returns to investors while directing new capital towards projects that would create new job opportunities to improve the standard of living of Palestinian people." It has a number of subsidiaries and affiliates in the tourism, poultry, electronics, real estate, telecommunications, and financial industries (one subsidiary operates the Palestinian stock exchange). Its various businesses have invested over $500 million since 1993. Its outlook, however, was dependent on both Israeli goodwill and the expectation of a "deepening of the peace process," based on which it expected "a substantial peace dividend, with the whole region likely to witness a macroeconomic resurgence" (all quotes from www.padico.com). Instead its businesses have stagnated as the economy of the territories has declined since the beginning of the al'Aqsa Intifada in September 2000.

SEE ALSO Aqsa Intifada, al-; Oslo Accords.

PALESTINE LIBERATION ARMY:
At the time of its first meeting in 1964, the Palestine National Council (PNC) decided that the Palestine Liberation Organization (PLO) must equip itself with a regular military force, called the Palestine Liberation Army (PLA). This resolution was modified at the fourth session of the PNC (held in Cairo in July 1968), where the influence of al-Fatah came to the fore. Thereafter the PLA came under the authority of the executive committee of the PLO, led by Yasir Arafat, whose duty it would be to "encourage the enrolment of Palestinians in Arab military academies and institutions, so as to acquire military training; to mobilize all the Palestinian forces and energies in preparation for the fight for liberty." Officially the PLA was comprised of four contingents or brigades based in different Arab countries: "Ain Jalut" in Egypt, "Qadisiya" in Iraq, "al-Badr" in Jordan, and "Hattin" in Syria. On 19 February 1969, the executive committee of the PLO created the Palestinian Armed Struggle Command (PASC) for the purpose of coordinating the actions of the PLA with those of other Palestinian armed forces. During the Arab-Israel War (1973), some of its units participated in combat against the

Israel Defense Force. In 1983, during the sixteenth meeting of the PNC in Algiers, the organization's name was changed to the Palestinian National Liberation Army (PNLA). This change reflected the desire of Arafat to tighten the ranks among combatants in each of the different movements, after some Palestinian forces based in Lebanon, commanded by Tariq al-Khudra, had rallied to Syria. The elements that had remained loyal to Arafat were integrated into the PNLA, under the command of General Ahmed Afanah. In 1994, following the establishment of the Palestinian Authority, some of the PNLA members joined the ranks of the new Palestinian Police, while others decided to remain in the army of their host country.

SEE ALSO Arab-Israel War (1973); Arafat, Yasir; Fatah, al-; Palestine Liberation Organization; Palestinian Armed Struggle Command; Palestinian Authority; Palestinian National Council.

PALESTINE LIBERATION FRONT (1961): Group of intellectuals founded by the Palestinian writer Shafiq al-Hut in 1961, based in Lebanon (not to be confused with the guerilla groups of the same name founded in 1965 and 1977). The Palestine Liberation Front (PLF)—which was later called the PLF–Path of Return or PLF–PR—recruited for the Palestine Liberation Army (PLA).

SEE ALSO Hut, Shafiq al-; Palestine Liberation Army.

PALESTINE LIBERATION FRONT (1965): Palestinian freedom fighter (*fida'iyyun*) group founded by Ahmad Jibril in 1965, based in Syria. The Palestine Liberation Front (PLF) was merged into the Popular Front for the Liberation of Palestine (PFLP) in 1967. Not to be confused with the groups of the same name founded in 1961 or 1977.

SEE ALSO Popular Front for the Liberation of Palestine.

PALESTINE LIBERATION FRONT (1977): Palestinian movement (*Jabhat al-Tahrir al-Filastiniya*) founded in April 1977. The Palestine Liberation Front (PLF) came out of a split in the Popular Front for the Liberation of Palestine–General Command (PFLP–GC), caused by the opposition of some of its members to Syrian influence in the organization. Iraqi in allegiance, the PLF was headed by its political leader, Muhammad Zaydan and a secretary general, Tal'at Ya'qub, flanked by Said Yusuf and Ali Zaydan. On

14 May 1977 the leadership of the Rejection Front, which had united opponents to the Israeli-Arab peace negotiations, decided to exclude Ahmad Jibril's PFLP–GC from its organization, replacing it with the PLF.

Having been established in Lebanon since the end of the 1970s, both movements' partisans entered a period of bloody confrontations. In the night of 12–13 August 1978, an attack generally believed to have come from the PFLP–GC on the headquarters of the PLF in Beirut caused nearly two hundred deaths. In 1981, having succeeded in solidifying its base among Palestinians, the PLF was admitted to the Palestine National Council (PNC). Between 1982 and 1983, when Palestinian forces were evacuating Lebanon, two currents surfaced in the movement. The first, headed by Muhammad Zaydan, was comprised of partisans of Yasir Arafat; the second, under the leadership of Tal'at Ya'qub, was made up of members who favored Syria. Ya'qub, after having created his own group (the PLF–Tal'at Ya'qub Faction), allied it with the Palestinian National Salvation Front (PNSF), which gathered together the Palestinian opposition. From November 1984, Zaydan, elected to the executive committee of the Palestine Liberation Organization (PLO), ardently supported the policies of Arafat.

A new tendency, represented by Abd al-Fattah Ghanim, until then a supporter of Tal'at Ya'qub, surfaced in the PLF. In September 1985, in spite of internal divergences in the movement, Zaydan was elected secretary general of the PLF. On the following 8 October, in reprisal for an Israeli air raid on the headquarters of the PLO, near Tunis, a PLF group carried out the hijacking of an Italian cruise ship, the *Achille Lauro,* during which a Jewish-American citizen was killed. The United States put out an international arrest warrant against Zaydan and the members of the commando. On 22 April 1987, the presence of the head of the PLF in Algiers at a meeting of the Palestine National Council (PNC) led the United States to protest to the Algerian authorities. Between 1986 and 1988, the leaders of different currents existing in the PLF tried in vain to unite their groups under a common banner.

In November 1988, after the death of Ya'qub, two new tendencies emerged in his movement: the first under the leadership of Abd al-Fattah Ghanim, pro-Libyan, the second, under Yusif al-Maqdah, pro-Syrian. On 15 November 1989, prodded by Arafat, the leaders of the different currents of the Front accepted the authority of Zaydan. On 30 May 1990, a PLF commando attempted a naval assault on Tel

Aviv, which failed. Arafat's refusal to condemn this action publicly caused the United States to reverse its decision to start talks with the leadership of the PLO. That August, when Iraq invaded Kuwait, the PLF came out in support of Baghdad. Hostile to the Israeli-Arab peace process, which had started in November 1991 with the Madrid Conference, the PLF leader, in spite of his supporting Arafat, declared his opposition to the Israeli-Palestinian Oslo Accords, signed on 13 September 1993, in Washington, D.C. Several members of the PLF joined the Palestinian opposition in the Alliance of Palestinian Forces (APF), while Zaydan decided, finally, to continue backing Arafat. In 2004 the principal leaders of the PLF are: Muhammad Zaydan (Abu al-Abbas, secretary general), 'Ali Ishaq (Abu Dunia, assistant secretary general), Ali Zaydan, Zuhdi Sammur, Bilal Qassem Dalkamoni, Muhammad Mahmud Qassem, Imad Yassin, and Marwan Bakr.

> **SEE ALSO** Alliance of Palestinian Forces; Arafat, Yasir; Jibril, Ahmad; Madrid Conference; Oslo Accords; Palestinian National Salvation Front; Popular Front for the Liberation of Palestine–General Command; Rejection Front; Zaydan, Muhammad 'Abbas.

PALESTINE LIBERATION FRONT–PATH OF RETURN

SEE Palestine Liberation Front (1961).

PALESTINE LIBERATION FRONT–TAL'AT YA'QUB FACTION

SEE Palestine Liberation Front (1977).

PALESTINE LIBERATION ORGANIZATION (PLO): Palestinian political institution (*Munadhdhamat al-Tahrir al-Filastiniya*).

Meeting in Jerusalem at its first congress on 28 May 1964, the Palestine National Council (PNC) created the PLO by adopting the Palestine National Charter and the PLO Fundamental Law, and becoming itself a member. As an umbrella organization for the Palestinian national struggle, the PLO replaced the moribund Arab Higher Committee, which had been presided over by Hajj Amin al-Husayni, and eventually became the most important of the Palestinian political organizations. Ahmad Shuqayri, a Palestinian lawyer and former assistant to the secretary general of the Arab League, was named chairman of the PLO executive committee.

The PLO platform was based on four principles: 1) rejection of the partition decreed by the United Nations General Assembly in 1947; 2) armed struggle

YASIR ARAFAT. THE HEAD OF THE PALESTINE LIBERATION ORGANIZATION (PLO) VISITS A REFUGEE CAMP IN WEST BEIRUT, LEBANON, IN 1982. THE MOST IMPORTANT POLITICAL ORGANIZATION OF PALESTINIAN RESISTANCE, THE PLO WAS FORCED OUT OF ITS BASE IN LEBANON BY ISRAEL'S INVASION. THE FORTUNES OF THE PLO AND ARAFAT IN THEIR STRUGGLES—BOTH ARMED AND DIPLOMATIC—FOR A PALESTINIAN STATE HAVE WAXED AND WANED EVER SINCE. (*AP/Wide World Photos*)

for the liberation of Palestine; 3) the fight against Zionism; and 4) ultimate establishment of an independent Palestinian state. The organization comprises three principal components: the Palestine National Council (PNC, *al-Majlis al-Watani al-Filastini*), with 300–600 members—roughly 30 percent from the resistance and guerrilla organizations that are members of the PLO, 20 percent from affiliated mass organizations and trade unions, 20 percent from the diaspora, and 30 percent independent members; the executive committee (EC, *al-Lajna a—Tanfidhiya*), with 15 members elected by the PNC, similar to a cabinet-style government, who direct the bureaucracy and apply policies adopted by the PNC; and the Central Council (CC, *al-Majlis al-Markazi al-Filastini*), with 50–70 members who act as a constitutional council to oversee the functions of the executive committee.

Although the Central Council serves a consultative role, acting as an intermediary legislative entity between the PNC and the EC, it can use its veto to sanction the action of the executive committee. The executive committee supervises the PLO's departments or ministries. It meets at the request of its members; and in the past has met often in Tunis, sometimes in Baghdad. During the deliberations of the EC, a quorum of two-thirds of its members is required, although decisions can be made by a simple majority of those present. Because of regional disturbances, the headquarters of the PLO has been moved successively from Jerusalem to Amman (1967), Beirut (1970-71), Tunis (1982), and Ramallah (1995). The PNC was originally headquartered in Cairo, then moved to Damascus (1979), Amman (1984), and Gaza (1996).

At first considered merely a tool of the Arab League, the PLO became truly independent in 1969. Defeat of the Arab forces in the 1967 War discredited the leadership of both the Arab states and the PLO; Shuqayri resigned in 1967 and was replaced by another lawyer, Yahya Hammuda. When the *fida'yyun* groups, primarily al-Fatah, increased guerrilla attacks against Israel, they earned the respect of the Arab public, receiving many new recruits and greater financial assistance from the Gulf states. On 4 February 1969 Yasir Arafat, head of al-Fatah, was elected chairman of the PLO executive committee, and since then, al-Fatah has been the dominant element within the PLO. Arafat has followed a pragmatic course designed to balance internal differences and further move the PLO toward its single overriding goal.

At times other leaders and organizations have disagreed with Arafat's strategies, leaving the organization and later rejoining it; but the PLO's core membership has remained stable. It includes all the major Palestinian liberation movements, encompassing a diversity of orientations. The largest groups are the centrist al-Fatah, the Marxist Popular Front for the Liberation of Palestine (PFLP), the PFLP–General Command (PFLP–GC), and the Marxist-Leninist inspired Democratic Front for the Liberation of Palestine (DFLP).

In July 1969, the PLO was invited for the first time to attend a meeting of nonaligned countries that took place in Belgrade. Confronted by internal rivalry and affected by regional political changes, there was much dissidence within the PLO, reflecting ideological cleavages among the Palestinian movements. These disagreements came to a head in 1970 when the PFLP launched a violent campaign to sabotage and overthrow the monarchy in Jordan, the base of PLO activity, provoking the government to strike back brutally during what became known as "Black September" 1970. The result of this conflict was the PLO's expulsion from Jordan and transfer to Lebanon, where it had already compelled the government there to grant it a degree of autonomy in governing and providing for the large population of Palestinian

refugees in Lebanon, and in defending them from many Lebanese enemies.

On 26 October 1974, a year after the 1973 War, the PLO was recognized at the Arab League summit in Rabat as the "only legitimate representative of the Palestinian people." On the following 13 November Arafat made a historic speech before the United Nations (UN) General Assembly, after which the PLO obtained observer status at the UN. With the exceptions of Israel and the United States, the international community thereafter recognized the PLO as the representative of the Palestinian people.

The Lebanese Civil War began in 1975, threatening Lebanese sovereignty and contributing to the destabilization of Lebanese politics. PLO operations in that country were partly to blame for the war because they were so extensive that the organization was often referred to as a "state within a state," and parts of southern Lebanon were known as "Fatahland." These operations included not only military organizations and activities, but civilian institutions that provided security and social services to hundreds of thousands of Palestinians who had no other resources within a Lebanese population that was largely hostile to them. Both for these reasons, and for the need to defend its people and maintain its operations, the PLO became a major participant in the war.

In September 1976, Palestine, represented by the PLO, was given full membership in the Arab League. The following year saw the famous journey of Egyptian president Anwar al-Sadat to Jerusalem, followed by the Camp David Accords in 1978, and the Israeli-Egyptian peace treaty in 1979. This treaty led to a schism in the Arab world that affected the PLO because, besides returning the Sinai Peninsula to Egypt, it provided for negotiations toward a future settlement of the Palestinian-Israeli issue "on the basis of" UN Security Council Resolution 242 of 1967, and contained a vague Israeli plan for Palestinian "autonomy" within restricted zones in the West Bank and Gaza without committing Israel's removal of settlements. The other signatories, Egypt and the United States, agreed with Israel's view of Resolution 242—that despite calling for complete Israeli withdrawal from the Occupied Territories, it did not apply to the West Bank and Gaza Strip. Jordan, which was part of the Camp David negotiations, and the PLO, which was not (although there were Palestinian representatives on the Jordanian delegation), along with the entire Arab world, rejected the treaty. In effect, Israel had removed Egypt, which was strong enough to threaten it, from the Arab-Israel dispute while conceding nothing to the Palestinians.

With the Egyptian threat neutralized by the treaty, Israel began aiding and subsidizing Lebanese who were hostile to the Palestinians; and in June 1982 Israel invaded Lebanon to attack the PLO directly in an attempt to destroy it. A cease-fire mediated by the United States in August obliged Arafat and his followers to leave Lebanon, which they agreed to do after receiving an American promise to protect Palestinian refugees. Under the protection of a multinational force, the leadership of the much weakened PLO and about 14,000 fighters went to Tunis where the remnants of the organization found itself cut off from both the Palestinian territories and Palestinian refugees in Lebanon. Within days of the PLO's withdrawal, the Israelis abetted the Phalange by invading two adjacent refugee camps in Beirut, perpetrating the Sabra and Shatila Massacre and leaving the entire community vulnerable. Later in 1982 the United States proposed a Palestinian-Israeli settlement, the Reagan Plan, based on the same Israeli autonomy plan as was in the Camp David Accord, again refusing to allow the PLO a part in the negotiations.

In late 1983 Arafat sought to restore the PLO in Lebanon; Syria, which under President Hafiz al-Asad had entered the Lebanese war in 1976 and wanted to control the PLO, thwarted him by helping Fatah-Intifada, a breakaway group founded by Saʿid Musa Muragha (Abu Musa), to defeat him. Asad, wanting Syria to replace Egypt as the primary deterrent to Israeli power—and as the leading state of the Arab world—aided opponents of Arafat's policies, led by former PNC president Khalid al-Fahum, to organize the Palestinian National Salvation Front (PNSF) in March 1985. Gathering together the Fatah-Intifada, the PFLP–GC, the Palestine Liberation Front (PLF), al-Saʿiqa, the Palestinian Revolutionary Communist Party (PRCP), and some members of the PFLP, the PNSF strove to constitute an alternative to the PLO. The DFLP and the balance of PFLP members, opposed to foreign interference in Palestinian affairs, refused to join because of Syrian backing. Riven by personality conflicts and ideological divergences, the PNSF was a failure and had faded away by 1989.

Meanwhile, the policies of the PLO in Tunis began to evolve away from armed struggle toward political action. Despite this change, the Israelis bombed PLO headquarters in an attempt to kill Arafat on 1 October 1985. At the 17th congress of the PNC in Algiers in April 1987 there was a reconciliation among the principal Palestinian movements, including al-Fatah, the DFLP, the PFLP, and the PCP.

Then in December of the same year the first Intifada broke out; and a new, younger leadership began to form within the Occupied Territories, forcing the leadership of the PLO to adapt and revise its strategy again. Many members of PLO organizations in the territories joined the Unified National Leadership of the Uprising (UNLU), the network of leadership committees that rose spontaneously early in the Intifada. Using the argument of "popular legitimacy," the Intifada proclaimed the state of Palestine, with Jerusalem as the capitol, at the 18th PNC congress in Algiers on 15 November 1988.

From that time the leadership of the PLO launched a diplomatic offensive, particularly in Western countries, and especially the United States. In December 1988 Arafat renounced terrorism and declared before the UN General Assembly the PLO's acceptance of Israel's right to exist. The United States rewarded him by opening a diplomatic dialogue. Israel, however, neither acknowledged nor responded to this declaration. Consequently, in the crisis beginning in July 1990 that led to the Gulf War of 1991, and in spite of the reservations of a majority of the PLO cadres, Arafat decided to throw his support behind Iraq.

He may have felt that Saddam Hussein would be able to change the balance of power in the region, but the decision was a disaster for the PLO and the Palestinians. The immediate results were the persecution, expulsion, and impoverishment of the large Palestinian community in Kuwait, reducing a population of about 350,000 before the war to about 30,000 after it. The earnings of this community had supported many family members in the territories and camps, and the PLO had collected taxes from it for the Palestinian National Fund. Arafat's support of Iraq also cost the PLO and Palestinians the financial aid they had been receiving from the Arab states (mainly Saudi Arabia) and Arab diplomatic support for the PLO in international affairs. The PLO, therefore, responded positively in September 1991 to the American-Soviet proposal for a Middle East peace conference, which opened in Madrid on 30 October 1991.

The PLO, which Israel considered a terrorist organization, was not permitted a delegation, but Palestinian representatives, advised by a committee that consulted with the PLO, were included in the Jordanian delegation. The negotiations were unproductive, however, blocked by a combination of intransigence on the part of the Israeli Likud government and Palestinian resentment of the format for the negotiations and distrust of the American negotiators, some of whom were associated with the Israeli lobby in Washington. When a new Labor government in Israel repealed the prohibition against dealing with the PLO, Arafat was able to seek talks outside of the Madrid conference. This led to the Oslo Accords and Declaration of Principles of 1993, embodying Israeli recognition of the PLO and containing a plan for partial autonomy of the Palestinian territories in anticipation of a treaty on their definitive status. In May 1994, under the terms of the Oslo Accords, the PLO created the Palestinian Authority (PA), an interim government responsible for putting the autonomy into effect, presided over by Arafat. Most PLO departments were moved to the PA, except for the political department which remained in Tunis headed by Faruq Qaddumi. On 7 July 1998 the UN upgraded the status of the PLO, according it the right to participate in political debates in the General Assembly. That same year the PNC altered the Palestine National Charter to conform to the provisions of the Oslo Accords.

In the early twenty-first century, many of the PLO's functions have been absorbed into the PA. The primary independent purpose of the PLO is to conduct negotiations with Israel, although there has been little talk between them since the start of the al-Aqsa Intifada in 2000. The PLO also oversees affiliated mass organizations such as the General Unions, civic organizations such as the Red Crescent Society, and various social service organizations that serve the Palestinian refugee population in Lebanon, Jordan, and camps in the Occupied Territories.

In October 2004, the removal of the seriously ill 75-year-old Arafat to France for medical treatment, and the uncertainty of his recovery, set off a wave of uncertainty and political maneuvering within the leadership of the PLO. Arafat's demise will leave a vacuum at the center of Palestinian political institutions. Initial speculation over the succession centered on PLO general secretary and former PNA prime minister Mahmud Abbas, PNA prime minister Ahmad Qurai, and security chiefs Jibril Rajub and Muhammad Dahlan. Abbas is the most senior of Arafat's collaborators, and the chief of the commission established to run the PLO's affairs in his absence (other members are Qurai and PNC chairman Salim Zanoun). Qurai has little independent support, and Rajub and Dahlan have made many enemies. They face potential competition from a younger generation of leadership that has been alienated from the PLO establishment by its ineffectiveness and corruption, as well as from outside organizations like HAMAS that have opposed PLO policies toward Is-

rael but have refrained from attacking or disrupting the PLO as long as Arafat, a living national symbol, remained in control. When Arafat is gone, there will likely be a struggle for power among the various factions: The established PLO leadership, the younger generation of secular leadership, and the Islamic organizations that have been keeping alive the al-Aqsa Intifada in the face of PLO opposition.

SEE ALSO Abbas, Mahmud Rida; Aqsa Intifada, al-; Arab Higher Committee; Arab-Israel War (1967); Arab-Israel War (1973); Arafat, Yasir; Asad, Hafiz al-; Black September 1970; Camp David Accords; Dahlan, Muhammad; Democratic Front for the Liberation of Palestine; Fahum, Khalid al-; Fatah, al-; Fatah-Intifada; Gaza (City); Gulf War (1991); HAMAS; Husayni, Hajj Amin al-; Hussein, Saddam; Intifada (1987–1993); Israel Labor Party; Israeli Settlements; League of Arab States; Likud; Musa Muragha, Sa'id; Oslo Accords; Palestine; Palestine National Charter; Palestine National Council; Palestine Red Crescent Society; Palestinian National Fund; Palestinian National Salvation Front; Palestinian Revolutionary Communist Party; Phalange; Popular Front for the Liberation of Palestine; Qaddumi, Faruq; Qurai, Ahmad Sulayman; Rajub, Jibril; Reagan Plan; Resolution 242; Sabra and Shatila; Sadat, Anwar al-; West Bank.

PALESTINE NATIONAL CHARTER: Also known as the Palestinian National Covenant; in Arabic, *al-Mithaq al-Watani* (or *al-Qawmi*) *al-Filastini*. A document written to accompany the founding of the Palestine Liberation Organization (PLO), that enumerates its purposes and intentions. It was written by Ahmad al-Shukayri and adopted at the first meeting of the Palestine National Council (PNC) in May and June 1964, and revised by the PNC in July 1968. The differences between the 1964 and 1968 versions of the Charter reflect the differences between the politics of two eras—before and after the Arab-Israel War (1967)—among Palestinians and in the Arab world. Both versions claim Palestine as the homeland of the Palestinian people, who have exclusive rights over it; both reject the legitimacy of Zionism, the Balfour Declaration, and the Mandate and call for Palestinian self-determination; both call for the complete liberation of Palestine (and therefore, by implication, the elimination of the Israeli state); both define Palestinian identity (and include Jews "of Palestinian [i.e. pre-Zionist] origin," as the 1964 version puts it);

both proclaim a belief in Arab unity. Neither version calls for a Palestinian state, but the 1964 version projects Palestinian self-determination somewhat ambiguously within the framework of a prospective sovereign Arab nation, to which the structural relationship of a Palestinian entity is not made clear; in the 1968 version, the commitment to Arab nationalism is perfunctory and the liberation of Palestine for Palestinians is the overriding goal. In the 1964 version, the PLO specifically disavows sovereignty over the West Bank and Gaza Strip, then under the control of Jordan and Egypt, respectively; the 1968 version declares a "Palestinian . . . national revolution" and rejects "intervention, trusteeship and subordination." In the 1964 version there is no mention of armed struggle or any specific means of liberation; in 1968, armed struggle is "the only way to liberate Palestine" and is insisted upon throughout.

On 24 April 1996, in the context of the Oslo peace process, the PNC voted to amend the Charter, canceling all the clauses that contradicted both the spirit of the peace process and the content of the letters of mutual recognition that had passed between Israel and the PLO in September 1993, particularly Article 22 regarding the character of Zionism. In December 1998, while United States president Bill Clinton was visiting Gaza, the PNC and the Palestinian Legislative Council (PLC), by a show of hands, ratified the annulment of the anti-Israeli clauses of the Palestine National Charter. The full official English text of the 1964 Charter may be found at www.mfa.gov.il/MFA; the 1968 text may be found at www.miftah.org and many other sites.

SEE ALSO Arab-Israel War (1967); Gaza Strip; Palestine Liberation Organization; Palestine National Council; Palestinian Legislative Council; West Bank.

PALESTINE NATIONAL COUNCIL: The legislative, policymaking body (*al-Majlis al-Watani al-Filastini*) of the Palestine Liberation Organization (PLO); the equivalent of a national parliament before the creation of the Palestinian Authority and its Palestinian Legislative Council (PLC). Its existence was formulated and authorized at an Arab League summit in January 1964 and it held its inaugural meeting in East Jerusalem in May and June 1964. The PNC represents all Palestinian people, those living in occupied Palestine as well as outside of Palestine, as well as the various constituent organizations of the PLO. At its 1964 meeting it adopted the Palestine National Charter and the PLO Fundamental Law that constituted the PLO, of which it became a part. Members

of the PNC, whose number has grown over the years from 430 to 669 as of 2004, are elected directly for a period of three years. The council meets once a year or by special convocation of the executive committee of the PLO and one-fourth of the council members. The PNC is headed by a president, assisted by two vice presidents and a secretary. The PNC held its meetings in Cairo until 1977, when it broke with Egypt over President Anwar al-Sadat's diplomatic overtures to Israel. Delegates have since met in Algiers.

On 15 November 1988, at the nineteenth session of the PNC, Yasir Arafat, basing himself on UN Resolution 181, issued a Proclamation of the State of Palestine (known as the Algiers Declaration), with Jerusalem as its capital. On 24 April 1996, in the framework of the Israeli-Palestinian peace process launched in Madrid in 1991, the PNC met in special session in Gaza, and decided to amend the Charter by removing all statements denying Israel's right to exist. Six articles were dropped, among which Article 9, calling for "armed struggle" to liberate Palestine; Article 21, which rejected all negotiated compromise; and Article 22, which compared Zionism to Nazism and described the State of Israel as an arm of "international imperialism." Demanded by the Israelis, this historic modification was adopted by a vote of 504 in favor, 54 against, 14 abstentions, and 27 absent. Among the latter were the Popular Front for the Liberation of Palestine (PFLP) and Democratic Front for the Liberation of Palestine (DFLP) representatives, both movements opposed to the Oslo Accords.

SEE ALSO Arafat, Yasir; Oslo Accords; Palestine Liberation Organization; Palestine National Charter; Palestinian Authority; Palestinian Legislative Council; Proclamation of the State of Palestine; Sadat, Anwar al-.

PALESTINE NATIONAL COVENANT
SEE Palestine National Charter.

PALESTINE RED CRESCENT SOCIETY: Medical and social services agency of the Palestine Liberation Organization (PLO) created in Amman in December 1968, to meet the medical care and sanitation needs of the Palestinian people. Established in the Palestinian territories, where it works with the Ministry of Health of the Palestinian Authority and other nongovernmental organizations and in countries where Palestinians have taken refuge, the Palestine Red Crescent Society (PRCS) has adopted a program whose goal it is to affirm the national identity of its

PALESTINE NATIONAL COUNCIL. MEMBERS OF THE POLICYMAKING BODY OF THE PALESTINE LIBERATION ORGANIZATION VOTE TO REAFFIRM AN EARLIER DECISION TO RESCIND PORTIONS OF THE PALESTINE NATIONAL CHARTER CALLING FOR THE DESTRUCTION OF ISRAEL. U.S. PRESIDENT BILL CLINTON WAS PRESENT FOR THE HISTORIC VOTE ON 14 DECEMBER 1998. THE EARLIER VOTE WAS ON 24 APRIL 1996. *(AP/Wide World Photos)*

people by giving it the means necessary to take charge of its sanitation, social, and humanitarian needs. The PRCS operates 15 hospitals, 130 ambulances, 69 public health clinics, and numerous other social service locations. It provides Palestinians with primary health care, emergency care, disaster assistance, clinical and rehabilitative medicine, and social services in the Palestinian territories, Lebanon, Syria, Jordan, and Egypt, and (until 2003) in Iraq. It also maintains offices in France, Italy, and Canada. Funding comes primarily through contributions from foundations, United Nations and foreign government aid organizations, humanitarian agencies, and similar sources. The PRCS is the largest Red Crescent organization in the Arab world, and is affiliated with the International Federation of the Red Cross/Red Crescent (IFRC). It is headquartered in al-Bireh, near Ramallah. In 2004, the honorary head of the PRCS is Yasir Arafat's brother, Dr. Fathi Arafat. The president and acting director general is Yunis al-Khatib.

SEE ALSO Palestine Liberation Organization; Palestinian Authority.

PALESTINE RED CROSS

SEE Palestine Red Crescent Society.

PALESTINIAN ACADEMIC SOCIETY FOR THE STUDY OF INTERNATIONAL AFFAIRS: An independent Palestinian academic institute that conducts and publishes research, seminars, conferences, and workshops on Palestinian issues in national, Arab, and international contexts, with affiliated and outside scholars. The Palestinian Academic Society for the Study of International Affairs (PASSIA) was founded in March 1997 by Mahdi Abdul Hadi and a group of intellectuals and academics in East Jerusalem. It is not affiliated with any government or political party. Its financial support comes from donations, sales of publications, foundation grants, and targeted grants from specialized agencies of some foreign governments, including those of the United States

(USAID), Canada, and Britain. It posts a great deal of useful information on its web site, www.passia.org.

PALESTINIAN AGENCY: Palestinian institution, founded in November 1996 in Geneva, for the purpose of supporting economic and cultural development of the Palestinian autonomous territories. The most important founders of this organization were wealthy businessmen of Palestinian origin, such as Abdul Mohsen Qattan, Jawid al-Ghossein, Abdul Majid Shoman, Hassib al-Sabbagh, and Munib al-Masri.

PALESTINIAN ASSEMBLY: Palestinian movement created in January 1995 at the initiative of the leadership of the Popular Front for the Liberation of Palestine (PFLP). Under the control of Bassam al-Shaq'a, the Palestinian Assembly wanted to draw Palestinian opponents of the Oslo Accords to its cause. On 25 May 1995 a communiqué of the ten groups belonging to the Palestinian opposition front Alliance of Palestinian Forces (APF) launched an appeal to strengthen this new movement, so as to function as a framework for an opposition front in the Occupied Territories. After a few promising statements, this organization was not heard from again.

SEE ALSO Alliance of Palestinian Forces; Oslo Accords; Popular Front for the Liberation of Palestine.

PALESTINIAN AUTHORITY: Interim Palestinian government, established under the terms of the Oslo Accords. It was created by a decree of 12 October 1993 of the Central Council of the Palestine Liberation Organization (PLO) and established in May 1994, in Gaza. The Palestinian Authority (PA)'s mandate was to administer the partial autonomy in the Occupied Territories for the five-year period specified in the Oslo Accords, at which time agreed-upon governmental powers and territory were to have been transferred and a final settlement negotiated. It was understood, though not stated, that the final settlement would result in the establishment of a sovereign Palestinian state. Under the Oslo Accords and subsequent agreements, the PA officially has control over both security and civil matters in certain designated ("A") areas and over civil matters only in other ("B") areas; Israel retains full control over the remaining ("C") areas. In practice the degree of Palestinian control of a given place has depended on whether the Israelis are in occupation at a given time. The PA maintains a number of armed Palestinian se-

curity forces (including a paramilitary police force), which report to Yasir Arafat directly, rather than through a PA chain of command. Some of these are responsible, essentially, for meeting Israel's "security needs" by controlling anti-Israel activity. They are the objects of frequent attack by Israel. Others are used to keep political opposition to the PLO leadership under control and are frequently deployed against Palestinian political organizations.

At the time of its establishment the PA administration was comprised of the following members: Yasir Arafat (president and minister of the interior; al-Fatah), Muhammad Zuhdi Nashashibi (Finance and Agriculture; Independent), Yasir Amr (Education and Teaching; Independent), Yasir Abd Rabbo (Culture; Fida), Ahmad Sulayman Qurai (Economy and Commerce; Fatah), Abdul Hafi al-Ashab (Communications; pro–Palestinian People's Party), Samir Ghosheh (Labor; Popular Front for the Liberation of Palestine), Intisar al-Wazir (Social Affairs; Fatah), Nabil Sha'th (Planning and Cooperation; Fatah), Zakariya al-Agha (Housing; Fatah), Elias Freij (Tourism; Independent), Riyad al-Za'nun (Health; Independent), Freih Abu Middein (Justice; Fatah), Saib Erekat (Local Communities; Fatah), Abdelaziz al-Haj Ahmad (Transportation), Azmi Shuaibi (Sports and Youth; Fida), Jamil Tarifi (Civil Service; Fatah), Sheikh Hasan Tahbub (Religious Affairs). Faysal al-Husayni was named minister without portfolio, in charge of the Jerusalem issue. In January 1996 elections were held for the presidency—Arafat won in a landslide—and for the newly created legislature, the Palestinian Legislative Council (PLC); in May, a cabinet reshuffle brought about the departure of some ministers who had just won seats and the arrival of others who until then had refused to be part of the PA, such as Hanan Ashrawi, named minister of higher education. In 1996 a Likud government was elected in Israel, headed by Benjamin Netanyahu, which did not believe in the Oslo peace process, and in fact the process has never recovered, changing the role of the PA. On 23 May 1997, an internal audit pegged the cost of management "errors" by the PA at $326 million, and a number of ministers were accused of embezzlement. On 5 August, the PA was reorganized again on the recommendation of the Legislative Council.

The International Monetary Fund and especially the European Union (EU), the largest outside financial contributor to the PA, have also been concerned over corruption and diversion of funds in the PA and have conducted investigations and demanded reforms, some of which have been made. It is known

Israel, West Bank, and Gaza Strip, 2000

— International border

[shaded] Areas in which the Palestinian Authority exercises various levels of control

[white] Areas under full Israeli control

• City

that millions of dollars of PA funds have gone either into the pockets of corrupt officials, their friends, and families, or to Palestinian groups outside the PA structure that have engaged in anti-Israel activities, including terrorism. Since these facts were uncovered, the EU has chosen to donate only in the form of specific grants for particular purposes. Corruption and ineffective and undemocratic government have also grown as issues among the Palestinian population, particularly since the beginning of the al-Aqsa Intifada in September 2000. Thanks to the increased violence and economic disruptions, the Israeli reoccupation and its continuing land confiscation, road and settlement building and the building of the "Apartheid wall," the people living in the occupied territories are increasingly angry, and younger people in particular have been alienated from the PA, seen as unrepresentative and ineffective, at best, against the Israelis.

In the spring of 2002 the Israelis invaded Ramallah, where the PA is headquartered, placed Arafat under house arrest, and destroyed buildings all around him, holding him hostage for months. In 2004, he is unable to travel, for fear the Israelis will prevent his return. In April 2003 Arafat bowed to American and Israeli pressure and appointed a (figurehead) prime minister, Mahmud Abbas, who was replaced by Ahmad Qurai in September. In the summer of 2004 there were a number of kidnappings of and threats to PA officials by a variety of groups. The most serious incident came in July when a revolt was threatened in Gaza if Arafat did not withdraw the appointment of his brother as security chief there. After several days, he did.

SEE ALSO Abbas, Mahmud Rida; Agha, Zakariya al-; Aqsa Intifada, al-; Arafat, Yasir; Ashrawi, Hanan; Fatah, al-; Erekat, Saib Muhammad; Netanyahu, Benjamin; Oslo Accords; Palestinian Legislative Council; Palestine Liberation Organization; Qurai, Ahmad Sulayman; Sha'th, Nabil Ali Mohamed; Wazir, Intisar al-.

PALESTINIAN AUTONOMOUS TERRITORIES: Those parts of the Israeli-occupied Palestinian territories (the West Bank and Gaza Strip) that, under the terms of the Oslo Accords and subsequent agreements, actually came under the control of the Palestinian Authority between 1994 and the Israeli reoccupation in 2002.

SEE ALSO Gaza Strip; Oslo Accords; West Bank.

PALESTINIAN AUTONOMY: The concept from the time of the Camp David negotiations that Palestinians will be allowed to govern themselves, in areas determined by negotiated agreement(s), under the effective supervision of the Israelis, for a specified period, after which there will be a "final status" settlement in which they may be allowed to declare (limited) legal sovereignty under the terms of further negotiated agreement(s). It is the compromise at the center of the Israeli-Palestinian Oslo peace process. The idea of autonomy came up seriously for the first time in 1978 during the Camp David negotiations between Israel and Egypt, which, in their second phase, specified that "full autonomy will be accorded for five years to the populations of the West Bank and Gaza. The Israeli military government and its civil administration will cease to exert their functions as soon as autonomous authorities shall have been freely elected by the inhabitants of these regions." Furthermore, it was anticipated that in the three years following the transitional period negotiations would start on the future of the West Bank and Gaza. No text took up the question of the future of Jerusalem.

On 25 May 1979, as required by the Israeli-Egyptian Peace Treaty, Cairo and Tel Aviv began negotiations on West Bank and Gaza Strip autonomy. There was no Palestinian participation in these negotiations. The opposition to the Camp David Accords of the only acknowledged representative Palestinian body, the Palestine Liberation Organization (PLO), and the intensification of Israeli colonization of the Occupied Territories, rendered the dialogue futile. In April 1980 Egypt proposed, in vain, that a regime of autonomy first be established in the Gaza Strip. Thirteen years later, on 13 September 1993, in Washington, D.C., Israel and the PLO signed the Declaration of Principles on transitional and partial autonomy for the Gaza Strip and the West Bank, excluding Jerusalem. It was specified that the objective of Israeli-Palestinian negotiations would consist, notably, in "establishing an interim Palestinian self-government authority . . . for the Palestinian people in the West Bank and in the Gaza Strip for a transitional period not exceeding five years, leading to a permanent settlement based on UN Security Council Resolutions 242 and 338." This agreement, known as the Oslo Accords, was followed by an Israeli-Palestinian agreement on the institution of Palestinian autonomy, signed on 4 May 1994, in Cairo.

SEE ALSO Gaza Strip; Oslo Accords; Palestine Liberation Organization; West Bank.

PALESTINIAN AUTONOMY COUNCIL

SEE Palestinian Legislative Council.

PALESTINIAN BROADCASTING CORPORATION: The broadcasting arm of the Palestinian Authority (PA). It operates both radio (Voice of Palestine) and television stations from its offices and studios in Ramallah. (It is not a monopoly; there are commercial broadcasters in the Palestinian territories, as well as ground and satellite stations available from other countries.) It began operations in 1994 and is under the direct control of Yasir Arafat rather than the PA Ministry of Information. It has been criticized for adhering to the official view, and has been accused by Israel of inciting violence and antisemitism.

SEE ALSO Arafat, Yasir; Palestinian Authority.

PALESTINIAN CENTER FOR HUMAN RIGHTS (PCHR): Independent Palestinian nongovernmental human rights organization founded in 1995 by Raji Sourani, a prominent human rights lawyer and activist. Its goals include "protection and respect of human rights and support of the rule of law according to the Universal Declaration of Human Rights and all the other human rights agreements; assisting in the development of democratic institutions and civil society according to international standards; supporting the rights of Palestinian people as recognized by international law." In addition to providing legal aid to victims, PCHR documents human rights violations (by Israeli or Palestinian authorities) and releases its findings in published reports and studies. The organization also works with other rights organizations and nongovernmental organizations (NGOs), organizes conferences, and conducts training workshops. PCHR is based in Gaza City and most of its activity is conducted in the Gaza Strip. It holds special consultative status with the United Nations Economic and Social Council and is an affiliate of the International Commission of Jurists, the Fédération Internationale des Ligues des Droits de l'Homme (FIDH), and the Euro-Mediterranean Human Rights Network. PCHR maintains a web site at www.pchrgaza.org.

SEE ALSO Gaza (City); Sourani, Raji.

PALESTINIAN COMMON BATTLE FRONT

SEE Palestinian Popular Struggle Front.

PALESTINIAN DECLARATION OF INDEPENDENCE

SEE Proclamation of the State of Palestine.

PALESTINIAN DEMOCRATIC ASSEMBLY: Palestinian movement created in January 1992, following dissension in the Palestinian People's Party (PPP), under the impetus of George Hazbun, vice president of the confederation of unions of the West Bank. This group has not been very widely known.

SEE ALSO Palestinian People's Party.

PALESTINIAN DEMOCRATIC UNION: This Palestinian political party (*Al-Ittihad al-Dimuqrati al-Filastini*; its acronym backward, "fida," means "sacrifice") was born of a split in the Democratic Front for the Liberation of Palestine (DFLP) in 1990–1991. It was founded in September 1991 and led by Yasir Abd Rabbo, former assistant secretary general of the DFLP and later minister of culture in the Palestinian Authority, and joined by others from the Popular Front for the Liberation of Palestine (PFLP) and the Palestine Communist Party (PCP) (soon to be the Palestinian People's Party [PPP]). At first representing itself as "the" DFLP, the group took the name Palestinian Democratic Union (PDU) in 1993. The PDU is a constituent member of the Palestine Liberation Organization (PLO), and is represented on the PLO executive committee and in the Palestine National Council (PNC). It represents a reformist tendency within the PLO and has campaigned for the democratization of Palestinian political life. The PDU directs its activity toward the "independence of the Palestinian people and its right to return to its native land, while backing the democratic aspirations of the Palestinians." Fervent but critical in its advocacy of the Israeli-Palestinian peace process that began with the Madrid Conference of 1991, the PDU has supported the policies of Yasir Arafat, although it has criticized the internal functioning of the PLO. The headquarters of the PDU is in Ramallah. In 2004, its principal figures are Rabbo and Saleh Raf'at (secretary general).

SEE ALSO Abd Rabbo, Yasir; Democratic Front for the Liberation of Palestine; Palestinian Authority; Palestine Liberation Organization.

PALESTINIAN ECONOMIC COUNCIL FOR DEVELOPMENT AND RECONSTRUCTION: Palestinian administrative structure established on 4 November 1993 by decree of the executive committee of the Palestine Liberation Organization (PLO) for the purpose of managing economic aid meant for the economic development of the Palestinian autonomous territories in the context of the Oslo Accords. While the advisory council was under the authority of Yasir Arafat's presidency, the executive committee of the organiza-

tion was chaired by Ahmad Sulayman Qurai, assisted by Hassan Abu Libdeh. On 25 January 1994 the Palestinian Economic Council for Development and Reconstruction (PECDAR) published a proposed Palestinian Development Plan for a seven-year period. PECDAR was supplanted by a new organization, the Ministry of Planning and International Cooperation (MOPIC). After MOPIC established itself as the administration responsible for donor coordination efforts and planning, PECDAR became an implementing agency for small- and medium-scale infrastructure projects (many, if not most, in association with the World Bank).

SEE ALSO Arafat, Yasir; Oslo Accords; Palestinian Autonomous Territories; Qurai, Ahmad Sulayman.

PALESTINIAN GENERAL UNIONS: "Popular organizations" affiliated with the Palestine Liberation Organization (PLO). These represent important sectors of Palestinian society, based on shared profession, skills, or interest, and in some cases act as umbrella organizations for smaller groups. Most have branches outside the Palestinian territories; in fact most were originally organized outside Palestine, to serve Palestinians in the diaspora and to incorporate them into the PLO's activities. Some are older than the PLO itself. They are formally constituted as democratic organizations, with constitutions, bylaws, and elected leaders, but in practice their policies conform to the direction of the PLO leadership. (None, however, has a monopoly in its area of Palestinian society.) All are represented in the Palestine National Council (PNC). Some operate important social programs and have had a significant role in the national struggle, which is their primary purpose. As of 2004, most are headquartered in Ramallah. The most significant have been the General Union of Palestinian Students (GUPS), the General Union of Palestinian Teachers (GUPT), the General Union of Palestinian Women (GUPW), the General Union of Palestinian Workers (GUPW), the General Union of Palestinian Writers and Journalists (GUPWJ), and the Higher Council of Palestinian Youth and Sports; other important general unions are those of Palestinian artists, artistic performers, doctors, economists, engineers, farmers and jurists.

SEE ALSO Palestine Liberation Organization; Palestine National Council.

PALESTINIAN INDEPENDENT COMMISSION FOR CITIZENS' RIGHTS: Autonomous human rights agency within the Palestinian Authority (PA) created in September 1993 at the urging of Hanan Ashrawi, who was its first commissioner general. To insure its independence, the commission is funded by contributions from outside the PA (mainly from European governments and foundations), and is controlled by a board of commissioners made up of Palestinians from both the territories and the diaspora, with public commitments to human rights and democracy. The commissioner general and executive director are appointed by the board, and staff members are not considered part of the PA civil service. The commission attempts to act as an ombudsman within Palestinian society, investigating and attempting to resolve complaints of abuses from Palestinian citizens against the PA. It monitors the activities of public institutions and tries to insure accountability; tries to safeguard freedom of expression and democratic participation in political decision making; reviews draft legislation and makes recommendations to insure conformity to international human rights standards; and familiarizes citizens with their rights and the means of defending them. The commission operates with sufficient independence that members of its staff and leadership have been arrested and jailed on several occasions. The commission also monitors and issues public statements and reports regarding the actions of the Israeli occupation authorities. In 2004, officers included Mamduh al-Aker, commissioner general, and Said Zeedani, director general. The board of commissioners included Ashrawi, Eyad Sarraj, Haydar Abd al-Shafi (all former commissioners general), Mahmud Darwish, and Nasir Aruri, among others.

SEE ALSO Abd al-Shafi, Haydar; Ashrawi, Hanan Daouda; Darwish, Mahmud.

PALESTINIAN INTERIM SELF-GOVERNMENT AUTHORITY

SEE Palestinian Authority.

PALESTINIAN ISLAMIC COMBAT MOVEMENT:
Palestinian Islamic splinter organization (*Harakat al-Mujahada al-Islamiya al-Filastiniya* in Arabic) created in Lebanon at the end of 1989 by Shaykh Ibrahim Ghonim, born of personal conflicts between Ghonim and Fathi Shiqaqi, who decided to organize the Palestinian Hizbullah. Backed by Iran in its struggle with Israel, the Palestinian Islamic Combat Movement (PICM) sometimes participated in operations mounted by the Lebanese Hizbullah. At the end of 1993, the PICM found itself much weakened by the departure of many of its members, who decided to

rejoin the ranks of the Palestinian Islamic Jihad of Shiqaqi.

SEE ALSO Hizbullah; Hizbullah–Palestine; Palestinian Islamic Jihad; Shiqaqi, Fathi.

PALESTINIAN ISLAMIC JIHAD:
Militant Palestinian fundamentalist Islamic group (*al-Jihad al-Islami al-Filastini,* in Arabic) that grew from an Islamic political current in the occupied Palestinian territories at the end of the 1970s, developed by a radical splinter group of the Muslim Brotherhood. Palestinian Islamic Jihad (PIJ) was born of the convergence of three events: the dissolution of the Islamic Liberation Party (ILP), the success of the Iranian revolution, and a split in the Islamic Collective (*al-Majma' al-Islami*) of Ahmad Isma'il Yasin. The PIJ is both a (Sunni) Islamist and a Palestinian nationalist group, and is therefore a descendant of the Islamic Liberation Party of Shaykh Taqi al-Din al-Nabhani.

From its beginnings the PIJ has advocated a *jihad* ("struggle; holy war" in Arabic) of liberation to create a state in the whole of Palestine, whose capital would be Jerusalem. Several of the early leaders of the PIJ, such as Fathi Shiqaqi, Ramadan Shallah, Abdelaziz Udeh, Muhammad al-Hindi, and Abdallah al-Shami, received a religious education in Egypt. In Jordan, Shaykh Asad Bayud Tamimi, former imam of the al-Aqsa Mosque in Jerusalem and former member of the ILP, made efforts to promulgate the ideas of this movement. The tendency backed by Shaykh Tamimi and his family became known as the Palestinian Islamic Jihad–Jerusalem faction. Between 1981 and 1983, Shiqaqi, Udeh, and Munir Shafiq joined the movement, to which they brought a radical nationalist coloring, particularly after the 1982 invasion of Lebanon by Israel. Thereafter, an armed branch was formed that conducted operations sometimes claimed in the name of the Islamic Jihad Brigades (*Sarayat al-Jihad al-Islami*), such as the incident in 1986 when jihadis threw hand grenades at an Israeli military ceremony at the Western Wall in Jerusalem. The leader of the Palestine Liberation Organization (PLO), Yasir Arafat, through the mediation of the leadership of the western sector of al-Fatah headed by Khalil al-Wazir (Abu Jihad), tried vainly to draw this movement into the ranks of al-Fatah and to convince its directors to join the PLO. At the end of 1987 and beginning of 1988, when the first Intifada was spreading and deepening in intensity, the PIJ and al-Fatah both attempted to take control of the revolt, as did HAMAS, which was formed by a group that broke away from the PIJ. (HAMAS immediately became the larger and more important organization, and remains so into the twenty-first century.) In February, a closer collaboration between their operations was discussed.

About this time, an Israeli commando in Cyprus assassinated three of the principal leaders of the Islamic Jihad Brigades, Bassam Sultan, Hassan Bheiss, and Marwan Kayyali, and then in Tunis, in April, al-Wazir, operations chief of the PLO. Four months later, Shaqaqi and Udeh were expelled by Israeli authorities to Lebanon. The development of the Intifada in the Occupied Territories, which PIJ claimed credit for, plus the expulsion of several dozen Islamic leaders to Lebanon, added to the popularity of the movement in the Palestinian population, and allowed the PIJ to obtain financial aid from Iran and Saudi Arabia. In Lebanon, the leaders of the PIJ developed contacts with fundamentalist pro-Iranian groups such as Hizbullah, as well as with radical Palestinian movements based in that country, such as the Popular Front for the Liberation of Palestine–General Command (PFLP–GC). In concert with Iranian leaders, the PIJ decided to create an organization meant to unite the diverse Palestinian Islamist groups. During August 1989 divergences between these different currents gave rise to two new movements: the Islamic Combatant Orientation (ICO; *al-Ittihad al-Islami al-Mujahid*), headed by Munir Shafiq, and the Palestinian Hizbullah, led by Sayed Baraka and Ahmed Mehanna, backed by Iran. Fathi Shiqaqi, editor of the weekly *al-Mujahid* and one of the founders of the PIJ, belonged to the latter movement. Rapidly, new divergences surfaced in the Palestinian Hizbullah, from then on in abeyance. Faced with this situation, Shaykh Tamimi, in Jordan, lay claim to the leadership of all the Palestinian movements connected to the Jihad, attracting to him a few of its members who were living in Lebanon. During November 1991, Abdelaziz Udeh and Fathi Shiqaqi decided to create the Palestinian Islamic Jihad–Shiqaqi-Udeh Faction in Lebanon, which was better known under the name Palestinian Islamic Jihad movement and which became the main organization in the Palestinian Jihad movement. Udeh became the spiritual guide of the movement, while Shaqaqi was its secretary general. At the same time, Munir Shafiq decided to leave Lebanon to go to Jordan, where he joined the ranks of al-Fatah. In December 1992, after the killing of an Israeli frontier guard, the Tel Aviv authorities expelled 415 men suspected of belonging to HAMAS and Islamic Jihad, to Lebanon, which only strengthened the determination of the members of the Jihad to fight against Israel.

In November 1993, opposed to the Oslo Accords, the Palestinian Islamic Jihad–Shiqaqi-Udeh Faction joined the Palestinian opposition in the Alliance of Palestinian Forces (APF). In 1994 and 1995, Shiqaqi's group organized a number of murderous anti-Israeli attacks in the Gaza Strip, where the new Palestinian Authority was responsible, in part, for security. On 2 November 1994, one of the most prominent military leaders of Jihad, Hani Abed, was assassinated by the Israelis at Khan Yunis, which led to bloody reprisals on the part of the movement. On 22 January, in the middle of Tel Aviv, a Jihad suicide bomber killed 19 people and wounded more than 60. Within the movement there surfaced tensions caused by an unprecedented problem: the intervention of Palestinian authorities in security matters in the autonomous territories. The latter were accused by some PIJ members of doing the Israelis' work, thereby betraying the Palestinian cause. In March, Shiqaqi was dismissed from his functions as secretary general of the movement. In May, the statements of Shaykh Abdallah al-Shami, in favor of a modification of the means used in the fight against Israel, caused him to be replaced as spokesperson of the movement in Gaza, by Shaykh Nafiz Azzam.

Fearing an infiltration by Palestinian and Israeli security services, the leaders of the movement undertook a significant reorganization. The Jihad office in Iran came under the authority of the Muhammad Saftawi, from a distinguished Palestinian family, and the leadership of the movement in Lebanon was strengthened by Sayed Baraka. The authoritarian methods of Shiqaqi caused a serious dispute between himself and Abdelaziz Udeh, which led to the expulsion of the latter from the PIJ. In September 1995, the dissidents of the PIJ decided to found their own movement, the Palestinian Islamic Front Party, thereby weakening the position of Shiqaqi. On 26 October, passing through Malta, Shiqaqi was assassinated by the Mossad. Three days later, he was replaced by Ramadan Abdallah Shallah. In mid-November 1999, two leaders of the movement, received by the Lebanese prime minister Selim Hoss, declared that the PIJ would no longer launch attacks against Israel from Lebanese soil. This declaration came in the middle of a series of attacks against Israel, attributed to the PIJ, and at a moment when the Israeli prime minister, Ehud Barak, had announced several times that he wanted the IDF to withdraw from South Lebanon by 7 July of the next year. In the autumn of 2000, the outbreak of the al-Aqsa Intifada in the Occupied Territories prompted the PIJ to pursue and intensify the armed struggle against Israel. Members of the movement, having joined a command group, coordinating the Intifada, carried out a number of bombings, leading to severe reprisals by the IDF, often in the form of "targeted killings."

SEE ALSO Alliance of Palestinian Forces; Fatah, al-; HAMAS; Hizbullah; Intifada (1987–1993); Intifada, al-Aqsa; Mossad; Muslim Brotherhood; Oslo Accords; Palestine Liberation Organization; Popular Front for the Liberation of Palestine–General Command; Shiqaqi, Fathi; Wazir, Khalil al-; Yasin, Ahmad Isma'il.

PALESTINIAN ISLAMIC JIHAD–BAYT AL-MAQDIS: Sub-group (*al-Jihad al-Islami al-Filastini–Bayt al-Maqdis*; Palestinian Islamic Jihad–Jerusalem) of the Palestinian Islamic Jihad whose name surfaced for the first time in February 1990, when it claimed responsibility for an attack on a bus filled with Israeli tourists in Isma'ilia, Egypt (the place where the Muslim Brotherhood was founded), that caused eleven deaths. Its principal leader was Shaykh Asad Bayud Tamimi, one of the founders of the Palestinian Islamic Jihad, who, taking advantage of disarray in the Jihad in Lebanon, tried to capture its leadership. The movement went on to claim credit for a number of attacks it had not really carried out. Opposing any negotiated resolution with Israel and advocating the liberation of the whole of Palestine, it received material support from Iran and Sudan. In October 1990 a disagreement between Tamimi and Ibrahim Serbal prompted the latter to form his own group, Palestinian Islamic Jihad–Kata'ib al-Aqsa. After the Gulf War, two factions appeared within Palestinian Islamic Jihad–Bayt al-Maqdis: one pro-Iraqi, the other pro-Iranian. These two new currents rose from a divergence between Shaykh Tamimi and Tala'at al-Tamimi. Within the larger Palestinian Islamic Jihad movement, the Bayt al-Maqdis faction is considered to be closest to al-Fatah. Some think that members of Force 17 joined its ranks in January 1993 in order to constitute a military branch called the Falcons of Islam. In Jordan, where the movement is based, the constant surveillance of the Jordanian services has kept its activities within the limits of strict legality.

SEE ALSO Fatah, al-; Palestinian Islamic Jihad; Palestinian Islamic Jihad–Kata'ib al-Aqsa.

PALESTINIAN ISLAMIC JIHAD–KATA'IB AL-AQSA: Splinter group (*al-Jihad al-Islami al-Filastini–al-Kata'ib al-Aqsa*; Palestinian Islamic Jihad–al-Aqsa Phalanx) of the Palestinian Islamic Jihad–Bayt al-Maqdis (itself a faction of Palestinian Islamic Jihad), led by Ibrahim Serbal. It originated in the discord be-

tween Serbal and Asad Tamimi, leader of the Bayt al-Maqdis faction. Its name surfaced for the first time on 21 October 1990 when it took responsibility for the killing of three Israelis in Jerusalem. In 1993 dissension between the principal leaders prompted the formation of two currents, one led by Serbal, the other by Fayiz al-Aswad. In October 1994 a new split, caused by Shaykh Husayn Anbar, led Aswad to quit the movement to live in Gaza with a few supporters. Weakened by internal bickering, this faction has lost its influence in the Palestinian community. Its headquarters is in Amman.

SEE ALSO Palestinian Islamic Jihad–Bayt al-Maqdis.

PALESTINIAN ISLAMIC JIHAD—SHIQAQI-UDEH FACTION: A faction within Palestinian Islamic Jihad (PIJ), formed in November 1991 by Abdelaziz Udeh and Fathi Shiqaqi. Opposed to the Oslo Accords, this group joined the Palestinian opposition bloc Alliance of Palestinian Forces in November 1993. Eventually it became the main current of the PIJ.

SEE ALSO Alliance of Palestinian Forces; Oslo Accords; Oslo Accords II; Palestinian Islamic Jihad; Shiqaqi, Fathi.

PALESTINIAN ISRAELIS: Palestinian Arab citizens of Israel; those Palestinians (and their descendants) who stayed in their homes during the Arab-Israel War (1948) or who returned and were allowed to stay. About 750,000 Palestinians became refugees in 1948; while about 150,000 stayed within the Israeli borders. Some fled and managed to return afterward, although all but 20,000–30,000 were expelled again. In late 1948 the Palestinians in Israel were 156,000, about 18 percent of the Israeli population; in 2004 they number more than 1.3 million (including the annexed areas of East Jerusalem and its suburbs), or about 20 percent of the population of Israel. Most are Sunni Muslim; almost 18 percent are Christians, and approximately 10 percent are Druze (and some unclassified). Until 1966 they were forbidden to travel without a special permit. Except for the Druze, Palestinian Israelis are exempt from military service. Otherwise they enjoy, theoretically, the same rights as other Israelis. Nevertheless, for many years, Palestinian Israelis have been treated as second-class citizens, discriminated against in education (Arabs are schooled in a separate, and less well-funded, system), housing (the government has granted only 1,000 permits to build new housing for Arabs since 1948), employment (unemployment among Palestinian Israeli men is estimated to be over 14 percent), and social provisions.

Between 1960 and 1980, the Palestinian Israeli population—whose land had been taken from them and thus had become mostly urban residents—reinforced a Palestinian nationalist feeling by voting for leftist Israeli parties (the largest, MAPAM and Labor, ran candidates on separate "Arab lists" into the 1970s). By the middle of the 1980s, after having long been rejected by both Israelis and Palestinians in the Occupied Territories, the Palestinian Israelis had started to feel more comfortable with their double nationality. They founded their own parties and started participating more actively in Israeli political life; this time also saw the rise of the Israeli Islamic Movement (IIM). At the time of the 1992 elections, Palestinian Israelis were the focus of much political maneuvering that aimed at persuading them to rally to the ranks of the two main Israeli political parties, Likud and Labor. After the ballot of 30 May 1996 that won them eleven seats in the Knesset for different Arab and mixed Arab and Jewish parties, the Palestinian Israelis became much more assertive about their rights. The Arab Democratic Party, specifically Palestinian, won four seats, while the other representatives belonged to the Democratic Front for Peace and Equality, the Labor Party, and Meretz. In March 1999, anticipating the general elections of the following May, Azmi Bishara, Democratic Front for Peace and Equality representative and founder of the National Democratic Alliance (NDA), announced his candidacy for the post of prime minister, becoming the first Arab to run for this office. Just before the vote he withdrew his candidacy and threw his support to the Labor candidate, Ehud Barak. On 18 May 1999, after the election, Palestinian Israelis had won a total of thirteen seats, divided between the Democratic Front for Peace and Equality, the NDA, the Unified Arab List, Meretz, and Israel United. Among these new representatives was Hussniya Jabara, the first Palestinian woman ever elected to the Knesset.

Between 1998 and 1999 two events evidenced the integration of the Arab community into Israel: the appointment of an Arab judge, Abdel Rahman Zoabi, to the High Court of Justice, and Rana Raslan's winning the title of Miss Israel. In 2000 Palestinian Israelis were represented in the Knesset by 13 seats that represented several parties: 5 for the Unified Arab Party, 2 for the Democratic Front for Peace and Equality, 1 for the National Democratic Assembly, 1 for the Arab Movement for Change, 2 for the Labor Party, 1 for Meretz, and 1 for Likud. Among them, Nawaf Masalha was deputy minister of foreign affairs and Salih Tarif, a Druze, chairman of the Rules Committee of the Knesset. In January 2001, the Arab community of Israel decided to boycott the elections of the following 6 February in protest against the policies of the Labor government of Ehud Barak. Labor went on to lose power, partly perhaps because of the drop in Arab support.

During the summer of 2001, when the Likud was back in power in a national unity government (in which Tarif was a minister without portfolio) and the al-Aqsa Intifada was intensifying in the Palestinian territories, two Palestinian Israeli deputies were the focus of an Knesset investigation. In November 2000, Azmi Bishara had gone to Damascus, where he met President Bashar al-Asad. One result of this visit was the organization of a trip that allowed Palestinian Israeli families to see their relatives who were refugees in Syria. In June 2001, the Knesset opened an inquiry about him, following remarks he had made that were thought to be anti-Israeli on the occasion of Hafiz al-Asad's death. Two months later the same charges were leveled against another Palestinian Israeli representative in the Knesset, Taleb al-Sanaa. On 7 November 2001 the Knesset lifted Bishara's parliamentary immunity, accusing him of incitement to terrorism and of organizing travel to a country at war with Israel. In 2002 Bishara and Ahmad Tibi were barred from running in the next election on the grounds that they had supported "terrorists" by denouncing the Israeli assault on Jenin that spring, but the Israeli Supreme Court overturned the ban shortly before the election in January 2003. Both Tibi and Bishara were returned to the Knesset.

Palestinian Israelis generally supported the Oslo Accords of 1993, and they have generally favored the establishment of a Palestinian state in the West Bank and Gaza Strip. But their belief in the good faith of Israeli governments has been decreasing. In October 2000, after the incident at the Haram al-Sharif that set off the al-Aqsa Intifada, Palestinian Israelis demonstrated in solidarity with the Palestinians of the territories. Police opened fire on the demonstrators and killed thirteen. A commission of inquiry was appointed, headed by Supreme Court Justice Theodor Orr, which issued a report in September 2003. The report deplored official neglect of underlying social issues and police overreaction, but also found that police "underreaction" to previous incidents, and "incitement" by Palestinian Israeli politicians such as Bishara, had also been at fault. Its major recommendations, however, were that to "remove the stain of discrimination," Israel must provide a more equitable system, specifically in the areas of land and housing allocation, education, state ministry budgeting, and employment. The government agreed to the recommendations (although it has yet to publish the report in Arabic).

SEE ALSO Arab Democratic Party; Arab-Israel War (1948); Barak, Ehud; Bishara, Azmi; Gaza Strip; Intifada, al-Aqsa; Israeli Islamic Movement; Knesset; National Democratic Alliance; West Bank.

PALESTINIAN LEGISLATIVE COUNCIL: Palestinian national parliament (*al-Majlis al-Tashri'i al-Filastini*) created under the Oslo Accords II as part of the Palestinian Authority (PA). The Palestinian Legislative Council (PLC) first convened on 21 March 1996, after the first and, as of 2004, only elections in the territories, held on a universal-suffrage basis on 20 January. Presided over by Ahmad Sulayman Qurai, the PLC was comprised of 88 deputies, 34 of whom were chosen from the Gaza Strip and 54 from the West Bank. Its first session took place in Gaza, and the first debates concerned the platform and investiture, on 27 June, of the PA. The majority of the members of the PLC, whether independent or belonging to al-Fatah, supported the policies of the PA, headed by Yasir Arafat. On 16 October, at the invitation of the Israel Communist Party, the Knesset received a delegation of nine members of the PLC. Among the ten committees in the PLC, the political committee was presided over by Hanan Ashrawi, and that of interior and security by Fakhri Shakoura. The principal task of the PLC was the elaboration of organizational laws for civil administration, in preparation for Palestinian statehood. It therefore devoted a major portion of its activity to developing a "Basic Law," amenable to giving the Palestinian state a true constitution. Meant to last for the period of transitional autonomy, the mandate of the PLC has been extended due to the stalling of the Israeli-Palestinian peace process.

SEE ALSO Arafat, Yasir; Ashrawi, Hanan Daouda; Gaza Strip; Oslo Accords II; Qurai, Ahmad Sulayman; West Bank.

PALESTINIAN MARTYRS WORKS SOCIETY
SEE SAMED.

PALESTINIAN NATIONAL AUTHORITY
SEE Palestinian Authority.

PALESTINIAN NATIONAL FRONT: Palestinian movement created in August 1973 in the West Bank, following the 11th congress of the Palestine National Council (PNC). Gathering together primarily leftist militants, the Palestinian National Front (PNF) wanted to mitigate the Palestine Liberation Organization (PLO)'s lack of representation in the Palestinian territories by attempting to establish a political dialogue with Israeli authorities that might look with favor on such an opening. The PNF disappeared in 1982, as suddenly as it had appeared on the Palestinian internal scene, following a hardening of Israeli policies toward the Occupied Territories. This movement has sometimes been confused with the Popular Resistance Front, a radical militant branch of the Palestine Communist Party (PCP).

SEE ALSO Palestine Communist Party; Palestine National Council; West Bank.

PALESTINIAN NATIONAL FUND: Palestinian organization established in 1964, conforming to Article 24 of the Palestine Liberation Organization (PLO) fundamental law, to finance the activities of the PLO in the political as well as military, social, and cultural areas. From 1984 to 1996, the Palestinian National Fund (PNF) was headed by Jawad Ghusayn. The PNF is responsible for managing financial aid coming from a variety of sources: funds from Arab states, contributions from wealthy Palestinians, and a "liberation tax" levied on Palestinians working in Arab countries.

SEE ALSO Palestine Liberation Organization.

PALESTINIAN NATIONAL SALVATION FRONT: Palestinian organization (*Jabhat al-Inqadh al-Watani al-Filastini,* in Arabic) created in March 1985 by Khalid al-Fahum, who, being opposed to the policies of Yasir Arafat, had resigned as president of the Palestine National Council (PNC). Backed by Syria and gathering together the Fatah-Intifada, the Popular Front for the Liberation of Palestine–General Command (PFLP–GC), the Palestine Liberation Front (PLF), al-Sa'iqa, the Palestinian Revolutionary Communist Party (PRCP), and a part of the Popular Front for the Liberation of Palestine (PFLP), the Palestinian National Salvation Front (PNSF) strove to constitute a true oppositional front to Arafat's Palestine Liberation Organization (PLO). The Democratic Front for the Liberation of Palestine (DFLP) and the Popular Front for the Liberation of Palestine (PFLP), opposed to all foreign interference in Palestinian affairs, refused to join because of the Syrian backing. Torn by personality conflicts and ideological divergences, the PNSF did not succeed in forming a viable opposition to the PLO, or proposing a real alternative to the policies of Arafat. From 1989 its activities were reduced to the publication of simple press communiqués. In 1993, after the signature of the Israeli-Palestinian Oslo Accords in September, Palestinian opposition forces formed a new front, the Alliance of Palestinian Forces (APF), which replaced the PNSF.

SEE ALSO Alliance of Palestinian Forces; Arafat, Yasir; Fahum, Khalid al-.

PALESTINIAN PEOPLE'S PARTY (*al-Hizb al-Sha'abi al-Filastini,* sometimes translated as Palestinian Popular Party): Name since October 1991 of the former Palestine Communist Party (PCP). The Palestinian People's Party (PPP) advocated a peaceful resolution of the Israeli-Palestinian problem. A member of the Palestine Liberation Organization (PLO) since 1987, this group supported the policies of Yasir Arafat. In January 1992 the party split; Georges Hazbun, vice president of the confederation of West Bank unions, resigned to found the Palestinian Democratic Assembly (PDA). In 1994, opposed to certain clauses of the Israeli-Palestinian Oslo Accords of 1993 and 1994, several figures in the PPP distanced themselves from the policies of Arafat. Its principal leaders have included: Bashir Barghuti (secretary general until 1998), Mustafa Barghuti (secretary general 1998–2003), Bassam al-Salhi (secretary general), Suleiman Najjab, Fu'ad Riziq, Abdul Majid Hamdan, Walid 'Awad, and Ghassan Khatib, Palestinian Authority minister of labor.

SEE ALSO Arafat, Yasir; Palestine Liberation Organization; Palestinian Democratic Assembly.

PALESTINIAN POPULAR PARTY

SEE Palestinian People's Party.

PALESTINIAN POPULAR STRUGGLE FRONT (*Jabhat al-Nidal al-Sha'abi al-Filastini,* in Arabic): Marxist-Leninist in inspiration and upholding Arab nationalism, the Palestinian Popular Struggle Front (PPSF) was created on 15 July 1967 in the West Bank, after the Arab defeat in the Arab-Israel War, which caused numerous splinters in al-Fatah. Its founder, Bahjat Abu Gharbiyya, a former member of the Ba'th Party in Ramallah, advocated continuing the struggle against Israel to recover the territories occupied by the Israeli army. In 1968 the PPSF emerged from clandestinity by opening an office in Jordan. In 1971 it joined with the Palestine Liberation Organization (PLO), and Abu Gharbiya was elected to its Execu-

tive Committee. Between 1971 and 1973 there were vain negotiations to merge the leading members of the PPSF in the ranks of al-Fatah. In November 1973, following the Arab defeat in the Arab-Israel War, the movement decided to leave the PLO and establish its headquarters in Syria, and its operational section in Lebanon. The following year, Ghosheh became secretary general of the PPSF. Seven years later, in 1981, the movement was admitted to the Palestine National Council (PNC). In 1983 the PPSF joined the Palestinian opposition alliance, the Palestinian National Salvation Front (PNSF).

From 1988, a new rapprochement with the PLO provoked much dissension in the PPSF, and certain members remained loyal to Syria. In April 1992, a dissident current supported by Damascus decreed that Ghosheh was no longer secretary general of the PPSF, and was replaced by Khalid Abdul Majid (Abu al-Abed), seconded by Muhammad Khalil al-Fitani (Abu Nayif). In October 1993, Ghosheh was alone in declaring himself in favor of the Israeli-Palestinian accord of the preceding 13 September, while the rest of the movement supported the faction led by Abdul Majid, an opponent of the peace process. (As for Abu Gharbiyya, he joined the Rejection Front in 1974 and stood as its candidate for speaker of the PNC in 1977, but lost to Khalid al-Fahum.)

SEE ALSO Arab-Israel War (1967); Arab-Israel War (1973); Fatah, al-; Palestine National Council; Palestinian National Salvation Front.

PALESTINIAN POPULAR STRUGGLE FRONT–ABDUL MAJID FACTION: Palestinian faction created in October 1993, following a split in the Palestinian Popular Struggle Front (PPSF) caused by the signing of the Israeli-Palestinian Oslo Accords that September. Syrian in allegiance, this faction joined the Palestinian opposition front, the Alliance of Palestinian Forces (APF), based in Damascus. Principal leaders include: Khalid Abdul Majid (Abu al-Abed) and Muhammad Khalil al-Fitani (Abu Nayif).

SEE ALSO Alliance of Palestinian Forces.

PALESTINIAN REVOLUTIONARY COMMUNIST PARTY: Palestinian political party (*al-Hizb al-Shuyu'i al-Thawri al-Filastini*) founded in 1982 by Arabi 'Awad. 'Awad, a teacher from Nablus, had been the secretary of the Jordan Communist Party (JCP) in the West Bank, the Palestinian successor to the pre-1948 Palestine Communist Party (PCP), which had included both Jews and Arabs. After a long period of imprisonment in Jordan, 'Awad was deported to Lebanon in 1973. In 1980 he founded the (Palestinian) Communist Organization of Lebanon as a branch of the JCP but it collapsed following a Palestinian-Jordanian split in that party. The Palestinian branch of the JCP (known as the Palestinian Communist Organization) renamed itself the Palestine Communist Party, and its central committee, changing its political orientation, now favored negotiating with Israel. The Palestinian Revolutionary Communist Party (PRCP), led by 'Awad, advocated continued armed struggle. In 1985, opposed to the policies of Yasir Arafat, the PRCP joined the Palestinian National Salvation Front, based in Damascus. At the beginning of the 1990s, weakened by the fall of communism in the Soviet Union, the PRCP tried to draw closer to Iran. Opposed to the 1993 Oslo Accords, this group joined the Palestinian opposition front, united in the Alliance of Palestinian Forces (APF).

SEE ALSO Alliance of Palestinian Forces; Arafat, Yasir; Palestinian National Salvation Front.

PALESTINIAN SECURITY SERVICES: Creation of Palestinian security agencies was provided for in the Oslo Accords II. In addition to those authorized by the Accords, the Palestinian leadership has created a number of others (precisely how many is not known), some of which have been incorporated into a formal government structure and others that seem to be independent. Most originated in entities overseen by the council of security of al-Fatah (*Jihaz al-Amn al-Qawmi al-Filastini*), directed by Salah Khalaf (Abu Ayad) and by the unified command of Palestine Liberation Organization (PLO) security (*al-Amn al-Muwahhad*). The ten main security and police forces are grouped in the General Security Services (GSS), an umbrella organization headed by a director general who reports to Yasir Arafat, the Palestinian Authority (PA)'s president.

They include Aerial Police (*al-Shurta al-Jawiya*), a very small unit with five helicopters. Civil Defense (*al-Difa'a al-Madani*), which provides fire and rescue services. Civil Police (*al-Shurta al-Madaniya*), which is a conventional police force of roughly 10,000 members; the main civil law enforcement agency. The Coast Guard (*al-Shurta al-Baharia*) is an anti-smuggling unit with about 1,000 members on the Gaza coast. County Guard (*Amn al-Mahafza*) provides security for the district governors and their offices.

General Intelligence (*Amn al-Mukhabarat al-Amm*) is the main state intelligence agency, with approximately 3,000 members. Headed by General Amin al-Hindi. Military Intelligence (*al-Istkhabarat al-Askariya*) provides preventive intelligence, de-

ployed against opponents of the PA and PLO. It is headed by Musa Arafat, Yasir Arafat's brother. The Military Police provides security for military installations and prisons; it is subordinate to Military Intelligence.

National Security (*Quwat al-Amn al-Watani*) is the largest security force, with a membership of more than 14,000. Preventive Security (*al-Amn al-Wiqa'i*) is probably the most powerful security force, with a membership of approximately 5,000. Formally headed by Musbah Saqr but actually directed by Muhammad Dahlan in the Gaza Strip and Jibril Rajub in the West Bank.

Two additional security forces are not part of the GSS and are directly under the command of Arafat. Presidential Security (*Amn al-Ri'asa*) provides security for Yasir Arafat, PA officials, and diplomats. Headed by Faisal Abu Sharah. Most of its estimated 3,000 members formerly belonged to Force 17. The second is Special Security (*al-Amn al-Khass*), which is headed by Abu Yusuf al-Wahidi. Its function is believed to be to gather information on other security services.

On 20 July 2004 Arafat yielded to both internal and international pressure to reorganize and reduce the number of security agencies. He issued a decree that converts the twelve forces enumerated above into three national, general, and domestic security and intelligence forces. As of 2004, it is not yet clear what the practical results of this decree will be.

SEE ALSO Dahlan, Muhammad; Fatah, al-; Hindi, Amin al-; Khalaf, Salah; Rajub, Jibril.

PALESTINIANS "FROM INSIDE"/ "FROM OUTSIDE": Expressions used to distinguish Palestinian political activists living under Israeli occupation in the West Bank and Gaza Strip from those living in exile. The terms became current during the first Intifada (1987–1993) to distinguish the mostly young leaders who arose in the early years of the uprising and improvised leadership structures to direct resistance activities, from the older leaders of established organizations, particularly al-Fatah and the Palestine Liberation Organization (PLO) who had lived in exile for years and were caught by surprise by the Intifada, and struggled to take control of it. The term became particularly widespread post–Oslo Accords and signified the differences that arose between the Palestinian leadership inside the Occupied Territories that developed during the Intifada and the PLO leadership that relocated from Tunis and elsewhere in the Arab world and became part of the Palestinian Authority in the West Bank and Gaza Strip.

SEE ALSO Gaza Strip; Intifada (1987–1993); Palestine Liberation Organization; West Bank.

PALESTINIAN STATEHOOD: The idea of statehood as the ultimate goal of the Palestinian national struggle emerged after the Oslo Accords of 1993. The Palestinian national movement had never been especially specific about the nature of the entity it was seeking to create, apart from its embodiment of the principle of Palestinian self-government. A future state was implicit in the various proposals put forth during the Mandate period (those plans that did not involve partition called for some form of power sharing between the Palestinian Arabs and what were thought of, hopefully, as Palestinian Jews). Statehood would have been the result of the partition plan voted by the United Nations in 1947, had it been accepted by both parties. The Palestine National Charter of 1964, which asserted the goals of the newly formed Palestine Liberation Organization (PLO), called for the liberation of Palestine from the Zionists and self-determination for the Palestinian people, but was ambiguous about the nature of the eventual Palestinian entity, leaving open the possibility of membership in a larger pan-Arab state. The 1968 revision of the Charter, written in changed political circumstances after the Arab-Israel War (1967), does not abandon the belief in "Arab unity," nor describe the Palestinian entity in detail, but makes clear that its goal is an independent, sovereign Palestine.

In 1974 the Palestine National Council (PNC) voted to establish a Palestinian "authority" on any liberated part of Palestine. In November 1988, the PNC voted to accept the "two-state solution"—it formally accepted the existence of Israel, and favored the creation of a Palestinian state in the West Bank and Gaza Strip. A Proclamation of the State of Palestine (the Algiers Declaration) was then issued. The Oslo Accords, which included the PLO's formal recognition of Israel (and the corresponding renunciation of its claim to 78 percent of Palestine), provided for the establishment of an "interim" Palestinian autonomous self-governing authority for a period of five years, at which time a "final settlement" would be negotiated. It was widely assumed that the final settlement would involve the creation of a universally recognized sovereign Palestinian state in the occupied territories, although the Accords do not say so. The Palestinian Authority (PA) was formally instituted in 1994. Since then, however, numerous issues, including inability to resolve the status of Jerusalem, continued confiscation of Palestinian land for Israeli settlements and "security needs," and the ongoing cantonizing of the West Bank, have brought serious negotiations to a standstill.

SEE ALSO Gaza Strip; Palestine Liberation Organization; Palestine National Charter; Palestinian Authority; Proclamation of the State of Palestine; West Bank.

PALET-NEWCOMBE ACCORDS

SEE Golan Heights.

PALMAH (acronym for Plugot Mahatz; Hebrew for "striking forces"): Special elite "combat units" of the Haganah. Founded in May 1941, this militia, composed of volunteers working in the kibbutzim, was headed by Yitzhak Sadeh and Yigal Allon. Most of its members were from "special night squads" or "midnight commandos" created by a British officer, Orde Wingate, and dissolved in 1938. After participating with the Haganah in combat against the Arab forces, the Palmah units were dissolved in May 1948, following the creation of the State of Israel.

SEE ALSO Haganah.

PAN-ARABISM: Nationalist movement, primarily in the Arab East or Mashriq, advocating the political union of all Arab peoples on the basis of their shared history, language, and culture. It arose from the Arab struggle against the Ottoman Empire before and during World War I, and from the struggle against French and British imperialism after the war. During the war promises of a sovereign Arab state were made by the British to Emir Husayn ibn Ali al-Hashem, the ruler of the Hijaz and an opponent of Ottoman rule, in return for his help against the Ottomans; instead, once the war was won, the British and French divided Syria, Lebanon, Iraq, Transjordan, and Palestine between them in accord with the Sykes-Picot Agreement. Further resentment was provoked by British encouragement of the Zionist movement, which brought to Palestine under imperial protection thousands of European settlers ambitious to create their own state. Arab politics increasingly focused on freeing the Arab lands from outside rule, and the idea of Arab unity was an emotionally powerful motivator.

In the 1940s the Ba'th Party, which was active in several countries, promoted the idea of a unitary Arab state from Morocco to Iraq. In the 1950s the success of the Egyptian revolution under Gamal Abdel Nasser, particularly after it successfully nationalized the Suez Canal while defying Britain, France, and Israel in the Suez War of 1956, made

Nasser an international hero and powerfully stimulated the Nasserist version of pan-Arabism. The joining of Egypt and (Ba'th-ruled) Syria in the United Arab Republic in 1958 marked a high point for pan-Arabism, but changing politics and conflicting interests doomed the experiment, which ended in 1961. The failure of the Arabs against Israel in the Arab-Israel War (1967) also discredited the pan-Arab idea. The actions of Saddam Hussein—whose launching of the Iran-Iraq War of 1980–1988 and claiming defense of the Arab homeland as a justification, and even more his invading Kuwait in 1990—split the Arab League (founded in 1945 as a pan-Arab institution), as well as the willingness of several Arab states to negotiate directly with Israel, have all but killed pan-Arabism as a serious political idea. A somewhat attenuated form of Arab "unity" remains a diplomatic ideal at the Arab League, but even that is diminished by the existence of smaller regional groups.

SEE ALSO Iran-Iraq War; Mashriq; Nasser, Gamal Abdel; Sykes-Picot Agreement.

PARLIAMENTARY ASSOCIATION FOR EUROPEAN-ARAB COOPERATION: European organization created in 1974 for the purpose of proposing solutions to Middle East conflicts. It is composed of 650 representatives of all political tendencies from 23 European countries.

PARTITION PLAN FOR PALESTINE, 1947

SEE Resolution 181.

PARTY OF GOD

SEE Hizbullah.

PASC

SEE Palestinian Armed Struggle Command.

PASDARAN: Iranian paramilitary organization (the name is Farsi for "Revolutionary Guards") founded in 1979, following the victory of the Iranian Revolution, to help the new Tehran regime apply Islamic law. Supervised by a special ministry, the Pasdaran was responsible also for foreign revolutionary Islamic activities. In the early 1980s the Pasdaran gave its support to the Lebanese Hizbullah against other Lebanese Muslim factions and in the struggle against Israeli occupation.

SEE ALSO Hizbullah.

PASSIA

SEE Palestinian Academic Society for the Study of International Affairs.

PATRIARCHS: From the Latin word *pater,* meaning "father." In the Jewish tradition this word designates the three "fathers" of the nation of Israel: Abraham, Isaac, and Jacob. Afterward, this title was given to the bishops of Rome, Alexandria, Jerusalem, Antioch, and Constantinople. Toward the end of the seventh century, the patriarch of Constantinople was recognized as the primate of the entire Orient.

SEE ALSO Abraham; Isaac; Jacob.

PBC

SEE Palestinian Broadcasting Corporation.

PCP

SEE Palestine Communist Party.

PDA

SEE Palestinian Democratic Assembly.

PDU

SEE Palestinian Democratic Union.

PEACE IN GALILEE

SEE Arab-Israel War (1982).

PEACE NOW (Shalom Achshav, in Hebrew): Israeli pacifist movement, the largest extra-parliamentary movement in Israel and the country's oldest peace movement. It was founded in March 1978, during the Israeli-Egyptian peace talks. When these negotiations faltered, a large group of reserve officers from the Israeli army published an open letter to the prime minister, calling on the government to make sure that the opportunity for peace was not lost. Tens of thousands of Israelis sent in support for the letter, leading to the establishment of an ongoing organization of citizens who view peace, compromise, and reconciliation with the Palestinian people and the Arab states as essential to the future of Israel.

This movement achieved prominence in 1982, when it organized massive demonstrations against the Israeli invasion of Lebanon and the involvement of Israeli forces in the massacres at the Sabra and Shatila Palestinian refugee camps in Lebanon. Its 1982 rally in Tel Aviv assembled over 250,000 demonstrators (by some estimates, 400,000). Peace Now also drew the attention and ire of right-wing extremists. In 1983, during a demonstration calling for the dismissal of then-minister of defense Ariel Sharon, a hand grenade was thrown at the demonstrators, killing activist Emil Grunzweig and wounding seven others.

A majority of Peace Now's membership is drawn from among Meretz Party voters, though it has declined suggestions to become an established political party itself, aiming instead for broad cross-party support. In August 1999, a former leader of the movement, Ya'el Tamir, was named minister of immigrant absorption in the Labor government of Ehud Barak.

After the assassination of Prime Minister Yitzhak Rabin and the subsequent decline of the peace process, Peace Now focused on its Settlement Watch project, monitoring and protesting settlement activities in disputed areas. It considers the occupation of Palestinian territory extremely harmful to Israel, both economically and morally. Peace Now condemns the use of violence on either side of the conflict. Discouraged by the violence of the al-Aqsa Intifada of September 2000 and the Israeli government's stiff military response, its members nonetheless have continued to campaign for peace, creating the Israeli-Palestinian Peace Coalition, and conducting joint activities with the Palestinian People's Campaign.

SEE ALSO Barak, Ehud; Tamir, Ya'el.

PEACE TECHNOLOGY FUND: A joint capital fund established in January 1998 as a partnership between the International Finance Corporation (an associated institution of the World Bank) and private Israeli, Palestinian, and international investors. The Peace Technology Fund (PTF) was initially capitalized at $65 million. Its purpose was to stimulate cooperation between Israeli and Palestinian investors, and to encourage through investment the creation of labor-intensive industries in the West Bank and Gaza Strip, thus helping to strengthen the Palestinian economy. The fund is frozen due to the al-Aqsa Intifada that began in September 2000.

SEE ALSO Gaza Strip; Intifada, al-Aqsa; West Bank.

PECDAR

SEE Palestinian Economic Council for Development and Reconstruction.

PELED, MATTITYAHU ("MATTI") (1923–1995): Israeli soldier, politician, peace activist. Mattityahu ("Matti") Peled was born in Haifa in 1923. He served as a platoon commander in the Palmach. After studying law in London, he returned in 1948 to serve in the Arab-Israel War. Peled served for twenty years as a career officer in the Israel Defense Forces, retiring in 1969. He then completed his doctoral degree and was appointed as lecturer at Tel Aviv University. Peled joined the Israeli Council for Israeli-Palestinian Peace in the mid-1970s, becoming deeply involved in the creation of a dialogue with Palestinian leaders, including Issam Sartawi, the Palestine Liberation Organization (PLO) representative in Paris. In 1983 and 1984, in defiance of Israeli law, he met several times with Yasir Arafat in Tunis and Geneva. Peled was elected to the Knesset in 1986 on the Progressive List of Peace, an Arab-Jewish party, serving one term. He died of cancer in March 1995.

PEOPLE OF THE BOOK (*Ahl al-kitab,* in Arabic): Word used in the Qur'an to designate communities whose religion is based on a revealed book, such as Jews, Christians, and Sabaeans.

PERES, SHIMON (born Perski, 1923–): Israeli political figure, prime minister of Israel (1984–1986 and 1995–1996). Born in 1923 in Poland, Shimon Peres emigrated to Palestine in 1934, where he joined the Zionist youth movement, Ha-No'ar Ha-Oved. Between 1941 and 1944, he was secretary general of this movement, participating in the creation of kibbutz Alumot. In 1947, he joined the Haganah, then led by David Ben-Gurion, who the next year, as prime minister of the new State of Israel, made him head of Israel's navy. In 1953 Ben-Gurion appointed him Director General of the Israeli Ministry of Defense, a position in which, among other achievements, he participated in secret arms negotiations with the French prior to the Sinai campaign of 1956 and was responsible for Israel's nuclear program.

In 1959 he was elected to a MAPAI seat in the Knesset, and was deputy minister of defense in the successive governments of David Ben-Gurion and Levi Eshkol from 1959 to 1965. He then left the Defense Ministry to help Ben-Gurion founded a new party, RAFI, of which he became secretary general. In 1968, he participated in the creation of the Israel Labor Party, formed through the merger of MAPAI, RAFI, and Ahdut ha-Avodah. The following year he was named minister without portfolio in the government of Golda Meir, responsible for economic development in the occupied territories. From this time on, he advocated the idea of the creation of an Israeli-Palestinian-Jordanian regional economic entity.

SHIMON PERES. THE ISRAELI FOREIGN MINISTER, A LIFELONG MODERATE WHO SERVED IN MANY GOVERNMENT POSTS (INCLUDING PRIME MINISTER FROM 1984 TO 1986), RECEIVES THE 1994 NOBEL PEACE PRIZE FOR HIS KEY EFFORTS TO BRING ABOUT THE OSLO ACCORDS BETWEEN ISRAEL AND THE PALESTINIANS. PRIME MINISTER YITZHAK RABIN AND PALESTINIAN LEADER YASIR ARAFAT WERE ALSO HONORED. (© *Photograph by Ya'acov Sa'ar. Government Press Office [GPO] of Israel*)

Between 1970 and 1974, Perez was minister of transport and communication, then of information. In 1974, he became defense minister in the government of Yitzhak Rabin; and in 1977, after Rabin's resignation as prime minister, he was elected to lead the Labor Party. It lost the next two elections; then in 1984, no party having a majority in the Knesset, a national unity government was formed, with Shimon Peres as prime minister and Yitzhak Shamir as foreign minister. Under a rotation agreement, in 1986 the two men switched roles. From 1988 to 1990,

Peres was deputy prime minister and foreign minister.

In the 1992 elections the Labor party regained power, and Peres was named foreign minister in the government of Yitzhak Rabin. In that capacity he negotiated the later stages of the Oslo Accords and convinced Rabin to support them. For his role in achieving this agreement, he, along with Rabin and Yasir Arafat, received the 1994 Nobel Peace Prize.

In November 1995, after the assassination of Yitzhak Rabin, Shimon Peres again became prime minister, serving until the following May, when Labor lost power to Likud. In June 1997, he was defeated by Ehud Barak in the election for chairmanship of the Labor party; but he continued as a member of the Knesset. On 6 July 1999 he was appointed minister of regional cooperation in the Barak government, serving until 2001. In July 2000 he was defeated in the election for the presidency of the State of Israel by his Likud rival, Moshe Katsav. In March 2001, after the defeat of Ehud Barak in the elections for prime minister, Peres agreed to join a government of national unity, led by the head of Likud, Ariel Sharon, in the capacity of deputy prime minister and foreign minister. In October 2002, however, Peres and other Laborites resigned from the Sharon government. In June 2003, after Labor's defeat under Amram Mitzna's leadership in the May elections, the party once again selected Peres as its leader.

SEE ALSO Ahdut Ha-Avodah; Ben-Gurion, David; Haganah; Israel Labor Party; MAPAI; Oslo Accords; Rabin, Yitzhak; RAFI Party.

PERETZ, AMIR (1954–): Israeli politician. Born in Morocco, Peretz immigrated to Israel at the age of four. In the 1980s Peretz became the head of Sderot Council. He was elected to the Knesset in 1988 as a member of the Labor Party. After serving as head of the Histradut's professional union, he was elected chairman of the Histradut in 1995. In January 1999 Peretz resigned from the Labor Party to found the Am Ehad (One Nation) Party, which that year won two seats in the Knesset. He is a member of the Peace Now movement.

PFLP

SEE Popular Front for the Liberation of Palestine.

PFLP–GC

SEE Popular Front for the Liberation of Palestine–General Command.

PFLP–SC

SEE Popular Front for the Liberation of Palestine–Special Command.

PFLP–SO

SEE Popular Front for the Liberation of Palestine–Special Operations.

PHALANGE: Lebanese Maronite Christian Party (*al-Kata'ib al-Lubnaniya* or *Phalange libanaise*; *kata'ib* is Arabic for "phalanx," or *phalange* in French; the party is sometimes referred to in English as the Kata'ib); founded in November 1936, by Pierre Jumayyil with Charles Hilu, George Naqqash, Shafiq Nasif, and Emile Yared. The Phalange was founded as a paramilitary youth organization modeled on the fascist political organizations Jumayyil had seen and admired at the Berlin Olympics of that year, particularly the Hitler Youth, one of whose rallies he had attended. From its founding (with about 300 members), the Phalange has aligned itself with France and the West. At first it supported the Mandate government, but in 1942 it advocated independence and was suspended by the authorities. It reactivated itself in 1943 when Lebanon became effectively independent. Also that year Lebanon's leading Maronite and Sunni Muslim politicians established the unwritten National Pact, which institutionalized religious communalism as the basis of Lebanese politics and set the relative political power within the state of the different religious communities. The National Pact fixed a ratio for allotting parliamentary seats (six Christian to five Muslim), and assigned the three highest state offices to representatives of three communities: the presidency to a Maronite, the prime ministry to a Sunni, and the speakership of the Chamber of Deputies to a Shi'a. (This distribution was based on a questionable census of 1932. No one from the Shi'a, Druze, Greek Orthodox, Melkite, or other community was consulted.)

The preservation of Maronite hegemony via the National Pact became the Phalange's primary cause, and it has remained opposed to any change that would result in a dilution of Maronite power. It also has opposed any political tendency, such as pan-Arabism, pan-Syrianism, communism, and pan-Islamism, that would compromise Lebanese sovereignty or the uniquely "Phoenician," non-Arab culture it believes distinguishes Lebanon. It has been right wing, authoritarian, anti-Palestinian, anti-Islamic, and thoroughly sectarian, although it has at times formed tactical alliances with Muslim organizations holding compatible positions. Between 1943

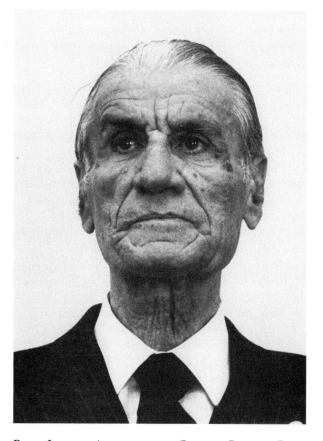

PIERRE JUMAYYIL. A FOUNDER OF THE CHRISTIAN PHALANGE PARTY IN LEBANON IN 1936, HE LED THE PARTY (UNDER VARIOUS NAMES) IN THE STRUGGLE FOR LEBANESE INDEPENDENCE WHILE RESISTING BOTH SYRIAN AND COMMUNIST INFLUENCE. IN 1975, ITS OPPOSITION TO THE PALESTINIAN PRESENCE IN SOUTH LEBANON TOUCHED OFF THE LONG LEBANESE CIVIL WAR. JUMAYYIL DIED IN 1984, TWO YEARS AFTER HIS SON BASHIR, THE PRESIDENT-ELECT, WAS ASSASSINATED. *(AP/Wide World Photos)*

and 1949, while it was primarily focusing on union activities, its first candidacies in legislative elections were failures. Dissolved on 20 July 1949, it was reborn on the following 3 August as the Lebanese Union, transformed in May 1951 into the Social Democratic Party, then into the Phalange Party the following year. At this time it had three deputies in parliament. In the 1958 crisis, the party backed the power in place, represented by the president, Camille Chamoun. Chamoun wanted the army to intervene against Muslim demonstrators, but the army commander, Fu'ad Chehab, refused to engage his forces in intercommunal fighting; Pierre Jumayyil stepped in to do so with the Phalange's considerable militia. As a result, in October 1958, Jumayyil became a minister in a multiparty government of national salvation, in which he held the public works, communications, health, national education and agriculture portfolios, under the new president, Chehab, who had been chosen largely because he had not taken sides in the civil war.

The party withdrew its support from Chehab (and his successor, the former Phalangist Charles Hilu), as his policies of administrative and (limited) economic reform, known as Chehabism, threatened the financial interests of Maronite oligarchs. In 1967, the Phalange sealed an alliance with two other Christian groups, Chamoun's National Liberal Party (NLP), and the National Bloc of Raymond Eddé, to form the Triple Alliance (al-Hilf al-Thulathi) in opposition to Chehabism. After the 1968 parliamentary elections, the Hilf coalition controlled the largest block of seats (the Phalange held nine). Lebanon then was being deeply affected by the Palestinian issue, which was beginning to destabilize its politics. Muslim and leftist Lebanese had always sympathized with the dispossessed Palestinians; Maronite Christians and conservatives, in general, had not. The outcome of the Arab-Israel War (1967), in which Lebanon had not participated, had made it clear that the Palestinian refugees in the country would not be returning to their homes, and armed Palestinian groups were organizing and carrying out anti-Israeli operations. Their activities tended to expose the government's weakness—it could prevent neither the guerrilla activities nor the Israeli reprisals they provoked—undermining its authority and polarizing the Lebanese. In January 1969 a new coalition cabinet that excluded right-wing Maronite parties, which opposed all reform, proclaimed its support for the Palestinian resistance, while allowing the army and police to attempt to repress political activity in the refugee camps. This resulted in fighting between government forces and Palestinian paramilitaries.

Eventually, under outside pressure, a formal agreement was made between the government and the Palestine Liberation Organization (PLO) giving Palestinians legal status and, in effect, ceding the PLO an autonomous state within the state. In 1970, after Jumayyil withdrew his candidacy, Sulayman Franjiyya, a nationalist and enemy of the PLO, was elected president. Further polarizing the situation was the arrival later that year and into 1971 of large numbers of Palestinians, including many PLO fighters, who had been expelled from Jordan in the wake of Black September 1970. Franjiyya's government, like Hilu's, did almost nothing to provide security against Israeli attacks on Lebanese territory in the south, which were indiscriminately hitting Lebanese—predominantly poor Shiites—as well as Pales-

tinian targets. Tens of thousands of South Lebanese Shiites migrated to Beirut to escape Israeli shelling, and little provision was made for them. Lebanon remained neutral in the Arab-Israel War (1973). Franjiyya, unable to use the army effectively against the Palestinians, encouraged the army to arm and train the Maronite militias. On 13 April 1975, unknown persons attempted to assassinate Pierre Jumayyil; in retaliation, Phalangists attacked a bus carrying Palestinian civilians through a Christian area of East Beirut, killing twenty-six. Fighting then broke out between armed factional groups and violence spread around the country: this was the beginning of the Lebanese Civil War of 1975–1990. The main antagonists at first were the Phalange and its militia, and the Lebanese National Movement (LMN), which loosely united fifteen organizations of the left around the Progressive Socialist Party (PSP) of the Druze leader Kamal Jumblatt and advocated reform of the Lebanese system. The PLO was aligned with the LNM and established a joint command with its militia. The Phalange was joined by other right-wing Maronite groups (soon to form an alliance, the Lebanese Front, and later a joint militia command, the Lebanese Forces [LF]), commanded by Bashir Jumayyil, son of Pierre.

In January 1976 the LF destroyed a Palestinian refugee camp and a Muslim neighborhood in East Beirut. In March Muslim troops of the Lebanese army mutinied and formed the Lebanese Arab Army, which joined with the LNM. It attacked Christian areas of Beirut and forced President Franjiyya to flee. In May Ilyas Sarkis, with Syrian support, was elected to become president in September at the end of Franjiyya's term. At the end of May, the LF was about to be defeated, and Syria, after having for months attempted to mediate a settlement, intervened militarily against the LNM and the Palestinians. This move was supported by Jordan, Israel, France, and the United States. By mid-August the Syrian forces had gained control and agreed to a cease-fire. A truce was agreed to and the Arab League sanctioned an Arab Deterrent Force (ADF) (consisting almost entirely of Syrian troops already in place) to be deployed to keep the peace. The ADF and Lebanese government authority did not extend to South Lebanon, largely controlled by the PLO, where Israel and Christian militias backed by Israel continued to attack. The diplomatic peace offensive by Egyptian president Anwar al-Sadat toward Israel in 1977 drove the Syrians closer to the PLO and away from the Sarkis government. By 1978 the Lebanese Forces (under control of the Phalange, the Lebanese Front alliance having deteriorated) were firmly allied with

Israel and operating independently of the government, and Syria switched its support to their opponents, the LMN.

After a PLO attack within Israel, the Israel Defense Force (IDF) invaded South Lebanon in March 1978, intending to destroy PLO bases and drive PLO fighters away from the border by creating a "security zone" on the Lebanese side. The Israelis organized, trained and armed a Christian militia called the South Lebanon Army (SLA) as their proxy to patrol the border area after they withdrew in October. In June 1978, Tony Franjiyya, son of Sulayman Franjiyya and a potential rival to Bashir Jumayyil for the presidency, was assassinated by an LF commando under directed by Samir Geagea. In November 1979, the principal figures in the political section of the Phalange were Pierre Jumayyil, Antoine Ayyub, Georges 'Omayra, Pierre Sayigh, Elie Karame, Munir al-Hajj, Karim Pakraduni, Ibrahim Najjar, Joseph Saadeh, Georges 'Aql, Edmond Rizq and Laura Jumayyil. On 31 January, the alliance with the NLP of Camille Chamoun was broken, following confrontations between the LF and the LDP's militia, the Tigers. Between 7 and 9 July, combat between members of the two parties caused more than 500 deaths, and the Tigers were decimated. In 1980 and 1981 there was also frequent fighting between the LF and the ADF, in which Israel at least once intervened significantly in support of the LF. In June 1982 the Israelis invaded Lebanon again, this time going as far north as Beirut and besieging the city for weeks, side by side with the LF, using artillery shelling and aerial saturation bombing, including phosphorus bombs, turning much of the city to rubble. A cease-fire was arranged by the United States, and a withdrawal of the PLO leadership along with about 13,000 PLO and Palestine Liberation Army (PLA) fighters to Tunis was arranged under the supervision of a Multinational Force (MF). Israel also meant to ensure that Bashir Jumayyil became president, and he was duly elected on 23 August. The MF left Beirut on 10 September. On 14 September Jumayyil was assassinated (by pan-Syrian nationalists). Israeli forces then moved in to help the LF secure the city. Two days later the IDF helped the LF enter the Sabra and Shatila Palestinian refugee camps and looked on passively as over three days they slaughtered approximately 1,500 to 3,000 civilians, ostensibly in reprisal for Jumayyil's assassination. On 20 September the MF was redeployed to Beirut. On 21 September Amin Jumayyil, Bashir's brother, was elected president, and at the end of September the Israelis left the city.

In May 1983, under pressure from the United States, Amin Jumayyil agreed to sign a peace treaty with Israel, which was actually ratified by parliament. Opposition to this treaty among Lebanese—and by the Syrians—was so great, however, that Jumayyil felt obliged to refuse to sign it. The Israelis, who had been protecting Jumayyil's government from its factional enemies, then withdrew their forces from the Shuf district southeast of Beirut, a largely Druze area held by the Phalange. Fighting broke out between the Phalange and the Druze militia directed by Walid Jumblatt, which had Palestinian and Syrian support. These were some of the biggest battles of the war. After several months the Phalange were expelled from the area. Jumayyil, with support from Syria, repudiated the agreement with Israel in March 1984. In August 1984 Pierre Jumayyil died; he was succeeded by Elie Karame, but his death set off power struggles within the Phalange and the LF. In March 1985, a split opened between the Lebanese Forces on one side and President Jumayyil and the Phalange on the other. An agreement had been reached for the LF to turn back to the government the public property, offices and functions it had taken over in its Beirut enclave during the war. Samir Geagea, a senior LF commander, had himself named chief of staff and proclaimed the LF independent of the Phalange. On 9 May, Geagea was ousted and Elie Hobeika was appointed to replace him. Hobeika tried to end the hostilities between his movement and Syria. In December Hobeika signed an agreement for peace and political reform with the leaders of the Shiite Amal and the Druze militia, but it never took effect because he lost control of the LF. Geagea revolted, and, after fighting between followers of the two men, Geagea took over command of the Lebanese Forces, evicting Hobeika and reestablishing the LF's ties with Israel. Hobeika, who had worked closely with the Israelis and had been one of the LF commanders in charge of the Sabra and Shatila massacre, organized a splinter LF under the protection of the Syrians. George Saade was elected head of the Phalange in 1987, succeeding Karame.

With the end of his presidential term in 1988, with no successor selected, Amin Jumayyil appointed General Michel Aoun as "interim president" and, having received death threats from Geagea, left Lebanon. Geagea supported the Ta'if Accords of 1989, causing a split in the LF; some members supported Aoun, who opposed the accords, and the two factions fought into October when the Syrians finally defeated Aoun's forces and ended the civil war. The same month, the head of the NLP, Dany Chamoun, former head of the Tigers militia and son of Camille

Chamoun, was assassinated by an LF commando. Both Geagea and Saade were included in the national unity cabinet formed in December 1990, but in March 1991 Geagea resigned to reconstitute the LF as a political party. In June 1991, Amin Jumayyil met with Shimon Peres in Brussels, and discussed the situation in South Lebanon. In 1992, he returned home and persuaded the Phalange party to boycott the parliamentary elections, the first since before the civil war; he was obliged, under government pressure, to cut his stay short. The LF Party also was unsuccessful in these elections; in 1994 the party was banned after the bombing of a church in Junieh in which ten people were killed, and responsibility for it, and for the assassination of Dany Chamoun and a number of other people were traced to Geagea. Geagea received a death sentence, commuted to life imprisonment, for the Chamoun killing, and remained in prison in 2004. A rump LF organization remains, run by Geagea's wife Strida. On 21 March 1998, Munir al-Hajj became head of the Phalange, following the death of George Saade. In July 2000 Amin Jumayyil returned to Lebanon again and campaigned to regain the leadership of the Phalange, but Karim Pakraduni was elected in 2002. Frustrated, Jumayyil formed a splinter group called the Phalange Base (al-Kata'ib al-Qa'ida). In July 2002 he was expelled from the party, and sued for insulting the leadership.

> SEE ALSO Arab Deterrent Force; Arab-Israel War (1967); Arab-Israel War (1973); Black September 1970; Chamoun, Camille; Franjiyya; Sulayman; Geagea, Samir; Hobeika, Elie; Israel Defense Force; Jumayyil, Bashir; Jumblatt, Kamal; Jumblatt, Walid Kamal; Lebanese Forces; Lebanese National Movement; Palestine Liberation Army; Palestine Liberation Organization; Pan-Arabism; Ta'if Accord.

PHILBY, HARRY ST. JOHN: Leading British explorer of Saudi Arabia who on occasion was involved in Palestinian affairs. He was born in 1885 in Sri Lanka (then Ceylon) and after distinguished studies at Cambridge in joined the Indian Foreign Office. In 1915 he left India to go to Iraq and served there in the Intelligence Service of the British army. Ten years later he left government service to become a merchant and to devote his life to the exploration of Arabia for which he is known. In 1930 he converted to Islam.

In 1929 Philby became involved, with Jewish dissenter Judah Magnes, in an ill-fated Arab-Zionist peace plan. Then in 1939 he developed a scheme under which his patron, Saudi ruler King Ibn Sa'ud,

might be persuaded to support the creation of a Jewish state in Palestine in exchange for Jewish political influence in London and in Washington, D.C. and financial compensation. This scheme would have been contingent on complete independence of the remaining Arab territory along with financial assistance to the Arabs; so although he proposed it to Zionist officials in London, nothing ever came of it.

PHOENICIANS: Maritime population, which, in the third millennium B.C.E., settled along the eastern coast of the Mediterranean, between Mount Carmel and the mouth of the Oronte, in the Land of Canaan. The Phoenicians founded many colonies and trading stations all around the Mediterranean. Excellent navigators, they disseminated the alphabet through the Mediterranean world, transmitting it to the Greeks.

> SEE ALSO Canaan.

PICCR

> SEE Palestinian Independent Commission for Citizens' Rights.

PICM

> SEE Palestinian Islamic Combat Movement.

PIJ

> SEE Palestinian Islamic Jihad.

PIKUAH NEFESH: Hebrew word meaning "saving an endangered life." Basic principle of Judaism, according to which saving a life takes precedence over any Torah commandment. In practice, the principle often used to override restrictions regarding Kashrut or Sabbath observance.

> SEE ALSO Torah.

PINES OPERATION: Military project in preparation between 1980 and 1981 by the Israeli defense minister, Ariel Sharon, and the general staff of the Israel Defense Force, headed by Raphael Eitan. This plan provided for the invasion of Lebanon, so as to neutralize, definitively, the terrorist actions of Palestinian movements in this country. Thereby deprived of the support of armed resistance, the Palestinian population of the territories would no longer be able to oppose the establishment of a limited autonomy, one that perpetuated the Israeli occupation. Israeli military experts, however, considered that this would be an opportunity to resolve the Syrian issue also: Either Damascus would decide to intervene, resulting in a sure defeat for the Syrian army, or Syria would not intervene, becoming scorned by the Arab world. In either case, the Syrian influence in Lebanon would be greatly reduced. When it was first presented to the Israeli government on 20 December, 1981, the plan was rejected, at least for the time being.

PISGA

SEE Palestinian Authority.

PLA

SEE Palestine Liberation Army.

PLC

SEE Palestinian Legislative Council.

PLF

SEE Palestine Liberation Front (1961); Palestine Liberation Front (1965); Palestine Liberation Front (1977).

PLF–PR

SEE Palestine Liberation Front (1961).

PLO

SEE Palestine Liberation Organization.

PMAL

SEE Popular Movement of Arab Liberation.

PNA

SEE Palestinian Authority.

PNC

SEE Palestine National Council.

PNF

SEE Palestinian National Front.

PNSF

SEE Palestinian National Salvation Front.

PO'ALEI AGUDAT ISRAEL: Ultra-Orthodox Israeli movement, created in Poland in 1922, and representing the workers of Agudat Israel. This group advocated the creation of a state of Israel based on the Torah. It was identified with Agudat Israel regarding religious matters, and in most elections, Po'alei Agudat

Israel (PAI) candidates ran on a joint electoral list with the Agudat. In 1960 PAI joined the coalition government, contrary to the advice of the Agudat Council of Sages.

SEE ALSO Agudat Israel.

PO'ALEI ZION (Workers of Zion): Labor Zionist political party founded in 1905 by Eastern European Jewish youth who went to Palestine. It tried to organize craftsmen into unions and initiated strikes to protest the conditions of employment in the Jewish farming colonies. Also, following the precedent set by Labor Zionist guard units formed in Eastern Europe to protect Jewish communities there during pogroms, this party established such units and their members were hired as guards on Jewish farms. Later, Po'alei Zion combined with Ahdut ha-Avoda after a split in MAPAI, and in 1948 the joint party united with MAPAM to run for the First and Second Knessets; Po'alei Zion's leader Moshe Erem and other members became Members of Knesset for MAPAM.

The name Po'alei Zion was also used by parties in the United States and other nations; Golda Meir, David Ben-Gurion, and Yitzhak Rabin all belonged to such groups in their teens.

SEE ALSO Ahdut ha-Avoda; MAPAI; MAPAM.

POGROM: Russian word meaning "attack" or "devastation." Historically, it designates mob attacks accompanied by pillage and murder that were perpetrated against the Jews of Russia—for example, in 1881–1882 and in 1903 at Kishinev. An important component of a pogrom is the usually silent complicity of the police and other authorities. Many Arab attacks on Jews in pre-1948 Palestine, such as those in 1908, 1920, 1921, 1922, and 1929, were labeled by some of the victims as "Arab pogroms."

POPULAR ARMY FRONT–RETURN BATTALIONS

SEE Aqsa Intifada, al-.

POPULAR FRONT FOR THE LIBERATION OF PALESTINE (PFLP): Palestinian movement (*al-Jabha al-Sha'biya li-Tahrir Filastin*, in Arabic) created in December 1967, in the wake of the Arab defeat in the Arab-Israel War (1967), by Dr. George Habash (b. 1925), Nayif Hawatma, and Ahmad Jibril. The Popular Front for the Liberation of Palestine (PFLP) was formed from the merger of Habash's Nasserist Arab Nationalist Movement (ANM) and Jibril's Palestine Liberation Front (PLF, 1965), and was more radical

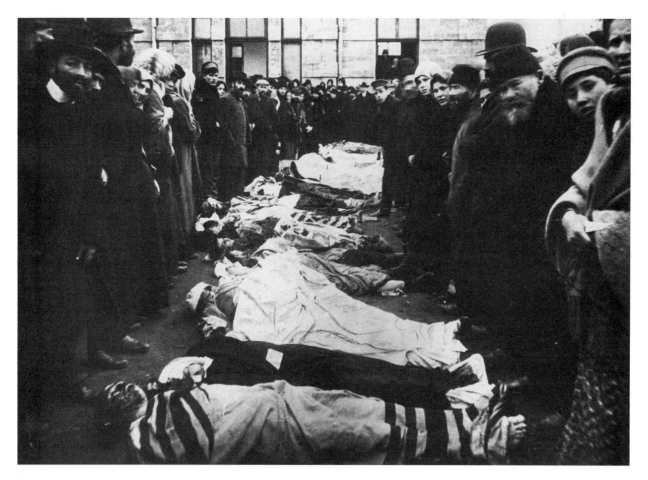

VICTIMS OF 1905 POGROM. IN LATE-NINETEENTH- AND EARLY-TWENTIETH-CENTURY RUSSIA, ANTI-SEMITIC MOBS REPEATEDLY ATTACKED JEWS, WITH THE ENCOURAGEMENT OR ACQUIESCENCE OF THE CZARIST GOVERNMENT. ONE RESULT WAS THAT MORE THAN FORTY THOUSAND JEWS FLED TO PALESTINE. THERE, WITH RISING ARAB NATIONALISM AND RESISTANCE TO ZIONISM, SIMILAR MOB ATTACKS TOOK PLACE REPEATEDLY IN THE DECADES BEFORE ISRAEL CAME INTO BEING. (© *Hulton-Deutsch Collection/Corbis*)

than either. It also attracted the dissidents of the groups Heroes of the Return of Fayiz Jabir and Revenge of Youth. Like the ANM advocating pan-Arabism, the PFLP opposed any negotiated solution with Israel. It espoused a strategy of mobilizing workers and peasants in a revolutionary grass-roots war of liberation. The second largest Palestinian movement after Yasir Arafat's al-Fatah, the PFLP established its headquarters in Damascus and affiliated with the Palestine Liberation Organization (PLO). In March 1968, Habash was jailed in Damascus, and returned to Jordan in early 1969. During his absence, Jibril quit the movement to create his own organization, the Popular Front for the Liberation of Palestine–General Command (PFLP–GC). In February 1969, a second break, initiated by Nayif Hawatima, gave rise to the Popular Democratic Front for the Liberation of Palestine (PDFLP), which later became the Democratic Front for the Liberation of Palestine

(DFLP). The PFLP engaged in hundreds of armed actions, mainly in the Gaza Strip, and became widely known for airplane hijackings.

On 30 August 1969, a Front commando led by Leila Khaled hijacked a TWA airliner en route from Rome to Tel Aviv via Athens. The commandos forced the plane to land near Damascus. In exchange for the passengers they obtained the release of thirteen Palestinians jailed in Israel; they also exploded a bomb in the cockpit of the aircraft. Khalid became a heroine of the Palestinian resistance. The PFLP moved from Syria to Jordan and played a critical role creating confrontations against the government of King Hussein. At the beginning of August 1970, coming out against the position of al-Fatah, Habash advocated the establishment of a "national democratic government" in Jordan. The PFLP multiplied provocations, meant to push the Jordanian forces toward confrontation. On 6–9 September 1970, PFLP commandos hijacked three Western airliners to a remote airstrip in the Jordanian desert, destroying them after the passengers were evacuated. On 16 September the king formed a military government and the next day launched an attack against Palestinian refugee camps, beginning a campaign of violent repression of Palestinian organizations. This was the beginning of Black September 1970. On 27 September, after ten days of fighting that caused nearly 4,000 Palestinian deaths, Egyptian president Gamal Abdel Nasser, at the behest of the Arab League, arranged a cease-fire. When fighting broke out again the following summer, the PLO was expelled from the country, from which it moved to Lebanon. The following year the PFLP mounted joint operations with the Japanese Red Army (JRA).

In 1972 the PFLP renounced operations outside Palestine. It also adopted a Marxist orientation and a more comprehensive social program. In 1974 when the PLO adopted the idea of a separate Palestinian state in the West Bank and Gaza Strip, the PFLP quit the PLO's executive committee and became the major force behind the creation of the Rejection Front. During the early period of the Lebanese Civil War of 1975–1990, the PFLP joined with al-Fatah against the Syrians, who at that point were supporting the Lebanese government. After Egyptian president Anwar al-Sadat launched his peace offensive toward Israel, breaking the Arab consensus, Syria and the PLO were reconciled. The PFLP rejoined the PLO executive committee in 1981. When the PLO was expelled from Lebanon in 1982, the PFLP moved to Damascus. In June 1983 the PFLP and the DFLP announced the creation of a common military and political command to coordinate the actions of the Palestinian resistance. In 1984, in order to counter the policies of Yasir Arafat, which were tending toward dialogue with Israel, the movement joined with the DFLP and the Palestine Liberation Front (PLF, 1977), in constituting the "Democratic Alliance," which lasted only around fifteen months because of personality conflicts.

In 1987, after the abrogation of the Jordanian-Palestinian Accord, the PFLP, along with the DFLP and the Palestine Communist Party (PCP), rejoined the Executive Committee of the PLO. In February 1993, there was radicalization of the movement at the PFLP congress; and following the signature of the Israeli-Palestinian Oslo Accords of 1993, the PFLP and the DFLP resigned once more from the Executive Committee of the PLO, joining with the Palestinian opposition front, the Alliance of Palestinian Forces (APF). In August 1994, in an effort to consoli-

date its common position against the Oslo Accords, the PFLP and the DFLP again announced the constitution of a common military command. In December 1994, the PFLP was the impetus behind the creation, at Amman, of a movement meant to unite opponents of the Oslo Accords, the Palestinian Assembly, under the leadership of Bassam al-Shaq'a. This entity, whose activities were very sparse, lasted only a few weeks. On 1 July 1996, the leadership of the PFLP announced it was withdrawing from the Central Council of the PLO.

Between 1996 and 1998, the PFLP strove to unify a new movement of credible opposition, principally with its main ally, the DFLP. During this time, the armed branch of the PFLP carried out some anti-Israel attacks, of which several were coordinated with the PFLP–GC. At the beginning of 1999, two currents surfaced in the PFLP: one led by Mustafa Zibri (Abu Ali Mustafa) and Abdul Rahim Malluh, which favored a rapprochement with the Palestinian Authority; the other, opposed to this rapprochement, was led by George Habash. The following June, the political bureau of the PFLP threw its support behind the project of unifying the Palestinian forces of the left, for the purpose of defending Palestinian interests, in negotiations on a final status for the Palestinian territories. In August, leaders of the PFLP, the DFLP, and al-Fatah met in Cairo to discuss reconciliation between the partisans and opponents of the Oslo Accords. In mid-February 2000, the political bureau of the PFLP rejoined the Executive Committee of the PLO. In April, Habash resigned as head of the movement, replaced three months later by al-Zabri, who had been residing in the Palestinian territories since the previous September. In November, while the al-Aqsa Intifada was raging in the Palestinian territories, the PFLP decided to become more involved in armed action against the Israelis. On 27 August 2001, al-Zabri was killed in his office in Ramallah by Israeli missiles in a "targeted killing," or assassination. On 3 October, Ahmad Sa'adat was chosen to head the PFLP, seconded by Abdul Rahim Malluh. Fourteen days later, in order to avenge the death of al-Zabri, a PFLP member assassinated Rehavam Ze'evi, Israeli minister of tourism. In 2004, Habash, who is in poor health, lives in Damascus.

SEE ALSO Alliance of Palestinian Forces; Aqsa Intifada, al-; Arab Nationalist Movement; Black September 1970; Fatah, al-; Habash, George; Hawatma, Nayif; Japanese Red Army; Jibril, Ahmad; Oslo Accords; Palestine Liberation Front (1965); Palestine Liberation Front (1977); Palestine Liberation

Organization; Palestinian Authority; Popular Front for the Liberation of Palestine–General Command; Rejection Front; West Bank.

POPULAR FRONT FOR THE LIBERATION OF PALESTINE–GENERAL COMMAND (PFLP–GC): Palestinian movement (*Al-Jabha al-Shaʿbiya li-Tahrir Filastni–Al-Qiyada al-ʿAmma*) created by Ahmad Jibril and Ahmad Zaʿrur in November 1968, after breaking with the Popular Front for the Liberation of Palestine (PFLP), claiming they wanted to concentrate on the struggle rather than politics. A radical, secular, socialist movement, the Popular Front for the Liberation of Palestine–General Command (PFLP–GC) advocated armed struggle and rejected any negotiated solution with Israel. It was backed by Syria, Libya, and Iran, who supplied them well with arms. Its headquarters was located in the suburbs of Damascus, while a section of its operational department was based in Lebanon. The PFLP–GC made itself known on 2 February 1970 when it destroyed a Swissair plane, killing 47 people, by placing a bomb aboard, which exploded in flight en route to Tel Aviv. From this date, the movement specialized in booby-trapped letters and suicide attacks. In April 1974 the PFLP–GC attacked a kibbutz at Kiryat Shimona, took hostages and attempted to trade them for 100 Palestinian prisoners. The operation failed and the guerrillas and 18 hostages were killed. In 1974, the PFLP-GC joined the Palestine Liberation Organization (PLO).

In 1977, the pro-Syrian policies favored by Jibril prompted Muhammad Zaydan to quit the PFLP–GC, to create the Palestine Liberation Front (PLF). Between 1978 and 1981, the PFLP–GC launched a campaign of armed actions against Israeli interests as well as Lebanese militia and other Palestinian splinter groups. During the 1980s, it participated in a number of attacks in liaison with the Irish Republican Army, the Armenian Secret Army for the Liberation of Armenia (ASALA), and Action Directe (a French terrorist organization). In 1982, when the PLO was expelled from Lebanon after the Israeli invasion, the PFLP–GC moved its headquarters to Damascus. In 1983, the PFLP–GC participated in a revolt against Yasir Arafat promoted by the Syrian regime; the resulting dissidence in the movement gave rise to the PFLP–GC–Temporary Command. In the following year, the PFLP–GC joined the Palestinian oppositional front, the Palestinian National Salvation Front (PNSF). A split in that movement, caused by Muhammad Shatta (Abu Jabir) and backed by al-Fatah, gave rise to the PFLP–GC–

Special Command. This new organization had its headquarters in Cyprus. In 1984 Jibril and the PFLP–GC was expelled from the PLO for its definitively pro-Syrian attitude. In April 1985, through the intermediary of the International Red Cross and the former chancellor of Austria, Bruno Kreisky, the PFLP–GC negotiated an exchange of three Israeli soldiers, whom they had captured in Lebanon in September 1982, for 1,187 Palestinians imprisoned in Israel.

In 1987 the movement effected a rapprochement with Iran, after which it retreated somewhat from its strictly secular orientation. In November of that year it staged a raid from South Lebanon into Israel by hang glider and killed six Israeli soldiers; this incident gave heart to many Palestinians and is said to have helped spark the first Intifada. In 1988 it established a radio station in Syria, Radio Jerusalem (*Idhaʾt al-Quds*), to broadcast into the occupied territories and encourage the resistance during the Intifada. Opposed to the Israeli-Palestinian Oslo Accords of 1993, the PFLP–GC joined the Alliance of Palestinian Forces (APF), and Ahmad Jibril made a death threat against Yasir Arafat, whom he accused of betraying the Palestinian cause. In 1994, an Islamic current, under the impetus of Mustafa Khamis, appeared in the movement, giving rise to a PFLP–Islamic GC. There was supposition that this new branch was created with Jibril's agreement to facilitate contacts of the PFLP–GC with Hizbullah and Palestinian Islamic Jihad. Thereafter, in the context of their opposition to the Oslo peace process, joint operations were mounted by the three movements. In December 1996, Khamis announced the creation of a new dissident party from the PFLP–GC, the Arab Union Party, which favored the policies of Arafat and was based in Jordan. Two trends exist within the movement: a radical wing, led by Jibril and, until his assassination by car bomb in 2002, his son Jihad, and a moderate wing, headed by the assistant secretary general of the movement, Talal Naji (Abu Jihad Talal). Weakened by financial crisis due to a reduction in external subsidies, as well as by personality conflicts and political dissension, the PFLP–GC has lost support in the occupied territories and has been largely inactive since the early 1990s.

SEE ALSO Alliance of Palestinian Forces; Arab Union Party; Fatah, al-; Intifada (1987–1993); Jibril, Ahmad; Palestine Liberation Front (1977); Palestine Liberation Organization; Palestinian National Salvation Front; Popular Front for the Liberation of Palestine; Zaydan, Muhammad.

POPULAR FRONT FOR THE LIBERATION OF PALESTINE–SPECIAL COMMAND: Palestinian armed group created in 1979, after the dissolution of the Popular Front for the Liberation of Palestine–Special Operations (PFLP–SO), caused by the death of Wadi Haddad. Backed by Syria and Iraq, this splinter group was led by Salim Abdul Salem (Abu Muhammad), seconded by Zaki Khalil Muhammad. Marxist-Leninist in ideology, this movement advocated the struggle against imperialism and Zionism as well as armed combat for the recovery of Palestinian land. The headquarters of the Popular Front for the Liberation of Palestine–Special Command (PFLP–SC) moved from Sidon, in South Lebanon, to Damascus, then to Baghdad, before finally winding up in South Yemen from the end of 1983. The PFLP–SC organized a number of attacks in the Middle East and in Europe, sometimes in liaison with European terrorist groups, such as the Basque group Homeland and Liberty (*Euskadi ta Askatasuna* [ETA]) and the Armenian Secret Army for the Liberation of Armenia (ASALA). The PFLP–SC ceased to exist at the end of 1989, most of its members rejoining the ranks of the Popular Front for the Liberation of Palestine–General Command (PFLP–GC).

> SEE ALSO Popular Front for the Liberation of Palestine–General Command; Popular Front for the Liberation of Palestine–Special Operations.

POPULAR FRONT FOR THE LIBERATION OF PALESTINE–SPECIAL OPERATIONS: Radical faction created in 1972 by Wadi Haddad, who split from the Popular Front for the Liberation of Palestine (PFLP) over the policies of George Habash, which he found too moderate. An organization with allegiance to Marxist-Leninism, backed by Iraq, the Popular Front for the Liberation of Palestine–Special Operations (PFLP–SO) cultivated ties with groups and movements that were ideologically close to it, such as the Japanese Red Army, and the German Baader-Meinhof group. The PFLP–SO became known for its participation in the hijacking of an Air France plane en route to Entebbe, Uganda, in 1976. In 1978, after the death of Haddad, the group was dissolved and its members scattered in three different movements: the 15 May Arab Organization, the Popular Front for the Liberation of Palestine–Special Command (PFLP–SC), and the Lebanese Armed Revolutionary Fraction (LARF).

> SEE ALSO Habash, George; Lebanese Armed Revolutionary Faction; Popular Front for the Liberation of Palestine; Popular Front for the Liberation of Palestine–Special Command.

POPULAR MOVEMENT OF ARAB LIBERATION: Palestinian movement founded at the end of 1973, following a split in al-Fatah caused by defeats in the Arab-Israel Wars of 1967 and 1973. Formed under the initiative of Naji ʿAllush, the Popular Movement of Arab Liberation (PMA), Marxist-Leninist in leaning, promoted the "unity of the Arab struggle for the defense of the Arab peoples, confronted by Zionism and capitalism." Opposing the policies of Yasir Arafat, the PMAL, at first allied with the Fatah Revolutionary Council of Abu Nidal, became completely autonomous in 1979, benefiting from the support of Syria, Libya, and Iraq. This movement, which has ceased all activity since 1991, was also known as the Arab Popular Liberation Front (APLF).

> SEE ALSO Arafat, Yasir; Nidal, Abu.

PORAT, HANAN (1943–): Israeli rabbi and politician. Hanan Porat was born in K'far Pines in Mandatory Palestine in 1943. Elected to the Knesset in 1981, he served until 1999 as a member of the National Religious Party and ha-Tehiyah. A proponent of the Greater Land of Israel, he became prominent in the settlement movement. Porat founded a yeshiva on the site of Rachel's Tomb in Bethlehem, which became the locus of clashes between Palestinians and the Israeli Defense Forces during the al-Aqsa Intifada beginning in October 2000.

> SEE ALSO Ha-Tehiyah; National Religious Party.

PORAZ, AVRAHAM (1945–): Israeli politician. Born in Romania in 1945, Avraham Poraz immigrated to Israel in 1950. He holds a law degree from the Hebrew University of Jerusalem. A member of the Knesset since 1988, Poraz has served on various committees, including Law and Justice, Ethics, and Finance. He is a member of the Shinui Party. In February 2003 Poraz was appointed minister of the interior.

PPP

> SEE Palestinian People's Party.

PPSF

> SEE Palestinian Popular Struggle Front.

PRCP

> SEE Palestinian Revolutionary Communist Party.

PRCS

> SEE Palestine Red Crescent Society.

PROCLAMATION OF THE STATE OF ISRAEL: Made on Friday, 14 May 1948, at 4 P.M., eight hours before the expiration of the British Mandate on Palestine, this proclamation marked the birth of the State of Israel. David Ben-Gurion, president of the Jewish Agency, read it before the members of the Jewish National Council, representing Palestinian Jewry (the "Yishuv") and world Zionism, meeting at the Tel Aviv Museum.

In part, the Proclamation declared: ". . . [W]e, members of the People's Council, representatives of the Jewish Community of Eretz-Israel and of the Zionist Movement, are here assembled on the day of the termination of the British Mandate over Eretz-Israel and, by virtue of our natural and historic right and on the strength of the resolution of the United Nations General Assembly, hereby declare the establishment of a Jewish state in Eretz-Israel, to be known as the State of Israel. We declare that, with effect from the moment of the termination of the Mandate being tonight, the eve of Sabbath, the 6th Iyar, 5708 (15th May 1948), until the establishment of the elected, regular authorities of the State in accordance with the Constitution which shall be adopted by the Elected Constituent Assembly not later than the 1st October 1948, the People's Council shall act as a Provisional Council of State, and its executive organ, the People's Administration, shall be the Provisional Government of the Jewish State, to be called 'Israel.' The State of Israel will be open for Jewish immigration and for the Ingathering of the Exiles; it will foster the development of the country for the benefit of all its inhabitants; it will be based on freedom, justice and peace as envisaged by the prophets of Israel; it will ensure complete equality of social and political rights to all its inhabitants irrespective of religion, race or sex; it will guarantee freedom of religion, conscience, language, education and culture; it will safeguard the Holy Places of all religions; and it will be faithful to the principles of the Charter of the United Nations. . . . We appeal—in the very midst of the onslaught launched against us now for months—to the Arab inhabitants of the State of Israel to preserve peace and participate in the upbuilding of the State on the basis of full and equal citizenship and due representation in all its provisional and permanent institutions. We extend our hand to all neighbouring states and their peoples in an offer of peace and good neighbourliness, and appeal to them to establish bonds of cooperation and mutual help with the sovereign Jewish people settled in its own land. The State of Israel is prepared to do its share in a common effort for the advancement of the entire Middle East. . . ."

SEE ALSO Ben-Gurion, David; British Mandate; Israel, State of.

PROCLAMATION OF THE STATE OF PALESTINE: Document, also known as the Algiers Declaration, proclaiming the existence of a sovereign state of Palestine "on our Palestinian territory," with Jerusalem as its capital. It was adopted on 15 November 1988 by the Palestine National Council (PNC), meeting in Algiers. The PNC also elected Yasir Arafat president of the embryonic state. These moves, made at Arafat's urging, were part of an ongoing strategy of Arafat's to gain enough international political leverage—specifically, American support—to bring about direct negotiations with Israel. The proclamation was an attempt to gain control of the first Intifada (1987–1993) in the occupied territories, then at its height. The PNC also voted to alter the Palestine National Charter, renouncing the use of terror and recognizing Resolutions 242 and 338 as a basis for an international peace conference. On 13 December 1988, Arafat gave a speech before the United Nations General Assembly, meeting in Geneva especially to hear him, in which he confirmed the Palestine Liberation Organization (PLO)'s recognition of Israel's right to exist and declared its renunciation of terrorism. These moves put the PLO in compliance with American conditions for discussions, and the United States was prompted to call for a "substantive dialogue" with the PLO.

SEE ALSO Arafat, Yasir; Intifada (1987–1993); Palestine National Charter; Palestine National Council.

PROGRESSIVE LIST FOR PEACE (ha-Reshimah ha-Mitkademet le-Shalom, in Hebrew): Israeli political bloc of the center-left, created in 1984 by some Jewish and Arab figures favorable to the creation of a Palestinian state. It advocated the right of self-determination for the two peoples. This party obtained a seat in the Knesset elections of 1988. Its influence waned with the departure of some of its members, principally Jews. In October 1993, while preparing for municipal elections, it formed a common list with HADASH and MAPAM. In the Knesset elections of May 1996, its principal leader, Mohammed Zaydan, was obliged to present his own list, which obtained no seats. The most prominent party members were Mohammed Zaydan, Said Azbarga, Ahmed Abu Freih, and Mohammed Miari.

SEE ALSO Democratic Front for Peace and Equality; Knesset; MAPAM.

PROGRESSIVE NATIONAL MOVEMENT

SEE Progressive List for Peace.

PROTESTANTS: Christians belonging to denominations that broke away from the Roman Catholic Church during the Reformation, or have been founded since that time, which deny the authority of the pope and view the Bible as the only source of revealed truth. Loosely, the term refers to any Christian not a member of the Roman Catholic or an Eastern church. Along with Catholicism and the Eastern Orthodox churches, Protestantism is one of the major branches of Christianity. There is, however, a wide range of beliefs and practices within Protestantism.

Protestant missionaries, based mainly in the United States and Britain, have been active in the Middle East since the nineteenth century, with the original goal of preaching the Gospel (the New Testament of the Bible) to Muslims. When Muslims proved unreceptive, these missionaries focused instead on indigenous Christian communities, which they considered unschooled in the Bible and in need of reform; as a result, Protestant congregations broke away from the Eastern Orthodox churches. Missionaries worked through benevolent service; they offered schools and medical care that were otherwise unavailable and had a major impact on increasing literacy. Among major Protestant establishments in Palestine were the American Colony and Schneller's Orphanage (both in Jerusalem) and the German Colony in Haifa and Jerusalem.

After World War I missions in the Middle East declined, in part because newly-independent states placed limits on them; and the percentage of Christians in the region, especially in Palestine, also declined during the last decades of the twentieth century. However, there has been a resurgence of enthusiasm for missionary work in recent years. The traditional Protestant denominations, employing new technologies such as the Internet and satellite television, have concentrated on alleviating human suffering and promoting social justice without proselytizing on behalf of a particular religious doctrine. U.S. conservative evangelic denominations, on the other hand, believe that salvation comes through Jesus Christ alone and feel a religious obligation to convert Muslims to that belief along with the provision of material aid. As a result, there have been Muslim attacks on missionaries, leading to objections from mainstream clergy who believe the evangelicals' actions not only are counterproductive, but endanger all Christians.

Another important aspect of the evangelicals' influence is their interpretation of the Bible, which they consider to be the literal Word of God, as sanctifying the expansion of Jewish settlement all over Palestine and beyond. This view is not shared by mainline Protestant denominations, which seek a peaceful resolution of the Israeli-Palestinian conflict satisfactory to all peoples of the region. The disagreement among Christians on this issue not only affects the relations between them in the Middle East, but has a significant impact on U.S. politics.

SEE ALSO Bible; Christianity; Eastern Orthodox Church; Roman Catholic Church.

PTF

SEE Peace Technology Fund.

PULSA DENURA: In Aramaic, "fire baton." Ceremony practiced by certain extremist rabbis, chanted in Aramaic and meant to fatally hex a person. It was originally performed by initiated kabbalists and thought to be effective only when at least ten pious Jews participated in it after a fast of three days. This ceremony was carried out on 2 October 1995, conducted by Rabbi Yossef Dayan, with twenty or so members of the Kach extremist party near the domicile of Prime Minister Yitzhak Rabin, whose death they desired. On 4 November, the latter was assassinated by Yigal Amir, an extremist Jew close to Kach who may have been aware of the ceremony, or at least of reports of it that appeared prior to the assassination.

On 14 September 2004, Rabbi Dayan declared on Israeli television that he would be prepared to carry out the ceremony again, to put a curse on Prime Minister Ariel Sharon, if the Gaza disengagement plan was not called off. Officials initiated an investigation of him on suspicion of incitement to murder.

SEE ALSO Amir, Yigal; Devekut; Eyal; Kach Party; Rabin, Yitzhak.

PUNDAK, RON (1955–): Born in Tel Aviv, Israel, in 1955, Ron Pundak holds a Ph.D. in Middle Eastern political history from the University of London. Dr. Pundak played a major role in creating the secret track of unofficial Israeli-Arab negotiations in Oslo in 1993, alongside Dr. Yair Hirschfeld and their Palestinian counterparts. He served as a member of the official Israeli negotiating team—guided by Shimon Peres and Yossi Beilin, and later by Yitzhak Rabin—until the signing of the Oslo Accords in September 1993. From 1995 to 2001 he served as executive director of the Economic Cooperation Foundation, a nonprofit, nongovernmental organization in Tel Aviv dedicated to building, maintaining, and supporting Israeli-Palestinian and Israeli-Arab cooperation in the political, economic, and civil-society arenas. Since July 2001 he has served as the director general of the Peres Center for Peace.

QADDUMI, FARUQ (Abu Lutf): Palestinian political figure, born in August 1931 at Kufr Qaddum, near Nablus; grew up in Haifa but returned to Nablus as a refugee in 1948. Faruq Qaddumi joined the Baʿth Party in 1949. He worked for the American oil company Aramco in Saudi Arabia, from 1952 to 1954, when he left to attend the American University of Cairo, from which he graduated in 1958 with degrees in economics and political science. In Cairo he belonged to the General Union of Palestine Students (GUPS). In 1959, with Yasir Arafat and Salah Khalaf, Qaddumi helped found the Palestinian Fatah movement. Between 1960 and 1966, while working at the Kuwaiti ministry of health, he was very active in furthering the Palestinian cause. Expelled from Kuwait, he went to Damascus, then to Cairo, finally settling in Amman.

During this period, Qaddumi and Salah Khalaf became friends of Gamal Abdel Nasser. In April, 1966, Qaddumi became Secretary General of Fatah. In 1969, Qaddumi was elected to the Executive Committee of the Palestine Liberation Organization (PLO), in charge of popular organizations. In May 1973, he was named head of the political department of the PLO, replacing Muhammad al-Najjar, who was assassinated in Lebanon by an Israeli commando. Combining the offices of head of Palestinian diplomacy and Secretary General of Fatah, he succeeded in obtaining the recognition of the PLO by the United Nations. Because of his connections with socialist countries, he was able to have PLO offices opened in numerous countries of Eastern Europe and Africa.

The Lebanese crisis became an occasion for him to demonstrate his talents at negotiation and diplomacy. While continuing to be vital in the political department of the PLO, Qaddumi maintained a great deal of influence in Fatah, of which he was one of the main leaders. In August 1989, at the fifth congress of Fatah, he consolidated his position near the top of the movement. He advocated maintaining the Fatah's role in revolutionary movement, while affirming the need for the PLO to have a central political role. On 1 June 1992, Yasir Arafat, hospitalized in Amman following a plane crash in Libya, designated Qaddumi as a member of the triumvirate, along with Mahmud Rida Abbas (Abu Mazen) and Khalid al-Hasan, in charge of the PLO in the interim. On 20 August 1993, when the coming accord with Israel was announced, he publicly expressed his reservations about its wisdom. As a result, on 13 September 1993, Qaddumi did not participate in the Washington ceremony, although it would have been expected that, as "foreign minister" of the PLO, he would have been the one to initial the accord, not Mahmud Abbas. In spite of his reservations about the Oslo accord, Faruq Qaddumi continued to participate in international negotiations, but when the Palestinian National Authority (PNA) was being set up in the Occupied Territories, he refused to go there, staying on as PLO foreign minister in Tunis. He was appointed director of the Palestinian Economic Council for Development and Reconstruction (PECDAR) but did not actively participate. Qaddumi remains head of the PLO political department and remains headquartered in Tunis.

> SEE ALSO Abbas, Mahmud Rida; Arafat, Yasir; Ba'th; General Union of Palestine Students; Hasan, Khalid al-; Khalaf, Salah; Nablus; Nasser, Gamal Abdel; Occupied Territories; Palestine Liberation Organization, Palestinian Economic Council for Development and Reconstruction.

QADI: ("judge," in Arabic.) In Islam, an educated shaykh responsible for deciding issues of Islamic law. In a civil context, a judge.

QA'IDA, AL-

> SEE International Islamic Front.

QANA 1996

> SEE Grapes of Wrath Operation.

QASM

> SEE Qassam.

QASSAM: Acronym for the Arab words *Quwat al-islamiya al-mujahida* (Islamic combatant force), designating the armed branch of an Islamic movement. Qassam is also the name given to a small, crude missile or artillery rocket with a range of about eight kilometers (five miles) developed by Hamas in the Gaza Strip.

> SEE ALSO Gaza Strip.

QASSAM, IZZ AL-DIN AL-: Syrian-Palestinian resistance fighter (1881–1935). Born in Jabla, Syria, and given a religious education in Latakia and at al-Azhar University in Cairo, Izz al-Din al-Qassam became a preacher in Syria. After 1920, he spoke out against French rule under the post-World War I Mandate, and was active in anti-French political resistance. Sentenced to death in the mid-1920s, he fled to Haifa, where he preached against the British and the Zionists. He founded, at the end of the 1920s, an activist group called the Black Hand, for the purpose of undertaking armed actions against Zionist colonists. In October 1935, he took to the countryside in the mountains near Jenin, at the head of a group of several hundred partisans. On 19 November, tracked

by British forces, Qassam was killed in battle in Ya'bad, becoming the first martyr of the Palestinian resistance. Almost sixty years later, both HAMAS and Palestinian Islamic Jihad named the armed branches of their movements, responsible for many attacks against Israel, after him.

> SEE ALSO Azhar, al-; HAMAS; Palestinian Islamic Jihad.

QASSAM IZZEDINE AL-

> SEE Qassam, Izz al-Din al-.

QIRYAT ARBA

> SEE Kiryat Arba.

QUDS, AL-: Arabic name (meaning "the holiness") of Jerusalem.

QUDS, AL- (Jerusalem): An independent daily, considered the most important of all local Palestinian newspapers, founded in 1951.

QUDS AL-SHARIF, AL-: Arab term designating the city of Jerusalem.

> SEE ALSO Jerusalem.

QUDS BRIGADE, AL-: An Iranian Islamic commando operating mainly in Lebanon. Affiliated with the *Pasdaran* (Revolutionary Guards) and supervised by the Iranian Special Services, it operates exclusively outside of Iranian territory.

QUDS COMMITTEE, AL-

> SEE Organization of the Islamic Conference.

QUDS FUND, AL-: Specialized institution of the Organization of the Islamic Conference, responsible for participating in the financing and upkeep of Muslim holy sites in Jerusalem. The Fund, created by the Jerusalem Committee, during the committee's fifteenth session held in January 1995 in Ifrane (central Morocco), seeks to raise funds to save the sites in the occupied side of Jerusalem, defend the Palestinians' rights over the city, support their resistance, and safeguard the city's history as well as its religious, cultural, and architectural heritage.

> SEE ALSO Organization of the Islamic Conference.

QUDS UNIVERSITY, AL-: Palestinian university with four campuses in East Jerusalem and nearby areas, created in 1984 from the confederation of four smaller institutions that had been founded in the 1970s. The university was fully unified into a single institutional structure in 1994. It now has ten faculties, including arts, science, medicine, health sciences, and law, with over 6,000 undergraduate and graduate students and a faculty and staff of more than 700. One campus, containing the main administrative offices, is in East Jerusalem, just outside the Old City; the largest campus is in Abu Dis, just beyond the city boundary. Other locations are in Ramallah and al-Bireh. The university's board of trustees includes internationally known academics, and its president since 1995 has been Sari Nusabaya, a well-known peace activist. It conducts numerous joint research projects with Israeli institutions, including the Hebrew University and Tel Aviv University, as well as with foreign universities.

Classes and attendance at al-Quds have been seriously affected by the difficulties placed in the way of Palestinian movement around the West Bank and into East Jerusalem: internal borders, checkpoints, closures, and curfews. Unlike Bir Zeit University, al-Quds has not been known for political activism, but it has been the target of Israeli harassment, particularly since Nusabaya became associated with it. In July 2002 Israeli police raided its administrative offices in East Jerusalem and carried away all files and computers, sealing the premises for several weeks. Earlier they had entered a university facility in Ramallah, smashed $200,000 worth of donated video equipment and vandalized the building. In September 2003 Israel announced that it was seizing a third of the Abu Dis campus to build a portion of its separation wall, which will cut off the town of Abu Dis from Jerusalem.

SEE ALSO Abu Dis; Bir Zeit University; Nusabaya, Sari; West Bank.

QUMRAN

SEE Dead Sea Scrolls.

QURAI, AHMAD SULAYMAN (Abu Ala): Palestinian political figure, born in 1937 at Abu Dis, in the suburbs of Jerusalem. An economist by education, at the time of the 1967 War, Ahmad Qurai was working for the Arab Bank in Saudi Arabia. The following year he joined Yasir Arafat's al-Fatah. In 1970 he was chosen to organize the Palestinian Martyrs' Works Society (SAMED), a set of business enterprises run from Beirut by the Palestine Liberation Organization (PLO) for the economic support of the Palestinian community in exile. It operated in most Palestinian communities in the Middle East outside the occupied territories and has been dormant since the founding of the Palestinian Authority (Qurai is still its head).

In August, 1987, Qurai was elected to the Central Committee of Fatah, and the following year he was chosen to be general director of the economics department of the PLO. In the framework of the Madrid peace process, launched in 1991, he participated in multilateral negotiations. With Mahmud Rida Abbas (Abu Mazen), he participated in secret negotiations with the Israelis, which resulted in the Oslo Accords of 1993. In February 1996, he was elected president of the new Palestinian Legislative Council (PLC), of the Palestinian Authority parliament. While carrying on his duties as the president of the Legislative Council, Ahmad Qurai also participated in the principal Israeli-Palestinian peace negotiations. On 5 September 2000, along with his counterpart in Israel, Knesset president Avraham Burg, he was invited to speak before the European Parliament on the subject of the Israeli-Palestinian peace process.

Between September and December 2001, while the al-Aqsa Intifada was continuing in the Palestinian territories, Qurai met several times with the Israeli Foreign Minister, Shimon Peres and European envoys Miguel Moratinos and Javier Solana, in an attempt to restart negotiations. On 23 January 2002, when the Intifada and Israeli reprisals were intensifying, Qurai went to Paris to participate in a colloquium organized by the French National Assembly, in which Burg and Moratinos also participated. During this meeting Qurai invited Burg to speak before the PLC, and Burg agreed. In a speech commenting on the seriousness of the situation in the Palestinian territories, Qurai appealed to the international community—and to the European Union in particular—to become more involved in the process. On the fringes of this meeting, Qurai met also with Peres, with whom he discussed various ways of restarting Israeli-Palestinian negotiations. In September 2003, Qurai was appointed prime minister in Arafat's Palestinian Authority government, replacing Mahmud Abbas. In mid-July 2004, as frustration grew not only with the Israeli occupation, but with the corruption and inaction of the Palestinian Authority and the PLO's old-guard leadership, and conditions in the Gaza Strip verged on chaos, Qurai offered his resignation, which Arafat refused. Qurai withdrew his resignation about a week later. Qurai, as prime minister of the PNA, is a possible successor to Arafat, but has been considered to be ineffective and corrupt, and does not command the level of support that would see

QUR'AN. THESE PAGES ARE FROM THE HOLY BOOK OF THE MUSLIMS, WHICH THEY BELIEVE TO BE THE WORD OF GOD, GIVEN TO THE PROPHET MUHAMMAD IN REVELATIONS THAT WERE COLLECTED IN THE MID-SEVENTH CENTURY, NOT LONG AFTER HIS DEATH. THE QUR'AN COMPRISES NEARLY 6,250 VERSES IN 114 CHAPTERS. (© *The Art Archive/Private Collection/Eileen Tweedy*)

him through the expected political struggle that would likely follow Arafat's demise.

SEE ALSO Abbas, Mahmud Rida; Aqsa Intifada, al-; Arafat, Yasir; Burg, Avraham; Fatah, al-; Oslo Accords; Palestine Liberation Organization; Palestinian Authority; Palestinian Legislative Council; Peres, Shimon.

QUR'AN: Sacred book of the Muslims (from the Arabic word meaning "recitation"), containing the revelations the Prophet Muhammad received from God over the period from 610 to 632 C.E., largely via the angel Jibra'il (or *Jibril*; Gabriel, in Arabic), first at Mecca, then at Medina. Muslims consider the Qur'an the word of God, from the heavenly Book, which was also the source of the Jewish and Christian scriptures. The written verses of revelation did not become one book until the reign of the Caliph Uthman (r. 644–652), some fifteen years after the death of Muhammad. At that time the writings of the prophet, which had been collected by his secretary, Zayd ibn Thâbit, started attracting a lot of attention. The Qur'an is comprised of 114 chapters (*suras*) in 30 equal sections (*juz'*), totaling nearly 6,250 verses (*ayat*). The Qur'an and Hadith (collection of authoritative traditions, based on what Muhammad did and said as a ruler) together form the Shari'a, the Islamic law and basis of all Muslim teaching. According to canonical norms, the Qur'an cannot be translated; to be understood, it must be read in Arabic. There are four Arabic designations for the Qur'an: *al-qur'an* (recited proclamation), *al-furqân* (discernment of true and false), *al-kitab* (the written book), and *al-dhikr* (recollection). The Qur'an presents many points of convergence, from both doctrinal and literary perspectives, with the Bible.

SEE ALSO Mecca; Muhammad.

R

RABBI: Title derived from Aramaic *rabban* (Hebrew *rav,*) which means "master," given by Jews to scholars familiar with sacred Jewish texts. In modern times there are two general categories of rabbis: those who are primarily teachers and scholars or serve on religious courts, and those who minister in synagogues and in the community, officiating at religious rituals, weddings, and funerals. Traditionally the title has been given only to men, but in recent times non-Orthodox Jews have begun to ordain women. Different Jewish denominations have different criteria for determining who is entitled to be called a rabbi; in the United States at present, there are four types: Reform; Reconstructionist, Conservative, and Orthodox. Only Orthodox rabbis are officially recognized in Israel, although those of other denominations exist there.

In modern Israel, despite an ostensible commitment to religious freedom, halakhah (Jewish religious law) governs in all matters related to the personal status of citizens, and Orthodox rabbinical interpretation of that law is dominant. Only Orthodox rabbis have the legal authority to perform marriages, divorces, and conversions and thus to determine who is entitled to immigrate (although marriages and conversions performed by other rabbis *outside* Israel are recognized by the state). Many Israeli rabbis are officials of the state ministry of religion and the office of the chief rabbinate, which is divided into Ashkenazic and Sephardic wings.

Though there are other rabbis in Israel, particularly within Hasidic and yeshiva circles, their authority is not official. During the last few decades, the official rabbis have steadily lost moral authority; secular Jews consider them irrelevant, while a small minority of ultra-Orthodox Jews, as well as a growing number of Reform (progressive) and Conservative (Masorti) Jews, look to their own rabbis for guidance.

SEE ALSO Ashkenazi; Bible; Halakhah; Haredi; Hasidism; Masorti; Orthodox Judaism; Reform Jew; Sephardim; Yeshiva.

RABBO

SEE Abd Rabbo, Yasir.

RABIN, YITZHAK (1922–1995): Israeli military and political figure, prime minister of Israel 1974–1977 and 1992–1995. Born in 1922 in Jerusalem, he studied at an agricultural school and became active in the Ahdut ha-Avodah movement in Galilee. In 1940 he joined the Haganah's commando unit, the Palmah, and became its chief operations officer in 1947. During the Israeli war of independence (1948), he directed the defense of Jerusalem and fought the Egyptians in the Negev. After the war he studied at the British army staff college, graduating in 1953, and became chief of staff of the Israeli Defense Force (IDF) in 1964. Under his command the IDF won an over-

YITZHAK RABIN. THE FORMER MILITARY LEADER WAS PRIME MINISTER OF ISRAEL FOR TWO TERMS, STARTING IN 1974 AND THEN IN 1989. RABIN TOOK NOTABLE STRIDES TOWARD PEACE WITH OTHER MIDDLE EASTERN COUNTRIES AND WITH PALESTINIANS. HE WAS AWARDED THE NOBEL PEACE PRIZE IN 1994 BUT ASSASSINATED A YEAR LATER BY YIGAL AMIR, A YOUNG ISRAELI EXTREMIST OPPOSED TO THE PEACE PROCESS. *(© Photograph by Ya'acov Sa'ar. Government Press Office [GPO] of Israel)*

whelming victory during the Six Day War of 1967, and he became a national hero.

In 1968 Rabin retired from the IDF and was appointed Israel's ambassador to the United States, a position he held until March 1973. This diplomatic experience led him to pursue a second career in politics; later in 1973 he was elected to the Knesset as a member of the Labor Party. He was minister of labor in the cabinet of Golda Meir, and after her resignation as prime minister, Rabin was chosen to succeed her. In June 1994 he became the first *sabra* (native-born) prime minister of Israel.

Early in his term, Rabin worked closely with U.S. Secretary of State Henry Kissinger, who helped Israel to reach disengagement agreements with Egypt and Syria. In July 1976 he ordered a bold raid to rescue hostages held by a Palestinian terrorist group on a hi-

jacked plane at Entebbe. However, the popularity of the Labor Party declined, in part because Rabin refused to meet National Religious Party (NRP) demands for greater control over the government by Orthodox Judaism. He was eventually forced to call for elections; but before they occurred, on 8 April 1977, he resigned as prime minister when the press revealed that his wife, Leah, had an illegal bank account in the United States. He thereupon lost the leadership of the Labor Party to Shimon Peres; however, he continued to hold a seat in the Knesset.

From 1984 to 1990 Rabin served as minister of defense in the two Likud-Labor coalition governments of that period, responding forcefully to the first intifada while proclaiming that there was no "military solution" to the Palestinian uprising. In 1985 he initiated the withdrawal of the IDF from most of Lebanon. In March 1990, the Labor Party having decided to quit the coalition, he resigned his position as defense minister. In 1992 he again became head of the Labor Party, which won the June Knesset elections, and on 13 July, for the second time, he became prime minister.

Three days later, Rabin announced the end of public subsidies for Jewish settlements in the occupied territories. Persuaded by his foreign minister, Shimon Peres, he gave the go-ahead to secret negotiations in Oslo, Norway, with the leadership of the Palestine Liberation Organization (PLO); and in September 1993, in Washington, he signed the Israeli-Palestinian Declaration of Principles (the Oslo Accords), which called for mutual recognition between Israel and the Palestinians and self-rule in Gaza and Jericho. In October 1994 he signed a full peace treaty with Jordan. For his role in the Oslo Accords, Rabin, together with Shimon Peres and Yasir Arafat, was awarded the 1994 Nobel Peace.

But Yitzhak Rabin's commitment to peace with the Palestinians, and the return of settled territories to them as its consequence, had earned him the hatred of Israeli extremists. On 4 November 1995, at the end of a peace rally in Tel Aviv, he was assassinated by a Jewish right-wing activist.

SEE ALSO Ahdut ha-Avodah; Entebbe; Haganah; Israel Labor Party; Intifada; Oslo Accords; Palmah.

RABIN-PELOSOFF, DALIA (1950–): Daughter of the former prime minister, Yitzhak Rabin, born in 1950. A lawyer by training, Dalia Rabin-Pelosoff performed her military service in an elite unit of the IDF. In March, 1999, she joined the ranks of the Center Party, created by Yitzhak Mordechai, former defense minister, who had resigned from the government of Benjamin Netanyahu, then head of Likud. As a result of the Knesset elections of the following May, which saw the victory of the Laborite, Ehud Barak, she was elected M.K.. A few weeks later, she became deputy speaker of the Knesset. At the beginning of 2001, Rabin-Pelosoff resigned from the Center Party, to create her own group, the New Way. On the following 7 March, she became deputy defense minister in the government of the leader of Likud, Ariel Sharon. This was the first time a woman had occupied this post.

SEE ALSO Barak, Ehud; Center Party; Knesset; Likud; Mordechai, Yitzhak; Netanyahu, Benjamin; Rabin, Yitzhak; Sharon, Ariel.

RAF: RED ARMY FACTION.

SEE Japanese Red Army.

RAFI PARTY (*Reshimat Po'alei Yisrael*): Israeli socialist party, created in 1965 by David Ben-Gurion, Moshe Dayan, and Shimon Peres, following a split in MAPAI. One of the sources of the rift was the Lavon Affair, a dispute over a 1954 espionage operation. The defectors also accused MAPAI of inflexibility and a failure to provide opportunities for younger leaders. In 1968, this group merged with MAPAI and the Ahdut ha-Avodah to create the Israel Labor Party (ILP).

SEE ALSO Ahdut ha-Avodah; Ben-Gurion, David; Dayan, Moshe; Israel Labor Party; Lavon Affair; MAPAI; Peres, Shimon.

RAJUB, JIBRIL (Abu Rami): Palestinian political figure, born in 1953 in Dura in the West Bank. In 1968, Jibril Rajub was arrested by the Israeli police and sentenced to life in prison for throwing a hand grenade at an Israeli army vehicle. In prison he learned Hebrew and English. In May 1985 he was released as part of a prisoner exchange and worked as a journalist for the magazine *Abir*. In January 1988, during the first Intifada, he was expelled to Lebanon, and from there he joined the leadership of the Palestine Liberation Organization (PLO) in Tunis.

Rajub became part of the Palestinian Security Services, functioning as an advisor to Khalil al-Wazir and liaison with some Intifada leaders in the Palestinian territories; after Wazir's assassination in April 1988, he became close to Yasir Arafat. At the end of December 1993, as part of the application of the Israeli-Palestinian Oslo Accords, he and Muhammad Dahlan went to Rome to meet with the Israeli general

Amnon Shahak to coordinate Israeli and Palestinian security activities. In May 1994, as part of the establishment of the Palestinian Authority, he was named director of the Palestinian Preventive Security Force for the West Bank, which was set up by the American Central Intelligence Agency (CIA). Rajub's position made him one of Israel's and the United States' main Palestinian interlocutors in the 1990s. He developed an independent power base in the West Bank in alliance with younger leaders of al-Fatah, including Marwan Barghuthi and Saib Erekat.

In 1997 rumors circulated about his taking control of the West Bank if Arafat's health failed, about his possible succession as head of the PLO, and even about a coup against Arafat. In late 1997 Rajub was suspended from the al-Fatah central committee for several months. He worked extensively with the Shin Bet and the CIA to prevent Palestinian attacks on Israel. In May 2001, eight months after the beginning of the al-Aqsa Intifada, he was wounded in an Israeli military attack on his home. In early 2002, Rajub fell out of favor with Arafat, who reportedly accused him of being an Israeli and American spy. In April 2002 the Israelis attacked his headquarters. Rajub escaped after turning over fifty Palestinian Islamists to the Israelis in a deal mediated by the CIA, for which he was widely condemned. In May when the Americans told Arafat he should reform his various security services with Rajub in charge, Arafat dismissed him, naming him governor of Jenin. In August 2003 Arafat named him head of his newly created National Security Council, supervising the chiefs of all Palestinian Security Services. In this post he was an effective opponent of the new prime minister, Mahmud Rida Abbas, who was appointed under American and Israeli pressure. Rajub remains committed to a two-state solution and was a member of the delegation that negotiated the Geneva Peace Initiative of 2003. Rajub is considered a possible successor to Arafat, though he would be opposed by Abbas and his ally, former interior minister Dahlan, among others. He is believed to have betrayed Barghuthi to the Israeli authorities and would not be acceptable to HAMAS, which, although opposed to the PLO, has refrained from attacking it as long as Arafat remained.

SEE ALSO Abbas, Mahmud Rida; Aqsa Intifada, al-; Arafat, Yasir; Barghuthi, Marwan; Dahlan, Muhammad; Fatah, al-; Geneva Peace Initiative of 2003; Intifada; Palestinian Security Services; Shin Bet; Wazir, Khalil al-; West Bank.

RAMADAN EVENING MEAL. A PALESTINIAN WOMAN AND HER CHILDREN IN THE OLD CITY OF JERUSALEM PREPARE THE EVENING MEAL DURING THE HOLY MONTH OF FASTING. ONE OF THE FIVE PILLARS OF ISLAM, FASTING IS BELIEVED TO FOSTER PIETY, AND ADULT MUSLIMS MUST ABSTAIN FROM FOOD OR DRINK BETWEEN SUNRISE AND SUNSET DURING RAMADAN. *(© Annie Griffiths Belt/Corbis)*

RAKAH (New Communist List): (*Reshimah Kommunistit Hadashah* in Hebrew): Israeli Arab communist party, formed in 1964 as an alternative to the overwhelmingly Jewish MAKI, which split over the issue of Arab nationalism. In the 1973 election the two communist parties, RAKAH and MAKI, ran together as Moked; but since then only RAKAH has borne the name "communist."

SEE ALSO Israel Communist Party; Moked.

RAK KACH ("only thus!"): Slogan/motto of the Irgun.

SEE ALSO Irgun.

RAMADAN (ramadhan): Ninth month of the Islamic calendar, lasting twenty-nine or thirty days. Ramadan is a month of fasting, which is one of the five obligations of Islam, and so between sunrise and sunset the believer abstains from smoking; partaking of food or drink; telling lies, gossiping and engaging in other unethical behavior; and engaging in sex. At sunset everyone breaks the fast, usually in a large meal with family and friends (*iftar*). The end of the month of Ramadan is celebrated with a feast, the *'Id al-Fitr*. Between the 27 and 28 Ramadan falls the Night of Destiny (*lailat al-qadr*), when according to a widespread belief everyone's fate is decided. For some this date marks the first revelation of the Qur'an to Muhammad.

SEE ALSO Hijra; 'Id al-Fitr; Islamic Calendar; Muhammad; Qur'an.

RAMATKAL: Hebrew word meaning the chief of staff of the Israeli army.

RAMÍREZ, ILYICH SÁNCHEZ (Carlos the Jackal; 1949–): Terrorist, born in Caracas, Venezuala, to a Communist lawyer who named his three sons Vladimir, Ilyich, and Lenin. After failing to obtain entrance to the Sorbonne, he was sent to Patrice Lumumba University in Moscow in 1967, where he became friendly with members of the Popular Front for the Liberation of Palestine (PFLP). In the spring of 1970 he left Moscow for Lebanon and then for a PFLP camp in Jordan. Between 1973 and 1984 he participated in many attacks in Europe, with a high cost in human lives (over 1,500 according to his own claims). On 30 December 1973 he committed his first assassination attempt, a failed one, against the owner of the British Marks and Spencer retail chain. On 15 September 1974 he threw a grenade into a Paris drugstore, causing two deaths and leaving thirty-four wounded. In early 1975 he participated in two attacks on Israeli airliners at Orly Airport. On 27 June 1975 he killed two French internal security officers (they were about to arrest him) as well as Michel Mukharbal, his Lebanese PFLP contact in France, who had betrayed him under interrogation.

On 21 December 1976 he participated in the kidnapping of eleven Organization of Petroleum Exporting Countries oil ministers (and fifty other people) to Algiers from their meeting in Vienna. The hostages were eventually released and Carlos had to answer to the PFLP for not killing the Saudi and Iranian oil ministers as he had been assigned to do. He was also suspected of having embezzled some of the ransom money and was expelled from the PFLP. After being arrested in Yugoslavia and expelled to Baghdad, he went to live in Aden, where he founded his own terrorist group, the Organization of Arab Armed Struggle, with some Arab and German terrorists. He established contacts with the East German and Romanian secret police and was hired by the Romanians to assassinate Romanian dissidents in France. In early 1982 the group attempted an attack on a French nuclear power plant.

After his then-wife, Magdalena Kopp, was arrested by the French police in February 1982, he mounted several attacks in France and Germany that were meant to persuade the French authorities to free her, including bombing a train on 29 March 1982 (5 dead, 27 wounded), an attack in Paris on 22 April (1 dead, 63 wounded), and twin attacks against the Paris-Marseille train and the Marseille railroad station on 31 December 1983 (5 dead, 50 wounded). Kopp was released in 1985 and joined Carlos in Damascus, and from there they went to Budapest. Expelled from Hungary later that year, they were denied refuge in Iraq, Libya, and Cuba but were allowed to stay in Damascus.

During this period Carlos's notoriety was such that terrorist incidents were frequently blamed on him if they could not otherwise be attributed (he was said to be a master of disguise); this was partly the result of his own boasting, which included taking credit for terrorist acts that he had had nothing to do with. The Syrians curtailed his activities until 1991, and he lived disguised as a Mexican businessman. He and Kopp had a daughter, and he was reportedly drunk most of the time. In 1991 the Syrians, newly allied with the United States over the Gulf War of 1991, expelled him; he was again denied refuge in several countries, finally entering Jordan with Syrian help; eventually he settled in Sudan during the summer of 1993.

On 14 August 1994, under pressure from the United States and France, the Sudanese police arrested him in Khartoum and handed him over to French authorities. In December 1997 he was convicted of the 1975 murder of the two French security officers and the Lebanese informer and sentenced to life imprisonment. In 2001 he married one of his French lawyers, and in 2003, a Muslim convert, he published a book in defense of terrorism, *Revolutionary Islam*. In 2004 his French wife published an unapologetic memoir about their relationship.

SEE ALSO Gulf War (1991); Organization of Petroleum Exporting Countries; Popular Front for the Liberation of Palestine.

RAMON, HAIM (1950–): Israeli politician, born in Jaffa. Haim Ramon was active in the Labor Party's Young Guard. A lawyer, he was elected to the Knesset in 1983, where he served on various committees, including law and justice, finance, and the house committee. He was chairman of the Labor faction of the Knesset from 1988 to 1992. Ramon was appointed minister of health in 1992 and served in that post until 1994. In July 1995 he was elected chairman of the Histradut; he left that position in November 1995, when he was appointed minister of the interior, a post he held until June 1996. From 1996 to 1999 he served as a member of the Knesset foreign affairs and defense committee. In July 1999 he was appointed minister without portfolio, with responsibility for Jerusalem, government reform, and liaison between the prime minister's office and the Knesset. He served as minister of the interior from August 2000 to March 2001.

SEE ALSO Israel Labor Party; Knesset.

RANTISI, ABD AL-AZIZ (1948–2004): Palestinian Islamist, born near Jaffa, in Palestine. In 1948, at the time of the first Israeli-Arab conflict, Abdul Aziz Rantisi and his family became refugees in the Khan

Yunis camp, in the Gaza Strip. After studying in Alexandria, Egypt, where he frequented the Muslim Brotherhood, he became a pediatrician and also started to teach religion at the Islamic University of Gaza. In 1973, with Shaykh Ahmad Yasin, Mahmud al-Azhar, and Ibrahim al-Yazuri, he participated in the creation of the Islamic Collective (al-Majmaʿ al-Islami), a charity helping the disadvantaged, supported by the Muslim Brotherhood.

In October 1987 the Israeli authorities banned him from working in hospitals because he refused to pay taxes to the "Israeli occupier." On 14 December, with Shaykh Yasin, Abdallah Darwish, Salah Shahada, and Ahmad Shamah, he participated in founding HAMAS. Between 1988 and 1990 he was imprisoned a number of times by the Israeli authorities, and in 1992 he was among the 417 Islamists banished to South Lebanon by Israel. During his expulsion, he was the spokesperson for those among the banished who belonged to HAMAS. On 15 December 1993, along with some hundred others, he was allowed to return to Israel, where as soon as he arrived he was again arrested. Freed on 21 April 1997, he returned to the political arena. On 9 April 1998 he was arrested by the Palestinian police for having accused the Palestinian Authority (PA) of being responsible for the death of Muhyaddin al-Sharif, a member of the armed branch of HAMAS. He was held until February 2000 without trial for the same killing. He was again arrested by the PA in July 2000 and held until December after having accused the leadership of treason for participating in that year's Camp David talks.

Over the next year he was arrested and released several times as the Palestinian authorities responded to Israeli demands that measures be taken against the Islamist movement. After December 2001, while the al-Aqsa Intifada was raging, he was frequently under house arrest. In 2003 he survived an Israeli attempt to assassinate him using helicopter-fired missiles. On 22 March 2004, following the Israeli assassination (by missile) of Shaykh Yasin, he became the head of HAMAS. On 17 April, in Gaza, Rantisi was assassinated the same way.

SEE ALSO Aqsa Intifada, al-; Arab-Israel War (1948); Camp David Accords; Camp David II Summit; Gaza Strip; HAMAS; Muslim Brotherhood; Palestinian Authority; Yasin, Ahmad Ismaʿil.

RASHIDUN, AL- ("the rightly guided," in Arabic): In Sunni Islam, the phrase "rightly guided caliphs" (al-khulafaʾ al-rashidun) designates the four successors of the prophet Muhammad: Abu Bakr, Umar (Omar), Uthman (Othman), and Ali.

SEE ALSO Muhammad.

RASUL: Arabic word meaning "messenger" in the sense of one receiving a divine message. For Muslims, the prophet Muhammad was such a *rasul*.

SEE ALSO Muhammad.

RATZ

SEE Movement for Civil Rights and Peace.

RAWABDEH, ABD AL-RAʾUF AL- (1939–): Jordanian political figure, born in Irbid. He received a bachelor of science in pharmacology from the American University of Beirut in 1962 and studied law at the University of Jordan from 1982 to 1983. Rawabdeh joined the Jordanian health ministry in 1962, becoming director of its pharmaceutical and supply department in 1968. In 1976, after having briefly served as administrative director of Yarmuk University, he was named communications minister, and two years later health minister, a post he filled for one year. From 1983 to 1989 he was the appointed mayor of the Jordanian capital, Amman. Between 1982 and 1985 he was on the governing board of the Jordanian Phosphate Mines Company. In 1989 he was appointed a parliamentary deputy and became minister of public works and habitat in the government of Tahir al-Masri. In February 1993 he created the Awakening (al-Yaqatha) Party, a center-right party, of which he was the secretary general. The following year he was elected deputy. In June 1994 he was named education minister in the government of Abd al-Salam Majali. He supported the 1994 peace treaty with Israel. Between 1995 and 1996 he was vice prime minister and minister of education. The following year he entered his party into a multiparty coalition, the National Constitutional Party, becoming deputy secretary general and head of its political section.

On 1 March 1999, following the accession of King Abdullah II to the Jordanian throne, he became prime minister and defense minister, replacing Fayiz al-Tarawneh. On 15 January 2000 he initiated a cabinet reshuffle, making the journalist Salih Qallab information minister. On the following 28 March he announced the creation of a royal commission for human rights, decided on by Abdullah II. Because the cabinet moved slowly in implementing the economic reforms requested by the king, on 18 June Rawabdeh resigned and was replaced by Ali Abu al-Raghib. In 2001 Rawabdeh was reelected to parliament. Having pulled his party out of the National Constitutional bloc, he once again represented the Yaqatha.

SEE ALSO Abdullah II ibn Hussein; Abu al-Raghib, Ali; Majali, Abd al-Salam; Tarawneh, Fayiz al-.

REAGAN PLAN: Peace plan presented on 1 September 1982 by U.S. President Ronald Reagan after the Israeli invasion of Lebanon and the subsequent expulsion of the Palestine Liberation Organization (PLO) following U.S. mediation. This plan provided for the creation of an autonomous Palestinian authority in the occupied territories, to be associated with Jordan.

The basic elements of the Reagan Plan included free elections of an autonomous Palestinian authority in the occupied territories; peaceful and orderly transfer of power from the Israeli government to the Palestinian inhabitants of the West Bank and Gaza over a period of five years, the final status of these territories to be a fully autonomous association with Jordan; an immediate freeze on the creation of new Israeli settlements in the West Bank and Gaza; negotiations on Jerusalem, which must remain undivided; and recognition by the Palestinians of the "right of Israel to a secure future," and by the Arab states of the reality of Israel. Also, President Reagan gave notice that the United States would support neither the creation of a Palestinian state in the West Bank and Gaza, nor the permanent annexation of these territories by Israel.

Israeli prime minister Menachem Begin rejected the plan and reiterated Israel's claim to the West Bank, while the Arab leaders showed little enthusiasm for it. Events in Lebanon soon drew U.S. attention from it, and it was never pursued.

SEE ALSO Arab-Israel War (1982); Begin, Menachem.

RED EAGLES: Armed militia of the Popular Front for the Liberation of Palestine. Inactive since 1994.

SEE ALSO Popular Front for the Liberation of Palestine.

REFORM JUDAISM: Form of Judaism originally developed in Germany in the nineteenth century and now dominant in the United States. (In other nations it is sometimes known as Progressive or Liberal Judaism.) This movement has modified traditional religious orthodoxy in the interests of greater adaptability to the moral, intellectual, and practical demands of modern life.

Because in Israel Orthodox Judaism dominates the government, society, and institutions such as marriage through its legal monopoly on religious affairs, the human rights of Israeli Reform Jews are limited. However, Knesset members have become more sensitive to the intensity of feeling that exists in the Diaspora regarding issues of religious freedom, in large part because of political campaigning by the Reform movement; as a result, steps have been taken toward reducing this discrimination.

SEE ALSO Masorti; Orthodox Judaism; Rabbi.

REJECTION FRONT [1]: Coalition of groups within the Palestine Liberation Organization (PLO), formed in November 1973 following the Arab defeat in the 1973 War to oppose any leadership strategy to seek negotiations with Israel. Formed through the impetus of the Popular Front for the Liberation of Palestine (PFLP) with the support of the Iraqi Ba'th Party, the front united the most radical of the Palestinian movements, including the PFLP, the Arab Liberation Front, the Popular Front for the Liberation of Palestine—General Command, the Palestinian Popular Struggle Front, and the Palestine Liberation Front (1977). Between 1974 and 1978 the Rejection Front contested all attempts, whether American, Arab, Palestinian, or Israeli, to start Israeli-Palestinian peace negotiations. Political changes after the Camp David Accords of 1978 drew the front's constituents back into the PLO and the front ceased to exist by 1980.

SEE ALSO Arab-Israel War (1973); Camp David Accords; Palestine Liberation Front (1977); Palestine Liberation Organization; Palestinian Popular Struggle Front; Popular Front for the Liberation of Palestine; Popular Front for the Liberation of Palestine–General Command.

REJECTION FRONT [2]: In October 1977 Egyptian President Anwar al-Sadat traveled to Jerusalem to negotiate peace with Israel. Between 2 and 5 December 1977 representatives of a number of Arab countries met in Tripoli, Libya, to oppose the move. Libya, Algeria, South Yemen, Syria, Iraq, and the Palestine Liberation Organization (PLO) were represented, having reconciled their differences. They constituted a second Rejection Front of Arab states (as distinct from the internal PLO Rejection Front [1], active since 1973). A final communiqué of this conference called for action to neutralize the effects of Sadat's move: a freeze in political and diplomatic relations with Egypt; nonparticipation in Arab League meetings held in Cairo; reconsideration of Egypt's membership in the Arab League; and opposition to any attempt to challenge the legitimacy of the PLO as representative of the Palestinian people. The PLO reaffirmed its rejection of UN Security Council Resolutions 242 and 338. In September 1981, meeting in Benghazi, Libya, the leaders of the front decided on a rapprochement with the Soviet Union and invited Arab countries to "reconsider their relations with the United States" and oppose, with all the means at their disposal, the accord of strategic cooperation that had been concluded between Washington and Tel Aviv. On 18 November 1981 the final communiqué from a meeting of the front at Aden stressed that "Arab solidarity should be based on a confrontation with Zionism and its ally, the United States." In June 1982 the Israeli invasion of Lebanon caused a schism in the front, resulting in its dissolution. Throughout the history of the Palestinian movement, the Arab response has been characterized by a lack of cohesiveness, due principally to a struggle for leadership and to political and ideological divergences.

> SEE ALSO League of Arab States; Palestine Liberation Organization; Rejection Front [1]; Resolution 242; Resolution 338; Sadat, Anwar al-.

RESOLUTION 32/40: Resolution passed on 2 December 1977 by the United Nations General Assembly, which, among other stipulations, fixed the date of 29 November as an "international day of solidarity with the Palestinian people."

RESOLUTION 51/26: Passed by the UN General Assembly on 4 December 1996, this resolution, "Peaceful Settlement of the Question of Palestine," expresses support for the Madrid/Oslo peace process, reaffirms the "right to self-determination" of the Palestinian people, the necessity for an "Israeli withdrawal" from the territories occupied since 1967, and the need to resolve "the problem of Palestinian refugees, with reference to UN Security Council Resolutions 194, 242, and 338." There were 152 votes for it, two against (United States and Israel), and four abstentions. Its preamble asserts the "illegal character" of the Israeli settlements and initiatives aimed at changing the status of Jerusalem.

> SEE ALSO Madrid Conference; Oslo Accords II; Resolution 194; Resolution 242; Resolution 338.

RESOLUTION 52/250: Adopted on 7 July 1998 by the UN General Assembly, this resolution raised the status of the Palestinian observer mission, allowing it to participate in the general debates of the Assembly and to coauthor projects aimed at resolving questions connected with Palestine and the Middle East. This new arrangement did not allow the Palestinian mission the right to vote, or to present a candidate.

RESOLUTION 181: Passed on 29 November 1947 by the UN General Assembly, this resolution provides for the partition of Palestine into two independent states, one Arab and the other Jewish, with an economic union between them and Jerusalem enjoying a special status. The General Assembly indicated that the British Mandate over Palestine should end as soon as possible. (Britain had already notified the United Nations that it would resign its mandate by 1 August 1948.) The resolution passed by thirty-three to thirteen, with ten abstentions. Voting in favor were Australia, Belgium, Bolivia, Brazil, Byelorussia, Canada, Costa Rica, Czechoslovakia, Denmark, Dominican Republic, Ecuador, France, Guatemala, Haiti, Iceland, Liberia, Luxemburg, Netherlands, New Zealand, Nicaragua, Norway, Panama, Paraguay, Peru, Philippines, Poland, South Africa, Soviet Union, Sweden, Ukraine, United States, Uruguay, and Venezuela. Voting against were Afghanistan, Cuba, Egypt, Greece, India, Iran, Iraq, Lebanon, Pakistan, Saudi Arabia, Syria, Turkey, and Yemen. Abstaining were Argentina, Chile, China, Colombia, El Salvador, Ethiopia, Honduras, Mexico, United Kingdom, and Yugoslavia.

> SEE ALSO British Mandate; Jerusalem.

RESOLUTION 185: Passed on 26 April 1948 by the UN General Assembly, when tensions were on the rise between Jews and Arabs, this resolution asked the Security Council to study measures that would guarantee the protection of Jerusalem and its inhabitants.

RESOLUTION 194: Passed by the UN General Assembly on 11 December 1948 after the 1948 War, this resolution resulted from the report of UN mediator Folke Bernadotte, who had been assassinated in September by terrorists from the Irgun, a Zionist militia. It establishes the UN Conciliation Commission (members: France, Turkey, and the United States), which is charged with carrying out instructions of the Security Council and conducting negotiations for a settlement; affirms that Jerusalem should have a special status under an "international regime" apart from the rest of Palestine, and that "all inhabitants of Palestine" should have the "freest possible access" to it; affirms that other holy places should be protected by the United Nations; and, affirming the Palestinians' right of return, resolves "that the refugees wishing to return to their homes and live at peace with their neighbours should be permitted to do so at the earliest practicable date, and that compensation should be paid for the property of those choosing not to return and for loss of or damage to property which, under principles of international law or in equity, should be made good by the Governments or authorities responsible; Instructs the Conciliation Commission to facilitate the repatriation, resettlement and economic and social rehabilitation of the refugees and the payment of compensation . . . "

The Conciliation Commission did eventually achieve an armistice, but none of the other provisions were ever put into effect. Clause 11, quoted above, provides the legal basis for the Palestinians' claim of a right of return.

SEE ALSO Arab-Israel War (1948); Bernadotte, Folke; Irgun.

RESOLUTION 237: Passed by the UN Security Council on 14 June 1967, immediately following the 1967 War, this resolution "*Calls* upon the Government of Israel to ensure the safety, welfare, and security of the inhabitants of the areas where military operations have taken place. . . . [and] *Recommends* to the Governments concerned the scrupulous respect of the humanitarian principles governing the treatment of prisoners of war and the protection of civilian persons in time of war contained in the Geneva Conventions of 12 August, 1949. . . ."

SEE ALSO Arab-Israel War (1967).

RESOLUTION 242: Passed unanimously by the UN Security Council on 22 November 1967, following the 1967 War, this resolution was drafted by the British ambassador, Lord Caradon, after exhaustive negotiation and discussion and was accepted by all belligerent states. It reads: "*The Security Council, Expressing* its continuing concern with the grave situation in the Middle East, *Emphasizing* the inadmissibility of the acquisition of territory by war and the need to work for a just and lasting peace in which every State in the area can live in security, *Emphasizing further* that all Member States in their acceptance of the Charter of the United Nations have undertaken a commitment to act in accordance with Article 2 of the Charter, 1. *Affirms* that the fulfillment of Charter principles requires the establishment of a just and lasting peace in the Middle East which should include the application of both the following principles: (i) Withdrawal of Israeli armed forces from territories occupied in the recent conflict; (ii) Termination of

all claims or states of belligerency and respect for and acknowledgement of the sovereignty, territorial integrity and political independence of every State in the area and their right to live in peace within secure and recognized boundaries free from threats or acts of force; 2. Affirms further the necessity (a) For guaranteeing freedom of navigation through international waterways in the area; (b) For achieving a just settlement of the refugee problem; (c) For guaranteeing the territorial inviolability and political independence of every State in the area, through measures including the establishment of demilitarized zones; 3. *Requests* the Secretary General to designate a Special Representative to proceed to the Middle East to establish and maintain contacts with the States concerned in order to promote agreement and assist efforts to achieve a peaceful and accepted settlement in accordance with the provisions and principles in this resolution; 4. *Requests* the Secretary General to report to the Security Council on the progress of the efforts of the Special Representative as soon as possible." Resolution 242 states the basic premise, land for peace, of all subsequent diplomatic proposals for settlement of the Arab-Israeli issue. In order to gain unanimous approval, however, it was artfully ambiguous regarding the extent of the land in question, leading to greatly differing interpretations later. It did not refer to the issue of Palestinian rights, mentioning the Palestinians only in the context of the "refugee problem." Although it was accepted by the belligerent states, it was rejected by the Palestine Liberation Organization, which had not been a party to the discussion and which continued to reject it until 1988.

SEE ALSO Arab-Israel War (1967); Palestine Liberation Organization.

RESOLUTION 253: Passed on 4 July 1967 by the UN General Assembly, following the 1967 War, this resolution declared invalid the measures taken by Israel to modify the status of Jerusalem and demanded that Israel rescind all measures already taken and abstain from further action that would change the status of the city.

SEE ALSO Arab-Israel War (1967); Jerusalem.

RESOLUTION 273: Passed on 11 May 1949 by the United Nations General Assembly, this resolution allowed Israel to become a member of the UN. There were 37 votes for, 12 against, and 9 abstentions, as follows: *In favor:* Argentina, Australia, Bolivia, Byelorussian SSR, Canada, Chile, China, Colombia, Costa Rica, Cuba, Czechoslovakia, Dominican

Republic, Ecuador, France, Guatemala, Haiti, Honduras, Iceland, Liberia, Luxembourg, Mexico, Netherlands, New Zealand, Nicaragua, Norway, Panama, Paraguay, Peru, Philippines, Poland, Ukrainian SSR, Union of South Africa, USSR, United States, Uruguay, Venezuela, Yugoslavia. *Against:* Afghanistan, Burma, Egypt, Ethiopia, India, Iran, Iraq, Lebanon, Pakistan, Saudi Arabia, Syria, Yemen. *Abstaining:* Belgium, Brazil, Denmark, El Salvador, Greece, Sweden, Thailand (Siam), Turkey, United Kingdom.

RESOLUTION 302: Adopted on 8 December 1949 by the UN General Assembly, this resolution creates the United Nations Relief and Works Agency for Palestine Refugees in the Near East.

SEE ALSO United Nations Relief and Works Agency for Palestine Refugees in the Near East.

RESOLUTION 338: Adopted unanimously by the UN Security Council on 22 October 1973, during the 1973 War, in an urgent session requested jointly by the United States and the Soviet Union, this resolution reads: "*The Security Council* 1. *Calls upon* all parties to the present fighting to cease all firing and terminate all military activity immediately, no later than 12 hours after the moment of the adoption of this decision, in the positions they now occupy; 2. *Calls upon* the parties concerned to start immediately after the cease-fire the implementation of Security Council resolution 242 (1967) in all of its parts; 3. *Decides* that, immediately and concurrently with the cease-fire, negotiations shall start between the parties concerned under appropriate auspices aimed at establishing a just and durable peace in the Middle East." Resolution 338 calls for the parties to implement Resolution 242 of 1967 immediately upon a ceasefire and begin negotiations for a permanent peace. (A ceasefire did begin almost immediately, but it was broken within hours.) Like Resolution 242, it does not deal with the Palestinian issue. These two resolutions have remained the legal foundation on which all subsequent proposals for an Arab–Israeli settlement have been based.

SEE ALSO Arab-Israel War (1973); Resolution 242.

RESOLUTION 425: Adopted 19 March 1978 by the UN Security Council on the initiative of the United States, following the Israeli invasion of Lebanon on 14 March, this resolution "1. *Calls* for strict respect for the territorial integrity, sovereignty and political independence of Lebanon within its internationally recognized boundaries; 2. *Calls upon* Israel immediately to cease its military action against Lebanese territorial integrity and withdraw forthwith its forces from all Lebanese territory; 3. *Decides* . . . to establish immediately under its authority a United Nations interim force for southern Lebanon for the purpose of confirming the withdrawal of Israeli forces, restoring international peace and security and assisting the Government of Lebanon in ensuring the return of its effective authority in the area. . ."

RESOLUTION 426: Passed on 19 March 1978 by the UN Security Council, this resolution approved the report of the secretary general on the application of Resolution 425 and decided that the United Nations Interim Forces in Lebanon would be created in accord with the mentioned report for an initial period of six months and renewed subsequently, if need be, by decision of the Security Council.

SEE ALSO Resolution 425; United Nations Interim Forces in Lebanon.

RESOLUTION 476 AND 478: Passed by the UN Security Council on 30 June and 20 August 1980, respectively, these resolutions deal with Israel's annexation of East Jerusalem. Resolution 476, citing five previous resolutions and the fourth Geneva Convention, and declaring again that "acquisition of territory by force is inadmissible," deplores Israel's "changing the physical character, demographic composition, institutional structure and the status" of Jerusalem, and declares itself "gravely concerned" over forthcoming Israeli legislation regarding the city. The resolution "*Reaffirms* the overriding necessity to end the prolonged occupation of Arab territories occupied by Israel since 1967, including Jerusalem" and "*Strongly deplores* the continued refusal of Israel, the occupying Power, to comply with the relevant resolutions of the Security Council and the General Assembly."

Resolution 478 was adopted after the passage in the Knesset on 30 July of the anticipated "basic law" formally extending Israeli sovereignty over East Jerusalem and surrounding territory and declaring Jerusalem the "capital of Israel." Referring to Resolution 476 and the fourth Geneva Convention, this resolution censures Israel for making that change as well as for its refusal to comply with previous UN resolutions, declares the law null and void, and asserts that Israel must rescind it. It also states that Israel's "action constitutes a serious obstruction to achieving a comprehensive, just and lasting peace in the Middle East" and calls upon all states with diplomatic missions in Jerusalem to withdraw them.

SEE ALSO Jerusalem; Knesset.

RESOLUTION 497 (UN Security Council): Passed on 17 December 1981 by the UN Security Council, this resolution declares "null and void and without international legal effect" the decision of Israel to "impose its laws, jurisdiction and administration in the occupied Syrian Golan Heights," and demands that Israel rescind its decision. The resolution was adopted unanimously.

SEE ALSO Golan Heights.

RESOLUTION 509: Passed unanimously by the UN Security Council on 6 June 1982, the day Israel invaded Lebanon, this resolution demands the immediate and unconditional withdrawal of the Israeli army from Lebanon.

SEE ALSO Arab-Israel War (1982).

RESOLUTION 520: Passed unanimously on 17 September 1982 by the UN Security Council, this resolution condemns Israeli violations of a ceasefire agreement. It notes and condemns the assassination on 14 September of Bashir Jumayyil, who had been about to take office as president. Then, "*Taking note* of Lebanon's determination to ensure the withdrawal of all non-Lebanese forces" and reaffirming several recent resolutions on the Lebanese situation, it "*Condemns* the recent Israeli incursions into Beirut in violation of the cease-fire agreements and of Security council resolutions," "*Demands* an immediate return to the positions occupied by Israel before 15 September 1982 . . ." and "*Calls again* for the strict respect for Lebanon's sovereignty, territorial integrity, unity and political independence under the sole and exclusive authority of the Lebanese Government through the Lebanese Army throughout Lebanon."

SEE ALSO Jumayyil, Bashir.

RESOLUTION 799: Passed on 18 December 1992 by the UN Security Council, this resolution, citing the fourth Geneva Convention and a number of previous UN resolutions, demands the immediate return of the more than 400 Palestinians who had just been banished to Lebanon by Israeli authorities. On 17 December 1992, during the first Intifada, Israel expelled these alleged HAMAS sympathizers from the Occupied Territories into the no-man's-land beyond the Lebanese border. The Israelis assumed they would proceed into Lebanon and exile, but instead they set up a camp in full view of the world's media and stayed there for months. They named their camp Return (al-Awdah).

SEE ALSO HAMAS; Intifada.

RESOLUTION 904: Passed unanimously on 18 March 1994 by the UN Security Council, three weeks after the massacre of twenty-nine Palestinians by an Israeli settler in Hebron, this resolution refers to the fourth Geneva Convention and to the Israeli-Palestinian Declaration of Principles of 1993 and vehemently condemns the Hebron massacre; demands that Israel adopt and apply measures, including confiscation of arms, to prevent illegal violent acts by Israeli settlers; demands that measures be adopted to guarantee the security and protection of Palestinian civilians in the entire occupied territory, including, among other recourses, a temporary international or foreign presence; entreats the cosponsors of the peace process, the United States and Russia, to pursue efforts to invigorate this process; and reaffirms its support for the peace process and demands that the Declaration of Principles be applied without delay. The resolution was voted on paragraph by paragraph, allowing the United State to abstain on two of them, one placing Jerusalem among the Occupied Territories, the other referring to "occupied territory" rather than "occupied territories."

SEE ALSO Oslo Accords.

RESOLUTION 997 AND 998: Adopted by the UN General Assembly on 2 and 4 November 1956, respectively, these resolutions dealt with the Suez War of 1956. They were brought before the General Assembly under the provisions of General Assembly Resolution 377 ("Uniting for Peace") of 1950, which allow urgent matters to be brought there for action in certain circumstances in case of "failure of the Security Council to discharge its responsibilities" (in this case, after a veto by Britain and France; in practice this tactic can work only when it has the support of the United States). Resolution 997 urged all belligerents to observe a ceasefire, urged the parties to the 1949 General Armistice Agreements (Egypt and Israel) to retreat to the armistice lines, and urged the reopening of the Suez Canal.

Resolution 998 provided for the creation of an "emergency international United Nations Force to secure and supervise the cessation of hostilities in accordance with all the terms of [Resolution 997]." A United Nations Emergency Force (UNEF)—the UN's first peacekeeping force—was set up within days and began operation in Egypt on 12 November. At first it had about 6,000 troops (the number was later reduced) from Brazil, Canada, Colombia, Denmark, Finland, India, Indonesia, Norway, Sweden, and Yugoslavia, commanded by a Canadian general. After the withdrawal of British, French, and Israeli troops, completed in March 1957, UNEF was deployed along the Egypt-Israel border until May 1967, when, during the tension that led to the 1967 War, it was withdrawn at the request of Egyptian President Gamal Abdel Nasser.

SEE ALSO Arab-Israel War (1967); Nasser, Gamal Abdel; Suez Crisis; United Nations Emergency Force.

RESOLUTION 1052: Passed by the UN Security Council on 18 April 1996, a week after Israel launched Operation Grapes of Wrath against the Lebanese Hizbullah, this resolution demanded the immediate cessation of hostilities by all concerned parties. The Security Council reaffirmed its commitment to the territorial integrity and sovereignty of Lebanon, as well as to the security of all states in the region. Finally, the council asked all states in the region to oversee the security and freedom of movement of the United Nations Interim Forces in Lebanon (UNIFIL) to allow it to fulfill its mandate without obstacle or interference ("deploring" the incident on the same day, 18 April, in which over a hundred civilians were killed when Israel shelled a UNIFIL compound). Operation Grapes of Wrath ended on 28 April.

SEE ALSO Hizbullah; United Nations Interim Force in Lebanon.

RESOLUTION 1154: Passed on 2 March 1998 by the UN Security Council at the apogee of an Iraqi-U.S. crisis, this resolution refers to Security Council Resolution 687 of 1991, which imposed economic sanctions and an arms inspection regime on Iraq at the end of the Gulf War of 1991 and endorses a recent "memorandum of understanding" between Iraq and the United Nations, which provided for International Atomic Energy Agency staff to inspect "presidential sites" in Iraq. The resolution urges that Iraq respect its "obligation" to accord immediate, unconditional, and unrestricted access to UN inspectors, and declares that "any violation would have the severest consequences for Iraq." The Council "notes that by its failure so far to comply with its relevant obligations Iraq has delayed the moment when the Council can" make a decision "to lift sanctions, which it reaffirms its intention to do."

SEE ALSO Gulf War (1991).

RESOLUTION 1373: Adopted by the UN Security Council on 28 September 2001, less than three weeks

after the terrorist attacks on New York and Washington, this resolution declares, among other provisions, that all states shall:

"(a) Prevent and suppress the financing of terrorist acts; (b) Criminalize the willful provision or collection, by any means, directly or indirectly, of funds by their nationals or in their territories with the intention that the funds should be used, or in the knowledge that they are to be used, in order to carry out terrorist acts; (c) Freeze without delay funds and other financial assets or economic resources of persons who commit, or attempt to commit, terrorist acts or participate in or facilitate the commission of terrorist acts; of entities owned or controlled directly or indirectly by such persons; and of persons and entities acting on behalf of, or at the direction of such persons and entities, including funds derived or generated from property owned or controlled directly or indirectly by such persons and associated persons and entities; (d) Prohibit their nationals or any persons and entities within their territories from making any funds, financial assets or economic resources or financial or other related services available, directly or indirectly, for the benefit of persons who commit or attempt to commit or facilitate or participate in the commission of terrorist acts, of entities owned or controlled, directly or indirectly, by such persons and of persons and entities acting on behalf of or at the direction of such persons[.]"

RESOLUTION 2253: Passed on 4 July 1967 by the UN General Assembly, this resolution declares "invalid" the "measures taken by Israel to change the status of the City" of Jerusalem and "*Calls upon* Israel to rescind all measures already taken and to desist forthwith from taking any action which would alter the status of Jerusalem." The vote was ninety-nine to zero, with twenty abstentions. The occasion was the passage of a law by the Knesset, after the conquest of East Jerusalem in the 1967 War, to apply Israeli law, jurisdiction, and administration to East Jerusalem. Although this act was referred to in public discussion as "annexation"—as, in practical terms, it was—annexation did not formally occur until 1980, when Israel unilaterally extended its sovereignty over East Jerusalem and surrounding territory; at that time the Security Council passed Resolutions 476 and 478.

SEE ALSO Arab Israel War (1967); Jersualem; Knesset; Resolutions 476 and 478.

RESOLUTION 2443: Resoution passed by the United Nations General Assembly on 19 December 1968, which created a "Special Committee to Investigate Israeli Practices Affecting the Human Rights of the Population in the Occupied Territories." The resolution expressed its concern at the violation of human rights in Arab territories occupied by Israel; drew the attention of the Government of Israel to the "grave consequences resulting from the disregard of fundamental freedoms and human rights in occupied territories;" called upon the Government of Israel to "desist forthwith from acts of destroying homes of the Arab civilian population"; and affirmed "the inalienable rights of all inhabitants who have left their homes as a result of the outbreak of hostilities in the Middle East to return home, resume their normal life, recover their property and homes, and rejoin their families."

Since its establishment the Special Committee has consistently been denied cooperation by the Government of Israel or access to the occupied territories. It has, however, received information from the governments of Egypt, Jordan, and Syria, much of it from witnesses having first-hand and recent experience of the human rights situation in the occupied territories. The Special Committee makes regular reports to the General Assembly on its evaluation of the situation and its recommendations. Its mandate has been regularly renewed from year to year.

RESOLUTION 2628: Passed by the UN General Assembly on 4 November 1970, following the bloody events of Black September 1970 in Jordan. Making reference to Security Council Resolution 242 and noting that it has not been implemented, this resolution deplores "the continued occupation of the Arab territories since 5 June 1967," "*Reaffirms* that the acquisition of territories by force is inadmissible and that, consequently, territories thus occupied must be restored," calls for "Withdrawal of Israeli armed forces from territories occupied" and "*Recognizes* that respect for the rights of the Palestinians is an indispensable element in the establishing of a just and lasting peace." The vote was fifty-seven to sixteen, with thirty-nine abstentions.

SEE ALSO Black September 1970; Resolution 242.

RESOLUTION 2649: Passed on 30 November 1970 by the UN General Assembly, this resolution condemned "governments which refused the right of self-determination to peoples who were recognized to have the right to it, notably the peoples of South Africa and Palestine."

RESOLUTION 3089: Passed on 7 December 1973 by the UN General Assembly, not long after the 1973 War; the primary subject is the financing and operation of the UN Relief and Works Agency for Palestine Refugees in the Near East. However, referencing the fourth Geneva Convention, Security Council Resolution 194, and a number of subsequent resolutions, it establishes an explicit connection between the Palestinians' right of return and their right to self-determination. The right of return is mentioned in several places but the clearest statement is in clause 3: "[The General Assembly] *Declares* that full respect for and realization of the inalienable rights of the people of Palestine, particularly its right to self-determination, are indispensable for the establishment of a just and lasting peace in the Middle East, and that the enjoyment by the Palestine Arab refugees of their right to return to their homes and property, recognized by the General Assembly in resolution 194 (III) of 11 December 1948, which has been repeatedly reaffirmed by the Assembly since that date, is indispensable for the achievement of a just settlement of the refugee problem and for the exercise by the people of Palestine of its right to self-determination."

SEE ALSO Arab-Israel War (1967); Resolution 194; Right of Return; United Nations Relief and Works Agency for Palestine Refugees in the Near East.

RESOLUTION 3236: Passed by the United Nations General Assembly on 22 November 1974, nine days after the Yasir Arafat addressed the General Assembly. In October, the Arab League had recognized the Palestine Liberation Organization (PLO) as "the only legitimate representative of the Palestinian people," and the UN was about to give the PLO observer status to allow it to take part in discussions on the Palestine issue for the first time. Arafat took the occasion to hint that the PLO might be willing to work for a political settlement, addressing this remark to the Israeli delegation: "I come carrying an olive branch and the rifle of a fighter for liberty; do not let the branch fall from my hand!" The resolution recognizes the Palestinians' right to a sovereign national state: "*The General Assembly, Having considered* the question of Palestine, *Having heard* the statement of the Palestine Liberation Organization, the representative of the Palestinian people, *Having also heard* other statements made during the debate, *Deeply concerned* that no just solution to the problem of Palestine has yet been achieved and recognizing that the problem of Palestine continues to endanger international peace and security, *Recognizing* that the Palestinian people is entitled to self-determination in accordance with the Charter of the United Nations, *Expressing its grave concern* that the Palestinian people has been prevented from enjoying its inalienable rights, in particular its right to self-determination, *Guided* by the purposes and principles of the Charter, *Recalling* its relevant resolutions which affirm the right of the Palestinian people to self-determination, 1. *Reaffirms* the inalienable rights of the Palestinian people in Palestine, including: (*a*) The right to self-determination without external interference; (*b*) The right to national independence and sovereignty; 2. *Reaffirms also* the inalienable right of the Palestinians to return to their homes and property from which they have been displaced and uprooted, and calls for their return; 3. *Emphasizes* that full respect for and the realization of these inalienable rights of the Palestinian people are indispensable for the solution of the question of Palestine; 4. *Recognizes* that the Palestinian people is a principal party in the establishment of a just and lasting peace in the Middle East; 5. *Further recognizes* the right of the Palestinian people to regain its rights by all means in accordance with the purposes and principles of the Charter of the United Nations; 6. *Appeals* to all States and international organizations to extend their support to the Palestinian people in its struggle to restore its rights, in accordance with the Charter; 7. *Requests* the Secretary-General to establish contacts with the Palestine Liberation Organization on all matters concerning the question of Palestine; 8. *Requests* the Secretary-General to report to the General Assembly at its thirtieth session on the implementation of the present resolution; 9. *Decides* to include the item entitled 'Question of Palestine' in the provisional agenda of its thirtieth session."

SEE ALSO Arafat, Yasir; League of Arab States; Palestine Liberation Organization.

RESOLUTION 3376: Adopted 10 November 1975 as part of the General Assembly's annual debate on the "Question of Palestine." The resolution reaffirms the provisions of General Assembly Resolution 3236 of 1974, including the right of return. It establishes a Committee on the Exercise of the Inalienable Rights of the Palestinian People, composed of twenty member states. The committee is mandated to recommend a program for the implementation of the rights of the Palestinian people.

SEE ALSO Resolution 3236; Right of Return.

RESOLUTION 3379: Adopted by the United Nations General Assembly on 10 November 1975 during the General Assembly's annual discussion of the "Question of Palestine." This resolution identified Zionism with racism. In part it was the result of a campaign by the Soviet Union to counter the American campaign condemning the Soviet Union for its treatment of its Jewish population (and the vote divided, in part, along Cold War lines). It gained wide support not only among Arab nations but among other Third World countries as well, most of which had long suffered from either exploitation or outright colonial occupation by Western powers, and from the racial ideologies that were associated with them. Moreover, Israeli cooperation with the apartheid regime in South Africa had long been a sore point—as was, two years after the 1973 War, Israel's increasingly close strategic alliance with the United States. Israel also maintained a firm refusal to recognize any legitimate representative of the Palestinians or consider any discussion with such a representative. (Israel's official position toward the Palestinians then was that there was no such people, as distinct from other Arabs; as Golda Meir famously put it in 1969, "It was not as though there was a Palestinian people in Palestine considering itself as a Palestinian people and we came and threw them out and took their country away from them. They did not exist.") The vote was seventy-two to thirty-five, with thirty-two abstentions. When the resolution passed, the Israeli ambassador, Chaim Herzog, tore up his copy of the draft at the podium. The resolution reads: "*The General Assembly, Recalling* its resolution 1904 (XVIII) of 20 November 1963, proclaiming the United Nations Declaration on the Elimination of All Forms of Racial Discrimination, and in particular its affirmation that 'any doctrine of racial differentiation or superiority is scientifically false, morally condemnable, socially unjust and dangerous' and its expression of alarm at 'the manifestations of racial discrimination still in evidence in some areas in the world, some of which are imposed by certain Governments by means of legislative, administrative or other measures,' *Recalling also* that, in its resolution 3151 G (XXVIII) of 14 December 1953, the General Assembly condemned, *inter alia,* the unholy alliance between South African racism and Zionism, *Taking note* of the Declaration of Mexico on the Equality of Women and Their Contribution to Development and Peace 1975, proclaimed by the World Conference of the International Women's Year, held at Mexico City from 19 June to 2 July 1975, which promulgated the principle that 'international cooperation and peace require the achievement of national liberation and independence, the elimination of colonialism and neo-colonialism, foreign occupation, Zionism, apartheid and racial discrimination in all its forms, as well as the recognition of the dignity of peoples and their right to self-determination,' *Taking note also* of resolution 77 (XII) adopted by the Assembly of Heads of State and Government of the Organization of African Unity at its twelfth ordinary session, held at Kampala from 28 July to 1 August 1975, which considered 'that the racist regime in occupied Palestine and the racist regime in Zimbabwe and South Africa have a common imperialist origin, forming a whole and having the same racist structure and being organically linked in their policy aimed at repression of the dignity and integrity of the human being,' *Taking note also* of the Political Declaration and Strategy to Strengthen International Peace and Security and to Intensify Solidarity and Mutual Assistance among Non-Aligned Countries, adopted at the Conference of Ministers for Foreign Affairs of Non-Aligned Countries held at Lima from 25 to 30 August 1975, which most severely condemned Zionism as a threat to world peace and security and called upon all countries to oppose this racist and imperialist ideology, *Determines* that Zionism is a form of racism and racial discrimination."

The resolution caused an uproar in the West, particularly in the United States. It was condemned by Israel as an international act of anti-Semitism "devoid of any moral or legal value," and increased distrust of the United Nations in Israel and the United States. It contributed to the feeling of the Israeli right that Israel was besieged and stiffened Israeli resistance to discussion or negotiation. It was annulled by General Assembly Resolution 4686 in 1991.

SEE ALSO Arab-Israel War (1973); Herzog, Chaim; Meir, Golda; Resolution 4686.

RESOLUTION 4686: Adopted by the UN General Assembly on 16 December 1991, this resolution nullified Resolution 3379 of 1975, the "Zionism is racism" resolution. By late 1991 the Soviet Union had collapsed and so had the South African apartheid regime. Earlier in the year the Gulf War of 1991 had been fought (under a UN resolution), causing division in the Arab world. In addition, Israel made its attendance at the Madrid Conference conditional on a repeal of Resolution 3379. Under considerable pressure from the United States, the members of the General Assembly voted 111 to 25, with 13 abstentions, to pass this resolution, given here in full: "The general assembly decides to revoke the determina-

tion contained in its resolution 3379 (XXX) of 10 November 1975."

SEE ALSO Gulf War (1991); Madrid Conference; Resolution 3379.

REVOLUTIONARY GUARDS

SEE Pasdaran.

REVOLUTIONARY PALESTINIAN COMMUNIST PARTY

SEE Palestinian Revolutionary Communist Party.

RHODES TALKS: Talks held on the island of Rhodes, Greece, formally ending the 1948 Arab-Israel War, and resulting in the signing of two general armistice agreements. On 24 February 1949 an armistice was signed between Israel and Egypt through Ralph Bunche's efforts as UN mediator. Although of a military nature, this first agreement conveys an implicit recognition of the Israeli state by an Arab government. Although it provided for demilitarized zones in the Nitzana-Abu Ageila sector, it did not specify Israeli shipping rights through the Suez Canal and the Straits of Tiran (a blockade was to last for thirty years). On 3 April, a second Rhodes armistice was signed between Israel and the Hashimite Kingdom of Jordan. The agreement left a number of issues unresolved, including Jewish access to the Western Wall in Jerusalem and Jordanian access to the south through the Bethlehem road, but it served as the framework of relations between the two states for nearly twenty years, until the Arab-Israel War of 1967.

SEE ALSO Arab-Israel War (1948); Arab-Israel War (1967).

RIGHT OF RETURN: Established by the State of Israel soon after its creation in 1948, the right of return enacted by the Knesset allows any Jew who so desires to live in Israel and obtain Israeli citizenship. This right was also requested by Palestinian political leaders, who demanded that Palestinians who had been forced to leave their land as a consequence of the various Israeli-Palestine wars be allowed to return home. This right of return, which now concerns 3.7 million Palestinians, principally refugees in neighboring Arab countries, is a source of anxiety for the Israeli authorities, who are afraid that allowing it would upset the country's demographic equilibrium between Palestinians and Israelis. Along with East Jerusalem, this problem is one of the main stumbling blocks in the Israeli-Palestinian peace negotiations, in particular as it concerns the refugees from 1948, whose right to return was affirmed by United Nations Resolution 194. Among Palestinians, renouncing the right of return has been considered tantamount to treason.

SEE ALSO Arab-Israel War (1948); Resolution 194.

ROAD MAP (2002): American-sponsored proposal for an Israeli-Palestinian peace settlement put forth by the so-called Quartet (the United States, the European Union, the United Nations and Russia) in April 2003; it was formally accepted by both sides, but never implemented. A revised version of a proposal floated, at the urging of British prime minister Tony Blair, in September 2002. The Road Map was issued as the United States and Britain took up the occupation of Iraq following the initial phase of the Iraq War of 2003, which had been justified, in part, as a step toward a general peace in the Middle East. The Road Map provided for the creation of a Palestinian state by 2005. It called for the Palestinians, again, to recognize Israel's right to exist; to renounce violence; and to reform the Palestinian Authority (PA), specifically to create the position of prime minister (to allow Israel to negotiate with someone other than Yasir Arafat). It called for Israel to remove curfews and roadblocks in the occupied territories; freeze settlement activity; dismantle "illegal" settlements (not defined; under international law all the settlements are illegal); and withdraw from territory seized from Palestinian autonomous areas since the beginning of the al-Aqsa Intifada in 2000. The Road Map was accepted by the PA, and a prime minister, Mahmud Rida Abbas (Abu Mazen), was appointed. The Israeli government of prime minister Ariel Sharon, fundamentally opposed to giving up any occupied territory or settlements, as well as to allowing a sovereign Palestinian state, publicly accepted the Road Map with reservations, but did nothing to implement it. Since then both sides have continued activities in violation of the Road Map and little progress has been achieved. In February 2004 Sharon announced his own plan of "unilateral disengagement" from the Gaza Strip, which involved dismantling Israeli settlements there and moving the approximately 7,500 to 8,000 settlers to the West Bank, while also removing four settlements in the West Bank. In September Sharon announced that he would not follow the Road Map, and added that once the disengagement from Gaza is complete, "it is very possible . . . there will be a long period when nothing else happens."

SEE ALSO Abbas, Mahmud Rida; Aqsa Intifada, al-; Arafat, Yasir; Gaza Strip; Iraq War; Palestinian Authority; Sharon, Ariel.

ROGERS PLAN: Proposal for an Arab-Israeli peace settlement put forward by American secretary of state William P. Rogers in December 1969. The plan was proposed in response to the outbreak of fighting between Israel and Egypt known as the War of Attrition (1969–70). It was also in response to Palestinian guerilla attacks across the Jordan, and to the ongoing futility of the Jarring Mission, a UN diplomatic effort begun shortly after the Arab-Israel War (1967) in an effort to realize the provisions of Security Council Resolution 242. At the same time the Nixon administration was making efforts to create a state of "détente" with the Soviet Union, which had broken off diplomatic relations with Israel over the war, and was supplying Egypt with fighter jets, missiles and other military material. The plan called for Israeli withdrawal from the occupied territories in return for recognition from Egypt and Jordan; like Resolution 242, it did not make specific reference to Palestinian rights but only called generally for a just solution to "the refugee problem."

Earlier in 1969 Rogers had made similar proposals in private discussions with Israel's ambassador, Yitzhak Rabin and prime minister, Golda Meir, without success, and the proposals had also been submitted for discussion with the Soviet Union, which had not responded by December. The plan was not met with favor by Egypt, Jordan or the other Arab states, none of whom wished to deal directly with Israel, but wanted to see a UN-imposed solution forcing Israel to evacuate the occupied territories in accordance with Resolution 242. Late in December the Rogers Plan was rejected by Israel, on the grounds that it would "prejudice the chances of establishing peace" by harming "Israel's sovereign rights and security in the drafting of the resolutions concerning refugees and the status of Jerusalem, and contain no actual obligation of the Arab States to put a stop to the hostile activities of the sabotage and terror organizations." Israel, which had already incorporated East Jerusalem and was establishing settlements in the Jordan Valley and elsewhere in the West Bank under the Allon Plan, was essentially rejecting the provisions of Resolution 242. At the same time, the United States continued to press Israel and Egypt to commit to a ceasefire, and one was agreed to in August 1970. The Palestinian guerilla activities in Jordan, and the efforts by that country's government to control them, eventually led to the events of Black September 1970.

CHURCH OF THE DORMITION. THIS ROMAN CATHOLIC CHURCH IS DEDICATED TO THE TRADITIONAL SITE WHERE THE VIRGIN MARY DIED. IT STANDS ON MOUNT ZION, THE TRADITIONAL LOCATION OF THE LAST SUPPER OF CHRIST. *(© Paul A. Souders/Corbis)*

SEE ALSO Allon Plan; Arab-Israel War (1967); Black September 1970; Jarring Mission; Meir, Golda; Rabin, Yitzhak; Resolution 242.

ROMAN CATHOLIC CHURCH: The church of Christians of the Latin rite, who accept the authority of the bishop of Rome (the pope). It is one of the three major branches of Christianity, the other two being the Eastern Orthodox churches and Protestantism. Although Roman Catholics are often referred to simply as Catholics, this is ambiguous, as in Arabic "Catholic" refers to the Melkites and some Anglican churches consider themselves Anglo-Catholic.

The Roman Catholic Church came into existence as a result of the schism between the Eastern and Western branches of Christianity that occurred in 1054. Under Pope Urban II it launched the First Crusade to take Jerusalem from the Muslims, who in

1009 had destroyed the Holy Sepulcher there; it succeeded in doing so in 1099 and a hierarchy under a Latin partriarchate was established in Jerusalem. More Crusades against the Muslims followed, with varying degrees of success, until 1291 when the Crusaders were driven out by the Mamluks. After that, only the Franciscan Brothers remained as custodians of Christian shrines.

The Latin patriarchate of Jerusalem was reestablished in 1847, and during that era missionaries engaged in education and nursing were sent to Ottoman Palestine. In 2004, a Roman Catholic community of over 60,000, with its own patriarch and diocesan clergy, exists in the West Bank and Jordan, although most other Roman Catholics in Palestine are scattered in small groups. There are many Catholic schools, most of them established in the nineteenth century, as well as a Catholic University in Bethlehem. As Palestine is the Christian Holy Land, it is a center for several Roman Catholic religious orders.

The Holy See (the papal headquarters, or Vatican) is an independent state that maintains diplomatic relations with sovereign nations. In June 1994 it established full formal relations with the State of Israel. Among the reasons for the long negotiations that preceded this event were the desire of the Roman Catholic Church to maintain control over, and access to, the Holy Places in Israel; its desire to protect the interests of Catholic communities there; concern over the legal status of the church under Israeli law; and fear that recognition of Israel would provoke retaliation against Catholics in the Arab world. On 10 November 1997 a formal agreement addressing some of these issues was signed in Jerusalem.

SEE ALSO Christianity; Eastern Orthodox Church; Melkites; Protestants.

ROSS, DENNIS B. (1948–): U.S. diplomatic envoy, born in San Francisco. A graduate of University of California-Los Angeles, Dennis Ross participated in the electoral campaigns of the Democrats Robert Kennedy and George McGovern. He began working at the Pentagon in 1972. Between 1985 and 1987, along with Martin Indyk, he was a member of the Washington Institute for Middle East Policy and a consultant to the National Security Council. He was a foreign affairs advisor in George W. Bush's presidential campaign. In 1988, after Bush was elected, he became one of the main assistants to Secretary of State James Baker, who was in charge of policy planning. A member of the presidential study group of the Washington Institute, he played an important role during the crisis that followed the collapse of the Soviet Union. He and Indyk became artisans of the Israeli-Arab peace process. It has been conjectured that without Ross, who was thought to be the éminence grise behind James Baker, the Madrid peace conference of November 1991 would never have taken place.

When Bill Clinton was elected, Ross remained at the State Department, which was headed by Warren Christopher. On 18 June 1993 he was named special coordinator of the peace process in the Middle East. He undertook numerous trips to try to advance Israeli-Palestinian negotiations, participating in working out the final details of various accords. In September he attended the sessions which resulted in the Israeli-Palestinian accord on principles signed by Yitzhak Rabin and Yasir Arafat in Washington. On 18 September 1994 he was in Damascus, then went on to Tel Aviv to prepare for Warren Christopher's upcoming trip. On 12 July 1995, during a round of visits in the Middle East, he was received by Arafat in the headquarters of the Palestinian Authority in Gaza. In October 1996 he was in Israel to participate in Israeli-Palestinian negotiations over the city of Hebron. In September 1998 he was in Israel again, trying restart the negotiations with the Palestinians, which had been blocked since Benjamin Netanyahu became prime minister. On 5 December 1999 he accompanied the new secretary of state, Madeleine Albright, on a visit to the Middle East at a time when Israeli-Palestinian negotiations were again stalled. Upon his arrival in Israel, together with Martin Indyk, undersecretary of state for the Middle East, he met with Arafat and then with Ehud Barak.

On 15 December he participated in Washington meetings between the Israeli foreign minister and the Syrian foreign minister Faruk al-Shara, which were meant to jumpstart the peace negotiations that had been interrupted since the spring of 1996. Between 13 February and 15 March 2000 he was in Israel several times to try to unblock the Israeli-Palestinian negotiations because the 13 February deadline for a general accord on the conflict had not been met. On 26 February he met with King Abdullah II of Jordan. On the following 2 May he participated in Israeli-Palestinian parleys in Elat, Israel, to speed up movement toward a general accord between the Israelis and the Palestinians. On 19 August, following the July failure of the Israeli-Palestinian summit at Camp David, he was in Alexandria to meet with the Egyptian foreign minister, Amr Mousa.

On 26 September he moderated a three-day secret Washington encounter between Palestinian and Israeli envoys in a vain attempt to restart the Israeli-Palestinian peace process. During November, when confrontations between Palestinians and Israelis were intensifying in the Palestinian territories, he was in Israel to meet with leaders of the two camps. At the beginning of 2001, after ten years devoted largely to the Israeli-Palestinian conflict, he resigned as U.S. special envoy to the Middle East to rejoin the Washington Institute for Near East Policy.

SEE ALSO Albright, Madeleine; Arafat, Yasir; Barak, Ehud; Camp David II Summit; Christopher, Warren; Indyk, Martin; Madrid Conference; Mousa, Amr Muhammad; Netanyahu, Benjamin; Palestinian Authority; Rabin, Yitzhak; Shara, Faruk al-.

ROTHSCHILD, EDMOND DE (1845–1935):
Banker, born in Paris. In 1882 Baron Edmond de Rothschild began to support Jewish emigration to Palestine, donating money to the Lovers of Zion pioneers, which allowed them to create several colonies. In 1891 he was joined by the financier Maurice de Hirsch in creating the Jewish Colonization Association. In 1900 Rothschild helped finance the Jewish National Fund and supported Eliezer Ben-Yehuda in his efforts to modernize Hebrew. A regent of the Bank of France, he participated in financing World War I.

SEE ALSO Lovers of Zion.

RUBINSTEIN, AMNON (1931–):
Israeli law professor and politician. Amnon Rubinstein was born in Tel Aviv and studied at the Hebrew University and the London School of Economics. In 1974 he founded the Shinui Party, a liberal, secular Zionist party that advocated electoral reform and the formulation of a written constitution. In 1992 Shinui joined MAPAM and the Citizens' Rights Party to form the Meretz Party, which won twelve seats in the Knesset. Rubinstein was a member of the Knesset from 1977 to 2002, serving on key committees, including foreign affairs and defense, economy, and ethics. In the National Unity government (1984–1988) he was minister of communications. From 1992 to 1996 he served as minister of education and culture and was responsible for the introduction of major legislation leading to educational reform. He retired from politics in 2002 to become dean of the law school of the Herzliya Interdisciplinary Centre.

SEE ALSO Knesset; MAPAM; Meretz Party; Shinui Party.

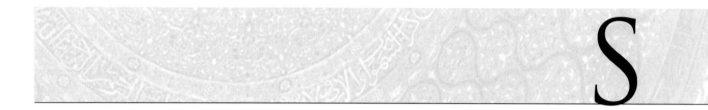

S

Sabra: From the Hebrew word *tsabar,* which means, in reference to cactus or the fruit of the Barbary fig tree, "sweet inside, under a prickly skin." By extension, this word is used to designate a Jew born in Israel, as opposed to immigrants.

Sabra and Shatila: Adjacent Palestinian refugee camps—actually a single area—in southern West Beirut, the site of a mass murder of Palestinian civilians during the Israeli invasion of Lebanon in 1982. From June through August, the Israelis bombed and shelled Beirut, where the Palestine Liberation Organization (PLO) and most of its fighters were trapped (destroying much of the city). A cease-fire was negotiated by the United States under which the Israelis withdrew from the city. After assurances were given that Palestinian civilians living in refugee camps would be protected, the PLO agreed to accept a safe passage, under protection of a multinational force, out of Lebanon; they were gone by 1 September. The Israelis' second goal in invading, after destroying the PLO, was to ensure the election of their ally and client, Bashir Jumayyil of the Phalange, as president of Lebanon.

Jumayyil was elected by the Lebanese parliament on 23 August. The multinational force withdrew on 10 September; on 11 September Israeli defense minister Ariel Sharon declared that "2,000 terrorists" remained in the Palestinian refugee camps in Beirut

("We even have their names," he claimed). On 12 September Sharon met with Jumayyil to arrange for the Phalange and its associated militia, the Lebanese Forces (LF) to "mop up" the camps. On 14 September a pan-Syrian nationalist assassinated Jumayyil. On 15 September, in violation of the cease-fire, Israeli troops once again entered Beirut, to help the Phalange and the LF take control of the city (the cease-fire agreement had assumed that the Lebanese army would take over West Beirut). As part of this operation the Israelis shelled the camps, and fired into them with small arms. On the following day, the Israel Defense Force (IDF), providing protection and logistical support, brought an LF force of 150 men under the command of Elie Hobeika into the camps, where from 6:00 P.M. on 16 September through 8:00 A.M. on 18 September, with Israeli forces surrounding them, the forces systematically killed approximately 1,500 to 3,000 civilians, and raped and injured an unknown number of others. Numerous people were "rounded up" and disappeared.

The massacre aroused strong reactions in Israel and the entire world. In Tel Aviv, 400,000 Israelis demonstrated in the streets to show their indignation, and the United States decided to interrupt its assistance to Israel for the construction of the Lavi bomber. The government of Prime Minister Menachem Begin (who himself had participated in the Deir Yassin massacre of 1948) was forced to appoint an investigative commission headed by the chief of the Israeli Supreme Court, Yitzhak Kahan. The Kahan Commission, reporting in February 1983, assigned "direct" responsibility for the massacre to the Phalangists, and "personal" but "indirect" responsibility to Defense Minister Ariel Sharon, as well as lesser degrees of "indirect" responsibility to IDF chief of staff General Rafael Eitan, Foreign Minister Yitzhak Shamir, and other officials, for "having disregarded the danger of acts of vengeance and bloodshed by the Phalangists against the population of the refugee camps" when allowing them into the camps, knowing their express hostility to Palestinians, and for allowing them to stay after being informed of the killings. It did not accept eyewitness accounts of Israeli direction of the action and did not question Sharon's assertion that there were "2000 terrorists" in the camps. An investigation by an unofficial International Commission of Enquiry headed by former United Nations assistant secretary general and Nobel Peace Prize winner Sean MacBride, held Israel responsible under the Geneva Conventions as an "occupying power," concluding that Israel both intended and enabled the massacre, and recommended a Nuremburg-style war crimes tribunal. (There was also an official investigation by a Lebanese military prosecutor, who absolved the Phalange of any responsibility and never issued a report, and several independent Palestinian investigations.)

After the Kahan report, Sharon was made to resign as defense minister, but remained in the government as minister without portfolio. Both Shamir and he went on to become prime minister. No one has ever been prosecuted, although there has been an effort to have Sharon tried for war crimes in Belgium, under that country's Universal Jurisdiction Law. The case was first brought in 2001 and has been the subject of several contradictory rulings by Belgian courts. As of 2004, the United States and Israel are bringing pressure on the Belgian government to amend the law.

SEE ALSO Begin, Menachem; Hobeika, Elie; Jumayyil, Bashir; Sharon, Ariel.

SABRA AND SHATILA MARTYRS GROUP: One of a number of small Palestinian resistance groups that sprung up in the Occupied Territories during the al-Aqsa Intifada, which began in late September 2000. These groups, collectively known as al-Tanzim ("organization"), are under the leadership of a younger generation of Palestinians who mainly grew up under the occupation. This group was named in honor of the victims of the Sabra and Shatila massacre at the Palestinian refugee camps in Beirut in 1982.

SEE ALSO Aqsa Intifada, al-; Tanzim, al-.

SADAT, ANWAR AL- (1918–1981): Egyptian military and political figure. Anwar al-Sadat was born in Mit Abu al-Kum, in Lower Egypt, the son of a government clerk. He graduated from the national military academy in 1938 as a communications officer and became friendly with Gamal Abdel Nasser, with whom he began to cultivate a network of officers opposed to the monarchy and British control of the country. Sadat also made contact with a number of clandestine groups working against the monarchy, including the Muslim Brotherhood. During World War II, Sadat was part of a cell within the army that collaborated with the Germans, in whom they saw an ally against the British. In October 1942 he was arrested by the British authorities for espionage on behalf of the Axis. Escaping from prison in 1944, he went underground with the Muslim Brotherhood until he was again arrested, accused of participating in the assassination of the finance minister, Amin Osman, in January 1946. After more than two years of imprisonment, he was released for lack of proof and expelled from the army.

In 1948 he launched on a career as a publisher with the review *al-Mussawar,* which failed; late the following year he was readmitted into the army with his old rank of captain. Reunited with his friend Nasser at his new posting in the Sinai, he joined the movement Nasser had founded, now called the Free Officers, which aimed to abolish the monarchy.

On 23 July 1952 Sadat participated in the coup d'état that overthrew King Faruq and Nasser assigned him to supervise Faruq's abdication. After the Free Officers took power, he became editor of the government's newspaper *al-Gumhuriya* (The republic) and a member of the Revolutionary Command Council. On 1 September 1954 he was on the tribunal charged with trying the Muslim Brothers who had attempted to assassinate Nasser, who by then had become president of the republic. In 1959 he became president (speaker) of the National Assembly, keeping that position until 1969.

From 1964 to 1966 he was one of Nasser's four vice presidents, and in 1969 he was appointed sole vice president. He presided over the 1969 Islamic summit meeting in Rabat that created the Organization of the Islamic Conference. When Nasser died of a heart attack in September 1970, Sadat was appointed interim president by the cabinet; his presidency was confirmed in a referendum in October (no other

ANWAR AL-SADAT. GAMAL ABDEL NASSER'S SUCCESSOR AS PRESIDENT IN 1970, SADAT LED EGYPT INTO THE ARAB-ISRAELI WAR OF 1973. HE ALSO CUT TIES WITH THE SOVIET UNION AND RENEWED RELATIONS WITH THE UNITED STATES. THEN, IN 1977, HE INITIATED CONTACT WITH ISRAEL; THE RESULTS INCLUDED THE HISTORIC CAMP DAVID ACCORDS, PEACE WITH ISRAEL (INCLUDING AN AGREEMENT TO RETURN THE SINAI PENINSULA TO EGYPT)—AND HIS ASSASSINATION BY EGYPTIAN EXTREMISTS IN 1981. *(AP/Wide World Photos)*

candidates were offered). He resolved the internal power struggle that followed in May 1971 by having his chief rival, the leftist Ali Sabri, whom he had appointed as one of two vice presidents, arrested on charges of plotting a coup. At the same time he moved to cultivate conservative religious elements by emphasizing his own religious beliefs and allowing the creation of Islamist political groups. To improve the depressed Egyptian economy, he instituted a liberal economic policy meant to attract foreign investment capital, backtracking on Nasser's policy of nationalization and directed development.

It was in part to counter the unpopularity of his domestic policies that Sadat made his most dramatic efforts in foreign affairs. Not long after taking office he signed the Egyptian-Soviet Friendship Treaty, which originated during the Nasser regime, but feeling that the Soviet Union gave him inadequate support in Egypt's continuing confrontation with Israel, he expelled thousands of Soviet technicians and advisers from the country in 1972. (He reconciled with the Soviet Union early in 1973, after which military aid resumed.) Frustrated by the Israeli refusal to negotiate the return of captured Egyptian territory, he also reconciled with Saudi Arabia and Syria and planned for a campaign to recapture it. Egypt and Syria launched the October 1973 War; the Egyptians achieved a tactical surprise in its attack on the Israeli-held Sinai Peninsula, and although Israel successfully counterattacked Sadat came out of the war with greatly enhanced prestige as the first Arab leader to retake some territory from Israel. Sadat successfully achieved two objectives with this war: showing that Egyptian armed forces were capable of fighting well against the Israelis and provoking the Americans to step in to mediate a peace settlement. Sadat agreed to an Israeli proposal to seek a treaty under U.S. rather than UN auspices and concluded agreements in 1974 and 1975 dealing with disengagement in the Sinai.

In October 1975, having opened the Suez Canal to international traffic after it had been closed for eight years, he became the first Egyptian president to visit the United States. He sought American aid and investment and abrogated the friendship treaty with the Soviet Union in 1976 when the Soviets refused to delay repayment of Egyptian debts. In late 1977 Sadat made his dramatic trip to Jerusalem to deliver a speech to the Knesset, in which he offered Israel peace, recognition, and security guarantees while warning that no "durable and just peace" could be achieved "in the absence of a just solution to the Palestinian problem," and insisting on a complete withdrawal from the occupied territories, "including Arab Jerusalem," because "any move to ensure our coexistence in peace and security . . . would become meaningless while you occupy Arab territories by force of arms." He did not claim to be speaking on behalf of all Arabs, but he declared that he was not seeking a separate peace.

Five days after returning from Jerusalem, Sadat convened a meeting in Cairo to attempt to obtain the support of the Arab countries for an international peace conference. These steps, which made the Egyptian president an honored figure internationally, led not to an international conference but to Camp David—the separate peace that Sadat claimed not to want, with no Israeli concessions regarding the Palestinians or the occupied territories. Sadat signed the

Camp David Accords in September 1978 and the subsequent peace treaty in March 1979. In October 1978 he and Israeli Prime Minister Menachem Begin were awarded the Nobel Peace Prize. The separate peace with Israel was unloved by Arabs and constituted a break with the entire Arab world. Members of the Arab League severed diplomatic relations; Egypt was suspended from the league and from the Organization of the Islamic Conference. It became highly dependent on American aid, which in turn affected Sadat's domestic policies.

In Egypt there was immense popular opposition to the treaty, with its perceived capitulation over the Palestinian issue, as well as to Sadat's economic liberalization. In the fall of 1974, about a year after the war, Sadat had introduced an intensified economic liberalization policy he called *infitah* ("opening up"). More foreign exchange was necessary to finance imports, and Sadat also wished to refinance Egypt's foreign debt. Largely at the behest of the World Bank, he reduced taxes and import duties, opened land and banking to foreign ownership, reduced protection for labor, reduced exchange controls, reduced food subsidies and price controls, and froze salaries. This policy brought inflation, increased the gap between rich and poor, created a whole new corrupt profiteer class (called *munfatihin*, "door openers") and brought tremendous hardship to the lower and middle classes. There were food riots in January 1977, which were suppressed violently by the army; 171 people died. Sadat referred to the rioters as "thieves."

In July of that year, a military expedition into Libya, organized to distract attention from internal problems, was opposed by most Egyptians. To retain control, Sadat governed in an increasingly autocratic and repressive manner, largely by decree and through rigged elections. He introduced legal limits on political activity. In June 1978 he had the leadership of the Wafd, an increasingly popular opposition party, arrested. He outlawed strikes, imposed censorship, repressed Palestinian political and economic activity in Egypt, and attempted to undermine the Palestine Liberation Organization. In January 1979, on an official visit to Sudan, he denounced Soviet intervention in Afghanistan and proposed that his country help the United States counter the "Soviet danger." In June 1979 he dissolved parliament and held a rigged election in which his own newly formed National Democratic Party gained the parliamentary majority. In May 1980, confronting a difficult economic situation and growing religious agitation, he appointed himself prime minister for the second time (the first had been in 1973–1974).

On 22 May 1981, a rigged referendum approved a constitutional amendment repealing the one-term limit for the presidency. In September 1981 he had nearly all activist dissidents and opposition political leaders imprisoned—some 1,500 to 2,000 people, among them the head of the Muslim Brotherhood—and dismissed Pope Shenouda III, head of the Coptic Church, who went into internal exile. When Sadat was assassinated by a group of young officers belonging to Egyptian Islamic Jihad, he was barely mourned; indeed his death was celebrated throughout the Arab world.

SEE ALSO Arab-Israel War (1973); Begin, Menachem; Camp David Accords; Eyptian Islamic Jihad; League of Arab States; Muslim Brotherhood; Nasser, Gamal Abdel; Organization of the Islamic Conference; Palestine Liberation Organization; Wafd.

SADR, MUSA AL-: Lebanese Shi'ite leader, born in March 1928 in Qom, Iran. Musa al-Sadr belonged to a family divided among three countries: Iran, Iraq, and Lebanon. After having followed religious studies in Iraq, then legal studies in Iran, Sadr returned to Qom, where he became an ulema. In this capacity, he gave conferences in theology and edited the review *Maktabi Islam*. In 1960 he was sent to Lebanon to replace Shaykh Abdul Hussein Sharafeddin, head of the Shi'ite community of Tyre. He soon became involved in social and political work aimed at reducing the social inequities that put the largely poor and disenfranchised Lebanese Shi'ite community at a considerable disadvantage. After participating in an Islamic-Christian dialogue in 1962, he made efforts to form a permanent committee of Muslim and Christian religious leaders of South Lebanon. After becoming a Lebanese citizen, he formed and headed the Supreme Islamic Shi'a Council (or Communal Council) in 1968–1969.

Having launched an appeal for a general strike on 26 May 1970, he was successful in establishing, at least temporarily, a dialogue with the Lebanese government over economic development of South Lebanon and the Baqaa Valley. Frustrated by a lack of results, however, Sadr in 1973 founded the Movement of the Disinherited, a branch of the Foundation of the Disinherited (*Mustadafin*), created in Iran in 1971. On 18 March 1974, he assembled at Baalbek some 100,000 people, ready to support him in his fight against poverty. In July 1975, confronted by the continued unresponsiveness of the government, the outbreak of communal fighting in the spring—the beginning of the civil war of 1975–1990—and the degradation of the situation in South Lebanon, Sadr and his fellow leaders decided to create an armed branch of the Movement, calling it AMAL ("Hope"), an acronym for Lebanese Resistance Brigade. Inspired by the al-Daʿwa movement, Sadr advocated jihad to establish an independent democratic republic in Lebanon that would protect the interests of the Shiʿites and support the struggle against Zionism. Despite this, he made efforts to maintain a moderate stance. AMAL did not engage in fighting in the early period of the civil war, and as a result lost considerable support to the Palestine Liberation Organization (PLO) and groups associated with the Lebanese National Movement (LNM). AMAL also endorsed Syrian intervention in 1976, which cost it more support. However, the mysterious disappearance of Sadr, along with two companions while on an official visit to Libya on 31 August 1978, transformed him into a popular hero and Shiʿa symbol (on the analogy of the Hidden Imam). It has always been assumed that Sadr was assassinated by the regime of Col. Muammar al-Qaddafi, but Libyan authorities have denied any responsibility in his disappearance, which prompted a period of tension between Libya and Iran.

SEE ALSO AMAL; Movement of the Disinherited; Shiʿite; Zionism.

SAFED (in Arabic, *Safad*; in Hebrew, *Tzefat*): City of Galilee; birthplace of Simon ben Yohai, presumed author of the Zohar. Safed is mentioned by the Roman historian Flavius; it was later an administrative center of the Mamluks. A city of mixed Arab and Jewish population, in the late eighteenth century Safed saw the influx of two large Jewish groups, the Hasidim and the followers of Rabbi Elijah Goan of Vilnius. In 1929 Arabs attacked and destroyed the Jewish quarter, which was rebuilt in the 1930s. In 1948 the Jewish population of the city was only 2,000, of a total population of 12,000. After the British evacuated in April 1948, Arab forces attacked Safed. When Palmakh forces launched a counterattack in May, most of the Arab population fled the city. Modern-day Safed (population 27,000) is considered a center of the arts and of Jewish mysticism.

SAID, EDWARD (1935–2003): Palestinian-American scholar, critic, and writer, born in 1935 in Jerusalem. At the end of 1947, Edward Wadie Said, with his family, left Palestine for Egypt, where his father ran a branch of the family business, and they were unable to return after the Arab-Israel War (1948). Said, raised as an Anglican, attended a British school in

Cairo and a prep school in the United States, where, in 1953, he obtained American nationality (his father had become a citizen through his service in the U.S. Army in World War I). After a brilliant student career at Princeton and Harvard, he became an academic literary critic. From 1963 until his death he was a professor of English and comparative literature at Columbia University in New York. By his own account, he was not politically engaged until the 1967 Arab-Israel War, a shock that caused him to reflect on the situation of the Palestinians. He soon became the best-known American advocate for the Palestinian cause, although he was never a spokesman for any Palestinian faction, from all of which he kept his distance.

From 1977 to 1991 he was an unaffiliated member of the Palestine National Council (PNC), and helped to write the proposed Palestinian constitution in 1988. In September 1993 just before the signing of the Israeli-Palestinian Declaration of Principles, he expressed openly his opposition to the Oslo Accords. He went on to publish many articles critical of the accords and the "peace process," which he felt were a disastrous capitulation—he called it "a Palestinian Versailles"—leaving the Palestinians defenseless against Israeli power, and obligating the Palestine Liberation Organization (PLO) to suppress the Palestinians on Israel's behalf. Before the Oslo Accords he had generally favored a two-state solution as an acceptable compromise, but the historical developments of the 1990s convinced him that the only fair solution was the creation of a binational state for both Jews and Palestinians. But he insisted that no solution would work, given the unequal power of the parties, unless Israelis faced up to and took responsibility for the injustice and cruelty of what they had done to the Palestinians, of dispossessing an entire people to establish another in their place, and then demonizing them as monstrous and inhuman for failing to accept their treatment quietly. He was a severe and articulate critic of the Israel and Zionist project, of America's imperial relation to the world, of craven and undemocratic Arab political leadership, and particularly of the policies and character of Yasir Arafat and the Palestinian leadership, whom he felt were corrupt and incompetent. (Arafat responded by banning Said's works in the territory ruled by the Palestinian Authority [PA].)

Said's work advocated, and embodied, what he called "worldliness," an understanding of the effects of theories and texts in the world, rather than as abstract intellectual exercises. He was also a highly accomplished musician; he published two books on music, and with his friend Daniel Barenboim, the Israeli conductor and pianist, founded the East-West Divan, a Palestinian-Israeli orchestra. He was the author of more than two dozen books and hundreds of articles, and from the mid-1990s until 2003 he wrote a monthly column for *al-Ahram,* the Egyptian newspaper. His 1978 book *Orientalism* reevaluated an entire historical tradition of European-American thought, examining the relation of political power to the representation of the world, and generated an entire field of cultural and postcolonial studies as well as informing the thinking of scholars in every area of cultural, social and historical work. Other significant books include *The Question of Palestine* (1979), *Covering Islam* (1981), *The World, the Text and the Critic* (1983), *Culture and Imperialism* (1993), *The Politics of Dispossession* (1994), *Representations of the Intellectual* (1994), *Peace and Its Discontents* (1995), *The End of the Peace Process* (2000), *Reflections on Exile* (2000) and *Humanism and Democratic Criticism* (2004). He published a memoir of his early years, *Out of Place,* in 1999. Edward Said was by general consent one of the most influential intellectuals of the late twentieth century. He died in New York on 25 September 2003.

SEE ALSO Arab-Israel War (1948); Arab-Israel War (1967); Palestine National Council.

SA'IQA, AL-: Palestinian movement ("Thunderbolt") created in 1967 by the Syrian Ba'th Party, after the Arab defeat in the Arab-Israel War that year. Under the leadership of Zuhayr Muhsin, al-Sa'iqa received the support of Syrian authorities anxious to counterbalance Iraqi influence on the Palestinian situation. Upholding pan-Arabism in general, al-Sa'iqa supported the creation of a secular Palestinian state under a socialist regime. Its first leader, Muhsin, one of the main rivals of Yasir Arafat for the leadership of the Palestinian resistance, was assassinated on 25 July 1979 in Cannes, France. Considered an elite paramilitary unit, al-Sa'iqa is also known as the "Vanguard of the People's War of Liberation," or as "Eagles of the Palestinian Revolution."

In September 1973 al-Sa'iqa carried out an attack in Austria on a train conveying Russian Jews for transfer to Israel. They held three hostages until the Austrian government agreed to close its transfer facility at Schönau. The perpetrators were released. Among other such incidents in which al-Sa'iqa participated in the 1970s were the March 1979 bombing of a kosher restaurant in Paris, which wounded twenty; the April 1979 bombings of the Israeli embassies in Nicosia and Ankara and a synagogue in Vi-

enna (no one was injured); and the July 1979 occupation of the Egyptian Embassy at Ankara. During the Lebanese Civil War (1973–1990), the movement sided totally with Syria against the Palestine Liberation Organization (PLO) and its Lebanese allies. In October 1983 the spokesperson of the movement, Farhan Abu al-Haija, exhorted Palestinian fighters to reject the authority of Arafat and to join the ranks of the Fatah-Intifada. In 1985 al-Sa'iqa quit the Executive Committee of the PLO and joined the Palestinian National Salvation Front (PNSF), becoming part of the Palestinian opposition. From 1990 on, most of its members were integrated into the Syrian army, reducing the activity of the movement to zero. In spite of having no presence in the Palestinian community, al-Sa'iqa joined the Palestinian opposition coalition, the Alliance of Palestinian Forces (APF), in 1993. The principal leaders of the movement included Isam al-Qadi (secretary general), Muhammad Khalifa (adjunct), Saleh Maani, Farhan al-Haija, Marwan Akari, Hassan Shahrur, and Majid Muhsin.

SEE ALSO Alliance of Palestinian Forces; Arab-Israel War (1967); Arafat, Yasir; Ba'th Party; Fatah-Intifada.

SALAAM: In Arabic, "peace, health" Shalom is its Hebrew equivalent.

SEE ALSO Shalom.

SALADIN (Salah al-Din Yusuf ibn Ayub; 1138–1193): Born in Tikrit, in Iraq, in 1138, died in Damascus in 1193. Kurdish in origin, Saladin was a lieutenant of the governor of Aleppo, Nur al-Din, who inspired him by his faith in holy war. Determined to realize the reunification of the Muslim empire, he conquered Egypt, where he founded the Ayyubid dynasty, by abolishing the Fatimid caliphate. The Ayyubids ruled in Syria, the Hijaz, as well as Mesopotamia (1171–1250), where they created many Sunnite schools. During his reign, Saladin, having defeated the crusaders at Hattin, in Palestine, just west of Lake Tiberius, on 4 July 1187, took Jerusalem, which led to the third Christian crusade (1188–1192). Saladin is an emblematic figure in the Arab world, standing for unity and independence.

SALAFIYYA: From the Arabic *salafi,* ancients. Name of the members of the *salafiya,* pan-Islamist, traditionalist and reformist movement, whose central personage at the end of the nineteenth century was Rashid Rida, a figure who inspired the Muslim Brotherhood. The salafiya ideology called for the renewal of Islam by a return to sources, which, according to this doctrine, would allow society to recover from the ills that beset it. Supplanted by the Muslim Brotherhood, this movement did not really succeed in emerging in Egypt until the beginning of the 1980s, owing to the constitution of a political program created by a dissident splinter group, al-Takfir wa al-Hijra. It has benefited from considerable support from Saudi Arabia.

SEE ALSO Muslim Brotherhood; Takfir wa al-Hijra, al-.

SALAMA, ALI HASSAN AL-

SEE Black September 1970.

SAMARIA: Region in the center of the West Bank, between Galilee to the north and Judea to the south. This is also the name of an ancient city of Palestine, whose destruction in 721 B.C.E., by Sargon II of Assyria, marked the fall of the Kingdom of Israel.

SAMARITAN: Around 932 B.C.E., after the death of King Solomon, there was a schism caused by the Samaritans that led to the constitution of two kingdoms: Israel to the north, and Judah to the south. After the city of Samaria fell in 721, which marked the end of the Kingdom of Israel, a part of the population was deported and replaced by Assyrian colonists, who gradually assimilated with the native peoples. Returning from exile, the Jews banished them from their community and from the Temple, since they considered them to be "half-Jews." Another schism occurred, resulting in the building of a rival temple on Mount Gerizim, north of Nabulus. Samaritans recognize only the Pentateuch and the Book of Joshua as sacred, while practicing their own special kind of Judaism. Currently, the Samaritan community counts some six to seven hundred people, who live on the slopes of Mount Gerizim, in the village of Kiryat Luza, or in Holon, on the outskirts of Tel Aviv.

SAMED: Palestine Martyrs' Works Society (originally Production Society for the Children of Palestinian Martyrs; *Jami'iyat 'amal abna' shuhada' falastin*), an organization set up and headed by Ahmad Qurai for the Palestine Liberation Organization (PLO) in Jordan in 1970 to provide vocational training and economic support for, at first, the children of those killed in the resistance, and after 1975, to all members of the Palestinian community in exile. It was moved to Beirut and reorganized in 1971. SAMED consisted of a set of business enterprises—crafts, lit-

tle factories and agriculture—that operated in most Palestinian communities in the Middle East outside the occupied territories. It has been dormant since the founding of the Palestinian Authority, but Qurai is still its head. SAMED publishes a scholarly economics journal called *Samed al-Iqtisadi* (SAMED Economist).

SEE ALSO Palestine Liberation Organization; Palestinian Authority.

SANHEDRIN: From the Aramaic *sanhedrin,* itself from the Greek *sunedrion,* meaning "assembly." Name of the supreme political, religious and judiciary tribunal of Judaism in Palestine, during the Roman Occupation.

SANJAK: A Turkish (presumably) word used by the Ottomans to designate an administrative subdivision of a province.

SANT' EGIDIO: Catholic community, founded in Rome, in 1968, by Andrea Riccardi, professor of religious history, for the purpose of educating young people about the situation of disinherited populations. Financed by subscription, and voluntary contributions, and with the support of the Vatican, this community developed a program of charitable activity in the world's most impoverished countries. In the Middle East Sant' Egidio was particularly concerned by the plight of the Palestinian refugees, and by the victims of repressive operations of the Israeli army. Becoming significant figures in humanitarian action, its leaders also launched into what they call "free lance diplomacy," participating in the peaceful resolution of conflicts. Therefore, in 1992, the Mozambique peace accords were concluded at the headquarters of the association, where, in January, 1995, the first encounter between all the parties in the Algerian dispute took place. On 3 September, 2001, the movement organized an encounter at Barcelona to discuss world peace, in which religious dignitaries of all confessions participated.

SARAYAT AL-JIHAD AL-ISLAMI

SEE Palestinian Islamic Jihad.

SARID, YOSSI (1940–): Israeli politician. Born in Rehovot, in Mandatory Palestine, Yossi Sarid had a brief career as a journalist before becoming active in the Israel Labor Party. He was elected to the Knesset in 1974. In 1984, after the formation of the Peres-Shamir unity government, Sarid resigned from the

Labor Party and joined the Movement for Civil Rights and Peace. In 1988 he was one of the founders of Meretz, a leftist party that advocated an active peacemaking process with the Palestinians, and he became party chair in 1996. Sarid was appointed minister of education in 1999, when Meretz was part of the Barak coalition government, and he served briefly until Meretz left the coalition in 2000. In the 2002 elections, the Meretz Party lost four of its ten Knesset seats, and Sarid resigned as party chair. He remained active in the Knesset.

SARRAJ, EYAD EL- (1944–): Palestinian psychiatrist and human rights activist, born in Beersheba in 1944; fled with his family to the Gaza Strip in 1948. Sarraj attended schools in Gaza, earned a medical degree at Alexandria University, a degree in psychology from the University of London and a doctorate at Harvard. Sarraj worked as a pediatrician and as a psychiatrist in Gaza and Bethlehem, and headed Mental Health Services in Gaza in 1981–1988. In 1989–1991, during the first Intifada (1987–1993), he took up a fellowship in the Refugee Studies Program at Oxford. Sarraj is the chairman of the Gaza Community Mental Health Program (GCMHP), which he founded in 1991. (The GCMHP provides services for those traumatized by the military occupation; its eight clinics are said to have treated ten percent of the population of the Gaza Strip.) As a prominent Palestinian human rights activist, he has criticized the policies and practices of both the Israelis and the Palestinian Authority (PA). As a public critic of Yasir Arafat, Sarraj has been jailed by the PA several times, tortured and threatened; in 1996 an international campaign was mounted to force the PA to release him. He is the author of numerous articles in newspapers and on the Internet, and travels frequently to lecture and promote the cause of human rights in Palestine and in the Arab world. Sarraj is on the board of commissioners of the Palestinian Independent Commission for Citizens' Rights (PICCR), and was its general commissioner (chairman) from 1995 to 2002. He is a member of the International Federation of Physicians for Human Rights, the International Rehabilitation Center for Torture Victims, and the Campaign against Torture.

SEE ALSO Arafat, Yasir; Gaza Community Mental Health Program (GCMHP); Gaza Strip; Intifada (1987–1993); Palestinian Authority; Palestinian Independent Commission for Citizens' Rights.

SARTAWI, ISSAM (1934–1983): Palestinian political leader, born in January 1934 in Acre; died in 1983.

Issam Sartawi and his family left Palestine in 1948, at the time of the first Arab-Israel War, to seek refuge in Iraq. He undertook a course of studies in medicine in the United States, choosing cardiology as a specialty. Following the Arab defeat of June 1967, he decided to join the Palestinian resistance, within which he became head of the Active Organization for the Liberation of Palestine (AOLP). Banished from Jordan after the events of Black September 1970, he sought refuge in Beirut, where he became acquainted with a small group of Palestinians that favored making contact with Israelis to resolve the Palestinian question. Among the group were Mahmud Abbas and Said Hamami. In July 1971 Sartawi decided to join al-Fatah. During the summer of 1976, in France, he participated in a number of secret meetings with Israelis who were in favor of an Israeli-Palestinian peace. On 4 January 1978, the assassination of Hamami by an Israeli commando in London strengthened him in his resolve to start negotiations with Israel.

The following May, through the mediation of the Swedish deputy to the Socialist International, he was able to meet with the Austrian chancellor, Bruno Kreisky. From then on, Sartawi traveled frequently to Vienna, where he encountered various Western political figures, arguing the Palestinian cause before them. In July 1979, in the company of Yasir Arafat, he was received by the president of the Socialist International, former West German chancellor Willy Brandt, and by Chancellor Kreisky. On 19 October 1979, at Vienna, he and the Israeli Aryeh Eliav were awarded the Peace Prize of the Kreisky Foundation, in honor of the risks they took to "further reconciliation between their two peoples." Between 1978 and 1982, Sartawi increased his efforts to try to get official Israeli-Palestinian negotiations started, prompting the anger of diverse radical currents, both Israeli and Palestinian. On 15 January 1983, in Tunis, he organized a meeting between Arafat and three Israelis: "Matti" Peled, Uri Avnery, and Yaacov Arnon. This meeting caused a wave of protests in Israel as well as among the Palestinians. On 10 April 1983, he was killed by a member of the Fatah Revolutionary Council of Abu Nidal during a preliminary meeting for the congress of the Socialist International, which was to take place in Portugal.

SEE ALSO Arafat, Yasir; Black September 1970; Fatah, al-; Fatah Revolutionary Council.

SATMAR: An ultra-Orthodox Hasidic sect, founded in New York in 1947 by Rabbi Joel Teitelbaum, passionately anti-Zionist and hostile to the existence of the State of Israel. Connected to the Neturei Karta movement, the Satmar, named after the Hungarian city of Szatmar, is a rival of the Lubavitch. While for the latter the creation of Israel was an act of God, for the Satmar the Jewish state cannot exist before the coming of the Messiah. By the 1960s the Satmar community in the Williamsburg section of New York City was the largest Hasidic community in the United States, and today it is the largest in the world. Most members outside the United States live in London; there are only about four hundred in Israel, migration to which is actively discouraged by the sect.

Rabbi Teitelbaum attracted worldwide Jewish attention on several occasions when he was the only prominent Jewish figure to categorically renounce the newly founded Jewish state and to lament Israel's victory in the Six-Day War. Considering it sinful for Jews to establish their own state prior to the arrival of the Moshiach (or Messiah), he publicly expressed this through sobbing and shouting; but his followers loved and admired him enough to tolerate the negative publicity they received. He died in 1977 and was succeeded by his nephew, Rabbi Moshe Teitelbaum, who holds Israel responsible for its wars with the Arabs.

SEE ALSO Hasidism; Lubavitcher Hasidim; Neturei Karta; Messiah; Moshiach.

SAUDI PEACE PLAN (2002): Plan for an Arab-Israeli peace settlement proposed by Crown Prince Abdullah of Saudi Arabia during the height of the al-Aqsa Intifada. It called for Israel to withdraw to its 1967 boundaries and accept the creation of an independent Palestinian state. In return the Arab states would recognize Israel and establish "normal relations" and security arrangements. The plan did not deal with the question of Palestinians' right to return; it called only for a "just solution" to the refugee problem. First floated publicly in February 2000, the plan was presented to the League of Arab States summit meeting in Beirut in March. It was endorsed by the Palestinian Authority (PA) in a statement read on the Arab satellite news channel al-Jazeera by Yasir Arafat (who was prevented by Israel from traveling out of the West Bank, and by Lebanese authorities from addressing the summit directly) and entered into the summit's minutes the next day by the Palestinian delegation. It was unanimously adopted by the member states in a closed session. In a declaration issued on 28 March, the last day of the summit, the League formally announced that in return for complete withdrawal from all occupied territories, including the Golan Heights; a "just solution to the

Palestinian refugee problem" under the terms of General Assembly Resolution 194 of 1948 (which called for the right to return or compensation for the refugees); and the establishment of a Palestinian state in the West Bank and Gaza Strip with East Jerusalem as its capital, the Arab states would "consider the Arab-Israeli conflict over, sign a peace agreement, and achieve peace for all states in the region." This was the first peace proposal put forth by the entire League of Arab States, and the first to offer immediate recognition and a peace treaty with every Arab state. The Israeli government of prime minister Ariel Sharon was opposed to returning any territory or withdrawing any of the almost 200 West Bank settlements, outposts, and colonies that had been established since 1967, with a population of 400,000. It did not reject the proposal out of hand, calling it a "very interesting development," but let it die.

SEE ALSO Aqsa Intifada, al-; Arafat, Yasir; Gaza Strip; Golan Heights; League of Arab States; Palestinian Authority; Resolution 194; Settlements; Sharon, Ariel; West Bank.

SAYERET: Hebrew word used to designate "special reconnaissance units" of the Israeli army. In the Israel Defense Force there are three principal sayeret—north, central, and south—all directly linked to the general staff. The first, called "Sayeret-Shaked," was formed in the 1950s by Commander Amos Yarkoni, his real name being Abdul Majid, so as to track the fida'iyyun infiltrating through the Negev, coming from Jordan and Egypt. The "Sayeret-Matkal" was formed in 1964, placed under the command of Avraham Arnan. Through the years, and by reason its success, this unit became a veritable "action" service of the Israeli general staff, carrying out a number of assassinations against Palestinian leaders. Between 1970 and 1973, the "Sayeret-Matkal" was headed by Ehud Barak, future prime minister. Finally the "Sayeret-Egoz," formed in 1970, was responsible for special operations in the northern sector of Israel, particularly on the border with Lebanon.

SEE ALSO Barak, Ehud.

SAYF AL-ISLAM: "Sword of Islam," an armed branch of the Palestinian Islamic Jihad created in 1991, whose principal leader was Khalid al-Ayyub.

SEE ALSO Palestinian Islamic Jihad.

SCHACH, ELIEZER (1898–2001): Israeli religious and political leader. Born on 22 January 1989 in the village of Wabolnick in Lithuania, Eliezer Schach was described as a "genius" at a young age. He migrated to Mandatory Palestine with his family in 1938. After studying at various yeshivas, he settled at Ponevezh Yeshiva. Rabbi Schach eventually became the standard-bearer for orthodoxy in Israel. Though he was an Ashkenazi, he was instrumental in forming the Sephardi Torah Guardians Party (SHAS) in the early 1970s. He was apparently in competition with Rabbi Ovadiah Yosef for influence over SHAS, and in 1988 founded a new party, Degel ha-Torah (Torah Flag), for the Ashkenazi ultra-orthodox. Though his rift with Yosef (and a highly publicized remark that Sephardi were not yet ready for leadership) eventually diminished his political influence, he remained the spiritual spokesman of the Ashkenazi and a prominent rabbinical authority until his death in 2001 at the age of 103.

SEE ALSO Ashkenazi; Degel ha-Torah; SHAS; Yosef, Ovadiah.

SECOND GULF WAR

SEE Gulf War (1991).

SEDER: Jewish Easter meal, celebrating the flight from Egypt of the Hebrew people. During the meal, participants recite the Haggadah, the book containing the story of the Exodus and the ritual of the Seder.

SELJUKS: Turkish dynasty that reigned over a part of central Asia from the eleventh to the thirteenth century. Between 1073 and 1092, the Seljuks conquered parts of Asia Minor, Kerman, Transoxiana, Damascus and Jerusalem. Their defeat of the Byzantine Empire opened Asia Minor to settlement by Turks. Seljuk power was based on a strong army and a well-organized administration. The Turkish practice of dividing the kingdom among heirs, family quarrels, the great number of vassals, and the Crusades led to the weakening of Seljuk power and the decline of the empire.

SEMED PROJECT: (Acronym, Southeast Mediterranean Development): A project for the coordinated development of the Southeast Mediterranean, initiated by Israel, Egypt and the Palestinian Authority, with the assistance of the European Union. Its purpose is to foster regional economic cooperation in the SEMED area, a coastal strip running from East of Lake Bardawil, through the Gaza Strip, up to and including Ashdod. A workshop was held in Cairo in 1995 to create a common vision for development of the area. Plans have focused on specific short- and medium-term projects that will attract private investors and create jobs, and have placed emphasis on development of the Gaza Strip to bring its facilities and standards in line with those of the other partners.

SEMITE: From "Shemi," Hebrew word from the name of Shem, son of Noah, who, according to Biblical tradition, was the eponymous ancestor of the Semites. Semites are people of the Middle East and Africa who speak one of the Semitic languages, which are branches of the Afro-Asiatic family. Examples of such languages are Amharic, Arabic, Aramaic, and Hebrew.

SEPHARDI: Descendants of Jews from the Iberian Peninsula, not including others of the lands in which they settled (although the term is used loosely to mean all Jews who are not part of the Ashkenazi culture). According to the dictionary the name derived from the Hebrew word "Sepharadh," which means "Spain;" the word "Sepharad" also appears in the Bible, but there is no scholarly consensus about the location to which it refers. By the Middle Ages, it was the term used by Jews to mean Spain, where during the tenth and eleventh centuries Spanish Judaism flourished under the Muslims. Even during the early centuries of Christian control there, Jews were involved in intellectual, cultural, and economic affairs. In the fifteenth century, however, they faced increasing persecution and violence; many were forced to flee or convert to Christianity, and in 1492 all Jews were expelled from Spain. Thereafter, communities of exiled Sephardi were established in many nations.

The Sephardi community has been one of the most disadvantaged in Israeli society. One of the main cleavages among Israelis opposes Sephardi to Ashkenazi, the former reproaching the latter with dominating the country. In September 1998, a historical study established that at the beginning of the existence of the State of Israel, the leaders, mostly Ashkenazi, decided to be selective about the eastern Jews (Sephardi) they were going to admit, receiving only those who would not represent a burden for the country. Disappointed by the promises of the Labor Party and by the attitudes of the Ashkenazim, a majority of the Sephardi rallied to Likud in 1977, thereby allowing the right-wing party to come to power after thirty years of Labor control. In May 1999, however, the Sephardi vote in the general elections caused the fall of the government of Benjamin Netanyahu, enabling the Labor Party to return to power. Tensions remain between Ashkenazi and Sephardi, but although the latter have not attained full equality in Israel, they have been politically active, especially through SHAS, and have increasingly occupied positions of influence.

SEE ALSO Ashkenazi; SHAS.

SEPHARDI TORAH GUARDIANS

SEE SHAS.

SEPTUAGINT

SEE Bible.

SETTLEMENT PARTY (*Mifleget ha-Hityashvut,* in Hebrew): Israeli political entity, formed in April, 1996, in anticipation of the coming Knesset elections. This movement was created uniquely to draw the attention of the Israeli government to the plight of Jewish settlers, who would lose everything, were there to be an Israeli withdrawal from the occupied territories. The Settlement Party obtained no seat in the Knesset.

SETTLEMENTS: Israeli colonies established in the Palestinian territories occupied by the Israeli Army in the Arab-Israel War (1967). The settlements were established by government policy and with substantial, and ongoing, state aid, infrastructure creation and military protection. The policy has been more or less aggressive, depending on the party in power. There are now more than 400,000 settlers in approximately 200 settlements in the West Bank, Gaza Strip and Golan Heights (before 1979 there were also settlements in the Sinai) including about 200,000 in the area immediately surrounding East Jerusalem.

Israeli colonization of these territories began immediately after the war. Before 1977 settlements were placed, in accordance with the Allon Plan, in and above the Jordan Valley, where the Palestinian population was small, and in a ring around East Jerusalem, which was incorporated into Israel just after the war. The Allon Plan anticipated an eventual treaty providing for a substantial portion of the West Bank to be annexed to Israel. This annexation included the Jordan Valley and the area between the river and Jerusalem, as well as the establishment of two autonomous Palestinian areas in the remainder—roughly eleven percent of Mandate Palestine, completely surrounded by Israel—which would have been administered by Jordan. The settlements were part of a strategy that was primarily defensive, though also acquisitive; it would have increased the amount of land controlled by Israel, but not the areas with the heaviest Palestinian population, and, it was believed, would have created a more easily defensible border.

HARADAR. THIS PHOTOGRAPH, C. 1994, SHOWS HARADAR, ONE OF THE LARGE NUMBER OF ISRAELI SETTLEMENTS ESTABLISHED IN VARIOUS PARTS OF THE OCCUPIED WEST BANK SINCE 1967. DISPUTES OVER THE SIZE, LOCATION, AND VERY EXISTENCE OF THESE SETTLEMENTS ARE AMONG THE MOST DIFFICULT ISSUES DIVIDING ISRAELIS AND PALESTINIANS WHO SEEK PEACE. *(© Morton Beebe, S.F./Corbis)*

After the Arab-Israel War (1973), ultraorthodox religious nationalist Jews were convinced that the Israel Defense Force (IDF) victories were messianic signs of the realization of a "Greater Israel" promised them by God. They founded the Gush Emunim movement, which regarded the Allon Plan as "minimalist." The Gush dedicated itself to establishing settlements throughout the occupied territories, and making it impossible to remove them in any future peace agreement. This movement was opposed by the Labor governments in power until 1977, but with the formation of a government that year led by the Likud—a party whose fundamental principle was the annexation of the occupied territories—their program became official state policy. A 1977 plan devised by housing minister Ariel Sharon—the Sharon Plan—proposed a line of settlements running north-south inside the Green Line in the western part of the West Bank. The Sharon Plan was enhanced by a another plan proposed by the World Zionist Organization in 1978, which called for settlements to be built around and in between towns in the most heavily populated Palestinian areas, dividing them from each other and thwarting "political and territorial continuity." These plans have been the basis of Israeli policy ever since. After 1967, approximately half the land in the West Bank was appropriated for settlements and military purposes, and by 1977 there were roughly 4,200 settlers in 36 settlements. Settlement building accelerated in the early 1980s, along with the confiscation of land, the building of roads, and all the legal and material measures necessary to create "facts on the ground," including financial incentives to potential settlers. By the time of the Oslo Accords of 1993, there were almost 200,000 settlers; after the Accords, new settlement activity, particularly expansion to accommodate "natural growth," was increased dramatically, and from 1994 to 2000 the number of settlers doubled. The 1990s also saw the building of roughly 250 miles of bypass roads, meant for Israeli use only, accompanied by further expropriation, crop destruction and house demolitions (construction is forbidden within fifty-five yards of such a road).

The religious settlers and their supporters believe that Jews must inhabit and control every part of Mandate Palestine (and, some of them, beyond), and a good many of them believe that Palestinians should be removed from it. The idea of "land for peace" is profoundly offensive to them and they have opposed any and all efforts to make a negotiated peace, even when the compromise keeps Palestinians virtually caged within noncontiguous "autonomous" zones under Israeli control. Ultraorthodox rabbis have ruled that settling *Eretz Yisroel* is a *mitzvah,* a religious imperative, and that dismantling settlements is contrary to religious law and must be resisted. This element in Israeli society is increasingly powerful, and has demonstrated that it can thwart or cripple government action. In mid-2004 it was mobilizing against Prime Minister Sharon's so-called Gaza "disengagement" plan.

Under international law, settlements are forbidden. The fourth Geneva Convention prohibits an occupying power from transferring its own citizens into occupied territory. Other humanitarian law forbids an occupying power to make changes in an occupied area unless for the benefit of the occupied population. Land expropriations have been carried out under Israeli laws and regulations, although Jor-

danian law remains the internationally recognized legal regime in the West Bank, as Egyptian law does in the Gaza Strip. Continued Israeli control of Palestinian land is not recognized as valid by the international community. The occupation, as well as changes in the status of the territories, is in violation of several UN resolutions, notably Security Council Resolution 242 of 1967, passed just after the 1967 War. The Resolution asserts "the inadmissibility of the acquisition of territory by war" and calls for the "withdrawal of Israeli armed forces from territories occupied." Israel rejects all such arguments, and by signing the Oslo Accords, the Palestine Liberation Organization (PLO) has effectively politically undermined them; under the Accords all matters affecting the status of the occupied territories have become subject to negotiation, including settlements, borders, security, water rights, the right of return for refugees, and the status of Jerusalem. Israel's overwhelming power, and the Palestinians' weakness, has made it impossible for the Palestinians to negotiate on an equal basis, or even to compel Israel to negotiate at all.

SEE ALSO Allon Plan; Arab-Israel War (1967); Arab-Israel War (1973); Gaza Strip; Golan Heights; Green Line; Gush Emunim; Israel Defense Force; Likud; Oslo Accords; Palestine Liberation Organization; Resolution 242; Sharon, Ariel; West Bank; World Zionist Organization.

SFEIR, NASRALLAH (1920–): Lebanese Maronite religious leader, born in May 1920, at Reyfun; Patriarch of the Maronite Catholic Church since April 1986. Considered to be a man of compromise and dialogue, his election seemed to exemplify the desire of the Maronite Church to mark its independence from certain Maronite leaders who, in the late 1980s, prosecuted an internal civil war within the Maronite community (within the Lebanese civil war of 1975–90). In September 1986, as president of the Council of Bishops and Patriarchs, Sfeir made an appeal for an end to the Lebanese war and for reestablishing the unity and sovereignty of an independent state. He appealed many times for dialogue between Christians and Muslims; in April 1987, on an official visit to Algiers, he received the head of the Palestine Liberation Organization (PLO), Yasir Arafat.

In 1988–1989 Sfeir made efforts as a mediator for a presidential election to take place, with a candidate able to win a national consensus. He opposed General Aoun for provoking the bloody confrontations between Christian militias meant to prevent implementation of the Ta'if Accords. On 6 November 1989, partisans of Aoun forced him to flee to the north of Lebanon, which was under Syrian control. (Aoun was defeated by the Syrians in late 1991 and fled the country.) In 1994 with the arrest of Samir Geagea, the last of the Phalange warlords, Sfeir became the most prominent leader of the Maronite community. On 1 April 1994, in his Easter sermon, Sfeir accused the Lebanese state of not treating the Lebanese Christians equitably, thereby violating the Ta'if Accords. In November, he was named a cardinal by Pope John Paul II. In May 1997, following the success of the latter's visit to Lebanon, Sfeir consolidated his position as the head of the Christian camp, confirming also his role of mediator with other Lebanese communities. On 22 August 2000, in the course of an interview with the *al-Nahar* newspaper during the Lebanese legislative elections, he reaffirmed his desire to see Lebanon free itself from Syrian influence, while maintaining special relations with Syria. (He had little to say about the Israeli occupation in South Lebanon.) On 4 August 2001, Sfeir visited the head of the Druze community, Walid Jumblatt, to show his support for the reconciliation between the Druze and Christian communities.

SEE ALSO Aoun, Michel; Arafat, Yasir; Druze; Jumblatt, Walid Kamal; Maronite; Phalange; South Lebanon; Ta'if Accords.

SHA'AB, AL- (*The People,* in Arabic): Palestinian daily paper based in Jerusalem Started in 1972, the paper has ties to the Palestine Liberation Organization (PLO).

SEE ALSO Palestine Liberation Organization.

SHAB: Arabic word meaning "adolescent" or "youth"; plural *shabab* (m.) or *shabiba* (f.). The term is used in the media to designate young Palestinians participating in the first Intifada or the al-Aqsa Intifada.

SEE ALSO Aqsa Intifada, al-; Intifada (1987–1993).

SHABAK

SEE Shin Bet.

SHABBAT (*sabbat, sabbath*): Holy day of rest for Jews, referring to the seventh day, in the course of which God rested after creating the world. Starting on Friday, just before sunset, shabbat ends with the appearance of the first stars on Saturday night.

SHABIBAT AL-FATAH: al-Fatah youth movement.

SEE ALSO Fatah, al-.

SHAFI ABD-AL, HAYDAR

SEE Abd al-Shafi, Haydar.

SHAHADA: Arab word used to designate the profession of faith of each Muslim, marked by the saying of the phrase: "There is no god but God, and Muhammad is His prophet." One of the five pillars of Islam.

SEE ALSO Muhammad.

SHAHID: Arab word meaning "martyr."

SHAHID, LEILA MOUNIB (1949–): Palestinian editor and diplomat, born in July 1949, in Beirut, to a family in exile from Acre (her father, Abbas Effendi [Abdul Baha], was one of the principal leaders of the Baha'i movement in Palestine). Shahid first got involved with the Palestinian issue in 1967, providing assistance to refugees in Lebanese camps. In 1970 she met the French writer Jean Genet and helped him during his journeys among the exiled Palestinians in the 1970s and 1980s about which he wrote in his book *Un captif amoureux* (1986; in English *Prisoner of Love,* 2003).

Between 1974 and 1977, following a stint as a journalist for a Lebanese weekly, Shahib studied sociology in France, where she was very active in the General Union of Palestine Students (GUPS). Between 1978 and 1988, she traveled widely in Europe and the Middle East, attending numerous conferences on the Israeli-Arab conflict, where she also happened to meet Israelis who were in favor of peace with the Palestinians. Between 1980 to 1984 she worked for the Society of United Moroccan Editors, and in 1986–1988 she worked for the Institute of Palestine Studies in Beirut and continues to be an editor of its journal *La Revue d'Etudes Palestiniennes,* now published in Paris. A member of al-Fatah, she represented the Palestine Liberation Organization (PLO) in Ireland in 1989, and in September 1990 she was designated the PLO representative in the Netherlands. During her tenure there, she developed relations with the lay Jewish community center in Brussels, which was working for Israeli-Arab peace. In 1992, working with the Israeli Shulamit Aloni among others, she participated in the creation of the Jerusalem Link: a Joint Venture for Peace, a women's association supporting the peace process in the Middle East. After representing the PLO in Denmark, Shahid was named in June 1993 to be the head of the general delegation of the PLO in Paris, a post she still holds. She is the PLO's only woman ambassador.

SEE ALSO Baha'i; Fatah, al-; General Union of Palestine Students; Palestine Liberation Organization.

SHAHIN, ABD AL-AZIZ (Shaheen, Ali Abu; Shahine, Abdu Aziz; 1938–): Palestinian political figure, born in Palestine. After secondary studies in Khan Younis, Gaza Strip, he moved to Saudi Arabia, where he worked in the ministry of health. In 1959 he joined Fatah, the new Palestinian movement created by Yasir Arafat, where he was active in the military section. In June 1967, in the course of an operation in which Arafat also participated, Shahin was captured by the Israelis, who kept him incarcerated until 1982. He is said to have led the Fatah organization inside the Israeli prisons. He lived at Dahaniya in the Gaza Strip until 1983, when he was rearrested for "illegal residence." In March 1984 Israel deported him to Lebanon. Two years later he sought refuge in Iraq. In 1988 he coordinated actions with the Western Sector of Fatah that were linked to the Intifada developing in the Occupied Territories. In August 1989 he was elected to the revolutionary council of Fatah. In 1992 he joined the leadership of the Palestine Liberation Organization in Tunis, where he became one of the leaders of the Western Sector, responsible for Palestinian actions in the Gaza Strip. In September 1993, in spite of his loyalty to Arafat, he opposed the Oslo Accords. Nevertheless he became the Palestinian Legislative Council deputy from Rafah in the Gaza Strip, and was minister of supply in the Palestinian Authority cabinet from 1996 to April 1993. While in that position he was accused, and is still widely suspected, of corruption—specifically, stealing food and medical supplies supplied by the United Nations Relief and Works Agency for Palestine Refugees in the Near East and reselling it on the black market. He retains Arafat's confidence and served as Fatah's representative at the all-faction negotiations in Gaza in 2002, a position he quit, accusing HAMAS of blocking an agreement.

SEE ALSO Arafat, Yasir; Fatah, al-; Gaza Strip; HAMAS; Intifada; Oslo Accords; Palestine Liberation Organization; Palestinian Authority; Palestinian Legislative Council; United Nations Relief and Works Agency for Palestine Refugees in the Near East.

SHAHRIT (from the Hebrew *chahar,* "dawn"): Morning prayer practiced by the Jews.

SHALOM ("peace," in Hebrew): The search for peace is a constant theme in the Bible, as well as in Hebrew liturgy and the Talmud. In the Kabbalistic tradition, Shalom is one of the names of "God, agent of universal harmony." The expression *shalom aleichem* (peace be with you) is close to the Arab phrase *al-salam alaykum* and means the same thing.

SEE ALSO Bible; Salaam; Talmud.

SHALOM ACHSHAV

SEE Peace Now.

SHAM, AL- ("left" or "north," in Arabic): Refers to the direction one takes to get to al-Sham from the Hijaz (western Arabian Peninsula), the original source of Arab culture. *Bilad al-Sham* is the early Arab name for Greater Syria, meaning the geographic area Syria, Lebanon, western Jordan, and Palestine. The name *Syria* (the Greek name for the city of Tyre; *Sur,* in Arabic), became current in the nineteenth century.

SHAMIR, YITZHAK (1915–): Israeli political figure, born in Rozhno, Poland. In 1934 Yitzhak Shamir (born Yzernitsky) joined Betar, the youth wing of the militant right-wing Zionist revisionist movement headed by Vladimir Jabotinsky. The following year he emigrated to Palestine, which was under the British Mandate. He enlisted in Irgun Zvai Le'umi (IZL, or ETZEL) in Tel Aviv, participating in terrorist attacks against the Arab population and British interests. In 1940 he joined the radical Abraham ("Ya'ir") Stern splinter group known as IZL-Bet and became chief of military operations. In December 1943, with Nathan Yalin-Mor and Israel Eldad, he reconstituted the Stern Group, which had been dormant since the death of its leader, renaming it LEHI. In July 1946 he was arrested by British military police following an attack on the King David Hotel in Jerusalem and was deported to Eritrea. He escaped a few months later, going to Djibouti.

In September 1948 a LEHI squad assassinated Count Folke Bernadotte, the UN mediator in Palestine. Outlawed by Israeli authorities, LEHI was dissolved and succeeded by a political organization, the Fighters' List, with Shamir at its head. Between 1955 and 1968 he was in the Mossad, the Israeli special intelligence service. In 1969, having quit Mossad, he entered politics, joining the rightist Herut Party led by his friend Menachem Begin. In July 1973 three small dissident groups in Herut joined with the Liberal Party and Herut to constitute a new right-wing parliamentary bloc, Likud.

YITZHAK SHAMIR. A FOLLOWER OF THE RADICAL NATIONALIST VLA-DIMIR JABOTINSKY AND A LEADER OF GROUPS ENGAGED IN VIOLENT AT-TACKS ON BRITISH AND ARAB TARGETS IN PALESTINE, SHAMIR LATER SERVED IN THE MOSSAD BEFORE ENTERING ISRAELI POLITICS IN 1969 AS AN ASSOCIATE OF MENACHEM BEGIN. HE SUCCEEDED BEGIN AS PRIME MINISTER IN 1983 AND, WITH A LIKUD-LABOR COALITION IN POWER, RETURNED TO THE OFFICE IN 1986. SHAMIR SERVED UNTIL 1992, TWO YEARS AFTER HE DISSOLVED THE UNITY GOVERNMENT. *(© Bettmann/Corbis)*

In October of the following year, as a Herut Knesset member, Shamir was critical of the policies of Yitzhak Rabin, who he argued was putting the existence of the Jewish state at risk through lax policies. In May 1977, ending thirty years of Labor hegemony, Likud came to power. The following month Begin became prime minister and Shamir was elected speaker of the Knesset.

In March 1980 he was named foreign minister in Begin's government. In the June 1981 Knesset elections, Likud won forty-eight seats and Labor won forty-seven. On the following 15 July, Begin, the head of Herut, became prime minister for the second time. In September 1983, weakened by his wife's recent death, his own illness, and criticism of the Israeli invasion of Lebanon, Begin resigned and Shamir replaced him as party leader and prime minister.

Within Likud, two currents surfaced, one led by David Levy and Ariel Sharon, the other by Shamir and Moshe Arens. In the Knesset elections of the following year, Likud won forty-one seats and the Labor Party won forty-four. The two parties constituted a National Unity government, agreeing that their leaders would alternate as prime minister. Shamir became deputy prime minister and foreign minister in the first cabinet headed by Shimon Peres. Two years later, in October 1986, he replaced Peres as prime minister. In the 1988 elections Likud won forty seats and the Labor Party thirty-nine. Another National Unity government was formed, headed by Shamir with Peres as finance minister.

On 13 March 1990 Shamir revoked the Labor ministers, breaking the agreement between the two parties. Two days later the Knesset censured the government by a vote of sixty to fifty-five, causing its dissolution. This was the first time an Israeli government was overthrown by a parliamentary majority. On 11 July, the Labor Party leader having failed to form a new government, Shamir formed one based on a union between Likud, the religious parties, and the extreme right. A few months later he was confronted by the Gulf War, during which the Palestinians in the Occupied Territories supported Baghdad. In response to Washington's demand, he agreed that Israel would not retaliate against a bombardment of Iraqi missiles. At the war's end, he agreed to participate in a peace conference on the Middle East, to take place in Madrid. In October 1991, he headed Israel's Madrid delegation, whose spokesperson was the rising star of Likud, Benjamin Netanyahu. During the conference, Shamir would not yield to any of the significant Arab proposals. The extremist parties, however, opposing any negotiations with the Palestinians, withdrew their support from the Shamir government. On 23 June 1992, weakened by internal divisions, the right lost the elections and was replaced in power by the left, which won 61 of the 120 seats in the Knesset. Shamir resigned from the government and backed Netanyahu as head of Likud. In December 1995, at the age of eighty, Shamir retired from Israeli politics.

SEE ALSO Arab-Israel War (1982); Begin, Menachem; Betar; Bernadotte, Folke; British Mandate; Eldad, Israel; Gulf War (1991); Herut Party; Irgun; Jabotinsky, Vladimir Ze'ev; Levy, David; Likud; Lohamei Herut Yisrael; Madrid Conference; Mossad; Netanyahu, Benjamin; Peres, Shimon; Rabin, Yitzhak; Sharon, Ariel; Stern, Abraham.

SHAMIR PLAN: Name of an Israeli proposal made on 14 May 1989 by Prime Minister Yitzhak Shamir. The four conditions Shamir fixed were: direct negotiations based on the principles of the Camp David Accords; no Palestinian state in the Gaza Strip and the region between Israel and Jordan; no negotiations with the Palestine Liberation Organization; and no change in the status of Judea and Samaria (West Bank) and the Gaza Strip. Otherwise, the Israeli proposal envisaged two phases: first a transitional period of five years; then in the third year of the transition at the latest, negotiations based on Resolutions 242 and 338 to result in a definitive solution. The Palestinians would be represented at the negotiating table by an elected delegation of Arab Palestinians residing in Judea and Samaria and in the Gaza Strip and satisfying the conditions fixed by the Israeli government; a peace treaty would be signed between Jordan and Israel.

SEE ALSO Camp David Accords; Gaza Strip; Judea and Samaria; Palestine Liberation Organization; Resolution 242; Resolution 338; Shamir, Yitzhak; West Bank.

SHAMSEDDIN, MUHAMMAD MAHDI (1933–2001): Lebanese Shi'ite religious leader. After studying theology in Iraq, Muhammad Mahdi Shamseddin returned to Lebanon in 1969. In 1975, along with Musa al-Sadr, president of the Supreme Islamic Shi'a Council, he participated in the creation of AMAL. Within the Supreme Islamic Shi'a Council, he often advocated a moderate line and came up against the intransigence of both the vice president, Abdul Amir Qabalan, and of Nabi Berri (another cofounder of AMAL). In February 1981 Shamseddin escaped an assassination attempt. In April 1984 he spoke in favor of deploying the United Nations Interim Forces in Lebanon in all of South Lebanon and also in favor of keeping Syrian forces in the country as long as the Israel Defense Force remained on Lebanese soil. That June, commenting on the Israeli occupation of Lebanon, Shamseddin demanded "the reapplication of the armistice agreement reached between Lebanon and Israel in March 1949, which, in itself, did not necessitate negotiations," and renewed his support for a Syrian presence in Lebanon as long as Israeli forces remained on Lebanese territory. In February 1988 he presided over a commission responsible for ending combat between AMAL and Hizbullah. In December he visited Tehran and was received by the leaders of the country. In January 1990 Shamseddin received an Iranian delegation, led by the Iranian ambassador to Syria, Muhammad Hassan Akhtari, which had come to discuss measures to end the fighting between AMAL and Hizbullah. In 18 March 1994 he

was elected president of the Supreme Islamic Shi'a Council. From then on he worked for a rapprochement between the Christian and Muslim communities in Lebanon. He died of cancer in Beirut.

SEE ALSO AMAL; Berri, Nabi; Hizbullah; Sadr, Musa al-; South Lebanon; United Nations Interim Force in Lebanon.

SHARA, FARUK AL- (1938–): Syrian political figure, born in Mharbé. Faruk al-Shara earned degrees in English literature and international law and became a Ba'th Party member. In the early 1970s, he ran the Syrian Airlines Agency in Dubai and London. In 1975 he joined the foreign ministry, where he became assistant director of the Western European desk. Between 1976 and 1979 he was Syrian ambassador to Italy. In January 1980 he was appointed foreign minister in the Qassem government. In July 1983, after the death of Iskandar Ahmed, he became interim information minister. On 11 March 1984, when the third Qassem government was formed, he was reappointed foreign minister, a post he has kept through all the succeeding governments. On 8 January 1985, at the Eighth Ba'th Regional Conference, he was elected a member of its central committee. In October 1991 he led the Syrian delegation to the Middle East Peace Conference in Madrid, where he advocated the Arab cause in the face of Israeli intransigence. His performance at the conference earned him the respect of Westerners and led him to play an important part in negotiations with Israel.

Shara's intelligence and his knowledge of the issues have made him a redoubtable negotiator. In the spring of 1994 he received American Secretary of State Warren Christopher, who was in charge of restarting the Israeli-Syrian talks. That December, al-Shara visited Washington, where he held an official meeting with Israeli Prime Minister Ehud Barak in an attempt to renew the Syrian-Israeli peace dialogue, which had been interrupted since the spring of 1996. He stated on this occasion, "Peace will doubtless pose questions for all of us, especially for the Arab world, which, after it reviews the last fifty years, may well ask itself if the Israeli-Arab conflict has only challenged Arab unity, or prevented it." Al-Shara kept his portfolio in the new government formed by Muhammad Mustafa Miro in March 2000. That June, following the death of President Hafiz al-Asad, al-Shara was elected to Ba'th Command, the highest authority of the party. In August he was by the side of the new Syrian president, Bashar al-Asad, when the American emissary Edward Walker paid a visit to Syria with the mission to restart Israeli-Syrian negotiations. That same month saw him in Egypt, where American emissary Dennis Ross was meeting with Amr Musa, the head of Egyptian diplomacy, to discuss the aftermath of the Israeli-Palestinian peace summit held in Camp David in July. On 13 December 2001, in a reshuffle of Muhammad Miro's government, he was named deputy prime minister and minister of foreign affairs.

SEE ALSO Asad, Bashar al-; Asad, Hafiz al-; Barak, Ehud; Baʿth; Camp David II Summit; Christopher, Warren; Madrid Conference; Musa, Amr Muhammad.

SHARANSKY, NATAN (1948–): Israeli political figure, born in the Ukraine, in the Soviet Union. Natan Scharansky graduated from the Moscow Institute of Physics and became an activist for human rights. He was imprisoned in 1973 for his opposition to the Soviet regime. In 1977, accused of "treason and espionage" on behalf of the American Central Intelligence Agency, he was sentenced to thirteen years of forced labor. His wife organized an international campaign that allowed him to be freed after nine years. In February 1986 he was exchanged for Eastern-bloc spies in Western custody. After a few weeks in Berlin, Sharansky emigrated to Israel, where he worked to integrate Soviet immigrants, who represented a considerable political bloc, into Israeli society. In 1988 he created the Zionist Forum of Soviet Union Jews, a center-right political grouping. He was courted by both Likud and the Labor Party. In June 1995, along with his friend Yuli Edelstein, he created the Israel be-Aliyah Party, which in the platform published on the following 1 November upheld "the inalienable rights of the Israeli people over the country of Israel, from the Mediterranean to the Jordan" and rejected the creation of a Palestinian state, while recommending autonomy for the Occupied Territories.

In the May 1996 parliamentary elections, Sharansky's party won seven seats in the Knesset. A few weeks later, Sharansky was named minister of commerce and industry in the government of Benjamin Netanyahu. Three years later he became minister of the interior in the Labor government of Ehud Barak. On 9 July 2000, opposing the Israeli-Palestinian summit in Washington, D.C. that Barak was participating in, Sharansky resigned his post in the Labor government. On 7 March 2001, after the election for prime minister, he was appointed minister of housing and construction in the cabinet of Likud's Ariel Sharon. In 2003 he became minister for diaspora, social, and Jerusalem affairs. In this capacity he has lec-

MOSHE SHARETT. ISRAEL'S FIRST FOREIGN MINISTER, FROM 1948 TO 1956, WAS ALSO ITS SECOND PRIME MINISTER, FROM 1953 UNTIL 1955, WHEN DAVID BEN-GURION RETURNED TO OFFICE AFTER NEW ELECTIONS. SHARETT TOOK A HARD LINE ON PALESTINIAN REFUGEES BUT LOST HIS MINISTERIAL POST WHEN HE URGED CAUTION IN RESPONSE TO TENSIONS WITH EGYPT IN 1956. (© Bettmann/Corbis)

tured widely on the topic of anti-Semitism and its connection to anti-Israel sentiment.

SEE ALSO Barak, Ehud; Israel be-Aliyah; Israel Labor Party; Knesset; Likud; Netanyahu, Benjamin; Sharon, Ariel.

SHARETT, MOSHE (1894–1965): Israel's first foreign minister and second prime minister. Born Moshe Shertok, he migrated with his family from Russia to Palestine in 1906. After attending school in Herzliyya and Tel Aviv, he entered the University of Istanbul to study law, but was drafted into the Turkish army at the outbreak of World War I. He graduated from the London School of Economics in 1924, then returned to Palestine as a journalist. In 1931 he became political secretary of the Jewish Agency Executive, where he began his long working relationship with David Ben-Gurion. In 1935 Sharett became director of the Jewish Agency's political department.

In 1947 Sharett was a representative of the Jewish Agency to the United Nations (UN) Special

Committee on Palestine, where he lobbied for UN support for the creation of a Jewish state in Palestine. In May 1948 he was named foreign minister in the Jewish provisional administration of the newly proclaimed State of Israel, and he held the post of foreign minister until 1956. In that capacity he introduced, in 1949, the principle of "nonidentification," which proposed that Israel pursue a diplomatic course of nonalignment. By 1951, however, the support of the Soviet Union for the Arab bloc made it clear that Israel's foreign policy would be aligned with the West.

When Prime Minister David Ben-Gurion resigned in December 1953, Sharett became prime minister, holding the post until 1955, when his cabinet was overturned by the withdrawal of the General Zionist Party. Ben-Gurion returned as prime minister after the November 1955 elections, and Sharett continued to serve as foreign minister. In 1956 tensions arose between them over a course of action regarding the Suez Canal Crisis, and Ben-Gurion asked for Sharett's resignation, replacing him with Golda Meir.

SEE ALSO Ben-Gurion, David; Meir, Golda; Suez Crisis.

SHARI'A ("way," in Arabic): Islamic religious law from the Qur'an and the Sunna. The Shari'a establishes laws concerning worship (*d"n, madhab*) as well as principles concerning human social and juridical behavior (*dunyâ, milla*). The Shari'a is interpreted and practiced differently by different schools of law and even by each Muslim.

SEE ALSO Qur'an; Sunna.

SHARIF (pl. *sharifs, shurafa;* "noble," in Arabic): Designates generally the descendents of Fatima, daughter of the prophet Muhammad and her husband 'Ali, the cousin of Muhammad. Every Sharif (for example, the members of the Jordanian Hashimite dynasty) traces his or her ancestry back to one of their sons, Husayn (Hussein) or Hasan.

SEE ALSO Fatima; Muhammad.

SHARM AL-SHAYKH

SEE Sharm al-Shaykh Summits.

SHARM AL-SHAYKH MEMORANDUM: On the night of 4–5 September 1999, Palestinian Authority (PA) President Yasir Arafat and Israeli Prime Minister Ehud Barak signed an accord at Sharm al-Shaykh, in Egypt, whose purpose was to open the way to final peace negotiations between Palestinians and Israelis. Ratified by King Abdullah II of Jordan, Egyptian President Husni Mubarak, and American Secretary of State Madeleine Albright, the signing of this accord came after long negotiations undertaken within the framework of the application of the Wye Plantation Agreements.

The major points in the agreement concerned: The speedy liberation of 200 Palestinian prisoners, followed on October 8 by 150 other prisoners, then by a number to be determined by a commission; negotiations on the final status of Palestinian territories, which were to be reinstated rapidly and to conclude with an agreement within a year's time; Israeli military withdrawal (a week after the agreement, 7 percent of the West Bank would change from Zone C to a Zone B; on November 15 another 3 percent would change from Zone C to Zone B and of 2 percent from Zone B to Zone A; on January 20 5.1 percent would change from Zone B and 1 percent from Zone C to Zone A); a "secure" passage to allow Palestinians to move between Gaza and the West Bank; a new port, which would be constructed at Gaza; Shuhada Street, along a Jewish enclave in Hebron, which would be opened to Palestinian circulation; cooperation on matters of security; and a renunciation of unilateral measures to change the status of the West Bank and Gaza Strip from what was defined in the accord.

On 9 September the Knesset approved the accord by a vote of fifty-four to twenty-three, with two abstentions. Ten Arab members of parliament voted in favor. On 6 January 2000 Israel transferred control of ten villages near Ramallah (West Bank) to the PA as part of the withdrawal from 5 percent of the West Bank that it had begun the evening before. On 7 February the Israeli withdrawal was contested, causing the transfer of authority to stop and negotiations to stall. On 21 March the Israel Defense Force retreated from 6.1 percent of the West Bank, allowing the PA to exercise control over 40 percent of the West Bank. On 16 October, after three weeks of violent Palestinian-Israeli confrontations in the Palestinian territories that caused more than a hundred deaths, an international summit was organized at Sharm al-Shaykh to try to arrange an accord to restore calm and to restart the Israeli–Palestinian dialogue.

SEE ALSO Abdullah II ibn Hussein; Albright, Madeleine; Arafat, Yasir; Barak, Ehud; Gaza Strip; Israel Defense Force; Knesset; Mubarak, Husni; Oslo Accords II; Palestinian Authority; Sharm al-Shaykh Summits; West Bank.

SHARM AL-SHAYKH SUMMITS: Situated south of the Sinai Peninsula, in Egypt, Sharm al-Shaykh has hosted several international meetings in the framework of the Israeli-Arab peace process. From 13 to 16 March 1996, under the sponsorship of U.S. president Bill Clinton, an international meeting on terrorism took place there, presented as the "summit of the peacemakers." Concerned by the terrorism unleashed against Israeli urban populations in early 1996—which, together with the assassination of Yitzhak Rabin in November 1995, had dangerously shaken the peace process—the twenty-nine leaders attending this summit, of which some twenty were heads of governments, were determined to formulate a common strategy in the struggle against terrorism. Following this meeting President Clinton went to Israel, where he finalized the U.S. Israeli accord on Islamic terrorism, providing for aid to Israel in the amount of 100 million dollars. To implement the resolutions made at this summit, a conference was organized at Washington for the following 30 March.

From 16 to 18 October 2000, a new summit was held at Sharm al-Sheikh eighteen days after the outbreak of the al-Aqsa Intifada in the Palestinian territories. In addition to Yasir Arafat and Ehud Barak, U.S. President Clinton, King Abdallah II of Jordan, European Union representative Javier Solana, UN secretary general Kofi Annan, and Egyptian president Hosni Mubarak attended this meeting. No accord was signed between the parties. Ehud Barak and Yasir Arafat committed themselves publicly to call for an end to the violence, to take concrete measures to end the current confrontations, and to prevent the recurrence of the recent events. The United States agreed, with the concurrence of the UN, to set up a fact-finding committee on the events of the preceding few weeks, a step that led to the Mitchell Report. On the following 27 December, a meeting between Yasir Arafat and Ehud Barak, scheduled to take place the next day at Sharm al-Sheikh, had to be canceled because of opposition that was mounting in both camps against the Clinton Plan known as "parameters for peace."

SEE ALSO Aqsa, Intifada, al-; Clinton, William Jefferson; Clinton Plan; Mitchell Report; Sharm al-Shaykh Memorandum.

SHARON, ARIEL: (born Scheinerman; called Arik): Israeli military and political figure, As of 2004, prime minister of Israel. Born in February 1928 at Kefar Malal, in Palestine. In 1942, barely fourteen years old, he joined the ranks of the Haganah. Six years later he started on a military career in the new Israeli

ARIEL SHARON. AS A MILITARY OFFICER AND THEN ISRAELI DEFENSE MINISTER, SHARON OFTEN ENGAGED IN EXTREMELY CONTROVERSIAL ACTIONS IN WARTIME AND AGAINST PALESTINIAN VILLAGES AND REFUGEE CAMPS. AN ARDENT SUPPORTER OF ISRAELI SETTLEMENTS IN OCCUPIED TERRITORIES, HE TOOK A HARD LINE ON NEGOTIATIONS WITH PALESTINIANS BOTH BEFORE AND AFTER HIS ELECTION AS PRIME MINISTER IN EARLY 2001—A FEW MONTHS AFTER HIS VISIT TO THE TEMPLE MOUNT IN JERUSALEM WAS BLAMED FOR PROVOKING A NEW PALESTINIAN INTIFADA. *(AP/Wide World Photos)*

army, the Israel Defense Force (IDF). In 1949 he commanded an intelligence unit of the Golani brigade, and in 1953 he headed a special anti-terror unit responsible for halting Palestinian incursions into Israeli territory. During the night of 14–15 October 1953, in reprisal for the murder of a woman and her daughters, the unit penetrated the village of Qibya, in West Jordan, where he ordered the dynamiting of forty-five houses, causing the death of sixty-nine persons. This action provoked widespread outrage, and Israel was condemned by the UN Security Council.

After his unit was disbanded, Ariel Sharon was transferred to a paratroop brigade, where between 1954 and 1955 he headed a battalion. In 1956, during the Suez-Sinai War, he ignored orders from army headquarters and occupied the Mitla Pass, which commanded the access to the Suez Canal. In the course of a confrontation with Egyptian troops, thirty-six of his men were killed. At the end of the conflict, accused of insubordination, he was tried and judged responsible for the death of these men; but he continued to advance in the IDF, for he had earned a reputation as a brilliant military strategist. Promoted to general in February of 1967, he commanded an armored division during the Six-Day War. Between 1969 and 1973, as chief of the southern command, he applied radical methods, demolishing thousands of homes in Gaza refugee camps to create roads for antiterror patrols.

In July of 1972, having vainly sought the position of Army chief of staff, he decided to quit the military for politics, registering as a member of the Liberal Party. With Menachem Begin and Yitzhak Shamir, he participated in the creation of the right-wing parliamentary group Likud. Mobilized in October 1973 during the Yom Kippur War, he commanded an armored division on the southern front. Once again ignoring orders, he crossed the Suez Canal, cutting the Egyptian Third Army off from its rear. This maneuver enabled the IDF to force the Egyptian army to surrender, and in the eyes of Israeli soldiers he became "Arik, King of Israel."

Elected a Likud representative in 1973, in 1975 Sharon became the security adviser for the Labor Party prime minister, Yitzhak Rabin. After arguing with the latter he decided to found his own party, Shlomzion, which in the May elections of 1977 won two seats in the Knesset. Shortly thereafter he rejoined Likud and was appointed minister of agriculture in the government of Menachem Begin. While in this office, his support for the development of Jewish settlements in the occupied territories impeded the Israeli-Egyptian peace negotiations. In June of 1981 he became defense minister, and a year later was the principal architect of the invasion of Lebanon (Operation "Peace in Galilee"), during which several hundred Palestinians were murdered by the Lebanese Christian militia at the refugee camps of Sabra and Shatila while the IDF observed, voicing no objection. On 11 February 1983, Sharon was judged culpable by a commission of inquiry headed by Israeli Supreme Court chief justice Yitzhak Kahan for not preventing the slaughter. He was forced to resign his post of defense minister, but remained minister without portfolio.

During the next decade Sharon served in several cabinet posts. Then in 1996 he was appointed national infrastructure minister by Benjamin Netanyahu; two years later he became foreign minister. After the election of Labor's Ehud Barak as prime minister in May 1999, Sharon succeeded Netanyahu as Likud leader. His visit to the Temple Mount in Jerusalem in September 2000 sparked Muslim riots and unleashed the anger of the Palestinians, prompting a revival of the Intifada known as al-Aqsa Intifada.

On 6 February 2001 Sharon was elected prime minister, with 62.5 percent of the votes, against his adversary from the Labor Party, incumbent prime minister Ehud Barak, whose peace policy had failed. A month later Sharon presented his cabinet, composed of 26 ministers belonging to eight different political parties, which allowed him to have a majority of 73 of the 120 seats in the Knesset. In his inauguration speech Ariel Sharon indicated that his cabinet would conduct negotiations with the Palestinians "so as to obtain political agreements, but not under the pressure of terrorism and violence." When the Intifada intensified in the Palestinian territories, he decided to reply to the violence with military operations of unprecedented brutality. This policy of "targeted responses," in other words the assassination of Palestinian leaders and militants, was vigorously criticized not only by Palestinians but also by the Israeli opposition and a part of the international community.

On 4 December 2001, when the terrorist actions of Hamas and Islamic Jihad were multiplying, Ariel Sharon decided to increase the operations of the IDF against the symbols of the Palestinian Authority of Yasir Arafat, whom he accused of supporting terrorism. Following a suicide bombing at a Netanya resort hotel in March 2002, Sharon ordered the invasion and reoccupation of West Bank cities under Operation "Defensive Shield." Israeli forces destroyed buildings and captured hundreds of Palestinians. In the 2003 elections, in an apparent endorsement of his policies, voters gave Likud 29.4 percent of the vote (thirty-eight seats in the Knesset), confirming Sharon's premiership.

Sharon continued his aggressive policies, making Palestinian leader Arafat a virtual prisoner in the ruins of his Ramallah headquarters. Under intense pressure from the United States, Sharon's cabinet voted in May 2003 to approve the internationally backed "Road Map" for peace. Sharon surprised many observers by apparently seeking a balance between the right-wing commitment to disputed territories and a more pragmatic approach to an eventual resolution of the conflict. In 2004 he presented a plan to disengage from settlements in Gaza and parts of the West Bank, in the face of strong opposition by a majority of his own Likud Party and the defection or firing of several members of his cabinet.

The Knesset voted to back Sharon's plan in October 2004. Likud called for a referendum, which Sharon rejected, causing a split in the ruling Likud.

SEE ALSO Aqsa Inlifada, al-; Haganah; Intifada (1987–1993); Likud; Road Map (2002); Shlomzion.

SHAS (*Shomrei ha-Torah ha-Sepharadim* in Hebrew, meaning "Sephardi Torah Guardians."): Ultra-Orthodox Israeli religious party, created in 1983 following a split within Agudat Israel that exemplifies the opposition that existed between Sephardim and Ashkenazim. SHAS, whose Sephardi electorate was positioned on the right, supported a greater Judaization of Israeli society while declaring itself in favor of territorial compromise with the Palestinians. When it was created the two religious authorities of SHAS, rabbis Ovadiah Yosef and Eliezer Schach, asked Arye Deri to turn the party into a real political force. Thereupon, as a result of the elections of 1984, SHAS won four seats in the Knesset and Deri was named director general of the ministry of the interior, the minister being the president of SHAS, Yitzhak Peretz, in the cabinet of Shimon Peres.

In only a few years, SHAS was able to greatly expand its educational and social network. In the elections of 1988, the party won six Knesset seats. Three of its members joined the government of Yitzhak Shamir: Arye Deri as minister of the interior, Yitzhak Peretz as minister of immigration, and Yosef Azran as deputy minister of finance. In 1990, tensions surfaced in the party between its principal leaders, resulting in the departure of Peretz, who created his own group, Moriah. In June of the same year, after a reshuffle in the Shamir cabinet, another SHAS member, Rafael Pinhasi, joined the government as communications minister.

In September 1993, Arye Deri, while he was the subject of legal proceedings for corruption, resigned his post in the ministry of the interior. The other SHAS ministers quit the government, rejoining it in March of the following year. In February 1995, the four SHAS ministers belonging to the cabinet of Yitzhak Rabin once more resigned, and the leadership of the party reproached the government for its lack of resolve in the struggle against terrorism. In the elections of May 1996, SHAS obtained ten Knesset seats, confirming its place in Israeli politics. Because of the party's strong support for the candidacy of Benjamin Netanyahu for the post of prime minister, two of its leaders joined his government: Eli Suissa as minister of the interior and Eli Ishai as minister of labor. In the municipal elections of 10 November 1998, the party won fifteen seats of the thirty-one in the municipality of Jerusalem, allowing it to strengthen its control over the religious institutions of the Holy City.

On 17 March 1999, after a difficult trial lasting several months, Arye Deri was judged guilty of corruption, abuse of confidence, and fraud during his term in the ministry of the interior and sentenced to four years in prison. After the May general elections, in spite of the trial of its leader, SHAS found itself in an even stronger position, with seventeen Knesset seats. On 15 June, with his condemnation obstructing negotiations on SHAS joining the Labor government of Ehud Barak, Deri resigned from his functions as head of the party. On 6 July six party members joined the government of Barak. On 21 June 2000, constant disagreement between the SHAS ministers and those of Meretz forced the latter to quit the government. On 9 July SHAS, with the National Religious Party (NRP) and Israel B'Aliyah, resigned from the Barak government, reproaching it for the concessions it was preparing to make to the Palestinians during the talks at Camp David. The departure of these three parties meant that the Barak cabinet commanded only a minority in the Knesset.

On 9 January 2001, in the elections for the post of prime minister, SHAS supported Likud's candidate, Ariel Sharon. On the following 7 March, after Sharon's victory, SHAS entered the new national unity government, obtaining five ministries (interior, labor, social affairs, health, and religion). In the 2003 elections it won eleven seats in the Knesset.

SEE ALSO Agudat Israel; Ashkenazi; Deri, Arye; Moriah; National Religious Party; Peres, Shimon; Peretz, Yitzhak; Rabin, Yitzhak; Shamir, Yitzhak; Schach, Eliezer; Sephardi; Suissa, Eli; Yosef, Ovadiah.

SHA'TH, NABIL ALI MUHAMMAD (Abu Rashid; 1938–): Palestinian politician, born in August 1938 to a wealthy commercial family of Safad, in British Mandatory Palestine. In 1948, at the time of the first Arab-Israel war, his family fled to Egypt. Sha'th was educated in Alexandria and the United States, where he received a Ph.D. in public administration from the Wharton School at the University of Pennsylvania. He returned to Egypt, becoming an Egyptian citizen, at the end of 1965 and headed the National Institute of Management Development in Cairo until 1969.

In 1967, after the Arab defeat in the June 1967 War, he joined the ranks of al-Fatah. In 1969, he settled in Lebanon, where he taught business administration at the American University in Beirut until 1976. In 1970 he became a member of the Palestine Liberation Organization (PLO) Central Committee and represented the PLO at the nonaligned nations summit at Lusaka, Zambia in September of that year. In August of 1973, Sha'th became director of the PLO's planning office. In this capacity he took numerous trips to the Gulf States and the United States, where he met with many political and economic leaders. In 1974, he showed himself to be a formidable negotiator at the time of his discussions with UN delegates, which led to the invitation extended to Yasir Arafat to address the General Assembly of the United Nations.

In 1975 Sha'th founded TEAM International, a large Beirut management consulting company. Three years later, he was elected to the Palestine National Council (PNC). Between 1982 and 1983 he was in the group of negotiators who were discussing a solution to the Palestinian situation in Lebanon with American authorities. In 1988 he emerged as one of the main Palestinian interlocutors in the initial proceedings that led to opening a dialogue between the United States and the PLO. In November, 1989, Sha'th became Yasir Arafat's economic and political counselor. Between 1990 and 1993, he participated in the many negotiations that resulted in the Oslo Accords with Israel. At the beginning of May, 1994, Sha'th was named minister of planning and the economy of the newly established Palestinian Authority (PA). That June, after a forty-five year exile, he settled in the Gaza Strip. In 1996 he was elected to the Palestinian Legislative Council (PLC) from Khan Yunis. He has, along with other senior PLO leaders, been credibly accused of corruption; a PLC commission demanded in 1997 that he be removed from office and prosecuted. No such action was taken. After the destructive Israeli reoccupation of 2002, Sha'th was named to head the PA's reconstruction effort. In April 2003 he was appointed the PA's foreign minister.

SEE ALSO Arab-Israel War (1967); Arafat, Yasir; Fatah, al-; Gaza Strip; Oslo Accords; Palestinian Legislative Council; Palestine Liberation Organization; Palestine National Council; Palestinian Authority.

SHAYKH ("old person," "religious scholar," in Arabic): A Muslim title implying respect for wisdom or leadership, or simply for age and experience, accorded to men who have achieved some standing in their community. Among Sufis, *shaykh* is the title of a group's spiritual director (*murshid*), who is responsible for initiating his disciples into the mystic way (*tariqa*).

SHEBAA FARMS: Territory of approximately 38.5 square miles situated on the Lebanese side of Mount Hermon (Jabal al-Shaykh) on the Lebanese-Syrian frontier; under Israeli occupation since 1967. At the beginning of May 2000, before the Israeli withdrawal from South Lebanon, the Lebanese authorities demanded that Israel also pull out of this area, citing the terms of UN Security Council Resolution 425. Israel claimed that the territory belonged to Syria and that evacuating it would be part of the application of Resolution 242, and therefore that an Israeli withdrawal would be tied to Israeli-Syrian peace talks. It is unclear whom the territory belongs to, but both Lebanese and Syrian officials suggest that Syria had officially given the territory to Lebanon in 1951. On 30 May 2000 Syria broke the stalemate by accepting its restitution to Lebanon at a later date, in the framework of an Israeli withdrawal from the Golan Heights.

SEE ALSO Resolution 242; Resolution 425; South Lebanon.

SHECHEM

SEE Nablus.

SHEETRIT, MEIR (1948–): Israeli politician. Born in Morocco in 1948, Meir Sheetrit migrated to Israel in 1957. He received a master's degree in political science from Bar-Ilan University. He was mayor of Yavneh from 1974 to 1987 and treasurer of the Jewish Agency from 1988 to 1992. First elected to the Knesset in 1981, he served on various committees, including the Finance Committee and the Education and Culture Committee. He became deputy speaker of the Knesset in 1996, then served as minister of finance from February 1999 to July 1999. He was appointed minister of justice in March 2001, and in February 2003 was appointed minister without portfolio.

SHEIK

SEE Shaykh.

SHEKEL (also spelled "sheqel"): Anciently, a Hebrew word designating the donation that was due to the Temple, and also a unit of weight corresponding to less than half an ounce. Currently it is the name of the national money of the State of Israel, the New Israel Shekel (NIS), which was introduced in 1985.

SHRINE OF HAZRAT IMAM ALI. A VIEW FROM THE COURTYARD SHOWS ONE OF THE HOLIEST PLACES TO SHI'ITE MUSLIMS, THE SITE OF THE TOMB OF THE FIRST IMAM, MUHAMMAD'S FIRST COUSIN AS WELL AS THE HUSBAND OF HIS FAVORITE DAUGHTER, FATIMA. LOCATED IN AN NAJAF, IRAQ, THIS MOSQUE WAS THE SCENE OF A LONG STANDOFF IN 2004 BETWEEN THE FORCES OF ANTI-AMERICAN CLERIC MOKTADA AL-SADR AND U.S. FORCES (AS WELL AS THOSE OF THE INTERIM IRAQI GOVERNMENT). *(© Shepard Sherbell/Corbis Saba)*

This replaced the "old" shekel, which in 1980 had replaced the Israeli pound, at a rate of one NIS per thousand. As of September 2004, the exchange rate was about 4.48 NIS per U.S. dollar and 5.51 NIS per Euro.

SHELI PARTY (Shelli): Israeli political party, founded in 1977 by retired general Matti Peled. Considered to be of the extreme left, the SHELI advocated a peace dialogue with the Palestinians. In the 1977 elections, the group won two seats in the Knesset. The party disbanded before the 1984 elections.

SEE ALSO Peled, Mattityahu ("Matti").

SHEMA ("hear. . ."): A shorthand name for the Shema-Israel (Hear O Israel) prayer.

SHI'A: Shi'a Muslims are the followers of Ali (*Shi'at Ali*), the cousin and brother-in-law of the prophet Muhammad, to whose descendants they believe leadership of the entire Muslim community rightfully belongs. Ali ibn Abi Talib succeeded the first three successors of Muhammad, but his rule was contested. The successor to Ali, Mu'awiyya, was succeeded by his son Yazid. The second son of Ali, Husayn, revolted against him and was martyred in 632 C.E.. Although they share with Sunnis the basic tenets of Islam, Shi'as have different doctrines, rituals, theology, and organization. Shi'as comprise the smaller of the two major branches of Islam. They are predominant in Iran and a majority in Iraq, but elsewhere in the Muslim world are a minority, making up around 15 percent of the world's Muslim population. They constitute a substantial minority in Kuwait, Bahrain, Saudi Arabia, Yemen, Lebanon, Pakistan, India, and Afghanistan. In many places Shi'as are subjected by Sunni majorities to discrimination and sometimes violence; in Iraq, where they are a majority, they have been suppressed for political reasons for decades.

SHIHABI, HIKMAT AL- (al-Shehabi; 1931–): Syrian career officer, born in Bab el-Hawa. Hikmat al-Shihabi began his career in aviation, training in the Soviet Union and the United States. In 1970 he earned a Soviet degree in intelligence services. In April 1971 he was named head of intelligence services of the Syrian Army, assisted by Colonel Ali Douba. Appointed a general the following year, he also supervised the department of military security. After the 1973 War, he led the Syrian delegation to the United States in April of 1974, negotiating the conditions of the Syrian–Israeli disengagement. On 12 August 1974 he was appointed chief of staff of the Syrian Army, replacing Yusuf Shakkur, who was promoted to deputy defense minister. In December 1983, while President Hafiz al-Asad was ill, Shihabi was part, along with General Tlass, of the committee in charge of running the country. In August 1984 he escaped an assassination attempt. Between 1994 and 1995 he was part of a delegation that traveled to the United States to discuss peace negotiations with Israel. In July 1998, after twenty-four years as army chief of staff, he resigned his post. He is thought of as an influential figure in the Syrian regime and has been considered several times for prime minister.

SEE ALSO Arab-Israel War (1973); Asad, Hafiz al-; Douba, Ali Issa Ibrahim.

SHI'ITE: A Shi'a Muslim may be referred to in English as a Shi'ite (or Shi'ite).

SEE ALSO Shi'a.

SHIKAKI, FATHI IBRAHIM

SEE Shiqaqi, Fathi.

SHIN BET (Sherutei ha-Bitahon, in Hebrew): Israeli General Security Service. Succeeding Shai, the Haganah intelligence service, Shin Bet was created in June 1948 and is responsible for the internal security of the State of Israel. Also nicknamed Shabak, it has been shaken by scandals that have revealed the extreme methods its members use in dealing with Palestinians. In December 1980 its head quit after an investigation revealed that members of his organization had been implicated in anti-Arab attacks. In April 1984 two Shin Bet agents killed two Palestinians who had hijacked an Israeli bus, beating them with rocks. In 1995 an inquest into the assassination of Yitzhak Rabin uncovered many failings in the functioning of Shin Bet, leading to the resignation of a number of its leaders. The directors of Shin Bet have been: Isser Harel (1948–1953), Amos Manor (1953–1963), Yosef Harmelin (1963–1974), Avraham Ahituv (1974–1981), Avraham Shalom (1981–1986), Yosef Harmelin (1986–1988), Jacob Peri (1988–1994), Karmi Gilon (1995–1996), Ami Ayalon (1996–2000), and Avraham Dichter (2000–).

SEE ALSO Haganah; Harel, Isser.

SHINUI PARTY ("Movement for Change," in Hebrew): Israeli center-left, ultra-secular political party, founded in 1974 by Amnon Rubinstein. Shinui stood for defending the interests of the Israeli middle class by supporting a liberal economy and advocated a peace process between Israel and the Arab countries. In the July 1981 elections the party won two seats in the Knesset. In 1988 the Shinui electoral program on the Palestinian question was based on three principles: "1) peace in exchange for the territories; 2) demilitarization of the territories and rectification of the1967 border; 3) creation of a Jordano-Palestinian confederation." In 1992 the party merged with RATZ (Movement for Civil Rights and Peace) and MAPAM to form the Meretz bloc. In that year's elections, Meretz obtained twelve seats in the Knesset, of which two went to Shinui. These seats were filled by Avraham Poraz and Amnon Rubinstein. On 18 May 1999, the day after the general elections in which the Labor Party leader Ehud Barak became prime minister, the Shinui list, headed by Yosef ("Tommy") Lapid, won six of the ten seats taken by Meretz. In 2003 it won sixteen seats.

SEE ALSO Lapid, Yosef (Tommy); MAPAM; Meretz Party; Movement for Civil Rights and Peace; Poraz, Avraham; Rubinstein, Amnon.

SHIQAQI, FATHI (1951–1995): Palestinian, born in the al-Shoura refugee camp in the Gaza Strip, where his family had sought shelter at the time of the 1948 War. Between 1974 and 1980, Fathi Shiqaqi was a student at Bir Zeit University in the West Bank, and then in Egypt, where he earned degrees in medicine and mathematics. The Arab defeat in the 1967 War impelled him to join the Muslim Brotherhood, whose ideas he disseminated, along with Abdulaziz Udeh, in the Palestinian community. In 1979, after the victory of the Iranian Islamic Revolution, he wrote a book in honor of the Ayatollah Khomeini (*Khomeini: The Islamic Solution and Alternative*), in which he advocated the application of Khomeini's ideas to the Palestinian problem. He founded the al-Tali'a al-Islamiyya association (Islamic Vanguard). In 1980 he was interrogated by the Egyptian authorities, who suspected him of planning an attack. The following year, he left Egypt for the Gaza Strip, where he began practicing medicine. He quickly joined the ranks of the Palestinian Islamic Jihad (PIJ) and became one of the principal leaders, along with Udeh. In 1983, with Munir Shafiq Asal, he created the Brigades of the Islamic Holy War. Imprisoned several times by Israeli authorities between 1984 and 1986, he was banished to Lebanon (together with Udeh) in August of 1988 and there established contacts with the pro-Iranian movements that were active in the country. He settled in Damascus, where he developed ties with leaders of the Shiʿite movements.

In 1990, after the founding of the Palestinian Hizbullah, he became editor of its press organ, *Al-Mujahid*. In November 1991, with Udeh, he formed a faction within the PIJ known as the Palestinian Islamic Jihad–Shiqaqi-Udeh Faction, which became the mainstream of that organization. In November 1993, opposing the Oslo Accords, his group became a member of the Alliance of Palestinian Forces, thereby joining the ranks of the Palestinian opposition. Between 1994 and 1995, his movement carried out a number of anti-Israeli attacks, but his authoritarianism provoked Udeh to resign. On 26 October 1995 he was assassinated by the Mossad in Malta as he was returning from a visit to Libya.

SEE ALSO Alliance of Palestinian Forces (APF); Arab-Israel War (1948); Arab-Israel War (1967); Bir Zeit University; Gaza Strip; Mossad; Muslim Brotherhood; Oslo Accords; Palestinian Islamic Jihad; West Bank.

SHIRAA, AL-: An Arabic-language pro-Syrian and pro-Iranian weekly newspaper, started in Beirut in 1982. This newspaper was notable for revealing, in 1986, American arms deliveries to Iran (the Iran-Contra scandal).

SHIRK: Arabic term indicating polytheism, the act of associating other divinities to God. This is considered the most serious sin in the Muslim religion.

SHLOMZION: Israeli political bloc, created by Ariel Sharon in 1977 after he quit the Likud coalition. After winning two seats in the Knesset elections of May 1977, Shlomzion merged with Likud.

SEE ALSO Likud; Sharon, Ariel.

SHOAH: Hebrew word meaning "catastrophe," "destruction"; preferred by many Jews and Israelis over the more common *Holocaust*. Designates the genocide carried out on the Jewish diaspora population during World War II.

SHOMAN, ABD AL-HAMID (1888–1974): Palestinian banker, born in 1888 in Beit Hanina near Jerusalem. Shoman immigrated to the United States in 1911 and returned to Jerusalem in 1929. In 1930 he founded the Arab Bank, today one of the largest banks in the Arab world (with branches all over the Middle East, South Asia, Africa and Europe). A conservative Palestinian nationalist, Shoman was an associate of Hajj Amin al-Husayni, the mufti of Jerusalem, in the 1930s, and was arrested twice by the British during the Palestine Arab Revolt of 1936–1939. In 1948 Shoman moved to Amman, Jordan, where the bank is now headquartered. The Abd al-Hamid Shoman Foundation in Amman supports scientific research and some arts institutions in Jordan and the Arab world. Shoman's son Abd al-Majid Shoman, who succeeded his father as chairman of the Arab Bank, was for at time the chairman of the Palestine National Fund of the Palestine Liberation Organization (PLO).

SEE ALSO Husayni, Hajj Amin al-; Palestine Arab Revolt (1936–1939); Palestine Liberation Organization.

SHULHAN ARUKH: Hebrew term designating the everyday precepts and practical commandments that every religious Jew must observe.

SHURA ("council," in Arabic): Arabic word designating the tradition of leaders consulting members of a community

SIAH (Israeli New Left; *ha-Smol ha-Israeli he-Hadash* in Hebrew): Israeli political movement, created at the beginning of 1969, uniting young leftists from different backgrounds. The Siah declared it was part of "the world movement of the new left, fighting against the political establishment, whether of the Capitalist West, or the Socialist East." As of 2004, Siah has won no seats in the Knesset.

SINGLETON-HUTCHESON COMMISSION

SEE Anglo-American Committee of Inquiry.

SIX-DAY WAR

SEE Arab-Israel War (1967).

SLA

SEE South Lebanon Army.

SNEH, EPHRAIM (1944–): Israeli brigadier general and politician, born in Tel Aviv. Ephraim Sneh received his medical degree from Tel Aviv Medical School and served as a medical officer in the Israel Defense Force (IDF). From 1978 to 1980 he commanded an elite IDF unit, and in 1981 commanded the Israeli security zone in southern Lebanon. From 1985 to 1987 Sneh served as head of the civil administration in the West Bank. Elected to the Knesset in 1992 on the Labor Party list, he served as a member of the foreign affairs and defense committee. Sneh was minister of health from 1993 to 1996, and in 1999 was appointed deputy minister of defense. In March 2001 he was appointed minister of transportation, serving until 2002. In 2004 he was chair of the Knesset subcommittee on defense policy and planning

SEE ALSO Israel Defense Force; Israel Labor Party; Knesset; West Bank.

SOCIALIST ZIONIST PIONEER PARTY

SEE Ahdut ha-Avodah.

SOURANI, RAJI (1953–): Palestinian human rights lawyer and activist, born in Gaza in 1953. Attended schools in Gaza and Bethlehem; studied law at Beirut Arab University and Alexandria University, where he earned his law degree in 1977. As a lawyer in private practice until 1991, Sourani worked as a defender of Palestinians in Israeli military courts. During this time he was frequently harassed by the Israelis and was imprisoned by them several times between 1979 and 1982, suffering beatings and torture. He was director of the Gaza Center for Rights and Law from 1991 until 1995, when he called for an investigation of the security courts operated by the Palestinian Authority (PA), only to be was arrested by the PA and dismissed from his job.

In 1995 he founded the Palestinian Center for Human Rights in Gaza, of which he remains the director. One of the most prominent human rights advocates in the Middle East, Sourani works to promote democracy, the rule of law, and the principles of human rights both domestically and internationally. He continues to be a severe critic of Israeli policies and to document Israeli actions in the occupied territories, and has also been critical of the PA for its human rights abuses. Sourani has worked with the Palestine Human Rights Information Center and other human rights NGOs. He is a board member of the International Federation of Human Rights and a member of the International Commission of Jurists. He has received a number of awards for his work, including a Robert F. Kennedy prize in 1991 and a Bruno Kreisky prize in 2002. In 2003 Sourani was selected for a human rights fellowship by the Oak Institute at Colby College in Maine, but was denied a visa to enter the United States.

SEE ALSO Palestinian Authority; Palestinian Center for Human Rights.

SOUSS, IBRAHIM (1945–): Palestinian writer and diplomat, born in August 1945 in Jerusalem. Souss studied in France and Britain and has degrees in political science and international relations. A former member of the Democratic Front for the Liberation of Palestine (DFLP), he joined the ranks of al-Fatah in 1966. Six years later, while a student in Paris, he was president of the General Union of Palestinian Students (GUPS) in France. Between 1975 and 1980, he was a member of the Palestinian delegation to United Nations Educational, Scientific, and Cultural Organization (UNESCO). In August 1978, after the assassination of Izz al-Din Kalak, Souss became head of the Palestine Liberation Organization (PLO) offices in Paris. During the following year he participated in the creation of the France-Palestine Association. In June 1992, Leila Shahid replaced him at the head of the general delegation of Palestine in Paris. In 1998 he was appointed assistant director general of the United Nations agency the International Labor Organization (ILO), with responsibility for ILO activities in the Arab states. Souss married Diana Tawil, a sister of Suha Tawil, wife of Yasir Arafat and daughter of Raymonda Hawa Tawil.

SEE ALSO General Union of Palestinian Students; Palestine Liberation Organization.

SOUTH LEBANON: Area between the Litani River and the Israeli border, the site of political contention and violence since the 1948 War, when Palestinian refugee camps were established there. The Palestinian presence was politically destabilizing in Lebanon, whose politics is communally based. The refugees were largely sustained by the United Nations Relief and Works Agency for Palestine Refugees in the Near East—little was done for them by the Lebanese government. Both Palestinians and Lebanese assumed that they would be returning home in the near future.

Lebanon did not take part in the 1967 War, but the aftermath affected the country deeply. It became clear that Palestinian refugees would not be allowed to return home, and increasingly angry and politicized Palestinians turned to armed guerrilla activities carried on across the border by groups based in the camps. Their activities in turn tended to polarize the Lebanese, undermining government authority, particularly in the south.

A December 1968 Israeli attack in Beirut in reprisal for an attack on an Israeli airliner in Athens by the Popular Front for the Liberation of Palestine, which was based in Lebanon, prompted a break between Lebanese supporters and opponents of the Palestinian resistance. In January 1969 a new coalition cabinet was formed that excluded right-wing Maronite parties. This government proclaimed its support for the Palestinian resistance while allowing the army and police organizations to take measures to repress political activity in the camps and reduce the activity of Palestinian guerrillas on Lebanese territory. Pressure brought by supporters of the Palestinians both inside Lebanon and in other Arab governments prompted negotiations, and in November accords were signed between the government and the Palestine Liberation Organization (PLO), establishing new legal relations between them. Palestinians now had the right to govern and police the camps themselves, to maintain military organizations in Lebanon, and to use them in the struggle against Israel. In effect, government ceded the Palestinians a kind of autonomous state within the state (often referred to as Fatahland.) Moreover, between the end of 1970 and the beginning of 1971, large numbers of Palestinians arrived in Lebanon, including many PLO fighters who had been expelled from Jordan in the wake of Black September 1970, further increasing polarization between Lebanese supporters and opponents of the Palestinians.

The opponents, a coalition of Maronites, nationalists, and conservatives, objected to the violation of Lebanese sovereignty represented by the Cairo agreement and particularly feared the consequences of Palestinian guerrilla activity against Israel; they also opposed increased Muslim access to power. The government did almost nothing to provide security against Israeli attacks on Lebanese territory in the south, which were striking Lebanese— predominantly poor Shi'ites in that area—as well as Palestinian targets indiscriminately. Tens of thousands of South Lebanese Shi'ites migrated to Beirut to escape Israeli shelling, and little provision was made for them.

Lebanon remained neutral in the October 1973 War; Maronite militias attacked the PLO and Palestinian civilians in South Lebanon. On 14 March 1978 the Israelis invaded and occupied Lebanon up to the Litani River in Operation Litani. On 19 March the UN Security Council passed Resolution 425, demanding an Israeli withdrawal "without delay" and providing for the creation of the UN Interim Forces in Lebanon (UNIFIL). The Israeli army withdrew

gradually after creating the South Lebanon Army (SLA), a largely Maronite force, to act in its stead. On 18 April 1979 SLA commander Major Saad Haddad proclaimed the creation of the Free State of Lebanon, leading to confrontations between the SLA and the Phalange-dominated Lebanese Forces (LF) militia, as well as between these and armed Lebanese Muslim groups.

Israel invaded Lebanon again on 6 June 1982 in Operation Peace for Galilee. After pushing through the UNIFIL lines, the Israeli army neutralized Syrian forces that were attempting to intervene. On 13 June, two days after the Israeli-Syrian ceasefire was concluded, the Israel Defense Force (IDF) joined with the Phalangist-dominated LF. The Israeli army undertook the siege of Beirut, where the Palestinians were dug in, backed by the Lebanese National Movement.

Israeli presence on Lebanese soil prompted the emergence of a Shi'ite resistance movement, the Hizbullah, which was based in the Bekáa Valley. A ceasefire was arranged by the United States, and a withdrawal of the PLO leadership and fighters to Tunis was arranged under the supervision of a Multinational Force; Israeli forces withdrew to the south.

One of Israel's goals was to ensure that Bashir Jumayyil, the Phalange leader and an asset of both the CIA and the Mossad, became president of Lebanon. Jumayyil was duly elected on 23 August. The Multinational Force left Beirut on 10 September. On 14 September Jumayyil was assassinated by pan-Syrian nationalists. Israel, in violation of the ceasefire, moved back to Beirut to secure the city for the Phalange. Two days later—on the grounds, according to Israeli defense minister Ariel Sharon, that there were "terrorists" inside—the IDF allowed the Phalangists to enter the adjacent Sabra and Shatila Palestinian refugee camps where from 16 to 18 September they slaughtered some 1,500 to 3,000 civilians. On 20 September the Multinational Force was redeployed to Beirut. On 21 September Amin Jumayyil, Bashir's brother, was elected president, and at the end of September the Israelis left the city.

In May 1983, under pressure from the United States, Jumayyil agreed to sign a peace treaty with Israel, which was ratified by parliament. Opposition to this treaty among Lebanese and Syrians was so great, however, that Jumayyil felt obliged to refuse to sign it. The Syrians would not negotiate, and the Israelis, who had been protecting Jumayyil's government from its factional enemies, withdrew their forces from the Shuf district southeast of Beirut, a largely Druze area held by the Phalange. Fighting broke out between the Phalange and the Druze militia directed by Walid Jumblatt, which had Palestinian and Syrian support, weakening the Phalange substantially in some of the biggest battles of the civil war. Israeli forces retired to South Lebanon, where, with the SLA, they remained in permanent occupation.

On 15 January 1985 the government of Israeli prime minister Shimon Peres announced a phased withdrawal of the Israeli army from South Lebanon. Six months later the withdrawal began, except from a territory of 850 square kilometers that Israel called a "security zone" along the Israeli border. Subject to constant attacks from Hizbullah, this zone was patrolled by around 1,300 Israeli soldiers, backed up by 2,600 men of the SLA. The purpose of the occupation was to protect Israeli territory from Hizbullah attacks, but these were not deterred.

The signing of the Ta'if Accord in October 1989 and the developments of succeeding months ended the Lebanese Civil War but did not resolve the situation in South Lebanon. In April and May 1993, during the Middle East peace process begun at the Madrid Conference in 1991, the Israeli government proposed to Lebanese authorities that they define, in general terms, an acceptable peace accord, but there was no consensus in Lebanon in favor of a peace treaty with Israel as long as Israel occupied Lebanese territory and the Palestinian issue was unresolved.

On 25 July 1993 Israel unleashed Operation Justice Is Done, targeting various Hizbullah positions. On 11 April 1996 Israel launched Operation Grapes of Wrath, a massive bombardment of South Lebanon, which led to the death of, among others, 103 Lebanese civilians killed when Israel shelled the camp of a UNIFIL unit where they had sought protection. After much negotiation and the intervention of several foreign leaders, a committee of surveillance of the ceasefire—made up of representatives of France, the United States, Syria, Lebanon, and Israel—was agreed upon. According to the terms of the arrangement, the belligerents promised to spare civilians on both sides of the Lebanese-Israeli frontier and not to launch operations from inhabited areas.

On 26 July the newly elected Israeli prime minister, Benjamin Netanyahu, proposed to restart Israeli-Syrian negotiations on the basis of a "Lebanon first" option, which would involve an IDF withdrawal from South Lebanon. Netanyahu knew the Syrians would reject this, since they had already made it clear to his predecessor, Shimon Peres, that a complete withdrawal from the Golan Heights was an absolute prerequisite for any agreement.

As expected, the Syrians demanded that negotiations be restarted from the point where they had been left the preceding February. For Syria, in control of the situation in Lebanon, the negotiations over South Lebanon were the only means at its disposal to pressure Israel for the restoration of the Golan Heights. On the other hand, the withdrawal of the Israeli army from South Lebanon was going to pose the question of the presence of 35,000 Syrian soldiers in Lebanon. (Syrian soldiers had entered Lebanon in May 1976 with the support of Jordan, Israel, France, and the United States, and were later authorized by the Arab League as the Arab Deterrent Force; their presence was no longer justifiable as an emergency measure.) In March 1998 the Israeli government renewed its proposal, based for the first time on the twenty-year-old UN Security Council Resolution 425 (which demanded Israeli withdrawal "without delay"), while adding one condition—that the Lebanese government oversee peace and security in this zone. The Lebanese authorities rejected the Israeli proposal, arguing that Resolution 425 was not negotiable. In May 1999 Ehud Barak was elected prime minister of Israel on a promise to withdraw Israeli troops from Lebanon, and in September he announced his commitment to do so before 7 July of the following year.

On 17 April 2000 Israel informed the United Nations of its intention to withdraw and declared itself willing to cooperate with the United Nations in the matter. On 1 May the Israeli army started evacuating its main positions near Marjayun, which prompted many desertions from the SLA. Between 17 and 20 May, an intense artillery duel took place between Hizbullah and the IDF. The following day, a weakened SLA abandoned five villages on the edge of the security zone, which were immediately occupied by their former inhabitants and by Hizbullah. From 22 to 24 May 2000 Israel withdrew its troops from South Lebanon, leading to the disbanding of the SLA; 1,200 men affiliated with SLA sought refuge in Israel, along with their families. On 23 June, on the recommendation of UN Secretary General Kofi Annan, the Security Council certified the withdrawal of Israeli forces behind the Blue Line. On 27 July 2000, the UN Security Council unanimously adopted Resolution 1310, extending the mandate of UNIFIL, which was deployed along the Israeli frontier on 5 August. On 9 August, a Lebanese army force of 9,000 was stationed in South Lebanon for the first time in 22 years.

The UNIFIL mandate has been extended every six months. Israel has not completely left Lebanese territory; it still holds the Shebaa Farms area, which it claims is Syrian territory but which Lebanon and Syria agree is Lebanese.

SEE ALSO Arab Deterrent Force; Arab-Israel War (1967); Arab-Israel War (1973); Barak, Ehud; Black September 1970; Blue Line; Golan Heights; Hizbullah; Jumayyil, Amin; Jumayyil, Bashir; Jumblatt, Walid Kamal; League of Arab States; Lebanese Forces; Lebanese National Movement; Madrid Conference; Maronites; Mossad; Netanyahu, Benjamin; Palestine Liberation Organization; Peres, Shimon; Phalange; Popular Front for the Liberation of Palestine; Resolution 425; Sabra and Shatila; Sharon, Ariel; Shebaa Farms; South Lebanon Army; United Nations Interim Forces in Lebanon; United Nations Relief and Works Agency for Palestine Refugees in the Near East.

SOUTH LEBANON ARMY: A Lebanese Maronite militia created, trained, and financed by Israel during its invasion of Lebanon in April 1978. It was commanded by Major Saad Haddad, a former Lebanese army officer. On behalf of Israel the South Lebanon Army (SLA) patrolled the border between Israel and Lebanon, keeping the Lebanese army and the Arab Deterrent Force out of the area. After Israel invaded Lebanon again on 6 June 1982 ("Operation Peace for Galilee"), the SLA operated as a part of the Israel Defense Force (IDF). An agreement was signed on 17 May 1983 between the Lebanese and Israeli governments, stipulating the creation of a "security zone" on the Lebanese side of the border, which remained under Israel's control. The SLA remained deployed there at the insistence of Israel. In March 1984, after the death of Major Haddad, the Israelis recruited the retired Lebanese general Antoine Lahad to replace him. In this security zone, Israeli forces numbered around 1,400 soldiers and those of the SLA around 2,600 men, and an Israeli administration was set up. From 1985 on, South Lebanon became an area of frequent confrontation between the Lebanese Hizbullah on one side, and the IDF and SLA on the other, causing hundreds of deaths.

In the mid-1990s the occupation of South Lebanon became a domestic political issue in Israel. Ehud Barak was elected prime minister in 1999 largely on a promise to withdraw Israeli forces. On 17 April 2000 the Israeli government informed the United Nations of its decision to withdraw its troops from South Lebanon before 7 July, causing unease in the SLA. Israeli leaders refused to disarm SLA soldiers as long as they had not received guarantees of their security. On 9 May, Lebanese prime minister Salim al-Hoss rejected Lahad's request for amnesty for himself and his soldiers. By the time of the final Israeli withdrawal on 24 May, about half the SLA's men and their families, including Lahad, chose to seek refuge in Israel. The remainder stayed in Lebanon, accepting thereby to be tried by Lebanese military justice (over 800 were sentenced to long terms in prison). On 5 August, the "blue helmets" of the United Nations Interim Forces in Lebanon were deployed in the former South Lebanon security zone.

SEE ALSO Barak, Ehud; Arab Deterrent Force; Hizbullah; Hoss, Salim, al-; United Nations Interim Forces in Lebanon.

SPECIAL OPERATIONS GROUP

SEE Hawari Group.

SSNP

SEE Syrian Social Nationalist Party.

STAMINA OPERATION: Code name for the retreat of the Israeli army from South Lebanon, realized between 22 and 25 May 2000.

SEE ALSO South Lebanon.

STAR OF DAVID: Hexagram formed by two equilateral triangles opposed at their base and interlaced, figuring in blue on white background on the Israeli flag. This six-pointed star surfaced for the first time in a Kabbalistic text. In the sixteenth century, under the name "seal of Solomon," it became the symbol of Judaism. It is called in Hebrew *Magen David*, or "David's shield."

STERN, ABRAHAM (1907–1942): Jewish underground leader. Born in Poland, Abraham Stern migrated in 1924 to Mandatory Palestine, where he studied at the Hebrew University. He later began doctoral studies in Florence, Italy. Stern served in the Haganah beginning in 1929, then left in 1931 to form the Irgun Zva'i Le'umi (IZL), through which he smuggled weapons into Palestine. He returned to Palestine in 1939, following publication of the British White Paper, to organize resistance to the British. In 1940 he left the Irgun in a dispute over ideology and tactics, forming a new group, Lohamei Herut Yisrael, or LEHI, which became known as the "Stern Gang." LEHI carried out a campaign of anti-British propaganda and terror attacks. Abraham Stern was killed by members of the British Criminal Investigation Division (CID) on 12 February 1942.

SEE ALSO Irgun; Lohamei Herut Yisrael; White Papers on Palestine.

STERN GROUP

SEE Lohamei Herut Yisrael.

SUBLIME PORTE: Name given traditionally to the headquarters of the Sultan's government in Constantinople and designating, by extension, the Ottoman Empire.

SUEZ CANAL: Canal linking the Mediterranean Sea to the Red Sea. It extends 101 miles from Port Sa'id in the north to Suez in the south, and since 1870 has been one of the world's most heavily used shipping lanes. Built between 1856 and 1869, it was the result of a plan initiated by former French diplomat Ferdinand de Lesseps, who convinced Egyptian viceroy Muhammad Sa'id Pasha to grant the Suez Canal Company, incorporated as an Egyptian stock company with headquarters in Paris, the right to operate a maritime canal for ninety-nine years after completion of construction. Although shares were offered widely, 52 percent were bought by the French and nearly half the rest by Sa'id Pasha. Some of the early construction work was done by Egyptian peasants forced to dig with picks and baskets; later it was taken over by European laborers with dredgers and steam shovels.

The canal soon became a main route for steamships because it reduced travel and cargo transport time between Europe and East Africa, South Asia, China, Japan, and the East Indies, avoiding the long passage around the Cape of Good Hope. It was administered by the Suez Canal Company until nationalized by Egypt under Gamal Abdel Nasser in 1956. The canal was closed from 1956 to 1957 and from 1967 to 1975 because of the Arab-Israel conflict, and until 1975, Egypt prevented its use by Israel or ships supplying Israel. At present it is especially important for transport of crude oil from the Persian Gulf, although some of the newest tankers are too large to use it except when empty.

SEE ALSO Suez Crisis.

SUEZ CRISIS: One of the most serious international crises of the twentieth century, triggered by Egyptian president Gamal Abdel Nasser's nationalization of the Suez Canal on 26 July 1956. As the canal was under Egyptian sovereignty and compensation to its foreign shareholders was promised, this move was entirely legal. But Britain and France viewed it as a blow to their prestige and political standing in the Middle East. A few days after Nasser's announcement, they made plans for an invasion of Egypt to regain control of the canal, which were strongly opposed by the United States despite its agreement on the need to assure international access to it.

On 2 August a Franco-Anglo-American statement reaffirmed the international character of the canal and invited its main users to a meeting. On 16 August, a conference opened in London, where American Secretary of State Foster Dulles proposed creating an international organization responsible for control and management of the Suez Canal. On 9 September President Nasser rejected the Dulles Plan, and his position was supported by the Soviet Union. Three days later, France and Great Britain, with the approval of the United States, created an association of users of the canal, which, on 15 September, Nasser declared he would not recognize. Four days later, a second conference opened in London. On 14 October 1956 the United Nations Security Council defined the right of passage through the Suez Canal. On 22 October, at Sèvres, France, there was a secret meeting of British, French and Israeli political and military leaders, which concluded with an agreement for a French-Israeli-British military alliance to retake control of the Suez Canal, after which France launched "Operation Musketeer."

The preceding April, France and Israel had signed an accord allowing Israel to obtain French arms. Although the British wanted to keep the Suez Crisis separate from the Arab-Israeli conflict, France wanted Israeli assistance and in fact wished to induce Israel to attack first; it therefore speeded up the delivery of these arms. On 29 October, the Israeli Army, under the leadership of General Moshe Dayan, started "Operation Kadesh" against Egypt. The 7th Armored Brigade routed the Egyptian forces, freeing access to the Suez Canal, and the Gaza Strip was rapidly brought under the control of the Israel Defense Force (IDF). By 1 November, the artillery support of the French-British forces had incapacitated the Egyptian Air Force. The next day, President Nasser decreed martial law and seized French and English assets on Egyptian soil. On 3 November the Egyptian Army sunk several ships, thereby blocking the Suez Canal. Syrian troops arrived in Jordan, while Israelis took over strategic Egyptian positions on the Gulf of Aqaba. On 5 November, Franco-British paratroopers descended on Port Said and Port Fuad and took control of the northern entry to the Suez Canal, allowing the expeditionary corps to begin establishing control over the whole length of the canal. At this point, Soviet Prime Minister Nikolai Bulganin gave an ultimatum to Tel Aviv, London, and Paris, demanding the immediate withdrawal of their troops from Egyptian soil.

Under pressure from Washington and threats from Moscow, France, Great Britain and Israel accepted a cease-fire and agreed to withdraw. On 15 November, UN soldiers moved into the Sinai desert. On 22 December, the Franco-British forces completed their evacuation of Port Said. On 5 January 1957, U.S. President Dwight Eisenhower presented his Middle East foreign policy, based essentially on economic aid and military assistance; but on 19 January, the leaders of Saudi Arabia, Egypt, Jordan and Syria, gathered in Cairo, rejected the Eisenhower Plan. On 21 January, the UN General Assembly adopted a resolution demanding the departure of Israeli troops from Egypt. Although Israel had hoped to hold on to the Gaza Strip and the entrance to the Gulf of Aqaba, heavy American pressure and the threat of UN sanctions moved Prime Minister David Ben-Gurion to withdraw Israeli forces. On 6 March, the IDF evacuated the Gaza Strip and Sharm el-Sheikh, making way for UN units.

On 8 April 1957, the Suez Canal was reopened to maritime traffic. In July, the Soviet Union began delivering large quantities of arms to Egypt. On 21 August, 1958, the United Nations General Assembly, at the initiative of the member states of the Arab League, approved a resolution demanding that the Middle East be kept out of the quarrels between the United States and the Soviet Union. The Suez war is generally considered a major blunder on the part of Britain and France, for it led to the loss of their positions in the Middle East and marked the end of British and French colonialism, as well as increasing U.S. power in Middle Eastern affairs. Egyptian President Nasser, on the other hand, emerged as the uncontested leader of the Arab people.

SEE ALSO Nasser, Gamal Abdel; Suez Canal.

SUEZ WAR

SEE Suez Crisis.

SUFISM

SEE Tasawwuf.

SUISSA, ELI (1956–): Israeli politician. Born in Morocco in 1956, Eli Suissa migrated to Israel that same year. He received his rabbinical ordination from Yeshivat Kfar Hassidim and joined the SHAS Party shortly after it was founded. Suissa served as minister

of the interior from 1996 until July 1999, served in rotation as minister of religious affairs, then as minister of national infrastructures from July 1999 until his resignation in July 2000. He was appointed minister without portfolio in March 2001, responsible for Jerusalem affairs.

SULEIMAN, OMAR MAHMUD (1935–): Egyptian military figure, born in 1935, in Cairo, Omar Suleiman began a career in the military in 1955. In 1978, he became head of the strategic planning section of the operational center of Egyptian armed forces. After earning a degree in political science, between 1986 and 1988 he was assistant director of the Egyptian Military Intelligence Department (MID). Appreciated by President Husni Mubarak, he was named director general of the MID in August 1989. General Ghayati replaced him in November of the following year. A few months later, Suleiman took over the leadership of the General Intelligence Service (GIS).

In October 1993 there was talk he was being considered for the position of vice president of the Republic, or, if not, as special advisor to the presidency. Two years later, in November, he was named special advisor to President Mubarak, while continuing to head the GIS. From then on, Suleiman was in charge of sensitive dossiers, like that of the Israeli-Arab peace process, and that of the Palestinian question, while participating in the negotiations between Yemen and Eritrea in their dispute over the Hanish Islands. On 10 January 2001, in the context of the intensification of the al-Intifada in the Palestinian territories, he met with the director of the Central Intelligence Agency (CIA), George Tenet. In 2003 he met with Palestinian leader Yasir Arafat and Premier Mahmud Abbas as part of a bid to broker a truce between radical militants and Israel.

SEE ALSO Aqsa Intifada, al-; Mubarak, Husni.

SULTANATE: Mandate and jurisdiction of the sultan, a title born by sovereigns through a number of Muslim dynasties. From 1517, the Ottoman sultan of Istanbul also assumed the title and functions of the caliph, as spiritual and temporal head of Islam.

SEE ALSO Caliph.

SUNNA: Arabic word meaning "the way" or "the path," signifying Islamic tradition or custom. It refers to the ways and sayings of the prophet Muhammad, upon which laws, decisions, and judgments not deriving directly from the Qur'an are based. These are collected and codified in the Hadith.

SEE ALSO Hadith; Qur'an.

SUNNI ISLAM: Follower of the majority branch of Islam, based on the sunna and the community consensus it aroused. Sunnis are those who recognize the legitimacy of the first four caliphs succeeding Muhammad, and adhere to one of the four juridical Sunni schools (*madhhab*): Hanafi, Malik, Shafi'i, and Hanbali. They make up about 85 percent of the world's Muslims, and the Shi'a make up the remaining 15 percent.

SEE ALSO Muhammad; Sunna.

SYKES-PICOT AGREEMENT: On 30 January 1916, an exchange of letters, started on 17 July 1915, between the British high commissioner in Egypt, Henry McMahon, and the sheriff of Mecca, Hussein ibn Ali, came to light. From a perusal of this material it can be understood that Great Britain was committing itself to support the creation of an independent Arab state extending from Persia in the east to the Persian Gulf and Indian Ocean in the south, and to the Red Sea and Mediterranean in the west. On 29 November 1917, after the October Revolution took place in Russia, Leon Trotsky made public the contents of several diplomatic documents that had been secret until then, including the Sykes-Picot Agreement. Mark Sykes (for Great Britain) and Georges Picot (for France) had signed an agreement, ratified by Russia, in view of a partition of the Ottoman Empire, allied with Germany during World War I. According to this document France would be granted Cilicia and the region of Adana, the oil-rich region of Mosul (Iraq), a coastal strip of Lebanon-Syria, and the zone corresponding to present-day Syria. Great Britain would be granted Lower Mesopotamia and the territories east of the Jordan. Palestine would be internationalized, and the two ports of Saint-John of Acre and Haifa would revert to Great Britain.

SEE ALSO Mecca.

SYNAGOGUE: From the Greek word *sunagoge*, meaning "meeting"; in Hebrew, *Beth Knesset*, meaning "assembly, house where people assemble." With origins dating back to the sixth century B.C.E., this building served as a place for meeting, teaching, and prayer. It always points toward Jerusalem.

SYRIA: In the latter years of the Ottoman Empire, Syria was part of an administrative region that included Lebanon and Palestine (including western Jordan). In the last year of World War I, Greater Syria was occupied by forces commanded by Emir Faysal ibn Husayn al-Hashem, son of Sharif Husayn of Mecca and a leader of the British-sponsored Arab Revolt. Faysal was welcomed by the notables of Greater Syria, who were largely Arab nationalists, and was chosen by the National Assembly to be Syria's king. France, which was awarded a League of Nations mandate over Syria (without Palestine) in the postwar peace settlement, occupied the country and expelled Faysal in July 1920 (he was later installed by the British as king of Iraq). The French detached an enlarged Lebanon from Greater Syria and created the current borders of Syria in 1924. After it adopted a constitution for a sovereign Syria in 1928, the French dissolved the National Assembly and imposed a constitution in 1930. After much public protest, an agreement was reached in 1936 to grant independence in 1939, but it was suspended and martial law imposed at the beginning of World War II.

In June 1941, British and Free French forces captured Lebanon and Syria from the Vichy government, and the Free French, under political pressure, proclaimed the independence of both in November. After the war, however, France attempted to reimpose itself; but by then Syria had been allowed to join the United Nations, and France was persuaded to leave the country in 1946. Syria participated in the Arab-Israel War (1948) against Israel, sending one ill-prepared brigade into Galilee. Its failure contributed to the instability of the Syrian government. In March 1949 a coup d'état installed a military regime headed by Colonel Husni al-Za'im, who was assassinated the next year in another coup. Za'im was the first of five coup-installed leaders from 1949 to 1954, when a coalition of civilian parties and military officers took power and held a free parliamentary election with universal suffrage, the first in the Middle East. A centrist government was formed; under pressure from the public and from leftist groups such as the Ba'th Party, the country's largest, it legislated social reforms. Political tension led to the cancellation of elections in 1957.

Syria was weak, unstable and vulnerable to outside threats, from the West and particularly from subversive actions of conservative and royalist Iraq, whose own stability was threatened by the existence of left-leaning Arab governments. The less radical faction of the Ba'th was faced with the prospect of forming a government with either the conservatives or the communists. This faction promoted the idea of a federation between Syria and the larger, more populous and more powerful Egypt, then at the height of its Nasserist prestige in the Arab world. The

National Assembly voted for union, and Egyptian president Gamal Abdel Nasser was persuaded to accept, though on terms decidedly favorable to Egypt.

The United Arab Republic (UAR) was created in February 1958, with Nasser as president and Cairo as its capital. Structured as a unitary state rather than a federation, it featured structural changes and policy measures that alienated politically important elements of Syrian society—landholders, the middle class, politicians, and the officer corps. Later changes to state structures such as abolition of local autonomy, and the planned unification of currencies, furthered centralized control, and government policies were based primarily on Egyptian conditions. Dissatisfaction grew, and there was growing talk of secession. In September 1961, Syrian army officers staged a coup d'état in Damascus and Nasser chose not to fight it. The UAR was dissolved in September 1961. There followed two years of extreme political tension among those advocating the maintenance of a nationalized economy, those favoring a mixed economy, and those advocating a return to the *status quo ante*.

In March 1963 there was another Ba'thist military coup by a group of officers led by Salah Jadid and Hafiz al-Asad. Under this regime, the Ba'thist government pursued socialist reforms at home and opposed conservative Arab governments abroad. Jadid became the regime's leader in 1966, after three years of internal struggles. He confronted Israel over its Jordan River diversion project of the early 1960s, as well as Israel's escalating attacks on Syria's borders, which had been demilitarized under the armistice agreement of 1949. Jadid gave his support to the Palestinian guerrilla resistance groups that had begun to emerge, including al-Fatah and the Palestine Liberation Army (PLA). These activities were critical in igniting the Arab-Israel War (1967). After the war, Jadid's government established a Ba'thist Palestinian group, al-Sa'iqa, while continuing to assist the others. The failure of the Arab armies, and particularly the Israeli occupation of the Golan Heights, caused internal dissension within the regime between Jadid's leftist faction and the nationalist faction led by Asad. When Jadid sent troops to assist the Palestinians in Jordan during Black September 1970, Asad, who was defense minister, refused to provide air cover. A power struggle followed, and in November 1970 Asad's faction overthrew Jadid's government and established the regime that remains in place today. It has followed a more conservative policy domestically, in pursuit of political stability, and has been more cautious and prag-

matic abroad, while attempting to build Syria into a regional power. In 1972 Asad formed a Ba'thist-led national coalition of nationalist parties. Syria participated in the Arab-Israel War (1973) against Israel, in collaboration with Anwar al-Sadat's Egypt, in an attempt to recover occupied territory, some of which was regained in the disengagement agreement in 1974.

In 1975 Syria and Jordan formed a joint command to coordinate their military and political activities against Israel. In late May 1976, after having attempted for months to mediate a settlement in the Lebanese civil war (1975–1990), Asad sent Syrian troops to intervene, saving the Maronite-dominated government from defeat at the hands of a coalition of leftist Lebanese parties and the Palestine Liberation Organization (PLO). This move was opposed by Egypt and Iraq but supported by Jordan, Israel, France and the United States, and was later ratified by the League of Arab States. The Syrians then held the balance of power in Lebanon except for the south, largely controlled by the PLO (parts of it were known as "Fatahland"), where Israel and Israeli-backed Christian militias continued to attack. The peace offensive by Sadat toward Israel in 1977 drove the Syrians closer to the PLO and away from the government side. Good relations with the PLO did not last after Israel, undeterred by Syria, invaded Lebanon in 1982 and forced the PLO's expulsion. Syrian forces remained involved in the civil war to prevent Lebanon, or a potential breakaway Maronite state, from coming under the control of Israel, and to prevent leftist groups from gaining control and forming an alliance with Iraq. Syria still keeps approximately 25,000 troops in Lebanon.

When Asad intervened in Lebanon on the Christian side, Islamic groups in Syria, led by the Muslim Brotherhood, which were already hostile to the secular-oriented Ba'th and the Alawis who dominated it, began a campaign of violent opposition, including acts of terrorism and assassinations. It lasted several years, surviving brutal repression, until in 1982 Asad sent in the special forces to put an end to a state of virtual rebellion in the cities of Aleppo and Hama. Ambushed in Hama, the army attacked the city with full force, including tanks and artillery. The regime regained control after the killing of an estimated 10–20,000 people (and 1,000 soldiers) and the destruction of much of the city.

After Sadat's trip to Jerusalem in 1977, Syria became a member of the Rejection Front [2]. After the Egyptian–Israeli peace treaty of 1979, Asad worked to make Syria militarily equal to Israel, supplied by the Soviet Union. In the Iran-Iraq War of 1980–1988, Syria supported Iran, cutting the Iraqi oil pipeline running through Syria and receiving oil from Iran in return, as well as financial support from Saudi Arabia. In 1990, during the crisis that led to the Gulf War of 1991, Asad attempted to persuade Saddam Hussein to withdraw his troops from Kuwait; he then joined the anti-Iraq coalition led by the United States, sending troops to Saudi Arabia. In October 1991 Syria agreed to participate in the Madrid Conference on the condition that Israel agree to discuss the Golan Heights in bilateral negotiations afterward. The Israeli-Syrian negotiations of 1994–2000 achieved nothing. In June 2000 Asad died. He was succeeded by his son Bashshar al-Asad, who lifted the state of emergency that had been in effect since 1963 and otherwise liberalized Syrian public life, though he has governed cautiously since. He has been less inclined to interfere in Lebanon and has followed his father's policies of not directly confronting Israel and not offending the United States. Syria maintains good relations with Iran and continues to support the Lebanese Hizbullah, a major Lebanese religious movement/militia/political party, regarded by Washington as a terrorist organization. Since the September 2001 attacks on the United States, Syria has cooperated with Washington on intelligence matters. Syria voted to approve the November 2002 UN Security Council resolution demanding that Iraq meet its obligation to allow continued weapons inspections, but opposed the American war in Iraq in 2003. Syrian relations with Israel have been frozen since the failure of the Oslo Accords II negotiations and the radicalization of Israeli and American policies toward the Palestinians.

SEE ALSO Alawite; Arab-Israel War (1948); Arab-Israel War (1967); Arab-Israel War (1973); Asad, Bashshar al-; Asad, Hafiz al-; Fatah, al-; Black September 1970; Golan Heights; Gulf War (1991); Hizbullah; Hussein, Saddam; Iran-Iraq War; Israeli-Syrian Negotiations (1994–2000); Madrid Conference; Maronite; Muslim Brotherhood; Nasser, Gamal Abdel; Oslo Accords II; Palestine Liberation Army; Palestine Liberation Organization; Rejection Front [2]; Sadat, Anwar al-; Sa'iqa, al-; United Arab Republic.

SYRIACS: Also known as Assyrians; there are communities of Syriacs in Palestine, in Syria, and in a worldwide diaspora. The Syriac Orthodox Church, whose patriarch resides in Jerusalem, is said to have been founded by Thomas the Apostle in 33 C.E. There is also a Syriac Catholic Church affiliated, like the Maronite Catholic Church, with the Roman Catholic Church. The Syriac (or Assyrian-Aramaic) language is used in the liturgy of all three churches.

SYRIAN SOCIAL NATIONALIST PARTY (SSNP; in Arabic, *al-Hizb a—Suri al-Qawmi al-Ijtima'i*): Syrian socialist political party. Under the name *Parti Populaire Syrien* (Syrian Popular Party), a name that is still in use, the SSNP was created in November 1932 by Antun Sa'ada, a Maronite Christian, during the French Mandate in Beirut. The SSNP was a pan-Syrian party whose ideology and organization owed much to contemporary European fascism. It opposed both the independence of Lebanon from Syria and pan-Arab nationalism, advocating instead "the rise of the Syrian nation" within its "natural" borders.

Sa'ada's conception of "Syria" included the traditional area of Greater Syria (*Bilad al-Sham*)—Syria, Lebanon, western Jordan, and Palestine—as well as eastern Jordan, Iraq, Kuwait, part of Iran, part of Turkey, the Sinai Peninsula, and Cyprus.

As a party of secular nationalism, it counted members of all ideologies. Between 1935 and 1937 many were arrested, prompting others to leave Lebanon. Legally authorized in April 1944, the SSNP was at that time led by Nehmé Tabet, aided by Fayez Sayegh; but after two years of exile in Brazil, Sa'ada returned to Lebanon in 1947 and retook the leadership of the party, moving it toward confrontation with the Lebanese government.

After an attack on the party by the Phalange in 1949, Sa'ada attempted an armed rebellion that led to the arrest of hundreds of party members. Sa'ada fled to Syria, but was betrayed by Syrian president General Husni al-Za'im who handed him over to Lebanese authorities; he was executed by them on 8 July 1949. Za'im's betrayal provoked a coup d'état in Syria on 14 August, removing the general from power.

The SSNP, which had particpated in the overthrow, moved its headquarters to Damascus under the leadership of Georges Abdul Massih, and nine of its members were elected to the Syrian parliament. Between 1950 and 1958, the party increased its activities in Lebanon, opposing the Communists and Arab nationalists. On 22 April 1955 a SSNP member assassinated the Syrian assistant chief-of-staff, Ba'thist Adnan Malki; this resulted in Syria banning the party and expelling its members from the country. In 1961, the SSNP participated in an attempted coup d'état in Lebanon and was declared illegal in that country as well, but by 1970 the party had been reinstated in Lebanon, and Abdallah Saʿada was elected to its head.

During the Lebanese civil war (1975–1990) the SSNP split into factions. One of these, headed by Inʿam Raad, tried to combine a form of Marxism with the semi-fascist SNP ideology; this group joined the Lebanese National Movement (LNM), an alliance of leftist secularist groups. Two more factions sufaced in 1984: one was pro-Syrian and led by Isam Mahayri, the second was pro-Libyan and headed by Daud Baz.

The parliamentary block of the SSNP proposed the abolition of confessionalism in Lebanon in 1992, and supported Islamic resistance against the Israeli presence in South Lebanon. On 5 August 2001, for the first time in 47 years, the SSNP organized a public meeting in Damascus, presided over by its secretary general Jubran Arbadji.

SEE ALSO Phalange.

T

TAGAR ("challenge", in Hebrew): International Zionist organization for students on university campuses, founded in 1983 as an expansion of the Betar Zionist Youth Movement. Its original aim was to counter anti-Israel propaganda during the Lebanon war. Today this, along with fostering a positive image of Israel and strengthening links among Israeli youth, are its main objectives. Among other activities it offers tours to Israel and opportunities for students to spend time volunteering there.

SEE ALSO Betar.

TAʾIF ACCORD: Agreement among factions that led to the end of the Lebanese Civil War (1975–90). In May 1989 the Arab League sponsored a tripartite commission composed of the heads of state of Algeria, Saudi Arabia and Morocco to resolve the civil war in Lebanon, which had lasted almost fifteen years. In July the commission made several proposals that were rejected out of hand by Syria. In September the commission asked representatives of the various factions remaining in the Lebanese Chamber of Deputies (last elected in 1972) to meet in Taʾif, Saudi Arabia, to discuss its proposals. After a month of negotiations, a compromise agreement, the National Unity Charter, known as the Taʾif Accord, was signed on 22 October.

The accord stipulated reducing the powers of the Lebanese president in favor of the prime minister,

who would become executive head of government, and the Council of Ministers (cabinet); and increasing the number of seats in Parliament (to 128 from 99) with equal proportions of Christians and Muslims. (Seats had previously been apportioned based on the fiction of a Christian majority. Lebanon is now approximately 70–75 percent Muslim.) The presidency would still be reserved for a Christian and the prime ministry for a Sunni Muslim. The sectarian basis of Lebanese politics was left unchanged. The accord also provided for disarming the sectarian militias as soon as a new president was elected and ratified the presence in Lebanon of the Syrian Army, whose 1976 mandate from the Arab League had expired in 1982, after several extensions.

The text of the accord, in spite of the opposition of the so-called "interim president," General Michel Aoun, was ratified by the Lebanese Parliament on 5 November 1989. On 4 November 1989 the parliament elected Rene Muawad president; he was assassinated on 22 November. On 24 November Ilyas al-Hrawi was elected, and a new national unity government was installed in December 1989. In August 1990 the parliament amended the constitution according to the provisions of the accord. The Taʾif Accord allowed the Lebanese to have a duly elected president again, after a gap of more than a year, and to begin to isolate the factions that wished to prolong the war. Aoun's forces continued to oppose the settlement until October, when, during the crisis leading to the Gulf War of 1991, the Syrian army defeated them. More than 25,000 Syrian troops remain in Lebanon, and no Lebanese government initiative can take place without Syrian approval.

SEE ALSO Aoun, Michel; Arab League; Gulf War (1991).

TAKFIR WA AL-HIJRA, AL-: Egyptian Islamicist movement ("Condemnation and Migration" in English), founded at the end of the 1960s by Ahmad Shukri Mustafa, then in prison. Mustafa was inspired by the writings of Sayyid Qutb (1906–1966), a radical Islamicist and propagandist for the Muslim Brotherhood, whose ideas he shared. This organization became known in July 1977 when it kidnapped and murdered an Islamic moderate and former Egyptian minister of the Waqf, Muhammad al-Dhahabi. In March 1978, four hundred members of the group were arrested, and five leaders, including Mustafa, were hanged.

SEE ALSO Muslim Brotherhood; Waqf.

TALA'I AL-FATAH

SEE Egyptian Islamic Jihad.

TALA'I AL-ISLAMIYYA, AL-

SEE Shiqaqi, Fathi.

TALAL, HUSSEIN IBN

SEE Hussein ibn Talal.

TALAL IBN ABDULLAH (1909–1972; King of Jordan, 1951–1952): Talal was the son of King Abdullah I ibn Hussein of Jordan, and acceded to power when Abdullah was assassinated in July 1951. During his brief reign he promulgated a constitution for Jordan that provided for a partly-elected legislature and restrictions on the power of the monarch. Diagnosed as a schizophrenic, he was deposed in August 1952 (with his acquiescence) in favor of his 17-year-old son Hussein ibn Talal, who had been groomed for the throne by his grandfather. Talal lived out the remainder of his life in a sanatorium in Turkey.

SEE ALSO Abdullah I ibn Hussein; Hussein ibn Talal.

TALMUD: Rabbinical work, constituted of the ensemble of Torah commentaries, written (Mishnah) and oral (Gemora). This is a veritable reading manual of Torah, in which sometimes diverging views may be expressed. There are two versions of the Talmud: the Palestinian, so-called of Jerusalem, and the more important one, from Babylonia. The author of the Mishnah, Juda Hanassi (second century C.E.), ignored the apocalyptic traditions of the Torah, keeping only the commandments. This written compilation attracted a number of commentaries, which were assembled to create the Gemora. The Talmud proclaims three interdictions that must never be infringed, even at the cost of one's life: incest, idolatry, and murder.

SEE ALSO Torah.

TAMI (Movement for the Traditions of Israel, in Hebrew *Tnu'at Masoret Israel*): Name of an Israeli political group, arisen from a splinter in 1981, in the National Religious Party. Founded by Aharon Abuhatzeira, TAMI attracted Sephardim, while benefiting from the financial support of the wealthy Swiss banker Nissim Gaon. As a result of the elections of June 1981, this party won three Knesset seats. The following year, TAMI was weakened by a corruption scandal involving its principal leader, Abuhatzeira, former minister of religious affairs. In 1983, TAMI Knesset Members backed, successfully, the candidacy of Laborite Chaim Herzog to the post of president of the State of Israel. In October 1983, TAMI joined the rightist government of Yitzhak Shamir, obtaining the portfolio of labor, taken by Aharon Uzan. In March 1984 the leadership of the party decided to withdraw its support from the Shamir government, anticipating the results of the next scheduled elections, in which the Labor Party won 44 seats against 41 for Likud. As a result of this ballot, nevertheless, TAMI obtained only one seat, filled by Abuhatzeira. Four years later, just before the elections of November 1988, the latter rejoined Likud, leading to the disappearance of TAMI from the Israeli political arena.

SEE ALSO Abuhatzeira, Aharon; National Religious Party; Shamir, Yitzhak.

TAMIR, YA'EL (1954–): Israeli scholar and politician. Ya'el (Yuli) Tamir was born in Israel in 1954 and received her doctoral degree from Oxford University. A professor of political philosophy at Tel Aviv University and a research fellow at the Hartman Institute of Jewish Studies, she is the author of numerous books and articles on various subjects, including liberalism, feminism, and nationalism. Tamir was also one of the founders of the Peace Now movement. From 1980 to 1985 she was an active member of the RATZ Party and since 1995 a member of the Labor

Party. Tamir served as minister of immigrant absorption from August 1999 to March 2001.

SEE ALSO Peace Now.

TANZIM, AL-: "Organization" (plural: *tanzimat*). A loosely organized network of groups of Palestinian militants in the Occupied Territories who surfaced in the first Intifada (1987–1993) and continue to be active in the al-Aqsa Intifada. It is said to have been run by Mustafa Barghuthi until his arrest in 2003. Information about the tanzim is limited and contested, and it is said that there are *tanzimat* for each of the PLO factions. The best-known is probably the al-Aqsa Martyrs Brigade, associated with al-Fatah.

SEE ALSO Aqsa Intifada, al-; Barghuthi, Mustafa; Fatah, al-; Intifada (1987–1993).

TARAWNEH, FAYIZ AL- (1949–): Jordanian political figure born in 1949 in Amman. Al-Tarawneh was the son of Ahmad al-Tarawneh, who held a number of ministerial posts in Jordanian governments. Educated in the United States, with a degree in economics, al-Tarawneh became assistant to the chief of protocol at the Jordanian royal court in 1971. Between 1980 and 1984, he was secretary to the prime minister, then became advisor for economic affairs. In January 1988, he was named minister for presidential affairs of the Jordanian council. In December of that year he became supply minister, a post that he kept until the fall of the Rifaʿi government in April 1989. After concentrating on business affairs for a few years, al-Tarawneh was named Jordanian ambassador to the United States in December 1992. In this capacity, he participated in Israeli-Jordanian peace negotiations and in multilateral consultations on the Israeli-Arab peace process, becoming one of the main crafters of the Israeli-Jordanian peace treaty of 1994. On 19 March 1997, al-Tarawneh was named foreign minister in the government of Abd al-Salam Majali. On 17 February 1998, during a reshuffling of the cabinet, he was appointed chief of the royal court of King Hussein. On 19 August he was named prime minister, replacing Majali, three days after Hussein delegated the regency to Prince Hassan. On 1 March 1999, three days after the accession of King Abdallah II ibn Hussein, al-Tarawneh resigned, replaced by Abd al-Rawuf al-Rawabdeh. In January 2000, he was again appointed chief of the royal court, replacing Abdul Karim Kabariti. In 2004 he was relieved of this post and appointed by the king to the Jordanian Senate.

SEE ALSO Abdallah II ibn Hussein; Hassan of Jordan; Kabariti, Abdul Karim; Majali, Abd al-Salam; Rawabdeh, Abd al-Rawuf al-.

TASAWWUF: Literally, "becoming a sufi"; the way of being of the spiritual and ethical ideals implied in the body of ascetic and mystical rules of the sufi Muslim orders; often rendered in English as "sufism." The word "sufi" comes from the Arabic *suf,* "wool," from the traditional ascetic clothing worn by holy men in the Arab world. Tasawwuf developed in Islam in the seventh century, inspired by the nightly vigils in a cave of the Prophet Muhammad, and by the contemplative practice of Christian hermits. The sufis established themselves in Al-Kufa, then Basra, and finally Baghdad, which became the movement's center in the second half of the ninth century. After the fall of the Abbasid caliphate, Cordoba became a center of mysticism, notably under Muhyi al-Din ibn Arabi. The sufis are organized in orders (*tariqas*), of which some, like the Qadiriyya or the Naqshbandiyya, have disciples on several continents. The great sufi orders have been and are still politically and religiously significant. They include: the Suhrawardiya; the Naqshbandiyya; the Kubrawiya; the Khalwatiya; the Tidjaniya; the Mawlawiya (whose members are known as the whirling dervishes); the Alawiya; the Bektashiya; the Jazuliya; the Muridiya;, the Qadiriya; the Rahmaniya; the Rifaiya; the Shadhiliya; the Shaykhiya; the Darqawiya; the Idrishiya; and the Sanusiya.

TAWHID AL-ISLAMI, HARAKAT AL-: Lebanese Sunni Islamicist group ("Islamic Unity Movement" in English), formed from the unification of three smaller groups in 1982 in Tripoli by Shaykh Said al-Shaaban (1928–1998). Shaaban had studied at al-Azhar University in Cairo where he was a member of the Muslim Brotherhood. He taught in Algeria, Iraq and Morocco. During the Lebanese civil war (1975–1990) this group supported the Lebanese National Movement (LNM)–Palestine Liberation Organization (PLO) alliance and remains a supporter of the Palestinian cause. It controlled Tripoli in 1983–1985, imposing its version of *sharia,* or Islamic law, but was ousted after a violent fight with the Syrians and their Lebanese allies in November 1985. Many of its members were imprisoned in Syria and were released only gradually through 2000. In recent years al-Tawhid, now led by Shaaban's son Bilal, has grown close to the Syrians.

SEE ALSO Azhar, al-; Lebanese National Movement; Muslim Brotherhood; Palestine Liberation Organization; Sunni Islam.

DERVISHES. THIS ILLUSTRATION DEPICTS SUFI DERVISHES DANCING. SUFISM (TASAWWUF IN ARABIC) ENCOMPASSES ASCETIC AND MYSTICAL MOVEMENTS WITHIN ISLAM, DATING BACK TO THE RELIGION'S EARLIEST PERIOD BUT EVOLVING EVER SINCE. (© *Bodleian Library, Oxford University*)

TAWIL, RAYMONDA HAWA (1939–): Palestinian journalist, born in 1939 into a Greek Orthodox family at Acre. Following the Arab defeat in the Arab-Israel War (1967), she decided to devote herself to the Pal-

estinian cause. In 1978, with journalist Ibrahim Karain, Tawil created the Palestine Press Service in Jerusalem, which, besides its newsgathering activities, provided Palestinian stringers for foreign news

TEL AVIV. ISRAEL'S SECOND-LARGEST CITY, LOCATED ON THE MEDITERRANEAN COAST, BOASTS A POPULATION OF MORE THAN 400,000. FOUNDED IN 1909 BY EARLY ZIONIST SETTLERS IN PALESTINE, TEL AVIV WAS THE FIRST CAPITAL OF THE STATE OF ISRAEL, FROM 1948 TO 1950. IT MERGED WITH THE MUCH OLDER CITY OF JAFFA IN 1950, BECOMING TEL AVIV–JAFFA. *(© Royalty-Free/Corbis)*

organizations. In September 1979, she published a book, *My Country, My Prison,* which won the Mamud Hamshari prize the following year, awarded by the Franco-Arab Solidarity Association. In 1983, with Ibrahim Karain, she brought out a new magazine in Jerusalem, *al-Awdah (The Return).* For many years Raymonda Tawil was harassed by the Israeli administration, and was put under house arrest several times. In November 1991, her daughter Suha married Yasir Arafat. Tawil and Suha now live in Paris.

SEE ALSO Arab-Israel War (1967); Arafat, Yasir Muhammad.

TEKUMAH PARTY (Resurrection or renaissance, in Hebrew): Small religious-Zionist political party, a faction of the National Union party. It was formed from the parliamentary group Emunim that had been established toward the end of the Fourteenth Knesset by MKs Zvi Hendel and Hanan Porat, who had left the National Religious Party; Uri Ariel, the

chairman of the movement; Yaakov Katz; Benny Katzover; and others. It joined forces with Herut and Moldet to form the National Union (Ihud ha-Le'umi) list for the 1999 Knesset elections, but continued to exist independently and ran in the 2003 Jerusalem municipal elections. The main difference between Herut and Tekumah is the religious orientation of the latter.

Tekumah strongly supports Jewish settlement activity and, anticipating the possibility of future compromise with Palestinians, in September 2004 it took part in a campaign to make policemen and soldiers aware that they are permitted not to "take part in the uprooting of Jews from their homes."

SEE ALSO National Union.

TEL AVIV: A coastal city founded in Ottoman Palestine in 1909. As Jewish settlers arrived in Palestine in the late nineteenth century, they found it difficult to find affordable homes in the overcrowded residential areas of Jerusalem and Jaffa. Ahuzat Bayit, the building society, purchased beachfront property and underwrote the construction of Tel Aviv's first houses in 1909. Initially planned as a residential suburb of Jaffa, Tel Aviv expanded rapidly. By 1935 the population had grown from 2,000 (in 1909) to 120,000, and the city included businesses, factories, and the headquarters of Histradut, the umbrella trade union organization. In 1948 David Ben-Gurion proclaimed Israel's statehood at a meeting held in the Tel Aviv Museum. In 1950 Jaffa was incorporated with Tel Aviv into the twin city of Tel Aviv-Jaffa. The population of central Tel Aviv reached 350,000 by the early twenty-first century, but the population of greater Tel Aviv, with its sprawling suburbs and outskirts, was 2.5 million.

TEL AVIV UNIVERSITY: The largest university in Israel, Tel Aviv University was founded in 1956, when the Tel Aviv School of Law merged with the Institute of Natural Sciences and the Institute of Jewish Studies. The university offers programs in the arts and sciences within nine faculties: engineering, exact sciences, humanities, law, life sciences, management, medicine, social services, and visual and performing arts. It also houses ninety research institutes. The university includes in its mission a commitment to social concerns and to the peace process. In 2002 it enrolled approximately 26,000 students.

TELEM EMANA: Israeli religious political party, founded in April 1996, by Rabbi Yosef Azran, a dissident from the ultra-orthodox SHAS Party, former deputy minister of finance in 1988, and deputy speaker of the Knesset in 1992. Sephardi in observance, with ideas close to Likud, this group was formed in anticipation of the Knesset elections of May 1996, as a result of which it obtained no seats.

TEMPLE MOUNT

SEE Haram al-Sharif.

TEMPLE MOUNT FAITHFUL: Israeli extremist religious movement, founded in 1967 (and still headed) by Gershon Salomon. Its objectives are to liberate the Temple Mount in Jerusalem from Islamic occupation; to remove what it views as "pagan shrines," which it suggests should be relocated to Mecca; to consecrate the Temple Mount so that it can become the moral and spiritual center of the Jewish people as the chosen people of God; to built the Third Temple (the Temple of Solomon) in accordance with the words of the Hebrew prophets; to make Jerusalem the undivided capital of the State of Israel; to "reject

false 'peace talks' which will result in the dividing of Israel and the breaking of God's covenant"; and to support the settlements in Jerusalem, Judea, Samaria, and the Golan Heights, which it considers holy because "God commanded the people of Israel to settle the land completely." According to this group, "Israel is not permitted to give any of this land to any group for any purpose since the land is a grant to Israel from God Himself. Any division of the Land and the giving of it to another people represents a breach of the Covenant with God."

In 1990, a violent confrontation between the group and Muslims at Temple Mount led to a confrontation with Israeli police, which left twenty-one Muslims dead. The group has at various times attempted to lay a cornerstone for the Third Temple, but has been prevented from doing so by Israeli police because of the likelihood that riots would be provoked. This issue was taken all the way to Israel's Supreme Court, which in 2001 allowed the stone to be moved temporarily to the gates of the site but ruled that in the interests of religious peace, it could not be placed on the Temple Mount itself. The group, though small, conducts marches and demonstrations when permitted to do so and has received a good deal of publicity.

SEE ALSO Haram al-Sharif.

TEMPORARY INTERNATIONAL PRESENCE IN HEBRON (TIPH): A United Nations civilian observer mission stationed in the city of Hebron, in the West Bank, charged with "monitor[ing] and report[ing] on misconduct by either side in the conflict. TIPH is not allowed to intervene directly in incidents and has no military or police functions." Personnel are supplied by Denmark, Italy, Norway, Sweden, Switzerland and Turkey. TIPH was first deployed in May 1994 after the murder of twenty-nine Muslim worshipers in the Ibrahim Mosque by an American-Israeli settler in February. It was withdrawn in August when the Israeli and Palestinian authorities could not agree on an extension of its mandate. A second, provisional, mission was established in May 1996 pending the IDF's withdrawal, and a new accord of 15 January 1997 provided for a full-scale mission with 180 members. This mission was deployed that February and remains in place. Its mandate is renewed every six months.

SEE ALSO Hebron; West Bank.

TENUAT HA-TEHIYAH

SEE Ha-Tehiyah.

Suicide Bombing. Israeli police and paramedics work at the scene of an explosion in April 2002, at a bus stop next to a crowded outdoor market in Jerusalem. Deliberate acts of terrorism against civilian populations have increased dramatically during the Second Intifada. *(AP/Wide World Photos)*

TERRORISM: Violence against civilians for the purpose of intimidation, revenge for perceived grievances, or the achievement of political goals. No definition of terrorism exists in international law. The application of the term to a violent and sometimes spectacular act is subject to debate because persons who perform such acts claim justification by invoking their right to defend themselves against an identifiable oppressor. There are often no objective criteria by which to determine whether a given act constitutes terrorism or legitimate resistance.

For example, the Palestine Liberation Organization (PLO) has been perceived by Israelis and by most of the world as a terrorist group, whereas it sees itself as an idealistic national liberation movement and was so viewed by allies such as the Soviet Union. Attempts have been made to establish international conventions that criminalize intentional violence against civilians whether a government or a nonstate group is responsible; but major nations, including both Israel and the United States, insist that the defi-

nition of terrorism must be limited to nonstate groups that target civilians. Whether or not a consensus is ever reached on what constitutes terrorism, violent acts perceived by their victims as terrorism are likely to continue.

THABITUN ALA AL-MABDA, AL-: "Those Constant for the Principle," an Islamist faction that appeared within the Popular Front for the Liberation of Palestine (PFLP-GC) in 1994.

SEE ALSO Popular Front for the Liberation of Palestine.

THIRD WAY (*ha-Derekh ha-Shlishlit*, in Hebrew): Israeli political party, created on 13 February 1996, anticipating the Knesset elections for the following May. In fact, this group had been in existence since 1994, as a radical current within the Labor Party, headed by Avigdor Kahalani, Yehuda Harel, and Emanuel Zissman. Presenting itself at this time as a forum for reflection, this movement expressed its support for the peace process, under the condition that Israel maintained its control over the Occupied Territories. In January 1995, a "council" was formed within the movement, uniting many figures on the left and in the center, so as to promote the proposition of a referendum on the return of the Golan Heights to Syria. In the context of an eventual peace accord with Syria, Third Way favored keeping Israeli control over the Jewish villages that had been established in the Golan, as well as over water sources, and also a security line on the heights. As a result of the elections of 29 May 1996, Third Way won four seats, and its leader, Kahalani, was named internal security minister in the government led by the head of Likud, Benjamin Netanyahu. For the scheduled general elections of May 1999, the party did not succeed in constituting an electoral list; and most of its members threw their support to the new Center Party, headed by Yitzhak Mordechai, which allowed this bloc to obtain six seats. Not presenting itself at the elections, the Third Way disappeared from the Israeli political scene.

SEE ALSO Center Party; Golan Heights; Israel Labor Party; Kahalani, Avigdor; Netanyahu, Benjamin.

THUNDERBOLT

SEE Sa'iqa, al-.

TIBI, AHMAD (1958–): Palestinian Israeli political figure, born in 1958 at Taibeh, near Tel Aviv. A medical doctor, with a degree from the Hebrew University in Jerusalem, Ahmad Tibi had very good relations with a number of Israeli personages, including former president Ezer Weizman. He developed into an important intermediary between the Israeli leaders and the head of the Palestine Liberation Organization (PLO), Yasir Arafat, whom he came to know in 1984, through Raymonda Hawa Tawil, a prominent Palestinian journalist (and Arafat's future mother-in-law). In September 1993, in the context of the Oslo Accords signed in Washington that month, he became a special advisor to Arafat. In June of 1994, on the advice of an advisor to the Israeli government, Michael Ben Yair, according to whom contacts with a representative of the PLO were prohibited, Israeli prime minister Yitzhak Rabin, decided to stop using Tibi as a liaison. In March, 1996, anticipating Israeli general elections scheduled for the following May, he founded the Arab Movement for Change (AMC). With ambitions to become one of the leaders of the Palestinian Israeli camp, he envisaged constituting a common electoral list with the Democratic Front for Peace and Equality and the Arab Democratic Party (ADP). After this project fell through, he changed the name of his movement to "Arab Alliance for Progress and Renewal," hoping, in vain, to obtain the support of the ADP and the Islamists. On 21 May of the same year he decided to withdraw his candidacy from the elections, calling on his supporters to vote for the Israeli Labor Party. In February 1999, he resigned his functions as advisor to Yasir Arafat to present himself as a candidate at the scheduled Israeli elections in May, on the list constituted by Azmi Bishara, the Democratic National Alliance, known as "Balad." In that election, in which Laborite Ehud Barak was voted in as prime minister, Balad obtained two seats, which were allotted to Bishara and Tibi. In 2002 Bishara and Tibi were barred from running in the next election on the grounds that they had "supported terrorists" by denouncing the Israeli assault on Jenin that spring. The Israeli Supreme Court overturned the ban shortly before the election in January 2003. Both Tibi and Bishara were reelected to the Knesset.

SEE ALSO Arab Democratic Party; Arab Movement for Change; Arafat, Yasir Muhammad; Barak, Ehud; Bishara, Azmi; Democratic Front for Peace and Equality; Democratic National Alliance; Oslo Accords; Palestine Liberation Organization; Palestinian Israelis; Rabin, Yitzhak; Tawil, Raymonda Hawa; Weizman, Ezer.

TIKVA (*ha Tikva*, hope, in Hebrew): Israeli political bloc essentially for immigrants from Ethiopia. Founded in January 1999 in anticipation of elections scheduled for the following May, this party proposed defending the interests of the Ethiopian community, which was badly integrated into Israeli society. Its founder, Ephraim Yona, is a former Likud militant. Tikva secured no Knesset seats in the 1999 or 2001 elections and did not run in 2003.

SEE ALSO Knesset; Likud.

TIPH

SEE Temporary International Presence in Hebron.

TLAS, MUSTAFA (Abu Firas; 1932–): Syrian general, born in May 1932 at Rastan. In 1952, Mustafa Tlas started on a military career, joining the same unit as his later friend, Hafiz al-Asad. In December 1959, both were part of a group of officers attached to the Egyptian army, as part of the attempted integration of the United Arab Republic (UAR). They stayed in Egypt until September 1961, when the UAR was dissolved. The shunting aside of the Ba'thists by the Syrian government relegated them to subordinate positions. In April 1962, as members of a Ba'thist underground committee, they participated in the "free officers" rebellion, demanding the resumption of the alliance with Egypt. Arrested and imprisoned, they were freed on 8 March 1963, after the Ba'th Party took over the government in a coup d'état. Rejoining the Syrian army, Mustafa Tlas was assigned to the military tribunal of Homs. Between 1964 and 1966 he was in command of the Fifth Armored Division in this city. In February 1968, Tlas was promoted to general, and named army chief of staff and defense vice minister, the defense minister being Hafiz al-Asad. A member of the military committee of Ba'th, headed by Asad, Tlas supported the latter in his differences with the civil committee of the party. On 13 November 1970, he participated in the coup that put Asad in power. On 22 March 1971, when the latter had been elected president of the Republic, Tlas was named defense minister.

Tlas played a significant role in the rapprochement between Syria and Jordan. On 13 May 1972, with his Soviet counterpart, he signed an important accord for military cooperation between the Soviet Union and Syria. In January 1978, he was named lieutenant general, a rank that had not existed until then in the Syrian army. In November 1983, when Asad was ill, he was among those to whom the latter entrusted the government in the interim, and also preventing the president's brother Rif'at al-Asad from trying to seize power. In September 1984, Tlas became vice prime minister, responsible for defense. Since the death of Hafiz al-Asad, Mustafa Tlas has remained one of the main supports of the Syrian regime, someone on whom the new president, Bashshar al-Asad, relies. On 7 March 2000, he was named vice prime minister and defense minister in the government of Muhammad Miro. In 1983 Tlas published a book called *The Matzo of Zion,* a work founded on the classic Christian "blood libel" against the Jews.

SEE ALSO Asad, Bashshar al-; Asad, Hafiz al-; Ba'th; United Arab Republic.

TORAH (*Tora, Thora*; "doctrine", in Hebrew): The book of Jewish scripture on which religious law (Halakhah) is based. According to Jewish tradition the Torah was given by God himself to the Jewish people through the intermediary Moses. Scholars, however, believe that it is an assembly of diverse an-

cient texts relating to the Exodus to Sinai. The Torah consists of the first five books of the Hebrew Bible. Ancient Jewish translations of these books into Greek were the basis of the Christian Old Testament, and are referred to as the Pentateuch (Law of Moses), which is a collection of five texts: Genesis (*Bereshit,* in Hebrew), Exodus (*Shemot*), Leviticus (*Vayiqr'a*), Numbers (*Bamidbar*) and Deuteronomy (*Devarim*). Modern Hebrew versions of the Torah exist both as a printed book within the larger printed Hebrew Bible and as a handwritten scroll used in synagogue rituals.

Although some ultra-Orthodox rabbinic sages regard the Torah as being older than the creation of the world, a representation of the principle at the heart of reality, most modern Jewish scholars view it in the light of European intellectual traditions of the eighteenth and nineteenth centuries. Some interpret it not as a set of laws demanding obedience but as an expression of unchanging moral and ethical values. Others perceive it as the record of profound personal religious experiences. For the majority, it embodies the unique Jewish spiritual and cultural experience as it has developed through the ages. The Torah is the foundation of religious and historical Judaism, its fundamental affirmation being the oneness of God. Thus the study of the Torah remains a powerful unifying force in world Jewry.

Many Orthodox Jews interpret the Torah (especially Genesis 15 and 17) as containing pledges and commandments amounting to a covenant between God and the Jewish people, as descendants of Abraham, including God's promise of the Holy Land to the Jews.

SEE ALSO Bible; Moses; Talmud.

TORAH FRONT

SEE United Torah Judaism Party.

TRANSJORDAN

SEE Jordan.

TSAHAL

SEE Israel Defense Force.

TUFAYLI, SUBHI ALI AL- (1948–): Lebanese Shi'ite religious leader, born in Brital in the Beqaa Valley. Tufayli studied theology in Najaf, Iraq, between 1965 and 1972, and briefly in Qom, Iran. A member of the al-Da'wa Party, he returned to Lebanon to teach. In June 1982, following the Israeli invasion of Lebanon,

TORAH. A JEW AT THE WESTERN WALL IN JERUSALEM TOUCHES HIS PRAYER SHAWL TO THE TORAH. BELIEVED BY JEWS TO BE THE LAW GIVEN BY GOD TO MOSES FOR THE JEWISH PEOPLE, IT CONSISTS OF THE PENTATEUCH, OR FIVE BOOKS OF MOSES, COMPRISING GENESIS, EXODUS, LEVITICUS, NUMBERS, AND DEUTERONOMY; AND, IN A BROADER SENSE, ALL THE INTERPRETATIONS OF SCRIPTURE COLLECTIVELY CALLED THE MIDRASH. *(© Paul A. Souders/Corbis)*

he joined the Pasdaran (Revolutionary Guards) who had been sent from Iran, becoming one of their principal figures. In February 1985 he was named head of Hizbullah for the Beqaa. As president of the movement's military commission he was in charge of coordinating operations in Lebanon with Tehran. He advocated radical policies towards the West and was believed to be involved in planning the attacks and kidnappings of Westerners that Hizbullah carried out in Lebanon. In 1986, backed by ʿAbbas al-Mussawi, he headed the mainstream of Hizbullah, facing a challenge from a faction led by Hasan Nasrallah. On 21 November 1988 he escaped a car-bomb assassination attempt. On 12 November 1989 he spoke out against the Taʾif Accord, which had been signed a few days earlier. On 26 November he was named secretary general of Hizbullah, a post that had just been created.

From this time on, his disagreements with the spiritual mentor of the movement, Muhammad Fa-

dlallah, as well as with Hasan Nasrallah, started to become more serious and sometimes translated into bloody confrontations between their respective partisans. On 29 March 1990 he escaped a second assassination attempt. In May 1991 he was removed from the leadership of Hizbullah and replaced by Abbas al-Mussawi. After al-Mussawi's death in February 1992, Nasrallah became secretary-general of the movement. Thereafter, Tufayli affirmed the necessity of continuing the fight against Israel, even if Israel withdrew from South Lebanon, but he opposed the policy of integrating Hizbullah into Lebanese political life for fear that it would lead to the disappearance of the movement. In November 1993 he became head of the Union of Muslim Ulamas (Tajamuʿ al-ʿUlama al-Muslimin) of the Beqaa, hoping to turn this movement into a party capable of competing with Hizbullah. Denouncing the Lebanese government's lack of any real social policy, on 4 July 1997 he launched the "revolt of the hungry" (Thawrat al-Jaʿan), calling on inhabitants of the Beqaa not to pay their taxes.

Confronted by this internal opposition, the leadership of Hizbullah gradually shunted him aside, succeeding despite a number of demonstrations that he organized in his support. On 23 January 1998 Tufayli was expelled from Hizbullah. Shortly afterward the Lebanese army, with the approval of Syria, moved on Tufayli. Bloody confrontations took place between his supporters and the army, in the course of which Khodr Tlays, a deputy partial to Tufayli, was killed. Tufayli sought refuge in his fief of Brital. Since then, his stock of arms has been seized and his radio station destroyed; he is under observation by government security forces, who have occasionally threatened to arrest him, and his following has shrunk; he has engaged in very little public activity.

SEE ALSO Fadlallah, Shaykh Muhammad Husayn; Hizbullah; Nasrallah, Hasan; Pasdaran; Taʾif Accords.

TZOMET PARTY (Junction; Movement for the Zionist Renaissance, in Hebrew): Ultranationalist Israeli party, founded in October 1983 by General Rafael Eitan (called Raful), former army chief of staff of the Israel Defense Force (IDF) for the Operation Peace for Galilee. Partisan of the ideology of Greater Israel, this party was on the extreme right of the Israeli political spectrum. Shortly after it was created, Tzomet allied with ha-Tehiyah, but very rapidly there was discord between the leaders of the two groups, prompting a separation. For the election campaign of 1988, which took place in the shadow of the first Intifada, Tzomet presented the following platform: (1) No land currently under Israel sovereignty will be returned; (2) The solution to the Palestinian problem is to be found on the other side of the Jordan; (3) Israeli jurisdiction must extend to the West Bank and the Gaza Strip; (4) the creation of an Israeli constitution; modification of the electoral law so as to make the Jewish deputies more representative; active Arab representation in the Israeli administration; reduction of the role of the state; (5) separation of religion and the state. As a result of the vote, this party won two seats, taken by Rafael Eitan and Yoach Tziddon.

Between June 1990 and December 1991, Eitan was minister of agriculture in the government of Yitzhak Shamir, becoming outspoken in favor of Jewish settlements. The leader of Tzomet resigned from the Shamir government after the latter agreed to participate in negotiations with the Palestinians. In June 1992, in spite of the electoral defeat of the Israel right, Tzomet obtained eight seats in the Knesset. A poll indicated that more than 17 percent of army conscripts voted for this party. Parleys were arranged to discuss an eventual entrance of Tzomet into the government of the Laborite Yitzhak Rabin. Meretz threatened to withdraw from the governmental coalition, and Rabin renounced this plan. In February 1994, a split in the party, prompted by Gonen Segev, who criticized the authoritarianism of the head of Tzomet, gave rise to a new grouping, Yad. Thereby Tzomet lost three seats. In February 1996, anticipating elections for the following May, Tzomet presented a common list with Likud, with Benjamin Netanyahu at the top of it. On the following 7 March, the Gesher Party joined the Tzomet-Likud alliance, with Eitan accepting third position on the party list, behind Netanyahu and David Levy. After the ballot, Tzomet had won 5 seats, with the Likud-Gesher-Tzomet parliamentary bloc obtaining 32 seats of the 120 in the Knesset. On the following 18 June, two Tzomet members joined the Netanyahu government: Rafael Eitan (as deputy prime minister and minister of agriculture and the environment) and Moshe Peled (as deputy minister of education). During their term in office, while the government seemed to be on verge of making progress in the negotiations with the Palestinians, ministers Eitan and Peled were adamant in their opposition to any concessions to the latter. In January 1999, after he announced a month earlier his candidacy for the post of prime minister, Eitan abandoned this idea. On the following 17 May, having obtained no seats in the scheduled general elections, Tzomet disappeared from the Israeli political scene.

SEE ALSO Gesher "Bridge" Party; Greater Israel; Ha-Tehiyah; Rabin, Yitzhak; Shamir, Yitzhak.

U

UIA

SEE Universal Israelite Alliance.

UJA

SEE United Jewish Appeal.

ULAMA

SEE Alim.

ULEMA

SEE Alim.

ULPAN: Absorption center; where new Jewish immigrants are taught basic Hebrew language and the rudiments of life in their new Israeli homeland.

ULTRA-ORTHODOX: Jewish religious faction affirming the strict and literal application of Biblical law. This faction includes religious extremists who are hostile to the state of Israel because, believing that Jews should have waited for the Messiah to proclaim it, they see it as a secular abomination. In accordance with their interpretation of strict Halakhah, some are hostile to those who recognize the state and work and lobby for its governance, and some believe that all the occupied territories should be retained in fulfillment of what they understand as God's promise.

SEE ALSO Chabad; Lubavitcher Hasidim; Neturei Karta; Satmar.

UMM (*Om*): Arabic word meaning "mother of."

UMMA: Arabic term for the Muslim community.

UMMA AL-ARABIYYA, AL-: Arab term originally designating the whole Arab community; it has become an Arabic intellectual concept suggesting a unity of values, traditions, history, and language. Great Britain had attempted to use the idea of a "Great Middle East Arab State" as a means to weaken the Ottoman Empire, but Arab unity became a mobilizing regional political theme at the end of World War I when the oil needs of France, the United States, and Great Britain preferred a lack of unity among the Arab states. This in turn led to the rise of a new feeling of national identity in the Arab community, al-Umma al-Arabiyya.

SEE ALSO Umma.

UMM JIHAD

SEE Wazir, Intisar al-.

UMRA: Arab word designating the "lesser pilgrimage" made by Muslims to Mecca. Umra can occur at anytime of the year except during the period of the "great pilgrimage" (*hajj*). During Umra, the pilgrim is exempted from certain obligations, but is not excused from making the "great pilgrimage."

SEE ALSO Hajj.

UNIATE CHURCHES: A group of Eastern-rite churches that broke from the Greek (or Eastern) Orthodox Church and affiliated with the Roman Catholic Church. These churches accept Roman Catholic doctrine and acknowledge the primacy of the Roman Catholic pope, but retain their own customs and forms of hierarchy and liturgy. Uniate churches include the Syrian Catholic, Armenian Catholic, Chaldean Catholic and Greek Catholic Churches, which affiliated with Rome in the sixteenth and seventeenth centuries, and the Maronite Catholic Church, which affiliated with Rome in 1182.

UNIFIED NATIONAL LEADERSHIP OF THE UPRISING (UNLU)

SEE Intifada (1987–1993).

UNIFIED TORAH LIST

SEE Unified Torah Judaism Party.

UNITED ARAB LIST (al-Laʿiha al-Arabiyya al-Muwahhada, in Arabic; Ha-Reshimah Ha-Aravit Ha-Meʾuhedet, in Hebrew): Israeli electoral alliance formed in September 1993 in anticipation of municipal elections and uniting a number of Israeli Arab candidates of diverse views under the leadership of Abed Quseibi. In April 1996, in preparation for the Knesset elections of 29 May, when for the first time Knesset members and the prime minister were to be elected on separate ballots, the list was reconstituted under the impetus of Abdulmalik Dehamshe. On it were joined the Israeli Islamic Movement, to which Dahamshe belonged, and the Arab Democratic Party of Abdul Wahab Darawshe. The list won four deputy seats in the Knesset, which were taken by Darawshe, Talib al-Sanaa, Tawfiq Khatib, and Dehamshe, the first Islamist ever to sit in the Knesset. On 18 May 1999, following the general elections, which saw the victory of the Labor Party's leader, Ehud Barak, the United Arab List consolidated its position by winning five seats, two of which went to the Israeli Islamic Movement. Before 2001, the United Arab List generally supported the Labor Party, which officially advocates a peace accord with the Palestinians. In the February 2001 election for prime minister, faced with a choice between the incumbent, Ehud Barak, and Ariel Sharon of Likud, the leadership recommended abstention. In the Knesset elections of 2001, United Arab List won five seats; in the 2003 elections, two seats. The United Arab List favors the creation of a Palestinian state in the West Bank and Gaza Strip, with East Jerusalem as its capital, and the dismantling of all Israeli settlements. Within Israel it favors full civil rights for Palestinian Israelis, making Israel a "state of all its citizens."

SEE ALSO Arab Democratic Party; Barak, Ehud; Darawshe, Abdul Wahab; Dehamshe, Abdulmalik; Gaza Strip; Israeli Islamic Movement; Israel Labor Party; Likud; Sharon, Ariel; West Bank.

UNITED ARAB REPUBLIC (UAR): After the Suez Crisis and Egypt's successful defiance of the imperial West, Egypt's prestige and that of its leader, Gamal Abdel Nasser, were extremely high in the Arab world. In Syria, which was weak, politically unstable, and vulnerable to outside threats from the West and particularly from the subversive actions of conservative and royalist Iraq, whose own stability was threatened by the existence of left-leaning Arab governments. The idea of a federation between the two countries appealed to many, particularly the socialist, pan-Arabist Baʿth Party, which was the country's largest party; other elements favored it as a way to prevent leftists, such as the left wing of the Baʿth, from getting into power. The Syrian National Assembly called for union with the larger, more populous and more powerful Egypt; Nasser eventually agreed, but only on strict conditions. As a result, the United Arab Republic was proclaimed on 1 February 1958 and confirmed in a referendum on 21 February. It was structured as a unified state, not a federation; its capital was Cairo; its leader was Nasser; and it had a one-party political system. The military was unified under Egyptian command, with Syrian officers in subordinate positions, and banks, major industries, and large landholdings were nationalized. In 1960 the National Assembly was dissolved and replaced with a new, appointive body.

In March 1958, Nasser also formed a union between Egypt and Yemen, called the United Arab States. The same month the UAR was formed, as a conservative counterweight, King Hussein of Jordan and his cousin King Faysal II of Iraq announced a federation of their kingdoms, the Arab Union. It failed five months later when the Iraqi monarchy was overthrown and Faysal was assassinated. After the revolution in Iraq, Nasser held discussions with the new regime about joining the UAR, but nothing came of them. The American decision to send troops to Lebanon during the 1958 civil war there was, in part, a response to these developments.

Nasser's structural changes and policy measures alienated politically important elements of the Syrian population: the landholders, the middle class, the politicians, and the officer corps. Later changes to state structures, such as abolition of local autonomy and the planned unification of currencies, furthered centralized control, and government policies were based primarily on Egyptian conditions. Dissatisfaction and resentment grew—there was a feeling that, rather than union, the UAR was more like an Egyptian occupation—and there was growing talk of secession. In September 1961 Syrian army officers staged a coup d'état in Damascus, and Nasser decided not to fight it. On 28 September Syria withdrew from the UAR. In December Nasser ended the union with Yemen, which had had no more success than the Syrian experiment. Egypt continued to use the name United Arab Republic until 1971, after Nasser's death.

SEE ALSO Hussein ibn Talal; Nasser, Gamal Abdel; Suez Crisis.

UNITED HEBREW RESISTANCE

SEE Irgun; Lohamei Herut Yisrael.

UNITED JEWISH APPEAL: The primary organization through which U.S. Jews support Jews in other parts of the world. The United Jewish Appeal (UJA) was founded in 1939, when the United Palestine Appeal merged with the American Jewish Joint Distribution Committee and the National Refugee Service. Most of the funds raised by the UJA go to the United Israel Appeal, which operates through the Jewish Agency in Israel. In 1999 the UJA, the United Israel Appeal, and the Council of Jewish Federations merged to form the United Jewish Communities, which that year was reported to have raised $524 million.

UNITED NATIONS EMERGENCY FORCE (UNEF): Military force created on 7 November 1956 by the UN General Assembly following the Suez-Sinai War of 1956, to allow the evacuation of Israeli, French, and British troops from Egyptian territory.

Composed of 6,000 men, commanded by Canadian General E.L.M. Burns headquartered in Ballah, this force operated on the Egyptian side of the Egyptian-Israeli frontier of 1949. On 19 May 1967, at the request of Egyptian President Gamal Abdul Nasser, the UNEF evacuated from Egyptian territory a few weeks before the start of the 1967 War.

SEE ALSO Arab-Israel War (1967); Nasser, Gamal Abdul; Suez Crisis.

UNITED NATIONS EMERGENCY FORCE II (UNEF II): Military Force created on 25 October 1973 by UN Security Council Resolution 340 following the Arab-Israel War that started on 6 October 1973, to allow the Israelis to evacuate the Suez Canal zone and the Sinai.

SEE ALSO Arab-Israel War (1973).

UNITED NATIONS INTERIM FORCE IN LEBANON (UNIFIL): Military unit created in 1978 by the United Nations to restore peace in Lebanon. Under Security Council Resolutions 425 and 426, adopted on 19 March 1978 following the invasion of South Lebanon by Israel, UNIFIL was given a mandate to confirm the withdrawal of Israeli forces, restore international peace and security, and assist the government of Lebanon in assuring the return of its effective authority in the area. The mandate has been extended every six months since then, most recently by Security Council Resolution 1553 of 29 July 2004.

UNIFIL was deployed over an area of 680 km with around 400,000 inhabitants. Since March 1978, when Israel occupied South Lebanon, UNIFIL has been a powerless witness of the nonobservance of various UN resolutions. It was "shoved aside" in May 1982 by Israeli forces, engaged in Operation "Peace in Galilee." The Israeli army occupied a "security zone" of around 850 km in South Lebanon after its partial retreat of 1985. A UNIFIL post at Qana was bombarded by Israeli artillery, on 18 April 1996 during Operation "Grapes of Wrath," causing over a hundred deaths among the Lebanese refugees that were under UNIFIL protection.

On 27 July 2000, a month after the withdrawal of the Israeli forces from South Lebanon, the Security Council unanimously passed Resolution 1310, renewing the mandate while calling on the government of Lebanon to proceed with the deployment of a significant number of Lebanese armed forces as soon as possible. On 30 January 2001, in Resolution 1337, it reduced the number of UNIFIL troops from 5,800 to 4,500, thereby signifying disapproval of the Lebanese government, which did not seem in a hurry to reestablish its authority over the area vacated by the IDF. This resolution also expressed concern about the violation of the withdrawal line set by the UN and urged both parties to fulfill the commitments they had made to respect it. Subsequent resolutions have continued to express such concern, reduce troops, and emphasize the interim nature of UNIFIL.

On 31 August 2004 UNIFIL had a force of 1995 troops, representing seven different countries, assisted by some 50 military observers from United Nations Truce Supervision Organization (UNTSO) and a civilian staff of over 400. In resolution 1559, adopted on 2 September 2004, the Security Council declared that it was "gravely concerned" at the continued presence of armed militias in Lebanon that prevented the Lebanese government from exercising full sovereignty over it territory, and called for their disbanding and disarmament. It also declared its support for a "free and fair electoral process" in Lebanon's upcoming presidential election.

SEE ALSO United Nations Truce Supervision Organization.

UNITED NATIONS RELIEF AND WORKS AGENCY FOR PALESTINE REFUGEES IN THE NEAR EAST (UNRWA): Relief and development agency of the United Nations, created by General Assembly Resolution 302 of 8 December 1949. UNRWA was created in the aftermath of the 1948 War to provide social services and emergency aid to Palestinian refugees for what was imagined to be a temporary period. Its mandate has been extended repeatedly. It runs the Palestinian refugee camps in the West Bank, Gaza Strip, Lebanon, Syria, and Jordan; it provides schooling, health care, and other social services to over four million registered refugees. It is the UN's largest operation in the Middle East, and its staff of more than 25,000 is made up largely of refugees. Funding comes almost entirely from voluntary contributions from governments and the European Union, rather than from UN assessments.

Some statistics give an idea of the scope of UNRWA's operations. The 59 camps it runs contain 663 schools, covering the first through the ninth grades, plus five secondary schools in Lebanon, with a total enrollment of 491,978, half of whom are girls, and a total staff of 15,814. They also contain eight vocational and technical training centers, with an enrollment of 5,131. The agency's 122 primary health care facilities have a staff of 3,642; medical and dental patient visits and consultations totaled 8,829,639 between July 2003 and June 2004. UNRWA also operates 64 women's program centers and 37 community rehabilitation centers. Between the 1991–1992 fiscal year and 30 June 2004, the agency funded 5,398 poverty alleviation projects and made 76,668 small enterprise loans with a total value of $85,442,882 U.S. The total budget for 2003–2004 was $350,968,000 U.S.

The al-Aqsa Intifada, which began in September 2000, has brought violence, curfews, and closures in the Occupied Territories, and imposed heavy new demands on the UNRWA's services. The agency estimates that more than 50 percent of the population is without work, and that between 50 percent and 60 percent live with an income of less than $2 U.S. per day. The United Nations estimates that almost two million Palestinians, 62 percent of the population, have inadequate access to food, shelter, or health services. In 2002 a U.S. Agency for International Development study reported that malnutrition and anemia had increased among Palestinian children to emergency levels. The UNRWA has increased its food aid, feeding almost 220,000 families in the West Bank and Gaza in 2004. The agency has also assisted thousands of refugees whose homes have been damaged or destroyed by Israeli military operations, and it is rebuilding the Jenin and Rafah refugee camps. Increases in the demand for health services have been comparable. Schooling has been radically disrupted in many areas, with teachers and students often unable to reach their schools. To cover these increased needs, the agency has made several emergency appeals for additional funds since 2001, and has also cut back on services; schoolbooks and materials, for instance, are no longer provided free of charge. These appeals have not been as successful as the agency had hoped, and the agency is experiencing serious financial problems.

The UNRWA has been controversial, however, at least among supporters of Israel. As evidence that it is not "neutral" or "unbiased" but "anti-Israel"—indeed "pro-terrorist"—detractors have cited the facts that the agency supports people in the camps on the assumption that they have a right to return (an assumption the United Nations supports), rather than inducing them to disperse to other Arab states; that the agency employs Palestinians; and that the agency has criticized Israeli attacks on the camps. They argue that violent resistance groups have recruited and trained in the camps. Critics have also accused UNRWA of being complicit with corrupt Palestinian officials who have stolen food and medicine from the agency and sold them on the black market.

SEE ALSO Aqsa Intifada, al-; Arab-Israel War (1948); Gaza Strip; Resolution 302; Right of Return; West Bank.

UNITED NATIONS SPECIAL COMMISSION ON IRAQ (UNSCOM): Agency of the United Nations, created by Security Council Resolution 687 of 3 April 1991, following the Gulf War of 1991, to oversee the elimination of Iraq's non-nuclear weapons of mass destruction and ballistic missiles with a range greater than 150 kilometers (57.92 miles), and to assist the International Atomic Energy Agency in eliminating nuclear weapons development programs. Its mandate was to carry out inspections, take possession of weapons or materials, and destroy them or render them harmless. With a great deal of resistance from Iraq, the passage of a number of additional Security Council resolutions, and U.S. interference in the process, UNSCOM carried out its mandate, a fact it was able to confirm only after the occupation of Iraq by the United States and Britain during the Iraq War of 2003.

SEE ALSO Gulf War (1991); Iraq War (2003).

UNITED NATIONS TRUCE SUPERVISION ORGANIZATION (UNTSO): A peacekeeping operation originally established in May 1948 to assist the United Nations Mediator and the Truce Commission in supervising the observance of the truce in Palestine. Since then, it has been given additional assignments in the Middle East; UNTSO military observers remain in various areas to monitor ceasefires, supervise armistice agreements, prevent isolated incidents from escalating and assist other UN peacekeeping operations. Among its tasks have been supervision of the General Armistice Agreements of 1949, and observation of the ceasefire in the Suez Canal area and the Golan Heights following the Arab-Israeli war of June 1967.

At present, UNTSO assists and cooperates with the United Nations Disengagement Observer Force (UNDOF) on the Golan Heights in the Israel-Syria sector, and the United Nations Interim Force in Lebanon (UNIFIL) in the Israel-Lebanon sector. UNTSO is also present in the Egypt-Israel sector in the Sinai. It maintains offices in Beirut and Damascus. As of 31 August 2004 its staff consisted of 153 military observers from 23 different nations, supported by 89 international civilian personnel and 121 local civilians.

SEE ALSO United Nations Interim Force in Lebanon.

UNITED TORAH JUDAISM PARTY (Yahadut ha-Torah; also known as United Torah List): Israeli parliamentary bloc formed in 1973 by an alliance between several ultra-orthodox religious group, such as Degel ha-Torah, Po'alei Agudat Israel and Agudat Israel.

After winning five seats in the Knesset, this bloc enabled the religious parties to remain unavoidable partners in Israeli political life, a phenomenon well established in Israel's long history of coalition governments. Confronted with divergences among its members, United Torah Judaism brought them together on the single issue of respect for the status quo by signing an agreement in 1948 between the Israeli government and the religious movements.

On 30 May 1996 the bloc won four seats in the Knesset—occupied by Meir Porush and Shmuel Halpert for Agudat Israel, and Avraham Ravitz and Moshe Gaoni for Degel ha-Torah. Three years later the bloc was renamed United Torah List, and won five seats in the general elections of 17 May 1999, which gave victory to Labor Party leader Ehud Barak. A few weeks later, United Torah List agreed to support the Barak government in exchange for lowering the quota of orthodox students in the army, but on the following 5 September, United Torah List quit the coalition government of Ehud Barak.

After the election of Prime Minister Ariel Sharon in mid-March 2001, United Torah List refused to join a national unity government judging that the posts it was offered were insufficient, but did agree to support it in the Knesset. Led by Avraham Ravitz, United Torah List often joined SHAS, Moriah, and the National Religious Party (NRP) in a bloc known as the Torah Front. In the 2003 elections, United Torah List received 4.3 percent of the vote (five Knesset seats).

SEE ALSO Agudat Israel; Barak, Ehud; Degel ha-Torah; Knesset; Moriah; National Religious Party; Po'alei Agudat Israel; Sharon, Ariel; SHAS.

UNIVERSAL ISRAELITE ALLIANCE: Jewish organization founded in Paris on 17 May 1860 for the purpose of opening up Judaism to the world. The statement its originators made that day was meant to be understood in the tradition of the Declaration of the Rights of Man (and of the Citizen), and aimed at organizing Judaism on a universal basis, by dissociating the individual citizen from the individual member of any specific community.

UNLU

SEE Intifada (1987–1993).

UNRWA

SEE United Nations Relief and Works Agency for Palestine Refugees in the Near East.

UNSCOM

SEE United Nations Special Commission on Iraq.

UNTSO

SEE United Nations Truce Supervision Organization.

VA'AD LEU'MI: Hebrew for National Council; constituted in Tel Aviv in April 1918 to function as a provisional government for the Jewish community of Palestine. It answered to an elected assembly, the "Assefat ha-Nivrharim," and had jurisdiction over spheres of internal communal interest until 1948. It functioned along with the Zionist Executive, which was responsible for political relations with the British Mandate authorities.

VANGUARD OF THE PEOPLE'S WAR OF LIBERATION
SEE Sa'iqa, al-.

VANGUARDS OF THE CONQUEST
SEE Egyptian Islamic Jihad.

VARASH (*Va'ad Rashei Ha Sherutim,* the Committee of the Chiefs of Services): Coordinating commission for Israeli security services. Varash is responsible for coordinating the activities of Israel's three main intelligence services: military intelligence (*Agaf Modi'in,* or Aman); the Mossad (*HaMossad Le-Modi'in U'LeTafkidim Meyuhadim,* Institute for Intelligence and Special Tasks); and the General Security Service (GSS). Mossad and the GSS operate under the auspices of the prime minister's office, and coordinate intelligence gathering and assessment with Aman through Varash.

SEE ALSO Aman; Mossad.

VENICE SUMMIT: In a general declaration of principles released at the European summit, meeting in Venice on 13 June 1980, the member countries of the Community affirmed that the Palestinian people should be able to exercise their right to self-determination, and that their representative, the Palestine Liberation Organization, should be associated with the Middle East peace process.

VISHNITZ: Great Hasidic dynasty, founded by Menachem Mendel Ben Hayyim Hager (1830–1884); became one of the basic elements of the Agudat Israel Party.

SEE ALSO Agudat Israel.

VOICE OF PALESTINE (VOP; Sawt al-Filastin): The official radio broadcasting service of the Palestinian Authority (PA), operated by the Palestinian Broadcasting Corporation (PBC) from stations in Ramallah and Gaza. The current operation was created in 1994 with the establishment of the PA. Previously the Palestine Liberation Organization had operated a Voice of Palestine radio service in other Arab countries from facilities made available to it by local governments. It operated in Cairo until 1970, when it was shut down by President Gamal Abdel Nasser; it has also operated from Baghdad and Beirut. Israel

463

has accused the Voice of Palestine of "inciting violence." In 1997 the Israeli government began jamming VOP broadcasts. On 13 December 2001, during the al-Aqsa Intifada, Israel bombed the PBC radio and television transmitter in Ramallah. On 19 January 2002 it blew up the building housing its offices and studios. Both the VOP and the other PBC stations continued to broadcast from borrowed commercial facilities in the West Bank.

SEE ALSO Aqsa Intifada, al-; Nasser, Gamal Abdel; Palestine Liberation Organization; Palestinian Authority; Palestinian Broadcasting Corporation; West Bank.

W

WAFA: Palestine News Agency (Wakalat al-Anba'
al-Filastiniya; WAFA is both an acronym and a word
meaning "trust"), the official news outlet of the Palestine Liberation Organization, created in 1972 in
Beirut. After 1982, following the expulsion of the
Palestinians from Lebanon to Tunisia, its headquarters was in Tunis. On 20 July 1994, with the creation
of the Palestinian Authority, the agency moved to the
Gaza Strip.

> SEE ALSO Gaza Strip; Palestine Liberation
> Organization; Palestinian Authority.

WAFD: In November 1918, at the end of World War
I, the Egyptian Legislative Assembly charged a delegation (*wafd*), led by Sa'd Zaghlul, with demanding
of the British high commissioner that they be allowed to petition the British government for Egyptian independence. The high commissioner's refusal
led to the formation of a coalition to agitate for independence. Some of the group's leaders were expelled.
Widespread demonstrations and uprisings in 1919
led the British to grant nominal independence in
1922; the Wafd organized itself as a nationalist political party in 1924 and dominated Egyptian political
life until the fall of the monarchy in 1952. In December 1922, King Fu'ad, needing the backing of the
party to promulgate a new constitution, drew close
to the Wafd, which continued nevertheless to demand an end to the British occupation. In January

1924 the party won the legislative elections and
Zaghlul formed the first constitutional government
of Egypt.

The new prime minister soon clashed with the
king, who wanted to retain all his prerogatives. Following the assassination of the British commander
of the Egyptian army and under pressure from the
British, Zaghlul resigned on 24 November 1924. Out
of power for nine years, the Wafd returned to the
government in November 1934 through the initiative of the British who, threatened by Italian designs
on the Red Sea, needed a strong Egyptian government behind them. Negotiations led by Mustafa al-
Nahhas (known as Nahhas Pasha), the successor to
Zaghlul, who had died in 1927, resulted in a treaty,
signed on 26 August 1936, in which Great Britain
recognized the independence of Egypt. After Nahhas
resigned as prime minister, a scission in the party led
to the creation, on 3 January 1938, of the Sa'dist
party.

On 4 February 1942, in the midst of World War
II, Britain forced a Wafdist anti-German government
on King Faruk. After the victory of his party in the
legislative elections, Nahhas returned to power in
January 1950. The Wafd remained at the head of the
government until the revolution of July 1952, which
saw the fall of the Egyptian monarch. The new regime, put into place by the Free Officers movement,
suspended the constitution and dissolved all political

parties, including the Wafd. Twenty-five years later, on 4 February 1978, under the impetus of Fuad Serag al-Din and Ibrahim Farag, the Wafd was officially reconstituted and renamed the Neo-Wafd (*al Wafd al-Gadid*). The new party adopted "socialism as economic and social system, but without foreign ties," while recognizing Islamic law (shari'a) as the "original source" of the law. As an opposition party, criticizing the regime of Anwar al-Sadat, the group found itself under pressure to cease its activities. After Sadat's assassination in November 1981, the coming to power of Husni Mubarak allowed the Neo-Wafd to resume its activities. Having made a strategic alliance with the Muslim Brotherhood in the 1984 elections, the Neo-Wafd won fifty-eight seats and by 1990 emerged as the main opposition force in Egypt. It boycotted the 1993 elections. It has become the party of a small minority.

SEE ALSO Mubarak, Husni; Muslim Brotherhood; Sadat, Anwar al-; Shari'a.

WAHHABIS: Followers of a conservative, puritan, orthodox Sunni Muslim movement, Wahhabiya, or Wahhabism, founded in the eighteenth century in Arabia by Muhammad ibn Abd al-Wahhab (1703–1792). After schooling in Iraq and Iran, Wahhab returned to Arabia around 1739, where he began preaching and composed his best known work, *Kitab al-Tawhid* (*Treatise on Divine Unity*). Wahhabi was adopted by the Sa'ud clan after his marriage to a daughter of Muhammad ibn Sa'ud in 1744, and Wahhabi doctrine later became the official state religion of Saudi Arabia. Fiercely opposed to Shi'ism, Wahhabism rejects all rationalist exegesis of the Qur'an and of the shari'a. Wahhabis, who are distinguished by their austerity, reject poetry, music, and laughter. Wahhabism has influenced the Muslim Brotherhood and the Salafiyya current. Contemporary radical Islamist movements have also been inspired by Wahhabism, partly through its uncompromising religious ideology and partly through the lavish subventions of the Saudis, who have established madrasas (religious schools) and supported radically conservative social groups all over the Muslim world.

SEE ALSO Muslim Brotherhood; Qur'an; Salafiyya; Shari'a.

WAILING WALL

SEE Western Wall Disturbances.

WAKALAT AL-ANBA' AL-FILASTINIYA

SEE WAFA.

WALI: Usually translated as "saint," a *wali*, in Islam, is a holy person, someone who is close to God, *wali Allah*. A *wali* may be a very pious person or spiritual master, or someone living or dead who is believed to have the power to intercede with God. Strict schools of Muslim thought do not believe there can be such a thing as a *wali*, since every Muslim has equal access to God through the Qu'ran. Although the practice is not sanctioned by scripture, the tombs of many *awliya'* (*walis*, plural) have become popular shrines.

WAQF: Muslim public religious trust or endowment (plural, *awqaf*). It may consist of any kind of income-producing property used for the benefit of the community: to maintain schools, colleges, hospitals, mosques, shrines, charities, or any such public institution or activity. The literal meaning of the Arabic word is "prevention" or "stopping," in the sense of preventing some significant property from ever being owned by any private interest, or from being sold or disposed of. (Private individuals may also create a *waqf* for the benefit of family or charity, but the word as used here refers to a communal foundation.) Control of *awqaf* confers political influence and has often been the subject of contention between religious and state authorities and is either controlled or regulated by the state. At some times and places the *awqaf* have been in control of a major portion of a community's property. In Iran in the 1930s, for instance, *awqaf* controlled a sixth of all agricultural land. In contemporary Palestine/Israel, properties controlled by a *waqf* include the Haram al-Sharif (which rightly includes, according to many Muslims, the Western Wall).

SEE ALSO Haram al-Sharif.

WASHINGTON ACCORD

SEE Oslo Accords II.

WASHINGTON SUMMIT: Meeting of Palestine Liberation Organization leader Yasir Arafat, King Hussein of Jordan, Israeli Prime Minister Benjamin Netanyahu, and Egyptian Foreign Minister Amr Musa, sponsored by U.S. President Bill Clinton. The meeting lasted from 1 to 3 October 1996; its purpose was to restart Israeli-Palestinian peace negotiations, blocked since the Israeli right wing came to power.

SEE ALSO Arafat, Yasir; Hussein ibn Talal; Musa, Amr Muhammad; Netanyahu, Benjamin; Palestine Liberation Organization.

WATAN: Arabic word meaning homeland or country.

PRECIOUS RESOURCE. A SWEET-WATER RESERVOIR, PART OF ISRAEL'S NATIONAL WATER SYSTEM, FLANKS THE ROAD TO ʿAFULA, IN THE JEZREEL VALLEY IN NORTHERN ISRAEL. FRESH WATER IS AN ESSENTIAL BUT RELATIVELY RARE RESOURCE IN LARGE PARTS OF THE MIDDLE EAST, INCLUDING ISRAEL. (*© Hanan Isachar/Corbis*)

WATER: Water is an indispensable resource in the Middle East both for development and for the survival of its people. It carries such importance that historically it has been a major reason for both conflict and cooperation, both war and peace. In fact, along with poverty, water distribution is one of the two most serious problems in the Middle East. Natural conditions render storage capacities to be quite modest, whether natural or artificial, and hydrographic and aquiferous resources are dispersed unequally. Faced with the inexorable decrease of water resources, there is general agreement that a plan for regional management should be established, with each country doing its best to set aside historical and political claims.

WAZIR, INTISAR AL- (Umm Jihad; 1941–): Palestinian political figure, born in Gaza City. In 1959 Intisar al-Wazir became the first woman member of Fatah, where she made the acquaintance of Khalil al-Wazir, a movement leader, whom she married two years later. From 1963 to 1965 the couple lived in Algiers, where Khalil al-Wazir was the Fatah representative. An ardent militant, upholding the place of women in the Palestinian resistance, Intisar al-Wazir was one of the founders of the General Union of Palestinian Women, of which she was secretary-general from 1980 to 1985. In the 1960s she helped to found such Palestine Liberation Organization (PLO) social service organizations as the Social Affairs Committee, the Martyrs' Families Organization, and the Committee for Prisoners and the Injured, which is responsible for helping the families of dead or imprisoned *fidaʾiyyun*. In 1974 she became a member of the Palestine National Council. In 1978 she obtained a degree in history from the University of Damascus. In 1981 she joined the revolutionary council of Fatah. On the night of 14–15 April 1988, when she and her husband had been living in Tunis for six years, an Israeli commando assassinated her husband in front of her. That same year she was elected to the PLO Executive Committee. In August 1989, at the fifth congress of the movement in Tunis, she joined the Fatah Central Committee. In 1995 she returned to the Gaza Strip after thirty years in exile and was appointed social affairs minister of the Palestinian Authority. In January 1996 she was elected a deputy from Gaza City in the new Palestinian Legislative Council.

SEE ALSO Fatah, al-; Gaza Strip; General Union of Palestinian Women; Palestine Liberation Organization; Palestine National Council; Palestinian Legislative Council; Wazir, Khalil al-.

WAZIR, KHALIL AL- (Abu Jihad; 1935–): Palestinian resistance figure, born in Ramla. At the time of the 1948 War, he was expelled with his family. They settled in the Burayj refugee camp in the Gaza Strip, where he attended a school run by the United Nations Relief and Works Agency for Palestine Refugees in the Near East. He is said to have joined the Muslim Brotherhood in 1951. Around this time he is also said to have received military training either in Gaza or in Egypt. In 1954 he made the acquaintance of Yasir Arafat and also formed a commando unit in Gaza, which carried out sabotage against the Israelis, for which he was briefly imprisoned by the Egyptians. In 1955 he became secretary of the General Union of Palestinian Students in Gaza. In 1956 he enrolled at the University of Alexandria but did not complete his education. From 1959 to 1963 he worked as a teacher in Kuwait, where in December 1959 he participated with Arafat in the creation of Fatah. In 1962 he married Intisar al-Khalil, an ardent Fatah militant. In November 1963 he became head of the first Fatah diplomatic mission, in Algiers. The following year, he traveled to China, North Vietnam, and North Korea, establishing contacts, and took part in the meeting of the Palestine National Council at which the Palestine Liberation Organization (PLO) was founded.

When the Fatah Central Committee decided to begin military action against Israel, Wazir was appointed deputy commander of Fatah's military wing. In March 1965 he moved to Damascus, where he acted as the liaison between underground fighters in Israel and the PLO. In May 1966 he was arrested by Syrian authorities, who released him after thirty days. In 1968, following the Arab defeat in the 1967 War, he became deputy commander of the PLO military forces and was put in charge of Fatah (*al-jihaz al-gharbi*) operations launched against Israel from the occupied territories. In 1970 he participated in the Black September 1970 confrontations in Jordan, after which, like most of the fida'iyyun, he was banished to Lebanon. Between 1971 and 1982, during the Lebanese Civil War and inter-Palestinian conflicts, his activities at the head of Palestinian forces were crucial to Arafat's survival. In 1982 he followed the latter into exile in Yemen, and then to Tunisia.

The Israeli invasion of Lebanon forced a change in Wazir's approach to fighting Israel; instead of direct military challenge from outside, he now favored popular resistance from within, and he organized local resistance committees in the Occupied Territories, which later were the institutional base for the first Intifada, which began in late 1987. According to his colleagues, Khalil al-Wazir had been planning to go to Baghdad in April 1988 to attend an intra-Palestinian meeting to coordinate the Intifada, but on the night of 14–15 April he was assassinated in his villa near Tunis by an Israeli commando. His death weakened Arafat's position in the PLO. A member of the central committee of Fatah, Khalil al-Wazir had been one of the principal military leaders of the Palestinian resistance and he was very close to Arafat. He was much admired in the Palestinian community, as well as being greatly respected by many Arab political figures. No hint of the corruption that was indulged in by other senior members of the PLO leadership ever clung to him.

SEE ALSO Arab-Israel War (1948); Arab-Israel War (1967); Arafat, Yasir Muhammad; Black September 1970; Fatah, al-; Gaza Strip; General Union of Palestinian Students; Intifada (1987–1993); Khalil, Intisar al-; Muslim Brotherhood; Palestine Liberation Organization; Palestine National Council; United Nations Relief and Works Agency for Palestine Refugees in the Near East.

WEIZMAN, EZER (1924–): Israeli military and political figure, eleventh president of Israel (1993–2000). Born in 1924 in Haifa into one of the most illustrious Jewish families, Ezer Weizman was the nephew of Israel's first president, Chaim Weizmann. In 1942 he enlisted in the (British) Royal Air Force, where he became a pilot, and in 1946–1947 studied aeronautics in Britain. He was one of the founders of the Israeli Air Force (IAF); in 1950 was named its chief of operations, and in 1956 its commander. In 1966 be became the Israel Defense Force (IDF) head of operations and deputy chief of staff.

In 1969 Weisman resigned from the IDF to start on a political career, joining Herut Party. He served as leader of the GAHAL bloc and as minister of transportation in the National Unity government. He resigned in 1970 to go into private business, but continued to be active in Herut, for a short time serving as president of its executive committee. In 1977 when Herut, GAHAL and other right-center groups formed the Likud bloc, he was campaign manager; and after its victory he became defense minister in the government of Herut leader Menachem Begin. He supervised the invasion of Lebanon in 1978 and later that year, was a moderating influence at the Camp David peace talks. However, his increasing support of a moderate view caused conflict with Likud, and in 1980 he resigned from the cabinet. The following November, he was expelled from Herut for having voted against the policies of the Begin government in the Knesset.

In 1984 Weizman formed his own centrist party, Yahad, which backed the electoral campaign of the Labor Party and won three Knesset seats in the election. He was then appointed minister without portfolio in the National Unity government. In January 1985 he was appointed coordinator of Arab affairs. In 1986 he and his party Yahad joined the Labor Party; and when it joined the National Unity government with Likud in 1988, he served as minister of science and technology. In January 1989 he came out openly for direct dialogue with the Palestine Liberation Organization (PLO), provoking outrage in the government. Accused of secret meetings with the PLO, in 1990 he resigned his seat in the Knesset; but in 1993, as Labor Party candidate, he was elected president of the State of Israel, taking office on 14 May.

In 1996, in an attempt to restart the Israeli-Palestinian peace process, Weizer invited Yasir Arafat to his own home, causing outrage in Israeli political circles. Nevertheless, he was reelected to the presidency in 1998. In 2000, however, he was alleged to have received large sums of money as bribes in the late 1980s and early 1990s, and although no formal charges were brought against him, the scandal forced him to resign. He left office on 10 July 2000.

SEE ALSO GAHAL Party; Herut Party; Israel Labor Party; Likud.

WEIZMANN, CHAIM (1874–1952): Zionist leader and Israeli statesman, first president of the State of Israel. He was born in November 1874 in Belorussia, and from early youth was a convinced Zionist. He earned his doctorate in chemistry at the University of Freiburg in 1899 and taught at the University of Geneva from 1900 to 1904. The following year he left Switzerland for England, where he took a position at the University of Manchester. Naturalized a British citizen in 1910, he directed the laboratories of the British Admiralty from 1916 to 1919. Throughout these years, he participated in Zionist activities.

CHAIM WEIZMANN. A NOTED CHEMIST AND LEADER OF THE WORLD ZIONIST CONGRESS, WEIZMANN WAS INFLUENTIAL IN WINNING BRITISH ACCEPTANCE OF A JEWISH HOMELAND IN PALESTINE (WHICH CAME IN A LETTER THAT BECAME KNOWN AS THE BALFOUR DECLARATION). IN THE FINAL YEARS OF HIS LIFE, FROM 1949 TO 1952, WEIZMANN SERVED AS THE FIRST PRESIDENT OF THE STATE OF ISRAEL.

In 1917, Weizmann was instrumental in persuading the British foreign secretary, Lord Balfour, that a Jewish state in Palestine would serve British interests in the Middle East. The Balfour Declaration, which promised British support for establishment of a Jewish homeland, was a turning point in modern Jewish history. In 1918, Weizmann headed the Zionist Commission to Palestine. He also led the Zionist delegation to the Paris Peace Conference at the end of that year, and in 1920–1922 he negotiated the document that laid the legal foundation for the Jewish National Home.

As president of the World Zionist Organization (WZO) from 1920 to 1931 and 1935 to 1946, Weizmann continued to promote policies that strengthened the position of Jews in Palestine; but he was disappointed by the slow progress of Zionist development there. He became simultaneously president of the Jewish Agency, the official liaison with the British authorities; however, the Palestinian riots of

1929 and subsequent decline in British support for Zionism led him to resign in protest from the presidency of both organizations.

Returning to head the movement in 1935, he helped to bring about the Palestine Royal Commission's recommendation for partition of Palestine, successfully persuading a majority of the Zionist Congress to accept partition in principle. But the British government reversed its initial approval and issued a White Paper that limited Jewish immigration. Thereafter, Weizmann's influence gradually decreased because of his opposition to the radical policies of rising WZO leaders. After his term as president ended in 1946, he remained actively involved and helped persuade U.S. president Harry Truman to support the establishment of Israel in 1948. Weizmann served as the new nation's first president, which at that time was a largely ceremonial post that he found frustrating. He died on 9 November 1952.

SEE ALSO Balfour Declaration; Jewish Agency for Israel; White Papers on Palestine; World Zionist Organization.

WEST BANK: The area of Mandatory Palestine inside the 1949 armistice line west of the Jordan River, including East Jerusalem, not controlled by Israel at the end of the 1948 War. Covering an area of 2,270 square miles, the West Bank was controlled by the Jordanians following the war and occupied by Israel following the 1967 War. Its principal cities, in addition to East Jerusalem, are Bethlehem, Hebron, Jericho, Nablus, Ramallah, Tulkarm, and Jenin. The West Bank was a part of the Arab state whose creation was proposed in the partition plan adopted by the United Nations by General Assembly Resolution 181 of 29 November 1947. Referred to by many Israelis as "Judea and Samaria," it was opened to settlement by the Israeli government and is home to several hundred thousand Israeli settlers. In 1978, Palestinians in the West Bank and Gaza showed strong opposition to the Camp David Accords, which led to Israeli military and administrative repression. In 1982 the majority of Palestinian mayors were discharged and replaced by Israeli administrators. This measure, combined with the departure of Palestinian forces from Lebanon, moved a group of young West Bank intellectuals to oppose the Israeli occupation openly, a move that resulted in a great number of arrests.

In December 1987 the Intifada broke out in the Gaza Strip and spread to the West Bank. On the following 15 November, at a meeting of the Palestine

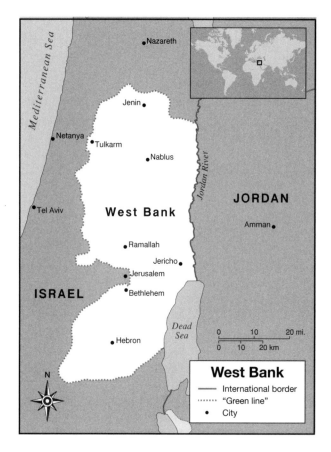

National Council in Algiers, Yasir Arafat proclaimed the creation of a Palestinian state with Jerusalem as its capital. In May 1994 the Oslo Accords led to the establishment of the Palestinian Authority and Jericho became the first autonomous territory under its control. The following year, the Oslo Accords II allowed approximately one-third of the West Bank to recover partial autonomy and the Israel Defense Force started withdrawing from the principal cities, with the exception of Hebron. According to the Israeli-Palestinian Declaration of Principles signed on 13 September 1993 in Washington, D.C., the "definitive and permanent" status of the West Bank and Gaza should have been decided by the end of 1999. In late September 2000 a new uprising, the al-Aqsa Intifada, broke out in the Palestinian territories. In 2002 Israel reinvaded and reoccupied many West Bank cities. Israel has also increased its confiscations of Palestinian property, increased its restrictions on Palestinian movement and economic activity, increased Israeli settlement, and begun to construct a "separation wall" between Jewish and Palestinian areas inside the Green Line.

SEE ALSO Aqsa Intifada, al-; Arab-Israel War (1948); Arab-Israel War (1967); Arafat, Yasir; British Mandate; Camp David Accords; Gaza Strip; Intifada (1987–1993); Jordan River; Oslo Accords; Oslo Accords II; Palestine National Council; Palestinian Authority; Resolution 181.

WESTERN WALL DISTURBANCES: The Western (Wailing) Wall, or Kotel, in Jerusalem is a site sacred to both Muslims and Jews. It is a wall on the west side of a hill (the Temple Mount), on top of which is the Haram al-Sharif. Its original purpose is unknown; it may have been a retaining wall or a part of a Roman-era building. For Muslims, the entire hill, including the wall, is part of the Haram; for Jews, the wall is a remnant of the Second Temple. In the 1920s, use of the site was governed by an arrangement that had been enforced by Ottoman authorities and continued by the British Mandatory government. It was owned by the Muslim community and although Jews were permitted access to it they were not allowed to adapt it in any way for religious ceremonies.

In 1928 Zionist institutions were rapidly growing stronger after several years of stagnation; Jewish immigration was up, the economy of the Jewish community was expanding, and Jewish political militancy was increasing. Efforts were even made to purchase the wall. On 23 September of that year, on the eve of Yom Kippur, the highest Jewish holy day, Jews gathered at the wall to pray placed a screen to separate the men from the women in the traditional way. Muslims asserted that this was a forbidden "innovation" and complained to the British authorities, who removed the screen. The authorities attempted to find a compromise, but the situation was too charged and became a political issue for both sides over the next few months; for the Zionists it became part of a campaign for expanded rights. On 15 August 1929 a group of right-wing Zionists from the Revisionist faction, raising the Zionist Star of David flag, staged a demonstration at the wall; Muslims staged a counterdemonstration the next day, destroying slips of paper containing prayers, which had been put into the crevices in the wall by the Jews.

Over the next few weeks violence broke out. Palestinians attacked Jews—mainly religious and non-Zionist—in Jerusalem, Hebron (killing 64) and Safad; Jews attacked and killed Palestinians in several cities. In all 116 Palestinians and 133 Jews died in the riots, although many of the Palestinian deaths were caused by shots fired into crowds by British troops and police. The disturbances inspired fresh political organizing among the relatively unorganized Pales-

THE WESTERN WALL. JEWS PRAY AT THE SYMBOLICALLY IMPORTANT REMNANT OF THE ANCIENT RETAINING WALL FOR THE SECOND TEMPLE OF JERUSALEM (WHERE THE DOME OF THE ROCK, AT UPPER LEFT, NOW STANDS). *(© Corbis)*

tinians. The Arab Executive demanded an end to Jewish immigration and land purchases and the creation of a democratic government. The British government, while refusing on principle, established commissions to study the matter. The Shaw Commission studied the causes of the violence; the Hope-Simpson Commission studied the land situation and its effect on the Palestinians. The findings of these commissions led to the Passfield White Paper of 1930, which called for limiting immigration and land purchases and for changing Britain's policy toward the Palestinians—90 percent of the population—who had until then been considered merely "non-Jewish communities" by a government whose policies were based on establishing a "Jewish National Home." The recommendations of the White Paper were never implemented.

SEE ALSO Arab Executive; British Mandate; Haram al-Sharif; Hebron; Ottomans; White Papers on Palestine.

WHITE PAPERS ON PALESTINE: British policy statements on Palestine issued from 1922 to 1939. The British government ruled Palestine under a League of Nations mandate from 1922 until 1948. Policy statements, called "command papers" or "white papers," were issued during this time in an attempt to deal with the tensions and violence between Arabs and the Jewish communities there.

The British government faced conflicting pressure from Zionists, who wanted implementation of the promises made in the Balfour Declaration concerning establishment of a Jewish homeland in Palestine, and the Arabs, who wanted annulment of the Balfour Declaration and independence under an Arab-majority government. The first major British white paper, the Churchill White Paper of June 1922, attempted to placate both by stating that the Jewish national home existed by right, yet that Jewish immigration would be limited and Arabs would have self-government with a majority in a council to be elected in the near future. Neither side was satisfied.

The next white paper, issued in on 19 November 1928, and four more issued in 1930 centered on conflict at the Western (Wailing) Wall in Jerusalem. The first of these affirmed that no benches or screens could be brought to the wall by Jews, since they had not been allowed during Ottoman rule; but there were Arab attacks against Jews there as well as in several other towns, and religious tension added to the Arab's growing fears of physical displacement. The second argued that the government must issue clear statements safeguarding Arab rights and regulating Jewish immigration and land purchase. The third recommended the appointment of a special commission to assess the problems facing landless Arab peasants and the prospects for expanded agricultural cultivation. Finally, the Hope-Simpson report recommended a drastic reduction in Jewish immigration on the grounds of insufficient cultivatable Arab land and widespread Arab unemployment; and the simultaneous Passfield White Paper endorsed stricter controls on Jewish immigration, asserting for the first time that the British government had equal obligations to both communities. Chaim Weizmann, head of the Jewish Agency, threatened to resign if the Passfield White Paper was implemented. The resignation threat produced the 1931 MacDonald Letter (called the "Black Letter" by the Arabs) which undid the anti-Zionist thrust of the Passfield White Paper.

One of the most important white papers was the Palestine Royal Commission Report of July 1937. Also known as the "Peel" Commission, it had been sent to investigate the causes of the Palestinian-Arab rebellion that had erupted in April 1936. After many months of hearing evidence, the commissioners came to the radical conclusion that the Mandate was no longer workable as originally conceived, and that the rival Jewish and Arab communities might find peace only if the land were partitioned into a Jewish state and an Arab state (the latter to be annexed to Transjordan). While the Zionist leadership was pleased with the proposal, in principle, to create a Jewish state, the Arabs rejected the plan as a violation of their majority status and claims to Arab sovereignty. The rebellion resumed, and the British gradually retreated from the idea of partition, especially after a further investigation (the Woodhead Commission Report of November 1938) suggested the near-impossibility of drawing acceptable boundaries between proposed Jewish and Arab areas.

The white paper of 17 May 1939 sought to establish a new British policy for Palestine on the eve of an imminent world war. After lengthy but unfruitful discussions in London between the Jewish Agency, Arab governments, and Palestinian Arabs, the government issued the "MacDonald" white paper that repudiated the concept of partition. In an attempt to satisfy Arab demands for independence, it proposed the development of self-governing institutions in a single independent state that would not be dominated by either Arabs or Jews. The white paper also limited Jewish immigration to seventy-five thousand over five years, with subsequent immigration to require Arab approval, and limited purchase of land by Jews. This paper, which reversed earlier promises to the Zionists and the recommendations of the Peel Commission, was received with anger by Jews throughout the world, especially since it came just at the time when many were seeking to escape from the Nazis in Europe.

SEE ALSO Balfour Declaration; British Mandate; Jewish Agency for Israel; Weizmann, Chaim; World Zionist Organization.

WJC

SEE World Jewish Congress.

WOLFOWITZ, PAUL (1943–): U.S. deputy secretary of defense. Paul Wolfowitz was born on 22 December 1943. He received a bachelor's degree in mathematics from Cornell University in 1965 and a doctorate in political science from the University of Chicago in

1972. He worked from 1973 to 1977 in the Arms Control and Disarmament Agency, participating in Strategic Arms Limitation Talks, and joined the Pentagon in 1977 as deputy assistant secretary of defense for regional programs. He served as assistant secretary of state for East Asian and Pacific Affairs, then as U.S. ambassador to Indonesia. From 1989 to 1993, Wolfowitz served as undersecretary of defense for policy, then in 1994 became dean and professor of international relations at Johns Hopkins University. In March 2001, Wolfowitz was sworn in as U.S. deputy secretary of defense. An early advocate of "preemptive" U.S. strikes against Iraq, he is considered a hawkish neoconservative. Wolfowitz supports a pro-Israel policy, yet he has publicly acknowledged the sufferings of the Palestinian people, for which he was heckled at a pro-Israel rally in 2002.

WORLD ISLAMIC FRONT FOR HOLY WAR AGAINST JEWS AND CRUSADERS (*al-Jabha al-Islamiiya al-Alamiya li-Jihad al-Yahoud wa al-Salibiyyin*): Radical Islamic movement gathering together a number of international extremist groups. Its existence was announced by a communiqué published on 12 February 1998, carrying the signatures of Osama Bin Ladin; Abu Yasir Rifai Ahmad Taha, of al-Jami'a al-Islamiyya; Ayman Zawahri, of the Egyptian Islamic Jihad; Mir Hamza, of the *ulamas* of Pakistan; Fazlur Rehman Khalil, of the Pakistani Harakat al-Ansar; and Shaykh Abdul Salam Muhammad, of the Pakistani Islamic Jihad. The communiqué called for jihad against the Americans. The movement has been regarded as being either identical to the International Islamic Front or else part of it.

> **SEE ALSO** Alim; Bin Ladin, Osama; Egyptian Islamic Jihad; International Islamic Front; Jihad; Jami'a al-Islamiyya, al-; Zawahri, Ayman Muhammad al-.

WORLD JEWISH CONGRESS (WJC): Institution founded in Geneva on 13 August 1936 for the defense of the cultural and religious rights of Jews throughout the world and to strengthen the unity of the Jewish people. The WJC represents 70 Jewish communities in the world and is one of the nongovernmental organizations in attendance at the United Nations, UNESCO, the Council of Europe, and the Commission for European Unity.

WORLD ZIONIST ORGANIZATION (WZO): Organization that turned the idea of establishing a Jewish state into a reality. The WZO has played a major role in sensitizing Jewish communities, dispersed throughout the world, to the issue of a national renaissance. It was created in 1897 at the first Zionist congress, in Basel, and was open to all Jews who accepted its goals and paid a small membership fee. Although it was originally organized on a regional basis, political parties developed within it. During the era of the British mandate in Palestine, it functioned as a quasi-government of the Jewish community there, serving as the Jewish Agency for which the mandate provided until 1929 and remaining the dominant power within that agency when it expanded to include non-Zionists. It therefore played a significant role in the creation of the Jewish national home.

After the establishment of the State of Israel in 1948, many of the WTO's functions were taken over by the Israel government, for which it became a foreign propaganda, economic support and political mobilization arm. It has remained active in the diffusion of information on Israel and the collection of funds, but in 1952 the Jewish Agency was given responsibility for development and settlement of the land and for the absorption of immigrants. Since 1960 only organizations, rather than individuals, have been eligible for WZO membership.

> **SEE ALSO** Zionism.

WYE PLANTATION ACCORDS

> **SEE** Oslo Accords II.

WYE RIVER ACCORDS

> **SEE** Oslo Accords II.

WZO

> **SEE** World Zionist Organization.

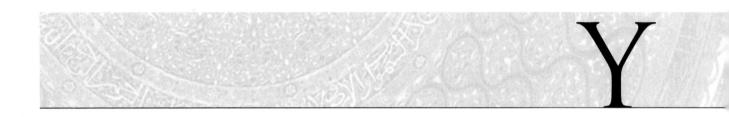

Y

YAD (also Ya'ad, Yehud, Yud; Hebrew for ensemble, union): Israeli political bloc created in February 1984 following a split in the extreme right party, Tzomet.

First constituted in 1984 by Ezer Weizman, Yad won two seats in the legislative elections of that year, following which Weizman was named minister without portfolio in the national union government headed by Shimon Peres. Four years later Yad was dissolved, after which its leaders decided to join the Labor Party. The revival of Yad in 1994 resulted in the Tzomet losing three seats in the Knesset.

Yad was envisioned as a nationalist and liberal party, although its proposals were sometimes vague. It saw itself as upholding the "spirit of the Camp David accords" and supported Jewish settlement in the occupied territories. In July 1994 two of the party's leaders, Gonen Segev and Alexander Goldfarb, joined the government of Yitzhak Rabin as minister of energy and deputy minister of housing respectively. During their mandate they tried to support the development of Jewish settlements and advocated holding a referendum before Israeli withdrawal from the Golan Heights. Weakened by a power struggle among its leaders, and by a judicial procedure involving one of its officials, Yad progressively lost influence. After failing to obtain any seats in the Knesset elections of 1996, Yad disappeared from Israeli politics.

SEE ALSO Golan Heights; Knesset; Peres, Shimon; Tzomet Party; Weizman, Ezer.

YAD VASHEM: Hebrew for an everlasting name [Isaiah 56:5]. Name of an Israeli institution founded in 1953 to honor the memory of the martyrs and heroes who died during the Shoah.

SEE ALSO Shoah.

YAHADUT: Hebrew for Judaism.

YAHADUT HA-TORAH

SEE United Torah Judaism Party.

YAHUD: Arabic word for Jew.

YAMIN ISRAEL (Right of Israel, in Hebrew; sometimes spelled Yemin Israel): Israeli political group of the extreme right, a splinter from Moledet, founded in November 1995 by Shaul Gutmann. It calls itself a party, but was disqualified from registering as a party by the Israeli Supreme Court because its stated principles would violate the democratic rights of non-Jewish citizens and perhaps incite racism. Presently it is attempting to create an "incorporated front" of extraparliamentary nationalist groups.

Yamin Israel believes that the essence of Israel as a Jewish state must be the nation's paramount principle, and that therefore an oath to this effect should be a prerequisite for participating in elections or holding public office. It also advocates adoption of a new constitution, including reforms proposed by the Foundation for Constitutional Democracy and supported by other parties, but going further to integrate them into a "comprehensive system based on Jewish ideas and values." It believes the right of Jews to settle throughout Palestine is absolute and that the presence of non-Jews is undesirable. In addition, it favors a market economy and privatization of national resources and assets. In 2004, Paul Eidelberg is the president of Yamin Israel; other current leaders include Eleonora Shifrin, Felix-Azriel Kochubievsky, Victoria Vexelman, Shlomo Markov, Yaakov Segal, Israel Hanukoglu, Konstantin Danovich, Miriam Adahan, Yrachmiel Elias, and Ya'akov Golbert.

YARMUK: Name of a tributary on the eastern bank of the Jordan river; location of an important battle in August 636 between the Byzantine armies of Heraclius and the victorious Arab-Islamic troops. Also the name of a Palestine Liberation Organization military brigade.

SEE ALSO Palestine Liberation Organization.

YASIN, AHMAD ISMA'IL (1936–2004): Palestinian Islamic activist, born in the village of al-Jura near Ashqelon. Shaykh Yasin was the founding father and spiritual guide of HAMAS. In 1948, during the first Israeli-Arab conflict, he and his family became a refugees in the Gaza Strip, where four years later, as a result of an accident, he became hemiplegic for life. In 1956 he went to Egypt to study Arabic literature and religion, and there he joined the Muslim Brotherhood. He returned to Gaza, teaching religion and preaching for a number of years, and in 1973 he created the Islamic Collective (al-Majma'a al-Islami), sponsored by the Muslim Brotherhood, and became active in charity work. He was assisted by Ibrahim al-Yazuri, Abd al-Aziz Rantisi, and Mahmud Zahhar.

Yasin became one of the guiding lights of the Palestinian Islamic movement. In October 1983 he was arrested by Israeli authorities and sentenced to thirteen years in prison for possession of arms and constitution of armed cells. In 1985, as part of a prisoner exchange between the Popular Front for the Liberation of Palestine—General Command and Israel, he was released and placed under house arrest in Gaza. The Palestinian Islamic movement, in the meantime, had become radicalized under the influence of some of Yasin's close collaborators. On 14 December 1987, with six other Muslim Brothers, he

SHAYKH AHMED YASIN. IN 1987, THIS MEMBER OF THE RADICAL MUSLIM BROTHERHOOD FOUNDED THE ISLAMIC RESISTANCE MOVEMENT, OR HAMAS, DEDICATED TO ARMED STRUGGLE AGAINST ISRAEL FOR CONTROL OF ALL OF PALESTINE. THE SPIRITUAL LEADER OF HAMAS, SHAYKH YASIN WAS KILLED BY AN ISRAELI MISSILE ATTACK ON 22 MARCH 2004. *(AP/Wide World Photos)*

published a communiqué supporting the Intifada that had just broken out in the Gaza Strip and announcing the creation of the Islamic Resistance Movement (Harakat al-Muqawima al-Islamiyya), or HAMAS. HAMAS rejected any compromise with Israel, preaching jihad for Islamic recovery of the whole of Palestine; it played an important role in the Intifada and was classified by Israel as a terrorist organization.

In May 1989 Yasin was again arrested and on 15 October was sentenced to life in prison. From his prison cell he continued to direct HAMAS and maintain its unity. On 1 October 1997, following a failed Mossad assassination attempt on Jordanian soil against a HAMAS representative, King Hussein of Jordan obtained his release, as well as that of some twenty other prisoners who held Jordanian passports. After passing through Amman to undergo medical examinations, Yasin arrived in Gaza on 6 October, where he was welcomed as a returning hero. On 2 May 1998 he launched an appeal to Palestinian Authority (PA) President Yasir Arafat asking him to join the "resistance front" against Israel. On 25 June, after a long tour through the Gulf countries, Iran, Syria, Egypt, and Sudan, Yasin returned to Gaza in spite of some administrative difficulties. In an interview he declared his opposition to HAMAS participation in a PA national unity cabinet and called for jihad against Israel. On 29 October he was assigned to house arrest by the PA following an attack in Gaza by members of his movement. In July 1999, following Israeli Prime Minister Ehud Barak's appeal for a "peace of the brave," he replied that HAMAS wanted a peace restoring the rights of the Palestinians, the end of Israeli occupation, the dismantling of the Jewish settlements, and the restitution to Jerusalem of its Islamic character.

In 2000 he criticized the PA for taking part in the Camp David talks in July. At the same time, however, he announced that if the Israelis stopped attacking Palestinian civilians HAMAS would stop attacking Israeli civilians, and that if the Israelis pulled out of the West Bank and Gaza Strip HAMAS would observe a truce. With the outbreak of the al-Aqsa Intifada in the Palestinian territories in October 2000, HAMAS and the PA reconciled. In November 2000 HAMAS joined the resistance committees on which national and Islamic forces coordinated their local actions.

At the beginning of 2001, when the Intifada was intensifying in the Palestinian territories, Yasin reaffirmed HAMAS's determination in the struggle, intensifying its campaign of suicide bombings against Israeli civilians, leading to many Israeli reprisal operations. In September 2003 the Israelis attempted to assassinate Yasin by bombing a house they believed he was in. On 22 March 2004 they succeeded in killing him in a helicopter-fired missile attack.

SEE ALSO Aqsa Intifada, al-; Arab-Israel Conflict (1948); Arafat, Yasir; Barak, Ehud; Camp David II Summit; Gaza Strip; HAMAS; Intifada (1987–1993); Jihad; Muslim Brotherhood; Palestinian Authority; Popular Front for the Liberation of Palestine–General Command; Rantisi, Abd al-Aziz; West Bank.

YATOM, DANI (1945–): Israeli military figure. Born in Israel in 1945, Dani Yatom started his military career in 1963. Between 1966 and 1973 he was in the *Sayeret Matkal*, a special unit attached to the Israel Defense Force (IDF) general staff. On 8 May 1972 he took part in the storming of a Sabena Airlines plane that had been taken over by Palestinian terrorists at

DANI YATOM. A CAREER MILITARY OFFICER, YATOM WAS THE FIRST PUBLICLY NAMED HEAD OF MOSSAD, ISRAEL'S INTELLIGENCE SERVICE, FROM 1996 TO 1998. YATOM HAS ALSO SERVED AS A GOVERNMENT ADVISER ON DEFENSE MATTERS. (© *Corbis Sygma*)

the Tel Aviv Airport. At his side were Ehud Barak, Benjamin Netanyahu, and Amnon Lipkin-Shahak. From 1983 to 1985, Yatom served as advisor to Defense Minister Moshe Arens. Two years later, he was appointed head of the planning department of the IDF general staff. In December 1990, Yatom became commander-in-chief of the central military region of Israel, replacing General Yitzhak Mordechai. By 1992 he had risen to become chief of the central command, military secretary to the prime and defense ministers in Prime Minister Yitzhak Rabin's cabinet. There, he rapidly became Rabin's closest confidant and most trusted counselor.

In February 1994 Yatom temporarily assumed command of the central military region, replacing General Tamari, who was killed in a helicopter accident. Among Yatom's biggest challenges in this position was dealing with the massacre of twenty-nine Muslims by a Jewish settler in Hebron. On the following 12 April, Yatom was replaced by General Ilan Biran, and he resumed his duties with the prime minister. In December 1994, Yatom became a member of the Israeli delegation, which, in the context of the Israeli-Palestinian peace process, went to Washington, D.C., to participate in parleys with Syrian representatives. On 2 June 1996 Yatom became head of Mossad, replacing Shabtai Shavit. In February 1998 a series of failures in his service forced him to resign this post.

In July 1999 Yatom became security adviser to Prime Minister Ehud Barak. Considered as the éminence grise of the new prime minister, Yatom's particular mission was to restart the Israeli-Syrian negotiations, which had been stalled since April 1996. In November 1999, Yatom—as Barak's chief of staff—traveled to Paris to meet Jordan's King Abdullah and discuss Israel's issues with Syria. In July and October 2000, Yatom took part in the Middle East peace summits at Camp David with Barak and Yasser Arafat, and presided over by U.S. president Bill Clinton. Although President Clinton's October summit objectives included a cease-fire and a plan to eventually return to the peace discussions that had broken down that July, Yatom conceded that that the situation was very complicated and the talks were going very slowly—and soon after talks broke down again. A discreet personage, Yatom has been considered as a perfectionist, someone well acquainted with the subtleties of power.

SEE ALSO Arens, Moshe; Barak, Ehud; Israel Defense Force; Lipkin-Shahak, Amnon; Mordechai, Yitzhak; Mossad; Netanyahu, Benjamin; Sayeret.

YEDIOT AHARONOT (Hebrew for "latest news"): Israeli daily newspaper. Founded in 1939 by the Moses family who remain its owners, the *Yedioth Aharanot* is a truly independent newspaper that has remained free of constraints despite any current government. Its politics are considered to be center-right with a tendency to support the Labor Party. In September 1995 the editor-in-chief was forced to resign after it was revealed that he was involved in an incident of telephone-tapping that included directors of another daily newspaper, the *Ma'ariv.*

YEHUD: Hebrew word meaning Judean, from the land of Judea. By extension designates the Jewish state in the Persian empire.

YEHUDI: Hebrew word for Jew.

YEKKIS: Mildly derisive term applied to German immigrants, supposedly pedantic and perfectionist in nature, who began arriving in Palestine in the 1930s, but resisted assimilation.

YELLIN-MOR, NATAN (1913–1980): Israeli underground leader. Born as Nathan Friedman-Yellin in Grodno, Poland, Natan Yellin-Mor became active in the Polish branch of Betar, then in the Irgun Zva'i Le'umi. With Abraham Stern, he edited the Irgun's Polish newspaper, *Di Tat.* He then left for Palestine with Stern, joining Stern's underground organization, Lohamei Herut Yisrael (LEHI), which conducted a campaign of propaganda and terror attacks against the British. After Stern's death in 1942, Yellin-Mor assumed leadership of LEHI, as part of a triumvirate, along with Israel Eldad and Yitzhak Shamir. Yellin-Mor was tried and convicted in 1949 for the 1948 assassination of United Nations emissary Count Folke Bernadotte. The sentence, however, was commuted in exchange for Yellin-Mor's vow to refrain from further terrorist activities. As a leader of the Fighters Party, LEHI's political entity, he was elected to the Knesset in 1949. In later years Yellin-Mor embraced the politics of the left, renouncing Zionism and advocating the creation of an Arab-Jewish socialist state.

SEE ALSO Lohamei Herut Yisrael; Stern, Abraham.

YESHIVA (pl. *yeshivot*): A school for the study of Jewish sacred texts. A fundamental element of the Jewish religious world, these schools were basic religious institutions of Palestine and Babylonia, where clarification and compilation of ancient texts led to the creation of the Talmud. Modern yeshivot are intended for all Jews who wish to increase their knowledge of Judaism as well as those preparing to be ordained as rabbis. Although they were once only for males, many now admit women. Some, which are often called day schools in North America, offer secular studies in addition to intensive religious study.

In Israel, yeshivot are of two types: those that embrace Zionism, whose students combine military service with study, and those that do not, whose students are exempt from military service. Some of the former have played a significant role in promulgating annexationist or messianic ideologies at the expense of the Palestinians in Jerusalem or the territories.

SEE ALSO Talmud.

YISHUV (Settlement or community, in Hebrew): The Jewish community in Palestine before the establishment of the State of Israel. The Yishuv was divided into two sections: the Old Yishuv, Jews of communities established prior to the start of the Zionist movement; and the New Yishuv, consisting of Zionists who came to Palestine in the hope of establishing a

YESHIVA. ISRAELI BOYS WEARING DECORATED SKULLCAPS CALLED KIPPOT, OR YARMULKES, STUDY—ESPECIALLY SACRED TEXTS—IN A YESHIVA, OR JEWISH DAY SCHOOL, IN THE GALILEE. THE STYLES OF THE HEADGEAR SOMETIMES INDICATE POLITICAL OR RELIGIOUS AFFILIATION. *(© Annie Griffiths Belt/Corbis)*

national Jewish homeland. The two had different cultures and aims and their members were often antagonists.

Members of the Old Yishuv came to Ottoman Palestine from Eastern Europe, starting in the late eighteenth century and continuing through the nineteenth. Pious men and scholars concerned by the waning of traditional Jewish culture in Europe, their goal was a routine centered upon study, prayer, and observance of religious commandments, based on medieval European ways of life. The communities and schools they established were funded by wealthy Jews in Europe and the United States who were supportive of this aim; but as their numbers grew, these funds became inadequate and most lived in poverty.

When Zionism emerged in Europe in the 1880s, Zionists, too, began to sponsor immigration to Palestine; but the goal of the newcomers was a self-supporting secular, egalitarian society based on productive labor and a Hebrew cultural renaissance, fueled by a vision of political change. They wanted

to cut ties with tradition and build modern independent Jewish state. So the two lifestyles clashed, and the social change brought about by the new threatened to overwhelm the old—a situation exacerbated by the fact that both competed for funding.

After World War I, when Palestine came under the British mandate, British policy recognized the Yishuv as a religious community; but in practice, it encouraged the Zionists' establishment of national-style institutions. These began with the election of a national council (Va'ad Le'umi), which administered the community. Many members of the Old Yishuv refused to participate in the elections because they objected to female suffrage and to the secular aims of Zionism. Most Zionists, on the other hand, refused to obey traditional Jewish laws, such as the one requiring land to lie fallow every seventh year. There was, of course, some overlap, as some newcomers were strongly religious and some members of the older communities embraced new ways; but on the whole the Yishuv became largely Zionist in its outlook, providing the foundation upon which the State of Israel was created. From the time of the first Zionist congress of 1897 to the UN plan for partition of Palestine in 1947, the Yishuv grew from 40,000 to 600,000 persons, from 27 to 300 agricultural settlements and from land holdings of 204,000 to 1,800,000 dunams.

SEE ALSO Balfour Declaration; Dunam; Herzl, Theodor; Jewish Agency for Israel; Va'ad Le'umi; Weizmann, Chaim; World Zionist Organization; Zionism.

YOM HA-ATZMA'UT: Hebrew name of the holiday celebrating the independence of the State of Israel on 14 May 1948.

YOM HA-SHOA: "Holocaust remembrance day"; on the anniversary of the Warsaw ghetto uprising (27 Nisan on the Hebrew calendar), which is usually in the middle or at the end of April.

YOM HA-ZIKARON: "Day of remembrance of soldiers fallen in the wars of Israel." Preceding Yom Ha-Atzma'ut, the independence holiday; falls between the end of April and beginning of May.

YOM KIPPUR: Name of the Jewish holiday termed "the Great Forgiveness" (also Expiation or Purification). Celebrated on the tenth day of Tishri (20 September–12 October) when every Jew accounts to God for his or her actions. Following Rosh ha-Shanah, this holiday is characterized by a complete fast of 24 hours and by the ceremony of *Kol Nidre*, during which all participate in a common repentance. The Egyptians and Syrians surprised the Israelis by launching a major Arab-Israeli war on Yom Kippur in 1973.

SEE ALSO Arab-Israel War (1973).

YOM KIPPUR WAR

SEE Arab-Israel War (1973).

YOSEF, OVADIAH (1920–): Israeli religious and political leader. Born in Baghdad, Ovadiah Yosef lived in Mandatory Palestine from childhood and became a rabbi by the time he was twenty years old. Although he was deputy chief rabbi of Cairo in 1948, he returned to Israel in 1950 to become a religious judge. Chief Sephardic rabbi of Israel from 1973 to 1983, he formed the ultra-Orthodox Sephardic SHAS Party in 1983 with other former members of the Ashkenazi-dominated Agudat Israel Party. In 2003 SHAS won eleven Knesset seats (8.2 percent of the vote). Yosef continues to be the ruling force behind the SHAS Party.

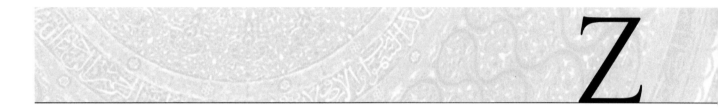

ZAKAT: Arab word designating the religious tax (2.5 percent of personal wealth) every Muslim (male and female) and Muslim community owes. According to the Qur'an the purpose of the zakat is to purify goods and the defilement of sin. It is one of the five obligations of Islam.

SEE ALSO Islam; Muslim.

ZAKI, ABBAS

SEE Mish'al, Sharif Ali.

ZAWAHRI, AYMAN MUHAMMAD, AL- (1952–): Egyptian Islamist, descended from an illustrious Cairo family. His grandfather was the imam of the al-Azhar Mosque and his great-uncle was secretary-general of the Arab League. When still very young, Ayman al-Zawahri joined the Muslim Brotherhood. After earning a degree in surgery, he left the Muslim Brotherhood and joined Egyptian Islamic Jihad. In October 1981, following the assassination of Anwar al-Sadat, he was arrested and imprisoned for three years. While in prison he established himself as one of the principal leaders of the Egyptian Islamic Jihad, representing its most radical current. Freed in October 1984, he practiced surgery for a time. In May 1985 he left Egypt, first going to Saudi Arabia and then to Pakistan to support the Afghan resistance against the Soviet army. At the end of 1986, with Osama bin Ladin, he created al-Qa'ida, the International Islamic

Front, where he was responsible for recruitment and logistical support of the Afghan resistance.

By 1992 he appears to have quit the Egyptian Jihad in order to found his own movement, Tala'i al-Fatah (Vanguard of the Conquest), a name already used by the Egyptian Islamic Jihad. In November 1995 he claimed responsibility for the attack on the Egyptian Embassy in Islamabad, which caused seventeen deaths. On 12 February, at Peshawar, he and Osama bin Ladin created the World Islamic Front for Jihad against Jews and Crusaders. On April 18 1999, with eight members of Egyptian Jihad, he was condemned to death in absentia by the Egyptian High Court of Military Justice. On September 25 2001 a "priority international arrest warrant" was issued against him, charging him and bin Ladin with masterminding the attacks of 11 September 2001 against the United States, which caused several thousand deaths. Zawahri is also under indictment in the United States for bombing the U.S. embassies in Tanzania and Kenya in 1998. After the 11 September attacks, he issued a public statement, on tape, in which he condemned Israeli crimes against the Palestinians and American complicity in them. Zawahri's whereabouts are unknown, although he is thought to have fled with bin Ladin into the Afghan mountains after the September 11 attacks.

SEE ALSO Bin Ladin, Osama; Egyptian Islamic Jihad; International Islamic Front; League of

Arab States; Muslim Brotherhood; Sadat, Anwar al-; World Islamic Front for Jihad against Jews and Crusaders.

ZAWIYA: Arab word designating a place of prayer; a hall; may or may not be attached to a mosque; often conjoined to the tomb of a Muslim saint where the faithful assemble. Historically related to Sufi practices.

SEE ALSO Mosque.

ZAYDAN, MUHAMMAD ʿABBAS (Abu al-ʿAbbas; 1943 or 1948–2003): Palestinian political figure, born in Palestine. After fleeing with his family to Syria in 1948, at the time of the 1948 War, Muhammad ʿAbbas Zaydan went to Egypt, where he studied in Cairo. In 1965 he joined the Palestine Liberation Front (PLF) of Ahmad Jibril, then followed Jibril when he merged his PLF into the Popular Front for the Liberation of Palestine (PFLP), headed by George Habash. In 1968 he followed Jibril again when he quit the PFLP to create the Popular Front for the Liberation of Palestine–General Command (PFLP–GC). In 1977 Jibril's resolutely pro-Syrian policy prompted Zaydan to quit the PFLP–GC, along with Talʿat Yaʿqub, Ali Zaydan, and Said al-Yussuf, to found the Palestine Liberation Front (1977), with headquarters in Baghdad. Yaʿqub was named secretary-general of the new PLF and Zaydan its political leader; their movement joined the Rejection Front [1], from which the PFLP–GC had just been expelled, leading to bloody confrontations between their respective members. In 1983, after Palestinian forces evacuated Lebanon, two tendencies surfaced in the PLF: one was pro-Syrian and headed by Yaʿqub, the other was pro-Yasir Arafat and supported by Zaydan. Zaydan remained leader of the PLF, and Yaʿqub formed his own movement. In November 1984 Zaydan was elected to the Palestine Liberation Organization (PLO) executive committee, accentuating his break with the Yaʿqub faction.

In September 1985 he became secretary-general of the PLF. On 8 October, in response to an Israeli raid on the PLO headquarters near Tunis, a commando of his movement took the passengers of an Italian ship, the *Achille Lauro*, hostage. A Jewish U.S. citizen, Leon Klinghoffer, was killed during the operation. Italy later tried Zaydan in absentia and he was convicted and sentenced to life in prison. Until 1999 he lived in Tunisia, Yugoslavia, and Iraq. On 22 April 1987 his presence at the Palestine National Council meeting in Algiers prompted a U.S. protest to the Algerians. In May, when Arafat was urging unity in the

PLO, Zaydan reconciled with Talʿat Yaʿqub. On 30 May 1990 a PLF commando attempted to stage a naval raid on Tel Aviv, leading to a halt in the dialogue with the PLO that U.S. authorities had just started. The following September Zaydan was expelled from the PLO Executive Committee and replaced as PLF representative by Ali Ishaq.

In spite of his support for Arafat, he was hostile to the peace process launched at the Madrid Conference of 1991 and opposed the Oslo Accords of 1993. After several members of his movement joined the opposition front, the Alliance of Palestinian Forces, Zaydan supported Arafat. In 1999 Zaydan returned to the Gaza Strip after agreeing to support the Oslo peace process, apologizing for Klinghoffer's death and receiving immunity from Israeli prosecution. In 2002, during the al-Aqsa Intifada, he returned to Iraq and from there directed his supporters' actions in the Palestinian territories. In April 2003 he was captured by American forces in Iraq during the Iraq War of 2003 and died in custody in March 2004, apparently from cardiovascular disease.

SEE ALSO *Achille Lauro;* Alliance of Palestinian Forces (APF); Aqsa Intifada, al-; Arab-Israel War (1948); Arafat, Yasir; Gaza Strip; Habash, George; Iraq War; Jibril, Ahmad; Madrid Conference; Oslo Accords; Palestine Liberation Front (1965); Palestine Liberation Front (1977); Palestine Liberation Organization; Palestine National Council; Popular Front for the Liberation of Palestine; Popular Front for the Liberation of Palestine–General Command; Rejection Front [1].

ZEʾEVI, REHAVAM (1926–2001): Israeli military and political figure, founder of the right-wing Moledet Party. He was born in 1926 in Jerusalem and joined the ranks of the Haganah when he was very young. Then, after the creation of the Israeli army, in 1948, he began a career in the military. From 1964 to 1968 he was Chief of the Department of Staff in the Israeli General staff. Between 1969 and 1972, he served as the Commander of Israel's Central Military District, where he was responsible for security in the West Bank. He retired in September 1973 but rejoined the army the following month at the beginning of the Yom Kippur War and served for several more months as the Chief of the Department of Staff.

Zeʾevi next served as a consultant on combating terrorism to Prime Minister Yitzhak Rabin, and the following year became Rabin's advisor on intelligence. In March 1977 he resigned from this position, and in 1981 was appointed director of the Haʾaretz museum in Tel Aviv. In February, 1988, during the first Intifada in the occupied territories, he announced the creation of a new party, Moledet, which advocated the transfer of the Palestinian population to Arab countries. As a result of the elections of the following June, his party won two seats in the Knesset. Five months later, he was named minister without portfolio in the government of Yitzhak Shamir. In 1992, after publicly expressing his disagreement with the policies of the government on negotiations with the Palestinians, he resigned his ministerial post. Moledet joined with Herut and Tekumah to form the National Union group in 1999.

On 7 March 2001, after the election of Ariel Sharon to the post of prime minister, Rehavam Ze'evi became minister of tourism. On the following 17 October, having resigned from the government two days earlier, he was assassinated by a Popular Front for the Liberation of Palestine (PFLP) squad in reprisal for the August killing of the leader of that movement. He was the only major Israeli politician to die in the Israeli-Palestinian conflict.

SEE ALSO Haganah; Moledet; National Union; Popular Front for the Liberation of Palestine.

ZIONISM: An international movement for the establishment of a Jewish homeland, formally founded in 1897 although initiated in the 1880s. The word "Zionist," which was coined in 1890 by Nathan Birnbaum, is derived from "Zion," one of hills of ancient Jerusalem, in the Bible sometimes applied to Jerusalem itself.

From the beginning, Zionism had both religious and secular aspects. Religious Jews believe that the land of Israel was given to the Jews by God, that their right to it is inalienable, and that their return to it was promised by God in biblical prophecies. However, not all of them have agreed with the idea of establishing a Jewish state by human agency before the return of the Messiah; before the 1930s many opposed it, and even today a few consider it blasphemous.

For secular Jews, on the other hand, Zionism was a political movement. Born of the continual oppression and persecution to which the Jews of Eastern Europe were subjected, it was triggered by the 1881–1884 pogroms in Russia. At that time, a few Jews began moving to Palestine; Rishon Le-Zion, the first Jewish agricultural colony, was established near Jaffa in 1882. Books and pamphlets proposing a Jewish homeland circulated among Europeans Jews, most notably "The Jewish State" by Theodor Herzl. The first world Zionist Congress, which was convened by Herzl and held in August of 1897 in Basel, endorsed the concept and began making plans, after which it became known worldwide. At first Jews of all political and religious persuasions joined to form the movement and worked together toward its goals. Later, dissention developed and Zionism split into factions. Socialist Zionism, favored by many secular Jews, was among the main branches.

Support for Zionism grew among Jews grew throughout the early twentieth century. The Holocaust, followed by the problem of refugees after World War II, convinced the vast majority, as well as many non-Jews, that a Jewish homeland in Palestine was urgently needed. Although not all of them approved of the radical tactics of some Zionists, in 1948 the movement achieved its aim through the creation of the State of Israel. Since that time, most Jews throughout the world have considered themselves Zionists in the sense that they support the existence of that state; but there are differences among them as to what Zionism entails.

The international Zionist movement continues to support Israel by such means as encouraging immigration and the investment of private capital, mobilizing public opinion in Israel's favor, and fundraising. However, since Israel occupied the West Bank and Gaza Strip during the Six-Day War of 1967, there has been opposition, both within Israel and elsewhere, to the view that there should be no compromise with the Palestinians.

The term "Zionist" is now also applied to groups in the Christian Zionism movement. Some fundamentalist and evangelical Protestants believe that according to Biblical prophecies, the return of the Jews to the Holy Land and the building of the Third Temple are necessary preconditions for Jesus to return and reign on Earth, and that by supporting Israel, they are helping to fulfill God's plan. This is a distinct, and much less widespread, view than the general belief of most Christians that the Jews have a right to a homeland in Israel; and it has political consequences, as these groups are adamantly opposed to any peace plan involving compromise.

SEE ALSO Balfour Declaration; Herzl, Theodor; Jewish Agency for Israel; Weizmann, Chaim; World Zionist Organization; Yishuv.

ZU ARTZENU (Hebrew for "this is our land"): Israeli nationalist movement of the extreme right, created in December 1993, following the Israeli-Palestinian Accords, which was signed in Washington, D.C. Zu Artzenu united settlers opposed to the dismantling of Jewish settlements in the West Bank. In the course of the summer of 1995, after months of dormancy, the movement, headed by Moshe Feiglin, returned to the Israeli political scene by supporting demonstrations against the government of Yitzhak Rabin. Its leadership, alluding to the Israeli-Palestinian Accords, accused the prime minister of "selling Israel to the Arabs and pushing the country towards war." At the beginning of September, the Israeli police arrested the principal leaders of the organization, who were accused of inciting revolt among the settlers in the Occupied Territories. On 14 September, Zu Artzenu organized a large demonstration against the Israeli-Palestinian peace process, during which some fifty people were injured. On 4 November, Jewish extremist Yigal Amir assassinated Prime Minister Yitzhak Rabin. Amir was later found to have connections to branches of Kach, Eyal, and Zu Artzenu. The actions of the movement found support in the extremist party, Moledet, of Rehavam Ze'evi. In March 1996, anticipating the Knesset elections of the following May, Zu Artzenu leader Rabbi Benyamin ("Benny") Elon appeared on the electoral list of Moledet. On 29 May, when Likud leader Benjamin Netanyahu was elected prime minister, Moledet gained two seats, one of which was taken by Rabbi Elon. From then on, befitting to the government's policy favoring Israeli settlements, the movement consolidated its position in the settler community. At the beginning of 1999, some of Zu Artzenu's members, essentially Russian in origin, decided to join the ranks of Israel Beiteinu.

SEE ALSO Elon, Benjamin; Eyal; Israel Beiteinu; Kach Party; Likud; Moledet; Netanyahu, Benjamin; Rabin, Yitzhak; West Bank; Ze'evi, Rehavam.

ZU'BI, MAHMUD AL- (Zo'bi; 1938–2000): Syrian political figure; born at Khirbat al-Ghazalah, Syria, to a wealthy Sunni family of Khirbat Ghazal. Mahmud al-Zu'bi obtained a degree in agronomical engineering in 1963 from the University of Cairo and was named director of the Syrian agricultural center of Ghab a few months later. He was in charge of agrarian reform in the Ghab valley from 1964 to 1968 during which time he joined the Ba'th Party and became a member of the council of agronomical engineers. In 1971 he was elected to the Syrian peoples council (Parliament), and occupied the posts of regional secretary of the Ba'th party and assistant secretary general of the national bureau of agriculture from 1971 to 1973. From 1973 to 1976 he directed the Society for Investment in the Euphrates, responsible for the agricultural development of a large part of Syria. He was elected acting member of the regional command of the Ba'th Party in March 1975, and four years later become a full member in charge of the peasant office. In 1981 Zu'bi was elected president of the Syrian peoples council, serving until October 1987 when President Hafiz al-Asad named him prime minister in place of Abdul Rawuf al-Kasem.

On 29 June 1992 Zu'bi was asked by the Syrian president to form a new government. During his first term the Syrian economy revived, and Syrian isolation among Arab nations and within the world ended. While Zu'bi was serving his second term, President Hafiz al-Asad and his designated successor, Asad's son Bashar, launched a campaign against corruption that touched many Syrian leaders. Himself accused of corruption, Zu'bi resigned from his post of prime minister on 7 March 2000; he was expelled from the Ba'th Party on the following 13 May and committed suicide eight days later.

SEE ALSO Asad, Bashshar al-; Asad, Hafiz al-; Ba'th.

TIMELINE OF MODERN ARAB-ISRAELI HISTORY

1878 First Jewish settlement in Palestine. Petah Tikvah, several miles outside Tel Aviv, is founded by a group of religious Jews from Jerusalem. By 1882, the Jewish population in Palestine is about 24,000.

1881 Russian czar Alexander II assassinated by revolutionaries. Hundreds of thousands of Jews flee the pogroms (1881–1884) in Russia and Eastern Europe. The Russian Zionist movement, Hibbat Zion (Love of Zion), establishes the first European Jewish farming colonies in Palestine. Because the settlers speak many different languages, Hebrew is revived and used as a common tongue.

1881–1903 First *Aliyah*. About 30,000 to 40,000 Jews, mostly Eastern European fleeing the pogroms, settle in Palestine during this first wave of immigration.

1896 Publication of *Der Judenstaat* (The Jewish State). Book written by Theodor Herzl, primarily as a response to European anti-Semitism, claiming that both the world and Jews need a Jewish state. At the First Zionist Congress, the author establishes the Zionist Organization (later known as the World Zionist Organization), which forms the foundation of the Zionist movement.

1897 First Zionist Congress, Basel, Switzerland. Meeting of Jewish leaders to discuss the ideas in *Der Judenstaat* of establishing a Jewish state. Issues the Basel Programme, which calls for a "home for the Jewish people in Palestine secured by public law."

1901 Fifth Zionist Congress. Establishes the Jewish National Fund (JNF) to raise funds and buy land in Palestine for Jewish settlers. By the early 2000s, the JNF owns about 14% of the land in Israel.

1903 Sixth Zionist Congress, Uganda proposal. A Zionist homeland is proposed in Uganda in East Africa by Herzl and Great Britain. The suggestion bitterly divides the congress because many Jews trace their homeland back to biblical territories (Palestine) and want to establish a state there.

1903–1914 Second *Aliyah*. About 35,000 to 40,000 Jews, mostly socialist-Zionists, immigrate to Palestine and establish the kibbutz and Zionist labor movements.

1905 Failed revolution in Russia. Pogroms (1903–1906) force thousands of Jews to flee Eastern Europe. Tens of thousands settle in Palestine.

485

1914–1918 World War I. As a result of the Allies' victory, lands previously under Ottoman rule are divided between France and England; Palestine lands under British rule.

1915–1916 Husayn-McMahon correspondence. Series of ten letters between Sharif Husayn ibn Ali, a leader of the Arab nationalist movement and king of the Hijaz, and Sir Henry McMahon, Britain's high commissioner in Egypt. British pledge support for Arab independence in exchange for an Arab revolt against the Ottomans and an alliance between the sharif and Britain.

1915 Sykes-Picot Agreement. Secret agreement between the French and British that divides Middle Eastern lands between the two countries after World War I. Formally known as the Anglo–Franco–Russian agreement, Britain receives common-day Iraq, Jordan, Israel, and Palestine; France receives common-day Syria and Lebanon.

1916 Balfour Declaration. Letter drafted by Zionist leaders of the British government calling for the establishment of a Jewish homeland in Palestine. This declaration is in direct conflict with the Husayn-McMahon correspondence (1915–1916), which called for an independent Arab state.

1916–1919 Arab revolt against Ottomans. Arab nationalist movement against Turkish rule of what is now Syria, Lebanon, Iraq, and most of the Arabian Peninsula. Backed by British supplies and led by Husayn ibn Ali and his four sons, the Arabs gain control of Mecca and other Ottoman garrisons, thus proclaiming their independence.

1917–1918 British troops occupy Palestine to secure a sea and land route to India.

1917–1922 Russian revolution and civil war. Pogroms (1919–1921) force many Jews to flee Russia, and thousands settle in Palestine.

1918 Muslim-Christian Association formed. Palestinian nationalist organization opposed to Zionism.

1919 Paris (Versailles) Peace Conference. Produces the Treaty of Versailles (1920), which ends World War I and establishes the League of Nations and the mandate system of lands surrendered by Germany. The Treaty of Sèvres (1920) virtually dismantles the Ottoman Empire. Britain gains control of Palestine.

1919 King-Crane Commission. U.S. president Woodrow Wilson sends two representatives, Henry C. King and Charles R. Crane, to Palestine and Syria to gather local reactions to rule under Britain and France. They find that the Palestinians and Syrians are opposed to the mandate system, perceiving it as a form of colonial rule, and want national independence for their countries. Zionists also oppose. British and French disregard the report.

1919–1924 Third *Aliyah*. About 35,000 Jews, mostly from Poland and Russia, immigrate to Palestine in response to the Russian Revolution.

1920 San Remo (Italy) Conference. Palestine and Iraq are assigned to Britain and Syria and Lebanon are assigned to France as Class A mandates, or trusteeships. Independence is promised only when the British or French determine that political systems are developed enough to be admitted to the League of Nations.

1921 Faisal I ibn Hussein—Amir Faisal—expelled from Syria by the French. A leader of the Arab revolt for nationalism from the Ottomans and king of Syria (1920) and Iraq (1921–1933), Faisal is forced to leave Syria shortly after he is appointed constitutional monarch by a congress of Arab nationalists.

1921 British accept Emir Abdullah as client ruler of Transjordan, install Faysal in Iraq. Britain grants the Palestinian Mandate east of the Jordan River to Abdullah II, who forms the Hashemite Kingdom of Transjordan. Jewish settlement is outlawed.

1922 Churchill White Paper. Policy paper by British government on the tensions between Arab and Jewish communities in Palestine. The statement claims equal protection and rights to both groups: Jewish immigrants should continue to settle in Palestine and have the right to do so; Arabs should not be subordinated by the immigration; and immigration should be economically sustainable by the region.

1922 British and French Mandates confirmed. League of Nations confirms British Mandate in Palestine, Transjordan, and Iraq. Syria and Lebanon are given to French Mandate.

1924–1930 Fourth *Aliyah*. Due to tough economic conditions, about 80,000 Jews from Poland immigrate to Palestine.

1929 Zionist demonstrations over prayer rights at Western (Wailing) Wall; Palestinian attacks on Jews. At the Western (Wailing) Wall, a holy site to both Jews and Muslims, Zionists protest when the British tear down a partition they had built to separate men and women. Palestinians attack religious Jewish communities, and Jews riot, killing Palestinians. British and police open fire in an attempt to stop the violence. About 250 people die that year.

1930 Passfield White Paper. Policy paper by British government on tensions between Arab and Jewish communities in Palestine finds that Arabs fear their economic, political, and national future is obstructed by Jewish immigration and land ownership, which results in violence against the Jews. Recommends clear policy statements protecting Arab rights and regulating Jewish immigration and land purchase.

1930 Shaw Commission. Commission of inquiry by British government on the violence between Arabs and Jews at the Western (Wailing) Wall in Palestine, 1929. Finds that Arabs are hostile toward immigrating and land-owning Jews because they pose a threat to the future of their economic and political stability and control. Calls for a policy that limits Jewish immigration.

1930 Sir John Hope-Simpson White Paper. Policy paper by British government on the tensions between Arab and Jewish communities in Palestine. Calls for drastic reduction in the number of Jewish immigrants and restrictions on land purchase because of widespread Arab unemployment and lack of farmable land.

1931 MacDonald Letter. Written by British prime minister Ramsay MacDonald (1924, 1929–35) to Zionist leader and future president of Israel, Chaim Weizmann. The letter reaffirms British support for Arab and non-Arab people in Palestine while expressing a responsibility to establish Jewish homeland in the region.

1931–1939 Fifth *Aliyah*. About 225,000 Jews, mostly educated and professional, immigrate to Palestine to flee the Nazis's increasing hold over Germany.

1933 Nazi accession to power in Germany. Anti-Semitic policies lead many Jews to flee Eastern Europe. At first, Nazis support the immigration to Palestine, as it helps their ethnic cleansing policies. However, once the Jewish population seeks statehood, Hitler sees a possible threat in the eastern European refugees.

1933–1945 Holocaust in Europe. Anti-Jewish policies of the Third Reich (Nazi Germany, 1933–1945) that include land and rights seizures; forced migrations into ghettos, work camps, and concentration camps; and the systematic genocide of six million Jews. Hundreds of thousands of Jews flee Europe to Palestine, as both legal immigrants and refugees.

1936 General strike and formation of the Arab Higher Committee. Palestinians strike against the British and the Jewish economy, determined to continue until Jewish immigration ceases, land sales are prohibited to Jews, and a national government and elected assembly are established. Five days into the strike, Palestinians form the Arab Higher Committee to present Arab demands to the British government.

1936–1939 Palestinian insurrection ("Arab Revolt"). Revolt against British support for a Jewish homeland in Palestine. Beginning with the general strike in 1936, the revolt escalates to full combat with the British and Jewish population from 1937–1938. About 10% of the adult male Palestinian population is killed, injured, or detained; the revolt has disastrous consequences for the Palestinian economy and leadership.

1937 Peel Commission Report. British Royal Commission Report that outlines solutions to tensions and unrest between the Arab Palestinians and Jewish immigrants. It concludes that the mandate system cannot work without repressing the Arab population and recommends that Palestine be divided into two nations, one Jewish and one Arab. The Jewish Agency accepts the plan, but opposes the borders and insists that the Palestinian population be deported from the Jewish state. The Palestinians' Arab Higher Committee denounces the plan, arguing that they have 70% of the population and 90% of the land and that Palestine should remain a unified state.

1937 Bludan Conference. Meeting of delegates from Syria, Palestine, Lebanon, Transjordan, Iraq, Egypt, and Saudi Arabia to discuss the Peel Commission. They reject the recommendation of splitting Palestine into Jewish and Arab states and call for a boycott of Jewish goods and British goods if the commission is carried out.

1938 Publication of *The Arab Awakening*. Book written by George Antonius, an Egyptian-born Christian and member of the British Palestine Administration. Discusses, from an Arab point of view, the origins of Arab nationalism, the significance of the Arab Revolt (1916), and the consequences of the British mandate system of dividing the Arab world after World War I.

1938 Woodhead Partition Commission. British report that retracts the Peel Commission's suggestion to partition Palestine.

1939 London (St. James/Roundtable) Conference. British host discussions between Arabs and Jews of Palestine on the future political situation in the Mandate. Talks held through British intermediaries, as the Arabs and Jews will not meet face-to-face. The Arabs call for the end of the mandate system, the creation of an independent Arab state, an end to Jewish immigration and land sales to Jews, and minority rights for Jews. The Jews call for an increased immigration to Palestine, especially with Hitler's rise to power and growing anti-Semitism in Europe.

1939 MacDonald White Paper. Policy paper issued by the British government outlining Britain's proposals from the London Conference on the post-Mandate government of Palestine. It calls for Jewish immigration to be limited to 75,000 over five years, after which Arab approval will be needed, limited land purchase by Jews, and promised self-government for Palestinians within ten years. Jews will have minority rights. Because of the outbreak of World War II, this policy is largely unimplemented.

1939–1945 World War II. British and French fight to secure their interests in the Middle East from the Germans. At the end of the war, Britain and France maintain control of the region.

1942 Biltmore Conference. New York City conference of about 600 American Zionists, plus many from around the world. They demand implementation of the Balfour Declaration (1916), which calls for a Jewish homeland, denounce the 1939 MacDonald White Paper as "cruel" in its quota of Jewish immigration to Palestine during a time of persecution and genocide in Hitler's Germany, and declare that there will never be peace in the world without a Jewish homeland. Sponsorship for Jewish immigration to Palestine shifts from Britain to the United States.

1943 National Pact in Lebanon, effective independence established. Christian and Muslim leaders come together to negotiate terms of a government independent of French influence in Lebanon.

1945 Arab League (League of Arab States) established. Formed to express the economic and security needs of Arab states. First founded with 7 Arab states; In 2004, it has 22 members.

1946 Anglo-American Committee of Inquiry. American and British collaboration formed to address the Arab-Israel conflict and Jewish refugees and survivors of the Holocaust.

1946 Morrison-Grady Plan for Palestine. Report by Britain's Herbert Morrison and United States' Henry Grady calling for a semi-autonomous Palestine divided into Jewish and Arab regions. Limits Jewish immigration to 100,000 in the first year, then to be determined by Britain, with Britain controlling the military, foreign relations, immigration, and customs. Rejected by both the Jews and Arabs.

1946 Anglo-American Conference (second Bludan Conference). Arab League meets to discuss Anglo-American Committee of Inquiry report. They criticize American interference in Palestine, suggest a boycott of Jewish goods, and vow to help the Palestinian Arabs.

1946 France leaves Syria and Lebanon; British end Mandate over Transjordan.

1947	United Nations votes partition plan (Resolution 181). Award Jews a homeland in Palestine. With one-third of the population and 7% of the land ownership, Jews are awarded 55% of Palestine. The plan is violently rejected by Arab Palestinians.
1948	Dayr Yasin (Deir Yasin) massacre. Surprise attack and massacre on Palestinian village outside Jerusalem kills 105 to 205 people and leaves the village in ruins. Conducted by Jewish paramilitary units, National Military Organization (led by Menachem Begin) and Fighters for the Freedom of Israel.
1948	British Mandate on Palestine expires on 14 May. British relinquish Mandate. Next day Jews proclaim the independent State of Israel. David Ben-Gurion, the Zionist leader, becomes Israel's first prime minister. Neighboring Arab countries send in troops to combat the Jews as British depart.
1948–1949	Arab-Israel war; known as *Nakba* to the Arabs and the War of Independence to the Jews. In Arabic, *Nakba* means "disaster" or "catastrophe." This war over the establishment of an Israeli state in Palestine results in the displacement of 700,000 to 750,000 Arabs (more than half the Arab population in the Mandate), confiscation of property, massacres, and the loss of a Palestinian homeland and society. Neighboring Arab countries (Lebanon, Syria, Jordan, Egypt, and Iraq) come to the aid of the Palestinians. Israel extends its boundaries by about 2,500 square miles.
1948	Count Folke Bernadotte assassinated; UN General Assembly passes Resolution 194. Bernadotte, a United Nations mediator in Israel and Palestine, proposes a truce between Arabs and Jews, which is broken and restored several times. In the two versions of the Bernadotte Plan for Arab-Israeli Settlement, boundaries are proposed in which Jerusalem goes to Transjordan (version 1) or is placed under United Nations control (version 2). Displaced Palestinians are offered repatriation or compensation for resettlement. Israel is to be recognized as an independent state. Both Arabs and Israelis reject his plan. On September 17, Bernadotte is gunned down by the Israeli group LEHI in Jerusalem.

1948	All-Palestine government; Palestine declaration of independence. In response to the formation of the Israeli state, the Palestinians declare the need for an Arab government to represent and defend their interests. It is backed by surrounding Arab countries, but ultimately is ineffective.
1949	General armistice agreements between Israel and Egypt, Jordan, Syria, and Lebanon. Peace agreements, sponsored by the United Nations and mediated by Ralphe Bunche, put an end to the 1948 Arab-Israel War.
1951	King Abdullah I is assassinated by a group of disgruntled Palestinians thought to have been working for Egypt's intelligence agency. In 1950, Abdullah I had held a conference in which it was proposed that the East and West Banks of Palestine were to be part of Jordan with parliamentary representation. The proposition was adopted unanimously and Abdullah became king of Palestine.
1953	Revolution in Egypt. Led by Nasser and the Free Officers, the coup overthrows the monarchy of King Farouk installed by the British. A republic is formed.
1954	Lavon Affair. Also known as the "mishap." Israeli-trained espionage group of Egyptian Jews are caught in mid-sabotage. They claim orders came from the head of the Intelligence Division of the Israeli Defense Forces, Colonel Benjamin Gibli, who in turn cites orders from Pinchas Lavon, the minister of defense. Lavon's involvement cannot be proven. The scandal extends into the 1960s and ultimately leads to the temporary withdrawal of David Ben-Gurion from politics in 1963.
1954	Moshe Sharett becomes prime minister of Israel when Ben-Gurion resigns.
1955	David Ben-Gurion elected prime minister of Israel for the second time.
1956	Arab-Israel War; Suez Crisis and War. The United States, Britain, and the World Bank pull out support for loans to Egypt after ties between Egypt and the Soviet Union grow closer. Egypt retaliates by nationalizing the Suez Canal Company, of which Britain is the largest shareholder. In response, Britain and France declare war on Egypt with support

and troops from Israel. Under pressure by the United States, Britain, France, and Israel accept a cease-fire after about ten days of fighting.

1958 Founding of United Arab Republic (UAR). The UAR combines Syria and Egypt from 1958–1961 and poses a threat to the West with Nasser's pan-Arab mission and anti-Western stance.

1958 Civil war in Lebanon, U.S. intervention. Sparked by the killing of a journalist, but rooted in grievances of political access, corrupt elections, elitist politics, and representation in government. Lebanon's president, Camille Chamoun, blames the UAR for inciting the violence and requests military intervention by the United States on his behalf.

1958 Revolution in Iraq. Hashemite monarchy, installed by British in 1921, violently overthrown in military coup led by the Free Officers. The revolution's goals are to rid the region of imperialistic forces and promote social and cultural reform. It results in a republican government and a foreign policy of nonalignment.

1959 Al-Fatah (Palestinian Liberation Movement) founded. Palestinian nationalist movement founded by Yasir Arafat. Its mission is to liberate Palestine by Palestinians, not by outside Arab assistance, through methods of armed struggle, not negotiation.

1961 Dissolution of UAR. Syria becomes increasingly dissatisfied with its diminishing role in the government; the Ba'thist party is dismissed and Nasser's policies seem more like an occupation than a collaboration. Syria's contingency in the army mounts a coup, which is met by little resistance from Nasser.

1963 Levi Eshkol becomes prime minister of Israel upon Ben-Gurion's resignation.

1964 Palestine Liberation Organization (PLO) and Palestine National Council (PNC) founded; Palestine National Covenant approved. Formed as a result of the first Arab Summit in Cairo, the PLO's mission is to be an organized representative body of Palestinian nationalism and liberation. The PNC is its parliamentary branch. The Covenant

calls for a liberation of Palestine by the Palestinians and the end of Israel.

1967 Arab-Israel War, also known as the Six-Day War. Issues left simmering from the British Mandate period—Palestinian refugees, water rights, and border with Arab States, arms race, growing Arab nationalism, and Israel's right to exist—lead to war between Israel and Syria, Jordan, Iraq, and Egypt. As a result of the war, Israel increases its land mass by almost three times and includes Egypt's Gaza Strip and Sinai Peninsula, Jordan's West Bank and East Jerusalem, and the Golan Heights from Syria.

1967 UN Security Council Resolution 242. The "land for peace resolution" calls for peace in the region based on Israel's withdrawal from lands won during the 1967 war and a recognition of secure boundaries. Little progress is made on the resolution.

1967 Popular Front for the Liberation of Palestine (PFLP) founded. Unites three groups: Heroes of the Return, the National Front for the Liberation of Palestine, and the Independent Palestine Liberation Front. Mission based on Palestinian national sovereignty, Arab unity, opposition to the State of Israel, and Marxist-Leninist ideology, borrowing some of Fidel Castro's methods. Second in importance and influence to al-Fatah.

1968 Palestine National Charter revised. After the Arab defeat in the 1967 war, the charter is revised to emphasize an Arab Palestinian homeland, national sovereignty, and self-determination. Calls for armed struggle to gain liberation.

1969 Democratic Front for the Liberation of Palestine (DFLP) founded. Marxist-Leninist group organized to liberate Palestine.

1969 Golda Meir becomes prime minister of Israel upon Eshkol's death.

1970 "Black September." Term used by some Palestinians (PLO and PFLP) to describe their defeat in the Jordanian Civil War. They had staged attacks against Israel from the Jordanian border since 1967, which provoked Israeli counter-attacks. The Jordanian army wins after ten days and thousands of casualties, many of which are civilian Palestinian refugees. A radical Palestinian terrorist group founded by members of al-Fatah takes this name.

1970 Gamal Abdel Nasser dies. President of Egypt from 1956–1970 and figurehead of pan-Arab nationalism, Arab socialism, and anti-Israel policies dies of a heart attack.

1971 PLO expelled from Jordan. At the end of the Jordanian Civil War (1970–1971), the Jordanian army ousts the PLO from the country, pushing them into southern Lebanon.

1973 Arab-Israel War, also known as the October War, Yom Kippur War, or Ramadan War. Caused by failure to resolve territorial disputes from the 1967 war. After diplomatic efforts fail, Egypt and Syria, backed by Soviet Union arms, plan a secret two-front attack on Israel, which is supported by United States weapons. A cease-fire is called when the United States proclaims a military alert in response to the Soviet Union's offer to send troops to Egypt. The war results in thousands of dead and injured and a dependence on the Soviet Union (Egypt) and the United States (Israel) for military support.

1973 UN Security Council Resolution 338. Passed during the cease-fire of the 1973 war. Calls for an immediate end to military operations, implementation of Resolution 242 (from 1967), and a start to peace negotiations.

1974 Yitzhak Rabin elected prime minister of Israel. First native-born prime minister. Makes major strides in diplomacy with Jordan and Palestine. Shimon Peres succeeds him in 1977 after a financial scandal.

1974 PLO implicitly accepts two-state solution. At the PNC in 1974, the PLO modifies its goal of liberating all of Palestine and focuses on creating a Palestinian state in the West Bank and Gaza.

1974 UN and Arab League accept PLO as sole legitimate representative of Palestinians. Yasir Arafat makes first appearance at the UN proposing peace.

1974 Suez I, or Sinai I, agreement between Israel and Egypt. Cease-fire agreement ending the 1973 war; moderated by U.S. Secretary of State Kissinger. Israeli troops pull back west from the Suez Canal and east on the Sinai front of the canal. Three buffer security zones are created for Israel, Egypt, and the UN.

1975 Suez II, or Sinai II, agreement between Israel and Egypt. Cease-fire agreement ending the 1973 war moderated by U.S. secretary of state Kissinger. Israel withdraws troops an additional 12 to 26 miles and the UN occupies buffer zone.

1975 UN General Assembly Resolution 3379. Equates Zionism with racism.

1975–1990 Lebanese Civil War. Series of domestic disruptions in southern Lebanon where the PLO is based and many Palestinian refugees live. Much fighting occurs in the region between Israelis and Palestinians.

1977 Menachem Begin elected prime minister of Israel. First right-wing prime minister. His term is marked by diplomacy with Egypt.

1978 First Israeli invasion of Lebanon. Israel backs the Lebanese Forces, a coalition of right-wing militias, and Syria backs the Palestinians. Israel invades to rid the region of pro-Palestinian groups and PLO training camps and occupies a strip of land called "the security zone."

1978 Camp David Accords. Peace negotiations between Israel and Egypt, mediated and hosted by the United States. Calls for the implementation of UN Security Council Resolution 242 "land for peace" principle whereby Israel will return the Sinai to Egypt (pre-1967 borders) in exchange for peace. Palestine and Lebanon oppose the accords. The establishment of an autonomous Palestinian state in the West Bank and Gaza is not achieved. The accords mark the first time an Arab nation officially recognizes the statehood of Israel.

1979 Egypt-Israel peace treaty. Treaty signed by Egypt and Israel as a result of the Camp David Accords. The two agreements include "A Framework for Peace in the Middle East" and "A Framework for the Conclusion of a Peace Treaty between Egypt and Israel."

1979 Revolution in Iran. Overthrow of Mohammad Reza Shah Pahlavi, the last monarch of the 450-year old Safavid dynasty. The shah had used the secret police to repress dissident voices during a period of social, economic, and cultural change. Its leader, Ayatollah Khomeini, opposed the shah's alliance with the United States and his support of Israel. A religious Islamist state replaces the monarchy.

1980–1988 Iran-Iraq War (First Gulf War). Iraq launches a surprise attack on Iran in 1980 because, according to Iraq, Iran was plotting raids across the border. Missile attacks and raids last for eight years, mostly on Iraqi soil, taking hundreds of thousands of lives. The UN Security Council intervenes in 1987 when international ships are threatened in the Gulf.

1981 Anwar al-Sadat assassinated. President of Egypt and successor to Nasser killed by three Egyptian soldiers discontented that Sadat did not ensure a liberated Palestine at the Camp David Accords and by Egypt's deteriorating economic condition.

1982 Second Israeli invasion of Lebanon ("Operation Peace for Galilee"). A PLO rocket attack on Israel prompts Israel to invade Lebanon and rid the area of PLO forces and Syrian troops. Israeli forces reach Beirut and the conflict takes over 20,000 lives. The U.S. mediates and expels PLO and Syrian troops from Beirut.

1982 Sabra and Shatila massacre. From 800 to 2000 Palestinian refugees, mostly women, children, and the elderly, are massacred at the Sabra and Shatila refugee camps by the Phalange (Lebanese Christian militias). Israeli troops, which had invaded West Beirut and surrounded the camps, stand back while the massacres take place. Defense Minister Ariel Sharon is found indirectly responsible for the killings.

1982 PLO expelled from Lebanon. Although the mission of the Israeli invasion is to wipe out the PLO in Beirut, they succeed in transplanting the PLO to Tunis, Tunisia.

1983 Yitzhak Shamir becomes prime minister of Israel.

1984 Shimon Peres becomes prime minister of Israel.

1986 Yitzhak Shamir becomes prime minister of Israel for second time.

1987–1994 First Intifada. Palestinian uprisings in the West Bank and Gaza against Israeli policies of land and property seizure and demolition, censorship, restricted travel and construction, and military tribunals instead of civilian courts. The uprisings escalate from labor strikes, boycotts against Israeli goods, demonstrations, and Palestinian youths throwing stones at Israeli troops in 1987 to riots and violence in 1994. More than 20,000 people die.

1987 HAMAS founded. Palestinian liberation group with the mission of establishing an Islamic Palestinian state. Employs methods of terror and violence.

1988 Algiers Declaration. Palestinian statehood proclaimed at PNC meeting.

1990 Iraq occupies Kuwait. After eight years of fighting with Iran, Iraq is left in severe debt. Accuses Kuwait of overproduction of oil to lower the price per barrel, which is seen as an act of war. U.S. forces are sent to protect Gulf states, particularly Saudi Arabia, under the operation Desert Shield.

1990 Ta'if Accord ends Lebanese Civil War. Morocco, Saudi Arabia, and Algeria make recommendations to Lebanon and Syria to end the war and establish Syria and Lebanon's relationship with Israel.

1991 Multinational war against Iraq ("Operation Desert Storm," Second Gulf War). A major five-week air offensive and 100-hour ground campaign, led by the United States, drives the Iraqis out of Kuwait.

1991 UN General Assembly Resolution 4686. Revokes Resolution 3379, which equates Zionism with racism.

1991–1993 Madrid Peace Conference. U.S.-led and -mediated talks between Israel, Syria, Jordan, Egypt, and Palestine. First time Israeli, Palestinian, and Arab diplomats (except Egypt) meet for public peace talks. Arab states recognize Israel as a nation.

1992 Yitzhak Rabin elected prime minister of Israel for second time.

1993 Oslo Accords I; Palestinian-Israeli "Declaration of Principles." Secret talks between PLO and Israel resulting in a land-for-peace agreement. PLO and Israel agree to recognize each other and sign the "Declaration of Principles," which outlines sovereignty for

Palestinians in Gaza and the West Bank for five years. PLO gives up claims to territory won by Israel in the 1967 war.

1994 Hebron massacre. U.S.-born Israeli settler opens fire on Palestinian worshippers at the al-Haram al-Ibrahimi mosque, killing 29.

1994 Cairo Agreement. Outlines Israel's withdrawal from parts of the West Bank and Gaza. A five-year plan is laid out for further Israeli withdrawals, negotiations on Jerusalem, settlements, refugees, and Palestinian sovereignty.

1994 Institution of Palestinian Authority. Autonomous Palestinian government set up in the West Bank and Gaza, chaired by Yasir Arafat and comprised of other PLO ministers.

1995 Oslo Accords II (Taba Accord). Set the stage for Palestinian elections, security, economic relations, and legal and civil matters. The accords do not lead to peace. Instead, escalating violence and terrorism rack the area in the late 1990s and into the 2000s.

1995 Prime Minister Yitzhak Rabin assassinated. Israeli prime minister killed by Jewish extremists who are opposed to his peace negotiations with Palestine. Shimon Peres succeeds him.

1996 First Palestinian elections for PLO president and Palestinian National Congress. Arafat wins election for president.

1996 Benjamin Netanyahu elected prime minister of Israel. Netanyahu's Likud Party campaigns against the Olso Accords and Peres and Rabin's peace process with Palestine.

1998 Wye River Memorandum. Document produced by talks between Israel and the United States after an 18-month stagnation of the peace process. Calls for Israel to hand over 80% of Hebron and outlines further withdrawals from the West Bank.

1999 Ehud Barak runs on a Labor platform and is elected prime minister of Israel. Barak, running on a platform of bringing peace between Israel and Syria, Lebanon, and Palestine, wins the election and resumes peace talks with Palestine.

2000 Israel withdraws from Lebanon. Barak calls the army out of the region, except for the area of the Shab'a Farms, which Israel main-

tains is Syrian territory and therefore can occupy with troops.

2000– Second Intifada (al-Aqsa Intifada). In reaction to Ariel Sharon's tour of the al-Aqsa mosque (Islam's third holiest shrine) with 1000 riot police, Palestinians take to the streets in demonstration. Israeli police shoot live ammunition and rubber bullets at the crowd, killing six. Fundamentally, the Palestinians rise up against the dead-end peace process. They are against the Israeli occupation of the West Bank and Gaza, the growing number of settlements in the area, land seizures, home and property destruction, and restricted travel.

2001 Israeli-Palestinian negotiations at Taba. U.S.-mediated talks that lay the final plans for Israeli withdrawals and Palestinian refugees. Time runs out on the accords before the details can be agreed upon and the proposals are not followed through.

2001 Ariel Sharon elected prime minister of Israel. Sharon advocates harsh punishments for Palestinian terror groups and campaigns against the Oslo peace accords. He wants a Greater Israel and encourages the settlements in the West Bank and Gaza. Violence escalates and Israel re-occupies almost all of the West Bank during Sharon's time in office.

2001 Palestinians claim Zionism is racist. At the World National Conference Against Racism, Palestinians claim that they are victims of crimes against humanity and the Zionist movement is racist.

2003– U.S.-UK war against, and occupation of, Iraq. Without UN support, the United States, Britain, and a coalition of countries send troops into Iraq to depose Saddam Hussein. Although the stated mission is to remove weapons of mass destruction from Iraq, none are found.

2004– Israel to withdraw unilaterally from Gaza Strip. Announcement made by Israeli prime minister Ariel Sharon in February seen as source of clashes with settlers, bitter disagreements in Israel, and potential split within Likud. On 26 October, the Knesset approves Sharon's plan, which calls for Gaza's complete evacuation by end of 2005.

2004	In mid-October, Yasir Arafat grows increasingly weak with an unknown illness. On 29 October he is allowed to leave his compound in Ramallah to seek medical help. He is taken to a military hospital outside Paris for diagnosis and treatment.
2004–	Yasir Arafat dies 11 November from an unknown illness. Mahmud Abbas sworn in as PLO chairman. Rawhi Fattuh sworn in as interim president of the Palestinian Authority. Faruq Qaddumi named al-Fatah leader.

TIMELINE OF THE ARAB-ISRAELI CONFLICT

1897	First Zionist Congress discusses plans to establish a Jewish state in Palestine.
1914–1918	World War I; the Ottoman Empire is defeated.
1916	Sykes-Picot Agreement divides Ottoman Arab lands into zones controlled by either the French or the British.
1917–1918	Palestine comes under British control, as British troops move northward from their bases in Egypt.
1917	Britain issues the Balfour Declaration, supporting "the establishment in Palestine of a national home for the Jewish people, . . .it being clearly understood that nothing shall be done which may prejudice the civil and religious rights of existing non-Jewish communities in Palestine. . ."
1920	League of Nations at San Remo divides Arab lands into mandates, which are supposed to eventually create nation states for the indigenous peoples. Britain holds the Mandate for Palestine.
1922	British create the Amirate of Transjordan out of Mandatory Palestine east of the River Jordan. The Jewish national home provisions of the Balfour Declaration will be applied only west of the Jordan.
1933	Adolf Hitler begins his rise to power in Germany. Jewish immigration to Palestine increases.
1936–1939	The Arab Revolt against British pro-Zionist policy and in a quest for an independent Arab state in Palestine.
1946	Hostilities in Palestine escalate and include Jewish terrorism against Britain. U.S. president Harry S. Truman expresses support for partition and a "viable Jewish state in an adequate area of Palestine."
1947	The United Nations General Assembly Resolution 181 recommends the partition of Palestine into Jewish and Arab states, with greater Jerusalem to be an international city. The resolution is adopted by a vote of 33-13-10, but rejected by Arab and Muslim delegates.
1948	Israel declares statehood as the British Mandate over Palestine ends. Arab armies attack Israel. The resulting war leaves Jerusalem divided and 650,000 Palestinians refugees. UN Resolution 194 declares that refugees should be allowed to return to their homes, and establishes a commission to facilitate their repatriation or compensation.

1949	An armistice is signed at Rhodes between Israel and Egypt. Similar agreements with Lebanon, Jordan, and Syria follow. U.N. conference at Lausanne produces no agreement between Israeli and Arab delegations.
1949– 1950	Israel holds 77 percent of the former Palestine. Jordan annexes East Jerusalem and the West Bank. Egypt controls the Gaza Strip. The United Nations Relief and Work Agency is established. Jews from several Arab countries begin migration into Israel.
1956– 1957	Egyptian president Gamal Abdel Nasser's nationalization of the Suez Canal leads to military action by Israel, Britain, and France. U.S. President Dwight D. Eisenhower threatens economic sanctions against Israel and succeeds in forcing Israel's withdrawal from Sinai and Gaza. United Nations puts UNEF [Emergency Force] along the Egyptian-Israeli frontier.
1964	The Palestinian Liberation Organization (PLO) is established.
1967	Israel captures the Golan Heights, the Gaza Strip, the West Bank, and East Jerusalem from Syria, Egypt, and Jordan. As many as 600,000 Palestinians become refugees. UN Resolution 242 calls for Israeli withdrawal and establishes the "land for peace" principle.
1969– 1970	Israel begins establishing settlements in disputed areas. Egypt's War of Attrition against Israel, with Soviet aid, leads to the Rogers Plan, which uses UN Resolution 242 as the basis for negotiations.
1973	Egypt and Syria attack Israel. No territorial changes result. UN Resolution 338 calls for negotiations between the parties. Minor border changes result as U.S. helps to broker disengagement agreements.
1977	Menachem Begin and the Likud coalition win Israeli elections. Settlements in Occupied Territories increase. Egypt's president Anwar al-Sadat goes to Israeli Knesset in the first efforts toward an Arab-Israeli peace treaty.
1978	Negotiations between Sadat and Begin are brokered by U.S. president Jimmy Carter at Camp David, Maryland, and result in the Camp David Accords, followed in 1979 by the first peace treaty between Israel and one

of its Arab neighbors. The Arab League expels Egypt. Israel invades Lebanon in response to terror attacks and in an attempt to clear out Palestinian fighters along the border.

1980	The Israeli government declares Jerusalem its capital. Ambassadors are exchanged between Israel and Egypt.
1981	Israel annexes the Golan Heights, captured from Syria in 1967. Sadat is assassinated by Islamic fundamentalists.
1982	Israel invades Lebanon a second time, laying siege to Beirut. The PLO moves its headquarters from Beirut to Tunis. The Reagan Peace Initiative and the Fez Summit Peace Proposal are launched.
1987	Palestinian uprising, known as the Intifada, begin in Gaza and spread to the West Bank. Over the next several years, several thousand Palestinians and hundreds of Israelis are killed in the fighting.
1988	The Palestinian National Council (PNC) accepts UN Resolutions 242 and 338, tacitly recognizing Israel, and declares a Palestinian state. The United States government begins dialogue with the PLO.
1991	The Gulf War begins in January. Later that year, a Middle East peace conference opens in Madrid between Israel and Arab nations, including, Jordan, Lebanon, and Syria. Palestinian representative participate, for the first time, in such an international forum as part of the Jordanian delegation.
1992	The administration of U.S. president George H. W. Bush stops $10 billion in U.S. loan guarantees to Israel in an attempt to curtail the spread of Israeli settlements into disputed areas.
1993	The Oslo Process begins during the administration of U.S. president Bill Clinton. Palestinian leader Yasir Arafat and Israeli prime minister Yitzhak Rabin meet at the White House. The PLO and Israel sign the Declaration of Principles, outlining a plan for Palestinian self-rule in the Occupied Territories.
1994	The Cairo Accords between the PLO and Israel establish Palestinian self-rule in Gaza and Jericho but allow Israeli settlements to remain in place. Jordan and Israel sign a

peace treaty with Clinton in attendance. Arafat, Shimon Peres, and Rabin receive the Nobel Peace Prize.

1995 The Interim Agreement on the West Bank and the Gaza Strip, known as Oslo II, establishes three areas in the West Bank, one under direct Palestinian control, one under both Palestinian civilian control and Israeli security, and one under Israeli control. Rabin is assassinated in Tel Aviv.

1996 Benjamin Netanyahu is elected Israel's prime minister. Israel launches Operation Grapes of Wrath in southern Lebanon. Arafat, Jordan's King Hussein, Netanyahu, and Clinton participate in a political summit in Washington, DC to negotiate for peace.

1997 The Hebron Protocol divides the city of Hebron. Palestinians protest the building of an Israeli settlement, Har Homa, on a hill overlooking East Jerusalem.

1998 The Wye River Memorandum is signed but not implemented.

1999 The PLO postpones a declaration of statehood. Ehud Barak, newly elected prime minister of Israel, pledges to work for peace. The Sharm al-Shaykh memorandum is signed between Israel and the PLO. Clinton attends a PNC meeting in Gaza to witness the elimination of Palestine National Covenant clauses calling for the destruction of Israel.

2000 Israeli Army withdraws from South Lebanon. At the Camp David II meetings in July, Clinton chairs negotiations between Arafat and Barak. Negotiations break down. The al-Aqsa Intifada begins, fueled by Ariel Sharon's visit to the Temple Mount/Haram al–Sharif.

2001 Sharon is elected prime minister of Israel.

2002 Israeli troops reoccupy Palestinian areas in response to a terrorist suicide bombing of elderly people celebrating Passover at a resort hotel. Arafat is placed under house arrest in his Ramallah compound. The Church of the Nativity in Bethlehem is stormed by armed Arab Palestinians. A Saudi peace plan, endorsed by the Arab League, promises recognition of Israel in exchange for ending occupation of all Arab lands. UN Resolution 1397 affirms a two-state vision for Israel. U.S. president George W. Bush announces a plan for a "viable Palestinian state next to a secure Israel." Israel begins construction of a highly controversial "security fence" around the West Bank in response to suicide bombing inside Jewish civilian population areas.

2003 The United States invades and begins its occupation of Iraq. The Road Map for Peace, sponsored by the "Quartet" (U.S., U.N., Russia, and the European Union), is released.

2004 Ariel Sharon's government promotes a plan that involves Israeli evacuation of the Gaza Strip and the abandonment of the settlements there. In October the Knesset votes to back Sharon's plan to remove Israeli troops, as well as twenty-one settlements from Gaza and four small settlements from the northern part of the West Bank. The vote—sixty-seven for, forty-five against, and seven abstentions—marks the first time in twenty years that the parliament had favored the withdrawal of Jewish settlers from the region. Sharon rejects a call for a referendum by the Likud which creates turmoil in the Knesset.

2004 In mid-October, Yasir Arafat, suffering from an unknown illness, is allowed to leave his compound in Ramallah to seek diagnosis and treatment in France. Israeli prime minister Ariel Sharon states that if Arafat dies, he will not allow Arafat to be buried in Jerusalem.

2004– Yasir Arafat dies 11 November from an unknown illness. Mahmud Abbas sworn in as PLO chairman. Rawhi Fattuh sworn in as interim president of the Palestinian Authority. Faruq Qaddumi named al-Fatah leader.

ADAR: Name of the sixth month of the Hebrew calendar, corresponding to the period between the end of the month of February and the beginning of the month of March. A second month of Adar is added every 3rd, 6th, 8th, 11th, 14th, 17th and 19th years of the calendar's nineteen-year cycle to align with the lunar calendar.

AGHA: Socio-political title of authority. Agha ("chief," "master") was associated with certain administrators in the Ottoman empire. It is also used in other settings, such as among Kurds.

ALMENOR: Name of the central platform in a synagogue, from which the rabbi officiates. Also called a bima.

AMIR: Political title. See dictionary entry "Emir."

ASHUR: Islamic tithe. Also called zakah or zakat, ashur (from the Arabic word for "ten") is a charitable tithe prescribed in Islam. In North Africa, ashur also denotes the tenth month of the Islamic calendar, Muharram.

AV: Eleventh month of the Hebrew calendar, corresponding to the period between the end of July and the beginning of August. The destruction of the Temple of Solomon is commemorated on the 9th of Av (*Tish'a b-Av*).

BAR-MITZVA: "Son of the commandment," in Hebrew. Jewish religious ceremony celebrating the passage from adolescence to majority and one's admission into the adult community. During the ceremony the 13-year old "mitzva" reads from the Torah and puts on phylacteries, symbolic of the commandments to which he will henceforward submit. The equivalent of bar-mitzva for young women is the bas-mitzva, which is celebrated at the age of 12.

BEIT MIDRASH: School of rabbinical studies, generally attached to a synagogue.

BETH: Also "beir, bait, bayt, beit." Hebrew word meaning "house," often figuring in composite names such as Bethel (house of God), Bethlehem (house of bread) or Beth Din (house of the law).

BEY: Political title. Bey is a Turkish term often translated as "prince." In the Ottoman empire's administration and military, it was given to mid-level officers. In modern Turkey, it is often used as a suffix to a man's first name as a polite form of address.

BINT: Arabic, "girl." Female children in the Arab world sometimes are referred to by making reference to their father. Thus, "so-and-so, bint [daughter] so-and-so."

CASBAH: Old quarters of an Arabic city. From the Arabic *qasaba* ("divide," "cut up"; also, "citadel" or "capital"), it is a term often used by Europeans to denote the older, native quarters of a town, as distinct from the newer areas in which foreigners lived.

DARB: Street or path. Has come to refer to a neighborhood, especially in Morocco.

DEY: Political title. The Turkish word for maternal uncle, the position of dey originally was military, but came to denote administrative power as well. Deys were found in North Africa, especially Tunisia and Algeria, from the late seventeenth through the early nineteenth centuries.

DHU AL-HIJJAH: Name of the twelfth month of the Islamic calendar.

DHU AL-QI'DAH: NAME OF THE ELEVENTH MONTH OF THE ISLAMIC CALENDAR.

DINAR: Monetary unit. Dinar is derived from the Greek "dinarion" and the Latin "denarius." During the early Islamic period, it was a type of gold coin. Currently it serves as the currency of Algeria, Bahrain, Iraq, Jordan, Kuwait, Libya, and Tunisia.

DIRHAM: Monetary unit. During the early Islamic period, the dirham was a type of silver coin. Currently it is used in Morocco, Libya, the United Arab Emirates, and Jordan.

EFFENDI: Honorific title. The origins of this title are Greek, and refer to a man of property or education. During the late Ottoman period, it was used as a sign of respect for middle class males as well as for some bureaucratic positions. Another form of the word, effendum, is still used in Egypt to mean "mister" or "sir."

EXILARCH: "Leader of the exile" (rosh ha-gola, in Hebrew; resh galonta, in Aramaic). Lay head of some Jewish communities settled outside of Israel.

FEDDAN: Unit of surface area. Deriving from an Arabic term for a yoke of oxen, it referred to the amount of land such animals could farm. Thus the actual surface area called a feddan varied from region to region. In Egypt, where it remains the standard unit of surface area today, it equals 4,200.883 square meters, slightly more than one acre.

FELLAH: Peasant. Fellah (also fallah; plural: fallahun, but more commonly fallahin following colloquial usage) derives from the Arabic verb *falaha* ("cultivate"). It refers to small scale, subsistence level cultivators in Arab countries, but can be used, often derisively, by urbanites to refer to the rural population generally.

GENTILE: Word used by Jews, from the time of the end of the Second Temple (between 19 and 70 C.E.) to designate non-Jews, then used by Christians to designate pagans.

GHAZEL: Type of poetic form. The word is Arabic (ghazal; "flirtation" or "love poem"), and is also seen as gazel or ghazal. A lyrical poetic mode often expressing romantic love or eroticism, the form passed into Turkish, Persian, and Urdu poetry as well.

GOY: (*Goi,* pl. *goyim*) "Nation or people" in Hebrew. Word used by Jews currently to designate "gentiles", that is, non-Jews.

HAZAN: Hebrew word used to designate the performer of a Jewish religious office, especially having to do with chanting prayers and teaching children.

HESHVAN: Name of the second month of the Hebrew calendar, corresponding to the end of October and the beginning of November.

HOCA: Honorific title. Hoca is a Turkish word derived from the Persian *khwaja*. In the Turkish speaking parts of the Ottoman empire, it denoted religious scholars and certain administrative bureaucrats. It is still used in modern Turkey to refer to teachers and religious scholars. See also "khawaja."

HOFSHI: Hebrew word meaning "free." By extension designates a secular Jew.

HOSAINIYEH: Place of a certain type of religious ceremony. In Iran, it is a place where the martyrdom of the Imam Husayn ibn Ali is commemorated, especially on Ashura, the tenth day of the Islamic month of Muharram. It refers to the death of Husayn, grandson of the prophet Muhammad, in 680 at the hands of the Umayyads at Karbala, in Iraq. Traditionally, a hosainiyeh was a different structure than a mosque, and was a populist institution rather than one under the control of the Islamic clerics.

INQILAB: Revolution or uprising. In modern Arabic political usage, the term inqilab is usually used to connote a sudden seizure of political power, often via a military coup d'état. In Persian, the term means "revolution," such as the 1979 revolution in Iran.

IYAR: Name of the eighth month of the Hebrew calendar, corresponding to late April and early May.

JUMADA AL-AWWAL: Name of the fifth month of the Islamic calendar.

JUMADA AL-THANI: Name of the sixth month of the Islamic calendar.

KADDISH: Hebrew word, from Aramaic, meaning "sanctification." Prayer of praise, addressed to

God and recited periodically in the course of a synagogue service, by men in mourning. Also called the prayer of the dead.

KARA: Hebrew term designating someone who reads and interprets sacred writings without the help of commentaries.

KAZA: Ottoman administrative unit. Kaza is a Turkish word derived from the Arabic *qada*. By the late Ottoman empire, a province (*vilayet*; Arabic: *wilaya*) was divided into governorates called *sanjaks* (Arabic singular: *sanjaq*) or *livas* (Arabic singular: *liwa*). These in turn were divided into smaller units called kazas. Kaza can also refer to the judgment of a *qadi*, or judge. See also "liwa," "qa'immaqam," and "vilayet."

KHAN: Highway inn for travelers, or a warehouse for merchandise. Khans were built as rest stops for travelers and caravans. A khan was also an urban complex for storing merchandise and hosting merchants.

KHANJAR: Type of Arabic dagger. A khanjar usually refers to a slightly curved, double edged dagger that tapers to a point. The hilt is often decorated.

KHATIB: Islamic preacher. A khatib is the religious official who delivers the sermon during Friday prayers in a mosque, usually from a raised pulpit called a minbar. See also "minbar."

KHAWAJA: Honorific title of Persian origin. In Egypt and parts of the Fertile Crescent, khawaja was a title used to denote a non-Muslim, both foreigners as well as native Christians and Jews. The term comes from the Persian *khwaja*. See also "hoca."

KHAWR: Natural harbor; also part of place names. The term is used in the Persian/Arabian Gulf region.

KHEDIVE: High-level title used in Egypt from 1867–1914. Khedive is a Persian word for a high prince that was used by the governors of Ottoman Egypt from 1867–1914 to replace the title "pasha" carried by other governors in the empire. It was first used by Isma'il Pasha, grandson of Muhammad Ali, who secured this right from the Ottoman sultan in order to differentiate and elevate himself from other provincial governors. The term was replaced with "sultan" by the British, who occupied Egypt starting in 1882. See also "pasha."

KIDDUSH: Blessing pronounced at a meal, or during Jewish religious holidays.

KIDDUSH HA-SHEM: Hebrew word for Jewish martyrs in general.

KIPPAH: ("yarmulka" in Yiddish) Skullcap worn by observant Jews, as a sign of submission to God.

KISLEV: Word for the third month of the Hebrew calendar, corresponding to the period between the end of November and the beginning of December. On 25 Kislev, the holiday of Hanukkah is celebrated.

KORAN: See dictionary entry "Qur'an."

LAILAT AL-QADR: Muslim holiday, celebrated on 27 Ramadan, commemorating the night of Qur'anic revelation.

LIRA: Ottoman monetary unit. The lira, or pound, was named after an Italian silver coin, and was the currency used in the Ottoman empire. Modern Turkey, Syria, and Lebanon continue to use the lira as their national currencies.

LIWA: Ottoman administrative unit. During the late Ottoman empire, a province (*vilayet*; Arabic: *wilaya*) was divided into liwas (called liva in Turkish). A liwa was also called a sanjak (Arabic: *sanjaq*). These in turn were divided into smaller units called qadas or kazas.

LUTI: Term implying deviation from moral standards. In Iran during the late nineteenth and early twentieth centuries, the term originally referred to a member of a chivalrous brotherhood. It later assumed more negative connotations implying drunkenness and moral deviation. In parts of the modern Arab world, luti is a term used for a homosexual. Some surmise that the term derives from the biblical figure Lot, son of Noah.

MAJLES: Legislature or parliament. Majles is the Persian form of the Arabic *majlis* (in Turkish, *meclis*), which is derived from the verb *jalasa* ("to sit"). It can mean a meeting, or sitting, in a number of senses, both private and public. In the public realm, it became the term used for legislatures in the Middle East and North Africa once these began to emerge in the nineteenth century. It can also refer to an appointed consultative body.

MALIK: "King" in Arabic. Malik derives from the Arabic verb *malaka* ("to own"). It has been used in the modern Arab world to mean king.

MA'PALIM: Illegal Jewish immigrants to Palestine. Ma'palim (Hebrew, "the daring ones") were Jewish immigrants who entered Palestine in violation of immigration quotas established by the British Mandate in Palestine, especially after the 1939 White Paper. The Zionist community in Palestine established the clandestine organization Mossad le-Aliyah Bet in 1938 to assist Jews fleeing Nazi persecution in Europe in reaching Palestine. British forces intercepted many maʿpalim and interned them in camps in Cyprus, including the 4,515 passengers aboard the ship *Exodus,* whose detainment in 1947 helped turn international sentiment against British rule in Palestine.

MENORAH: Hebrew word for the seven-branch candelabra, principal object of worship in the Jewish temple. Its shape was inspired by a plant known in antiquity under the name of moriah. When the first temple of Jerusalem was destroyed, the candelabra disappeared with all the other sacred objects.

MEZUZAH: Little case in wood or metal, containing a verse of the Torah, attached to the frame of the door to a house.

MIKVAH: Purifying bath, a practice of Orthodox Jews.

MINBAR: Pulpit in a mosque. In a mosque, the sermon (*khitab*) is delivered by the preacher (*khatib*) from a raised pulpit called a minbar, derived from the Arabic *nabara* ("to raise the voice"). See also "khatib."

MINHA: Hebrew word for "offering." Name of the Jewish afternoon prayer.

MINYAN: Hebrew word meaning "number." A quorum of ten adult males is required for Jewish public prayer.

MITNAGDI: Hebrew word used to designate a Jew who is opposed to the Hasidic movement.

MITZVA: Practical commandments of Judaism. According to tradition, the Torah contains 613 commandments, of which 248 are "positive" (obligations) and 365 are "negative" (interdictions).

MOSLEM See the dictionary entry "Muslim."

MUEZZIN: The one who calls Muslims to pray. A muezzin (Arabic: *muʾadhdhin*) calls the Muslim faithful to pray, usually from a minaret. The call to prayer must be in Arabic, even though most of the world's Muslims do not speak Arabic.

MUHARRAM: Name of the first month in the Islamic calendar. The first of Muharram is New Year's Day; the tenth of Muharram, the Feast of Ashura, commemorates at once the meeting of Adam and Eve, the end of the deluge, and the death of Husayn. Among the Shiʿa, Ashura is celebrated in distress, since they commemorate on this day only the death of Husayn. Before the Islamic epoch, the month of Muharram corresponded to a period of sacred repose. Concerning New Year's Day, the Iranians continue to celebrate the "Naw Rouz" (new light), the Sassanid New Year's Day, having survived the coming of Islam, which falls after the spring equinox, 21 March.

MUKHTAR: Chief or headman. Deriving from the Arabic word *khatara* ("to choose" or "select"), a mukhtar ("selected one") was an official appointed by the Ottoman authorities to serve as a go-between between the government and a tribe, village, or urban quarter. The function was part of the Ottomans' centralization efforts, efforts that included attempts to undercut traditional religious figures who had maintained levels of local influence. The position is still found in parts of the Arab world.

MULAI: Title and form of address. In Arabic, "my lord." Also mawlai, mawlay. A form of address formerly used when speaking to a king, sultan, or caliph. It is still used in Morocco when referring to the crown prince.

MUTASARRIF: Ottoman provincial official. A mutasarrif was the recipient of taxes from sub-provincial governorates in the Ottoman empire. By the late Ottoman era, the term denoted the government-appointed head of a governorate, or sanjak (also liwa). See also "liwa."

NARGHILA: Water pipe. A narghila (also called *arghila, qalyan,* and *shisha*) is a water pipe used in the Middle East and North Africa to smoke tobacco, usually flavored tobacco called *tombac.* They are commonly seen in all-male coffee houses.

NISSAN: Month of the Hebrew calendar, occurring between late March and early April. The holiday of Pesach (Passover) is celebrated from 15 to 21 Nissan. Yom ha-Shoah (Holocaust Remembrance Day), observed on 27 Nissan, is a national day of mourning in memory of Jews who died in the Holocaust during World War II.

OASIS: Watered area surrounded by desert. An oasis is a fertile area, watered by wells, that is found in the midst of a desert. They can be small or large.

PESH MERGA: Kurdish, "those who face death." Modern term used to denote armed Kurdish fighters. It first appeared during the Kurdish war against the Iraqi government that began in 1962.

QAʾID: Arabic for "leader." Arabic term denoting political leadership.

QAʾIMMAQAM: Ottoman provincial official. The term itself is Arabic, and was the title given by Ottoman authorities to the official appointed to head a subgovernorate called a kaza (also qada). See also "kaza," "liwa," and "vilayet." It was also used to denote a low ranking military officer.

QANAT: Canal. A qanat (also qana) can mean an underground water channel for irrigating fields, but can also denote a surface level canal, both small and large (such as the Suez Canal).

QAT: Plant with mildly stimulant effect. The leaves of the qat (also khat) plant, Catha edulis, are chewed in southwestern Arabia and eastern Africa for their mildly stimulant effect. Similar to the stimulant qualities of caffeine, qat is chewed in the company of others as an important form of social gathering. In this regard, gathering together to chew qat is akin to gathering in a coffee house to drink coffee or tea.

QIBLA: Direction of Islamic prayer. The qibla is the direction in which Muslims must pray. The first qibla was Jerusalem, but this was quickly changed in the seventh century to the direction of Mecca. Muslims around the globe all pray in the direction of Mecca.

QIRSH: Monetary unit. The Arabic word qirsh, and Turkish word ghurush or kuruş, is translated as piastre, itself the Italian name for the medieval peso duro. The qirsh was introduced into the Middle East in the early seventeenth century and became a unit of Ottoman currency equivalent to one-hundredth of a lira. It is still used as a small unit of currency in parts of the Middle East.

RABI AL-AWWAL: Name of the third month of the Muslim calendar. The 12th of this month is celebrated as the anniversary of the birth of the prophet Muhammad. In the Maghreb, this holiday is called *al-Mawled* (*Muled, Mulud*).

RABI AL-THANI: Name of the fourth month in the Muslim calendar.

RAJAB: Name of the seventh month of the Muslim calendar, during which, on the 27th, the Muslims commemorate the ascension of the prophet Muhammad. During this month, some believers also celebrate the birth of Zaynab, eldest daughter of the Prophet.

RAMADAN: Ninth month of the Islamic calendar, lasting twenty-nine or thirty days. Ramadan is a month of fasting, which is one of the five obligations of Islam, and so between sunrise and sunset the believer abstains from smoking; partaking of food or drink; telling lies, gossiping and engaging in other unethical behavior; and engaging in sex. At sunset everyone breaks the fast, usually in a large meal with family and friends (*iftar*). The end of the month of Ramadan is celebrated with a feast, the *'Id al-Fitr*. Between the 27 and 28 Ramadan falls the Night of Destiny (*lailat al-qadr*), when according to a widespread belief everyone's fate is decided. For some this date marks the first revelation of the Qur'an to Muhammad.

ROSH HA-SHANAH: (*Rosh Hashana*; head of the year, in Hebrew) Jewish New Year's Day, celebrated on the first and second days of the month of Tishri (September-October). This holiday, after which, for a period of ten days, every Jew shows penitence, is extended by the additional day of *Yom Kippur*. On the afternoon of the first day the *tashlih* occurs, a purification ceremony. In the Old Testament, Rosh ha-Shanah was called *Yom Teru'ah* (Day of the Trumpet), since the new moon on that day was announced by the sound of the shofar.

SAFAR: Name of the second month of the Islamic calendar.

SAYYID: Arabic word for "master," "lord," "chief," or "mister." Prior to the coming of Islam, sayyid (plural: sada or asyad) was used in Arabia to denote a tribal chief. After the coming of Islam, it assumed a particular meaning: descendants and certain relatives of the prophet Muhammad. The term sayyid thereafter came to denote the direct descendants of the Prophet through his two grandsons, Hasan and Husayn, the sons of the union of the Prophet's daughter, Fatima, and his son-in-law (and cousin), Ali. In some part of the Arab world, notably in the Hijaz region of Arabia and parts of the Fertile Crescent, sayyid came to denote those who were part of the lineage of Husayn, while the term *sharif* denoted those descendant from Hasan. Sayyids were held in high social esteem. However, the terms sayyid or sid (also, "sidi": "my lord") have also been used in a variety of Islamic societies as a form of address for holy men and religious figures. It also is the modern Arabic equivalent of "mister."

SEVEN SISTERS: Group of Western oil companies in the Middle East. The Seven Sisters were a cartel of Western oil companies that dominated the Middle Eastern oil industry from 1930–1970. They were: Standard Oil of New Jersey (Exxon), British Petroleum, Royal Dutch Shell, Chevron, Texaco, Mobil, and Gulf Oil. They increasingly lost power starting in the 1950s and 1960s as Middle Eastern countries began nationalizing their oil industries. With the merger of Chevron and Gulf in 1986, the number of "sisters" dropped to six, which remain important companies in the fields of oil refining and distribution.

SHAʿABAN: Name of the eighth month of the Islamic calendar. According to a belief dating back to the 10th century, for every Muslim, the night of 14–15 of this month is considered as the "night of destiny," in the course of which everyone finds out what the year to come has in store. Others think this "revelation" occurs on the night of 27–28 Ramadan.

SHAWAL: Tenth month of the Islamic calendar, following the month of Ramadan. On the 1st of this month Muslims celebrate the end of the fast (*Id el-Fitr*).

SHEVAT: Name of the fifth month of the Hebrew calendar, corresponding to the period between the end of January and the beginning of February.

SHUTTLE DIPLOMACY: Term denoting a diplomatic intermediary shuttling back and forth between countries in an effort to arrange an agreement among contending countries. The term was first raised to the level of public discourse to describe the efforts of American secretary of state Henry Kissinger to bring about a disengagement of forces after the October 1973 Arab–Israeli war. Kissinger had to shuttle back and forth between the capitals of Egypt, Syria, and Israel, carrying his proposals, because the parties could not agree to meet together.

SITT: Arabic for "lady." Sitt is often used in female royal titles.

SIVAN: Nine month of the Hebrew calendar, corresponding to the period between the end of May and the beginning of June. On 6 Sivan the holiday of the first fruits takes place (Shavuot).

TAMMUZ: Name of the tenth month of the Hebrew calendar, corresponding to the period between the end of June and the beginning of July.

TAQLID: Islamic legal term. In Sunni Islam, the term taqlid came to mean "deference" or "imitation," in the sense that religious jurisprudents were obliged to defer to the doctrinal precedents of their respective schools of law (the Shafiʿi, Hanbali, Hanafi, and Maliki schools). This, then, reduces the realm of individual interpretation (*ijtihad*). In Shiʿite Islam, however, the position of marja al-taqlid is quite different, and denotes an elite jurist who is spiritually empowered to employ *ijtihad.*

TARIQA: Sufi order or brotherhood. Tariqa is an Arabic word derived from the term meaning "the way." It is used to denote sufi mystical orders.

TELL: Hill or mound. The Arabic word *tall* means a hill, and is used to describe such geographical features. In archeological parlance, however, it refers to a mound containing ancient archeological remains. Finally, it also refers to a large region of North Africa from Morocco to Tunisia.

TEVET: Name of the fourth month of the Hebrew calendar, corresponding to the period between the end of December and the beginning of January.

THALWEG LINE: Maritime boundary. The thalweg principle of international law, whereby a river or some other body of water constitutes an international border, was most notably used in the Middle East in the case of the border between Iraq and Iran.

TISHRI: Name of the first month in the Hebrew calendar, corresponding to the period between the end of September and the beginning of October. On 1 and 2 Tishri the holiday of Rosh ha-Shana falls, on the 10th that of Yom Kippur, and on the 21st, Simhat Torah.

TISHRIN: Arabic term for the tenth and eleventh months of the Gregorian calendar. In the modern Arab world, Tishrin al-Awwal ("First Tishrin") refers to the Gregorian (Western) month of October, while Tishrin al-Thani ("Second Tishrin") refers to November. Some Arab countries, notably Saudi Arabia, do not use the Gregorian calendar but only the Islamic (hijri) calendar. It is also the name of a newspaper in Syria, named after the initial Arab victories in the October 1973 Arab-Israeli war.

TU B'SHVAT: Name of the Jewish holiday, called "of the trees," celebrated on 15 Shevat, month corresponding to the period between the end of January and the beginning of February.

TURKMEN: Turkic peoples in Turkmenistan, Iran, and Afghanistan. The Turkmen are speakers of Western Oghuz Turkic, and were originally pastoral nomads. They lived east of the Caspian Sea and west of the Amu Darya (Oxus) River. In addition, Turkmen minorities today reside in Iraq, Syria, and Turkey.

URF: Arabic customary law. Urf refers to largely unwritten tribal or customary codes that govern social relations, in contradistinction to Islamic law (*shariʿa*) or state legal codes (qanun).

USTADH: Arabic for "teacher" or "master." This term (also ostad or ustaz) is used to denote a teacher or professor, but can also be used as a polite form of address for any educated person.

Uzi: Type of Israeli firearm. The uzi is a short submachine gun designed by the Israeli army office Maj. Uziel Gal, after whom it is named.

Vali: Ottoman provincial governor. The term vali is the Turkish and Persian rendition of the Arabic *wali,* referring to someone who has been deputized to exercise authority. It meant "governor." The Mamluks assigned valis to their smallest administrative units, whereas in Iran and later in the Ottoman empire, a vali was the governor of the largest type of administrative unit. In the Ottoman empire, a vali was head of a *vilayet,* or province. See also "kaza," "liwa," and "vilayet."

Vilayet: Ottoman Turkish term for province. A vilayet, from the Arabic word *wilaya,* was the largest administrative unit within the Ottoman empire. See also "vali."

Vizier: Type of government official; "minister." Under the Ottomans, the vizier (Arabic: *wazir;* Turkish: *vezir*) served as a government minister. The vezir-i azam, or grand vizier, was the functional equivalent of a prime minister under the sultan. The Ottomans replaced the term with *vekil* (Arabic: *wakil*) in the 1830s, although *wazir* is still in use to denote a government minister in the Arab world.

Za'im: Arabic for "boss" or "leader." Usually used in an informal manner to denote a strong leader. It is also used as a military rank in some Arab countries.

Abbas, Mahmoud. *Through Secret Channels: The Road to Oslo.* Readings. Reading, UK: Garnet, 1995.

Abed, George T. *The Economic Viability of a Palestinian State.* Washington, DC: Institute for Palestine Studies, 1990.

Abu-Amr, Ziad. *Islamic Fundamentalism in the West Bank and Gaza: Muslim Brotherhood and Islamic Jihad.* Bloomington: University of Indiana Press, 1994.

AbuKhalil, Asʿad. *Bin Laden, Islam, and America's New "War on Terrorism."* New York: Seven Stories, 2002.

———. *Historical Dictionary of Lebanon.* Lanham, MD: Scarecrow Press, 1998.

———. "Lebanon." *Political Parties of the Middle East and North Africa,* edited by Frank Tachau. Westport, CT: Greenwood, 1994.

Aburish, Said K. *Arafat: From Defender to Dictator.* New York: Bloomsbury, 1998.

———. *Saddam Hussein: The Politics of Revenge.* New York: Bloomsbury, 2000.

Adelson, Roger. *London and the Invention of the Middle East: Money, Power, and War, 1902–1922.* New Haven, CT: Yale University Press, 1995.

Ahmed, Leila. *Women and Gender in Islam: Historical Roots of a Modern Debate.* New Haven, CT: Yale University Press, 1992.

Alexander, Yonah. "Popular Front for the Liberation of Palestine." *Palestinian Secular Terrorism.* Ardsley, NY: Transnational Publishers, 2003.

Algar, Hamid. "A Brief History of the Naqshbandi Order." In *Naqshbandis: Cheminements et situation actuelle d'un ordre mystique musulman,* edited by Marc Gaborieau, Alexandre Popovic, and Thierry Zarcone. Istanbul and Paris: Editions Isis, 1990.

Almog, Oz. *The Sabra: The Creation of the New Jew,* translated by Haim Watzman. Berkeley: University of California Press, 2000.

Alterman, Jon. *New Media, New Politics?: From Satellite Television to the Internet in the Arab World.* Washington, DC: Washington Institute for Near East Policy, 1998.

Amery, Hussein A., and Aaron T. Wolf, eds. *Water in the Middle East: A Geography of Peace.* Austin: University of Texas Press, 2000.

Anderson, Benedict. *Imagined Communities: Reflections on the Origin and Spread of Nationalism,* revised edition. London and New York: Verso, 1991.

Arian, Alan, and Michal Shamir. *The Elections in Israel, 1996.* Albany: State University of New York Press, 1999.

Arian, Asher. *The Second Republic: Politics in Israel.* Chatham, NJ: Chatham House, 1998.

Armstrong, Karen. *Jerusalem: One City, Three Faiths.* New York: Ballantine, 1997.

Arnow, David. "The Holocaust and the Birth of Israel: Reassessing the Causal Relationship." *Journal of Israeli History* 15, no. 3 (autumn 1994): 257–281.

Aronoff, Myron. *Israeli Visions and Division: Cultural Change and Political Conflict.* New Brunswick, NJ: Transaction Books, 1990.

Aronson, Geoffrey. *Israel, Palestinians, and the Intifada: Creating Facts in the West Bank.* London and New York: Kegan Paul, 1990.

Aronson, Shlomo. *The Politics and Strategy of Nuclear Weapons in the Middle East.* Albany: State University of New York Press, 1992.

Aruri, Naseer H. *The Obstruction of Peace: The United States, Israel, and the Palestinians.* Monroe, Maine: Common Courage, 1995.

Arzt, Donna E. *Refugees Into Citizens: Palestinians and the End of the Arab-Israeli Conflict.* New York: Council on Foreign Relations, 1997.

Ashrari, Hanan. *This Side of Peace: A Personal Account.* New York: Simon and Schuster, 1995.

Avruch, Kevin, and Walter P. Zenner, eds. *Critical Essays on Israeli Society, Religion and Government.* Albany: State University of New York Press, 1997.

Awaisi, Abdal-Fattyah Muhammad al-. *The Muslim Brothers and the Palestine Question, 1928–1947.* New York: I. B. Tauris, 1998.

Baker, Raymond William. *Sadat and After: Struggles for Egypt's Political Soul.* Cambridge, MA: Harvard University Press, 1990.

Bar-On, Mordechai. *The Gates of Gaza: Israel's Road to Suez and Back, 1955–1957.* New York: St. Martin's Press, 1994.

———. *In Pursuit of Peace: A History of the Israeli Peace Movement.* Washington, DC: U.S. Institute of Peace, 1996.

Bar-Siman-Tov, Yaacov. *Israel and the Peace Process, 1977–1982: In Search of Legitimacy for Peace.* Albany: State University of New York Press, 1994.

Bass, Warren. *Support Any Friend: Kennedy's Middle East and the Making of the U.S.-Israel Alliance.* Oxford and New York: Oxford University Press, 2004.

Beaumont, Peter. "Water Policies for the Middle East in the Twenty-first Century: The New Economic Realities." *International Journal of Water Resources Development* 18, no. 2 (2002): 315–334.

Beinin, Joel, and Joe Stork. *Political Islam: Essays from Middle East Report.* Berkeley: University of California Press, 1997.

Ben-Eliezer, Uri. *The Making of Israeli Militarism.* Bloomington: Indiana University Press, 1998.

Ben-Rafael, Eliezer, and S. Sharot. *Ethnicity, Religion and Class in Israeli Society.* Cambridge and New York: Cambridge University Press, 1991.

Ben-Rafael, Eliezer. *Crisis and Transformation: The Kibbutz at Century's End.* Albany: State University of New York Press, 1997.

———. *Jewish Identities: Fifty Intellectuals Answer Ben-Gurion.* Leiden, Netherlands: Brill, 2002.

Benvenisti, Meron. *City of Stone: The Hidden History of Jerusalem.* Berkeley: University of California Press, 1997.

Ben-Yehuda, Nachman. *The Masada Myth: Collective Memory and Mythmaking in Israel.* Madison: The University of Wisconsin Press, 1995.

Berg, Nancy E. "Transit Camp Literature: Literature of Transition." In *Critical Essay on Israeli Society, Religion, and Government: Books on Israel,* Vol. 4, edited by Kevin Avruch and Walter P. Zenner. Albany: State University of New York Press, 1997.

Berkowitz, Michael. *Western Jewry and the Zionist Project, 1914–1933.* New York: Cambridge University Press, 1997.

Bickerton, Ian J., and Carla L. Klauser. *A Concise History of the Arab-Israeli Conflict.* 2d ed. Englewood Cliffs, NJ: Prentice-Hall, 1995.

Binur, Yoram. *My Enemy, My Self.* New York: Penguin, 1990.

Black, Ian, and Benny Morris. *Israel's Secret Wars: A History of Israel's Intelligence Services.* New York: Grove Press, 1991.

Bohn, Michael K. *The Achille Lauro Hijacking: Lessons in the Politics and Prejudice of Terrorism.* Dulles, VA: Brassey's, 1999.

Bose, Meena, and Rosanna Perotti, eds. *From Cold War to New World Order: The Foreign Policy of George H. W. Bush.* Westport, CT: Greenwood, 2002.

Boyd, Douglas A. *Broadcasting in the Arab World: A Survey of the Electronic Media in the Middle East,* 3d edition. Ames: Iowa State University Press, 1999.

Brentjes, Burchard. *The Armenians, Assyrians, and Kurds: Three Nations, One Fate?* Campbell, CA: Rishi, 1997.

Brom, Shlomo, and Yiftah Shapir, eds. *The Middle East Military Balance, 2001–2002.* Cambridge, MA, and London.: MIT Press, 2002.

Brooks, David B., and Ozay Mehmet, eds. *Water Balances in the Eastern Mediterranean.* Ottawa: International Development Research Centre, 2000.

Brown, Nathan. *Palestinian Politics after the Oslo Accords: Resuming Arab Palestine.* Berkeley: University of California Press, 2003.

Brynen, Rex. *Sanctuary and Survival: The PLO in Lebanon.* Boulder, CO.: Westview Press, 1990.

Brynen, Rex; Bahgat Korany; and Paul Noble, eds. *Political Liberalization and Democratization in the Arab World,* 2 volumes. Boulder, CO: Lynne Rienner, 1995.

Burdett, Anita, ed. *The Arab League: British Documentary Sources, 1943–1963.* Slough, UK: Archive Editions, 1995.

Burrows, William E., and Robert Windrem. *Critical Mass: The Dangerous Race for Superweapons in a Fragmenting World.* New York: Simon and Schuster, 1994.

Caplan, Neil. *Futile Diplomacy,* Vol. 4: *Operation Alpha and the Failure of Anglo-American Coercive Diplomacy in the Arab-Israeli conflict, 1954–1956.* Totowa, NJ; London: Frank Cass, 1997.

Carey, Roane. *The New Intifada: Resisting Israel's Apartheid.* London: Verso, 2001.

Carroll, James. *Constantine's Sword: The Church and the Jews, a History.* Boston: Houghton Mifflin, 2002.

Caspi, Dan, and Yehiel Limor. *The In/Outsiders: The Mass Media in Israel.* Cresskill, NJ: Hampton Press, 1999.

Cassese, Antonio. *Terrorism, Politics, and Law: The Achille Lauro Affair.* Princeton, NJ: Princeton Univ. Press, 1989.

Chomsky, Noam. *The Fateful Triangle: The U.S., Israel and the Palestinians.* 2d ed. Boston: South End, 1999.

Choueiri, Youssef M. *Arab Nationalism: A History: Nation and State in the Arab World.* Oxford and Malden, MA: Blackwell, 2000.

Christison, Kathleen. *Perceptions of Palestine: Their Influence on U.S. Middle East Policy.* Berkeley: University of California Press, 1999.

Ciment, James. *Palestine/Israel: The Long Conflict.* New York: Facts on File, 1997.

Cobban, Helena. *The Israeli-Syrian Peace Talks, 1991–1996 and Beyond.* Washington, DC: Institute of Peace Press, 1999.

———. *The Palestinian Liberation Organisation: People, Power, and Politics.* Cambridge and New York: Cambridge University Press, 1984.

Cohen, Avner. *Israel and the Bomb.* New York: Columbia University Press, 1998.

Corbin, Jane. *The Norway Channel: The Secret Talks that Led to the Middle East Peace Accord.* New York: Atlantic Monthly Press, 1994.

Cubert, Harold. *The PFLP's Changing Role in the Middle East.* London: Frank Cass, 1997.

Davila, James R., ed. *The Dead Sea Scrolls as Background to Postbiblical Judaism and Early Christianity: Papers from an International Conference at St. Andrews in 2001.* Boston, MA: Brill, 2003.

Davis, Joyce M. *Martyrs: Innocence, Vengeance, and Despair in the Middle East.* New York: Palgrave, 2003.

Dawisha, Adeed. *Arab Nationalism in the Twentieth Century: From Triumph to Despair.* Princeton, NJ: Princeton University Press, 2003.

Deeb, Marius. *Syria's Terrorist War on Lebanon and the Peace Process.* New York: Palgrave Macmillan, 2003.

Diskin, Abraham. *The Last Days in Israel: Understanding the New Israeli Democracy.* London: Frank Cass, 2003.

Divine, Donna Robinson. *Politics and Society in Ottoman Palestine: The Arab Struggle for Survival.* Boulder, CO: Rienner, 1994.

Doumain, Beshara. *Rediscovering Palestine: Merchants and Peasants in Jabal Nablus, 1700–1900.* Berkeley: University of California Press, 1995.

Dowty, Alan. *The Jewish State: A Century Later.* Berkeley: University of California Press, 2001.

Drezon-Tepler, Marcia. *Interest Groups and Political Change in Israel.* Albany: State University of New York Press, 1990.

Dumper, Michael. *Islam and Israel: Muslim Religious Endowments and the Jewish State.* Washington, DC: Institute for Palestine Studies, 1994.

———. *The Politics of Sacred Space: The Old City of Jerusalem in the Middle East Conflict.* Boulder, CO: Lynne Rienner Publishers, 2002.

Dupuy, Trevor N. *Elusive Victory: The Arab-Israeli Wars, 1947–1974,* 3d edition. Dubuque, IA: Kendall/Hunt, 1992.

Eban, Abba. *Personal Witness: Israel through My Eyes.* New York: Putnam, 1992.

Eisenberg, Laura Zittrain, and Neil Caplan. *Negotiating Arab–Israeli Peace: Patterns, Problems, and Possibilities.* Bloomington: Indiana University Press, 1998.

Elad-Bouskila. *Modern Palestinian Literature and Culture.* London: Frank Cass, 1999.

Elmusa, Sharif S. *Water Conflict: Economics, Politics, Law, and the Palestian-Israeli Water Resources.* Washington, DC: Institute for Palestine Studies, 1997.

El-Nawawy, Mohammed, and Adel Iskander. *Al Jazeera: How the Free Arab News Network Scooped the World and Changed the Middle East.* Cambridge, MA: Westview Press, 2002.

Elon, Amos. *Herzl.* New York: Holt, Rinehart, 1975.

Enderlin, Charles. *Shamir.* Paris: Orban, 1991.

————. *Shattered Dreams: The Failure of the Peace Process in the Middle East, 1995–2002.* New York: Other Press, 2003.

Eshed, Haggai. *Reuven Shiloah: The Man behind the Mossad,* translated by David and Leah Zinder. London: Frank Cass, 1997.

Fahmy, Ninette. *The Politics of Egypt: State-Society Relationship.* New York; Routledge, 2002.

Falk, Richard. "Azmi Bishara, the Right of Resistance, and the Palestinian Ordeal." *Journal of Palestine Studies* 31, no. 2 (winter 2002): 19–33.

Farsoun, Samih K., and Christina Zachharia. *Palestine and the Palestinians.* Boulder, CO.: Westview Press, 1996.

Feiler, Gil. *From Boycott to Economic Cooperation: The Political Economy of the Arab Boycott of Israel.* London: Frank Cass, 1998.

Fernea, Elizabeth Warnock, and Hocking, Mary Evelyn, eds. *The Struggle for Peace: Israelis and Palestinians.* Austin: University of Texas Press, 1992.

Finlan, Alistair. *The Gulf War 1991.* New York: Routledge, 2003.

Firro, Kais. *The Druzes in the Jewish State.* Leiden, Neth.: Brill, 2001.

Fleischmann, Ellen L. "Selective Memory, Gender and Nationalism: Palestinian Women Leaders in the British Mandate Period," *History Workshop Journal* 47 (1999): 141–158.

Fraser, T. G. *The Arab-Israeli Conflict.* New York: St. Martin's, 1995.

Freedman, Lawrence, and Efraim Karsh. *The Gulf Conflict, 1990–1991: Diplomacy and War in the New World Order.* Princeton, NJ: Princeton University Press, 1993.

Friedland, Roger, and Richard Hecht. *To Rule Jerusalem.* Cambridge: Cambridge University Press, 1996.

Friedman, Robert I. *Zealots for Zion: Inside Israel's West Bank Settlement Movement.* New York: Random House, 1992; New Brunswick, NJ: Rutgers University Press, 1994.

Friedman, Thomas L. *From Beirut to Jerusalem.* New York: Farrar, Straus & Giroux, 1991.

Fry, Michael, and Miles Hochstein. "The Forgotten Middle East Crisis of 1957: Gaza and Sharm el Sheikh." *International History Review* 15 (1993): 46–83.

Gal, Allon. *David Ben-Gurion and the American Alignment for a Jewish State.* Bloomington: Indiana University Press, 1991.

Gawyrch, George W. *The Albatross of Decisive Victory: War and Policy Between Egypt and Israel in the 1967 and 1973 Arab-Israeli Wars.* Westport, CT: Greenwood Press, 2000.

Geddes, Charles L., ed. *A Documentary History of the Arab-Israeli Conflict.* New York: Praeger, 1991.

Gerner, Deborah J. *One Land, Two Peoples: The Conflict over Palestine,* 2d edition. Boulder, CO: Westview Press, 1994.

Gilbert, Martin, ed. *The Illustrated Atlas of Jewish Civilization: 4,000 Years of Jewish History.* New York: Macmillan, 1990.

————. *Israel: A History.* New York: Morrow, 1998.

Glock, Albert. "Archaeology." In *Encyclopedia of the Palestinians,* edited by Philip Mattar. New York: Facts On File, 2000.

Glubb, John Bagot. *The Changing Scenes of Life: An Autobiography.* London: Quartet, 1983.

Golani, Motti. *Israel in Search of A War: The Sinai Campaign, 1955–1956.* Brighton and Portland, OR: Sussex Academic Press, 1998.

Goldberg, Harvey E., ed. *Sephardi and Middle Eastern Jewries: History and Culture in the Modern Era.* Bloomington: Indiana University Press, 1996.

Goldschmidt, Arthur, Jr. *A Concise History of the Middle East,* 4th edition. Boulder, CO: Westview Press, 1991.

Gollaher, David L. *Circumcision: A History of the World's Most Controversial Surgery.* New York: Basic Books, 2000.

Gordon, Haim, ed. *Looking Back at the June 1967 War.* Westport, CT: Praeger, 1999.

Gorman, Anthony. *Historians, State and Politics in Twentieth Century Egypt: Contesting the Nation.* London and New York: Routledge Curzon, 2003.

Government of Palestine. *A Survey of Palestine for the Information of the Anglo-American Committee of Inquiry* (1946), 2 vols. Washington, DC: Institute for Palestine Studies, 1991.

Gowers, Andrew, and Tony Walker. *Behind the Myth: Yasser Arafat and the Palestinian Revolution.* London: W. H. Allen, 1990.

Greilsammer, Ilan. "The Religious Parties." In *Israel's Odd Couple: The 1984 Knesset Elections and the National Unity Government,* edited by Daniel J. Elazar and Shmuel Sandler. Detroit: Wayne State University Press, 1990.

Grossman, David. *Sleeping on a Wire: Conversations with Palestinians in Israel.* New York: Farrar, Straus & Giroux, 1993.

Haddadin, Munther J. *Diplomacy on the Jordan: International Conflict and Negotiated Resolution.* Boston: Kluwer Academic Publishers, 2001.

Haidar, Aziz. *Education, Empowerment and Control: The Case of the Arabs in Israel.* Albany: State University of New York Press, 1994.

Halamish, Aviva. *The Exodus Affair: Holocaust Survivors and the Struggle for Palestine,* translated by Ora Cummings. Syracuse, NY: Syracuse University Press, 1998.

Halper, Jeff. *Between Redemption and Revival: The Jewish Yishuv of Jerusalem in the Nineteenth Century.* Boulder, CO: Westview Press, 1991.

Halpern, Ben, and Reinharz, Jehuda. *Zionism and the Creation of a New Society.* New York: Oxford University Press, 1998.

Hart, Alan. *Arafat: A Political Biography.* Bloomington: Indiana University Press, 1989.

Hatina, Meir. *Islam and Salvation in Palestine: The Islamic Jihad Movement.* Tel Aviv: Tel Aviv University, 2001.

Hazan, Reuven. *Reforming Parliamentary Committees: Israel in Comparative Perspective.* Columbus, OH: Ohio State University, 2001.

Heiberg, Marianne, and Geir Ovensen. *Palestinian Society in Gaza, West Bank and Arab Jerusalem: A Survey of Living Conditions.* Oslo, Norway: FAFO Institute for Applied Social Science), 1993.

Heilman, Samuel C. *Defenders of the Faith: Inside Ultra-Orthodox Jewry.* New York: Schocken, 1992.

Heller, Joseph. *The Birth of Israel, 1945–1949: Ben-Gurion and His Critics.* Gainesville: University Press of Florida, 2000.

———. *The Stern Gang: Ideology, Politics, and Terror, 1940–1949.* Portland, OR, and London: Frank Cass, 1995.

Herb, Michael. *All in the Family: Absolutism, Revolution, and Monarchy in the Middle Eastern Monarchies.* Albany: State University of New York Press, 1999.

Hersh, Seymour. *The Samson Option: Israel's Nuclear Arsenal and American Foreign Policy.* New York: Random House, 1991.

Hertzberg, Arthur, ed. *The Zionist Idea: A Historical Analysis and Reader.* Philadelphia: Jewish Publication Society, 1997.

Herzog, Chaim. *Living History: A Memoir.* London: Weidenfeld and Nicolson, 1997.

Hetzron, Robert, ed. *The Semitic Languages.* New York: Routledge, 1998.

Hilal, Jamil. "PLO Institutions: The Challenge Ahead." *Journal of Palestine Studies* 89 (1993): 46–60.

Hiro, Dilip. *Sharing the Promised Land: A Tale of the Israelis and Palestinians.* New York: Olive Branch, 1999.

Hitti, Philip K. *History of the Arabs: From the Earliest Times to the Present,* revised 10th edition. New York: Palgrave Macmillan, 2002.

Hourani, Albert. *History of the Arab Peoples.* Cambridge, MA: Belknap Press of Harvard University, 2002.

Hroub, Khaled. *Hamas: Political Thought and Practice.* Washington, DC: Institute for Palestine Studies, 2000.

Ilan, Amitzur. *Bernadotte in Palestine: A Study in Contemporary Humanitarian Knight-Errantry.* London: Macmillan, 1989.

———. *The Origin of the Arab-Israeli Arms Race: Arms, Embargo, Military Power and Decision in the 1948 Palestine War.* New York: New York University Press; London: Macmillan, 1996.

Inbar, Efraim. *Rabin and Israel's National Security.* Washington, DC: Woodrow Wilson Center

Press; Baltimore, MD: Johns Hopkins University Press, 1999.

Institute for Palestine Studies. *The Palestinian-Israeli Peace Agreement: A Documentary Record.* Washington, DC: Institute for Palestine Studies, 1994.

———. *United Nations Resolutions on Palestine and the Arab-Israeli Conflict, 1947–1998.* 4 vols. Washington, DC: Institute for Palestine Studies, 1988-99.

Jaimoukha, Amjad. *The Circassians: A Handbook.* New York: Palgrave, 2001.

Jankowski, James. *Nasser's Egypt, Arab Nationalism, and the United Arab Republic.* Boulder, CO: Lynne Rienner Publishers, 2002.

Jayyusi, Salma Khadra, ed. *Anthology of Modern Palestinian Literature.* New York: Columbia University Press, 1992.

Jumayyil, Amin. *Rebuilding Lebanon's Future.* Lanham, MD: University Press of America, 1992.

Kaikobad, Kaiyan Homi. *The Shatt-al-Arab Boundary Question: A Legal Reappraisal.* New York: Oxford University Press; Oxford: Clarendon Press, 1988.

Kamali, Mohammad Hashim. *Principles of Islamic Jurisprudence.* Cambridge: Islamic Texts Society, 1991.

Kamalipour, Yahya R, and Hamid Mowlana, eds. *Mass Media in the Middle East: A Comprehensive Handbook.* Westport, CT: Greenwood Press, 1994.

———. *Mass Media in the Middle East.* Westport, CT: Greenwood Press, 1994.

Kaminer, Reuven. *The Politics of Protest: The Israeli Peace Movement and the Palestinian Intifada.* Brighton, UK: Sussex Academic Press, 1996.

Kark, Ruth. *Jaffa: A City in Evolution, 1799–1917,* translated by Gila Brand. Jerusalem: Yad Izhak Ben-Zvi Press, 1990.

Katz, Yossi. *Partner to Partition: The Jewish Agency's Partition Plan in the Mandate Era.* London and Portland, OR: Frank Cass, 1998.

Kawar, Amal. *Daughters of Palestine: Leading Women of the Palestinian National Movement.* Albany: State University of New York Press, 1996.

Kennedy, Valerie. *Edward Said: A Critical Introduction.* Malden, MA: Blackwell; Cambridge: Polity Press, 2000.

Khalaf, Issa. *Politics in Palestine: Arab Factionalism and Social Disintegration, 1939–1948.* Albany: State University of New York Press, 1991.

Khalidi, Rashid. *Palestinian Identity: The Construction of Modern National Consciousness.* New York: Columbia University Press, 1997.

Khalidi, Rashid; Lisa Anderson; Muhammad Muslih; et al., eds. *The Origins of Arab Nationalism.* New York: Columbia University Press, 1991.

Khan, Saira. *Nuclear Proliferation Dynamics in Protracted Conflict Regions: A Comparative Study of South Asia and the Middle East.* Aldershot, UK, and Burlington, VT: Ashgate, 2002.

Kimche, David. *The Last Option: After Nasser, Arafat, and Saddam Hussein—The Quest for Peace in the Middle East.* New York: Charles Scribner's Sons; Maxwell Macmillan International, 1991.

Kimmerling, Baruch, and Joel S. Migdal. *Palestinians: The Making of a People.* New York: Free Press, 1993.

———. *The Palestinian People: A History.* Cambridge, MA: Harvard University Press, 2003.

Kolars, John. "The Spatial Attributes of Water Negotiation: The Need for a River Ethic and River Advocacy in the Middle East." In *Water in the Middle East: A Geography of Peace,* edited by Hussein A. Amery and Aaron T. Wolf. Austin: University of Texas Press, 2000.

Kurzman, Dan. *Soldier of Peace: The Life of Yitzhak Rabin, 1922–1995.* New York: HarperCollins, 1998.

Kyle, Keith. *Suez.* London: Weidenfeld and Nicolson, 1991.

Landau, David. *Who Is a Jew? A Case Study of American Jewish Influence on Israeli Policy.* New York: American Jewish Committee, Institute on American Jewish-Israel Relations, 1996.

Lahav, Pnina. *Judgment in Jerusalem: Chief Justice Simon Agranat and the Zionist Century.* Berkeley: University of California Press, 1997.

Lapidus, Ira M. *A History of Islamic Societies,* 2d edition. Cambridge and New York: Cambridge University Press, 2002.

Laqueur, Walter, and Barry Rubin, eds. *The Israel-Arab Reader: A Documentary History of the Middle East Conflict,* 6th revised edition. New York and London, Penguin Books, 2001.

Laqueur, Walter, and Judith Tydor Baumel, eds. *The Holocaust Encyclopedia.* New Haven: Yale University Press, 2001.

Laskier, Michael M. *Israel and the Maghreb: From Statehood to Oslo.* Gainesville: University Press of Florida, 2004.

Lesch, Ann Mosely. *Transition to Palestinian Self-Government: Practical Steps toward Israeli-Palestinian Peace.* Bloomington: Indiana University Press, 1992.

Lesch, Ann Mosley, and Dan Tschirgi. *Origins and Development of the Arab-Israeli Conflict.* Westport, CT: Greenwood Press, 1998.

Lesch, David W., ed. *The Middle East and the United States: A Historical and Political Reassessment,* 3d edition. Boulder, CO: Westview, 2003.

Livingstone, Neil C., and David Halevy. *Inside the PLO: Covert Units, Secret Funds, and the War against Israel and the United States.* New York: Morrow, 1990.

Lorch, Netanel. *Shield of Zion: The Israeli Defense Forces.* Charlottesville, VA: Howell Press, 1991.

Lockman, Zachary. *Comrades and Enemies: Arab and Jewish Workers in Palestine, 1906–1948.* Berkeley: University of California Press, 1996.

Lowi, Miriam. *Water and Power: The Politics of a Scarce Resource in the Jordan River Basin.* Cambridge and New York: Cambridge University Press, 1993.

Lucas, W. Scott. *Divided We Stand: Britain, the US, and the Suez Crisis.* London: Hodder & Stoughton, 1991.

Lukacs, Yehuda, ed. *The Israeli-Palestinian Conflict: A Documentary Record, 1967–1990.* Cambridge: Cambridge University Press, 1992.

Lunt, James. *Glubb Pasha: A Biography.* London: Harvill, 1984.

Lustick, Ian S. *For the Land and the Lord: Jewish Fundamentalism in Israel.* New York: Council on Foreign Relations, 1988.

———. *Arab-Israeli Relations: A Collection of Contending Perspectives and Recent Research.* 10 vols. Hamden, Conn.: Garland, 1994.

Luz, Ehud. *Parallels Meet: Religion and Nationalism in the Early Zionist Movement, 1882–1904,* translated by Lenn J. Schramm. Philadelphia: Jewish Publication Society, 1988.

Ma'oz, Moshe, and Gabriel Sheffer, eds. *Middle Eastern Minorities and Diasporas.* Brighton, UK: Sussex Academic Press, 2002.

MacDonald, Eileen. *Shoot the Women First.* New York: Random House, 1991.

Magnes, Judah Leon. *The Magnes-Philby Negotiations, 1929: The Historical Record.* Jerusalem: Magnes Press, Hebrew University, 1998.

Mahler, Gregory S. *Politics and Government in Israel: The Maturation of a Modern State.* Boulder, CO: Rowman and Littlefield, 2004.

Makovsky, David. *Making Peace with the PLO: The Rabin Government's Road to the Oslo Accord.* Boulder, CO: Westview Press, 1996.

Marr, Phebe. "The Iran-Iraq War: The View from Iraq." In *The Persian Gulf War: Lessons for Strategy, Law, and Diplomacy,* edited by Christopher C. Joyner. Westport, CT: Greenwood Press, 1990.

Massad, Joseph A. *Colonial Effects: The Making of National Identity in Jordan.* New York: Columbia University Press, 2001.

Masud, Muhammad Khalid; Brinkley Messick; and David S. Powers, eds. *Islamic Legal Interpretation: Muftis and Their Fatwas.* Cambridge, MA: Harvard University Press, 1996.

Mattar, Philip. "The PLO and the Gulf Crisis." *Middle East Journal* 48, no. 1 (winter 1994): 31–46.

The Mufti of Jerusalem: Al-Hajj Amin al-Husayni and the Palestinian National Movement, revised edition. New York: Columbia University Press, 1992.

McCarthy, Justin. *The Population of Palestine: Population History and Statistics of the Late Ottoman Period and the Mandate.* New York: Columbia University Press, 1990.

McGowan, Daniel, and Marc H. Ellis, eds. *Remembering Deir Yassin: The Future of Israel and Palestine.* Brooklyn, NY: Olive Branch Press, 1998.

Medoff, Rafael, and Chaim I. Waxman. *Historical Dictionary of Zionism.* Lanham, MD: Scarecrow Press, 2000.

Mernissi, Fatima. *The Veil and the Male Elite: A Feminist Interpretation of Women's Rights in Islam.* Reading, MA: Addison-Wesley, 1991.

Meyers, Eric M., ed. *Galilee through the Centuries: Confluence of Cultures.* Duke Judaic Studies Series, vol. 1. Winona Lake, IN: Eisenbrauns, 1999.

Miller, Anita; Jordan Miller; and Sigalit Zetouni. *Sharon: Israel's Warrior-Politician.* Chicago: Academy Chicago, Olive, 2002.

Mintz, Jerome R. *Hasidic People: A Place in the New World.* Cambridge, MA: Harvard University Press, 1992.

Mishal, Shaul, and Avraham Sela. *The Palestinian Hamas: Vision, Violence, and Coexistence.* New York: Columbia University Press, 2000.

Mitchell, John, et al. *The New Economy of Oil: Impacts on Business, Geopolitics, and Society.* London: Earthscan, 2001.

Momen, Moojan. *An Introduction to Shi'i Islam: The History and Doctrines of Twelver Shi'ism.* New Haven, CT: Yale University Press, 1985.

Moosa, Matti. *The Maronites in History.* Syracuse, NY: Syracuse University Press, 1986.

Morris, Benny. *Israel's Border Wars, 1949–1956: Arab Infiltration, Israeli Retaliation, and the Countdown to the Suez War.* Oxford: Clarendon Press, 1993.

————. *Righteous Victims: A History of the Zionist–Arab Conflict, 1881–1999.* New York: Alfred A. Knopf, 1999.

Moussalli, Ahmad. *Historical Dictionary of Islamic Fundamentalist Movements in the Arab World, Iran, and Turkey.* Lanham, MD: Scarecrow Press, 1999.

Moderate and Radical Islamic Fundamentalism: The Quest for Modernity, Legitimacy, and the Islamic State. Gainesville: University of Florida Press, 1999.

Munthe, Turi, ed. *The Saddam Hussein Reader.* New York: Thunder's Mouth Press, 2002.

Muslih, Muhammad Y. *The Origins of Palestinian Nationalism.* New York: Columbia University Press, 1988.

Mutahhari, Morteza. *Jihad: the Holy War in Islam and the Legitimacy in the Qur'an,* translated by Mohammad Salman Tawhidi. Tehran, Iran: Islamic Propagation Organization, 1998.

Nashashibi, Nasser Eddin. *Jerusalem's Other Voice: Ragheb Nashashibi and Moderation in Palestinian Politics, 1920–1948.* Exeter, UK: Ithaca, 1990.

Nassar, Jamal R. *The Palestine Liberation Organization: From Armed Struggle to the Declaration of Independence.* New York: Praeger Publishers, 1991.

Neff, Donald. *Fallen Pillars: U.S. Policy towards Palestine and Israel.* Washington, DC: Institute for Palestine Studies, 1995.

Netanyahu, Benjamin. *A Place Among the Nations: Israel and the World.* New York: Bantam Books, 1993.

Newman, D. "Boundaries in Flux: The Green Line Boundary between Israel and the West Bank." *Boundary and Territory Briefing* 1, no. 7 (1995).

Newman, David, ed. *The Impact of Gush Emunim: Politics and Settlement in the West Bank.* New York: St. Martin's Press, 1985.

Newman, David. *Population, Settlement and Conflict: Israel and the West Bank.* Update Series in Contemporary Geographical Issues. New York: Cambridge University Press, 1991.

Oren, Michael B. *Six Days of War: June 1967 and the Making of the Modern Middle East.* New York: Ballantine, 2003.

Pappé, Illan. *The Israel-Palestine Question.* London: Routledge, 1999.

Parker, Richard B., ed. *The Six-Day War: A Retrospective.* Gainesville: University Press of Florida, 1996.

Peres, Shimon. *Battling for Peace: A Memoir.* New York: Random House, 1995.

Peres, Shimon, and Robert Littell. *For the Future of Israel.* Baltimore, MD: Johns Hopkins University Press, 1998.

Peretz, Don. *Intifada: The Palestinian Uprising.* Boulder, CO: Westview Press, 1990.

————. *Palestinians, Refugees, and the Middle East Peace Process.* Washington, DC: United States Institute of Peace Press, 1993.

Peters, F. E. *Mecca: A Literary History of the Muslim Holy City.* Princeton, NJ: Princeton University Press, 1994.

————. *The Hajj: The Muslim Pilgrimage to Mecca and the Holy Places.* Princeton, NJ: Princeton University Press, 1994.

Peterson, Erik R. *The Gulf Cooperation Council: Search for Unity in a Dynamic Region.* Boulder, CO: Westview Press, 1988.

Postel, Sandra. *Pillar of Sand: Can the Irrigation Miracle Last?* New York: Norton, 1999.

Quandt, William B. *Peace Process: American Diplomacy and the Arab-Israeli Conflict Since 1967,* revised edition. Berkeley, CA: Brookings Institution Press, 2001.

Rabin, Leah. *Rabin: Our Life, His Legacy.* New York: Putnam, 1997.

Rabinovich, Itamar. *The Brink of Peace: Israel and Syria, 1992–1996.* Princeton, NJ: Princeton University Press, 1998.

Ranstorp, Magnus. *Hizb'allah in Lebanon: The Politics of the Western Hostage Crisis.* New York: Palgrave Macmillan, 1997.

Raswamy, P. R. Kuma, ed. *Revisiting the Yom Kippur War.* London and Portland, OR: Frank Cass, 2000.

Raviv, Dan, and Yossi Melman. *Every Spy a Prince: The Complete History of Israel's Intelligence Community.* Boston: Houghton Mifflin, 1990.

Rebhun, Uzi, and Chaim I. Waxman, eds. *Jews in Israel: Contemporary Social and Cultural Patterns.* Hanover, NH: University Press of New England/Brandeis University Press, 2004.

Reeve, Simon. *One Day in September: The Full Story of the 1972 Munich Olympics Massacre and the Israeli Revenge Operation "Wrath of God."* New York: Arcade Books, 2001.

Reinhart, Tanya. *Israel/Palestine: How to End the War of 1948.* New York: Seven Stories Press, 2002.

Reiter, Yitzhak. *Islamic Endowments in Jerusalem under British Mandate.* London: Frank Cass, 1996.

Rogan, Eugene L., and Avi Shlaim, eds. *The War for Palestine: Rewriting the History of 1948.* New York: Cambridge University Press, 2001.

Rogers, Peter, and Peter Lydon, eds. *Water in the Arab World: Perspectives and Prognoses.* Cambridge, MA: Division of Applied Sciences, Harvard University, 1994.

Rolef, Susan Hattis, ed. *Political Dictionary of the State of Israel,* 2d edition. New York: Macmillan, 1993.

Ron, James. *Frontiers and Ghettos: State Violence in Serbia and Israel.* Berkeley: University of California Press, 2003.

Ross, Dennis. *The Missing Peace: The Inside Story of the Fight for Middle East Peace.* New York: Farrar, Straus & Giroux, 2004.

Rossoff, Dovid. *Safed: The Mystical City.* Spring Valley, NY, 1991.

Rouhana, Nadim. *Palestinian Citizens in an Ethnic Jewish State.* New Haven, Conn.: Yale University Press, 1997.

Rouyer, Alwyn R. *Turning Water into Politics: The Water Issue in the Palestinian-Israeli Conflict.* New York: St. Martin's Press, 1999.

Roy, Sara. *The Gaza Strip: The Political Economy of De-Development,* 2d edition. Washington, DC: Institute for Palestine Studies, 2001.

Rubin, Barry. *Revolution until Victory? The Politics and History of the PLO.* Cambridge, MA: Harvard University Press, 1994.

Rubinstein, Amnon. *From Herzl to Rabin: The Changing Image of Zionism.* New York: Holmes and Meier, 2000.

Rubenstein, Danny. *The People of Nowhere: The Palestinian Vision of Home.* New York: Times Books, 1991.

Saad-Ghorayeb, Amal. *Hizbullah: Politics and Religion.* London: Pluto Press, 2002.

Sachar, Howard M. *A History of Israel: From the Rise of Zionism to Our Time,* 2d edition. New York: Knopf, 1996.

Said, Edward. *Edward Said: A Critical Reader,* edited by Michael Sprinker. Cambridge, MA, and Oxford, UK: Blackwell, 1992.

———. *End of the Peace Process: Oslo and After.* New York: Pantheon, 2000.

Sakr, Naomi. *Satellite Realms: Transnational Television, Globalization and the Middle East.* New York and London: I. B. Taurus, 2001.

Savir, Uri. *The Process: 1,100 Days that Changed the Middle East.* New York: Vintage, 1999.

Sayigh, Yezid. *Armed Struggle and the Search for State: The Palestinian National Movement, 1949–1993.* Oxford: Clarendon Press, 1997.

Schiff, Benjamin N. *Refugees unto the Third Generation: UN Aid to Palestinians.* Syracuse, NY: Syracuse University Press, 1995.

Schiff, Ze>ev, and Ehud Ya'ari. *Intifada: The Palestinian Uprising—Israel's Third Front.* New York: Simon and Schuster, 1990.

Schumacher, Gottlieb. *The Golan: Survey, Description and Mapping.* Jerusalem, 1998.

Seale, Patrick. *Abu Nidal: A Gun for Hire.* New York: Random House, 1992.

———. *Asad: The Struggle for the Middle East.* Berkeley: University of California Press, 1995.

Segev, Tom. *One Palestine, Complete: Jews and Arabs under the Mandate,* translated by Haim Watzman. New York: Metropolitan Books, 2000.

Seikaly, May. *Transformation of an Arab Society, 1918–1939.* New York: St. Martin's Press, 1995.

Selim, Mohammad El Sayed, ed. *The Organization of the Islamic Conference in a Changing World.* Giza, Egypt: Center for Political Research and Studies, Cairo University, 1994.

Shafir, Gershon. *Land, Labor and the Origins of the Israeli–Palestinian Conflict, 1882–1914,* revised edition. Berkeley: University of California Press, 1996.

Shafir, Gershon, and Yoav Peled. *Being Israeli: The Dynamics of Multiple Citizenship.* Cambridge, UK, and New York: Cambridge University Press, 2002.

Shapira, Anita. *Land and Power: The Zionist Resort to Force, 1881–1948.* Stanford, CA: Stanford University Press, 1999.

Shapland, Greg. *Rivers of Discord: International Water Disputes in the Middle East.* New York: St. Martin's Press; London: Hurst, 1997.

Sharkansky, Ira. *The Politics of Religion and the Religion of Politics: Looking at Israel.* Lanham, MD: Lexington Books, 2000.

Sharon, Ariel (with David Chanoff). *Warrior: The Autobiography of Ariel Sharon,* 2d Touchstone edition. New York: Simon & Schuster, 2001.

Sharoni, Simona. *Gender and the Israel-Palestinian Conflict: The Politics of Women's Resistance.* Syracuse, N.Y.: Syracuse University Press, 1995.

Shavit, Yaacov. *Jabotinsky and the Revisionist Movement, 1925–1948.* Totowa, NJ; London: Frank Cass, 1988.

Shemess, Moshe. *The Palestinian Entity, 1959–1974: Arab Politics and the PLO.* 2d ed. London: Frank Cass, 1996.

Shimoni, Gideon. *The Zionist Ideology.* Hanover, NH: Brandeis University Press/University Press of New England, 1995.

Shlaim, Avi. *Collusion across the Jordan: King Abdullah, the Zionist Movement, and the Partition of Palestine.* New York: Columbia University Press, 1988.

———. "The Rise and Fall of the All-Palestine Government in Gaza." *Journal of Palestine Studies* 20, no. 1 (autumn 1990).

———. *The Iron Wall: Israel and the Arab World since 1948.* New York: W. W. Norton, 1999.

Shlonsky, Ur. *Clause Structure and Word Order in Hebrew and Arabic: An Essay in Comparative Semitic Syntax.* New York: Oxford University Press, 1997.

Shultz, George P. *Turmoil and Triumph: My Years As Secretary of State.* New York: Scribner's, 1993.

Sifry, Micah L., and Christopher Cerf, eds. *The Gulf War Reader: History, Documents, Opinions.* New York: Times Books, 1991.

Silberstein, Laurence J., ed. *New Perspectives on Israeli History: The Early Years of the State.* New York: New York University Press, 1991.

Simon, Reeva S.; Michael M.Laskier; and Sara Reguer, eds. *The Jews of the Middle East and North Africa in Modern Times.* New York: Columbia University Press, 2002.

Slater, Robert. *Warrior Statesman: The Life of Moshe Dayan.* New York: St. Martin's, 1991.

Smith, Barbara J. *The Roots of Separatism in Palestine: British Economic Policy, 1920-1929.* Syracuse, N.Y.: Syracuse University Press, 1993.

Smith, Charles D. *Palestine and the Arab-Israeli Conflict.* New York: St. Martin's Press, 2004.

Smith, Pamela Ann. *Palestine and the Palestinians, 1876–1983.* New York: St. Martin's, 1984.

Smith, Peter. *The Babi and Baha'i Religions: From Messianic Shi'ism to a World Religion.* Cambridge and New York: Cambridge University Press, 1987.

Sofer, Sasson. *Begin: An Anatomy of Leadership.* New York and Oxford, UK: Blackwell, 1988.

Sprinzak, Ehud. *Brother against Brother: Violence and Extremism in Israeli Politics from Altalena to the Rabin Assassination.* New York: Free Press, 1999.

Stern, Jessica. *Terror in the Name of God: Why Religious Militants Kill.* New York: Ecco, 2003.

Sternhell, Ze'ev. *The Founding Myths of Israel: Nationalism, Socialism, and the Making of the Jewish State.* Princeton, NJ: Princeton University Press, 1998.

Stillman, Norman A. *The Jews of Arab Lands in Modern Times.* Philadelphia: Jewish Publication Society, 1991.

Swedenburg, Theodore. *Memories of Revolt: The 1936–1939 Rebellion and the Palestinian National Past.* Fayetteville: University of Arkansas Press, 2003.

Takkenberg, Lex. *The Status of Palestinian Refugees in International Law.* Oxford, UK: Clarendon, 1998.

Tejirian, Eleanor H., and Reeva Simon. *Altruism and Imperialism: Western Cultural and Religious Missions in the Middle East.* New York: Columbia University Press, 2002.

Telhami, Shibley. *Power and Leadership in International Bargaining: The Path to the Camp David Accords.* New York: Columbia University Press, 1990.

Tessler, Mark. *A History of the Israeli-Palestinian Conflict.* Bloomington: Indiana University Press, 1994.

Teveth, Shabtai. *Ben-Gurion's Spy: The Story of the Political Scandal that Shaped Modern Israel.* New York: Columbia University Press, 1996.

Touval, Saadia. *The Peace Brokers: Mediators in the Arab-Israeli Conflict, 1948–1979.* Princeton, NJ: Princeton University Press, 1982.

Troen, Selwyn Ilan. *Imagining Zion: Dreams, Designs, and Realities in a Century of Jewish Settlement.* New Haven, CT: Yale University Press, 2003.

Troen, Selwyn Ilan, and Moshe Shemesh. *The Suez-Sinai Crisis, 1956: Retrospective and Reappraisal.* New York: Columbia University Press; London: Frank Cass, 1990.

Victor, Barbara. *Army of Roses: Inside the World of Palestinian Women Suicide Bombers.* Emmaus, PA: Rodale, 2003.

———. *A Voice of Reason: Hanan Ashrawi and Peace in the Middle East.* New York; Harcourt Brace, 1994.

Wallach, Janet, and John Wallach. *Arafat: In the Eyes of the Beholder.* New York: Lyle Stuart, 1990.

Wasserstein, Bernard. *The British in Palestine: The Mandatory Government and the Arab-Jewish Conflict, 1917–1929,* 2d edition. Oxford, UK, and Cambridge, MA: B. Blackwell, 1991.

Waterbury, John. *The Nile Basin: National Determinants of Collective Action.* New Haven, CT: Yale University Press, 2002.

Weaver, Many Anne. *A Portrait of Egypt: A Journey through the World of Militant Islam.* New York: Farrar Straus Giroux, 1999.

Wiktorowicz, Quintan. *The Management of Islamic Activism: Salafis, the Muslim Brotherhood, and State Power in Jordan.* Albany: State University of New York Press, 2000.

Wilson, Jeremy. *Lawrence of Arabia.* Stroud, UK: Sutton, 1998.

Wilson, Mary C. *King Abdullah, Britain, and the Making of Jordan.* Cambridge and New York: Cambridge University Press, 1987.

Wistrich, Robert S. *Antisemitism: The Longest Hatred.* New York: Pantheon, 1991.

Wolfe, Michael, ed. *One Thousand Roads to Mecca: Ten Centuries of Travelers Writing About the Muslim Pilgrimage.* New York: Grove Press, 1997.

Wright, Richard. *The Color Curtain: A Report on the Bandung Conference.* Jackson: University Press of Mississippi, 1995.

Yahil, Leni. *The Holocaust: The Fate of European Jewry, 1932–1945.* New York: Oxford University Press, 1990.

Yaqub, Salim. *Containing Arab Nationalism: The Eisenhower Doctrine and the Middle East.* Chapel Hill: University of North Carolina Press, 2004.

Yergin, Daniel. *The Prize: The Epic Quest for Oil, Money and Power.* New York: Simon and Schuster, 1991.

Zerubavel, Yael. "The Historic, the Legendary, and the Incredible: Invented Tradition and Collective Memory in Israel." In *Commemorations: The Politics of National Identity,* edited by John R. Gillis. Princeton, NJ: Princeton University Press, 1994.

———. *Recovered Roots: Collective Memory and the Making of Israeli National Tradition.* Chicago: University of Chicago Press, 1995.

Zipperstein, Steven J. *Elusive Prophet: Ahad Ha'am and the Origins of Zionism.* Berkeley: University of California Press, 1993.